JUDICIAL DECISIONS ON THE LAW
OF INTERNATIONAL ORGANIZATIONS

Judicial Decisions on the Law of International Organizations

Edited by
CEDRIC RYNGAERT
IGE F DEKKER
RAMSES A WESSEL
and
JAN WOUTERS

OXFORD
UNIVERSITY PRESS

OXFORD

UNIVERSITY PRESS

Great Clarendon Street, Oxford, OX2 6DP,
United Kingdom

Oxford University Press is a department of the University of Oxford.
It furthers the University's objective of excellence in research, scholarship,
and education by publishing worldwide. Oxford is a registered trade mark of
Oxford University Press in the UK and in certain other countries

Published in the United States of America by Oxford University Press
198 Madison Avenue, New York, NY 10016, United States of America

British Library Cataloguing in Publication Data
Data available

Library of Congress Control Number: 2015959802

ISBN 978–0–19–874362–0 (Hbk)
ISBN 978–0–19–874361–3 (Pbk)

Printed and bound by
CPI Group (UK) Ltd, Croydon, CR0 4YY

Contents

List of Abbreviations

ABH	Arab British Helicopter Company
ACHR	American Convention on Human Rights
ACP Group	African, Caribbean, and Pacific Group of States
ALQ	Arab Law Quarterly
AMF	Arab Monetary Fund
AOI	Arab Organization for Industrialization
ARE	Arab Republic of Egypt
ARIO	Articles on the Responsibility of International Organizations
ARS	Articles on Responsibility of States for Internationally Wrongful Acts
ASDI	Annuaire Suisse de Droit International
CAP	Common Agricultural Policy
CBB	College van Beroep voor het Bedrijfsleven
CFI	Court of First Instance
CJEU	Court of Justice of the European Union
CPIUN	Convention on Privileges and Immunities of the United Nations
Dutchbat	Dutch battalion under the command of the United Nations in operation United Nations Protection Force
EC	European Community
ECHR	European Convention on Human Rights
ECJ	European Court of Justice
ECOSOC	United Nations Economic and Social Council
ECR	European Court Reports
ECSC	European Coal and Steel Community
ECtHR	European Court of Human Rights
EEC	European Economic Community
EMRO	Eastern Mediterranean Regional Office
ESA	European Space Agency
EU	European Union
EUI	European University Institute
FPR	Rwandan Patriotic Front
FRCP	Federal Rules of Civil Procedure
FRY	Federal Republic of Yugoslavia
FSIA	Foreign Sovereign Immunities Act
FYROM	Former Yugoslav Republic of Macedonia (Macedonia)
GA	General Assembly
GCEU	General Court of the European Union
ICC	International Criminal Court
ICC	International Chamber of Commerce
ICCPR	International Covenant on Civil and Political Rights
ICJ	International Court of Justice
ICJ Rep	Reports of the International Court of Justice
ICTR	International Criminal Tribunal for Rwanda
ICTY	International Criminal Tribunal for the Former Yugoslavia
IDI	Institut de Droit international
IFAD	International Fund for Agricultural Development

IFOR	Implementation Force
ILC	International Law Commission
ILM	International Legal Materials
ILO	International Labour Organisations
ILR	International Law Reports
IO	International organization
IOIA	International Organizations Immunities Act
IOs	International organizations
IPGRI	International Plant Genetic Resources Institute
ITC	International Tin Council
KFOR	Kosovo Force
MINUAR	United Nations Assistance Mission for Rwanda
MNF	Multinational Force in Iraq
MOU	Memorandum of Understanding
NAB	NATO Appeal Board
NAC	North Atlantic Council
NATO	North Atlantic Treaty Organization
OJ	Official Journal (of the European Union)
ONUC	United Nations Operation in the Congo
OPEC	Organization of the Petroleum Exporting Countries
PCIJ	Permanent Court of International Justice
Publ.	Publication(s)
R2P	Responsibility to protect
SC	Security Council of the United Nations
SFOR	Stabilization Force
S/RES	Resolution of the UN Security Council
TEU	Treaty on European Union
TFEU	Treaty on the Functioning of the European Union
TRIPS	Trade-Related Aspects of Intellectual Property Rights (Agreement on)
UAE	United Arab Emirates
UK	United Kingdom
UN	United Nations
UNAT	United Nations Administrative Tribunal
UNEF	United Nations Emergency Force (for the Middle East)
UNESCO	United Nations Educational, Scientific and Cultural Organization
UNGA	United Nations General Assembly
UNICITRAL	United Nations Commission on International Trade Law
UNITAF	Unified Task Force
UNMIK	United Nations Interim Administration Mission in Kosovo
UNOSOM	United Nations Operation in Somalia
UNPROFOR	United Nations Protection Force
UNRRA	United Nations Relief and Rehabilitation Administration
UNSC	United Nations Security Council
US(A)	United States (of America)
VCLT	Vienna Convention on the Law of Treaties
WEU	Western European Union
WHA	Assembly of the WHO
WHL	Westland Helicopters Ltd
WHO	World Health Organization
WLR	Weekly Law Reports

Table of Cases

Page numbers in **bold** refer to the pages where the cases have been discussed in detail

PERMANENT COURT OF INTERNATIONAL JUSTICE (PCIJ)

INTERNATIONAL COURT OF JUSTICE (ICJ)

EUROPEAN COURT OF HUMAN RIGHTS (ECTHR)

EUROPEAN COURT OF JUSTICE (ECJ)

**Court of Justice (formerly European Court of Justice) and General Court
(formerly Court of First Instance (CFI))**

INTERNATIONAL CRIMINAL TRIBUNAL FOR
THE FORMER YUGOSLAVIA (ICTY)

INTERNATIONAL CRIMINAL TRIBUNAL FOR RWANDA (ICTR)

WORLD BANK ADMINISTRATIVE TRIBUNAL

WTO APPELLATE BODY AND WTO PANEL

ARBITRAL AWARDS

NATIONAL COURTS

Austria

Belgium

US Federal Appeals Court Cases

US Federal District Court Cases

List of Contributors

Christiane Ahlborn is a researcher at the Amsterdam Centre for International Law, University of Amsterdam.

Ana Sofia Barros is a Ph.D. candidate at the Leuven Centre for Global Governance Studies, University of Leuven.

Laurence Boisson de Chazournes is Professor of International Law and International Organization at the University of Geneva.

Kristen Boon is Professor of Law and Director of International Programs at Seton Hall University.

Catherine Brölmann is Associate Professor of Law at the University of Amsterdam.

Gian Luca Burci is Legal Counsel at the World Health Organization.

Agnes Chong is a Ph.D. candidate at the University of Hong Kong.

Lydia Davies-Bright is a researcher at the University of Nottingham.

Ige Dekker is Head of the Utrecht University School of Law and Vice-Dean of the Faculty of Law, Economics, and Governance at Utrecht University.

James D. Fry is Associate Professor of Law and Director of the LLM Programme at the University of Hong Kong.

Andrzej Gadkowski Ph.D. in international law, researcher at the Public International Law and International Organization Department of the Faculty of Law at the University of Geneva.

Peter Hilpold is Professor of Law at the University of Innsbruck.

Kenneth Keith is professor emeritus, Victoria University of Wellington, New Zealand.

Jan Klabbers is Martti Ahtisaari Academy Professor at the University of Helsinki.

Pieter-Jan Kuijper is Professor of the Law of International (Economic) Organizations at the University of Amsterdam.

Tobias Lock is a Lecturer in EU Law at the University of Edinburgh.

Brianne McGonigle Leyh is Associate Professor of Law at Utrecht University.

Aleksandar Momirov is Senior Policy Advisor on the Rule of Law at the Embassy of the Kingdom of the Netherlands in Belgrade, Serbia.

Blanca Montejo is a Political Affairs Officer at the United Nations Office of Legal Affairs.

Thore Neumann, University of Basel.

Jed Odermatt is a Ph.D. candidate at the Leuven Centre for Global Governance Studies at the University of Leuven.

Paolo Palchetti is Professor of International Law at the University of Macerata.

Anne Peters is Professor of Public International Law and Constitutional Law at the University of Basel.

Jakob Quirin is an Associate Legal Officer at the World Health Organization Office of the Legal Counsel.

Tom Ruys is Professor of Public International Law at Ghent University.

Cedric Ryngaert is Professor of Public International Law at Utrecht University.

Aurel Sari is Senior Lecturer in Law at the University of Exeter.

Kirsten Schmalenbach is Professor of Public International Law and European Union Law at the University of Salzburg.

Pierre Schmitt is a Postdoctoral Researcher at the Leuven Centre for Global Governance Studies, University of Leuven.

Tulio Scovazzi is Professor of International Law at the University of Milano-Bicocca.

Otto Spijkers is Assistant Professor of Public International Law at Utrecht University.

Antonios Tzanakopoulos is Associate Professor of Public International Law and Fellow in Law at St. Anne's College, University of Oxford.

Harmen Van der Wilt is Professor of International Criminal Law at the University of Amsterdam.

Santiago Villalpando is Legal Officer in the Codification Division of the Office of Legal Affairs of the United Nations in New York and Adjunct Professor at New York University.

Ramses Wessel is Professor of International and European Law and Governance at the University of Twente.

Nigel D. White is Professor of Public International Law at the University of Nottingham.

Chanaka Wickremasinghe is Legal Counsellor at the Foreign Commonwealth Office.

Jan Wouters is Director of the Leuven Centre for Global Governance and the Institute for International Law, Professor of International Law and the Law of International Organizations at the University of Leuven.

General Introduction

Cedric Ryngaert, Ige F Dekker, Ramses A Wessel, and Jan Wouters

Concomitant with the rising relevance of international organizations in international affairs, and the general turn to litigation to settle disputes, international institutional law issues have increasingly become the subject of litigation, before both international and domestic courts.

While there are a number of textbooks introducing the law of international organizations, the judicial treatment of this sub-field of international law has not been given the attention due to it. This book aims to fill that gap. Specifically, it contains excerpts of the most prominent international and domestic judicial decisions that are relevant to the law of international organizations, as well as—most importantly—comments thereto. The book does not seek to replace relevant textbooks; rather, it complements them by providing in-depth analysis of judicial decisions, which often receive only cursory, non-systematic treatment in textbooks.

Methodologically speaking, the book contains case-notes regarding about fifty judicial decisions of international and domestic courts. Each case-note consists of five sections, discussing (1) the relevance of the case, (2) the facts, and (3) the legal question; giving (4) a relevant excerpt of the judicial decision; and (5) commenting on the decision. The commentaries are written by leading experts in the field, both scholars and practitioners. They are opinionated and critically engage with the decision in question, with commentators' and stakeholders' reactions thereto, and with later decisions, codifications, or reports. The commentaries have been reviewed by the editors.

While the cases typically address different topics rendering any categorization somewhat arbitrary, the book is divided into seven parts, which correspond to classic categories of international institutional law: (1) legal status (personality), (2) legal powers, (3) institutional structures and position of members, (4) legal acts, (5) obligations, (6) responsibility and accountability, and (7) immunity. Per part, the editors have written an introductory section that presents and contextualizes the legal issues. This allows for a better and more coherent understanding of the bundle of case-notes per part.

Judicial decisions from a variety of courts have been selected: the International Court of Justice and its predecessor, the Permanent Court of International Justice, the Court of Justice of the European Union, the international criminal tribunals, and assorted domestic courts. Although the need to ensure a sufficient degree of diversity of courts and tribunals was taken into account, the selection of cases is ultimately mainly based on the innovative character of the judicial decisions for the law of international organizations in general, regardless of the specific organizational context which formed the factual background for the decision. Every decision is included for the significance of its contribution to the development of the law of international organizations, and thus for marking, to a greater or lesser extent, an advancement in international institutional law thinking. The editors have decided not to include international staff cases before assorted international tribunals, as such cases concern rather specific issues of international labour and administrative law rather than international institutional law.[1]

Despite the important role which courts play in advancing international institutional law, the editors consider it appropriate to add a caveat: one has to admit that this legal area has predominantly been developed 'out of court', and more particularly on the basis of institutional and state practice[2] and advisory practice of legal counsel of international organizations.[3] But even then, courts may play a role as an arbiter of the legality of certain developments and interpretations, and as a provider of legal certainty. For instance, art. 27(3) of the UN Charter—the provision dealing with the UN Security Council's decision-making procedure—has been interpreted by the members of the UN Security Council itself as not requiring affirmative votes by the permanent members for a resolution in non-procedural matters to be adopted; voluntary abstentions would suffice. This institutional practice was later confirmed by the International Court of Justice,[4] thereby dispelling any lingering doubts as to its lawfulness.

However this may be, there is no denying that the body of judicial rulings with respect to the law of international organizations is eventually rather limited. This is a consequence of the incomplete character of international law, which lacks a compulsory mechanism to settle disputes between international actors. In international institutional law, this incompleteness is brought into even starker relief, as at the international level international organizations do not—as a general rule—have access to dispute settlement mechanisms, nor are there venues where affected actors can sue organizations. In contentious cases, the International Court of Justice only has jurisdiction over inter-state disputes, whereas the jurisdiction of the European Court of Human Rights extends only to—again—inter-state disputes, and applications brought

---

[1] See for further reading: O. Elias (ed.), *The Development and Effectiveness of International Administrative Law* (Brill 2012); F.C. Amerasinghe, 'International Administrative Tribunals', in C.P.R. Romano, K.J. Alter, and Y. Shany (eds), *The Oxford Handbook of International Adjudication* (Oxford, Oxford University Press 2014), pp. 316–38; O. Elias and M. Thomas, 'Administrative Tribunals of International Organizations', in C. Giorgetti, *The Rules, Practice, and Jurisprudence of International Courts and Tribunals* (Brill 2012), pp. 159–90.

[2] See in respect of the United Nations, the *travaux préparatoires* of the San Francisco Conference establishing the United Nations, UNCIO Vol. 13, at 831 *et seq.* ('in the course of the operations from day to day of the various organs of the Organization, it is inevitable that each organ will interpret such parts of the Charter as are applicable to its particular functions').

[3] See *inter alia* H.C.L. Merillat (ed.), *Legal Advisers and International Organizations* (Oceana Publications 1966); United Nations Office of Legal Affairs (ed.), *Collection of Essays by Legal Advisers of States, Legal Advisers of International Organizations and Practitioners in the Field of International Law* (United Nations Publications 1999); J. Wouters and J. Odermatt (eds), *Legal Advisers in International Organizations* (Elgar Publishers, forthcoming); R. Zacklin, 'The Role of the International Lawyer in an International Organization', in C. Wickremasinghe (ed.), *The International Lawyer as Practitioner* (British Inst of Intl & Comparative 2000), pp. 57–68.

[4] ICJ, *Legal Consequences for States of the Continued Presence of South Africa in Namibia (South West Africa) notwithstanding Security Council Resolution 276 (1970)*, Advisory Opinion, [1971] ICJ Rep 16, 22.

by individuals against states. At the level of domestic courts, international organizations are often shielded by immunities from jurisdiction and enforcement; these obstacles may render domestic litigation a non-starter for injured parties.

In spite of these—often inherent—procedural limitations, issues of international institutional law *have* come up before courts, both domestic and international. Notably, the International Court of Justice, while not having jurisdiction over organizations in contentious matters, has the competence to 'give an advisory opinion on any legal question at the request of whatever body may be authorized by or in accordance with the Charter of the United Nations to make such a request'.[5] Many, if not most advisory opinions pertain to legal issues of internal institutional organization of the UN (system), or the relations between an organization belonging to the UN system and its member states. Some of these decisions have been extremely important to ensure the proper functioning of the UN, for example, the 1962 advisory opinion in *Certain Expenses*, which declared that UN peacekeeping operations are lawful and that their costs are part of the regular expenses of the organization, and to be borne by all the member states.[6] Other decisions have set the terms of the debate in general international law: thus, for instance, the International Court of Justice's landmark ruling on the international legal personality of the UN in its 1949 advisory opinion *Reparation for Injuries* has had a profound impact on debates regarding the legal status of international organizations, and even of non-state actors in general, where it held that '[t]he subjects of law in any legal system are not necessarily identical in their nature or in the extent of their rights, and their nature depends upon the needs of the community'[7] and further developed the doctrine of *implied powers*.

Judicial decisions on issues of international institutional law may also emanate from international organizations which have a constitutional structure that allows an independent judicial body to review acts of other organs of the organization. The UN and its specialized agencies do not have such a structure, but the European Union (EU) does. Its Court of Justice (CJEU) has developed an intricate body of case-law, in particular on the division of competences between the organization and its member states, and between different institutions of the organization. Insofar as these CJEU cases have seminal importance for general institutional law, they have been included in this book.

Relevant judicial decisions have also been rendered by international dispute settlement mechanisms in inter-state disputes, to the extent that such disputes concern the relationship between a state and an organization of which it is a member. The court will then be called upon to pronounce itself on whether the claim really concerns an act attributable to a state, or rather to an international organization on which this state

---

[5] United Nations, *Statute of the International Court of Justice*, 18 April 1946, art. 65(1).

[6] ICJ, *Certain Expenses of the United Nations (Article 17, paragraph 2, of the Charter)*, Advisory Opinion, [1962] ICJ Rep 151. Not all ICJ opinions have been followed, however. See for an early assessment: K.L. Penegar, 'Relationship of Advisory Opinions of the International Court of Justice to the Maintenance of World Minimum Order', (1965) 113 *University of Pennsylvania Law Review* 529 (discussing, *inter alia*, the *Admissions Cases*).

[7] ICJ, *Reparation for Injuries Suffered in the Service of the United Nations*, Advisory Opinion, [1949] ICJ Rep 174, 178.

has conferred competences—in which case it will have to decline jurisdiction. A number of such cases, often pertaining to responsibility questions, have been decided by the International Court of Justice and the European Court of Human Rights.

Finally, regardless of the immunities which international organizations may be said to enjoy before domestic courts, there is a substantial amount of domestic case-law relevant to the law of international organizations. Plaintiffs and accountability advocates have continued to exert pressure on domestic courts to decline the immunity of international organizations on the ground that such immunity is not functionally necessary for the organization, or violates the plaintiffs' right of access to a remedy. These pressures have obviously generated their own case-law, which, given the variety of courts involved, shoots in various directions. A body of domestic case-law has also been generated as a result of plaintiffs targeting state action taken in an international institutional context, for example, member state implementation of international sanctions, or wrongful action committed by national troop contingents in the context of UN peacekeeping or peace-enforcement operations. To determine whether domestic courts have jurisdiction over such cases, just like the international courts mentioned earlier, these courts have to ascertain whether the impugned acts are attributable to a state or rather an international organization. In so doing, they touch on issues of institutional or operational division of competences between states and organizations.

Ultimately, many of the judicial decisions discussed in this book pertain to the scope and limitations of the powers of international organizations. The legal status of an organization may be considered to be a function of the powers it actually exercises, its institutional structure, and the allocation of powers to and between various organs. International organizations, as is well-known, can only perform legal acts that fall within their powers; they have international obligations that dovetail with the powers conferred on them, they are responsible for action committed in the exercise of their competences, and they enjoy immunities insofar as these are necessary for the performance of their functions as they flow from the powers given to them. The centrality of the concept of 'powers' is by no means coincidental. This concept reflects in an outspoken way the fundamental different visions of the legal nature of international organizations: as state-driven entities established on the basis of a conferral of powers by member states, or as relatively autonomous entities with inherent competences to realize their purposes and functions. And not unimportantly, these different principles at the same time functionally determine all actions of organizations, including their limits. Small wonder then that legal disputes often pertain to the question whether the powers that organizations actually exercise are in keeping with the principle of conferral, or whether impugned conduct was carried out within the scope of an organization's powers.

Courts have not shirked from ruling on these matters, sometimes affecting the balance of powers between states and organizations, or between organs of organizations. States and organizations may not always welcome such judicial decisions, as they may be viewed as meddling in international and national affairs. But for an international system to be based on the rule of law, an independent and impartial judicial control over organizational decisions is called for. This applies with particular force where international organizations and states pass the responsibility buck, and leave third parties clamouring for accountability in the cold.

This book is aimed at students of the law of international organizations in the broad sense, not only university and college students, but also legal practitioners—offices of legal counsel of the organizations, litigators, judges, diplomats, and national and international civil servants—as well as academic researchers. It is hoped that the commentaries prove insightful to all of them, and contribute to the solution of extant questions of international institutional law. The editors would like to extend their thanks to all contributors, as well as to Ana Sofia Barros for her invaluable editorial assistance.

1

Legal Status (Personality)

In an international legal system that was set up around states, it is not surprising that the question of the international legal status of international organizations continues to pop-up, both in legal doctrinal debates and in judicial proceedings. The question of the legal status of international organizations is connected to their coming of age as autonomous legal subjects (leaving aside the question of whether they can be anything else). After all, it is only because of the acceptance of a distinction between the organization and its members that rights and duties of international organizations become relevant.

At the same time, it is the very tension between the organization and its members that seems to underly most of the debates in international institutional law. Text books often refer to the Janus-faced nature of international organizations: they are created by and composed of states, while at the same time in need of a certain autonomy. In order for states to become a *member* of something, there needs to be something. States make the rules from which international organizations draw their competences; in turn international organizations may be created to make rules to limit the freedom of the exact same states. International organizations are both creations and creators.

It is in particular the *institutionalization* of the legal order and the autonomy of international organizations that has led not only to the adoption of 'international decisions' (the products of law-making by international organizations), but also to questions related to their responsibilities and immunities. Literature on the law of international organizations and their role in the international legal order is quite extensive, and has been booming over the past decade. There is no doubt that states continue to be influential—and frequently clearly decisive—in relation to the role and function of the international organizations they created for certain purposes. Yet, as has been noted by many over the past years, the law-making functions of many international organizations made us aware of the existence of—perhaps not the emergence of a world government[1]—but at least of global governance 'beyond the state' in what is sometimes normatively framed as a 'world community'.[2] International organizations

---

[1] Yet, see the clear reference to 'global government' J.P. Trachtman, *The Future of International Law: Global Government* (Cambridge, Cambridge University Press 2013). Elsewhere I address the consequences of this line of reasoning for the structure of the international legal order in more detail: R.A. Wessel, Revealing the Publicness of International Law', in E.J. Molenaar, P.A. Nollkaemper, S. Nouwen, and C. Ryngaert (eds), *What's Wrong With International Law?* (Leiden/Boston, Martinus Nijhoff Publishers 2015) pp. 449–66.

[2] But see M. Koskenniemi, 'The Subjective Dangers of Projects of World Community', in A. Cassese (ed.), *Realizing Utopia: The Future of International Law* (Oxford, Oxford University Press 2012), pp. 3–13; as well as the other contributions in Part 1 of this volume under the heading 'Can the World Become a Global Community'?

have found their place in global governance, and are even considered 'autonomous actors', following an agenda that is no longer fully defined by their Member States[3]—which has caused the latter to devote much of their time and energy to responding to what has been termed the 'Frankenstein problem'.[4]

It is therefore no coincidence that we start this collection of cases by addressing the legal status of international organizations. This question is closely connected to the question of the organizations' legal personality. Basically, the legal status question concerns an organization's subjectivity under international law. It has to do with the entity's legal *existence*. Once that can be established one may say that an international organization enjoys legal personality: it can have legal rights and duties (or at least one right or duty).

Literature on the legal personality of international organizations is abundant and the classic debates never seem to reach a unified conclusion. Can international organizations exist without legal personality, or is legal personality a (perhaps *the*) feature to distinguish it from a more loosely organized international conference? Can international organizations have a 'partial' legal personality, or is the partiality related to their competences only? Perhaps the most pragmatic solution would be to follow Klabbers' (somewhat circular) notion that 'as soon as an organization performs an act which can only be explained on the basis of international legal personality, such an organization will be presumed to be in possession of international legal personality.'[5]

The cases analysed in this Part do not provide all the answers. In fact, most of the time they form the source of the debates in academic circles as well as in Court rooms. This may be particularly true for the question of whether the United Nations could bring a claim against a (non-member) state (*Reparation*, Wessel). The fact that the UN was not merely a centre 'for harmonizing the actions of nations' reflects the foundation of international institutional law. In 1949 the International Court of Justice well understood the importance of the concept of legal personality and apart from solving a practical issue, its Advisory Opinion is full of references which indeed later formed the building blocks of the subdiscipline called the law of international organizations (such as the attribution of competences, implied competences, the importance of the objectives of an organization, or subsequent practice).

In a similar vein as the *Reparation* case defined the legal status of the UN, the *ERTA* case can be seen as a founding case in relation to the international legal competences of the European Union (*ERTA*, Klabbers). This case revealed the EU's (or in fact at that time the European Community's) external competences, on which—as in the case of the UN—not too much was regulated in the founding treaty. Again, implied

---

[3] N.D. White and R. Collins (eds), *International Organizations and the Idea of Autonomy: Institutional Independence in the International Legal Order* (Abingdon, Routledge 2011).

[4] A. Guzman, 'International Organizations and the Frankenstein Problem', (2013) *European Journal of International Law* 999–1025; Cf. also J. Klabbers, *An Introduction to International Organizations Law* (3rd edn, Cambridge, Cambridge University Press 2015).

[5] Klabbers (n. 4); and more extensively J. Klabbers, 'Presumptive Personality: the European Union in International Law', in M. Koskenniemi (ed.), *International law Aspects of the European Union* (The Hague, Kluwer Law International 1998), pp. 231–53.

competences were derived from both objectives and existing express competences. *ERTA* made clear that the European Community had become an international organization that was not only competent to regulate its own member states, but that it could (and in fact should) also engage in legal relations with third states on those matters: whatever the EU can do internally, it can also do externally.

The question to which extent the separate legal personality of an international organization is consistent with the possibility of members being held responsible for the conduct of the organization became apparent in domestic proceedings in the United Kingdom in the 1980s (*International Tin Council*, Palchetti). The judgment of the House of Lords is still leading in debates on the extent to which membership of an international organization can entail responsibility for the acts of the organization. This was also one of the central questions in the discussions in the International Law Commission that led to the 2011 Articles on the Responsibilities of International Organizations.

The distinction between domestic and international legal personality that was made by the House of Lords in the *Tin Council* case, returned in the 1990s in a case before the same court (*Arab Monetary Fund*, Schmalenbach). The case is interesting because it reveals the influence of a dualistic (UK) approach to the legal status of international organizations. Rather than following the 'objective' approach to international organizations of which the state is not a member—which was for instance used by the ICJ in the *Reparation* case—the Lords took recourse to the United Kingdom's own rules on conflict of laws in order to recognize the Arab Monetary Fund as a corporate body established under the laws of the United Arab Emirates.

Like states, international organizations are abstract entities; they act through their organs. In discussing their legal status, one will have to remain aware of the fact that decisions are always taken by organs on the basis of the internal institutional rules of the organization. In two EU cases the relationship between the institutions and the organization was further developed (*Algera*, and *France v Commission*, Klabbers). The Court made clear that questions of international personality should be related to the organizations and not (necessarily) to the organs ('institutions' in EU jargon) of the organization. Here we see an interesting parallel between statehood and 'organizationhood' that is present in other debates as well (e.g. on international responsibility): we should in principle see the organization as a unity.

But, if that is the case, member states would be offered possibilities to hide behind the organizational veil and would perhaps find reasons to evade their individual responsibilities under international law. The question of how and when this veil can or should be pierced, returned when Macedonia was denied membership of NATO due to the fact that the organization could not reach a unanimous decision on that point (*FYROM v Greece*, Barros). The reason for a lack of consensus was that one member state, Greece, blocked Macedonian membership as a result of their differences of opinion concerning the correct use of the name of that state. The ICJ argued that the veil of an international organization must, when relevant, be lifted, in order for (member) states to be directly addressed by international law.

In the present Part in this collection this tension forms a thread that links the different cases together. Accepting a separate legal status of international organizations is a logical consequence of the fact that international organizations were established as separate entities. The states that created these organizations became members of these new entities and in that capacity willingly subjected themselves to the rules of the organization. The moment they take their 'seat' they are in fact part of the organization's institutional structure. Yet, both in a practical and a conceptual sense it is difficult to deny the fact that member states remain states. Allowing them to hide behind the institutional veil would not only imply a denial of their individual international legal responsibilities, but also of political realities.

1.1 *Reparation for Injuries Suffered in the Service of the United Nations*, Advisory Opinion, [1949] ICJ Rep 174

Ramses A. Wessel

Relevance of the case

The fact that this collection of case notes starts with the *Reparation* case will not come as a surprise to most of our readers. Ever since the International Court of Justice delivered its opinion in 1949, the case has featured in most introductory lectures on the law of international organizations and in the leading textbooks. Indeed, the relevance of the case cannot be underestimated as it deals with the recognition of international organizations (in this particular case the United Nations) as entities enjoying a legal position in the international legal order in distinction from their Member States. The question of the legal status of international organizations did recur in later opinions and judgments,[1] but the ground rules were clearly laid down in 'Reparation'.

Despite the fact that questions on the legal status had previously been addressed,[2] the mainstream view on subjects of international law was that these could only be states. So, not just the question of legal personality, but also the notion of international organizations being more than a structure 'for harmonizing the actions of nations' can be seen as having influenced the further development of the law of international organizations. And, finally, the *Reparation* case has become known for its clear acceptance of the existence of *implied powers*.

I. Facts of the case

Count Folke Bernadotte, the UN mediator officially charged with bringing peace to the Palestinian region at the time of the creation of the state of Israel, was shot by Israeli militants belonging to a Zionist group on 17 September 1948 when his small convoy was stopped. The chief UN observer Colonel Andre Serot was also wounded and both men were dead on arrival at the hospital. Bernadotte was a Swedish aristocrat and diplomat who acted as a United Nations Security Council mediator in the Arab-Israeli conflict of 1947–48. Ironically, Bernadotte was known for his negotiation of the release of about 31,000 prisoners from German concentration camps during the Second World War, including 450 Danish Jews from Theresienstadt released on 14 April 1945.

---

[1] See the other cases reviewed in this section as well as, for instance, *Interpretation of the Agreement of 25 March 1951 Between the WHO and Egypt*, Advisory Opinion, [1980] ICJ Rep 73.

[2] For instance, in relation to the League of Nations (cf. J.F. Williams, 'The Status of the League of Nations in International Law', in *Chapters on Current International Law and the League of Nations* (London/New York, Longman, Green, and Co 1929)).

II. The legal question

In Resolution 258 (III) of 3 December 1948 the UN General Assembly submitted the
following legal questions to the ICJ for an advisory opinion:

I.   In the event of an agent of the United Nations in the performance of his duties
     suffering injury in circumstances involving the responsibility of a State, has the
     United Nations, as an Organization, the capacity to bring an international claim
     against the responsible de jure or de facto government with a view to obtaining
     the reparation due in respect of the damage caused (a) to the United Nations,
     (b) to the victim or to persons entitled through him?

II. In the event of an affirmative reply on point I (b), how is action by the United
     Nations to be reconciled with such rights as may be possessed by the State of
     which the victim is a national?

III. Excerpts

When the Organization brings a claim against one of its Members, this claim will be
presented in the same manner, and regulated by the same procedure [as in the case
of States].

But, in the international sphere, has the Organization such a nature as involves the
capacity to bring an international claim? In order to answer this question, the Court
must first enquire whether the Charter has given the Organization such a position
that it possesses, in regard to its Members, rights which it is entitled to ask them
to respect. In other words, does the Organization possess international personality?
This is no doubt a doctrinal expression, which has sometimes given rise to controversy. But it will be used here to mean that if the Organization is recognized as having that personality, it is an entity capable of availing itself of obligations incumbent
upon its Members.

The Charter has not been content to make the Organization created by it merely
a centre 'for harmonizing the actions of nations in the attainment of these common ends' (Article 1, para. 3). It has equipped that centre with organs, and has
given it special tasks. It has defined the position of the Members in relation to the
Organization by requiring them to give it every assistance in any action undertaken
by it (Article 2, para. 5), and to accept and carry out the decisions of the Security
Council; by authorizing the General Assembly to make recommendations to the
Members; by giving the Organization legal capacity and privileges and immunities in the territory of each of its Members; and by providing for the conclusion
of agreements between the Organization and its Members. Practice—in particular
the conclusion of conventions to which the Organization is a party—has confirmed
this character of the Organization, which occupies a position in certain respects in
detachment from its Members, and which is under a duty to remind them, if need
be, of certain obligations. It must be added that the Organization is a political body,
charged with political tasks of an important character, and covering a wide field
namely, the maintenance of international peace and security, the development of
friendly relations among nations, and the achievement of international co-operation

in the solution of problems of an economic, social, cultural or humanitarian character (Article 1); and in dealing with its Members it employs political means. The 'Convention on the Privileges and Immunities of the United Nations' of 1946 creates rights and duties between each of the signatories and the Organization (see, in particular, Section 35). It is difficult to see how such a convention could operate except upon the international plane and as between parties possessing international personality.

In the opinion of the Court, the Organization was intended to exercise and enjoy, and is in fact exercising and enjoying, functions and rights which can only be explained on the basis of the possession of a large measure of international personality and the capacity to operate upon an international plane. It is at present the supreme type of international organization, and it could not carry out the intentions of its founders if it was devoid of international personality. It must be acknowledged that its Members, by entrusting certain functions to it, with the attendant duties and responsibilities, have clothed it with the competence required to enable those functions to be effectively discharged.

Accordingly, the Court has come to the conclusion that the Organization is an international person. That is not the same thing as saying that it is a State, which it certainly is not, or that its legal personality and rights and duties are the same as those of a State. Still less is it the same thing as saying that it is 'a super-State', whatever that expression may mean. It does not even imply that all its rights and duties must be upon the international plane, any more than all the rights and duties of a State must be upon that plane. What it does mean is that it is a subject of international law and capable of possessing international rights and duties, and that it has capacity to maintain its rights by bringing international claims.

Whereas a State possesses the totality of international rights and duties recognized by international law, the rights and duties of an entity such as the Organization must depend upon its purposes and functions as specified or implied in its constituent documents and developed in practice.

The Charter does not expressly confer upon the Organization the capacity to include, in its claim for reparation, damage caused to the victim or to persons entitled through him. The Court must therefore begin by enquiring whether the provisions of the Charter concerning the functions of the Organization, and the part played by its agents in the performance of those functions, imply for the Organization power to afford its agents the limited protection that would consist in the bringing of a claim on their behalf for reparation for damage suffered in such circumstances. Under international law, the Organization must be deemed to have those powers which, though not expressly provided in the Charter, are conferred upon it by necessary implication as being essential to the performance of its duties. This principle of law was applied by the Permanent Court of International Justice to the International Labour Organization in its Advisory Opinion No. 13 of July 23rd, [p. 183] 1926 (Series B., No. 13, p. 18), and must be applied to the United Nations.

Having regard to the foregoing considerations, and to the undeniable right of the Organization to demand that its Members shall fulfil the obligations entered into by them in the interest of the good working of the Organization, the Court is of the opinion that, in the case of a breach of these obligations, the Organization has the capacity to claim adequate reparation, and that in assessing this reparation it is authorized to include the damage suffered by the victim or by persons entitled through him.

Accordingly the question is whether the Organization has capacity to bring a claim against the defendant State to recover reparation in respect of that damage or whether, on the contrary, the defendant State, not being a member, is justified in raising the objection that the Organization lacks the capacity to bring an international claim. On this point, the Court's opinion is that fifty States, representing the vast majority of the members of the international community, had the power, in conformity with international law, to bring into being an entity possessing objective international personality, and not merely personality recognized by them alone, together with capacity to bring international claims.

[On question II] In such a case, there is no rule of law which assigns priority to the one or to the other, or which compels either the State or the Organization to refrain from bringing an international claim.

Although the bases of the two claims are different, that does not mean that the defendant State can be compelled to pay the reparation due in respect of the damage twice over. International tribunals are already familiar with the problem of a claim in which two or more national States are interested, and they know how to protect the defendant State in such a case.

IV. Commentary

Legal personality has become a key—and much debated—issue in the law of international organizations. This should not come as a surprise as the popular narrative presents the possession of legal personality as a necessary requirement for international organizations to act in a legal sense. Also in the classic case under review here, the Court basically argued that in order for it to be able to assess the possibility of bringing a claim, it should first establish whether the Organization has legal personality. At the same time, these days international personality is seen as a characteristic of an international organization (see also the *WHO-Egypt* case mentioned above). In that narrative it only makes sense to talk about an international organization when it occupies a distinctive legal position from its founders; and it is this distinct legal position that is often equated with possessing legal personality (or, what amounts to the same thing: being a legal person). It is the latter narrative that seems to be dominant these days and the 'autonomy' of international organizations (and the related constitutional questions) have started to spark new debates.[3]

In fact, the notion of international institutions not being merely centres 'for harmonizing the actions of nations' (in the words of the Court) seems to be at the root of most current debates on postnational rule-making, global administrative law, the exercise of public authority, informal international lawmaking, and global constitutionalism. The (in)famous *volonté distincte* of international organizations (well-known as the idea by Schermers and Blokker that international organizations have 'a will of

---

[3] cf. R. Collins and N. White, *International Organizations and the Idea of Autonomy* (Abingdon, Routledge 2011).

their own'), triggered debates on how to control these creations.[4] This reveals that legal personality is not just about the capacity to bring claims or to engage in other legal actions; it is part of the defining nature of international organizations.

In 1949 the International Court of Justice well understood the importance of the concept of legal personality. While the question arose out of a practical problem (is the UN legally competent to bring an international claim), the legal-philosophical dimension was clear from the outset. The Court no doubt knew Kelsen's argument that, if we talk about rights and duties, '[t]here must exist something that "has" the duty or the right'.[5] The Court, at least at first, thus enquires 'whether the Charter has given the Organization such a position that it possesses, in regard to its Members, rights which it is entitled to ask them to respect'. It directly relates legal personality to the subjective will of the creators of the UN to endow the organization with certain rights, duties, and functions and even seems to equate this to its separate legal status ('In other words, does the Organization possess international personality?'). Since legal personality was not explicitly mentioned by the founders of the UN, it is derived from the (perceived) objectives ('it could not carry out the intentions of its founders if it was devoid of international personality') and even from subsequent practice ('It is difficult to see how such a [concluded] convention could operate except upon the international plane and as between parties possessing international personality'). The idea of a legal personality as a threshold (the organization cannot act legally when it is devoid of legal personality, so we first have to establish or construct it) has been contested ever since.[6] The main point of criticism seems to be that international organizations *do* act and that these actions can or should have legal consequences irrespective of whether or not the legal personality problem has been solved.

In a way, the approach of the ICJ in the *Reparation* case (let's look at what the organization is supposed to do and what it is actually doing and derive legal personality from that) has become quite common in legal doctrinal approaches to the question of legal personality. A similar approach was used by the European Court of Justice in the *ERTA* case (Case 22/70), and also by scholars attempting to define the international legal status of other international organizations, such as the European Union.[7]

In legal scholarship the tendency to construct or prove legal personality on the basis of the (implied) will of the founders, met with objections from those with a preference for objective facts. Yet, it has been noted that both approaches to the legal status of international organizations are flawed and difficult to work with in practice.[8] The intention of the founders may not only be difficult to establish, but it may also have changed since the creation of the organizations. In the case of the UN, any reference in

---

[4] cf. the reference to Mary Shelley in J. Klabbers, *An Introduction to International Organizations Law* (Cambridge, Cambridge University Press 2015).

[5] H. Kelsen, *General Theory of Law and State* (New York, Russell & Russell 1945), at 93.

[6] See for instance J. Klabbers, 'The Concept of Legal Personality', (2005) *Ius Gentium* 35–66.

[7] cf. R. A. Wessel, 'The International Legal Status of the European Union', (2007) *European Foreign Affairs Review* 109–29.

[8] cf. T. Gazzini, 'Personality of International Organizations' in J. Klabbers and Å. Wallendahl (eds), *Research Handbook on the Law of International Organization* (Cheltenham UK, Northampton US, Edward Elgar 2011), pp. 33–55.

the Charter was deliberately omitted as it was considered superfluous. It was held that the international personality of the UN 'will be determined implicitly from the provisions of the Charter taken as a whole'.[9] Taking 'the objective fact of its existence'[10] as proof of international legal personality equally meets with some problems. After all, if legal personality implicitly follows the establishment of a legal entity, how do we deal with organizations in which the 'distinct will of its own' is virtually absent because of a largely intergovernmental set-up? And, can we really assume legal personality when the only thing states meant to do was to create a light international framework to facilitate their co-operation (and would this not violate the fundamental rule of international law that states are in principle free to decide what they wish to agree on)?

In practice—and despite their flaws—both theoretical approaches play a role in the establishment of the legal status of an international organization and a more pragmatic approach seems to have become dominant, phrased by Klabbers as: 'as soon as an organization performs an act which can only be explained on the basis of international legal personality, such an organization will be presumed to be in possession of international legal personality.'[11]

All in all, the present author would maintain that the concept of legal personality is first and foremost relevant to settle the separate status of the international entity in the international legal order. And this is indeed what the ICJ started with. More in general, Bekker once defined legal personality as 'the concrete exercise of, or at least the potential ability to exercise, certain rights and the fulfilment of certain obligations'.[12] Earlier, I have argued that it is in particular about the *potential* ability rather than about the concrete exercise of powers.[13] The distinction between *legal personality* and *legal capacity* is illuminating in this respect: the first concerns a *quality*, the second is an *asset*. Where international personality thus means not much more than being a subject of public international law, capacity is concerned with what the entity is potentially entitled to do (and where *implied powers* may come in). The rather formal approach is apparent in the work of a number of other authors as well who have stressed that 'the concept of personality does not say anything about the qualities of the person' and that 'it is a mistake to jump to the conclusion that an organization has personality and then to deduce specific capacities from an *a priori* conception of the concomitants of personality'.[14] It follows from this approach that there is not much sense in speaking of a 'partial legal personality' of international organisations. Neither can we say that a particular international entity 'to some extent' possesses

  [9] 13 UNCIO Doc. 803, IV/2/A/7 (1945), at 817.
  [10] Seyersted, 'International Personality of Intergovernmental Organizations. Do Their Capacities Really Depend Upon Their Constitutions?', (1964) *Indian Journal of International Law* 1–121.
  [11] J. Klabbers, 'Presumptive Personality: the European Union in International Law', in M. Koskenniemi (ed.), *International Law Aspects of the European Union* (The Hague, Kluwer Law International 1998), pp. 231–53.
  [12] P. H. F. Bekker, *The Legal Position of Intergovernmental Organizations: A Functional Necessity Analysis of Their Legal Status and Immunities* (Dordrecht, Martinus Nijhoff Publishers 1994), p. 53.
  [13] R. A. Wessel, 'Revisiting the Legal Status of the European Union', (1999) *European Foreign Affairs Review* 507–37.
  [14] I. Detter, *Law-Making by International Organizations* (Stockholm, Norstedt & Söners Förlag 1965), p. 21.

legal personality. The possession of legal personality ('being a legal person') is a binary phenomenon: you either have it or you do not. Competences, on the other hand, seem to depend on what was attributed to the organization, although a case could be made for the existence of competences inherent to the enjoyment of legal personality, such as perhaps the conclusion of certain international agreements or (at least in the eyes of the ICJ) bringing an international claim.

The idea that international organizations by definition are legal persons (and that this in fact would distinguish them from less-institutionalised phenomena such as international conferences) seems to have become more accepted. Not only can this notion be derived from case-law of the ICJ,[15] but it has also become part of the definition of an international organization in the ILC's 2011 Articles on the Responsibility of International Organizations as: 'an organization established by a treaty or other instrument governed by international law and possessing its own international legal personality'.

Indeed, and returning to the *Reparation* case, this may also explain the link between legal personality and the other notion contributing to the fame of the case: *implied powers*. The Court argued that: 'Whereas a State possesses the totality of rights and duties recognized by international law, the rights and duties of an entity such as the Organization must depend upon its purposes and functions as specified *or implied* in its constituent documents and developed in practice.' As Rama-Montaldo held, 'It is very important to note the objective manner in which the Court proceeded in determining the personality of the organization. The personality could not be implied from the functions; its foundation was not a by-product of functional necessity but a logical relationship between certain presuppositions and certain legal effects.'[16]

This latter observation on the objective existence of international legal personality seems to be in line with some views on the question of a need for recognition by third states. According to the Court, 'fifty States, representing the vast majority of the members of the international community, had the power, in conformity with international law, to bring into being an entity possessing objective international personality'. While the Court relates the objectivity to an acceptance by 'the vast majority', one (later) judge held that it would seem that recognition by other international actors is never a prerequisite for the possession of international legal personality: 'If the attributes are there, personality exists. It is not a matter of recognition. It is a matter of objective reality'.[17] The practice of dealing with third states may be the proof of an (implicit) attribution of international competences by the member states, rather than the source of legal personality. On the other hand, the practical value of capacities on the international plane can only be established in case third states are willing to enter

---

[15] See the *WHO-Egypt* case (n. 1), at 90: '[I]nternational Organisations are subjects of international law and, as such, are bound by any obligations incumbent upon the under general rules of international law.'

[16] M. Rama-Montaldo, 'International Legal Personality and Implied Powers of International Organizations', (1970) 44 *British Yearbook of International Law* 111, 126. *Reparation* was not the first reference to implied powers. See *Interpretation of the Greco-Turkish Agreement of 1 December 1926*, Advisory Opinion, [1928] Publ. PCIJ, Series B, no. 16.

[17] R. Higgins, *Problems & Process: International Law and How We Use It* (Oxford, Clarendon Press 1994) p. 48.

into a legal relation with the international entity at stake—underlining the clear political dimension of all this.

The conclusion may be that—apart from cases where the separate legal personality of organs of international organizations is being discussed—the question of legal personality has perhaps come quite close to the question of whether an international entity could be regarded as an international organization. In fact, in the *Reparation* case, the International Court of Justice seemed to have followed the same line of reasoning. It based its conclusions on a number of criteria, which were regrouped by Amerasinghe[18] in a helpful way:

1. The entity must be an association of states or international organisations or both (a) with lawful objects and (b) with one or more organs which are only subject to the authority of the participants in those organs acting jointly. Brownlie[19] pointed to the additional requirement that the association needs to be 'permanent'.

2. There must exist a distinction between the organization and its members in respect of legal rights, duties, powers, and liabilities, etc. on the international plane as contrasted with the municipal or transnational plane, it being clear that the organisation was 'intended' to have such rights, duties, power and liabilities.

Indeed, sixty-five years after *Reparation for Injuries*, not only the question of the international legal personality of the UN, but of international organizations in general may seem outdated. At the same time, the acceptance of legal personality as a key element of the separate legal position of an international organization, both vis-à-vis its own members as well as towards non-members and individuals has never been more important, as for instance reflected in debates on the accountability and responsibility of international organizations, on the legislative functions of international organizations and on their role in global governance in general.

---

[18] C. F. Amerasinghe, *Principles of the Institutional Law of International Organizations* (2nd edn, New York, Cambridge University Press 2005), p. 83.

[19] I. Brownlie, *Principles of Public International Law* (4th edn, Oxford, Clarendon Press 1990), p. 681.

1.2 Case 22/70, *Commission v Council* (*European Road Transport Agreement*), Court of Justice of the EC, [1971] ECR 263

Jan Klabbers

Relevance of the case

It is difficult to overstate the relevance of the *ERTA* case for the development of the EU. If *Van Gend & Loos* established that the EU was a new legal order whose acts could be directly effective in its member states, and *Costa v ENEL* established the supremacy of EU law over the law of the member states, *ERTA* marked the beginning of the EU's role in global affairs by creating an almost unlimited power for the EU to act externally, regardless of the silence of the treaties in this matter, and often pre-empting the member states from taking individual action. Thus, *ERTA* (often referred to under its French acronym *AETR*) is generally considered as an essential component in the process of the development of the EU from intergovernmental organization to constitutional entity, and justifiably so.[1]

I. Facts

After attempts in the early 1960s to create a pan-European regime (extending beyond the EU) relating to road transportation had come to naught, the issue was picked up again in 1967, sponsored by the UN Economic Commission for Europe. In the meantime, the EU had adopted internal legislation on road transportation. After the Council had reached an agreement in March 1970 as to how the (then six) member states should behave in connection with the conclusion of the agreement, the Commission started proceedings against the Council, aiming to get the relevant Council proceedings annulled. In the Commission's view, the power to conclude an agreement such as ERTA had come to rest exclusively with the EU: art. 75 of the EEC Treaty (as it then was) created a general transport power for the EU and had to be read so as to also encompass treaty-making powers in the field of transport. Hence, there would be no independent treaty-making power left for the member states, contrary to what the Council assumed when it adopted its proceedings in March 1970. The Council, on the other hand, claimed that the EU could only act on the basis of powers conferred upon it, and since the treaties contained no express provision on external transport policy, the matter was rightly left to the member states, acting on instructions from the Council.

[1] Seminal is E. Stein, 'Lawyers, Judges, and the Making of a Transnational Constitution', (1981) 75 *American Journal of International Law* 1–27.

II. Legal question

Quite a few issues were raised by the case, including the legal status of Council proceedings and the question of the EU's international legal personality. Technically, the legal question before the Court was whether or not the Council proceedings should be annulled, and the Court approached the matter in this way: as a request for annulment. It ended up dismissing the Commission's application and rejecting its submissions. The main question, however, boiled down to this: does the Treaty endow the EU with the power to engage in external relations, including treaty-making, in the field of transport? And if so, does it do so at the exclusion of the member states?

III. Excerpts

12 In the absence of specific provisions of the Treaty relating to the negotiation and conclusion of international agreements in the sphere of transport policy—a category into which, essentially, the AETR falls—one must turn to the general system of Community law in the sphere of relations with third countries.

13 Article 210 provides that 'The Community shall have legal personality'.

14 This provision, placed at the head of Part Six of the Treaty, devoted to 'General and Final Provisions', means that in its external relations the Community enjoys the capacity to establish contractual links with third countries over the whole field of objectives defined in Part One of the Treaty, which Part Six supplements.

15 To determine in a particular case the Community's authority to enter into international agreements, regard must be had to the whole scheme of the Treaty no less than to its substantive provisions.

16 Such authority arises not only from an express conferment by the Treaty—as is the case with Articles 113 and 114 for tariff and trade agreements and with Article 238 for association agreements—but may equally flow from other provisions of the Treaty and from measures adopted, within the framework of those provisions, by the Community institutions.

17 In particular, each time the Community, with a view to implementing a common policy envisaged by the Treaty, adopts provisions laying down common rules, whatever form these may take, the Member States no longer have the right, acting individually or even collectively, to undertake obligations with third countries which affect those rules.

18 As and when such common rules come into being, the Community alone is in a position to assume and carry out contractual obligations towards third countries affecting the whole sphere of application of the Community legal system.

19 With regard to the implementation of the provisions of the Treaty the system of internal Community measures may not therefore be separated from that of external relations.

20 Under Article 3 (e), the adoption of a common policy in the sphere of transport is specially mentioned amongst the objectives of the Community.

21 Under Article 5, the Member States are required on the one hand to take all appropriate measures to ensure fulfilment of the obligations arising out of the Treaty

or resulting from action taken by the institutions and, on the other, hand, to abstain from any measure which might jeopardize the attainment of the objectives of the Treaty.

22 If these two provisions are read in conjunction, it follows that to the extent to which Community rules are promulgated for the attainment of the objectives of the Treaty, the Member States cannot, outside the framework of the Community institutions, assume obligations which might affect those rules or alter their scope.

23 According to Article 74, the objectives of the Treaty in matters of transport are to be pursued within the framework of a common policy.

24 With this in view, Article 75 (1) directs the Council to lay down common rules and, in addition, 'any other appropriate provisions'.

25 By the terms of subparagraph (a) of the same provision, those common rules are applicable 'to international transport to or from the territory of a Member State or passing across the territory of one or more Member States'.

26 This provision is equally concerned with transport from or to third countries, as regards that part of the journey which takes place on Community territory.

27 It thus assumes that the powers of the Community extend to relationships arising from international law, and hence involve the need in the sphere in question for agreements with the third countries concerned.

28 Although it is true that Articles 74 and 75 do not expressly confer on the Community authority to enter into international agreements, nevertheless the bringing into force, on 25 March 1969, of Regulation No 543/69 of the Council on the harmonization of certain social legislation relating to road transport (OJ L 77, p. 49) necessarily vested in the Community power to enter into any agreements with third countries relating to the subject-matter governed by that regulation.

29 This grant of power is moreover expressly recognized by Article 3 of the said regulation which prescribes that: 'The Community shall enter into any negotiations with third countries which may prove necessary for the purpose of implementing this regulation'.

30 Since the subject-matter of the AETR falls within the scope of Regulation No 543/69, the Community has been empowered to negotiate and conclude the agreement in question since the entry into force of the said regulation.

31 These Community powers exclude the possibility of concurrent powers on the part of Member States, since any steps taken outside the framework of the Community institutions would be incompatible with the unity of the Common Market and the uniform application of Community law.

[...]

69 The Commission claims that in view of the powers vested in the Community under Article 75, the AETR should have been negotiated and concluded by the Community in accordance with the Community procedure defined by Article 228 (1).

70 Although the Council may, by virtue of these provisions, decide in each case whether it is expedient to enter into an agreement with third countries, it does not enjoy a discretion to decide whether to proceed through intergovernmental or Community channels.

71 By deciding to proceed through inter-governmental channels it made it impossible for the Commission to perform the task which the Treaty entrusted to it in the sphere of negotiations with third countries.

72 In the absence of specific provisions in the Treaty applicable to the negotiation and implementation of the agreement under discussion, the appropriate rules must be inferred from the general tenor of those articles of the Treaty which relate to the negotiations undertaken on the AETR.

73 The distribution of powers between the Community institutions to negotiate and implement the AETR must be determined with due regard both to the provisions relating to the common transport policy and to those governing the conclusion of agreements by the Community.

74 By the terms of Article 75 (1), it is a matter for the Council, acting on a proposal from the Commission and after consulting the Economic and Social Committee and the Assembly, to lay down the appropriate provisions, whether by regulation or otherwise, for the purpose of implementing the common transport policy.

75 According to Article 228 (1), where agreements have to be concluded with one or more third countries or an international organization, such agreements are to be negotiated by the Commission and concluded by the Council, subject to any more extensive powers which may have been vested in the Commission.

76 As a subsidiary point, since the negotiations took place under the auspices of the United Nations Economic Commission for Europe, the first paragraph of Article 116 has also to be taken into account. By the terms of that paragraph, from the end of the transitional period onwards, Member States shall 'proceed within the framework of international organizations of an economic character only by common action', the implementation of such common action being within the powers of the Council, basing its decisions on proposals submitted by the Commission.

77 If these various provisions are read in conjunction, it is clear that wherever a matter forms the subject of a common policy, the Member States are bound in every case to act jointly in defence of the interests of the Community.

78 This requirement of joint action was in fact respected by the proceedings of 20 March 1970, which cannot give rise to any criticism in this respect.

79 Moreover, it follows from these provisions taken as a whole, and particularly from Article 228 (1), that the right to conclude the agreement was vested in the Council.

80 The Commission for its part was required to act in two ways, first by exercising its right to make proposals, which arises from Article 75 (1) and the first paragraph of Article 116, and, secondly, in its capacity as negotiator by the terms of the first subparagraph of Article 228 (1).

81 However, this distribution of powers between institutions would only have been required where negotiations were undertaken at a time when the vesting of powers in the Community had taken effect, either by virtue of the Treaty itself or by virtue of measures taken by the institutions.

82 In this connexion it must be borne in mind that an earlier version of the AETR had been drawn up in 1962, at a period when, because the common transport policy was not yet sufficiently developed, power to conclude this agreement was vested in the Member States.

83 The stage of negotiations of which the proceedings in question formed part was not aimed at working out a new agreement, but simply at introducing into the version drawn up in 1962 such modifications as were necessary to enable all the contracting parties to ratify it.

84 The negotiations on the AETR are thus characterized by the fact that their origin and a considerable part of the work carried out under the auspices of the Economic Commission for Europe took place before powers were conferred on the Community as a result of Regulation No 543/69.

85 It appears therefore that on 20 March 1970 the Council acted in a situation where it no longer enjoyed complete freedom of action in its relations with the third countries taking part in the same negotiations.

86 At that stage of the negotiations, to have suggested to the third countries concerned that there was now a new distribution of powers within the Community might well have jeopardized the successful outcome of the negotiations, as was indeed recognized by the Commission's representative in the course of the Council's deliberations.

87 In such a situation it was for the two institutions whose powers were directly concerned, namely, the Council and the Commission, to reach agreement, in accordance with Article 15 of the Treaty of April 1965 establishing a Single Council and a Single Commission of the European Communities, on the appropriate methods of cooperation with a view to ensuring most effectively the defence of the interests of the Community.

88 It is clear from the minutes of the meeting of 20 March 1970 that the Commission made no formal use of the right to submit proposals open to it under Articles 75 and 116.

89 Nor did it demand the simple application of Article 228 (1) in regard to its right of negotiation.

90 It may therefore be accepted that, in carrying on the negotiations and concluding the agreement simultaneously in the manner decided on by the Council, the Member States acted, and continue to act, in the interest and on behalf of the Community in accordance with their obligations under Article 5 of the Treaty.

91 Hence, in deciding in these circumstances on joint action by the Member States, the Council has not failed in its obligations arising from Articles 75 and 228.

92 For these reasons, the submission must be rejected.

IV. Commentary

ERTA is a strange and puzzling decision,[2] for a variety of reasons. There is, first, the technical point: the Court dismissed all the Commission's submissions, finding in the end that no violation of art. 75 by the Council had occurred. Yet, this is not why the case is so often invoked, discussed, and analyzed. Instead, people refer to *ERTA* as support for the proposition that the EU has certain external powers granted by implication which, curiously enough, would seem to suggest that the Council actually did do something contrary to art. 75 when it adopted its proceedings in March 1970.

This seeming contradiction is solved by the court in twofold fashion. First, it stipulates that art. 75 still leaves a considerable role for the Council, albeit not for the

---

[2] See for example the critical comments by P. Koutrakos, *EU International Relations Law* (Oxford, Hart 2006) pp. 77–88.

individual member states. The point is made with great subtlety, but is really vital: the Court distinguishes the Council from its members (the member states). The member states cannot act individually any more, but the Council can. To the extent that the Council took a decision (instructing the member states how to act), it had done nothing wrong. Second, to quell all remaining doubts, the Court introduces a temporal element: when the ERTA negotiations first started, in the early 1960s, the matter clearly fell within the Council's jurisdiction. The later negotiations were presented as continuations of those earlier ones (paras 82–5); therefore there was no new agreement, and therefore all that had happened was that in the meantime the Council's freedom had been hemmed in by means of internal legislation (Regulation No 543/69). This was, in a sense, dictated by circumstances: it would have been awkward, to say the least, to present the prospective treaty partners with the situation in which their negotiating partners (the Six) had all been replaced by the EU.[3]

Indeed, as a matter of fact, the Court could have stopped at Regulation No 543/69. In the case at hand, a regulation had been adopted which gave the EU the power to conclude transport agreements with third states—end of story. The Court, however, must have sensed that the issue was of greater relevance than the mere circumstance of a road transport agreement, and must have felt the need to make a statement of principle about the powers of the EU.[4] Moreover, stopping at Regulation No 543/69 would have been difficult to reconcile with the idea that the Council had gradually lost some of its powers; it would have suggested that after 1969, the Council actually had done something wrong, and this was a conclusion the Court wanted to avoid.

Hence, the Court needed to express itself in more general terms, and could not base its position on a transport regulation alone. And thus the Court set out to launch its own version of the implied powers doctrine.

The implied powers doctrine has been recognized as being of relevance to international organizations since the Permanent Court of International Justice (PCIJ) first made reference to it in the 1920s, in a case involving the exchange of Greek and Turkish populations.[5] In this early decision, the PCIJ opted for a narrow approach to implied powers: an implied power, so it suggested, is a power that is necessary to give effect to an expressly granted power. Simply put: the power to take the dog for a walk would necessarily have to include the power to put the dog on a leash, since otherwise the power to walk the dog could not be realized. In this limited version, the implied powers doctrine is beyond controversy, and has a long pedigree in federal thought.

Two decades later, the ICJ greatly expanded the scope of the implied powers doctrine by suggesting that powers can be implied not only if needed to give effect to express powers, but can also be implied if needed to secure the functioning of the

---

[3] The point is well made by P.J. Kuijper, 'Raad/Commissie (AETR)', in T.W.B. Beukers, H.J. van Harten, and S. Prechal (eds), *Het recht van de Europese Unie in 50 klassieke arresten* (The Hague, Boom 2010), pp. 44–51, at 48, note 16.

[4] Few provisions in secondary legislation could be expected to be as to-the-point as art. 3 of Reg. No. 543/69. As much is suggested by A.G. Dutheillet de Lamothe, at 291.

[5] *Interpretation of the Greco-Turkish Agreement of 1 December 1926*, Advisory Opinion, [1928] Publ. PCIJ, Series B, no. 16. See generally J. Klabbers, *An Introduction to International Organizations Law* (2nd edn, Cambridge, Cambridge University Press 2015), p. 57.

organization.[6] In *Reparation for Injuries*, it felt that the UN had the power to bring a claim on behalf of its employees because otherwise the UN would not be able to function properly. Apart from the hyperbole involved in the finding (surely the UN can achieve a lot even without being allowed to act on behalf of its employees), this was a considerable stretching of the notion, way beyond the PCIJ's version of the doctrine. Accordingly, it came with a word of warning from one of its dissenting judges (not coincidentally perhaps the US judge on the bench, who had been steeped in federal thought during his forty years in the US administration): too broad a notion of the implied powers may be unjustifiable, and may result in the organization losing legitimacy in the eyes of its member states.[7]

In *ERTA*, the CJEU devised yet another version, arguably even more far-reaching than the *Reparation* version: it held that the EU's power to conclude external agreement was implied because it was necessary not so much to allow the EU to function properly, but in order to safeguard 'the unity of the Common Market and the uniform application of Community law' (para. 31).

In order to reach this conclusion, the Court took five distinct but related steps. First, it observed that the treaties were silent on the role of the EU in the conclusion of agreements on transport policy with third states. Since the treaties were silent, it was imperative to look at the general system of the EU's law on external relations (para. 12).

Second, the Court started by assigning international legal personality to what was at the time still the EEC. This, so the Court claimed, followed from the terse statement in what was then art. 210 EEC, according to which the 'Community shall have legal personality'. It followed from this personality that the EU would have the general capacity to conclude treaties (paras 13–14). Curiously though, any type of argument is missing: there is no reference to any concept of legal personality under international law, or how international legal personality is usually created or established. Much less is there any discussion about the circumstance that art. 211 further specifies the scope of the EU's personality under the laws of its member states, and thus art. 210 could just as easily have been interpreted as a general grant of domestic (as opposed to international) legal personality.[8]

Having just established that the EU has international legal personality and thus also a general treaty-making capacity under international law, the Court's third step, in para. 15, is to lay down a method for determining whether a specific treaty-making power has been granted. This, so the Court holds, depends on the entire scheme of the Treaty as well as on its substantive provisions.

This paved the way for its fourth step: internal EU measures cannot be separated from external action (para. 19). Whatever the EU can do internally, it can also do externally: *in foro interno, in foro externo*, as it is sometimes put.

---

[6] *Reparation for Injuries Suffered in the Service of the United Nations*, [1949] ICJ Rep 174. See generally also J. Klabbers, *An Introduction* (n. 5), 56–63.

[7] See *Reparation* (n. 6), per Hackworth J., at 198.

[8] See similarly F.G. Jacobs, 'Direct Effect and Interpretation of International Agreements in the Recent Case Law of the European Court of Justice', in A. Dashwood and M. Maresceau (eds), *Law and Practice of EU External Relations: Salient Features of a Changing Landscape* (Cambridge, Cambridge University Press 2008), pp. 13–33, at 13 (noting that art. 210 EEC was concerned with domestic personality, and that it 'would have been uncharacteristically presumptuous of the Treaty to purport to confer international legal personality on the Community'.)

And if this was not yet enough, any remaining gaps in the argument would be closed with the help of the fifth step. The Court invoked the EU's very own *deus ex machina*, the principle of fidelity (*Gemeinschaftstreue*), at the time laid down in art. 5 EEC: the member states must abstain from any measure which might jeopardize the attainment of the EU's objectives. These five steps together inexorably lead to the conclusion that the EU has an implied power to conclude agreements in the field of transport and, what is more, the member states are pre-empted from acting: not only had they transferred a legislative internal power to the EU, this also affected their external prerogatives. And even if this were too radical an interpretation of the treaties, there was always art. 5 to fall back on: any individual member state action would necessarily run afoul of the principle of fidelity.

Viewing the case from the perspective that *ERTA* was meant to safeguard EU law rather than be 'merely' concerned with the division of powers between the EU and its member states also helps to make sense of the otherwise curious circumstance that the Court did not resort to the general 'additional power' clause of what was art. 235 EEC: if necessary for the attainment of the objectives of the EU, the Council can unanimously agree on new powers. This was the designated route for the creation of powers additional to those already created in the treaties, and was the preferred solution in the eyes of Advocate-General Dutheillet de Lamothe: if the EU wants to conclude external transport agreements, it can do so on the basis of art. 235 EEC.[9] The fact that the Court paid little attention to this possibility suggests that at its heart *ERTA* is not so much about a conflict concerning powers, but a conflict concerning the integrity and unity of EU law—and for this art. 235 offers no solace.

Given that *ERTA* marks the emergence of the EU as a player on the international scene, and given its tacit reliance on general concepts of international law, it is astonishing that the entire judgment makes no reference to international law whatsoever. There is no discussion of what international legal personality means in international law: whether it can indeed be derived from a terse and not very explicit treaty provision, or whether it can indeed serve, as the Court seems to suggest, as a threshold condition for legal capacity under international law. It is not even the case that there is a flawed discussion—there is no discussion whatsoever. Likewise, despite its pedigree in international law, there is no discussion of the implied powers doctrine as established by the PCIJ or developed by the ICJ; there is, indeed, nothing about the very notion of powers of international organizations. All this signifies, it would seem, a reluctance on the part of the EU to be seen as somehow being captured by international law: if *Van Gend & Loos* rubber-stamped the existence of a new legal order, then *ERTA* continues it: the EU is neither international organization nor state and, importantly, therewith also not directly subjected to international law. The EU has always been happiest straddling this fence: it is neither a classic international organization nor a state. It is not a regular creature of international law, and can thus pick and choose its own preferred elements of international law.[10]

---

[9] See *ERTA*, per AG Dutheillet de Lamothe, at 293: 'Article 235 exists precisely to vest in the Community whatever powers it may need.' Article 235 EEC is currently art. 352 TFEU.

[10] See generally J. Klabbers, 'Straddling the Fence: The EU and International Law', in A. Arnull and D. Chalmers (eds), *Oxford Handbook of EU Law* (Oxford, Oxford University Press, 2015) pp. 52–71.

The *ERTA* decision has proved to be immensely influential, in two ways. One, it is still seen as the basis for well-nigh the entire external relations edifice of the EU: *ERTA* solved (if that is the word to use) most relevant legal issues simply by proclaiming that when in doubt, powers accrue to the EU. Second, there is what may be referred to as the spirit (not to say ghost) of *ERTA*: *ERTA* pioneered the use of the principle of fidelity, and it is this principle that has come to play an influential role also in cases not involving strict delimitations of competences. Thus, in the *Open Skies* cases, addressing powers in the field of air transport agreements with third states, the Court consistently upheld the position that even if it would be difficult to ascribe powers to the EU, the exercise of powers by member states would be irreconcilable with the principle of fidelity. Likewise, in cases involving investment treaties concluded by member states, even a merely potential, hypothetical disharmony between such treaties and EU law would mean that the member states act in violation of the principle of fidelity.

In the end, the Court skillfully found a middle ground between international law and domestic law by, essentially, ignoring both. The judgment has a high Münchhausen content: the Court creates the edifice of EU law by pulling itself up by its own bootstraps. Put differently, the EU has implied powers in the field of external relations under EU law because otherwise EU law could not be EU law. There is no explicit attempt to connect the implied powers doctrine to its counterpart in international law; nor is there any explicit attempt to justify it, or the concomitant idea of pre-emption, in terms of domestic (federal) thought.[11]

In later cases and opinions, the Court has time and again fallen back on its *ERTA* doctrine; it is still considered the basis of the EU's external implied powers. The EU's political taskmasters have attempted to codify the doctrine in Lisbon, but have done so in a less than fully systematic manner. Article 3 TFEU and art. 216 TFEU both refer, albeit in slightly different terms, to the exclusive treaty-making competences of the EU. Article 216 specifies that these may be explicitly mentioned in the treaties, something art. 3 omits. Both articles suggests that exclusive treaty-making competences can be derived from internal legislation or the necessity to exercise an internal competence, or when the conclusion of an external agreement by the EU can come to affect EU law (art. 3(2) TFEU). This latter point is unfortunate, in that it departs from the *ERTA* situation: in *ERTA*, the prospect of affecting EU law came from treaties concluded by member states, not by the EU itself.

In international law terms, *ERTA* has been less influential: its peculiar rendition of the implied powers doctrine has not been much followed in other international organizations, and understandably so: the decision is premised on the unique nature of EU law, and its logic can thus not easily be transplanted to different settings.[12] This however takes nothing away from its constitutional significance in the development of EU law.

---

[11] Kuijper suggests that the Court follows the ICJ's methodology in *Reparation for Injuries* to a large extent and borrowed the idea of pre-emption from federal thought, but acknowledges with respect to the former that there is no explicit reference. See P.J. Kuijper, 'Raad/Commissie (AETR)' (n. 3), at 45.

[12] See for example V. Engström, *Constructing the Powers of International Institutions* (Leiden, Martinus Nijhoff 2012), who discusses *ERTA* but, justifiably, does not pay it a huge amount of attention.

1.3 *Maclaine Watson & Co. Ltd v International Tin Council,* 26 October 1989, United Kingdom House of Lords, 81 ILR 670

Paolo Palchetti

Relevance of the case

The present case is one of the first in which a court was squarely confronted with the problem of determining whether the separate legal personality of an international organization is consistent with the possibility of members being held responsible for the conduct of the organization. The House of Lords denied that, as a general rule, members are responsible, concurrently and subsidiarily, for the wrongful conduct of the organization. Its judgment showed the uncertainties surrounding this legal question and marked the beginning of an intense debate which is still ongoing.

I. The facts of the case

The International Tin Council was an international organization established, at the relevant time, under the 1981 Sixth International Tin Agreement. The members comprised twenty-three states and the European Economic Community. The purpose of the organization was to provide for adjustment between world production and consumption of tin and to prevent excessive fluctuations in the price of tin. To this end, the ITC managed a buffer stock.

In 1985 the supported price of tin collapsed and the Tin Council suspended its activities, owing debts estimated at several million Pounds Sterling. Since the organization was insolvent, creditors initiated proceedings against the members in domestic courts of different states and before the European Court of Justice.

Among the several proceedings instituted before UK courts, the two most interesting cases brought against the members were initially decided, respectively on 24 June 1987 and on 29 July 1987, by the Commercial Court (*JH Rayner [Mincing Lane] Ltd v Department of Trade and Industry and Others*) and by the High Court, Chancery Division (*Maclaine Watson & Co Ltd v Department of Trade and Industry*). All claims were struck out. In its judgment of 27 April 1988 the Court of Appeal, in a non-unanimous decision, dismissed the appeals.

Before the House of Lords the plaintiffs advanced various alternative submissions. Under the first submission they argued that the Tin Council did not have separate legal personality under English law and that therefore the contracts concluded by the organization were to be considered as contracts concluded jointly by all members of the organization. Secondly, even if the organization possessed separate legal personality, the members were to be regarded as responsible, concurrently or subsidiarily, for the debt incurred by the organization. Thirdly, it was argued that the International Tin Council had acted as an agent of its members. The last submission related to the receivership action, by which the creditor aimed at enforcing the claims of the International Tin Council against its members.

II. The legal question

The case raises two distinct, albeit interrelated, questions. The first one concerns the nature of the legal personality enjoyed by the International Tin Council before UK courts. The problem is whether the effects stemming from the possession of a separate legal personality is to be assessed by reference to international law or by reference to the domestic law of the forum state. Article 16 of the Sixth International Tin Agreement provided that the Council 'shall have legal personality'. On the other hand, the 1972 International Tin Council (Immunities and Privileges) Order, a domestic act which gave effect in English law to the International Tin Council-United Kingdom Headquarters Agreement, established that the Council was to have 'the legal capacities of a body corporate'. Confronted with two distinct sets of rules, both substantially recognizing that the Council possessed separate legal personality, the House of Lords was called upon to decide whether the nature of such personality had to be determined by reference to international law, as claimed by the plaintiffs, or whether the legal effects of the personality had rather to be assessed in the light of UK law.

The other legal question relates to the international responsibility of the members for the conduct of the organization. In fact, this is the question to which the judgment of the House of Lords is usually associated, although, admittedly, it was only slightly addressed by the UK court. Since the Council had no assets from which the creditors could seek recovery on their claims, proceedings were instituted against the members for the debts incurred by the organization. The question was therefore relatively straightforward: can states or international organizations, under international law, be held responsible, concurrently or subsidiarily, for the obligations of the organization of which they are members?

III. Excerpts

Lord Templeman[…]

The appellants submitted that if Parliament had intended to do more than endow 23 sovereign states and the E.E.C. trading in this country with a collective name, then Parliament would have created the I.T.C. a body corporate. But the Government of the United Kingdom had by treaty concurred in the establishment of the I.T.C. as an international organisation. Consistently with the treaty, the United Kingdom could not convert the I.T.C. into an United Kingdom organisation. In order to clothe the I.T.C. in the United Kingdom with legal personality in accordance with the treaty, Parliament conferred on the I.T.C. the legal capacities of a body corporate. The courts of the United Kingdom became bound by the Order of 1972 to treat the activities of the I.T.C. as if those activities had been carried out by the I.T.C. as a body incorporated under the laws of the United Kingdom. The Order of 1972 is inconsistent with any intention on the part of Parliament to oblige or allow the courts of the United Kingdom to consider the nature of an international organisation. The Order of 1972 is inconsistent with any intention on the part of Parliament that creditors and courts should regard the I.T.C. as a partnership between 23 sovereign states and the E.E.C. trading in the United Kingdom like any private partnership. The Order of 1972 is inconsistent with any intention on the part of Parliament that contracts made by the I.T.C. with metal brokers, bankers, staff, landlords, suppliers of goods and services and others, shall be treated by those creditors or by the courts of the United Kingdom as contracts entered into by 23 sovereign states and the E.E.C. The Order of 1972 conferred on the I.T.C. the legal capacities of a body corporate. Those capacities include the power to contract. The I.T.C. entered into contracts with the appellants.[…]

The third argument described as submission B(2) is that a rule of international law imposes on sovereign states, members of an international organisation, joint and several liability for the default of the organisation in the payment of its debts unless the treaty which establishes the international organisation clearly disclaims any liability on the part of the members. No plausible evidence was produced of the existence of such a rule of international law before or at the time of I.T.A.6 in 1982 or thereafter. The appellants submitted that this House was bound to accept or reject such a rule of international law and should not shrink from inventing such a law and from publishing a precedent which might persuade other states to accept such law.

My Lords, if there existed a rule of international law which implied in a treaty or imposed on sovereign states which enter into a treaty an obligation (in default of a clear disclaimer in the treaty) to discharge the debts of an international organisation established by that treaty, the rule of international law could only be enforced under international law. Treaty rights and obligations conferred or imposed by agreement or by international law cannot be enforced by the courts of the United Kingdom. The appellants concede that the alleged rule of international law must imply and include a right of contribution whereby if one member state discharged the debts of the I.T.C., the other member states would be bound to share the burden. The appellants acknowledge that such right of contribution could only be enforced under international law and could not be made the subject of an order by the courts of the United Kingdom. This acknowledgment is inconsistent with the appellants' submission B(2). An international law or a domestic law which imposed and enforced joint and several liability on 23 sovereign states without imposing and enforcing contribution between those states would be devoid of logic and justice.

Lord Griffiths[…]

I can only hope that the assurance given on behalf of the Government in 1944 still holds true because it seems to me that the obvious just solution is that the governments that contributed to the buffer stock should provide it with funds to settle its debts in the same proportion that they contributed to the buffer stock. But this end must be pursued through diplomacy and an international solution must be found to an international problem; it can not be solved through English domestic law.

Lord Oliver of Aylmerton[…]

Whilst it is, of course, not inaccurate to describe article 4 of the Order as one which 'recognises' the I.T.C. as an international organisation, such 'recognition' is of no consequence in domestic law unless and until it is accompanied by the creation of a legal persona. Without the Order in Council the I.T.C. had no legal existence in the law of the United Kingdom and no significance save as the name of an international body created by a treaty between sovereign states which was not justiciable by municipal courts. What brought it into being in English law was the Order in Council and it is the Order in Council, a purely domestic measure, in which the constitution of the legal persona is to be found and in which there has to be sought the liability of the members which the appellants seek to establish, for that is the act of the I.T.C.'s creation in the United Kingdom.[...]

It is contended that there is a rule of international law that where sovereign states by treaty bring into being an international organisation which is intended to engage in commercial transactions, the member states are liable, secondarily, for the organisation's debts to third parties (whether states or individuals) unless (a) the treaty expressly excludes such liability and (b) the exclusion is brought to the notice of third parties. Now assuming that such a rule could be established, I can see that it might be said that it forms part of English law and that reference to the treaty would not be precluded by the non-justiciability rule inasmuch as such reference would be solely for the purpose of seeing whether it contained an express exclusion of liability and thus of determining whether the rule—on this hypothesis now part of domestic law—applies. Such an argument cannot run, nor indeed has it, I think, been advanced in precisely these terms. If such a rule exists, it is at highest a rule of construction, and however the matter is looked at, the question of liability or no liability stems from an unincorporated treaty which, without legislation, can neither create nor destroy rights under domestic law.

I accordingly concur in the reasoning of Ralph Gibson L.J. and would hold that submission B(2) falls at the first hurdle. But even if this were wrong, I am clearly of opinion that the majority of the Court of Appeal were right to reject it for the other reasons which they gave.

First and foremost, the 'authorities' to which your Lordships were referred, which consisted in the main of an immense body of writings of distinguished international jurists, totally failed to establish any generally accepted rule of the nature contended for. Such writings as tended to support the supposed rule were in publications taking place since the affairs of the I.T.C. came before the courts in 1986 and express simply the views of particular jurists about what rule of international law ought to be accepted. They were, in any event, unclear as to whether the liability suggested was primary or secondary, whether it was joint or several, and whether it was to be contributed to equally or in some other proportions. It was indeed submitted that it was not only open to your Lordships but was your Lordships' duty to decide these points as, indeed, Nourse L.J. had opined in the Court of Appeal. For my part, I cannot accept this. A rule of international law becomes a rule—whether accepted into domestic law or not—only when it is certain and is accepted generally by the body of civilised nations; and it is for those who assert the rule to demonstrate it, if necessary before the International Court of Justice. It is certainly not for a domestic tribunal in effect to legislate a rule into existence for the purposes of domestic law and on the basis of material that is wholly indeterminate.

In an endeavour to establish acceptance of the supposed rule, attention was drawn to some 16 treaties establishing international organisations which contained provisions expressly excluding liability on the part of the members, but there was a very large number of similar treaties which did not and the Court of Appeal found it impossible to make any useful deduction from them. So do I. Equally—although for the reasons given I do not think that the question arises—I have been unable to accept the suggestion that there can be found in the terms of the treaty itself indications of an intention that the member states should assume liability for the I.T.C. debts. Indeed, such indications as there are seem to me to point in the contrary direction and to indicate that any liability assumed was merely to the I.T.C. itself and existed only to the extent prescribed.[...]

I agree with Millett J. and with the Court of Appeal that, however the matter is approached, any claim of the I.T.C. against the member states for indemnity must ultimately rest upon I.T.A.6. This is an issue which is not justiciable by your Lordships and it is therefore unnecessary to decide whether, in any event, any such claim would also be precluded by [an] act of state non-justiciability. I would accordingly dismiss this appeal also.

IV. Commentary

Does the separate legal personality of an international organization preclude that the members can be held responsible, due to their membership, for the conduct of such an organization? When, in 1989, the House of Lords rendered its judgment in the present case, this question had already been addressed by other tribunals. In an interim award rendered in 1984, an arbitral tribunal had recognized that the four member states of the Arab Organization for Industrialization could incur responsibility for the acts of the organization—a decision which was reversed by Swiss courts a few years later.[1] However, perhaps because of the numbers of states involved and of the amount of debts incurred by the organization, the cases which originated from the failure of the International Tin Council contributed more than others to highlight the importance of the question concerning the responsibility of the members of an organization.

The possession of a separate legal personality is a necessary requirement for an international organization to be responsible for a wrongful act.[2] Absent a separate legal personality, the conduct of the organization is to be attributed to the members, which have to bear responsibility for it. On the other hand, the fact that an organization possesses legal personality is not incompatible, at least in principle, with the possibility that members are to be considered, simply because of their membership, concurrently or subsidiarily responsible for the acts of the organization.

The present case did not directly concern the question of whether members of an organization are responsible under international law. It related to the civil liability arising out of the non-fulfilment of obligations contracted by the International Tin Council with private parties under UK law. However, the fact that the claims directed against the organization or its members are made under the domestic law of a state does not imply that the question of the concurrent or subsidiary responsibility of

[1] For the interim award of the Arbitral Tribunal see *Westland Helicopters Ltd v Arab Organization for Industrialization, United Arab Emirates, Kingdom of Saudi Arabia, State of Qatar, Arab Republic of Egypt, and Arab British Helicopter Company,* Arbitration, 5 March 1984, 80 ILR 600. For the decision of the Swiss Federal Supreme Court, see *Arab Organization for Industrialization and others v Westland Helicopters Ltd,* Swiss Federal Supreme Court (First Civil Court), 19 July 1988, 80 ILR 652.

[2] See art. 2 of the Articles on the Responsibility of International Organizations (hereinafter ARIO). Report of the International Law Commission on the Work of its Sixty-Third Session, Official Record of the General Assembly, 66th Sess., Supp. 10 (A/66/10), 2011, p. 73.

the members must also be addressed as a matter of domestic law. Since this question relates to the status of an entity which was set up by an international instrument and which exists as a subject of international law, a better approach is to regard it as a matter to be governed by reference to international law.[3] This would also avoid that the question of the responsibility of the members of a given organization could receive different answers by domestic courts of different states.

Before the House of Lords the plaintiffs advocated the view that the responsibility of the members of the International Tin Council had to be assessed by reference to international law. However, the House of Lords took a strict dualist approach according to which the nature of the legal personality enjoyed by an international organization before UK courts was to be assessed by reference exclusively to domestic law. According to the House of Lords it was the 1972 International Tin Council (Immunities and Privileges) Order which, by conferring on the organization the capacities of a body corporate, 'created' the organization for the purposes of English law.[4] The non-justiciability principle also played a role for excluding the possibility of taking into account the nature of the International Tin Council under international law.[5]

The approach of the House of Lords on this point can be criticized for having introduced too rigid a distinction between the legal personality of the Tin Council under UK law and its personality under international law.[6] Such an approach might have been influenced by the fact that, under the UK legal order, international rules on the domestic legal personality of a given international organization are not given direct effect. The recognition of legal personality presupposes the adoption of a domestic act providing for such personality.[7] It might also be suggested that the House of Lords preferred to rely primarily on domestic law, rather than to refer to international law, because of the uncertainties as to the content of the international rule governing the question of the responsibility of the members of an organization. In this respect, it will be interesting to see whether, and to what extent, in future cases raising these type of issues, domestic courts will be willing to rely on the rules set forth in the ARIO adopted in 2011 by the International Law Commission. Significantly, some domestic courts have already referred to the ARIO, although, admittedly, not in relation to the question of the concurrent or subsidiary responsibility of the members.[8]

---

[3] See art. 4(b) of the 1995 Resolution of the Institut de droit international on 'The legal consequences for member states of the non-fulfilment by international organizations of their obligations toward third parties', Annuaire de l'Institut de Droit International, Session de Lisbonne Vol. 66-II, 1995, p. 447. See also P. Klein, *La responsabilité des organisations internationales* (Brussels, Bruylant 1999), p. 428, and C.F. Amerasinghe, *Principles of the Institutional Law of International Organizations* (2nd edn, Cambridge, Cambridge University Press 2005), p. 412.

[4] For this assessment, see the opinion of Lord Oliver of Aylmerton, 81 ILR, p. 708. See also the opinion of Lord Templeman, p. 678.

[5] See, in particular, the opinion of Lord Oliver of Aylmerton, ibid., p. 713.

[6] R. Higgins, *Problems and Process: International Law and How We Use It* (Oxford, Oxford University Press 1994), pp. 47–8.

[7] On the process through which legal personality of international organizations is recognized in the UK legal order and in the domestic legal orders of other states, see P. Klein and P. Sands, *Bowett's Law of International Institutions* (6th edn, London, Sweet & Maxwell 2009), p. 481ff.; A. Reinisch, *International Organizations before National Courts* (Cambridge, Cambridge University Press 2000), p. 49ff.

[8] See, for instance, the cases referred to in the Commentary to art. 7 ARIO, in Report of the International Law Commission on the Work of its Sixty-Third Session (n. 2), p. 92.

The approach taken by the House of Lords in analyzing the legal consequences attached to the separate personality of the International Tin Council explains why much of its reasoning focused exclusively on English law. It remains, however, that the judgment also contains several important references to international law aspects of the problem. Moreover, some of the arguments developed with regard to English law offer interesting elements if considered from the perspective of international law.

The main issue of international law raised by the plaintiffs, and addressed, albeit rapidly, by the judgment, concerned the existence of a rule of general international law according to which, in the absence of an express provision in the constitutive treaty excluding or limiting the responsibility of the members, they are responsible, jointly and severally, for the breach by the organization of its obligations to third parties. The evidence relied upon by the plaintiffs to support the existence of such a rule mainly consisted of the writings of jurists and the fact that a number of international treaties establishing international organizations contain clauses excluding or limiting the responsibility of the members. The House of Lords did not regard these elements as being sufficient to establish a general rule recognizing the responsibility of the members. This conclusion, in itself, is hardly objectionable. Indeed, it would be difficult not to agree with Lord Oliver's observations that the writings of distinguished international jurists, at the end, 'express simply the views of particular jurists about what rule of international law ought to be accepted', or that it is 'impossible to make any useful deduction' from treaty clauses expressly excluding liability on the part of the members.[9] While the House of Lords was right in stressing the lack of practice supporting the rule advocated by the plaintiffs, no elements were offered to prove the existence of the opposite rule, namely the rule excluding that members, solely by reasons of their membership, can be held responsible for the conduct of the organization. The House of Lords simply did not find it necessary to address this point. Since the two main points made in the judgment are, first, that the International Tin Council enjoyed separate legal personality under international law,[10] and secondly, that there is no general rule establishing the responsibility of the members, one is left with the impression that, according to the House of Lords, attribution of separate legal personality to the organization is decisive of the issue of the responsibility of the members. Be that as it may, the indication that one may safely infer from the judgment is that, as a general rule, when an international organization is recognized separate legal personality under international law, membership alone cannot entail for the members responsibility for the acts of the organization. This basic proposition was later assumed as the starting point in the works conducted on this matter by the Institut de droit international[11] and by the International Law Commission,[12] both referring to the judgment of the House of Lords as an important precedent.

---

[9] 81 ILM, p. 715.

[10] See, in particular, the observation of Lord Oliver of Aylmerton, 81 ILM, p. 703.

[11] See art. 6(a) of the 1995 Resolution of the Institut de droit international, *Annuaire de l'Institut de Droit International*, Session de Lisbonne Vol. 66-II, 1995, p. 449.

[12] The ARIO do not include a residual rule on the non-responsibility of the members for acts of the organization. However, as the Commentary makes clear, 'such a rule is clearly implied. Therefore, membership does not as such entail for member States international responsibility when the organization commits an internationally wrongful act'. Report of the International Law Commission on the Work of its Sixty-Third

The fact that membership alone does not entail responsibility of the members for the acts of the organization does not rule out the possibility that members accept to bear such responsibility. Lord Oliver admitted this possibility, although he was 'unable to accept the suggestion that there can be found in the terms of the treaty itself indications of an intention that the member states should assume liability for the I.T.C. debts'.[13] While in the present case the only form of acceptance which was contemplated by the plaintiffs and by the judges was an acceptance which resulted from the terms of the treaty establishing the organization, acceptance may also be expressed in other ways. As the International Law Commission put it, 'acceptance may be expressly stated or implied and may occur either before or after the time when responsibility arises for the organization'.[14] Moreover, the fact that the constitutive instrument contains a clause providing for the responsibility of the members does not necessarily imply that members have accepted to bear responsibility in relation to third parties. Such clauses may well have been intended as producing effects only towards the organization. This point was rightly stressed by Lord Oliver when he observed that, under the treaty provisions referred to by the plaintiffs, 'any liability assumed was merely to the I.T.C. itself and existed only to the extent prescribed'.[15]

According to one of the arguments advanced by the plaintiffs, the members of the Tin Council were to bear responsibility for the debts incurred by the organization because the latter, when contracting with third parties, had acted as agent for its members.[16] While this argument, as well as the House of Lords' assessment of it, was entirely based on English law, one aspect deserves to be mentioned because it raises an interesting issue when considered from the perspective of international law. In order to demonstrate the existence of a principal-agent relationship, plaintiffs relied on the way in which the International Tin Council conducted its operations under its constitutive treaty, stressing that the organization operated under the 'immediate direction' of its members.[17] From the viewpoint of international law, direction and control over a specific conduct of the organization could give rise to the responsibility of the members if that conduct amounts to a breach of an obligation also incumbent on them.[18] However, the situation envisaged by the plaintiffs' argument is one in which direction and control over the conduct of the organization result from acts taken within the framework of the organization and in accordance with the rules governing its management. It seems extremely unlikely that participation in the decision-making process of the organization could constitute a form of direction and control in the commission of a wrongful conduct by the organization. The ARIO specify that,

---

Session (n. 2), p. 164. For the opposite view, see I. Brownlie, 'The Responsibility of States for the Acts of International Organizations', in M. Ragazzi (ed.), *International Responsibility Today. Essays in Memory of Oscar Schachter* (Brill 2005), pp. 355–62.

[13] 81 ILM, p. 715.

[14] Report of the International Law Commission on the Work of its Sixty-Third Session (n. 2), p. 164.

[15] 81 ILM, p. 715.

[16] For an analysis of agency as a ground for attributing responsibility on members, see C.F. Amerasinghe, *Principles of the Institutional Law of International Organizations* (2nd edn, Cambridge, Cambridge University Press 2005), p. 419.

[17] 81 ILM, p. 717.   [18] See art. 59 ARIO (n. 2).

as a general rule, '[a]n act by a State member of an international organization done in accordance with the rules of the organization does not as such engage the international responsibility of that State under the terms of this article'.[19] This situation must be distinguished from the one in which a state is responsible for its own conduct taken in the framework of an international organization. As the International Court of Justice has recently recognized in its judgment in the *Application of the Interim Accord of 13 September 1995* case, the conduct of a state representative participating in the decision-making process of an organization is to be attributed to the state and, if it is contrary to an international obligation of that state, it gives rise to its international responsibility.[20]

A last point worth mentioning concerns the right of an international organization to be indemnified by its members for the debts incurred by it against third parties. In the present case one of the appellants sought the appointment of a receiver in order to receive and enforce the right vested in the International Tin Council to be indemnified by its members. Seen from an international law perspective, this raises the question of the obligation of members to assist the organization in discharging its duties to make reparation in cases when it incurs in international responsibility. Lord Griffiths appeared to allude to that obligation when he observed that 'it seems to me that the obvious just solution is that the governments that contributed to the buffer stock should provide it with funds to settle its debts in the same proportion that they contributed to the buffer stock'.[21] There is little doubt that in most cases one can infer from the rules of the organization an obligation of members to provide the organization with the funds to repair its debts.[22] Whether the existence of such an obligation can provide a real guarantee against the risk that third parties may fail to obtain the reparation owed to it by the organization is an altogether different matter. In most cases the organization will lack effective means for ensuring the enforcement of the obligation of members to put it in fund. Moreover, if the injured party is not a member of the organization, it has no legal means at its disposal to ensure the performance of this obligation by members.[23]

In an overall assessment of the different points addressed by the House of Lords in the case under analysis, it may safely be said that this judgment constitutes one of the most authoritative precedents in favour of the principle of non-responsibility of members for acts of the organization. When the judgment was rendered, many commentators shared the view of Lord Griffiths that 'the appellants have suffered a grave injustice',[24] and urged to fill what they perceived as a gap in the law of international

---

[19] See para. 2 of art. 59 ARIO. However, the DARIO's Commentary recognizes that direction and control may take place 'in borderline cases', adding that '[t]he factual context such as the size of membership and the nature of the involvement will probably be decisive'. Report of the International Law Commission on the Work of its Sixty-Third Session (n. 2), p. 159.

[20] *Application of the Interim Accord of 13 September 1995 (The Former Yugoslav Republic of Macedonia v Greece)*, Judgment, [2011] ICJ Rep 660.

[21] 81 ILM, p. 684.   [22] See also, in this respect, art. 40(2) ARIO.

[23] P. Palchetti, 'Exploring Alternative Routes: The Obligation of Members to Enable the Organization to Make Reparation', in Ragazzi (ed.), *Responsibility of International Organizations. Essays in Memory of Sir Ian Brownlie* (Leiden, Martinus Nijhoff 2013), pp. 303–12.

[24] 81 ILM, p. 683.

responsibility.[25] More than twenty years later the International Law Commission has attempted to fill this gap. Significantly, the solution adopted by the Commission confirms the approach taken by the House of Lords in 1989. The 2011 ARIO admit that members may be held responsible for an internationally wrongful act of the organization, but this possibility is restricted to rather exceptional situations. Obviously, the adoption of the ARIO does not put to an end the debate triggered by the failure of the Tin Council. This is the more so since, as the Commission itself has recognized, the fact that several draft articles 'are based on limited practice moves the border between codification and progressive development in the direction of the latter'.[26] In this respect, when one considers the question of the responsibility of members for the acts of the organization, it is a fact that the relevant practice still remains confined to very few cases.

---

[25] R. Sadurska and C.M. Chinkin, 'The Collapse of the International Tin Council: A Case of State Responsibility?', (1990) 30 *Virginia Journal of International Law* 890; C. Greenwood, 'The Tin Council Litigation in the House of Lords', (1990) 49 *Cambridge Law Journal* 13.

[26] Report of the International Law Commission on the Work of its Sixty-Third Session (n. 2), p. 70.

1.4 *Arab Monetary Fund v Hashim and others*, 21 February 1991, United Kingdom House of Lords, 85 ILR 1

Kirsten Schmalenbach

Relevance of the case

With the *Arab Monetary Fund (AMF)* case the House of Lords set a precedent for the recognition of the domestic legal personality of 'foreign' international organizations to which the United Kingdom is neither a party nor the host state. Instead of proceeding from the notion of an internationally and thus 'objectively' existing legal personality of international organizations, the House of Lords took recourse to the United Kingdom's rules on conflict of laws (international private law) in order to recognize the AMF as a corporate body established under the laws of the United Arab Emirates (UAE). The House of Lords' reasoning in the *AMF* case has to be evaluated in the light of the dualistic approach of UK law towards international law[1] that had already influenced the decision on the legal personality of the International Tin Council,[2] an international organization to which the United Kingdom was a member. Even though the AMF judgment is the outcome of UK legal peculiarities,[3] it has influenced the reasoning of other domestic courts in the matter of the domestic legal personality of 'foreign' international organizations.[4]

I. The facts of the case

The AMF was formed by a 1976 treaty among twenty-one Arab states[5] plus Palestine for the purpose of 'laying the monetary foundations of Arab economic integration and accelerating the progress of economic development in all Arab countries'.[6] It was designed as a regional counterpart to the International Monetary Fund for the Islamic Middle East. The founding instrument[7] grants the AMF independent legal personality and emphasises that the AMF shall have the right to own assets, enter into contracts,

---

[1] See A. Aust, *Modern Treaty Law and Practice* (2nd edn, Cambridge, Cambridge University Press 2007), pp. 189ff.

[2] *Re International Tin Council*, High Court, Chancery Division, judgment of 22 January 1987, [1988] 77 ILR 18–41; Court of Appeal, judgment of 27 April 1988, [1989] 80 ILR 181–90.

[3] cf. A. Reinisch/J. Wurm, 'International Financial Institutions Before National Courts', in: D. Bradlow/D. Hunter (ed.), *International Financial Institutions and International Law* (Alphen aan den Rijn, Kluwer Law International 2010), 103–36 (at 109).

[4] See for instance *In Re Jawad Mahmoud Hashim et al.*, United States Bankruptcy Court, District of Arizona, judgment of 15 August 1995, [1997] 107 ILR 405, in which the US court held (at 426) that 'The issue to which comity is given effect is whether the AMF is a juridical person (a corporation, a persona ficta, an entity capable of legal battle) under UAE law [...]. Once this has been decided, capacity follows under American law as a matter of "customary" law.'

[5] Jordan, United Arab Emirates, Bahrain, Tunisia, Algeria, Djibouti, Saudi Arabia, Sudan, Syria, Somalia, Iraq, Oman, Qatar, Kuwait, Lebanon, Libya, Egypt, Morocco, Mauritania, Yemen, and Comoros.

[6] Preamble of the Articles of Agreement of the Arab Monetary Fund of 27 April 1976.

[7] The Articles of Agreement of the Arab Monetary Fund, in force since 13 February 1977.

and litigate (the so-called Status Clause).[8] Headquartered in Abu Dhabi in the United Arab Emirates (UAE), the domestic legal personality of the AMF was established by UAE Federal Decree No. 35 of 1977. Investigations by the AMF's internal auditor into heavy financial losses led to the discovery of bank accounts in Luxembourg in the name of Mr Hashim, the AMF's former Director General. Mr Hashim was elected President and Director General of the AMF and served in this position from 1977 to 1982. In 1988 Mr Hashim was prosecuted and convicted in the UAE *in absentia* for fortyseven charges of embezzlement, forgery, and criminal breaches of trust, involving 80 million US dollars. At the time, Mr Hashim lived in the United Kingdom where he faced civil action instituted by the AMF. In the proceedings before the UK High Court, the defendant simultaneously challenged the domestic legal personality of the AMF and its capacity to institute legal proceedings before the UK High Court. The plaintiff AMF countered with two lines of argument. Firstly, English conflict of law rules recognized the existence of legal entities constituted under international law, and secondly, following Rules 171[9] and 174[10] in Dicey & Morris, the Fund was entitled to be recognized as an ordinary juridical entity established under the domestic foreign law of the UAE. Even though Hoffmann J had a clear preference for argument 1,[11] he found for the plaintiff on the basis of argument 2. This came about because during the proceedings, the plaintiff withdrew argument 1 under the impression that the House of Lords' *International Tin Council (ITC)* case anchored the ITC's domestic legal personality firmly in UK law (i.e. ITC Order of Council of 1972). In recognition of the AMF's legal personality granted by UAE law, Hoffmann J issued *ex parte* an order against Mr Hashim comprising an order for disclosure of his worldwide assets and a worldwide 'Mareva'[12] injunction preventing their dissipation.[13] The Court of Appeal however, reversed the High Court judgment on the grounds that in absence of a UK Order in Council granting the AMF domestic legal personality, the plaintiff lacked capacity to sue because it was created by a non-justiciable international treaty.[14] The *AMF* case was referred to the House of Lords which held by majority (Lord Bridge of Harwich, Lord Templeman, Lord Griffiths, Lord Ackner; dissenting: Lord Lowry) that the order of Hoffmann J was to be restored.

---

[8] Article 2 of the Articles of Agreement.

[9] Rule 171: The existence or dissolution of a foreign corporation duly created or dissolved under the law of a foreign country is recognised in England. *Dicey and Morris on the Conflict of Laws* (11th edn, London, Stevens 1987), Vol. 2, p. 1128.

[10] Rule 174: The capacity of a corporation to enter into any legal transaction is governed both by the constitution of the corporation and by the law of the country which governs the transaction in question. All matters concerning the constitution of a corporation are governed by the law of the place of incorporation. *Dicey and Morris* (n. 9), p. 1134.

[11] *Arab Monetary Fund (No. 3)*, High Court, judgment 14 November 1989, [1990] 3 WLR 139, 143 (Hoffman J).

[12] A temporary injunction that freezes the assets of a party pending further order or final resolution by the court; named after: *Mareva Compania Naviera SA v International Bulkcarriers SA* (1975) Court of Appeal, Civil Division.

[13] *Arab Monetary Fund (No. 3)*, High Court, judgment of 14 November 1989, [1990] 3 WLR 139, at p 142 (Hoffman J).

[14] *Arab Monetary Fund (No. 3)*, Court of Appeal, judgment of 30 April 1990, [1990] 3 WLR 139, at 166; see also: G. Marston, 'The Arab Monetary Fund: Legal Person or Creature from Outer Space?', (1991) 50 *Cambridge Law Journal* 211, 219.

II. The legal questions

The key issue of the *AMF* case is the identification of the proper legal basis for the acknowledgment of the legal personality of a 'foreign' international organization within a non-member state. In contrast to non-member states, member states conclude the constituent instrument that not only creates the organization but also attributes to it domestic legal personality. On the basis of this founding treaty member states are obliged to recognize the organization's domestic legal personality in accordance with the treaty's status clause.[15] Obviously, this is not valid for non-member states, for whom the 'foreign' organization is—at least on a formal level—a *res inter alios acta* and, in absence of an explicit or implicit recognition, of no legal relevance.[16] In the *AMF* case, the House of Lords was called upon to decide if the lack of an English legal instrument recognizing the domestic legal personality and capacities of the AMF must lead to the denial of its personality. As a solution to this difficult situation that harmonized with the United Kingdom's dualistic approach to such issues, the House of Lords applied English conflict of law rules that pointed at UAE Decree No. 35 as a source for the AMF's legal personality. This domestic law centred approach inevitably led to the follow-up question of whether or not international organizations enjoy multiple or parallel domestic legal personalities created by each single domestic legal order of its member states (in case of the AMF over twenty legal orders), a notion which exaggerates the conflict of laws solution to the point of deconstruction.

III. Excerpts

Lord Templeman[...]

I am unable to agree with my noble and learned friend, Lord Lowry, that [UAE] Federal Decree No. 35 only recognised an international organisation and did not create a corporate body. [...] (W)hen sovereign states enter into an agreement by treaty to confer legal personality on an international organisation, the treaty does not create a corporate body. But when the AMF Agreement was registered in the UAE by means of Federal Decree No. 35 that registration conferred on the international organisation legal personality and thus created a corporate body which the English courts can and should recognise.[...]

Although a treaty cannot become part of the law of the United Kingdom without the intervention of Parliament, the recognition of foreign states is a matter for the Crown to decide and by comity the courts of the United Kingdom to recognise a corporate body created by the law of a foreign state recognised by the Crown.[...]

---

[15] If the founding treaty does not explicitly impose an obligation on the member states of the international organization to grant domestic legal personality to the organization, some scholars argue that it is generally accepted that they are obliged under customary law to do so (see T. Gazzini, 'Personality of International Organizations', in: J. Klabbers/A. Wallendahl (eds), *Research Handbook on the Law of International Organizations* (Cheltenham, Edward Elgar 2011), pp. 33–55, at p. 45 with further references).

[16] cf. D. Sarooshi/A. Tzanakopoulos, 'United Kingdom', in: A. Reinisch (ed.), *The Privileges and Immunities of International Organizations in Domestic Courts* (Oxford, Oxford University Press 2013), pp. 275–90, p. 284.

(T)hough the Fund was incorporated by 21 states and has multiple incorporation and multiple nationality there is only one Fund with its head office in Abu Dhabi, one Board of Governors, one Executive Board of Directors and one Director-General. The domicile and residence of the Fund are in the UAE and nowhere else. [...] (T)here is only one Fund to which each of the member states accorded legal personality. [...] The Articles of Agreement which were annexed to the federal decree of the UAE and which thus became part of the law of the UAE are no different from the memorandum and articles of a limited liability company established under the law of England.

It is beyond dispute that if the Fund had been incorporated in the UAE and nowhere else the Fund would have been recognised in this country as a legal personality. If the Fund has been incorporated not only in the UAE but also in a number of friendly foreign states recognised by the government of this country, it still has legal personality and is capable of suing in this country.

[...]

It seems to me that it would be unthinkable for the courts of the United Kingdom applying the principles of comity to reach any other conclusion. It will be observed that the reply of the Foreign and Commonwealth Office stipulates that the international organisation for which recognition is sought must have acquired legal personality and capacity under the laws of one or more member states or the state wherein it has its seat or permanent location. This requirement is necessary because the courts of the United Kingdom cannot enforce treaty rights but they can recognise legal entities created by the laws of one or more sovereign states. A treaty cannot create a corporation but a sovereign state which is party to a treaty can, in pursuance of its obligations accepted under the treaty, create a corporation which will be recognised in the United Kingdom. A member state can create a corporation by signing and ratifying the treaty if in that member state a treaty is self-executing and becomes part of domestic law on signature and ratification. Another member state, such as the UAE, can only create legal personality by the legislative process which was adopted in the case of the AMF Agreement. In the present case the Fund was given legal personality and capacity by the law of the state wherein it has its seat or permanent location. There is every reason why the Fund should be recognised as a legal personality by the courts of the United Kingdom and no reason whatsoever why recognition should be withheld.

[...]

The *Tin* case left untouched the principle that the recognition of a foreign state is a matter for the Crown and the principle that, if a foreign state is recognised by the Crown, the courts of the United Kingdom will recognise the corporate bodies created by that state. In the *Tin* case the Tin Council was created a corporate body by the Order in Council. The USA were not a party to the ITC Treaty and did not altogether approve of its functions. But the USA nevertheless recognised the ITC as a corporate body once it had been created by the United Kingdom.

[...]

In the present case the English courts cannot identify and accept the right to sue of an international organisation which sovereign states by the AMF Treaty agreed to create. But the English courts can identify and accept the right to sue of a corporate body created by a sovereign state pursuant to the obligations accepted by that state in the treaty. In the *Tin* case there was the ITC Treaty, followed by the Order in

Council which created the ITC a corporate body. In the present case there is the AMF Agreement, followed by Federal Decree No. 35 which created the Fund a corporate body. Her Majesty's Government, through the Foreign and Commonwealth Office, has expressed its willingness to recognise an international organisation which has been incorporated by a foreign sovereign state.

Lord Lowry

[…]

At common law, with due respect to learned writers who have sought to maintain a different view, international organisations set up by treaty are not recognised as having legal status in our courts. Parliament's response to the emergence of such organisations was to pass a series of Acts starting with the Diplomatic Privileges (Extension) Act 1944. Statute law now recognises international organisations as having juridical personality in three instances. The International Organisations Act 1968, in regard to an organisation of which the United Kingdom and any other sovereign power are members, and also in regard to an organisation of which two or more sovereign powers (but not the United Kingdom) are members and which maintains or proposes to maintain an establishment in the United Kingdom, gives power to Her Majesty by Order in Council to *'confer on the organisation the legal capacities of a body corporate'* and also to confer certain privileges and immunities (consisting, in regard to the second type of organisation, of exemption from tax). […] A third recognised class consists of those international organisations which have been the subject of special Acts such as the Bretton Woods Agreements Act 1945 and the International Sugar Organisation Act 1973. Viewed as an international organisation, the Fund belongs to a fourth class, which continues to have no legal standing.

[…]

It seems to me to be wholly consistent with Lord Oliver's approach to have regard to the Arab Monetary Fund Agreement, not as creating rights and obligations enforceable by the English courts, but as casting light on, and indeed determining, the true nature of the independent juridical personality which exists under the laws of the signatory states, including Abu Dhabi and the United Arab Emirates, and under the laws of any other states which adopt the same approach as Swiss law. It was common ground that the recognition of the fund by Swiss law as a juridical person formed no basis for the English courts to treat it as such in accordance with (rule) 171 in *Dicey and Morris*. I can see no reason why the English courts should adopt a different attitude towards the Abu Dhabi and United Arab Emirates manifestation of the fund and a 'manifestation' is what it is: a persona ficta designed solely to give tangibility and visibility to something which would otherwise be intangible and invisible in the eyes of the law. This is wholly different from a foreign municipal juridical person whose existence is fully recognised under English law.

[…]

Before 1944 no international organisation, whatever its assets or trading interests might have been, would have enjoyed legal status in the courts of the United Kingdom. Now, by virtue of the legislation at present represented by the International Organisations Act 1968, the position has altered. But, even if regrettable, it need not be a matter for surprise if our legislation has not moved far enough or fast enough to embrace every international organisation. If the Fund cannot sue here and if that is an unacceptable result, it appears to me that the remedy is by way of legislation to amend the 1968 Act.

I would affirm the order of the Court of Appeal and dismiss the appeal with costs in this House.

IV. Commentary

The legal personality of international organizations under domestic law, consisting of passive and active legal capacities (e.g. the capacity to institute legal proceedings before domestic courts), is an essential prerequisite for the organization to fulfil its functions without interference from outside.[17] Devoid of domestic legal personality, the international organization would be dependent on its member states or other 'guardians' to act on its behalf within the domestic legal order, a notion that is evidently inconsistent with the idea of an independent and effective international organization. What appears to be an imperative necessity from the perspective of an international organization (and, as the case may be, its member states) can pose difficulties for domestic courts. Courts may find themselves forced to reject the domestic personality of the suing organization with reference to international law documents that do not explicitly grant domestic personality.[18] Similarly in cases where international treaties do assign to the international organization personality but, in the absence of ratification, the international duty to recognize the personality is not legally binding upon non-member states.[19] In both scenarios, numerous domestic courts have shown their willingness to directly apply international law but fail to identify the forum state's customary or conventional international duty to recognize the domestic legal personality of the international organization.[20] If under these conditions national legislation is not available that proactively recognizes the domestic legal personality of certain or all international organizations,[21] a court may decline the capacity of the organization to institute legal proceedings even though the national legal order bears monistic

---

[17] As A. Reinisch, *International Organizations Before National Courts* (Cambridge, Cambridge University Press 2000), indicates at p. 37f, domestic legal personality 'is a prerequisite not only for entering into legal relationships, but also for being a party to legal proceedings before domestic courts.'

[18] See in relation to intergovernmental fishery bodies J.E. Carroz/A.G. Roche, 'The Proposed International Commission for the Conservation of Atlantic Tunas', [1967] 61 *American Journal of International Law* 697f.

[19] cf. Reinisch (n. 17), at p. 41f.

[20] For the first scenario see for example *UNRRA v Daan*, District Court Utrecht, judgment of 16 June 1948, [1949] 16 ILR 337; *Branno v Ministry of War*, Italian Court of Cassation, decision of 14 June 1954, [1955] 22 ILR 756 (deriving the legal personality of NATO under Italian Law from its international personality); see also H. Schermers/N. Blokker, *International Institutional Law* (5th edn, Leiden, Martinus Nijhoff 2011), § 1595ff; for the second scenario see for instance *Republique italienne, Ministère italien des transports et Chemins de fer de l'Etât italian v Beta Holding et Autorité de sequester de Bâle Ville*, Swiss Federal Court, 1966, as discussed in L. Caflisch, 'La pratique suisse en matière de droit international public 1974', [1975] 31 ASDI 225.

[21] See for example the British Copyright, Designs and Patents Act of 1988, s. 168, para 4: 'An international organisation to which this section applies (by virtue of Order in Council) shall be deemed to have, and to have had at all material times, the legal capacities of a body corporate for the purpose of holding, dealing with and enforcing copyright and in connection with all legal proceedings relating to copyright.'

features. In strictly dualistic legal systems, such as that of the United Kingdom, the courts exclusively apply domestic law which transposes international law obligations into the domestic legal order for the purpose of democratic legitimacy and as the expression of legislative supremacy, respectively.[22] Again, legislative tardiness easily results in a detrimental situation for the organization, as Lord Lowry noted.

Irrespective of whether the respective forum state's legal order authorises courts to apply international law directly or not,[23] it is evident that courts of member states are rarely in the awkward position to search in vain for a legal basis of the organization's domestic legal personality. A range of court cases demonstrate that domestic courts of member states simply refer to the international status clause legally binding upon the forum state, often accompanied by the addendum that the legal personality has been recognized in one way or the other by domestic law.[24] The *Tin Council* case is an example how UK courts follow a strictly dualistic legal approach when discussing the legal personality of an international organization to which the United Kingdom is a member. In the Tin Council judgment of the House of Lords, Lord Templeman uncompromisingly rejected the idea of applying the statute of the Tin Council directly by stressing the non-justiciable nature of unincorporated international treaties even if the United Kingdom is a party to the treaty. Consequently the domestic legal personality of the Tin Council was the direct consequence of domestic legislation, that is the Order in Council pursuant to the International Organisation Act of 1968. Given that courts of member states rarely suffer from a shortage of international instruments or domestic legislation that indicate the member state's recognition of the organization's legal personality under domestic law, references to a customary obligation of member states to that effect are rarely made.[25]

It is evident that courts of non-member states are in a much more challenging position if the domestic legal personality of a 'foreign' international organization is of decisive weight in litigation.[26] The AMF case illustrates the struggle for both a legally sound and pragmatic solution. In 1978, about ten years before the AMF

---

[22] cf. *Re International Tin Council*, High Court, Chancery Division, judgment of 22 January 1987, [1988] 77 ILR 18–41, at 26.

[23] Regarding the direct application of international law in order to establish the domestic legal personality of an organization see for instance *Balfour, Gutherie & Co. et al. v United States et al.*, United States District Court N. D. California, judgment of 5 May 1950, [1950] 17 ILR 323 (resorting directly to art. 104 UN Charter: at p. 324); and *Manderlier v Organisations des Nations Unies and Etat Belge*, Brussels Civil Tribunal, judgment of 11 May 1966, [1972] 45 ILR 446 (also based on art. 104 UN Charter: at p 450); see also Reinisch (n. 17), at p 47f.

[24] For Belgium: *Mandalier v Organisation des Nations Unies and Etat Belge (Ministre des Affaires Etrangères)*, Civil Tribunal Brussels, judgment of 11 May 1966, [1972] ILR 446–55: with reference to art. 104 UN Charter; *Centre pour le développement industriel v X*, Civil Tribunal Brussels, Judgment of 13 March 1992, [1992] Actulité du droit 1377 at 1381: with reference to the Headquarters Agreement with Belgium, see Reinisch (n. 17), at p. 40. For Austria: *OPEC-Fonds Case*, Austrian Supreme Court, 10 Ob 53/04y, Judgment of 14 December 2004: with reference to the Headquarters Agreement with Austria. For The Netherlands: *UNRRA v Daan*, District Court Utrecht, Judgment of 16 June 1948, [1949] 16 ILR 337: with reference to the agreement establishing UNRRA. For Japan: *Shigeko Ui v United Nations University*, Tokyo District Court, Judgment of 21 September 1976, The Japanese Annual of International Law 23 (1980), p. 196 following: with reference to Headquarters Agreement.

[25] See further Reinisch (n. 17), at p. 42ff.

[26] In *International Association of Machinists v OPEC*, District Court of California, judgment of 18 September 1979, 477 F. Supp. 553 (C.D. Cal. 1979) the court took an easy way out: it had doubts whether

litigation, the general practical relevance of the legal personality of 'foreign' international organizations prompted an inquiry from the Bank of England to the Foreign
and Commonwealth Office in 1978. The Bank of England wanted to clarify the government's position concerning the legal personality and capacity in English law of
'entities set up by a group of foreign sovereign states by a treaty'. The Minister of
State for the Foreign and Commonwealth Office replied:[...] a bank or other entity
would enjoy legal personality and capacity in this country, without any formal statement by or on behalf of Her Majesty's Government, in the same way and to the same
extent as any other banking, commercial or other trading organisation established
in a country other than the United Kingdom and enjoying legal personality and
capacity in that country. It is considered that the legal personality and capacity in
this country of such a bank or other entity would be acknowledged by the English
Courts [...][27]

This executive statement sketches out the path followed by the House of Lords in the
AMF case,[28] which was at the same time constrained by the domestic law approach of
its recent Tin Council judgment of 1989. Given the lack of domestic legislation conferring legal capacities to the organization in question, the English conflict of laws rules
authorizes British courts to apply foreign status laws. In the light of the preceding
Tin Council jurisprudence, it came as no surprise that the House of Lords considered
the foreign *domestic* conferment of the AMF's legal capacities as crucial, not the 'foreign' international status rules (i.e. the AMF Articles of Agreement). While the AMF-
Articles of Agreement are non-justiciable before British courts, the United Kingdom
has internationally recognized the host state of the AMF's headquarters, namely the
UAE, and thus its laws. Hence the English conflict of laws rules allow UAE Decree No.
35 on the privileges and immunities of the AMF as a source of the organization's legal
capacity to institute legal proceedings in the United Kingdom.

The House of Lords' approach is without doubt a pragmatic solution.[29] It respected
the expectations of the British government with regard to the acknowledgement of
foreign organizations and left the 'self-perception' of the AMF as well as the 'dignity'
of its member states intact. The adequacy of the judgment is, however, an entirely
different matter. The most often voiced criticism of the judgment is that the House

---

OPEC could be legally served with process. Since the plaintiff and its counsel admitted that OPEC could
not be and had not been legally served, the court dismissed OPEC from the lawsuit and out of the case
entirely. However, reference can be also made to several cases where national courts explicitly or implicitly granted domestic legal personality to international organizations the forum state was not a member
of: In *Re Jawad Mahmoud Hashim* (n. 4); *International Tin Council v Amalgamet Inc.*, Supreme Court
New York City, judgment of 25 January 1988, 524 NYS 2d 971 (NY Supp. Ct). In the case *In re Poncet*,
Swiss Federal Tribunal, judgment of 12 January 1984, [1948] 15 ILR 346 the Swiss Federal Court had
admitted the UN as a defendant—however—without an argument. See also: C.F. Amerasinghe, *Principles
of the Institutional Law of international Organizations* (2nd edn, Cambridge, Cambridge University Press
2005), at p. 71f with further references.

[27] *'United Kingdom Materials on International Law'*, (1978) 49 *British Yearbook of International Law*
329, 347.
[28] Hoffmann J also referred to this statement before finding that the AMF existed as a legal person
under English Law (*Arab Monetary Fund (No. 3)*, High Court, judgment 14 November 1989, [1990] 3
WLR 139, at 146f.
[29] See also Reinisch/Wurm (n. 3), at p. 110.

of Lords ignored an international reality,[30] that is the AMF being an international actor and as such concluding contracts and fulfilling its functions in the real world which is geographically not necessarily confined to the territory of its member states. Indeed there is room for the argument that the British Government has implicitly recognized the international legal personality of the AMF and other 'foreign' international organizations in absence of an explicit denial. Another line of reasoning proceeds from the equally undisputable fact that international organizations are objective real life phenomena even for non-member states. Proceeding from this observation, Dame Rosalyn Higgins heavily criticised the AMF judgment as 'fanciful', because Lord Templeman searched for a piece of domestic law 'creating' (not even recognizing) the legal status of the organization and thus its existence under domestic law.[31] This criticism is especially obvious for those who advocate the objective international legal personality of international organizations[32] which transcend the dichotomy of member and non-member recognition and non-recognition. Irrespective of whether the international personality of the organization is either considered as implicitly recognized in consequence of executive action or as objectively existing as a real world phenomenon, the existence of domestic legal personality is easy to infer from the undisputed international personality: the latter is derived from the former given that both personalities are functionally linked and thus inseparable. Following on from this notion, domestic laws recognizing the domestic legal personality and capacities of international organizations have only declaratory value because the source of the legal status is international law alone.[33]

The theory of the declaratory character of the national conferment of domestic legal personality has its merits[34] but must necessarily fail to convince courts that adhere to the non-justiciable nature of international law without exception, as the House of Lords did. However, it is worth mentioning that Hoffmann J, as the judge of the court of first instance, leaned towards the first argument of the AMF counsel, later withdrawn in the wake of the Tin Council judgment, according to which English law recognizes the existence of legal entities constituted under international law.[35] This first submission had its inspirational source in the above cited answer of the Minister of State for Foreign and Commonwealth Office to the Bank of England of 1978: the English conflict of laws rules not only allow courts to apply the laws of foreign sovereign states that create legal persons but also international law when a group of foreign states create

---

[30] cf. Higgins, *Problems and Process: International Law and How We Use It* (Oxford, Clarendon Press 1994) p. 47f.

[31] Higgins (n. 30), p. 207.

[32] For example Seyersted, 'Objective International Personality of Intergovernmental Organizations, Do Their Capacities Really Depend upon the Conventions Establishing Them?', (1964) 34 *Nordisk Tidsskrift for International Ret* 1–112.

[33] Advocates of this declarative view are for instance K. Ahluwalia, *The Legal Status, Privileges and Immunities of Specialized Agencies of the United Nations and Certain Other International Organizations* (The Hague, Nijhoff 1964), p. 60; C. Jenks, 'The Legal Personality of International Organizations', (1945) 22 *British Yearbook of International Law* 267, 270ff.

[34] But is not uncontested, cf. Reinisch (n. 17), at p. 60 with further references.

[35] *Arab Monetary Fund (No. 3)*, High Court, Judgment of 14 November 1989, [1990] 3 WLR 139 at 143 (Hoffmann J).

an international organization and bestow it with legal capacities in *foro domestico*. Naturally, this executive opinion was not binding on the House of Lords, whereas the latter's diverging ratio in the AMF decision binds all lower English courts.[36]

The 'foreign' domestic law solution of the House of Lords, which was duly followed in the *Westland Helicopters* case[37] and served as a model for a US bankruptcy court in a subsequent case against Mr. Hashim,[38] produced a reasonable and practical result for the AMF and other 'foreign' international organizations that choose the United Kingdom as a place of business and legal action. Its weakness, however, lies not only in its blindness to international law, but also in the multitude of foreign domestic status laws that confer domestic legal personality and capacities to the organizations. The notion of 'pathological' multiple domestic legal personalities of one and the same organization deconstruct the foreign domestic law approach for those who consider the international AMF Article of Agreements the proper source of domestic personality and capacities. As the case may be, on the basis of their line of reasoning the House of Lords also rejected the 'multiple personality' notion. Even if a multitude of states have accorded legal personality to the international organization under their laws, the organization remains one and the same in the eyes of the House of Lords.[39] The multitude of domestic status laws only means that there is more than one factual basis upon which UK courts can recognize the legal personality of that organization under domestic laws. From this, it follows that domestic laws do not create the organization as a 'corporate body' within the national legal order but merely for the purpose of legal personality and capacities treat the organization as if it were one.[40]

---

[36] *Miliangos v George Frank (Textiles) Ltd*, House of Lords, judgment of 1 January 1975, [1976] AC 443, [1975] 1 WLR 758.

[37] *Westland Helicopters Ltd v Arab Organisation for Industrialisation*, High Court, Queens Bench Division, judgment of 3 August 1994, [1995] 10 ALQ 115 at 125ff.

[38] *In Re Jawad Mahmoud Hashim* (n. 4).

[39] But see Lord Templeman's references to the *Tin* case (n 22) in which he stated that the Tin Council was 'created a corporate body' by an Order in Council, [1991] 1 ALQ 90, 96.

[40] See G. Marston, 'The Arab Monetary Fund: Legal Person or Creature from Outer Space?', (1991) 50 *Cambridge Law Journal* 211 (n. 14), 220. Note also that this '*sui generis* personality' generates the effect that UK law governing UK corporations will not per se be applicable directly to international organizations, see D. Sarooshi/A. Tzanakopoulos (n. 16), at p. 286.

1.5 Cases 7/56 and 3/57–7/57, *Algera,* Court of Justice of the EC, [1957–8] ECR 39 and Case C-327/91, *France v Commission,* Court of Justice of the EC, [1994] ECR I-3641

Jan Klabbers

Relevance of the cases

The cases under discussion may deal with radically different topics (employment law in *Algera,* external relations and anti-trust in *France v Commission*) but have in common that both address the limits of the autonomy of the institutions of the EU. In both, the Court discussed how the institutions of the Union relate to the Union itself, and how this affects what it is they are allowed to do. In both also the issue of a revocation of a decision taken by one of the institutions was at issue, and it is often for the latter reason that *Algera* is remembered.[1] Both judgments have become classic examples (albeit minor classics perhaps) of the way the CJEU conceptualizes the EU's internal constitutional law.

I. Facts

The facts in *Algera* were rather complicated, but essentially boiled down to the following. Ms Dineke Algera and her four co-complainants (I will from now on just refer to Ms Algera) were temporarily employed by the Common Assembly of the European Coal and Steel Community, the forerunner of today's European Parliament. The Assembly aimed to streamline its personnel classifications and remunerations, moving from contracts to a public law system, and had in December 1955 issued an order bringing Algera (following her own acceptance hereof) under Staff Regulations, then still in the drafting stage. The drafting was to have been done, following art. 78 ECSC, by the Committee of Presidents of the institutions, representing and thus harmonizing the employment situation in all EU institutions at the time. Instead, the Assembly was the only one of the institutions to claim autonomous decision-making powers. It was understood that bringing Ms Algera within the ambit of the Staff Regulations entailed the offer of a permanent position. In June 1956 it became clear that she would have to accept a drop in salary and what she effectively held to be a demotion. She refused to accept this, at which point, on 12 July 1956, the offer of permanent employment was withdrawn and replaced by a temporary assignment.[2] Ms Algera went to Court claiming that the letter of 12 July 1956 should be annulled.

By contrast, the facts in *France v Commission* were considerably less complicated. In September 1991, the Commission of the EU had concluded an agreement with the US

---

[1] See for example H. Nehl, *Principles of Administrative Procedure in EC Law* (Oxford, Hart 1999), p. 6.

[2] Craig suggests that Ms Algera's involvement in industrial action may have had something to do with the chain of events. See P. Craig, *EU Administrative Law* (Oxford, Oxford University Press 2006), pp. 614–15.

on co-operation in anti-trust matters, therewith codifying and streamlining an informal practice that had continued for a number of years.[3] France complained before the Court that in doing so, the Commission had overstepped its competences: in the EU system, the conclusion of agreements was the sole prerogative of the Council, unless treaty-making powers had been explicitly delegated.

II. The legal question

In *Algera*, the Court was asked to annul the contested decision of 12 July 1956. This then revolved around the question whether a revocation by the administration is possible if creative of a vested right for an individual. In *France v Commission*, the Court was asked to declare that the 1991 agreement was void. The Court itself, without stating anything on the matter, must have realized that annulling an international agreement is not something that is within its jurisdiction; hence, it took the step of rephrasing the question so as declare void the act by which the Commission sought to conclude the agreement.[4] The latter is an internal EU act and can thus be annulled by the CJEU; the former, however, is an international act which cannot unilaterally be annulled—and perhaps cannot be annulled at all.[5]

III. Excerpts (*Algera*)

First of all, an error of reasoning which is liable to lead in this connexion to a vicious circle must be eliminated: it consists in asserting the existence of a vested right, and then inferring therefrom that that right cannot be revoked. In fact, if the right conferred by an administrative measure can be unilaterally revoked by the administration, then the simple fact is that it does not constitute a vested right.

The orders of 12 December 1955 declare that the applicants are brought within the ambit of the Staff Regulations, appoint them to certain 'grades' and fix their rank at certain specified steps of seniority.

If those orders are legal and valid in law, they constitute individual administrative measures giving rise to an individual right. The possibility of withdrawing such measures is a problem of administrative law, which is familiar in the case-law and learned writing of all the countries of the Community, but for the solution of which the Treaty does not contain any rules.

Unless the Court is to deny justice it is therefore obliged to solve the problem by reference to the rules acknowledged by the legislation, the learned writing, and the case-law of the member countries. It emerges from a comparative study of this

---

[3] For background, see generally A.D. Ham, 'International Cooperation in the Antitrust Field and in Particular the Agreement between the United States of America and the Commission of the European Communities', (1993) 30 *Common Market Law Review* 571–97.

[4] See *Commission v France*, para. 17.

[5] It is controversial in international law whether any acts can be annulled (and if so, by whom) for considerations other than violations of *jus cogens*. For brief discussion, see J. Klabbers, 'Straddling Law and Politics: Judicial Review in International Law', in R.St.J. MacDonald and D.M. Johnston (eds), *Towards World Constitutionalism* (Leiden, Martinus Nijhoff, 2005), pp. 809–35.

problem of law that in the six Member States an administrative measure confer-ring individual rights on the person concerned cannot in principle be withdrawn, if it is a lawful measure; in that case, since the individual right is vested, the need to safeguard confidence in the stability of the situation thus created prevails over the interests of an administration desirous of reversing its decision. This is true in particular of the appointment of an official. If, on the other hand, the administra-tive measure is illegal, revocation is possible under the law of all the Member States. The absence of an objective legal basis for the measure affects the individual right of the person concerned and justifies the revocation of the said measure. It should be stressed that whereas this principle is generally acknowledged, only the conditions for its application vary.

[...]

As regards the orders of 12 December 1955, this dispute raises the question, in relation to the provisions of the Treaty establishing the European Coal and Steel Community, whether the defendant could validly bring the applicants within the ambit of the Staff Regulations and determine their classification without the consent or the opinion of the Committee of Presidents provided for in Article 78 of the Treaty, or whether it could do so only with the said consent or the said opinion.

[...]

Examination of the problem as to whether the Common Assembly had authority to determine the salary of its officials on its own, or whether it could do so only with the participation of the Committee of Presidents provided for in Article 78 of the Treaty, leads to the following considerations:

(1) The institutions are autonomous within the limits of their powers (fourth paragraph of Article 6 of the Treaty). Thus, in its judgment in Case 1/55 *Kergall* v *Common Assembly,* the Court acknowledged that the Common Assembly had authority 'to organize its Secretariat as it wished and in the interests of the service'.

Moreover, the second subparagraph of Article 78 (3) merely creates an exception to the rule of autonomy laid down in the previous subparagraph and is therefore to be strictly construed. However, that does not prevent Article 78 (3) from giving the Committee of Presidents authority of its own as regards the number of servants and their salary scales: those factors must be 'determined in advance' by the said Committee.

That provision can be explained by the fact that only the Community has legal personality, and its institutions do not. From that springs the need to harmonize the life of the four institutions and to provide for financial and budgetary supervision, a task entrusted by Article 78 of the Treaty to the Committee of Presidents. It should be stressed that no other body has a power of preliminary supervision in financial matters.

(2) The second subparagraph of Article 78 (3) of the Treaty confers the power to determine the number of servants and their salary scales on the Committee of Presidents only to the extent to which they have not been fixed under another pro-vision of the Treaty or of an implementing regulation. Such is not the case in this instance. The supervision provided for by the Treaty would be ineffective if each of the institutions had power to issue internal regulations fixing the number or the sal-ary scales of its servants. Such an interpretation would lead to an absurd result. The

interpolated clause of the second subparagraph of Article 78 (3) refers only to those cases for which the Treaty lays down a special method for the fixing of a salary and to the eventuality of an implementing regulation based on such a provision of the Treaty. Any other interpretation would deprive Article 78 of its content and hence must be rejected.

Nor can the autonomy of the Common Assembly, as a Parliamentary Assembly, be said to conflict with the power conferred on the Committee of Presidents by Article 78 of the Treaty. In fact, that article applies to all the institutions of the Community without distinction; the fact that the Common Assembly has special powers changes nothing in that respect; its functional autonomy exists only within the limits of its powers, as laid down by the Treaty (last paragraph of Article 6).

(3) Therefore, the power attributed to the Committee of Presidents by Article 78 of the Treaty applies in this instance. However, two arguments have been submitted to the Court in relation to the extent of that power:

(a) According to the first argument, in order to carry out effective supervision, the Committee of Presidents must have a right of decision in financial matters.

[...]

According to another opinion, the theory of an implied power does not necessarily lead to the conclusion that the Committee of Presidents should have a right of decision in the sense described above, since it also has other means of exercising effective supervision.

[...]

In the event, the classification applied to the applicants by the orders of 12 December 1955 proves to be unlawful according both to the first argument and to the second: according to the first argument, because the Common Assembly had not previously obtained the consent of the Committee of Presidents; according to the second argument, because the Common Assembly had not previously submitted the classification to the Committee of Presidents for its opinion, which it should also have done pursuant to the fourth paragraph of Article 2 of its Rules of Internal Administration as well as according to Article 43 (3) of its Rules of Procedure.

(*Commission v France*)

15 The Court finds that, as is apparent from its actual wording, the Agreement is intended to produce legal effects. Consequently, the act whereby the Commission sought to conclude the Agreement must be susceptible to an action for annulment.

[...]

19 Article 228(1) of the EEC Treaty, in the version in force at the time of the events material to this case, provided as follows: 'Where this Treaty provides for the conclusion of agreements between the Community and one or more States or an international organization, such agreements shall be negotiated by the Commission. Subject to the powers vested in the Commission in this field, such agreements shall be concluded by the Council, after consulting the European Parliament where required by this Treaty.'

20 The French Republic argues that that provision expressly reserves to the Council the power to conclude international agreements. Consequently, by concluding the Agreement, the Commission, which is empowered merely to conduct negotiations in that field, exceeded its powers.

21 The Commission contends that the Agreement in fact constitutes an administrative agreement which it is competent to conclude. In view of the nature of the obligations which it lays down, failure to perform the Agreement would result, not in an international claim capable of giving rise to liability on the part of the Community, but merely in termination of the Agreement.

22 The Commission further points out that, in any event, Article IX of the Agreement, cited above, precludes the parties from interpreting its provisions in a manner inconsistent with their own laws (and, moreover, as regards the European Communities, with the laws of the Member States) or as requiring any change in their own laws.

23 As the Court has already found, the Agreement produces legal effects.

24 Next, it is the Community alone, having legal personality pursuant to Article 210 of the Treaty, which has the capacity to bind itself by concluding agreements with a non-member country or an international organization.

25 There is no doubt, therefore, that the Agreement is binding on the European Communities. It falls squarely within the definition of an international agreement concluded between an international organization and a State, within the meaning of Article 2(1)(a)(i) of the Vienna Convention of 21 March 1986 on the Law of Treaties between States and International Organizations or between International Organizations. In the event of non-performance of the Agreement by the Commission, therefore, the Community could incur liability at international level.

26 That being so, the question is whether the Commission was competent under Community law to conclude such an agreement.

27 As the Court explained in Opinion 1/75 [...] Article 228 uses the expression 'agreement' in a general sense to indicate any undertaking entered into by entities subject to international law which has binding force, whatever its formal designation.

28 Furthermore, as the Advocate General has pointed out in paragraph 37 of his Opinion, Article 228 constitutes, as regards the conclusion of treaties, an autonomous general provision, in that it confers specific powers on the Community institutions. With a view to establishing a balance between those institutions, it provides that agreements between the Community and one or more States are to be negotiated by the Commission and then concluded by the Council, after consulting the European Parliament where required by the Treaty. However, the power to conclude agreements is conferred on the Council 'subject to the powers vested in the Commission in this field'.

29 According to the French Government, those powers vested in the Commission are limited to agreements to be concluded by the Commission for the recognition of Community laissez-passer (Article 7 of the Protocol on the Privileges and Immunities of the European Communities). The French Government acknowledges that those powers may also extend to the conclusion of agreements which it describes as administrative or working agreements and which include, by way of example, the establishment of relations with the organs of the United Nations and the other international organizations referred to in Article 229 of the EEC Treaty.

30 The Commission, relying on what it describes as international administrative agreements, maintains, first, that the exception provided for in Article 228 should not be interpreted in the restrictive manner suggested by the French Government. It points out that, if those who drafted the Treaty had really sought to limit its power to conclude treaties, the French version of Article 228 would have conferred power

on the Council 'sous réserve des compétences *attribuées* à la Commission' and not '*reconnues* à la Commission'.

31 Instead, the use of the term 'reconnues' in the French version shows, according to the Commission, that it may derive its powers from sources other than the Treaty, such as the practices followed by the institutions. Moreover, reasoning by analogy from the third paragraph of Article 101 of the Euratom Treaty, the Commission considers that it can itself negotiate and conclude agreements or contracts whose implementation does not require action by the Council and can be effected within the limits of the relevant budget without giving rise to any new financial obligations on the part of the Community, provided that it keeps the Council informed.

32 That argument cannot be accepted.

33 First, the expression 'sous réserve des compétences reconnues à la Commission' derogates from the rule empowering the Council to conclude international agreements.

34 Second, according to the second subparagraph of Article 4(1) of the EEC Treaty, 'each institution shall act within the limits of the powers conferred upon it by this Treaty'. Consequently, the term 'reconnues' in the French version of Article 228 of the Treaty cannot have any meaning other than 'attribuées'.

35 Third, other language versions of Article 228 use terms suggesting that the powers in question are 'attribuées' rather than 'reconnues'. That is the case in particular as regards the versions in Danish ('som på dette område er tillagt Kommissionen'), German ('der Zuständigkeit, welche die Kommission auf diesem Gebiet besitzt'), Dutch ('van de aan de Commissie te dezer zake toegekende bevoegheden') and English ('the powers vested in the Commission in this field').

36 Fourth, and in any event, a mere practice cannot override the provisions of the Treaty.

37 It follows from the foregoing that the Commission cannot claim to derive from Article 228 of the Treaty powers analogous to those which it enjoys by virtue of the third paragraph of Article 101 of the Euratom Treaty.

38 First, as the Advocate General has pointed out in paragraph 26 of his Opinion, Article 101 provides for a procedure which is quite different from that referred to in Article 228 of the EEC Treaty.

39 Second, the EEC and the Euratom Treaties were negotiated simultaneously and signed on the same day; accordingly, if those negotiating the two treaties had intended to grant the Commission the same powers, they would have done so expressly.

40 The Commission's final argument against the French Government's plea is that its power to conclude international agreements is all the more clear-cut in the present case, since the EEC Treaty has conferred on it specific powers in the field of competition. Under Article 89 of the Treaty and Regulation No 17 of the Council of 6 February 1962, the first regulation implementing Articles 85 and 86 of the EEC Treaty … the Commission is entrusted with the task of ensuring the application of the principles laid down in Articles 85 and 86 of the EEC Treaty and the application of Council Regulation (EEC) No 4064/89 of 21 December 1989 on the control of concentrations between undertakings …

41 That argument cannot be accepted either. Even though the Commission has the power, internally, to take individual decisions applying the rules of competition, a field covered by the Agreement, that internal power is not such as to alter the

allocation of powers between the Community institutions with regard to the conclusion of international agreements, which is determined by Article 228 of the Treaty.

42 The plea alleging lack of competence on the part of the Commission to conclude the Agreement at issue must therefore be upheld.

IV. Commentary

There is one striking similarity about the two cases: in both, the legal personality of the EU (respectively as ECSC and EC) is invoked. The individual institutions lack legal personality and this, it seems, has a serious implication. Lacking personality, the Commission cannot enter into treaties under international law, so *France v Commission* suggests, or rather, it cannot be held responsible in its own right and thus its behavior will inevitably be attributed to the EU. Here then, legal personality under international law is at stake. *Algera*, by contrast, suggests that domestic legal personality is required in order to hire staff; this is something only the Community can do, and hence (or so it seems) the ECSC Treaty envisaged a harmonizing role for the Committee of Presidents. As so often with the CJEU, however, the reasoning is a little opaque: while it may well be the case that employees enter into a relationship with the ECSC rather than the Assembly, it might not necessarily follow that therefore harmonization among the institutions is required.

Algera is mostly cited as authority for the proposition that lawful administrative measures creating individual rights cannot be revoked at will by the administration, and that unlawful measures may only be revoked within a reasonable period of time. But there is more to *Algera* than this finding alone: it is also an early illustration of the problems of gap-filling and the Court's approach to it.[6] Where the Treaty contains no rules, the Court is 'obliged to solve the problem by reference to the rules acknowledged by the legislation, the learned writing and the case-law of the member countries'. Perhaps curiously, the Court fails to make any reference to international law, despite the existence, already at the time of the judgment, of a sizeable body of case-law from various staff tribunals of various international organizations. While the argument can be made that the civil service law of any international organization only applies within that organization, it also generally acknowledged that staff tribunals can and do take inspiration from each other.[7] Moreover, international civil service law is usually conceptualized as administrative law rather than as labour law, so in this light too the Court could have found inspiration and guidance in international civil service law. As so often, however, the Court by not looking at international law distanced itself from that body of law; the Court is happiest when it can cherry-pick international law, and has never aligned itself overtly with international law.[8]

---

[6] See T. Tridimas, *The General Principles of EC Law* (Oxford, Oxford University Press 1999), p. 10.

[7] For such a balanced assessment, see the first decision of the World Bank Administrative Tribunal in *De Merode v World Bank*, WBAT No. 1, judgment of 5 June 1981; note also how the CJEU's staff cases, including *Algera*, make a regular occurrence in the leading general treatise on the topic: C.F. Amerasinghe, *The Law of the International Civil Service* (2nd edn, Oxford, Oxford University Press 1994).

[8] See J. Klabbers, 'Straddling the Fence: The EU and International Law', in A. Arnull and D. Chalmers (eds), *Oxford Handbook of EU Law* (Oxford, Oxford University Press, 2015), pp. 52–71.

Indeed, fairly typical for its general attitude is how in *France v Commission* it used an international law argument to protect the EU. It correctly surmised that under international law, the EU would be held responsible for any possible breaches by the Commission of the anti-trust agreement in question: acts or omissions of the Commission would end up being attributed to the EU (para. 25). Hence, the conclusion could be drawn (again, plausibly) that there is no such thing as an administrative agreement in international law binding merely parts of the administration,[9] and it followed that if under international law the responsible actor would be the EU, then it would only be proper for the EU to follow the prescribed treaty-making procedures. Hence, the Court relied on international law in order to prevent the EU from being held responsible under international law. Here then, international law was utilized so as to help protect the EU, and bearing this in mind it should not come as a surprise that the Court decided the way it did.

The international law argument strengthened the Court's insistence that under EU law, the institutions can only act within the limits of their powers. This is a generally accepted starting point in the law of international organizations, and to see the Court endorse it is, as such, not very surprising. Interestingly though, the idea that institutions can only act within the limits of their powers is given a more restrictive interpretation than in international institutional law in general, with the Court noting that 'a mere practice cannot override the provisions of the Treaty' (para. 36). The precise import remains somewhat unclear: what exactly does the Court mean when it refers to a 'mere practice'?

The International Court of Justice, by contrast, has generally accepted an argument that practice taking place within an organization may elucidate the meaning of treaty provisions, and can even come to affect the meaning of a treaty provision.[10] Under art. 27 UN Charter, a valid decision by the Security Council requires the 'concurring votes' of the five permanent members of the Council. The practice grew, from the 1950s onwards, to treat abstentions as 'concurring votes', and this was accepted in 1971 in *Namibia*, with the ICJ holding that it 'evidences a general practice of [the] Organization'.[11] The ICJ stipulated the relevance of acceptance of the practice, and it could be argued that the Security Council's practice therefore went beyond being a 'mere practice', but even so, it would seem that generally the CJEU has been more reluctant than the ICJ in accepting informal change through practice; if anything, this again pays homage to the idea that the EU is reluctant to view itself as a regular international organization (whatever that may be).

---

[9] See generally J. Klabbers, *The Concept of Treaty in International Law* (Dordrecht, Kluwer 1996).

[10] For general discussion, see J. Arato, 'Treaty Interpretation and Constitutional Transformation: Informal Change in International Organizations', (2013) 38 *Yale Journal of International Law* 289–357.

[11] See *Legal Consequences for States of the Continued Presence of South Africa in Namibia (South West Africa) Notwithstanding Security Council Resolution 276 (1970)*, Advisory Opinion, [1971] ICJ Rep 16, para. 22. See also Jan Klabbers, *An Introduction to International Institutional Law* (2nd edn, Cambridge, Cambridge University Press 2009), pp. 209–10.

1.6 Application of the Interim Accord of 13 September 1995 (The Former Yugoslav Republic of Macedonia v Greece), Judgment, [2011] ICJ Rep 644

Ana Sofia Barros

Relevance of the case

The present case addresses the responsibility of states for their own conduct performed in an institutional setting. It marked perhaps the first time where the International Court of Justice (ICJ) so assertively decided upon the legality of member state participation in an international organization, by focusing on the individual conduct of the state in the process of decision-making. The Court's decision proves that the veil of an international organization's decision must, when relevant, be lifted, in order for (member) states to be directly addressed by international law.

I. Facts of the case

Following the break-up of the Socialist Federal Republic of Yugoslavia, the Former Yugoslav Republic of Macedonia (FYROM) applied for membership in several international organizations. FYROM became a member of the United Nations and various of its specialized agencies but did not succeed in applying for membership in non-United Nations affiliated organizations and institutions, mainly owing to disagreement between Greece and FYROM over the name of the latter.

This state of affairs led to the adoption on 13 September 1995 of the Interim Accord, whereby Greece agreed 'not to object to the application by or the membership of [FYROM] in international, multilateral and regional organizations and institutions of which [Greece] is a member', unless the Parties' divergences regarding the name would be at issue.

Despite the subsequent admission of FYROM in a number of international organizations, its candidacy for membership in NATO was thwarted—and thus an invitation to begin talks on accession to the organization was not extended to FYROM—on grounds related to the absence of a mutually acceptable solution to the name issue.

Understanding that Greece, in its capacity as a member of NATO, had objected and acted to prevent FYROM from receiving an invitation to proceed to NATO membership, FYROM instituted proceedings against Greece for a violation of its obligations under the Interim Accord. Greece objected to the Court's jurisdiction and the admissibility of the Application by claiming, among other reasons, that the decision to defer the invitation was not a unilateral act of Greece, but rather a collective decision taken by NATO 'unanimously'.

II. The legal question

The case touches upon the relationship between international organizations and their member states and the difficult question of identifying legally relevant state conduct in an institutional setting for the purpose of establishing state responsibility. In particular, the contention was raised as to whether a certain conduct was to be considered as a collective decision taken by NATO, or if it should rather be assessed independently of NATO's will, as an autonomous conduct of the member state. Drawing such a distinction is essential for attribution purposes: only by understanding the position of a member state *vis-à-vis* the international organization in the process of adoption of institutional acts may a certain act be attributed to one or to the other, as a subject of international law. Concomitantly, only then can the identified conduct be evaluated for its conformity with international legal rules.

The legal question raised by the present case is the following: can member state participation in institutional decision-making processes constitute, in its own right, a legally relevant fact against which compliance with the state's own international obligations may be judged?

III. Excerpts

39. By way of objection to the Court's jurisdiction in the present case and the admissibility of the Application, the Respondent claims that the object of the Application relates to the conduct of NATO and its other member States, because the decision to defer the invitation to the Applicant to join the Organization was a collective decision taken by NATO 'unanimously' at the Bucharest Summit, and not an individual or autonomous decision by the Respondent. Thus, it is argued that the act complained of is attributable to NATO as a whole and not to the Respondent alone. Moreover, in the view of the Respondent, even if the decision to defer the Applicant's admission to NATO could be attributed to the Respondent, the Court could not decide on this point without also deciding on the responsibility of NATO or its other members, over whom it has no jurisdiction. Accordingly, the Respondent argues that the interests of a third party would form the subject matter of any decision the Court may take. The Respondent further contends that, in accordance with the Monetary Gold case law, the Court 'will not exercise jurisdiction where the legal interests of an absent third party form "the very subject matter" of the jurisdiction'.

40. The Applicant, for its part, argues that its Application is directed solely at the Respondent's conduct and not at a decision by NATO or actions of other NATO member States. The Applicant claims that the Respondent's conduct is distinct from any decision of NATO. It contends that the Court does not need to express any view on the legality of NATO's decision to defer an invitation to the Applicant to join the Alliance.

[...]

42. By the terms of the Application, the Applicant's claim is solely based on the allegation that the Respondent has violated its obligation under Article 11, paragraph 1, of

the Interim Accord, which refers specifically to the Respondent's conduct, irrespective of the consequences it may have on the actual final decision of a given organization as to the Applicant's membership. The Court notes that the Applicant is challenging the Respondent's conduct in the period prior to the taking of the decision at the end of the Bucharest Summit and not the decision itself. The issue before the Court is thus not whether NATO's decision may be attributed to the Respondent, but rather whether the Respondent violated the Interim Accord as a result of its own conduct. Nothing in the Application before the Court can be interpreted as requesting the Court to pronounce on whether NATO acted legally in deferring the Applicant's invitation for membership in NATO. Therefore, the dispute does not concern, as contended by the Respondent, the conduct of NATO or the member States of NATO, but rather solely the conduct of the Respondent.

43. Similarly, the Court does not need to determine the responsibility of NATO or of its member States in order to assess the conduct of the Respondent. In this respect, the Respondent's argument that the rights and interests of a third party (which it identifies as NATO and/or the member States of NATO) would form the subject-matter of any decision which the Court might take, with the result that the Court should decline to hear the case under the principle developed in the case of the Monetary Gold Removed from Rome in 1943, is misplaced. The present case can be distinguished from the Monetary Gold case since the Respondent's conduct can be assessed independently of NATO's decision, and the rights and obligations of NATO and its member States other than Greece do not form the subject-matter of the decision of the Court on the merits of the case (Monetary Gold Removed from Rome in 1943 (*Italy v. France*; United Kingdom and United States of America) Preliminary Question, Judgment, I.C.J. Reports 1954, p. 19; East Timor (*Portugal v. Australia*), Judgment, I.C.J. Reports 1995, p. 105, para. 34); nor would the assessment of their responsibility be a 'prerequisite for the determination of the responsibility' of the Respondent (Certain Phosphate Lands in Nauru (*Nauru v. Australia*), Preliminary Objections, Judgment, I.C.J. Reports 1992, p. 261, para. 55). Therefore, the Court considers that the conduct forming the object of the Application is the Respondent's alleged objection to the Applicant's admission to NATO, and that, on the merits, the Court will only have to determine whether or not that conduct demonstrates that the Respondent failed to comply with its obligations under the Interim Accord, irrespective of NATO's final decision on the Applicant's membership application.

[...]

67. The first clause of Article 11, paragraph 1, of the Interim Accord obliges the Respondent not to object to 'the application by or membership of' the Applicant in NATO. The Court notes that the Parties agree that the obligation 'not to object' does not require the Respondent actively to support the Applicant's admission to international organizations. In addition, the Parties agree that the obligation 'not to object' is not an obligation of result, but rather one of conduct.

68. The interpretations advanced by the Parties diverge, however, in significant respects. The Applicant asserts that in its ordinary meaning, interpreted in light of the object and purpose of the Interim Accord, the phrase 'not to object' should be read broadly to encompass any implicit or explicit act or expression of disapproval or opposition, in word or deed, to the Applicant's application to or membership in an organization or institution. In the Applicant's view, the act of objecting is not limited

to casting a negative vote. Rather, it could include any act or omission designed to oppose or to prevent a consensus decision at an international organization (where such consensus is necessary for the Applicant to secure membership) or to inform other members of an international organization or institution that the Respondent will not permit such a consensus decision to be reached. In particular, the Applicant notes that NATO members are admitted on the basis of unanimity of NATO member States, in accordance with Article 10 of the North Atlantic Treaty. That provision states, in relevant part, as follows:

'The Parties may, by unanimous agreement, invite any other European State in a position to further the principles of this Treaty and to contribute to the security of the North Atlantic area to accede to this Treaty.' (North Atlantic Treaty, 4 April 1949, Art. 10, UNTS, Vol. 34, p. 248.)

69. The Respondent interprets the obligation 'not to object' more narrowly. In its view, an objection requires a specific, negative act, such as casting a vote or exercising a veto against the Applicant's admission to or membership in an organization or institution. An objection does not, under the Respondent's interpretation, include abstention or the withholding of support in a consensus process. As a general matter, the Respondent argues that the phrase 'not to object' should be interpreted narrowly because it imposes a limitation on a right to object that the Respondent would otherwise possess.

70. The Court does not accept the general proposition advanced by the Respondent that special rules of interpretation should apply when the Court is examining a treaty that limits a right that a party would otherwise have. Turning to the Respondent's specific arguments in regard to the first clause of Article 11, paragraph 1, the Court observes that nothing in the text of that clause limits the Respondent's obligation not to object to organizations that use a voting procedure to decide on the admission of new members. There is no indication that the Parties intended to exclude from Article 11, paragraph 1, organizations like NATO that follow procedures that do not require a vote. Moreover, the question before the Court is not whether the decision taken by NATO at the Bucharest Summit with respect to the Applicant's candidacy was due exclusively, principally, or marginally to the Respondent's objection. As the Parties agree, the obligation under the first clause of Article 11, paragraph 1, is one of conduct, not of result. Thus, the question before the Court is whether the Respondent, by its own conduct, did not comply with the obligation not to object contained in Article 11, paragraph 1, of the Interim Accord.

[…]

80. The Respondent stresses the absence of a formal voting mechanism within NATO. For that reason, the Respondent asserts that, irrespective of the statements by its government officials, there is no means by which a NATO member State can exercise a 'veto' over NATO decisions. The Respondent further maintains that its obligation under Article 11, paragraph 1, does not prevent it from expressing its views, whether negative or positive, regarding the Applicant's eligibility for admission to an organization, and characterizes the statements by its government officials as speaking to whether the Applicant had satisfied the organization's eligibility requirements, not as setting forth a formal objection. The Respondent further contends that it was 'unanimously' decided at the Bucharest Summit that the Applicant would not yet be invited to join NATO, and thus that it cannot be determined whether a particular State 'objected' to the Applicant's membership. According to the Respondent, 'Greece

did not veto the FYROM's accession to NATO … It was a collective decision made on behalf of the Alliance as a whole.' (Emphasis in the original.)

81. In the view of the Court, the evidence submitted to it demonstrates that through formal diplomatic correspondence and through statements of its senior officials, the Respondent made clear before, during and after the Bucharest Summit that the resolution of the difference over the name was the 'decisive criterion' for the Respondent to accept the Applicant's admission to NATO. The Respondent manifested its objection to the Applicant's admission to NATO at the Bucharest Summit, citing the fact that the difference regarding the Applicant's name remained unresolved.

82. Moreover, the Court cannot accept that the Respondent's statements regarding the admission of the Applicant were not objections, but were merely observations aimed at calling the attention of other NATO member States to concerns about the Applicant's eligibility to join NATO. The record makes abundantly clear that the Respondent went beyond such observations to oppose the Applicant's admission to NATO on the ground that the difference over the name had not been resolved.

83. The Court therefore concludes that the Respondent objected to the Applicant's admission to NATO, within the meaning of the first clause of Article 11, paragraph 1, of the Interim Accord.

IV. Commentary

The present case addresses the responsibility of states for their participation in international organizations. Member state responsibility has already been invoked before the ICJ[1] and other international[2] and domestic Courts[3] in cases mainly related to military operations conducted under the auspices of NATO and the UN. Although these cases differ from the present one in that they did not specifically regard member state participation in institutional decision-making processes,[4] they also involved the complex exercise of determining who, between the international organization and its members, is to be held responsible, and for what. In fact, assessing member state participation in institutional settings, whatever its form, necessarily entails a clear understanding of what exactly is the state's position *vis-à-vis* the undertakings of the international organization.

On the one hand, international organizations are endowed with international legal personality and the autonomy with which they act enables them to express a *separate will* from their members. This implies that organizations (rather than their members) may incur responsibility for any wrongful acts attributable to them. On the other

---

[1] In the *Legality of the Use of Force* cases, brought by the Federal Republic of Yugoslavia against ten NATO member states, for example, *Serbia and Montenegro v Belgium*, Preliminary Objections, Judgment, [2004] ICJ Rep 279.

[2] See, for example, the cases brought before the European Court of Human Rights: *Agim Behrami and Bekir Behrami v France*, App. No. 71412/01 and *Ruzhdi Saramti v France, Germany and Norway*, App. No. 78166/01, 2 May 2007, also commented on in this book.

[3] See, *inter alia, Nuhanovic v Netherlands*, Judgment, BZ9225, and *Mustafic v Netherlands*, Judgement, BZ9228, Supreme Court of The Netherlands, 6 September 2013, also commented on in this book.

[4] The issue has however been raised within the European human rights regime. See the case of *Matthews v United Kingdom*, ch. 6.3. in this book.

hand, member states do not just *disappear* behind the institutional veil, and thus, certain consequences related to the operations of an international organization may, after a closer look, have to be linked to member state acts. For this reason, the identification of legally relevant state conduct within a given institutional framework becomes critical, as it directly impacts upon the application of attribution rules, and thus, the establishment of responsibility.

The present case marked perhaps the first time where the ICJ so assertively decided upon the legality of member state participation in an international organization, by focusing on the individual conduct of the state in the process of decision-making. The Court's approach proves that the veil of an international organization's decision must, when relevant, be lifted, in order for (member) states to be directly addressed by international law.

On 3 April 2008, NATO publicly announced that FYROM would not be invited to begin accession talks to join the Alliance. In its press release, it stated: *'we agreed that an invitation to the former Yugoslav Republic of Macedonia will be extended as soon as a mutually acceptable solution to the name issue has been reached'* (emphasis added).[5] Such a statement could be viewed as the corollary of a legal decision taken by NATO as a whole, expressing the will of the organization—a will that is therefore distinct from the individual 'wills' of its member states.

From the viewpoint of the legal personality of international organizations, and their capacity to operate with autonomy and manifest a *volonté distincte*, the question at issue could theoretically be analyzed by focusing on NATO's decision not to invite the applicant to join the Alliance.[6] However, proof of wrongfulness would hardly be possible. The applicant was rather backed by an international law obligation imposing upon the respondent the duty 'not to object to the application by or the membership of [FYROM] in international, multilateral and regional organizations and institutions of which [Greece] is a member'.[7] Hypothetically then, and still from the perspective of NATO's legal personality, the applicant could have attempted to assert the respondent's responsibility for having exercised—through its dissent—direction or control over the act formally performed by NATO, in accordance with art. 59 of the International Law Commission's (ILC) Articles on the Responsibility of International Organizations.[8]

Seemingly bypassing the legal distinctness of NATO, the applicant concentrated the *locus* of responsibility on the individual conduct of the respondent which, through its state organs and agents,[9] had made clear—before, during, and after the Bucharest

---

[5] cf. NATO Press Release, 'Bucharest Summit Declaration Issued by the Heads of State and Government participating in the meeting of the North Atlantic Council in Bucharest on 3 April 2008', para. 20.

[6] The legal personality of international organizations has been the main reference point for discussions regarding member state responsibility, as the Tin Council litigation (ch. 1.3 in this book), and subsequent academic writings appositely demonstrate.

[7] cf. art. 11, para. 1 of the Interim Accord.

[8] Articles on the Responsibility of International Organizations, with commentaries, in Report of the Law Commission on the Work of its Sixty-Third Session, Official Record of the General Assembly, 66th Sess., Supp. 10 (A/66/10), 2011 (hereinafter ARIO). It should, however, be noted that the ILC discarded in art. 59(2) of the ARIO the possibility of establishing member state responsibility for the acts of international organizations due to the participation of the former in the process of decision-making.

[9] cf. Memorial at 123.

Summit—that it objected to the respondent's admission to NATO. As clarified by the applicant in its Memorial, the dispute did 'not require the Court to address the actions of any third states or any international organizations',[10] and thus, the action in question was attributable solely to the respondent, in accordance with art. 4 and the other provisions of Chapter II of the ILC's Articles on Responsibility of States for Internationally Wrongful Acts of 2001.[11]

As will be further explored, the understanding put forward by the applicant was embraced by the ICJ. This is particularly interesting given the intricacies characterizing the relationship between international organizations and their members, and notably, the way by which the former come to operate as corporate-like structures in decision-making processes. On the one hand, the formative role of their decision-making power allows international organizations to express a *volonté distincte* from their members; on the other hand, the prominence of member states as drivers and participants in institutional decisions is undeniable, making it sometimes unclear where the organization begins and its member states end.[12] The ambiguity stems in particular from the fact that states act in the framework of international organizations in a dual capacity, that is, as members of the organization, and as sovereign states pursuing their own national interests. By concentrating on the individual conduct of the respondent, and by judging it in accordance with its own international law obligations, the ICJ can be said to have based its decision on an account of the respondent as a sovereign state pursuing its national preferences—the exercise of voting rights, or the assumption of a concrete position in consensus decision-making, constituting a means to materialize such pursuit.

It could be claimed that the conclusion of a decision-making process, with the adoption of a decision by the organization, renders it unnecessary to assess the member state's *contribution* to that act, in that the latter would ultimately become diluted in the collective will informing the decision adopted.[13] This was one of the arguments put forward by the respondent to object to the ICJ's jurisdiction and the admissibility of the application.[14] The respondent repeatedly stressed that the action at issue was a 'collective decision taken by NATO and its organs'[15] wherein 'Greece had no individual or autonomous role to play'.[16] Alluding to the 'veil effect',[17] the respondent attempted to demonstrate that a consensus-based decision process, such as that of NATO, reflected the 'will of the organization and not the will of a given Member State'.[18] Accordingly, 'it is not possible and it is legally irrelevant ... to try to search out and individualise the ("real") author of the proposal on which the consensus is based. Such decisions are, by definition, not attributable to any individual State'.[19]

---

[10] cf. Memorial at 69–70.   [11] cf. Memorial at 87.

[12] cf. J. Klabbers, *An Introduction to International Organizations Law* (Cambridge, Cambridge University Press 2015), p. 310. See also I.F. Dekker and R.A. Wessel, Identities of States in International Organizations, *International Organizations Law Review*, 2016 (forthcoming).

[13] See N. White, *The Law of International Organisations* (Manchester, Manchester University Press 2005), pp. 30 and 31.

[14] cf. Counter-Memorial at 109–23.   [15] cf. Counter-Memorial at 109.

[16] cf. Counter-Memorial at 112.

[17] Which would stem directly from the recognition of the separate legal personality of international organizations (cf. Counter-Memorial at 117).

[18] cf. Counter-Memorial at 119.   [19] cf. Counter-Memorial at 120.

The metaphor of the 'veil' was employed to warrant the assertion that it prevented the member states 'from being held responsible for the conduct of the Organisation'.[20] This constitutes, however, a misplacement of the facts that formed the subject matter of the Court's decision.[21] By simply observing that the contention regarded the respondent's responsibility for its individual conduct and not for the decision of NATO, the Court easily circumvented the argumentation espoused by the respondent. Hence, the ICJ did not find it problematic to set a clear distinction between NATO's decision taken at the end of the Bucharest Summit and the respondent's behaviour prior to that moment.[22] The ICJ moreover asserted that it was not required to determine the responsibility of NATO nor that of its members in order to evaluate the conduct of the respondent.[23]

The Court's wide understanding of participation in decision-making facilitated the unfolding of the reasoning described above. Contrary to the respondent's submission that the non-objection clause could only be interpreted as requiring 'a specific, negative act', 'to the point of outright opposition',[24] such as a veto,[25] the ICJ observed that: 'nothing in the text of that clause limits the Respondent's obligation not to object to organizations that use a voting procedure to decide on the admission of new members.'[26] Hence, based on the evidence submitted by both parties, the ICJ concluded that the acts of the respondent were more than mere 'observations' (as claimed by the respondent cf. Counter-Memorial at 141), and were therefore tantamount to an 'objection'.[27] It is important to keep the Court's assertion in mind, as future contentions might well involve member state participation in decisions of international organizations where, despite the existence of voting rules, a formal vote has not taken place. Indeed, from the above it follows that also in instances of consensual decision-making, the position assumed by member states can be legally relevant for responsibility purposes.[28]

---

[20] cf. Counter-Memorial at 117.

[21] Such misplacement also led the respondent to invoke the 'Monetary Gold principle', in light of which the Court's decision would be precluded given that it would involve the legal interests of a third party, *in casu*, NATO or its other members, who were not parties to the proceedings and, in the case of the former at least, could not be parties thereto. (Counter-Memorial at 122–3).

[22] cf. Judgment, para. 42. In the 1948 *Admissions* case, see ch 3.3 in this book, the ICJ did not seem to stand so clearly as to the separateness between the UN and its members in what regarded the refusal, by UN Security Council members, of the application for membership of a few member states. This is for instance reflected in the following passage concerning the conditions for admission required by para. 1 of art. 4: '[a]ll these conditions are subject to the judgment of the Organization. The judgment of the Organization means the judgment of the two organs mentioned in paragraph 2 of Article 4, and, in the last analysis, that of its Members. The question put is concerned with the individual attitude of each Member called upon to pronounce itself on the question of admission'. (See *Conditions of Admission of a State to Membership in the United Nations (Article 4 of Charter)*, Advisory Opinion, [1948] ICJ Rep 57, 61).

[23] cf. Judgment, para. 43.   [24] cf. Counter-Memorial at 129.

[25] cf. Counter-Memorial, at 138.   [26] cf. Judgment at para. 70.

[27] cf. Judgment at paras. 81–3.

[28] The question could be raised as to whether the responsibility of member states, as envisaged in arts. 58 and 59 of the ARIO, could be engaged for their participation in consensual decision-making processes (n. 8). In fact, the ARIO *only* discarded the possibility of establishing member state responsibility for/in connection with the acts of the organization for conduct performed in accordance with the rules of the latter (see arts. 58(2) and 59(2)), without mention being made to state participation in informal institutional processes.

It remains to be seen whether the Court's reasoning only applies where, through its voting behaviour, the member state actually impedes institutional action—either on the basis of dissent or a veto. Next to this, could the responsibility of member states be established for a (wrongful) favourable vote? One can hardly claim that a favourable vote is determinant to the adoption of a decision, with the exception perhaps of international organizations with a small membership or those operating with a weighted voting system. Ultimately, it will all depend on the scope of the obligation under consideration, and on whether it imposes a particular course of action upon the state when participating in institutional decision-making processes. It is submitted that where the obligation at issue is one of conduct and not of result (as in the present case), the determining character of the vote is not a necessary element to consider.[29] As suggested by the applicant, the obligation 'not to object' also covered situations where the respondent's act 'would not have the effect of preventing membership (where unanimity is not required for membership decisions). In other words … it is the act of objection itself that is prohibited, irrespective of its consequences.'[30]

From the ICJ's assertions it follows that the decision of a state representative acting under the instructions of his home state can 'be held to be an act of his home State'.[31] Whilst the member state's vote/veto or consent/dissent, is to be considered as state conduct, it should be distinguished from the final decision adopted, which expresses the international organization's will. Accordingly, the final decision is attributable to the organization, whereas the position assumed by the state representative still refers to the state's own action and is thus attributable to it.[32]

Hence, it is possible to conclude that member state participation in the process of adoption of institutional acts can constitute, in its own right, a legally relevant fact. In the present case, the respondent was bound by a specific duty determining the contours of its participation in institutional settings and was thereby held responsible regardless of the final decision adopted by the organization as a whole. In general, therefore, any international legal regime can constitute a basis upon which to assess member state participation in institutional decision-making, as long as it entails obligations clearly conditioning the state's behaviour.[33] Authors have for instance suggested that

---

[29] cf. Judgment, at para. 70.   [30] cf. Memorial, at 81–2.

[31] I. Seidl-Hohenveldern, 'Responsibility of Member States of an International Organization for the Acts of that Organization', in *Collected Essays on International Investments and on International Organizations* (The Hague/Boston, Kluwer Law International, 1998), p. 66. The question of the significance of state participation in institutional decision-making processes was discussed by the Institut de Droit International in the framework of its work on the responsibility of member states for the acts of international organizations. See 'Draft Questionnaire', from June 1989 and 'Questionnaire', from September 1990, 'The legal consequences for member states of the non-fulfilment by international organizations of their obligations toward third parties', Annuaire de l'Institut de Droit International, Session de Lisbonne Vol. 66-I, 1995, pp. 289 and 301, respectively, and the following answers.

[32] See A. S. Barros and C. Ryngaert, 'The Position of Member States in (Autonomous) Institutional Decision-Making: Implications for the Establishment of Responsibility', (2014) 11 *International Organizations Law Review* 1, pp. 53–82.

[33] P. Palchetti, 'Sulla Responsabilità di uno Stato per il Voto Espresso in Seno ad Un'Organizzazione Internazionale', *Rivista di Diritto Internazionale*, XCV, 2012, pp. 356–61. The author provides a few examples of normative provisions that can be interpreted as requiring a particular course of action from states when acting as members of international organizations, such as: art. XXII(1)(2) of the Convention on International Liability for Damage Caused by Space Objects and art. 139(2) of the United Nations Convention on the Law of the Sea. Where there is no explicit reference to member state conduct, recourse

states' duty to prevent genocide or other R2P crimes may imply exercising the right to vote (or veto) in a certain manner.[34] At the end of the day, voting (or consenting) corresponds to the exercise of a right that, alike any other right recognised in international law, must be judged for its conformity with possible conflicting international obligations.

The case under analysis, quite progressively perhaps,[35] set new pathways for reflection when it comes to delineating the boundaries between international organizations and their members in decision-making processes. By clearly isolating the conduct of states when acting as members of international organizations, the ICJ reminds us that even after having transferred competences to a collective body, states cannot leave their international law obligations 'at home'.

---

must be made to rules of Treaty interpretation in order to determine the scope of the norm under consideration. Within the human rights regime, mention can be made of the opinions expressed by the UN Committee on Economic, Social, and Cultural Rights, in its General Comments and Concluding Observations, regarding the role of states as members of international organizations. See, for example, General Comment No. 19 on the Right to Social Security, UN Doc. E/C.12/GC/19 (2008), para. 58.

[34] See, for a critical account of such contention, P. Palchetti (n. 33), pp. 359–62 and the brief appraisal made by M. Vashakmadze, in B. Simma, D. Khan, G. Nolte, and A. Paulus (eds), *The Charter of the United Nations: A Commentary* (Oxford, Oxford University Press 2012), pp. 1232 and 1233.

[35] In his dissenting opinion, Judge Ad Hoc Roucounas stated that '[t]o uphold the Applicant's thesis means that, for the first time, the highest international court is ruling through a member State on the lawfulness of an act of a third-party international organization' (para. 22).

2

Legal Powers

'Legal powers' make it possible for international organizations to act and in so doing to become 'living' entities in the legal world as well as in social reality. A 'legal power' is neither more nor less than the ability to perform all kind of acts, that is buying or renting a building to accommodate the organization or the adoption by an organ of an organization of sanctions against a state. In international documents and literature legal powers are also termed 'capacities', 'competences', or even 'rights'. From a legal point of view the most important powers are those that confer on organs of an international organization the power to perform *legal* acts, that is the capacity to take decisions with a certain normative force; for instance the establishment by an international organization of a judicial organ for the settlement of disputes with its administrative staff, the approval of the budget by an organ of an international organization, the call of an international organization to its members to refrain from the use of nuclear weapons, the promise of an international organization to send doctors, nurses, and medical equipment to a disaster area, etc.

Of course, only international organizations with the status of an international legal person, as discussed in the First Part, can have legal powers. Holding otherwise would be problematic, because an international organization without international legal personality does not exist as a separate entity in the international legal system and cannot, as such, have or perform legal powers. At the same time, *having* certain legal powers is sometimes also seen as a strong indication that the international organization concerned does exist as an international legal person. As discussed, the International Court of Justice observed in its advisory opinion in the *Reparation for Injuries* case that the United Nations was entrusted with a whole range of specific legal powers, which could practically only be carried out if the organization did possess international legal personality.[1]

Legal powers define to a large extent the character and functioning of an international organization. There are (a lot of) international organizations with no other purpose than to co-ordinate the actions of their member states in certain policy areas and to that end dispose merely of *hortatory* powers, powers to *induce* or *recommend* their member states to carry out certain courses of action. Although such powers are regularly cast in rather vague terms and the scope or limitation of such powers is not always clear, the performance of such powers will usually not lead to disputes before (international) courts or tribunals. That is different with regard to international organizations with aims that go beyond the mere co-operation between the member

---

[1] See, International Court of Justice, *Reparation for Injuries Suffered in the Service of the United Nations*, Advisory Opinion, [1949] ICJ Rep 174, at 178–9.

states, such as the United Nations, some of its specialized agencies like the World Health Organization, and several regional organizations, with the European Union as the most outspoken one.

These 'supra-national' or 'integration' organizations have far-reaching legal powers in their fields of competence, related to, for instance, the elaboration or the creation of international rules, the implementation and maintenance of such rules, and/or the judicial or quasi-judicial settlement of disputes. The use of these powers can really affect, directly or indirectly, the position of the member states or of other actors, including citizens and private entities. And thus it is not surprising that, at least in some situations, the (intended) exercise of these powers, through for instance the (proposed) adoption of a decision by an organ of an organization, results in discussions, and even serious conflicts. Such conflicts can occur between member states inter se, between member states and the organ, or between organs of the organization and can be related to various 'constitutional' issues, such as the legal foundation(s) of the powers of the organization, the division of powers between organs of the organization, and, last but not least, the scope and limitations of the powers.

One can say, the stronger the powers of international organizations, the stronger the fear for improper use or misuse of those powers. To some extent the legal regime of powers itself can provide for certain guarantees in that respect, above all by formulating the power-conferring rules as precise as possible. However, other fields of international institutional law will be of utmost importance for the protection against improper use or misuse of powers, such as the regimes concerning decision-making, responsibility, and judicial remedies.

The controversies about the foundation and scope of the powers of international organizations are to some extent related to the differences in the approach of the legal character of international organizations.[2] According to the traditional school of thought—approaching international organizations primarily as state driven entities—the powers of international organizations are, explicitly or implicitly, *attributed* to them by the member states via the founding treaty and other constitutive instruments. Such an approach tends to favour a restrictive interpretation of the legal powers. The other school of thought views international organizations primarily as autonomous legal persons and maintains that their powers are *inherently* vested in the organizations themselves; they comprise all those powers—explicitly or implicitly stated—that are necessary to realize the objectives and functions of the organization. Because of the fundamental dual character of international organizations, namely as an alliance of states *and* as a relatively independent legal person, it seems self-evident to see the two aforementioned views on the foundations of the powers of international organizations as complementary rather than as mutually exclusive.

Be that as it may, the judgments and opinions of international courts on the legal powers of international organizations—including the four cases commented upon in

---

[2] See, J. Klabbers, *An Introduction to International Institutional Law* (2nd edn, Cambridge, Cambridge University Press 2009), pp. 64–73; N.D. White, *The Law of International Organisations* (2nd edn, Manchester, Manchester University Press 2005), pp. 80–9, 98–107.

this Part—can best be understood as attempts to find an adequate balance between the two approaches. That holds also true for the advisory opinion in the *Reparation for Injuries* case, which is extensively discussed in the former Part of this volume but is at least as important for the foundation and scope of the legal powers of international organizations. In its opinion from 1949, the International Court of Justice made the following—now famous—observation:

> Under international law, the Organisation must be deemed to have those powers which, though not expressly provided in the Charter, are conferred upon it by necessary implication as being essential to the performance of its duties.[3]

The recognition by the Court of the principle or doctrine of implied powers has been by far its most important decision for the development of the legal powers of, first, the United Nations and, gradually, nearly all international organizations. Also where the principle of attribution is expressly stated in the basic treaty as the legal foundation of its powers, such as in the Treaty on European Union,[4] claims of implied powers arise and are awarded. Not every situation is foreseeable and thus organizations—including their member states—are confronted with gaps in the legal power regime and with the question whether the powers of the organization should be extended without formally amending the basic treaty. Consequently, the doctrine of implied powers, in particular its foundation and scope, is among the most discussed issues of international institutional law, and also in legal practice. All the cases discussed in this Part are linked to the doctrine of implied powers, as holds true for some cases in other Parts of this volume.[5]

The doctrine of implied powers was not new in 1949. It was applied in some national legal systems and, more significantly, by the Permanent Court of International Justice in relation to a specific international organization, a Mixed Commission of Greece and Turkey for the settlement of some (territorial) issues. That as such was quite remarkable, given the strict positivistic legal approach of the Permanent Court towards international law. Only one year earlier the Permanent Court very clearly expressed its approach in the following sentence in its judgment in the *SS Lotus* case: 'Restrictions

---

[3] See [1949] ICJ Rep 174, at 182. The Court had to answer the question whether the organization had the legal power to maintain its rights by bringing international claims, in this case a claim against Israel to obtain reparation in respect of the damage caused by the killing of Count Bernadotte, at that time the Chief United Nations Truce Negotiator in the Middle East. The Court concluded (at 184): 'Upon examination of the character of the functions entrusted to the Organisation and of the nature of the missions of its agents, it becomes clear that the capacity of the Organisation to exercise a measure of functional protection of its agents arises by *necessary intendment* out of the Charter.'

[4] See, arts. 4(1) and 5(1) of the Treaty on European Union. In particular after the entry into force of the Lisbon Treaty, the legal regime of the European Union internal and external competences is quite complex. See for a general treatment of the competences of the European Union, including the implied powers doctrine, P. Craig and G. de Burca, *EU Law* (5th edn, Oxford, Oxford University Press 2011), pp. 73–102; and for different aspects: L. Azoulai (ed.), *The Question of Competence in the European Union*, (Oxford, Oxford University Press 2014).

[5] See *Prosecutor v Dusko Tadic*, Appeals Chamber of the International Criminal Tribunal for the Former Yugoslavia, 2 October 1995, IT-94-1-AR72: see *infra* Part 3; *Legal Consequences for States of the Continued Presence of South Africa in Namibia (South West Africa) Notwithstanding Security Council Resolution 276 (1970)*, advisory opinion, [1971] ICJ Rep 16: see *infra* Part 4.

upon the independence of States cannot [...] be presumed.'[6] Therefore it is worth-while to see how the Permanent Court formulated and applied the notion of implied powers in its opinion concerning the *Interpretation of the Greco-Turkish Agreement of 1 December 1926 (Montejo)*, the first case discussed in this Part. It is suggested that the Permanent Court in effect did nothing more than make an interpretation of an exist-ent power provision in the agreement concerned, and thus, if it applied implied pow-ers at all, it applied the doctrine in—what later is called—a *restricted* way by deducing the implied power from an expressly attributed power.

Already in the *Reparation for Injuries* case, the International Court of Justice made use of a wider and more flexible version of the implied powers doctrine by accepting the existence of a tacit power on the basis of a functional analysis of the objectives and tasks of the organization. Later, it had the chance to develop its liberal approach in a number of cases, of which three are commented upon in this section. In the first two opinions—*Effect of Awards of Compensation Made by the United Nations Administrative Tribunal (Keith)* and *Certain Expenses of the United Nations (Article 17, Paragraph 2, of the Charter) (Wouters and Odermatt)*—the Court accepted, *inter alia*, claims of competences of the General Assembly to establish an administrative tribu-nal and a peace-keeping force, notwithstanding the silence of the Charter as to those claims. The most controversial opinion in this regard certainly is given by the Court on request of the Assembly of the World Health Organization in the case of the *Legality of the Use by a State of Nuclear Weapons in Armed Conflict (WHO Opinion, Burci and Quirin)*. It is the first and until now sole case in which the Court, without abandon-ing its implied powers doctrine, clearly addressed—and enforced—restrictions to the extension of powers of international organizations.

The cases in this Part are not only chosen for their relevance to the implied pow-ers doctrine but also because of their significance for some other aspects of the legal powers of international organizations: the delegation of powers is addressed in the *Effect of Awards* case; the division of legal powers between organs of an international organization is a central element in the *Certain Expenses* case; the division of legal powers between the United Nations and one of its specialized agencies, the World Health Organization, is the subject of the *WHO Opinion*; and, finally, the doctrine of *ultra vires* acts of international organizations is, explicitly or implicitly, present in all the cases.

---

[6] Permanent Court of International Justice, *Case of the SS Lotus, France v Turkey*, Judgment 1927, Publ. PCIJ 1927, Series A, no. 10. The cited sentence is preceded by the following observations: 'International law governs the relations between independent states. The rules of law binding upon States therefore emanate from their own free will as expressed in conventions or by usages generally accepted as express-ing principles of law.'

2.1 *Interpretation of the Greco-Turkish Agreement of 1 December 1926*, Permanent Court of International Justice, Advisory Opinion, [1926] Publ. PCIJ, Series B, No. 16

*Blanca Montejo**

Relevance of the case

The present case is of relevance mainly in the context of the evolution of the powers and competencies of international organizations under public international law. This case marks the first time that a court, the Permanent Court of International Justice (the PCIJ), seemingly articulated the basic elements of the implied powers doctrine, thereby opening the door to a series of decisions that would culminate in the International Court of Justice's advisory opinion on the *Expenses* case.[1] By virtue of the present advisory opinion, the Court initiated a path towards consolidating the role of international organizations as international actors in their own right, with powers beyond those strictly attributed to them by their establishing treaties.[2] The case is also relevant in that it recognized very early on the existence of an independent and separate international legal personality of international organizations. Drawing on principles of domestic law,[3] the PCIJ articulated some of the main features of the international legal personality of international organizations that would then resonate with the International Court of Justice in its advisory opinion on the *Reparations* case.[4]

I. The facts of the case

After the First World War, the relationship between Greece and Turkey became extremely complex, particularly because of the traumatic consequences of the massive transfers of populations between the two countries that had occurred during the period of hostilities. The PCIJ was involved in a number of cases dealing with various aspects of that tense relationship.

In so far as it concerns the present case, it would suffice to note that a treaty was signed in 1923 in Lausanne to, among other things, regulate the orderly transfer of Greeks (Christians) in Turkey to Greece and Turks (Muslims) in Greece to Turkey.[5]

---

* Political Affairs Officer, Department of Political Affairs of the United Nations. Please note that the views expressed herein are exclusively those of the author and do not necessarily reflect the views of the United Nations.

[1] *Certain Expenses of the United Nations*, Advisory Opinion, [1962] ICJ Rep 151.

[2] Only one year before this opinion, the PCIJ concluded that international organizations were inherently limited in their powers by the scope of their establishing legal instruments (see *Jurisdiction of the European Commission of the Danube between Galatz and Braila*, 1927, PCIJ, Series B, No. 14).

[3] For an interesting discussion on this aspect, see E. Lauterpacht, *Collected Courses of The Hague Academy of International Law* (1976), pp. 404–6.

[4] *Reparation for Injuries Suffered in the Service of the United Nations*, Advisory Opinion, [1949] ICJ Rep 174.

[5] The Treaty of Lausanne was concluded, on 24 July 1923, by the British Empire, France, Italy, Japan, Greece, Rumania, and the Serb-Croat Slovene State, on the one hand, and Turkey, on the other. As

This 'Treaty of Lausanne' established a Mixed Arbitral Tribunal, with Greek and Turkish members, to deal with property issues ensuing from the transfer of populations from one country to another.[6] In addition to the Treaty of Lausanne, a further agreement was entered into by Greece and Turkey, also in Lausanne, but known as the Convention for the Exchange of Greek and Turkish Populations of 1923 (the Convention), which created a Mixed Commission for the Exchange of Greek and Turkish Populations to facilitate emigration and to liquidate certain categories of property (the Mixed Commission).[7]

According to art. 12 of the Convention, the duties of the Mixed Commission were to supervise and facilitate emigration, and to carry out the liquidation of the movable and immovable property. Most importantly, the Mixed Commission would have full power to take the measures necessitated by the Convention and to decide all questions arising therefrom.[8] The Convention was clear in that the decisions of the Mixed Commission would be taken by majority and that all disputes relating to property, rights, and interests which would be liquidated, would be settled definitely by the Commission.[9] Declaration No. IX related to Muslim properties in Greece, also concluded in Lausanne in 1923, assigned additional powers to the Mixed Commission.[10]

The Mixed Commission, however, did not function well. As it is documented in detail by Ladas in his work on the exchange of minorities after the First World War,[11] the Mixed Commission became a highly ineffectual body which rendered the work of the Commission 'practically nil'.[12] As a result, Greece and Turkey concluded yet another agreement on 1 December 1926, this time in Athens, to deal with difficulties in the implementation of the Treaty of Lausanne and Declaration No. IX (the Agreement of Athens).[13]

The Agreement of Athens assigned further powers to the Mixed Commission[14] and included a Final Protocol, which was concluded the same day. It was art. IV of that protocol that was brought to the Permanent Court for interpretation in the present case. Article IV provided as follows:

> '[a]ny questions of principle of importance which may arise in the Mixed Commission in connection with the new duties entrusted to it by the Agreement signed this day and which, when that Agreement was concluded, it was not already discharging, in virtue of previous instruments defining its powers, shall be submitted for arbitration

---

provided for in art. I, the entering into force of the Treaty would definitively re-establish peace between the parties and the respective nationals. The text of the Treaty of Lausanne can be found in L. Martin, *The Treaties of Peace 1919–1923*, Vol. II, New York, Carnegie Endowment for International Peace, 1924.

[6] See art. 59 of the Treaty of Lausanne.

[7] See art. 11 of the Convention. The text of the Convention can be found at the website of the Ministry of Foreign Affairs of Turkey (http://www.mfa.gov.tr).

[8] See art. 12 of the Convention.   [9] Ibid.

[10] The text of Declaration No. IX can be found in the website of the Ministry of Foreign Affairs of Turkey (http://www.mfa.gov.tr).

[11] S. Ladas, *The Exchange of Minorities* (New York, Macmillan 1932).   [12] Ibid., p. 369.

[13] *Accord entre la Grèce et la Turquie en vue de faciliter l'application de certaines dispositions du Traité de Lausanne et de la Déclaration No IX annexée à ce Traité*, 68 LNTS 11, 1927.

[14] Article 14 of the Agreement of Athens provided that '[it] shall be the duty of [the Mixed Commission] to apply the present Agreement'.

to the President of the Greco-Turkish Arbitral Tribunal sitting at Constantinople. The arbitrator's awards shall be binding.'[15]

A dispute arose concerning the interpretation of the Agreement of Athens, particularly concerning who were the beneficiaries of the Agreement.[16] While the Greek delegation to the Mixed Commission proposed to bring the question to arbitration, as provided for in the Final Protocol, the Turkish delegation argued that no recourse could be had to arbitration before the Mixed Commission decided that it was unable to find a solution to the dispute.

The Mixed Commission reached a twofold decision.[17] On the one hand, the matter would be brought to the President of the Greco-Turkish Arbitral Tribunal at Constantinople for arbitration, and the question of principle concerning the conditions of recourse to arbitration under the Final Protocol would be referred to the PCIJ for an advisory opinion. While no steps were ever taken to submit the actual dispute to arbitration, the Mixed Commission duly applied to the PCIJ through the agency of the League of Nations, for an advisory opinion.

II. The legal question

The formal legal question put before the Permanent Court was the interpretation of art. IV of the Final Protocol of the Agreement of Athens in so far as it concerned the conditions for appeal to the arbitrator. Significantly for the purposes of the present case, one should note that the PCIJ modified the formulation of the question addressed to it. While the Mixed Commission required the PCIJ's opinion on the conditions to which submission of a question to the arbitrator were subject, the Court concluded that the differences of opinion actually related to the question for whom it was to decide whether these conditions were fulfilled and by whom.[18] In other words, in the view of the Court, at stake was whether the Mixed Commission had the power (i) to determine whether a dispute was ripe for arbitration, and (ii) to submit such dispute to arbitration by the President of the Greco-Turkish Arbitral Tribunal. In considering the above, the Court also dwelled on whether the Mixed Commission had separate legal personality and, therefore, whether it had powers that could be exercised in its own right, that is, to the exclusion of those powers being exercised by the states parties to the Agreement of Athens.

III. Excerpts

[...]

In its written Memorial, the Turkish Government submitted that:

> 'the right to resort to proceedings before the President of the Greco-Turkish Mixed Arbitral Tribunal provided for in Article IV of the Final Protocol of the said Agreement

---

[15] The official text of the Agreement of Athens is in French. The text reproduced above is the translation by the Registry used by the PCIJ in its opinion.

[16] S. Ladas (n. 11), pp. 531–2.   [17] Ibid. p. 534.

[18] See *Interpretation of the Greco-Turkish Agreement of 1 December 1926*, 1928, PCIJ, Series B, No. 16, p. 15.

(1) may be exercised by the Mixed Commission as such, that is to say that it has power to refer a question to the single arbitrator, whilst leaving the conduct of the proceedings to the interested Parties;

(2) may not be exercised separately or jointly by the two States signatories of the Agreement except after a vote by the Mixed Commission establishing that the conditions laid down by Article IV of the Final Protocol are fulfilled and declaring itself incompetent to deal with the question which has arisen within it, this decision finally settling the question of jurisdiction as between the two arbitral bodies and being binding upon the President of the Greco-Turkish Arbitral Tribunal.'

[...]

On the other hand, the submissions of the representative of the Greek Government are, in his oral statement, summarized as follows:

(1) that the Mixed Commission, as such, has no right to refer a matter to the arbitrator, since the two contracting Parties have given it no such right under Article IV of the Final Protocol of the Agreement of Athens which is purposely silent on the subject. At the utmost, the Commission might, perhaps, appear;

(2) that neither has the Mixed Commission the right to settle by a preliminary decision the question, should it arise, of the jurisdiction or lack of jurisdiction of the arbitrator in each particular case—a question which must be exclusively reserved to the arbitrator himself, according to the basic principles of public international law;

(3) that the two Parties have the right jointly to have recourse to the arbitrator without such recourse being made subject to a previous decision of the Mixed Commission to the effect that the conditions laid down by Article IV of the Final Protocol are fulfilled. If the two Parties do not succeed in agreeing jointly to refer a matter to the arbitrator, either of them may do so unilaterally.

[...]

[T]he Court must observe that the conditions for this reference or submission are clearly defined by the actual terms of Article IV of the Final Protocol, so that in regard to this point no difference of opinion can be presumed to exist. According to this article, in order that a question may be submitted for arbitration to the President of the Greco-Turkish Mixed Arbitral Tribunal, it is necessary (1) that it should have arisen within the Mixed Commission; (2) that it should have arisen in connection with the new duties which were entrusted by the Agreement of Athens to that Commission and which the latter, when that Agreement was concluded, was not already discharging in virtue of previous instruments defining its powers; (3) that it should be a question of principle, and (4) that it should be of importance. There is no doubt that only when these four conditions are fulfilled can a matter be referred to the President of the Greco-Turkish Mixed Arbitral Tribunal.

[...]

In the eyes of the Court the meaning of this text [art. IV of the Final Protocol] is clear although, no doubt, a more satisfactory formula might have been found. It should, in particular, be noted that the article contains no express provision designed to settle the question by whom or when the questions with which the instrument deals may be referred to the President of the Greco-Turkish Mixed Arbitral Tribunal. But from the very silence of the article on this point, it is possible and natural to deduce that the power to refer a matter to the arbitrator rests with the Mixed Commission when that body finds itself confronted with questions of the nature indicated.

For, according to its very terms, Article IV of the Final Protocol expressly contemplates questions which may arise within the Mixed Commission; there can, therefore, be no doubt that only questions arising in the course of the deliberations of the Commission are contemplated. But, that being so, it is clear—having regard amongst other things to the principle that, as a general rule, any body possessing jurisdictional powers has the right in the first place itself to determine the extent of its jurisdiction—that questions affecting the extent of the jurisdiction of the Mixed Commission must be settled by the Commission itself without action by any other body being necessary.

[...]

According to the interpretation given above of Article IV of the Final Protocol, the right of reference can, however, only belong to the Mixed Commission; for it is a matter of determining the extent of its own competence. It follows logically that the Mixed Commission itself must also decide whether the various conditions required to make such reference possible are fulfilled; and it is simply necessary to add that, whatever the legal nature of these conditions may be, their appreciation and the decision whether they are duly fulfilled, both of which are left to the absolute discretion of the Commission, undoubtedly fall within the category of questions naturally arising in the course of the Commission's deliberations.

In this connection it should be observed that the question whether a given matter is one of principle, and especially whether it is of some importance, is essentially a question of appreciation, and that it must therefore, in the nature of things, be left to the decision of the Mixed Commission itself, which, being acquainted with the many and various matters coming before it, is alone in a position to say whether a given question does or does not fulfil the conditions mentioned in Article IV. This being so, if the Commission, after having freely considered the matter, comes to the conclusion that the question at issue is not of the nature contemplated by Article IV of the Final Protocol, it must itself decide that question; only if the Commission considers that the requisite conditions for the reference of the question to the arbitrator are present is it the duty of that body to refer it to him. This would only not hold good if the article contained a provision imposing this duty, for instance, on the States which signed the Final Protocol, on the individual members of the Commission, or on a group of such members, or a provision authorizing them to refer a matter to the arbitrator. But no such provision is to be found in the article.

The decision as to the presence of the conditions required for the reference of a given question to the arbitrator must be taken by the Mixed Commission, which must apply the general rule governing the performance of its duties; if consequently there exists between the members of the Commission a difference of opinion as to whether these conditions have or have not been fulfilled, the Commission is to decide this point and the question whether it will refer the matter to the President of the Greco-Turkish Mixed Arbitral Tribunal, by a majority vote. As regards the arbitrator, once he is satisfied that a question submitted to him has been referred to him by a decision of the Mixed Commission, he must decide this question and he may not revert to a consideration of the question of the presence of the conditions required by Article IV of the Final Protocol. This appears from the actual terms of the article, which provides for two clearly differentiated jurisdictions, one to decide whether the conditions required for the reference to the arbitrator of a question of principle of some importance are or are not fulfilled, the other to give judgment on this question of principle on its merits, once it has been established that the required conditions are fulfilled. Accordingly, the Court considers that a negative conflict of jurisdiction cannot arise between the Mixed Commission and the arbitrator.

[...]

It follows, in the opinion of the Court, that the restriction placed by that article on the general powers of the Mixed Commission cannot constitute an impediment to the fulfilment by the latter of the important duties assigned to it, but must be construed in such a way as to accelerate and facilitate the progress made by that body with its work. Speed must be regarded as an essential factor in the work of the Mixed Commission, both in the interest of the populations with which its work is concerned and in that of the Greek and Turkish Governments.

[...]

On the basis of the foregoing considerations, the Court feels obliged to observe that it is wrong to seek to attribute either to one of the members or to a group of Greek or Turkish members of the Mixed Commission, or again to one of the States signatories of the Final Protocol, the right to refer a question to the arbitrator, with a view to obtaining from him a decision, at all events as to whether a given question is to be regarded as a question of principle of some importance. Such a contention in fact is incompatible not only with the terms of Article IV of the Final Protocol, but also with the spirit which, as has been already pointed out, underlies all the relevant international instruments.

[...]

Even leaving aside considerations based on the spirit of these international instruments, the same result is arrived at, for an individual member or a group among the Greek or Turkish members within the Commission has no power to take action outside the Commission, and the same applies as regards the neutral members. This would still hold good even if all the Greek or all the Turkish members of the Commission could be regarded as constituting governmental delegations within it, a conception which has however already been rejected by the Court; for to accord to individual members of an organization constituted as a corporate body any right to take action of any kind outside the sphere of proceedings within that organization, would be clearly contrary to an accepted principle of law. In the absence of an express provision, therefore, it is impossible to accept such an abnormal state of things.

In this connection, another observation of some importance should be made: the situation of the States signatory to the Final Protocol is altogether singular as regards matters concerning the exchange of Greek and Turkish populations; this singularity obviously arises from the special nature of the Convention of Lausanne concerning the exchange of populations, as well as of Declaration No. IX of Lausanne and the Agreement of Athens. For, according to the provisions of these instruments, it does not rest with the contracting States themselves to apply and carry out, each for its own part and in the exercise of its sovereign rights, the clauses governing the matter in question; the application and carrying out of these clauses are entrusted as a whole to the Mixed Commission which acts in the interests of the two contracting States.

[...]

The Court, unanimously, is of opinion that to the question submitted to it as formulated at the beginning of this advisory opinion, the following answer should be given:

(1) It is for the Mixed Commission for the Exchange of Greek and Turkish Populations alone to decide whether the conditions enumerated in Article IV of the Final Protocol annexed to the Agreement concluded at Athens on December 1st, 1926, between the Greek and Turkish Governments, for the submission of the questions contemplated by that article to the President of the Greco-Turkish Mixed Arbitral Tribunal sitting at Constantinople, for arbitration, are or are not fulfilled.

(2) The conditions contemplated by the said Article IV having been fulfilled, the right to refer a question to the arbitrator contemplated by that article belongs to the Mixed Commission alone.

IV. Commentary

The advisory opinion of the PCIJ addresses fundamental questions about the powers and competencies of international organizations. The impact of the decision of the PCIJ is twofold: on the one hand, the PCIJ strengthened the notion by which international organizations enjoy international legal personality independent from their members, and on the other, the PCIJ elaborated seemingly for the first time in history, the doctrine of implied powers of international organizations.[19]

The decision is interesting in that although the parties defined the dispute as an admissibility matter (the conditions for appeal), the Court redefined it as a jurisdictional one (who had the power to determine admissibility and resort to arbitration).[20] For that reason, a case that was originally an international arbitration case actually became a case of relevance for international organizations.

For purposes of its analysis, the decision should be framed in its historical context. The early cases of the PCIJ had shown a certain hesitation on the part of the Court to establish a special status for international organizations beyond that of mere products of treaties.[21] Only one year prior to this decision, in the Commission of the Danube advisory opinion, the PCIJ had concluded that powers of international organizations were limited by the functions bestowed on them by their 'definitive statute'.[22] This notwithstanding, the PCIJ in the same decision recognized the ability of international organizations to exercise those functions which were not restricted by their statute, opening the door to further development.[23]

---

[19] J. Klabbers, 'Global Governance Before the ICJ: Re-reading the WHA Opinion', (2009) 13 *Max Planck Yearbook of United Nations Law* 1, 15.

[20] See for an interesting discussion on the concepts of admissibility and jurisdiction, J. Paulsson, 'Jurisdiction and Admissibility', in Liber Amicorum in honor of R. Briner *Global Reflections on International Law, Commerce and Dispute Resolution* (Paris, ICC Publishing 2005), pp. 602–17.

[21] See *Competence of the ILO to Regulate the Conditions of Labour of Persons Employed in Agriculture* and *Competence of the ILO to Examine Proposals for the Organization and Development of Methods of Agricultural Production*, 1922, PCIJ, Series B, Nos. 2 and 3, *Competence of the International Labour Organization to Regulate, Incidentally, the Personal Work of the Employer*, 1926, PCIJ, Series B, No. 13, and *Jurisdiction of the European Commission of the Danube between Galatz and Braila* (n. 2).

[22] See *Jurisdiction of the European Commission of the Danube between Galatz and Braila* (n. 2), p. 64.

[23] Ibid, p. 67.

In this case, the PCIJ went one step further and attributed to the Mixed Commission powers that had not been explicitly recognized by any of the relevant treaties.[24] Indeed, the PCIJ argued that while no provision gave express power to the Mixed Commission to submit disputes to arbitration, such power could be implied.[25]

In supporting its decision, the Court employed a variety of legal arguments. The Court emphasized the importance of the 'spirit' underlying the various international instruments regulating the role of the Mixed Commission. The Court also made reference to the textual interpretation of art. IV of the Final Protocol (or rather to the silence of the provision in this regard) and it finally evoked general principles of law (impliedly referring to domestic laws)[26] in support of the conclusion that the Mixed Commission was a 'body corporate' and thereby a separate legal entity from its members for all relevant purposes.[27]

Indeed, while the Court gave the 'spirit' underlying the Final Protocol a key role in arriving at a correct interpretation of its art. IV, it also considered that the text was a fundamental part of that reasoning. While acknowledging the deficient drafting of art. IV of the Final Protocol (and admitting that the article contained no express provision designed to settle the question at stake), the Court affirmed that the *meaning* of the text was clear.

The Court attributed to 'the very silence of the article on this point' the power to refer a matter to the arbitrator by the Mixed Commission.[28] In concluding its reasoning, the PCIJ sustained that as a general rule, any body possessing jurisdictional powers has the right to determine the extent of its own jurisdiction,[29] echoing the general principle of *compétence de la compétence*.[30]

The PCIJ added further that the Mixed Commission enjoyed such powers to the exclusion of its members. According to the PCIJ, the Mixed Commission was an international organization that had been conferred a series of powers with regard to the subject matter of the Convention and the Agreement of Athens. The conferring of such powers, in the view of the Court, entailed the actual relinquishment of the same by the states parties.

The PCIJ concluded that although the power to submit a 'dispute' in the sense of art. IV of the Final Protocol to arbitration was not provided for, it should be considered an implied power of the Mixed Commission to the extent that the exercise of such power was consistent with the 'spirit'[31] of the relevant treaties. The object and purpose of the Mixed Commission, as well as its effectiveness, justified the decision of the Court.

---

[24] V. Engström, 'Implied Powers of International Organizations: On the Character of a Legal Doctrine', (2003) 14 *Finnish Yearbook of International Law* 129.

[25] The Court further found that only the Mixed Commission and not the states parties to the relevant treaties could exercise those powers.

[26] See W. W. Bishop, *Collected Courses of The Hague Academy of International Law* (1965), p. 92.

[27] See E. Lauterpacht (n. 3), pp. 404–6.

[28] The Court went one step further and affirmed that there could be 'no doubt' that only questions arising in the course of the deliberations of the Commission were contemplated by art. IV.

[29] This conclusion would appear to be more akin to the 'inherent powers' doctrine than to the doctrine of implied powers. See in this regard, as cited by Klabbers in n. 19 above, F. Seyersted, *Common Law of International Organizations* (Leiden: Brill 2008), pp. 65–70; and J. Klabbers, 'On Seyersted and his Common Law of International Organizations', (2008) *International Organizations Law Review* 381–90.

[30] See H. Waldock, *Collected Courses of The Hague Academy of International Law* (1962), p. 60.

[31] See for a detailed recount of the Court's reliance on the 'spirit' of a number of provisions involved in the case, J.P. Fockema Andreae, *An Important Chapter From the History of Legal Interpretation* (Leyden, Sijthoff 1948). See also V. Engström, *Constructing the Powers of International Institutions* (Martinus Nijhoff 2012).

Ironically, the Mixed Commission proved to be a very inefficient body, marked more by its dysfunction than by its efficacy and the implied powers wished for by the Court were ultimately never exercised.

While the decision of the PCIJ is a fundamental milestone in the crystallization of the doctrine of implied powers, some authors have assessed the performance of the Court in critical terms. In Reisman's assessment, for instance, the choice for the Court was simple: either opt for an interpretation that would remove the impasse with some theoretical 'but improbable' risk of abuse by the President of the Greco-Turkish Arbitral Tribunal or elect an interpretation that would reinforce the paralysis, rendering the Mixed Commission essentially insignificant.[32] According to Reisman, the latter seemed to have happened, resulting in a decision reflective of 'a general misperception of the nature of the problem before it'.[33]

Reisman's assessment of the Court's stance in this case is partly correct in that it identifies a misperception in adjudicating the 'problem before it'. Indeed, the case dealt ultimately with the clarification of a poorly drafted dispute resolution clause of a treaty between two states. In refusing to confer any meaning to the word 'arbitration' of that clause, the Court ventured itself into a rather complex articulation of the powers of the Mixed Commission consistent with the 'spirit', rather than with the text, of the underlying treaties. The interpretation process followed by the Court is questionable under the principles of arts. 31 and 32 of the Vienna Convention on the Law of Treaties, more so, in that it did not seem to resort—at least not explicitly—to supplementary means of interpretation.[34]

This notwithstanding, it seems clear that the present case marked a change of mind in the Court, which had already been signaled in the Commission of the Danube advisory opinion.[35] According to the Court, although no provisions expressly indicated the power of the Mixed Commission to submit disputes to arbitration, such a power could be implied. In employing a teleological interpretation of the relevant treaties, the Court found justification to strengthen the powers of the Mixed Commission at the expense of the states parties to the Agreement of Athens and the President of the Greco-Turkish Arbitral Tribunal based in Constantinople.[36]

---

[32] W. M. Reisman, *Collected Courses of The Hague Academy of International Law* (1996), pp. 57–82.

[33] Ibid., p. 63.

[34] This is particularly so given Ladas's description of the object and purpose of art. IV of the Final Protocol. According to Ladas, 'the provision for reference to the arbitrator was included in the Agreement of Athens in order to do away with the difficulties that had repeatedly arisen in the Mixed Commission whenever a question of principle of some importance caused a difference of opinion ... To avoid these deadlocks seemed to be the principal consideration which inspired the adoption of art. IV of the Final Protocol.' See Ladas (n. 11), p. 538.

[35] See *Jurisdiction of the European Commission of the Danube Between Galatz and Braila*, (n. 2), pp. 64 and 67.

[36] Indeed, by virtue of this opinion, the latter was deprived of the power to examine his own competence. This risk did not materialize, however, since the Mixed Commission, as had happened in the past, was unable to reach agreement to transmit the question to the President of the Arbitral Tribunal for arbitration. Ultimately, the dispute was resolved upon the intervention of two particularly proactive commissioners. See for further details, Ladas (n. 11), pp. 539–45. It is also interesting (and disheartening) to read Ladas's account of the aftermath of the decision at p. 539: 'The opinion was communicated to the Council of the League of Nations, which took note of it on September 8, 1928, and ordered it communicated (sic) to the President of the Mixed Commission. In the meantime the new negotiations for the final liquidation of all pending questions were begun at Angora [now known as Ankara], and the opinion of the Court did not serve any practical purpose.'

2.2 *Effect of Awards of Compensation Made by the United Nations Administrative Tribunal* Advisory Opinion [1954] ICJ Rep 47

Kenneth Keith

Relevance of the case

This advisory opinion considers the powers of the General Assembly of the United Nations to establish a tribunal with authority to decide disputes brought by UN Secretariat members against the Secretary-General, as their employer, about employment matters. It also addresses the impact of the Tribunal's decisions on the power of the Assembly to adopt the budget of the United Nations. Underlying those issues is the principle of the independent international public service.

I. Facts

Eleven staff members of the UN Secretariat had been dismissed. They were United States nationals who had refused to answer questions put by an investigating committee of the US Senate about their membership of the Communist Party or their involvement in subversive activity. They had pleaded the protection against self-incrimination provided for in the Fifth Amendment of the US Constitution. They challenged their dismissals before the United Nations Administrative Tribunal, a body set up by the General Assembly to decide staff disputes. The relevant provisions of the Statute of the Tribunal appear in the extracts from the advisory opinion set out in section III below. Their challenges were successful and awards totalling 179,420 US dollars were made in their favour.

The Secretary-General submitted to the General Assembly, as part of the budget to be approved by it, a supplementary appropriation for the amount awarded. The Fifth Committee of the General Assembly, the Committee concerned with budgetary and administrative matters, then debated the question whether the Assembly was obliged to make provision for those awards in the budget. (The United States at that time met one-third of the UN regular budget.) The competing views were captured in part by the delegates of Australia and New Zealand, the former a barrister, an ex Foreign Minister, Australia's Ambassador in Washington and soon to be a Judge at the International Court of Justice, the latter a classicist, an early and long term member of the Secretariat of the League of Nations, and an original member of the New Zealand Department of External Affairs who had successfully proposed at San Francisco when the Charter was being drafted the inclusion of arts. 100 and 101. The Australian said this:

> My Delegation would have thought that there could be no question as to the competence of the General Assembly in this matter, for it is commonplace that every executive authority must obtain the authorization in the form of an appropriation from the legislative body before it can disburse public funds. I do not think that any member

of this Committee would attack the validity of the principle, which is an accepted thesis, I believe, in every country in the world, and it applies in a very special degree to an international organization such as the United Nations, which derives its funds from contributions by sovereign States. It is, indeed, precisely for this reason that the matter comes before the Fifth Committee. For at the very outset there is posed the vital question—whether the award of a tribunal set up by its authority, or whether any other outside authority can or should override the power of appropriation and its free exercise, without which no sovereign body may continue effectively to exercise its functions. However, it has been suggested by some delegations that the Assembly has no option but to make the necessary appropriations to meet without question the awards of the Administrative Tribunal. That is not a position with which my delegation can associate itself. It is our view that the Assembly has the authority to decline to accept findings of the Tribunal and has also the unquestionable authority to accept the findings of the Tribunal but to vary the awards the Tribunal has made.

The constitutional instrument of the United Nations is the Charter, which has established the General Assembly and the Secretariat as principal organs of the United Nations and which has marked out the powers of both. Neither has the power to extend or derogate from a power which the Charter has reposed in the other—or for that matter, in itself.

[...]

When we come to an award of compensation, the exercise by the Assembly of its appropriation power becomes a real issue. An award of the Tribunal may call not for passive acquiescence on the part of the Assembly, but for the exercise in a positive way of its appropriation power. Is it to be asserted that the Assembly, in stipulating in the Statute of the Tribunal that the United Nations shall pay compensation awarded, has foregone *pro tanto* its appropriation power? If so, by what authority did the Assembly strip itself of a power which the Charter has placed upon it. In the opinion of my Delegation there is no warrant for any such suggestion. We feel that the Assembly would have every justification for declining to exercise its appropriation power in any case in which it appeared to it that the Tribunal had acted unreasonably or improperly. [1]

The New Zealander by contrast said this:

There is of course nothing to prevent the Assembly deciding to amend the powers of the Tribunal if they are found to be excessive. Indeed we have been doing this during the past few days. Nevertheless any interference with awards that have already been made is, it appears to us, save in the most exceptional cases, a denial of justice and a departure from principle.

The principle that legislation should not be retroactive is one which is firmly entrenched in most municipal systems of law. May I compare the relationship between Assembly and Tribunal with the situation in those countries which do not have a fixed constitution rigidly defining the respective competence of the courts and the legislature. In my own country, for instance, Parliament is sovereign; it can make

---

[1] United Nations General Assembly, 5th Committee, 4 December 1953, 421st meeting, paras 21–38, pp. 291–3, quoted by the US representative before the Court, Pleadings pp. 312–13.

or unmake any law past or future. It can change the composition and competence of our courts overnight. But it would be a most grave decision for Parliament to use that power to pass legislation having retrospective effect and depriving individuals of the benefit of judgments they had been given in the courts.[2]

II. Legal questions

The difference of opinion, just illustrated, led to the General Assembly asking the International Court of Justice the following questions:

(1) Having regard to the Statute of the United Nations Administrative Tribunal and to any other relevant instruments and to the relevant records, has the General Assembly the right on any grounds to refuse to give effect to an award of compensation made by that Tribunal in favour of a staff member of the United Nations whose contract of service has been terminated without his assent?

(2) If the answer given by the Court to question (1) is in the affirmative, what are the principal grounds upon which the General Assembly could lawfully exercise such a right?

As will appear from the extracts from the opinion given by the Court, set out below, it ruled on the following issues:

(a) The scope of the question which it was to answer, stressing in particular that there was no suggestion that the Tribunal was not properly constituted or that it had acted outside its competence; one of the Judges in the majority would also have limited the reference in the question to those awards in respect of which there was no fundamental breach of procedural requirements.

(b) The power of the General Assembly to establish subsidiary bodies, in particular a tribunal with power to make awards binding on the United Nations. Is a body with those powers 'subsidiary'?

(c) The role of the principle of *res judicata*. See the passage from para. [21] of the ICJ Reports set out under section III below.

(d) The limits, if any, on the power of the General Assembly to determine its budget. The General Assembly adopts a regular budget every two years. Its exercise of its power to do that, under art. 17 of the Charter of the UN, is binding on the Members. They are obliged to pay the share of the expenses of the Organization as apportioned by the Assembly. In terms of the Assembly's power of consideration and approval consider the ongoing obligations of the Organization in respect of employees (including pensions), any loans it may have incurred, rental arrangements, service contracts, many of which will extend beyond the budget period. Comparable issues arise in national legislatures as they consider and approve their budgets.

(e) The principle of the independent international civil service. See Chapter XV of the Charter on the Secretariat, particularly arts. 100 and 101(3), considered by the Court, paras. 36–8. See also the lecture given by Dag Hammarskjöld, the Secretary-General, cited below.

---

[2] United Nations General Assembly, 5th Committee, 5 December 1953, 423rd meeting, paras 25–40, pp. 305–7, quoted by The Netherlands in its written statement to the Court, p. 106.

III. Excerpts[3]

[...]

[11] This examination of the first Question shows that the Court is requested to consider the general and abstract question whether the General Assembly is legally entitled to refuse to give effect to an award of compensation made by the Administrative Tribunal, properly constituted and acting within the limits of its statutory competence. The answer to this question depends on the provisions of the Statute of the Tribunal as adopted by the General Assembly on November 24th, 1949, and on the Staff Regulations and Rules as in force on December 9th, 1953. But the Court will also take into account the amendments which were made to the Statute on the latter date. The Court will first consider whether the Tribunal is established either as a judicial body, or as an advisory organ or a mere subordinate committee of the General Assembly.

[12] Article 1 of the Statute provides: 'A Tribunal is established by the present Statute to be known as the United Nations Administrative Tribunal.' This Tribunal shall, according to Article 2, paragraph 1, 'be competent to hear and pass judgment upon applications', whereupon the paragraph determines the limits of the Tribunal's competence as already mentioned above.

[13] Article 2, paragraph 3, prescribes:

'In the event of a dispute as to whether the Tribunal has competence, the matter shall be settled by the decision of the Tribunal.'

[14] Article 10 contains the following provisions:

'2. The judgments shall be final and without appeal.'
'3. The judgments shall state the reasons on which they are based.'

[...]

[16] [...] The independence of its members is ensured by Article 3, paragraph 5, which provides:

'No member of the Tribunal can be dismissed by the General Assembly unless the other members are of the unanimous opinion that he is unsuited for further service.'

[...]

[20] This examination of the relevant provisions of the Statute shows that the Tribunal is established, not as an advisory organ or a mere subordinate committee of the General Assembly, but as an independent and truly judicial body pronouncing final judgments without appeal within the limited field of its functions.

[21] According to a well-established and generally recognized principle of law, a judgment rendered by such a judicial body is *res judicata* and has binding force between the parties to the dispute. It must therefore be examined who are to be regarded as parties bound by an award of compensation made in favour of a staff member of the United Nations whose contract of service has been terminated without his assent.

---

[3] The numbers between brackets before each paragraph are added to the original text, following the reprint of the opinion in *Oxford Public International Law* (http://opil.ouplaw.com/view/10.1093/law:icgj/226icj54.case.1/law-icgj-226icj54).

[22] Such a contract of service is concluded between the staff member concerned and the Secretary-General in his capacity as the chief administrative officer of the United Nations Organization, acting on behalf of that Organization as its representative. When the Secretary-General concludes such a contract of service with a staff member, he engages the legal responsibility of the Organization, which is the juridical person on whose behalf he acts. If he terminates the contract of service without the assent of the staff member and this action results in a dispute which is referred to the Administrative Tribunal, the parties to this dispute before the Tribunal are the staff member concerned and the United Nations Organization, represented by the Secretary-General, and these parties will become bound by the judgment of the Tribunal. This judgment is, according to Article 10 of the Tribunal's Statute, final and without appeal. The Statute has provided for no kind of review. As this final judgment has binding force on the United Nations Organization as the juridical person responsible for the proper observance of the contract of service, that Organization becomes legally bound to carry out the judgment and to pay the compensation awarded to the staff member. It follows that the General Assembly, as an organ of the United Nations, must likewise be bound by the judgment.

[...]

[27] It is likewise the result of a deliberate decision that no provision for review of the judgments of the United Nations Administrative Tribunal was inserted in the Statute of that Tribunal. [...]

[28] The General Assembly could, when it adopted the Statute, have provided for means of redress, but it did not do so. Like the Assembly of the League of Nations it refrained from laying down any exception to the rule conferring on the Tribunal the power to pronounce final judgments without appeal.

[29] This rule contained in Article 10, paragraph 2, cannot however be considered as excluding the Tribunal from itself revising a judgment in special circumstances when new facts of decisive importance have been discovered; and the Tribunal has already exercised this power. Such a strictly limited revision by the Tribunal itself cannot be considered as an 'appeal' within the meaning of that Article and would conform with rules generally provided in statutes or laws issued for courts of justice, such as for instance in Article 61 of the Statute of the International Court of Justice.

[...]

[32] The Court must now examine the principal contentions which have been put forward, in the written and in the oral statements, by the Governments that take the position that there are grounds which would justify the General Assembly in refusing to give effect to awards of the Administrative Tribunal.

[33] The legal power of the General Assembly to establish a tribunal competent to render judgments binding on the United Nations has been challenged. Accordingly, it is necessary to consider whether the General Assembly has been given this power by the Charter.

[34] There is no express provision for the establishment of judicial bodies or organs and no indication to the contrary. However, in its opinion—*Reparation for Injuries Suffered in the Service of the United Nations*, Advisory Opinion: [1949] ICJ Reports 182—the Court said:

'Under international law, the Organization must be deemed to have those powers which, though not expressly provided in the Charter, are conferred upon it by necessary implication as being essential to the performance of its duties.'

[35] The Court must therefore begin by enquiring whether the provisions of the Charter concerning the relations between the staff members and the Organization imply for the Organization the power to establish a judicial tribunal to adjudicate upon disputes arising out of the contracts of service.

[36] Under the provisions of Chapter XV of the Charter, the Secretariat, which is one of the principal organs of the United Nations, comprises the Secretary-General and the staff. The Secretary-General is appointed by the General Assembly, upon the recommendation of the Security Council, and he is 'the chief administrative officer of the Organization'. The staff members are 'appointed by the Secretary-General under regulations established by the General Assembly'. In the words of Article 101(3) of the Charter, 'The paramount consideration in the employment of the staff and in the determination of the conditions of service shall be the necessity of securing the highest standards of efficiency, competence and integrity'.

[...]

[38] When the Secretariat was organized, a situation arose in which the relations between the staff members and the Organization were governed by a complex code of law. This code consisted of the Staff Regulations established by the General Assembly, defining the fundamental rights and obligations of the staff, and the Staff Rules, made by the Secretary-General in order to implement the Staff Regulations. It was inevitable that there would be disputes between the Organization and staff members as to their rights and duties. The Charter contains no provision which authorizes any of the principal organs of the United Nations to adjudicate upon these disputes, and Article 105 secures for the United Nations jurisdictional immunities in national courts. It would, in the opinion of the Court, hardly be consistent with the expressed aim of the Charter to promote freedom and justice for individuals and with the constant preoccupation of the United Nations Organization to promote this aim that it should afford no judicial or arbitral remedy to its own staff for the settlement of any disputes which may arise between it and them.

[39] In these circumstances, the Court finds that the power to establish a tribunal, to do justice as between the Organization and the staff members, was essential to ensure the efficient working of the Secretariat, and to give effect to the paramount consideration of securing the highest standards of efficiency, competence and integrity. Capacity to do this arises by necessary intendment out of the Charter.

[40] The existence of this capacity leads to the further enquiry as to the agency by which it may be exercised. Here, there can be no room for doubt.

[41] In Article 7 of the Charter, after naming the six principal organs, it is provided in paragraph (2):

'Such subsidiary organs, as may be found necessary may be established in accordance with the present Charter.'

Article 22 provides:

'The General Assembly may establish such subsidiary organs as it deems necessary for the performance of its functions.'

Further, in Article 101, paragraph 1, the General Assembly is given power to regulate staff relations:

'The Staff shall be appointed by the Secretary-General under regulations established by the General Assembly.'

[42] Accordingly, the Court finds that the power to establish a tribunal to do justice between the Organization and the staff members may be exercised by the General Assembly.

[43] But that does not dispose of the problem before the Court. Some of the Governments that take the position that there are grounds which would justify the General Assembly in refusing to give effect to awards, agree that the powers of the General Assembly, and particularly its power to establish regulations under Article 101, imply the power to set up an administrative tribunal. They agree that the General Assembly would be able to establish a tribunal competent to hear and decide staff grievances, to prescribe its jurisdiction, and to authorize it to give a final decision, in the sense that no appeal could be taken as of right. They nevertheless contend that the implied power does not enable the General Assembly to establish a tribunal with authority to make decisions binding on the General Assembly itself.

[44] In the first place, it is contended that there was no need to go so far, and that an implied power can only be exercised to the extent that the particular measure under consideration can be regarded as absolutely essential. There can be no doubt that the General Assembly in the exercise of its power could have set up a tribunal without giving finality to its judgments. In fact, however, it decided, after long deliberation, to invest the Tribunal with power to render judgments which would be 'final and without appeal', and which would be binding on the United Nations. The precise nature and scope of the measures by which the power of creating a tribunal was to be exercised, was a matter for determination by the General Assembly alone.

[45] In the second place, it has been argued that, while an implied power of the General Assembly to establish an administrative tribunal may be both necessary and essential, nevertheless, an implied power to impose legal limitations upon the General Assembly's express Charter powers is not legally admissible.

[46] It has been contended that the General Assembly cannot, by establishing the Administrative Tribunal, divest itself of the power conferred by paragraph (1) of Article 17 of the Charter, which reads:

'The General Assembly shall consider and approve the budget of the Organization.'

This provision confers a power on the General Assembly, for the exercise of which Article 18 requires the vote of a two-thirds majority. Accordingly, the establishment of a tribunal competent to make an award of compensation to which the General Assembly was bound to give effect would, it has been argued, contravene the provisions relating to the budgetary power. The Court is unable to accept this contention.

[47] The Court notes that Article 17 of the Charter appears in a section of Chapter IV relating to the General Assembly, which is entitled 'Functions and Powers'. This Article deals with a function of the General Assembly and provides for the consideration and approval by it of the budget of the Organization. Consideration of the budget is thus an act which must be performed and the same is true of its approval, for without such approval there can be no budget.

[48] But the function of approving the budget does not mean that the General Assembly has an absolute power to approve or disapprove the expenditure proposed to it; for some part of that expenditure arises out of obligations already incurred by the Organization, and to this extent the General Assembly has no alternative but to honour these engagements. The question, therefore, to be decided by the Court is whether these obligations comprise the awards of compensation made by the Administrative Tribunal in favour of staff members. The reply to this question must be in the affirmative. The obligatory character of these awards has been established by the considerations set out above relating to the authority of *res judicata* and the binding effect of the judgments of this Tribunal upon the United Nations Organization.

[49] The Court therefore considers that the assignment of the budgetary function to the General Assembly cannot be regarded as conferring upon it the right to refuse to give effect to the obligation arising out of an award of the Administrative Tribunal.

[50] It has also been contended that the implied power of the General Assembly to establish a tribunal cannot be carried so far as to enable the tribunal to intervene in matters falling within the province of the Secretary-General. The Court cannot accept this contention.

[51] The General Assembly could at all times limit or control the powers of the Secretary-General in staff matters, by virtue of the provisions of Article 101. Acting under powers conferred by the Charter, the General Assembly authorized the intervention of the Tribunal to the extent that such intervention might result from the exercise of jurisdiction conferred upon the Tribunal by its Statute. Accordingly, when the Tribunal decides that particular action by the Secretary-General involves a breach of the contract of service, it is in no sense intervening in a Charter power of the Secretary-General, because the Secretary-General's legal powers in staff matters have already been limited in this respect by the General Assembly.

[...]

[53] In the third place, the view has been put forward that the Administrative Tribunal is a subsidiary, subordinate, or secondary organ; and that, accordingly, the Tribunal's judgments cannot bind the General Assembly which established it.

[54] This view assumes that, in adopting the Statute of the Administrative Tribunal, the General Assembly was establishing an organ which it deemed necessary for the performance of its own functions. But the Court cannot accept this basic assumption. The Charter does not confer judicial functions on the General Assembly and the relations between staff and Organization come within the scope of Chapter XV of the Charter. In the absence of the establishment of an Administrative Tribunal, the function of resolving disputes between staff and Organization could be discharged by the Secretary-General by virtue of the provisions of Articles 97 and 101. Accordingly, in the three years or more preceding the establishment of the Administrative Tribunal, the Secretary-General coped with this problem by means of joint administrative machinery, leading to ultimate decision by himself. By establishing the Administrative Tribunal, the General Assembly was not delegating the performance of its own functions: it was exercising a power which it had under the Charter to regulate staff relations. In regard to the Secretariat, the General Assembly is given by the Charter a power to make regulations, but not a power to adjudicate upon, or otherwise deal with, particular instances.

[55] It has been argued that an authority exercising a power to make regulations is inherently incapable of creating a subordinate body competent to make decisions binding its creator. There can be no doubt that the Administrative Tribunal is subordinate in the sense that the General Assembly can abolish the Tribunal by repealing the Statute, that it can amend the Statute and provide for review of the future decisions of the Tribunal and that it can amend the Staff Regulations and make new ones. There is no lack of power to deal effectively with any problem that may arise. But the contention that the General Assembly is inherently incapable of creating a tribunal competent to make decisions binding on itself cannot be accepted. It cannot be justified by analogy to national laws, for it is common practice in national legislatures to create courts with the capacity to render decisions legally binding on the legislatures which brought them into being.

[56] The question cannot be determined on the basis of the description of the relationship between the General Assembly and the Tribunal, that is, by considering whether the Tribunal is to be regarded as a subsidiary, a subordinate, or a secondary organ, or on the basis of the fact that it was established by the General Assembly. It depends on the intention of the General Assembly in establishing the Tribunal, and on the nature of the functions conferred upon it by its Statute. An examination of the language of the Statute of the Administrative Tribunal has shown that the General Assembly intended to establish a judicial body; moreover, it had the legal capacity under the Charter to do so.

[...]

[59] The Court has accordingly arrived at the conclusion that the first Question submitted to it must be answered in the negative. The second Question does not therefore call for consideration.

[60] For these reasons, having regard to the Statute of the United Nations Administrative Tribunal and to any other relevant instruments and to the relevant records,

The Court is of opinion,

by nine votes to three,

that the General Assembly has not the right on any grounds to refuse to give effect to an award of compensation made by the Administrative Tribunal of the United Nations in favour of a staff member of the United Nations whose contract of service has been terminated without his assent.

[...]

IV. Commentary

The response of the General Assembly to the opinion was twofold: (a) to note the opinion and authorise payment of the awards and (b) to create the possibility, in effect, of judicial review by the Court of awards of the Tribunal on the following grounds:

'[T]hat the Tribunal has exceeded its jurisdiction or competence or that the Tribunal has failed to exercise jurisdiction vested in it, or has erred on a question of law relating to the provisions of the Charter of the United Nations, or has committed a fundamental error in procedure which has occasioned a failure of justice'[4].

The request would be made by a subsidiary organ of the General Assembly, a committee consisting of the member States, the representatives of which have served on the General Committee of the most recent regular session of the General Assembly. The General Assembly gave the new Committee the necessary authority under art. 96(2) of the Charter of the UN.

The Committee could be approached by a member State, the Secretary-General, or the person in respect of whom a judgment has been rendered by the Tribunal. In that context, Dag Hammarskjöld, the Secretary-General, identified as a fundamental principle 'that the staff member should have the right to initiate the review and to participate in it. Further, any review procedure should enable the staff member to participate on an equitable basis in such procedure, which should ensure substantial equality'.

The review procedure was used only three times and never with success between 1955 and 1995.[5] In 1995 the General Assembly, stating that the procedure had not proved to be a constructive or useful element in the adjudication of staff disputes within the Organization, decided to remove the provision for review. Fourteen years later, in a general recasting of the internal justice system of the UN, a two-tier system was established: the United Nations Disputes Tribunal and the United Nations Appeal Tribunal, the decisions of the latter being final and binding.

In the three review cases which did reach the Court procedural issues concerning the participation of the staff member in the procedure before the Court had to be addressed. As the Court read its Statute and Rules, the staff member could not make written submissions directly to the Court, but they had to be transmitted via the UN Secretariat (the employer), and the staff member could not appear at a hearing—which accordingly was not held. The same issues arose in respect of two similar challenges brought against rulings of the International Labour Organization Administrative Tribunal, most recently in the *IFAD* case.[6] In those two cases there was the further difficulty that only the employing agency could initiate the challenge process. By contrast the UNAT process gave officials along with the UN and member States access to the process which could lead to a request.

The Secretary-General's concern for the protection of the status of rights of UN Secretariat members was matched by his emphasis on their responsibilities as independent international civil servants. He addressed these broad matters in an outstanding lecture, given at Oxford University in 1961, shortly before his death in a plane crash in Northern Rhodesia where he was trying to resolve aspects of the crisis

---

[4] Resolution 957(X) of the General Assembly of the United Nations, adopted 8 November 1955.

[5] See for the legal history of the Administrative Tribunal: R. Gulati, 'The Internal Dispute Resolution Regime of the United Nations', (2011) 15 *Max Planck Yearbook of United Nations Law*, pp. 489–538.

[6] See *Judgment No. 2867 of the Administrative Tribunal of the International Labour Organisation Upon a Complaint Filed Against the International Fund for Agricultural Development*, Advisory Opinion [2012] ICJ Rep 10, paras 33–48.

in the Congo.[7] He emphasized the international composition and the international responsibilities of the international civil service. He found guidance in all the provisions of Chapter XV of the Charter and reviewed the pressures brought to bear on the Secretary-General in the previous fifteen years. The continual process of interpretation and clarification in the face of those pressures tended to affirm and strengthen the independence of the international civil service. These developments involved (1) the relation between the UN and member States in regard to the selection and employment of nationals and (2) the relation between the official, their own State, and the international responsibilities of the Organization. A major part of the lecture concerns the implementation of controversial political decisions in a manner fully consistent with the exclusively international responsibility of the Secretary-General. Where was he to find his guidance? Read this excellent address and also Hammarskjöld's closely related introduction to his 1960–61 *Annual Report of the Secretary-General*.[8]

The Court in this case, as in others, made use of the doctrine of implied powers (paras. 32–44). But on what basis is such an implication to be made? How is the particular implied power to be related to the powers expressed in the Charter, here the (apparently unfettered) power to consider and approve the budget (paras. 45–51)? How far does this doctrine go, bearing in mind the very wide scope of the purposes and principles of the UN? The authorizing of a peacekeeping force by the General Assembly? The creation of tribunals for other purposes?

If, as the Court says, the General Assembly does not have judicial functions conferred on it by the Charter how can it establish a 'subsidiary body' with such functions? Do art. 7(2) and 22 help (para. 54)?

Notice the use which the Court makes throughout the opinion of principle, for instance in respect of implied powers, the character of the judicial function, *res judicata*, and the independent international civil service.

While in form the Court answered the question using exactly the same words put to it, in substance, as it indicated in the first paragraph (para. 11) of the extract from the opinion set out above and in para. II it limited its answer; the tribunal had to be properly constituted and acting within its competence. That rewriting of the question is a frequent occurrence in advisory cases. To quote Judge Lauterpacht, it is a matter of common experience that a mere affirmation or denial of a question does not necessarily result in a close approximation to truth.[9] For recent examples of redrafting see the *IFAD* case[10] and the *Kosovo* case.[11]

---

[7] D. Hammarskjöld, *The International Civil Servant in Law and in Fact* (Oxford, Clarendon 1961).

[8] United Nations documents, GAOR (XVI) Supp. 1 A, A/4800/Add. 1.

[9] See *South West Africa* (Hearings) [1956] ICJ Rep 23, 37.   [10] See n. 6 above.

[11] See *Accordance with International Law of the Unilateral Declaration of Independence in Respect of Kosovo*, Advisory Opinion, [2010] ICJ Rep 403.

2.3 *Certain Expenses of the United Nations (Article 17, paragraph 2, of the Charter)*, International Court of Justice, Advisory Opinion, [1962] ICJ Rep 151

Jan Wouters and Jed Odermatt

Relevance of the case

The International Court of Justice's Advisory Opinion *Certain Expenses of the United Nations (Article 17, paragraph 2, of the Charter)* ('*Certain Expenses*' or 'opinion') is a landmark case in the history of the Court, although the Court defined its task narrowly and avoided delving into deeper issues of international law. On the face of it, the opinion is confined to the specific issue of the UN General Assembly's authority regarding the budget and expenses of the United Nations (UN), especially those related to the maintenance of international peace and security. Yet *Certain Expenses* has wider consequences: it provides rich jurisprudence for international law and the law of international organizations, including the powers of UN organs, treaty interpretation, the doctrine of *ultra vires*, and the Court's relationship with other UN organs.

I. Facts of the case

The request for an advisory opinion from the UN General Assembly (UNGA) came as part of a wider political and legal dispute about the funding of two UN peacekeeping missions. The UNGA had authorized the creation of the UN Emergency Force I (UNEF) in the wake of the Suez crisis, and UN Operations in the Congo (ONUC) related to the conflict in Central Africa. Partially as a result of these missions, the UN experienced a severe deterioration in its financial condition, and it became clear that it was facing 'imminent bankruptcy' if its financial issues could not be brought under control. One of the main issues was the unpaid obligations of various member States, including the Soviet Union, who had refused to accept certain special expenditures related to these two operations. The UNGA had treated these expenditures as normal expenses of the UN, which are apportioned to the various members of the organization according to art. 17(3) of the UN Charter. Certain member States had doubts regarding the legality of the UNGA's actions in the Middle East and Congo, and as such refused to pay for expenditures related to these operations. The request for an advisory opinion was an attempt to help resolve some of these legal issues regarding the UNGA's power to incur expenses related to peace and security.

II. The legal questions

The UNGA essentially asked whether certain expenses related to operations in the Congo and in the Middle East constituted 'expenses of the Organization' under art. 17(2) of the UN Charter. In order to define 'expenses of the Organization' it faced the question of whether there is a distinction to be made between a 'regular' ('administrative') and an 'operational' budget.

The Court was also asked to decide, indirectly, on the legality of the expenses incurred by the UNGA. The Court discussed whether it should take into account the rejection of a French amendment to the question which would have specifically asked the Court to judge whether certain expenses were 'decided on in conformity with the provisions of the Charter and, if so, do they constitute expenses of the Organization'. Did the rejection of this amendment preclude the Court from examining the legality of the UNGA resolutions concerned under the UN Charter?

The Court was called upon to decide on questions of jurisdiction, especially whether there were any compelling reasons why it should refuse to give an opinion in this instance. One argument put forward in this regard was that the question was essentially not a 'legal question' given the political nature of the dispute.

III. Excerpts[1]

[11] The power of the Court to give an advisory opinion is derived from Article 65 of the Statute. The power granted is of a discretionary character [...]...

[12] The Court finds no 'compelling reason' why it should not give the advisory opinion which the General Assembly requested by its resolution 1731 (XVI). It has been argued that the question put to the Court is intertwined with political questions, and that for this reason the Court should refuse to give an opinion. It is true that most interpretations of the Charter of the United Nations will have political significance, great or small. In the nature of things it could not be otherwise. The Court, however, cannot attribute a political character to a request which invites it to undertake an essentially judicial task, namely, the interpretation of a treaty provision.

[...]

[15] The question on which the Court is asked to give its opinion is whether certain expenditures which were authorized by the General Assembly to cover the costs of the United Nations operations in the Congo (hereinafter referred to as ONUC) and of the operations of the United Nations Emergency Force in the Middle East (hereinafter referred to as UNEF), 'constitute "expenses of the Organization" within the meaning of Article 17, paragraph 2, of the Charter of the United Nations.'

[...]

[19] The rejection of the French amendment does not constitute a directive to the Court to exclude from its consideration the question whether certain expenditures were 'decided on in conformity with the Charter', if the Court finds such consideration appropriate. It is not to be assumed that the General Assembly would thus seek to fetter or hamper the Court in the discharge of its judicial functions; the Court must have full liberty to consider all relevant data available to it in forming an opinion on a question posed to it for an advisory opinion. Nor can the Court agree that the rejection of the French amendment has any bearing upon the question whether

---

[1] The numbers between brackets before each paragraph have been added to the text. They are the same as in the reprint of the advisory opinion in *Reports of International Law* (Oxford, Oxford University Press).

the General Assembly sought to preclude the Court from interpreting Article 17 in the light of other articles of the Charter, that is, in the whole context of the treaty. If any deduction is to be made from the debates on this point, the opposite conclusion would be drawn from the clear statements of sponsoring delegations that they took it for granted the Court would consider the Charter as a whole.

[...]

[20] Turning to the question which has been posed, the Court observes that it involves an interpretation of Article 17, paragraph 2, of the Charter. On the previous occasions when the Court has had to interpret the Charter of the United Nations, it has followed the principles and rules applicable in general to the interpretation of treaties, since it has recognized that the Charter is a multilateral treaty, albeit a treaty having certain special characteristics. In interpreting Article 4 of the Charter, the Court was led to consider 'the structure of the Charter' and 'the relations established by it between the General Assembly and the Security Council'; a comparable problem confronts the Court in the instant matter. The Court sustained its interpretation of Article 4 by considering the manner in which the organs concerned 'have consistently interpreted the text' in their practice (Competence of the General Assembly for the Admission of a State to the United Nations, I.C.J. Reports 1950, pp. 8–9).

[...]

[24] The text of Article 17, paragraph 2, refers to 'the expenses of the Organization' without any further explicit definition of such expenses. It would be possible to begin with a general proposition to the effect that the 'expenses' of any organization are the amounts paid out to defray the costs of carrying out its purposes, in this case, the political, economic, social, humanitarian and other purposes of the United Nations. The next step would be to examine, as the Court will, whether the resolutions authorizing the operations here in question were intended to carry out the purposes of the United Nations and whether the expenditures were incurred in furthering these operations. Or, it might simply be said that the 'expenses' of an organization are those which are provided for in its budget. But the Court has not been asked to give an abstract definition of the words 'expenses of the Organization'. It has been asked to answer a specific question related to certain identified expenditures which have actually been made, but the Court would not adequately discharge the obligation incumbent on it unless it examined in some detail various problems raised by the question which the General Assembly has asked.

[25] It is perhaps the simple identification of 'expenses' with the items included in a budget, which has led certain arguments to link the interpretation of the word 'expenses' in paragraph 2 of Article 17, with the word 'budget' in paragraph 1 of that Article; in both cases, it is contended, the qualifying adjective 'regular' or 'administrative' should be understood to be implied. Since no such qualification is expressed in the text of the Charter, it could be read in, only if such qualification must necessarily be implied from the provisions of the Charter considered as a whole, or from some particular provision thereof which makes it unavoidable to do so in order to give effect to the Charter.

[26] In the first place, concerning the word 'budget' in paragraph 1 of Article 17, it is clear that the existence of the distinction between 'administrative budgets' and 'operational budgets' was not absent from the minds of the drafters of the Charter, nor from the consciousness of the Organization even in the early days of its history.

In drafting Article 17, the drafters found it suitable to provide in paragraph I that 'The General Assembly shall consider and approve the budget of the Organization'...

[...]

[29] Actually, the practice of the Organization is entirely consistent with the plain meaning of the text. The budget of the Organization has from the outset included items which would not fall within any of the definitions of 'administrative budget' which have been advanced in this connection...

[...]

[30] It is a consistent practice of the General Assembly to include in the annual budget resolutions, provision for expenses relating to the maintenance of international peace and security. Annually, since 1947, the General Assembly has made anticipatory provision for 'unforeseen and extraordinary expenses' arising in relation to the 'maintenance of peace and security'.

[...]

[33] In the light of what has been stated, the Court concludes that there is no justification for reading into the text of Article 17, paragraph 1, any limiting or qualifying word before the word 'budget'.

[34] Turning to paragraph 2 of Article 17, the Court observes that, on its face, the term 'expenses of the Organization' means all the expenses and not just certain types of expenses which might be referred to as 'regular expenses'. An examination of other parts of the Charter shows the variety of expenses which must inevitably be included within the 'expenses of the Organization' just as much as the salaries of staff or the maintenance of buildings.

[...]

[38] Passing from the text of Article 17 to its place in the general structure and scheme of the Charter, the Court will consider whether in that broad context one finds any basis for implying a limitation upon the budgetary authority of the General Assembly which in turn might limit the meaning of 'expenses' in paragraph 2 of that Article.

[39] The general purposes of Article 17 are the vesting of control over the finances of the Organization, and the levying of apportioned amounts of the expenses of the Organization in order to enable it to carry out the functions of the Organization as a whole acting through its principal organs and such subsidiary organs as may be established under the authority of Article 22 or Article 29.

[40] [...] [I]t has been argued before the Court that one type of expenses, namely those resulting from operations for the maintenance of international peace and security, are not 'expenses of the Organization' within the meaning of Article 17, paragraph 2, of the Charter, inasmuch as they fall to be dealt with exclusively by the Security Council, and more especially through agreements negotiated in accordance with Article 43 of the Charter.

[41] The argument rests in part upon the view that when the maintenance of international peace and security is involved, it is only the Security Council which is authorized to decide on any action relative thereto. It is argued further that since the General Assembly's power is limited to discussing, considering, studying and recommending, it cannot impose an obligation to pay the expenses which result from the implementation of its recommendations. This argument leads to an examination of the respective functions of the General Assembly and of the Security Council under

the Charter particularly with respect to the maintenance of international peace and security.

[...]

[43] The responsibility conferred is 'primary', not exclusive. This primary responsibility is conferred upon the Security Council, as stated in Article 24, 'in order to ensure prompt and effective action'. To this end, it is the Security Council which is given a power to impose an explicit obligation of compliance if for example it issues an order or command to an aggressor under Chapter VII. It is only the Security Council which can require enforcement by coercive action against an aggressor.

[44] The Charter makes it abundantly clear, however, that the General Assembly is also to be concerned with international peace and security. Article 14 authorizes the General Assembly to 'recommend measures for the peaceful adjustment of any situation, regardless of origin, which it deems likely to impair the general welfare or friendly relations among nations, including situations resulting from a violation of the provisions of the present Charter setting forth the purposes and principles of the United Nations'. The word 'measures' implies some kind of action, and the only limitation which Article 14 imposes on the General Assembly is the restriction found in Article 12, namely, that the Assembly should not recommend measures while the Security Council is dealing with the same matter unless the Council requests it to do so. Thus while it is the Security Council which, exclusively, may order coercive action, the functions and powers conferred by the Charter on the General Assembly are not confined to discussion, consideration, the initiation of studies and the making of recommendations; they are not merely hortatory. Article 18 deals with 'decisions' of the General Assembly 'on important questions'. These 'decisions' do indeed include certain recommendations, but others have dispositive force and effect. Among these latter decisions, Article 18 includes suspension of rights and privileges of membership, expulsion of Members, 'and budgetary questions'. In connection with the suspension of rights and privileges of membership and expulsion from membership under Articles 5 and 6, it is the Security Council which has only the power to recommend and it is the General Assembly which decides and whose decision determines status; but there is a close collaboration between the two organs. Moreover, these powers of decision of the General Assembly under Articles 5 and 6 are specifically related to preventive or enforcement measures.

[45] By Article 17, paragraph 1, the General Assembly is given the power not only to 'consider' the budget of the Organization, but also to 'approve' it. The decision to 'approve' the budget has a close connection with paragraph 2 of Article 17, since thereunder the General Assembly is also given the power to apportion the expenses among the Members and the exercise of the power of apportionment creates the obligation, specifically stated in Article 17, paragraph 2, of each Member to bear that part of the expenses which is apportioned to it by the General Assembly. When those expenses include expenditures for the maintenance of peace and security, which are not otherwise provided for, it is the General Assembly which has the authority to apportion the latter amounts among the Members. The provisions of the Charter which distribute functions and powers to the Security Council and to the General Assembly give no support to the view that such distribution excludes from the powers of the General Assembly the power to provide for the financing of measures designed to maintain peace and security.

[…]

[49] The Court accordingly finds that the argument which seeks, by reference to Article 11, paragraph 2, to limit the budgetary authority of the General Assembly in respect of the maintenance of international peace and security, is unfounded.

[…]

[55] […] In determining whether the actual expenditures authorized constitute 'expenses of the Organization within the meaning of Article 17, paragraph 2, of the Charter', the Court agrees that such expenditures must be tested by their relationship to the purposes of the United Nations in the sense that if an expenditure were made for a purpose which is not one of the purposes of the United Nations, it could not be considered an 'expense of the Organization'.

[56] The purposes of the United Nations are set forth in Article 1 of the Charter. The first two purposes as stated in paragraphs 1 and 2, may be summarily described as pointing to the goal of international peace and security and friendly relations. The third purpose is the achievement of economic, social, cultural and humanitarian goals and respect for human rights. The fourth and last purpose is: 'To be a center for harmonizing the actions of nations in the attainment of these common ends.'

[57] The primary place ascribed to international peace and security is natural, since the fulfilment of the other purposes will be dependent upon the attainment of that basic condition. These purposes are broad indeed, but neither they nor the powers conferred to effectuate them are unlimited. Save as they have entrusted the Organization with the attainment of these common ends, the Member States retain their freedom of action. But when the Organization takes action which warrants the assertion that it was appropriate for the fulfilment of one of the stated purposes of the United Nations, the presumption is that such action is not *ultra vires* the Organization.

[58] If it is agreed that the action in question is within the scope of the functions of the Organization but it is alleged that it has been initiated or carried out in a manner not in conformity with the division of functions among the several organs which the Charter prescribes, one moves to the internal plane, to the internal structure of the Organization. If the action was taken by the wrong organ, it was irregular as a matter of that internal structure, but this would not necessarily mean that the expense incurred was not an expense of the Organization. Both national and international law contemplate cases in which the body corporate or politic may be bound, as to third parties, by an *ultra vires* act of an agent.

[59] In the legal systems of States, there is often some procedure for determining the validity of even a legislative or governmental act, but no analogous procedure is to be found in the structure of the United Nations. Proposals made during the drafting of the Charter to place the ultimate authority to interpret the Charter in the International Court of Justice were not accepted; the opinion which the Court is in course of rendering is an *advisory* opinion. As anticipated in 1945, therefore, each organ must, in the first place at least, determine its own jurisdiction. If the Security Council, for example, adopts a resolution purportedly for the maintenance of international peace and security and if, in accordance with a mandate or authorization in such resolution, the Secretary-General incurs financial obligations, these amounts must be presumed to constitute 'expenses of the Organization'.

[…]

[81] This resolution, which was adopted by the requisite two-thirds majority, must have rested upon the conclusion that the expenses of UNEF were 'expenses of the Organization' since otherwise the General Assembly would have had no authority to decide that they 'shall be borne by the United Nations' or to apportion them among the Members. [...]

[...]

[100] [...] Consequently, the Court arrives at the conclusion that the question submitted to it in General Assembly resolution 1731 (XVI) must be answered in the affirmative.

[101] For these reasons, The Court is of opinion, by nine votes to five, that the expenditures authorized in General Assembly resolutions [...] constitute 'expenses of the Organization' within the meaning of Article 17, paragraph 2, of the Charter of the United Nations.

IV. Commentary

The Court's answer was that expenses authorized by the UNGA in relation to the ONUC and UNEF constituted 'expenses of the Organization' within the meaning of art. 17(2) of the UN Charter. Although the immediate outcome of the opinion was to clarify this legal question regarding the UNGA's budgetary authority, the opinion continues to have relevance in defining the powers of the UN organs, clarifying the Court's approach to treaty interpretation, the legal issue of *ultra vires* acts of international organizations, and the role of the Court in giving advisory opinions.

A. Powers of the UN organs

While the legal issue in this case is related to the relatively narrow question of the meaning of 'expenses', the dispute stemmed from a wider disagreement over the UN's increasing role in international peace and security, in particular by the UNGA. It has been noted that the opinion allowed, 'for the first time, express judicial approval of the practical transfer of responsibility for maintenance of peace from the Security Council to the General Assembly'.[2] The opinion acknowledges that while the UN Security Council has primary responsibility for the maintenance of international peace and security under the Charter, this role is not exclusive.[3] The Court points out that the Charter provides a role for the UNGA relating to international peace and security which is not limited to giving recommendations—'they are not merely hortatory'.[4]

The Court found that there was nothing in the distribution of powers among the UNSC and UNGA that precluded the latter from financing measures designed to maintain peace and security. The UNGA could exercise its powers in the field of peace and security, except where it was expressly precluded from doing so by an exclusive

---

[2] J. Fergusson Hogg, 'Peace-Keeping Costs and Charter Obligations—Implications of the International Court of Justice Decision on Certain Expenses of the United Nations', (1962) 62 *Columbia Law Review* 1236, 1238.

[3] *Certain Expenses*, Opinion, para. 43.   [4] Ibid., para. 44.

power of the Security Council. It is to these enforcement actions that the restrictive clause of art. 11(2) of the UN Charter applies. Yet upon examining the nature of the UNEF and ONUC operations the Court determined that they were not enforcement actions under Chapter VII of the UN Charter. In effect, the Court authorized a wider role for the UNGA in international peace and security. This is particularly significant since the UN Security Council was often unable to act due to the exercise of veto powers by that body's permanent members, particularly during the superpower rivalries of the Cold War.

B. Treaty interpretation

The case is also notable in that it further illustrates the Court's approach to treaty interpretation, particularly of the UN Charter.[5] The Court confirmed that the UN Charter is a multilateral convention, albeit one with certain special characteristics, and as such customary international law techniques of treaty interpretation apply. The Court found that expenditures could only be considered 'expenses of the organization' where they were carried out in order to fulfil the purposes of the UN. The Court examined the plain meaning of the text and found that expenses means 'the amounts paid out to defray the costs of carrying out its purposes, in this case, the political, economic, social, humanitarian and other purposes of the United Nations'.[6] The Court could not find any reason to differentiate between expenses of a 'regular' or 'administrative' nature. In coming to this conclusion, the Court found it relevant that art. 17(3) *does* use the limiting term 'administrative' whereas art. 17(2) does not. If the drafters had intended to limit the expenditure in art. 17(2) to administrative expenses only, they would have used similar limiting language.

The Court also analysed art. 17 in a wider context, taking into account the broader UN structure, and found that there was no limitation to the term 'expenses'. A distinction between 'administrative' and 'regular' expenses could only be made 'if such qualification must necessarily be implied from the provisions of the Charter considered as a whole, or from some particular provision thereof which makes it unavoidable to do so in order to give effect to the Charter'.[7] There is nothing in the Charter, particularly in the distribution of functions and powers to the UNSC and to the UNGA, to imply that the latter did not have power for the financing of measures related to peace and security.

To support this conclusion, the Court also took into account 'the manner in which the organs concerned "have consistently interpreted the text" in their practice'.[8] In particular, it noted that '[i]t is a consistent practice of the General Assembly to include in the annual budget resolutions, provision for expenses relating to the maintenance of international peace and security'.[9] The Court therefore relied upon the practice of

---

[5] J. Arato, 'Treaty Interpretation and Constitutional Transformation: Informal Change in International Organizations', (2013) 38 *Yale Journal of International Law* 318: 'What is extraordinary is the Court's method of interpretation.'

[6] *Certain Expenses*, Opinion, para. 24.   [7] Ibid., para. 25.   [8] Ibid., para. 20.

[9] Ibid., para.30.

the UN organs as a subsidiary means to support its conclusion. The opinion has been criticized for its reliance on the practice of UN organs as 'subsequent practice' of the parties in interpreting the UN Charter, especially by Judge Spender in his separate opinion.[10]

This raises the question of the probative value of 'organ practice' within the United Nations, and in international organizations generally. Article 31(3)(b) of the 1969 Vienna Convention on the Law of Treaties provides that subsequent practice may be taken into account as a means of interpretation if it 'establishes the agreement of the parties'. Yet when using 'organ practice' the Court did not examine the extent to which the practice of the UN organs actually reflected the consent of UN member States. The UNGA practice to which the Court referred did not represent unanimous decisions; on the contrary, some were strongly opposed by member States. The question is not whether organ practice should be used as an interpretive tool, but the weight that should be given to it. Here 'organ practice' was used as a subsidiary, supporting reason, rather than a primary tool of treaty interpretation.[11]

C. *Ultra vires*

Some states had argued that the operations authorized by the UNGA violated the UN Charter and should therefore be considered *ultra vires*. The Court had to determine whether it should examine the validity of the expenditures. In particular, the Court examined whether the French amendment to the text of the question constituted a relevant limit on the jurisdiction of the Court. The French amendment to the question, a proposal that was eventually defeated in the UNGA, would have requested the Court to answer whether the expenses were 'decided upon in conformity with the provisions of the Charter'.

The question of validity did arise through the Court's examination of art. 17(2) of the UN Charter. The expenditures under consideration could only be regarded as 'expenses of the organization' if they were to fulfil one of the goals of the UN, as set out in the UN Charter. The Court analysed whether the expenditures were undertaken in order to fulfil the purposes of the Organization. Since the expenditures were made in pursuance of an objective of the UN, namely the maintenance of peace and security, the expenditures were considered 'expenses of the Organization' according to art. 17(2) of the UN Charter.

The Court opined on the legal implications of a finding that the action was not in pursuance of the objectives and purposes of the UN, that is, a finding of *ultra vires*. The Court held that 'when the Organization takes action which warrants the assertion that it was appropriate for the fulfilment of one of the stated purposes of the United Nations, the presumption is that such action is not *ultra vires* the Organization'.[12] Even if action was carried out by the wrong organ, this does not mean that the expenses incurred would not be considered as expenses of the organization.[13] There is,

---

[10] *Certain Expenses*, Separate Opinion of Judge Sir Percy Spender, para. 55.
[11] J. Arato (n. 5), 295.   [12] *Certain Expenses*, Opinion, para. 57.   [13] Ibid., para. 58.

according to the Court, a difference between the validity of the UN's financial distribution among member States and the legal validity of the UN action. The resolutions authorizing budgetary expenses could be valid even if the operations concerned were not, since they had been taken by the wrong organ. The Court's narrow approach to the legal question put before it meant that the Court did not go into depth on these issues, leaving many important legal questions unanswered.[14]

One of the legal issues that one not addressed pertained to the UNGA's role in the field of collective security, particularly since the adoption of the 'Uniting for Peace' resolution. Under this resolution, when Security Council action in the maintenance of international peace and security is blocked by the veto of a permanent member, the UNGA shall consider the matter, and may make recommendations to member states, to restore international peace and security. A question that arises is whether the UN Security Council is the sole UN organ competent to act in the field of collective security. Supporters of the resolution argued that the UNSC has a 'primary responsibility' for the maintenance of peace and security (as indicated in art. 24(1) of the UN Charter), but not an exclusive one. The UNGA may exercise tasks in that field where the UNSC is unable to fulfil that function. Moreover, since this interpretation allows the UN to fulfil one of its main purposes, the maintenance of peace and security, the UN Charter should be read in a way that allows these aims to be achieved. The Court did not elaborate on the extent of the General Assembly's powers, particularly whether it could recommend coercive measures.[15] The opinion does not seem to prevent the UNGA from recommending such measures.

Certain Expenses is also an important opinion insofar as it relates to the limits of the 'implied powers' of international organizations. In determining whether the costs could be qualified as 'expenses of the organisation', the Court examined primarily whether they fit within the purposes of the UN. The Court acknowledged that these purposes are broad, but not unlimited. For instance, the exercise of powers must not affect the distribution of functions between UN organs. Nonetheless, by making a link between the purposes of the organization and legal powers, the Court can be criticized for developing an overly broad approach to implied powers. As President Winiarski points out in his dissenting opinion, '[t]he fact that an organ of the United Nations is seeking to achieve one of those purposes does not suffice to render its action lawful'.[16]

D. Role of the Court

The opinion also further elaborates on the role of the Court, especially its relationship with the other UN organs. Some UN member States had argued that the Court should decline to give an opinion since it was essentially a political, rather than a legal question. The Court notes that in most instances where it is requested to interpret the UN

---

[14] K.R. Simmonds, 'The UN Assessments Advisory Opinion', (1964) 13 *International and Comparative Law Quarterly* 854, 890.

[15] N. D. White, *The Law of International Organisations* (2nd edn, Manchester, Manchester University Press 2005) p. 103.

[16] *Certain Expenses*, dissenting opinion of President Winiarski, p. 230.

Charter, political questions necessarily arise; however, this does not deprive the question from its essentially juridical character. In principle, the Court will not refuse to give an opinion unless there is a 'compelling reason' for it not to do so.[17] Having found no such compelling reason, it proceeded to answer the question before it. In doing so, however, it interpreted the question before it in a narrow manner. It limited its opinion to the interpretation of art. 17 of the UN Charter[18] and did not elaborate on the related legal questions that arose from the underlying dispute.

The Court noted that there is no explicit power of judicial review for the Court in the UN Charter or the ICJ statute.[19] A proposal made at the San Francisco Conference to include such a power of judicial review in the Court's mandate was rejected. Nor was the Court given a general power to interpret the Charter in a manner like a domestic constitutional court. However, it has been recognized that the Court may play an incidental role in judicial review through exercising its judicial function and in its role as the principal judicial organ of the UN.[20] By narrowly interpreting the question in this case, and by not ruling on the legality of the conduct of the other organs, the Court can be seen as respecting the division of powers of the Charter.

---

[17] *Certain Expenses*, Opinion, para. 12.   [18] Ibid., para. 22.   [19] Ibid., para. 59.
[20] D. Akande, 'The International Court of Justice and the Security Council: Is there Room for Judicial Control of Decisions of the Political Organs of the United Nations?', (1997) 46 *International and Comparative Law Quarterly* 331.

2.4 *Legality of the Use by a State of Nuclear Weapons in Armed Conflict* International Court of Justice, Advisory Opinion of 8 July 1996, [1996] ICJ Rep 66

Gian Luca Burci and Jakob Quirin

Relevance of the advisory opinion

The advisory opinion contains important guidance on the delimitation of competence and co-ordination of international organizations, in particular those forming part of the UN system. The Court held by eleven votes to three that it did not have jurisdiction to give the advisory opinion 'which was requested of it'. The opinion marks an important step in the Court's jurisprudence in that it focusses not on an expansion of competence of international organizations as previous ICJ jurisprudence, but rather on the limits of this competence. The opinion is a succinct reminder of the tension between the goal to effectively and efficiently 'divide labour' between the mandates of the UN and the specialized agencies and the relative lack of mechanisms to enforce this division of labour.

I. Background

The World Health Organization (WHO), which requested the advisory opinion from the Court, is a United Nations specialized agency in the sense of art. 57 of the Charter. Its objective, as expressed in art. 1 of the WHO Constitution, is 'the attainment by all peoples of the highest possible level of health'. In May 1992, the World Health Assembly started engaging in a discussion of the legal aspects of the use of nuclear weapons. In May 1993, it passed resolution WHA46.40 to request an advisory opinion from the Court on the following question:

'In view of the health and environmental effects, would the use of nuclear weapons by a State in war or other armed conflict be a breach of its obligations under international law including the WHO Constitution?'

The vote on the resolution was taken by secret ballot. It obtained seventy-three affirmative votes from among the 164 member States at the time.[1] One-and-a-half years after resolution WHA46.40 was adopted the United Nations General Assembly requested the Court to give an advisory opinion on the question: 'Is the threat or use of nuclear weapons in any circumstances permitted under international law?'.

---

[1] For a detailed account of the events at WHO preceding the request see *Legality of the Use by a State of Nuclear Weapons in Armed Conflict*, Separate Opinion of Judge Oda, ICJ Rep 1996 pp. 88, 90 ff, 8 July 1996; see also L. Boisson de Chazournes/P. Sands, 'Introduction', in L. Boisson de Chazournes/P. Sands (eds), *International Law, the International Court of Justice and Nuclear Weapons* (Cambridge, Cambridge University Press 1999), pp. 1, 4ff.

Thus faced with two closely related requests for advisory opinions, the Court decided to hold public sittings and to hear, during those sittings, oral statements relating to both requests. Public sittings were mostly held in the first half of November 1995. Twenty States presented oral statements. WHO made a statement in which it laid out the procedural history of the request but maintained, in view of its divided membership, a position of 'strict neutrality'.[2] The Court gave distinct advisory opinions on the requests on 8 July 1996.[3]

II. The legal question

It was clear that the proceedings, as far as the WHO request was concerned, would strongly focus on whether the Court had jurisdiction. Jurisdiction hinged, in turn, on whether WHO acted *intra* or *ultra vires* through the decision to request the advisory opinion since art. 96, para. 2, of the UN Charter stipulates that a question asked by a specialized agency must be one arising within the scope of the activities of the requesting agency. This question had been intensely discussed within the WHO before the organization formally requested the opinion.

III. Excerpts

[...]

18. The Court will now seek to determine whether the advisory opinion requested by the WHO relates to a question which arises 'within the scope of [the] activities' of that Organization, in accordance with Article 96, paragraph 2, of the Charter. [...]

19. In order to delineate the field of activity or the area of competence of an international organization, one must refer to the relevant rules of the organization and, in the first place, to its constitution. [...]

20. [...] The functions attributed to the Organization are listed in 22 subparagraphs (subparagraphs (a) to (v)) in Article 2 of its Constitution. None of these subparagraphs expressly refers to the legality of any activity hazardous to health; and none of the functions of the WHO is dependent upon the legality of the situations upon which it must act. [...]

21. [...]

The question put to the Court in the present case relates [...] not to the effects of the use of nuclear weapons on health, but to the legality of the use of such weapons in view of their health and environmental effects. Whatever those effects might be, the competence of the WHO to deal with them is not dependent on the legality of the acts that caused them. Accordingly, it does not seem to the Court that the provisions of Article 2 of the WHO Constitution [...], can be understood as conferring upon the

---

[2] *Legality of the Use by a State of Nuclear Weapons in Armed Conflict*, Oral Statement by the WHO Legal Counsel, verbatim record of the public sitting held on Monday, 30 October 1995, at 10 a.m., at the Peace Palace, CR 1995/22, pp. 19, 20.

[3] For the Court's advisory opinion on the *Legality of the Threat or Use of Nuclear Weapons*, given on the same day upon the request of the United Nations General Assembly, see [1996] ICJ Rep 226.

Organization a competence to address the legality of the use of nuclear weapons, and thus in turn a competence to ask the Court about that.

22. World Health Assembly resolution WHA46.40, by which the Court has been seised of this request for an opinion, expressly refers, in its Preamble, to the functions indicated under subparagraphs (a), (k), (p) and (v) of Article 2 under consideration. [...] In the view of the Court, none of these functions has a sufficient connection with the question before it for that question to be capable of being considered as arising 'within the scope of [the] activities' of the WHO. The causes of the deterioration of human health are numerous and varied; and the legal or illegal character of these causes is essentially immaterial to the measures which the WHO must in any case take in an attempt to remedy their effects. In particular, the legality or illegality of the use of nuclear weapons in no way determines the specific measures, regarding health or otherwise (studies, plans, procedures, etc.), which could be necessary in order to seek to prevent or cure some of their effects. Whether nuclear weapons are used legally or illegally, their effects on health would be the same.

[...]

25. The Court need hardly point out that international organizations are subjects of international law which do not, unlike States, possess a general competence. International organizations are governed by the 'principle of speciality', that is to say, they are invested by the States which create them with powers, the limits of which are a function of the common interests whose promotion those States entrust to them. The Permanent Court of International Justice referred to this basic principle in the following terms:

> 'As the European Commission is not a State, but an international institution with a special purpose, it only has the functions bestowed upon it by the Definitive Statute with a view to the fulfilment of that purpose, but it has power to exercise these functions to their full extent, in so far as the Statute does not impose restrictions upon it.' (Jurisdiction of the European Commission of the Danube, Advisory Opinion, PCIJ, Series B, No. 14, p. 64.)

[...] In the opinion of the Court, to ascribe to the WHO the competence to address the legality of the use of nuclear weapons—even in view of their health and environmental effects—would be tantamount to disregarding the principle of speciality; for such competence could not be deemed a necessary implication of the Constitution of the Organization in the light of the purposes assigned to it by its member States.

26. The World Health Organization is, moreover, an international organization of a particular kind. As indicated in the Preamble and confirmed by Article 69 of its Constitution, 'The Organization shall be brought into relation with the United Nations as one of the specialized agencies referred to in Article 57 of the Charter of the United Nations'. [...]

As these provisions [arts. 57, 58, and 63 of the UN Charter] demonstrate, the Charter of the United Nations laid the basis of a 'system' designed to organize international co-operation in a coherent fashion by bringing the United Nations, invested with powers of general scope, into relationship with various autonomous and complementary organizations, invested with sectorial powers. The exercise of these powers by the organizations belonging to the 'United Nations system' is co-ordinated, notably, by the relationship agreements concluded between the United Nations and each of the specialized agencies. [...]

It follows [...] that the WHO Constitution can only be interpreted, as far as the powers conferred upon that Organization are concerned, by taking due account not only of the general principle of speciality, but also of the logic of the overall system contemplated by the Charter. If, according to the rules on which that system is based, the WHO has, by virtue of Article 57 of the Charter, 'wide international responsibilities', those responsibilities are necessarily restricted to the sphere of public 'health' and cannot encroach on the responsibilities of other parts of the United Nations system. And there is no doubt that questions concerning the use of force, the regulation of armaments and disarmament are within the competence of the United Nations and lie outside that of the specialized agencies. Besides, any other conclusion would render virtually meaningless the notion of a specialized agency; it is difficult to imagine what other meaning that notion could have if such an organization need only show that the use of certain weapons could affect its objectives in order to be empowered to concern itself with the legality of such use. It is therefore difficult to maintain that, by authorizing various specialized agencies to request opinions from the Court under Article 96, paragraph 2, of the Charter, the General Assembly intended to allow them to seise the Court of questions belonging within the competence of the United Nations.

For all these reasons, the Court considers that the question raised in the request for an advisory opinion submitted to it by the WHO does not arise 'within the scope of [the] activities' of that Organization as defined by its Constitution.

[...]

28. It remains to be considered whether the insertion of the words 'including the WHO Constitution' in the question put to the Court (which essentially seeks an opinion on the legality of the use of nuclear weapons in general) could allow it to offer an opinion on the legality of the use of nuclear weapons by reference to the passage in the question concerning the WHO Constitution. The Court must answer in the negative. Indeed, the WHO is not empowered to seek an opinion on the interpretation of its Constitution in relation to matters outside the scope of its functions.

[...]

29. Other arguments have nevertheless been put forward in the proceedings to found the jurisdiction of the Court in the present case. [...]

As the Court has stated, 'each organ must, in the first place at least, determine its own jurisdiction' [...] But likewise it is incumbent on the Court to satisfy itself that the conditions governing its own competence to give the opinion requested are met; through the reference made, respectively, by Article 96, paragraph 2, of the Charter to the 'scope of [the] activities' of the Organization and by Article X, paragraph 2, of the Agreement of 10 July 1948 to its 'competence', the Court also finds itself obliged, in the present case, to interpret the Constitution of the WHO [...] and in doing so the Court arrives at different conclusions from those reached by the World Health Assembly when it adopted resolution WHA46.40. [...]

32. For these reasons, THE COURT,

By eleven votes to three,

Finds that it is not able to give the advisory opinion which was requested of it under World Health Assembly resolution WHA46.40 dated 14 May 1993. [...]

IV. Commentary

Framed as a statement on the jurisdiction of the Court, the advisory opinion gives important guidance on the delimitation of competence and co-ordination of international organizations, in particular those forming part of the UN system. It is of particular importance not only for the WHO, which requested the opinion, but for all United Nations specialized agencies.[4] The advisory opinion is the second opinion requested by the WHO[5] and the fifth coming from a UN specialized agency in total.[6] The Court refused to give an advisory opinion requested from it for the first time,[7] having previously stated, albeit with regard to its discretionary power under art. 65 of the Statute ('may'), that requests for an advisory opinion 'in principle, should not be refused'[8] and that it would take 'compelling reasons'[9] for it not to give the requested opinion.

The Court's finding that it lacked jurisdiction to give the requested advisory opinion rests on the reasoning that one of the three conditions set out by art. 96, para. 2 of the Charter is not fulfilled, namely, that the opinion must be on a question 'arising within the scope' of activities of the requesting specialized agency.[10] The Court supports this conclusion with two arguments, both relying on an interpretation of the WHO Constitution and the UN Charter in accordance with art. 31 of the Vienna Convention on the Law of Treaties, but also with due regard to the particularities of

---

[4] J. Salmon, 'Quels sont les destinataires des avis?', in Boisson de Chazournes/Sands (eds) (n. 1), pp. 28, 31.

[5] The first one concerned the interpretation of the 'Agreement between the World Health Organization and the Government of Egypt for the purposes of determining the privileges, immunities and facilities to be granted in Egypt by the Government to the Organization, to the representatives of its Members and to its experts and officials' (WHO/Egypt host-country agreement) (Cairo, 25 March 1951, 223 UNTS 3058), see *Interpretation of the Agreement of 25 March 1951 Between the WHO and Egypt*, Advisory Opinion, [1980] ICJ Rep 73, 20 December 1980.

[6] Besides the first WHO request, the others are *Judgments of the Administrative Tribunal of the ILO upon Complaints Made against Unesco*, Advisory Opinion, [1956] ICJ Rep 77, 23 October 1956; *Constitution of the Maritime Safety Committee of the Inter-Governmental Maritime Consultative Organization*, Advisory Opinion, [1960] ICJ Rep 150, 8 June 1960 and *Judgment No. 2867 of the Administrative Tribunal of the International Labour Organization upon a Complaint Filed against the International Fund for Agricultural Development*, Advisory Opinion, [2012] ICJ Rep 10, 1 February 2012.

[7] The Permanent Court of International Justice had refused a request for an advisory opinion once, in the case *Status of Eastern Carelia*, Advisory Opinion, PCIJ Series B No. 5, 23 July 1923.

[8] *Interpretation of Peace Treaties with Bulgaria, Hungary, and Romania*, Advisory Opinion, First Phase, [1950] ICJ Rep 65, 71, 30 March 1950; see also *Certain Expenses of the United Nations (Article 17, paragraph 2, of the Charter)*, Advisory Opinion, [1962] ICJ Rep 151, 155, 20 July 1962; *Legal Consequences for States of the Continued Presence of South Africa in Namibia (South West Africa) notwithstanding Security Council Resolution 276 (1970)*, Advisory Opinion, [1971] ICJ Rep 16, 27, 21 June 1971.

[9] *Judgments of the Administrative Tribunal of the ILO upon Complaints Made against Unesco*, Advisory Opinion, [1956] ICJ Rep 77, 86, 23 October 1956; see also *Certain Expenses* (n. 8), 151, 155; *Namibia* (n. 8), 16, 27.

[10] The other two conditions which must be satisfied to found the competence of the Court are that the agency—in this case the WHO—is duly authorized, under the Charter, to request opinions from the Court and that the opinion requested is on a legal question. The Court concluded that in this case these conditions were fulfilled. *Legality of the Threat or Use of Nuclear Weapons* (WHO), [1996] ICJ Rep, paras 10–17.

interpreting the constituent instrument of an international organization.[11] The first argument is already introduced in para. 20 of the opinion, the second in para. 25.

The first argument has neither been widely reflected upon in the literature nor in the jurisprudence of the Court to date. In contrast, the second argument has both been discussed in the nearly twenty years since 1996 and also draws attention to a necessary corollary of the implied powers—jurisprudence of the Court.

A. Mandate

Under the first argument, the Court correctly observes that the WHO can address the effects of the use of nuclear weapons in armed conflict on health and the environment while remaining squarely within its mandate. Depending on the scale of use of nuclear weapons in an armed conflict, it can also be safely assumed that the WHO would, at least *ex post*, not focus its resources on determining the legality of, and responsibility for, the use of these weapons but would concentrate on directing and co-ordinating international efforts to alleviate peoples' suffering and to support the affected governments in that effort. To conclude from these facts that the legality or otherwise of the use of nuclear weapons in armed conflict 'in no way determines the specific measures, regarding health or otherwise' that the WHO can take in such a situation may, however, not be accurate.[12] Judge Shahabuddeen noted in his dissenting opinion that in 'the course of carrying out its activities, the WHO can be confronted with the constraining effects of the conduct of a member State. If that conduct constitutes a breach by that State of its obligations under the Constitution of the WHO, the latter could take or initiate appropriate remedial measures to remove any resulting impediment to the carrying out of its activities'.[13] This observation seems correct with the caveat that the WHO would, in choosing 'remedial measures', be limited by its constituent instrument like any other international organization. As noted in the general commentary to the draft articles on State responsibility, '(i)n carrying out their functions it may be necessary for international organizations to take a position on whether a State has breached an international obligation'.[14] This applies as much to the WHO as to any other international organization. For instance, in the aftermath of a use of nuclear weapons it may be highly relevant for the work of the WHO to

[11] On interpretation of the constituent instrument of an international organization, see C.F. Amerasinghe, *Principles of the Institutional Law of International Organizations* (Cambridge, Cambridge University Press 2005), pp. 24–61; D. Akande, 'International Organizations', in M.D. Evans (ed), *International Law* (Oxford, Oxford University Press 2014), pp. 248, 257; for a short account of the early approach of the Permanent Court of International Justice to interpretation of the constituent instruments of international organizations see J. Klabbers, *An Introduction to International Institutional Law* (Cambridge, Cambridge University Press 2009), pp. 53–5.

[12] cf. *Legality Nuclear Weapons* (WHO), Dissenting Opinion of Judge Koroma, [1996] ICJ Rep 172, 190–91: '[U]nduly formalistic and narrow view taken of the competence and scope of activities of the Organization'.

[13] *Legality Nuclear Weapons* (WHO), Dissenting Opinion of Judge Shahabuddeen, [1996] ICJ Rep 97, 98.

[14] 'Draft Articles on Responsibility of States for Internationally Wrongful Acts', General Commentary para. 4(b), in *Yearbook of the International Law Commission* 2001, Volume II, Part Two, United Nations 2007, p. 31.

assess (state) responsibility for the use and in order to do so, the WHO would need to concern itself with whether the use was legal.[15] Judge Weeramantry, in his dissenting opinion, gives more examples and makes the point that the Constitution obliges the WHO to prepare for the public health impact of a use of nuclear weapons and that the 'duty of preparedness for that eventuality' is all the greater if the use is, in the event, lawful.[16]

B. Principle of speciality

The second argument made by the Court merits further attention. The Court proceeds to it in para. 25 of the opinion where it states that international organizations 'are governed by the "principle of speciality", that is to say, they are invested by the States which create them with powers, the limits of which are a function of the common interests whose promotion those States entrust to them'.

The principle of 'speciality', of 'attributed powers', of 'conferral', or of 'conferred powers' is indeed an important principle of the law of international organizations, which lack the *Kompetenz-Kompetenz* of States.[17] The Permanent Court of International Justice had enunciated the substance of the principle of speciality in its opinion in the case concerning *Jurisdiction of the European Commission of the Danube*.[18] Quoting this opinion, the Court revisits and applies the principle in the opinion under review. In some contrast to its earlier jurisprudence, which focussed on expansion of the competences of international organizations under the 'implied powers'[19] doctrine, the Court highlights the limits of competence of an international organization, in this case that of the WHO. In para. 25, it comes to the conclusion that 'to ascribe to the WHO the competence to address the legality of the use of nuclear weapons [...] would be tantamount to disregarding the principle of speciality; for such competence could not be deemed a necessary implication of the Constitution of the Organization in the light of the purposes assigned to it by its member States'. The second half of this sentence is important. It highlights the rationale of the implied powers doctrine, which does not aim at extending an international organization's competence

---

[15] M. Bothe, 'The WHO Request', in Boisson de Chazournes/Sands (eds) (n. 1), pp. 103, 104.

[16] *Legality Nuclear Weapons* (WHO), Dissenting Opinion of Judge Weeramantry, [1996] ICJ Rep 101, 129–34; see also D. Akande, 'The Competence of International Organizations and the Advisory Jurisdiction of the International Court of Justice', (1998) *European Journal of International Law* 437, 447.

[17] N.M. Blokker, 'International Organizations or Institutions, Implied Powers', in Wolfrum (ed.), *Max Planck Encyclopedia of Public International Law* (Oxford, Oxford University Press 2009), para. 1.

[18] See *Jurisdiction of the European Commission of the Danube*, Advisory Opinion, PCIJ Series B, No. 14, p 64, 8 December 1927.

[19] *Reparation for Injuries Suffered in the Service of the United Nations*, Advisory Opinion, [1949] ICJ Rep 174, 182, 11 April 1949; see also *Effect of Awards of Compensation Made by the United Nations Administrative Tribunal*, Advisory Opinion, [1954] ICJ Rep 47, 57, 13 July 1954; *Certain Expenses* (n. 8), 151, 168, 20 July 1962; see also *Legality of Use of Force, Yugoslavia v United States of America*, Declaration of Judge Shi, [1999] ICJ Rep 927, 2 June 1999; the implied powers doctrine must be distinguished from the 'inherent powers' doctrine, on the difference between the two doctrines see Certain Activities carried out by Nicaragua in the Border Area and in the case concerning the *Construction of a Road in Costa Rica along the San Juan River, Costa Rica v Nicaragua/Nicaragua v Costa Rica*, Separate Opinion of Judge Cançado Trindade to the Joinder of Proceedings, 17 April 2013; for a critical assessment see Klabbers (n. 11), pp. 65–9.

beyond what its member States consented to. On the contrary, the implied powers doctrine aims 'to give effect to what (States) agreed by becoming parties to the constitutional treaty'.[20] Similarly, and as noted by the Court, the principle of speciality is a 'function of the common interests' which member States mandate an international organization to pursue. Both doctrines bear, in effect, close resemblance in that they both strive to give effect to the 'purposes' or 'common interests' guiding an international organization. These common interests are indeed not a one-way street, which can only justify an expansion of competence (through the implied powers doctrine). The common interest of States can also point in the other direction, that of limits on competence (through the principle of speciality), as in this case. Perhaps, the Court merely intended to draw attention to a necessary corollary to the implied powers doctrine in para. 25 of the opinion, rather than making 'backward steps in the development of the law of international organisations'.[21] At the same time, it may well be true that the decision is part of a broader dynamic also visible in the jurisprudence of the European Court of Justice since the 1990s,[22] in which the principle of implied powers loses prominence and international organizations are reminded of 'their main tasks as envisaged'.[23] In any case, the Court has not revisited the doctrine of 'implied powers' in the years since 1996 while the principle of speciality was argued before the Court by the International Fund for Agricultural Development (IFAD) in the proceedings regarding IFAD's request of an advisory opinion[24] and the Court briefly revisited it in 2010, when it confirmed, with regard to the Administrative Commission of the River Uruguay, that the principle 'also applies of course to organizations, which like CARU, only have two member States'.[25]

C. System of the UN Charter

The Court proceeds further in para. 26 where it argues that the WHO Constitution, 'can only be interpreted [...] by taking due account not only of the general principle of speciality, but also of the logic of the overall system contemplated by the Charter' and that the WHO's 'responsibilities are necessarily restricted to the sphere of public 'health' and cannot encroach on the responsibilities of other parts of the United Nations system'.[26] This reading of the principle of speciality by the ICJ in the advisory

---

[20] K. Skubiszewski, 'Implied Powers of International Organizations', in Y. Dinstein (ed), *International Law at a Time of Perplexity: Essays in Honour of Shabtai Rosenne* (Martinus Nijhoff 1989), pp. 855, 860. Skubiszewski also notes that 'intention referred to in the context of implication will in most cases indicate a purpose or a task that Member States wish to be fulfilled'.

[21] V. Leary, 'The WHO case: Implications for specialised agencies', in Boisson de Chazournes/Sands (eds) (n. 1), pp. 112, 127; see also Blokker (n. 17), para. 12.

[22] See Opinion 1/94, *Re WTO Agreement* [1994] ECR I-5267; Opinion 2/94, *Re European Convention on Human Rights* [1994] ECR I-5267; Case C-376/98, *Germany v European Parliament and Council* [2000] ECR I-8419.

[23] Klabbers (n. 11), pp. 70, 72.

[24] Judgment No. 2867 (n. 6), Written Comments of IFAD, para. 21, 11 March 2011.

[25] *Pulp Mills on the River Uruguay, Argentina v Uruguay*, Judgment, [2010] ICJ Rep 14, 53/para. 89, 20 April 2010.

[26] For a similar reasoning regarding the distribution of competences among the organs of the United Nations see *Certain Expenses* (n. 8), Dissenting Opinion of Judge Winiarski, [1962] ICJ Rep 227, 230.

opinion has attracted criticism.[27] It is inspired by the functionalist theories that under-
pinned the creation of the specialized agencies and that advocated the creation of a
system of international institutions with compartmentalized 'technical' (that is: not
political) mandates.[28] However, the Court's interpretation seems to take this idea too
far, given that it is in tension with the concept of public health expressed in the WHO's
Constitution and does not reflect the established practice of the WHO, as of other
institutions in the UN system.

Regarding the WHO's Constitution, it is of course correct that the WHO's responsibilities are in the sphere of public health.[29] The Constitution does not reveal a narrow
understanding of these responsibilities, however. In contrast to its earlier predeces-
sors, which were meant to focus on disease surveillance and control, the mandate of
the WHO is surprisingly broad. Building on the work of the so-called social medicine
movement, which had developed since the nineteenth century, a broad definition of
health was included in the preamble to the WHO Constitution and the 'functions'
of the WHO, enumerated in art. 2 of the Constitution, mention the 'improvement of
nutrition, housing, sanitation, recreation, economic or working conditions' as important factors of public health. Since the early days of the WHO it has been accepted that
these provisions give the WHO a mandate to work on what have become known as the
political and social 'determinants' of health.[30] These determinants are manifold: environmental pollution, discrimination against vulnerable groups, bad sanitation infrastructure, or entrenched unhealthy lifestyles in a population are examples. Working on
such determinants of health, the WHO necessarily touches on areas which are outside
a narrowly understood public health mandate. In order to adequately address the issue
of access to essential medicines, the WHO needs to concern itself with patent law and
its international regulation through the TRIPS Agreement and bilateral investment
treaties.[31] The WHO must equally deal with questions of investment and trademark
law in its work on reducing the disease burden caused by tobacco consumption.[32] The
transmission of human pathogens (viruses, bacteria) between countries for research
purposes raises the difficult legal question whether such pathogens are protected as a

---

[27] See, for instance, M. Bothe, 'The WHO Request', in Boisson de Chazournes/Sands (eds) (n. 1), p. 103;
N.D. White, 'The World Court, the WHO, and the UN System', in N.M. Blokker/H.G. Schermers (eds),
Proliferation of International Organizations—Legal Issues (Brill 2001), pp. 85–109.

[28] P. Klein, 'Quelques réflections sur le principe de spécialité et la "politisation" des institutions spé-
cialisées', in Boisson de Chazournes/Sands (eds) (n. 1), pp. 78, 87; E. Klein, 'Specialized Agencies', in
Wolfrum (ed.) (n. 17), paras 6, 80.

[29] For a detailed analysis of the WHO Constitution see G.L. Burci/C.-H. Vignes, *World Health
Organization* (London, Kluwer Law International 2004).

[30] See, O.P. Ottersen et. al., 'The political origins of health inequity: prospects for change', [2014] *The
Lancet* 630–67.

[31] On the former see J. Quirin, 'Art. 31bis', in P. Stoll/J. Busche/K. Arend (eds), *WTO—Trade-Related
Aspects of Intellectual Property Rights* (Leiden, Martinus Nijhoff 2009); H. Grosse Ruse-Kahn, 'The
International Law Relation between TRIPS and Subsequent TRIPS-Plus Free Trade Agreements: Towards
Safeguarding TRIPS Flexibilities?', (2011) *Journal of Intellectual Property Law* 1, available at
http://papers.ssrn.com; on the latter see UNITAID, The Trans-Pacific Partnership Agreement—
Implications for Access to Medicines and Public Health, available at http://www.unitaid.eu.

[32] See M. Davison, 'Plain Packaging of Tobacco and the "Right" to Use a Trade Mark', (2012) *European
Intellectual Property Review* 498–501; A.D. Mitchell/S.M. Wurzberger, 'Boxed In? Australia's Plain
Tobacco Packaging Initiative and International Investment Law', (2011) *Arbitration International* 623–51.

'genetic resource' under international environmental law.[33] It has also been reiterated that the WHO should pay close attention to fiscal policies as an 'underused lever for curbing of non-communicable diseases and injuries'.[34]

These few examples should suffice to show that the WHO is not only a stakeholder in the governance 'of' health but also in governance 'for' health. In this light one may put a question mark behind the Court's assessment that questions not narrowly related to public health such as those 'concerning the use of force, the regulation of armaments and disarmament' are necessarily excluded from the mandate of the WHO. To avoid confusion: if it was the Court's concern to guarantee an effective and efficient delivery of the utterly broad mandate of the UN and its specialized agencies, this concern can only be supported. Ten years after the Court gave its opinion, the report of the UN Secretary-General's High-level Panel on UN System-wide Coherence in the Areas of Development, Humanitarian Assistance, and the Environment asserted a 'proliferation of agencies, mandates and offices' and a general 'loss of cohesion'.[35] The various horizontal agreements between the specialized agencies are meant to counter such trends. Today, they are complemented by a number of more political initiatives, which are meant to integrate the work of institutions in the UN system.[36]

D. Hierarchy

In national administrative law contexts, a most important means to guarantee the effective and efficient achievement of objectives is hierarchy, expressed through authority/competence based on law.[37] The responsibility of institutions to discharge their functions is distributed in pyramidal systems with competence and authority gradually increasing from bottom to top. Conflicts over 'who does what' can be resolved through this institutional hierarchy. Such systemic hierarchy does not exist in the relations between the UN and its specialized agencies, which are more a network or an 'unwieldy system'[38] than a pyramid. It is certainly correct that the 'specialized agencies [...] to a certain extent come under [the United Nation's] power of coordination and supervision'.[39] Articles 17

[33] M. Wilke, 'A Healthy Look at the Nagoya Protocol—Implications for Global Health Governance', in E. Morgera/M. Buck/E. Tsioumani (eds), *The 2010 Nagoya Protocol on Access and Benefit-Sharing in Perspective* (Leiden, Martinus Nijhoff 2012), pp. 123–49.

[34] See G. Yamey et al., 'Global Health 2035 Report: A World Converging Within a Generation', [2013] *The Lancet* 1898–955.

[35] Report of the UN Secretary-General's High-level Panel on UN System-wide Coherence in the Areas of Development, Humanitarian Assistance, and the Environment, 9 November 2006, para. 10, available at http://www.un.org/events/panel/resources/pdfs/HLP-SWC-FinalReport.pdf.

[36] Since 1994, the 'human security' concept gained traction in the United Nations, which emphasizes the interconnectedness of economic, food, health, environmental, personal, community, and political challenges; see C. Ryngaert/M. Noortmann (eds), *Human Security and International Law* (Cambridge/Antwerp/Poland, Intersentia 2013); the Millenium Development Goals served a similar integrating purpose in that they broadly guided the work of many agencies in the UN system.

[37] See H. Dreier, *Hierarchische Verwaltung im demokratischen Staat* (Tübingen, Mohr Siebeck 1991), pp. 19–158; a trend away from hierarchy as a mode of governance in domestic contexts has been observed for a number of years now, see K.-H. Ladeur, 'The Changing Role of the Private in Public Governance—The Erosion of Hierarchy and the Rise of a New Administrative Law of Cooperation. A Comparative Approach', *EUI Working Paper LAW No. 2002/9*, available at http://hdl.handle.net/1814/187.

[38] White (n. 27), pp. 85, 93.

[39] B. Conforti, *The Law and Practice of the United Nations* (Leiden, Martinus Nijhoff 2010), p 349.

paras 3, 58, and 64 of the Charter and the various relationship agreements between the UN and its specialized agencies specify these powers.[40] However, the means by which the various mandates within the network can be co-ordinated are rather limited. Article 63 para. 2 of the Charter merely mentions 'consultation' and 'recommendations' by the Economic and Social Council in relation to the specialized agencies. On the one hand, this relative lack of co-ordinating power between the United Nations and the specialized agencies seems natural considering that States are interested in having multiple autonomous yet interlinked fora to implement their common interests. On the other hand, these circumstances are in some tension with the goal to effectively and efficiently 'divide labour' on the very broad normative mandates of the UN and the specialized agencies. The Court's advisory opinion is a succinct reminder of this state of affairs.

---

[40] On the relationship agreements, see W. Meng, 'Article 63 paras 1-36', in B. Simma/D.-E. Khan/ G. Nolte/A. Paulus (eds), *The Charter of the United Nations* (Oxford, Oxford University Press/C.-H. Beck 2012).

3

Institutional Structure and the Position of Members

This Part brings together two subjects, which are usually dealt with separately in textbooks on international institutional law. The heading 'institutional structure' is usually used to cover issues relating to the various organs of an international organization, such their composition, tasks, decision-making, and their mutual relations. 'The position of members' covers a variety of issues of states and other actors in relation to international organizations, such as different forms of membership, the admission of new members, the termination and suspension of membership, membership questions in case of the association and disintegration of states, and the representation of members.

Yet, there are strong links between both subjects. For instance, the admission of new members is often subject to procedures in which organs of the organization concerned have a role to play. The same holds true for the suspension or termination of membership. The link exists also very clearly and directly the other way around, in that, for instance, most organs of international organizations are composed of representatives of member states. And sometimes members are even seen and coined as an organ or as organs of the organization. Whether this designation is useful remains open for debate. What has to be underlined is that member states have more than one crucial function in relation to the institutional structure of international organizations. They are not only the 'masters' of the constituent instruments and thus the existence of the organization as such; they occupy at the same time seats in the governmental—and normally most important—organs of the organization and, in that capacity, bear responsibilities for the organization as a whole. In other words, the position of the member states in the institutional structure of international organizations reflects as such the fundamental dual structure of international organizations (compare the first two Parts in this book on legal personality and legal powers).

It may be argued that both organs and members are the buildings blocks of international organizations. While they, indeed, may coincide, at least theoretically the distinction is quite clear. This is also evidenced by the distinction that is usually made between so-called 'Boards' or 'Councils' and the 'Assembly' of an international organization. 'Board' (such as the UN Security Council) perhaps best represents the distinctive position of the organization vis-à-vis its member states. Alongside a central congress in the form of an 'Assembly' and a Secretariat, the Board completes the 'elementary triad'[1] forming the basis of the institutional structure of most

---

[1] H.G. Schermers and N.M. Blokker, *International Institutional Law* (Boston/Leiden, Martinus Nijhoff Publishers 2011), p. 293.

universal international organizations. Whereas the plenary general congress is usually the reflection of the 'agora' function of an international organization[2] and the
Secretariat has mainly administrative functions, Boards were created to allow organizations to act more effectively through a non-plenary organ that would meet more frequently than the general congress or which would even be in session on a 'permanent'
basis. The fact that not all members of the organization are represented in the Board
and that members may be selected on the basis of the knowledge of the field turns this
organ into a 'true' part of the institutional structure of the organization. While there
are good reasons also to view general congresses as 'true' organs of the organization
(in which the participating states obtain a new identity as 'member state', following
the rules and procedures of the organization and taking decisions that can be accred-
ited to the organization), the fact that Boards are in most cases non-plenary organs
strengthens the idea of autonomy.[3]

Issues relating to the institutional structure and the position of members are
only in rare instances the subject of cases before international courts. With regard
to the institutional structure two kind of issues stand out. The first one relates
to the relations between organs of international organizations, in particular the
division of powers and the question whether relations between main organs are
hierarchical or not. The division of powers was a central element in the *Certain
Expenses* case, discussed in Part 2 of this volume, in which the ICJ, *inter alia*, extensively considered the distinctive functions and powers of the General Assembly
and the Security Council for the maintenance of international peace and security.
It spelled out that both organs, to a certain extent, have concurrent powers, with
the Council having a primary responsibility in these matters but only a monopoly
on *mandatory* coercive action, leaving for the General Assembly a broad field of
discretionary power.

The first case in the present Part of this volume, concerning *Questions of Interpretation
and Application of the 1971 Montreal Convention arising from the Aerial Incident at
Lockerbie*, covering two contentious proceedings before the ICJ between Libya and the
United Kingdom/United States, could have had, at least potentially, far-reaching consequences for the relationship between two main organs of the United Nations (Davies-
Bright and White). The crucial legal question was whether the Court had the capacity
to review decisions of the Security Council of the United Nations and, eventually, could
judge that a resolution was not in conformity with the UN Charter and thus was taken
ultra vires. For several reasons, the Court did not get to pronounce itself as such on its
'constitutional' function as to the primary responsibility of the Security Council, but

---

[2] J. Klabbers, 'Two Concepts of International Organization', (2005) *International Organizations
Law Review* 277–93; as well as his 'Contending Approaches to International Organizations: Between
Functionalism and Constitutionalism', in J. Klabbers and Å. Wallendahl (eds), *Research Handbook on
the Law of International Organizations* (Cheltenham/Northampton, Edward Elgar Publishing 2011),
pp. 3–30.

[3] See in general also R. Collins and N.D. White, *International Organizations and the Idea
of Autonomy: Institutional Independence in the International Legal Order* (London/New York,
Routledge 2011).

the issue of judicial review by the Court was dealt with in the pleadings and in some of the separate and dissenting opinions.

As far as the validity of Security Council resolutions is concerned, the advisory opinion of the ICJ in the *Namibia* case—discussed in the next Part—may also be of relevance. There is some difference of opinion whether the Court asserted in this case a judicial review role or not. The fact is, that it made an interesting analysis of UN Security Council resolutions and their legal bases.

The second line of institutional questions concerns the power of organs of international organizations to create new organs. Such a power is certainly not an exception and its use is usually not contested because these new organs have a subsidiary status and have only certain delegated functions. Problems arise where the newly created organ has an autonomous status and is entrusted with functions that the parent organs do not have, that is in case a political organ creates a judicial one. The *Effect of Awards* case, discussed in Part 2 of this volume, concerned the United Nations Administrative Tribunal (UNAT), a judicial organ created by the General Assembly of the United Nations to settle disputes between the organization and its staff members. According to the International Court of Justice, the Assembly had the power to establish such a judicial organ with the capacity to take decisions, which were, under its Statute, 'final and without appeal' and thus binding on all the parties, including the General Assembly itself.[4]

Whether the Security Council has a similarly broad discretionary power to establish a judicial organ, and in particular an International Criminal Tribunal for the prosecution and trial of persons suspected of having committed serious international crimes, such as war crimes or crimes against humanity, is the question in the *Prosecutor v Dusko Tadic* case, discussed in this Part (Dekker and Wessel). A peculiar feature of this case is the fact that the question whether the creation of the tribunal was *intra vires* or not, was decided by the Appeal Chamber of the Tribunal itself. That the Chamber reached a positive conclusion did not come as a big surprise, but it is, in particular, its argumentation that has led to heated debates on the 'dynamic' powers of organs of international organizations.

With regard to the position of member states, two advisory opinions of the ICJ on the conditions and procedure with regard to the admission of new members are discussed in this Part. Both cases—*Conditions of Admissions of a State to Membership in the United Nations* and *Competence of the General Assembly for the Admission of a State to the United Nations*—can only be understood well against the background of the political situation in the first years after the Second World War, especially the fast development of the Cold War (Fry and Chong). At the same time, they are still of interest these days as they illustrate how courts try and uphold the interests of the United Nations as such in a very difficult political situation.

---

[4] See also *Application for Review of Judgment No. 158 of the United Nations Administrative Tribunal*, Advisory Opinion, [1973] ICJ Rep 166.

In the second opinion, the Court had the opportunity to pronounce itself for the first time on the relationship between the General Assembly and the Security Council. It made clear that both organs have their own responsibilities in the admission procedure and, although the Security Council is given only a hortatory role in that respect, it does not mean that that role can be disregarded by the General Assembly.

3.1 *Case Concerning Questions of Interpretation and Application of the 1971 Montreal Convention Arising from the Aerial Incident at Lockerbie (Libya Arab Jamahiriya v United States of America), Request for the Indication of Provisional Measures, Order of 14 April 1992, [1992] ICJ Rep 114*

Lydia Davies-Bright and Nigel D. White

Relevance of the case

In the early 1990s the UN Security Council (UNSC) was engaging more assertively in international affairs and pursuing a more activist role in maintaining international peace and security.[1] This was not received without criticism,[2] especially as the United Nations Charter does not contain explicit provisions for oversight, a balancing of powers, or a procedure, in the case of a conflict of interests, in situations where states disagree as to the path to resolution. The *Lockerbie* cases provided the Court with the opportunity to assert its role in providing judicial scrutiny over the actions and Resolutions of the UNSC.

The US government's response to the air-incident at Lockerbie was to pursue a UN-centred diplomatic approach, as opposed to a military reaction as with the 1986 Berlin bombing, in order to effect Libyan compliance.[3] Libya did not comply with the demands issued by the administration and so the US, together with the UK, sought UNSC action. The demands issued by the interested states arguably demonstrate an unwillingness to entertain any alternative to the conclusions of the investigators and also reveal the effect of the domestic political pressure on the governments to respond with strength to the incident. Libya attempted to rely on the provisions of the 1971 Montreal Convention, which was rebuffed by the US and UK. The successful resort to the UNSC raises the question of whether or not it is possible for the international system to deliver justice in such cases where parties are unwilling to comply with their treaty obligations and where there is no established practice of judicial review. By invoking the power of the UNSC, the UK and US departed from the consensual element of international law in a situation where a legal framework already existed and was applicable to the event in question.

---

[1] Such as in S/RES/678 (1990), which authorized member states to utilise 'all necessary means' to ensure compliance with the previous Resolutions dealing with Iraq's invasion of Kuwait.

[2] See, for example, B.H. Western, 'Security Council Resolution 678 and Persian Gulf Decision Making: Precarious Legitimacy' (1991) 83 *American Journal of International Law* 516; O. Schachter, 'United Nations Law in the Gulf Conflict', (1991) 85 *American Journal of International Law* 432; M. Weller, 'The Kuwait Crisis: A Survey of some Legal Issues', (1991) 3 *The African Journal of International and Comparative Law* 1, on UNSC action on Iraq's invasion of Kuwait.

[3] D.R. Andrews, 'A Thorn in the Tulip—A Scottish Trial in The Netherlands: The Story Behind the Lockerbie trial', (2004) 36 *Case Western Reserve Journal of International Law* 307.

I. Facts

On 21 December 1988 Pan Am Flight 103, bound for New York, fell from the sky onto the southern Scottish town of Lockerbie killing all 243 passengers and sixteen crew members on board, plus eleven people on the ground. On 13 November 1991, the Lord Advocate of Scotland issued warrants, on charges of murder, conspiracy to murder, and contravention of the Aviation Security Act 1982 (UK), for the arrest of Abdelbaset Ali al-Megrahi (a Libyan intelligence officer and head of security for Libyan Arab Airlines (LAA)) and Lamin Khalifa Fhima (LAA station manager to Luqa Airport in Malta). The US also issued charges against the two suspects on the same day. The charges centred on the allegation that the suspects had placed a bomb on board the flight that then exploded and caused the plane to crash. The Libyan government denied any involvement in the events leading to the incident and was not willing to surrender the accused or to admit general involvement in terrorist activities. As the suspects were present on Libyan territory, the government sought to rely on the 'extradite or prosecute' formula of the Montreal Convention 1971, to which all the states involved were parties.

On 30 December 1991, the UK and US issued a joint declaration, circulated to the UN General Assembly (UNGA) and UNSC, stating that 'Libya must surrender for trial all those charged with the crime'.[4] The two states also issued a declaration on terrorism and requested that Libya comply with their demands.[5] In January 1992, Libya attempted to call a special assembly of the UNGA denying UNSC competence in the matter and invoking the dispute settlement provisions in art. 14 of the Montreal Convention 1971, to which all the states involved were parties. On 2 January 1992 the UK and US began to seek support for a UNSC resolution calling on Libya to comply with their demands. The UNSC passed Resolution 731 on 21 January 1992 urging Libya to provide a 'full and effective' response to the 'requests' of the UK and US.[6]

II. The legal question

Together with requests for an indication of provisional measures of protection, Libya filed separate applications against the UK and US at the International Court of Justice (ICJ), invoking art. 14 of the Montreal Convention 1971 as the basis, claiming that the UK and US were attempting to bypass the provisions (and obligations) of the Convention by seeking sanctions. Libya claimed that it had sought the co-operation of the two states in conducting an investigation into the incident and the alleged offences, but had received no response.[7] The UK and US resisted Libya's application

---

[4] A/46/827 S/23308 (1991).   [5] A/46/828 S/23309 (1991).   [6] S/RES/731 (1992).

[7] *Questions of Interpretation and Application of the 1971 Montreal Convention Arising from the Aerial Incident at Lockerbie (Libyan Arab Jamahiriya v United States of America; Libyan Arab Jamahiriya v United Kingdom)*, Application Instituting Proceedings, 3 March 1992, http://www.icj-cij.org/docket/files/89/13253.pdf

to the ICJ to resolve jurisdictional issues and claimed that Libya had not tried arbitration. Three days after the completion of oral hearings on Libya's request for provisional measures, the UNSC adopted UNSC Resolution 748[8] under Chapter VII of the UN Charter imposing sanctions on Libya for failing to comply with UNSC Resolution 731 1992, which urged Libya to 'provide a full and effective response' to the requests of the UK and US. On 3 March 1992 the Libyan Arab Jamahiriya filed an application with the ICJ, in accordance with art. 40(1) of its Statute, against the governments of the United Kingdom and United States of America. Libya argued that the UNSC Resolutions made a 'grave legal mistake' in linking the alleged acts of two Libyan nationals to international terrorism generally[9] and asserted its rights under the 1971 Convention.

The extracts below are from the judgment of the ICJ in the case brought against the United States. The judgment in the case brought against the United Kingdom by Libya follows along the same lines.[10]

III. Excerpts

[...]

ORDER

41. Whereas the Court, in the context of the present proceedings on a request for provisional measures, has in accordance with Article 41 of the Statute, to consider the circumstances drawn to its attention as requiring the indication of such measures, but cannot make definitive findings either of fact or of law on the issues relating to the merits, and the right of the Parties to contest such issues at the stage of the merits must remain unaffected by the Court's decision;

42. Whereas both Libya and the United States, as Members of the United Nations, are obliged to accept and carry out the decisions of the Security Council in accordance with Article 25 of the Charter; whereas the Court, which is at the stage of proceedings on provisional measures, considers that prima facie this obligation extends to the decision contained in resolution 748 (1992); and whereas, in accordance with Article 103 of the Charter, the obligations of the Parties in that respect prevail over their obligations under any other international agreement, including the Montreal Convention;

43. Whereas the Court, while thus not at this stage called upon to determine definitively the legal effect of Security Council resolution 748 (1992), considers that, whatever the situation previous to the adoption of that resolution, the rights claimed by Libya under the Montreal Convention cannot now be regarded as appropriate for protection by the indication of provisional measures;

---

[8] 31 March 1992.

[9] Letters dated 20 and 23 December 1991 from France, the United Kingdom of Great Britain and Northern Ireland, and the United States of America, Decision of 11 November 1993 (3312th meeting): Resolution 883 (1993) repertoire. Available at https://www.un.org/en/sc/repertoire/93-95/Chapter%208/AFRICA/93-95_8-7-LETTERS%20FRANCE%20UK%20US.pdf

[10] *Case Concerning Questions of Interpretation and Application of the 1971 Montreal Convention Arising from the Aerial Incident at Lockerbie* (*Libya Arab Jamahiriya v United Kingdom*), Request for the Indication of Provisional Measures, Order of 14 April 1992, [1992] ICJ Rep 3.

44. Whereas, furthermore, an indication of the measures requested by Libya would be likely to impair the rights which appear prima facie to be enjoyed by the United States by virtue of Security Council resolution 748 (1992);

45. Whereas, in order to pronounce on the present request for provisional measures, the Court is not called upon to determine any of the other questions which have been raised before it in the present proceedings, including the question of its jurisdiction to entertain the merits of the case; and whereas the decision given in these proceedings in no way prejudges any such question, and leaves unaffected the rights of the Government of Libya and the Government of the United States to submit arguments in respect of any of these questions;

46. For these reasons,

THE COURT

By eleven votes to five,

Finds that the circumstances of the case are not such as to require the exercise of its power under Article 41 of the Statute to indicate provisional measures.

IN FAVOUR: *Vice-President* Oda, *Acting President; President* Sir Robert Jennings; *Judges* Lachs, Ago, Schwebel, Ni, Evensen, Tarassov, Guillaume, Shahabuddeen, Aguilar Mawdsley;

AGAINST: *Judges* Bedjaoui, Weeramantry, Ranjeva, Ajibola; *Judge* ad hoc El-Kosheri

[...]

DECLARATION OF ACTING PRESIDENT ODA

[...]

I do not deny that under the positive law of the United Nations Charter a resolution of the Security Council may have binding force, irrespective of the question whether it is consonant with international law derived from other sources. There is certainly nothing to oblige the Security Council, acting within its terms of reference, to carry out a full evaluation of the possibly relevant rules and circumstances before proceeding to the decisions it deems necessary. The Council appears, in fact, to have been acting within its competence when it discerned a threat against international peace and security in Libya's refusal to deliver up the two Libyan accused. Since, as I understand the matter, a decision of the Security Council, properly taken in the exercise of its competence, cannot be summarily reopened, and since it is apparent that resolution 748 (1992) embodies such a decision, the Court has at present no choice but to acknowledge the pre-eminence of that resolution.

[...]

SEPARATE OPINION OF JUDGE LACHS

[...]

The framers of the Charter, in providing for the existence of several main organs, did not effect a complete separation of powers, nor indeed is one to suppose that such was their aim. Although each organ has been allotted its own Chapter or Chapters, the functions of two of them, namely the General Assembly and the Security Council, also pervade other Chapters than their own. Even the International Court of Justice receives, outside its own Chapter, a number of mentions which tend to confirm its role as the general guardian of legality within the system. In fact the Court is the guardian of legality for the international community as a whole, both within and without the United Nations. One may therefore legitimately suppose that the intention of the founders was not to encourage a blinkered parallelism of functions but a fruitful interaction.

[...]

DISSENTING OPINION OF JUDGE BEDJAOUI

[...]

6. Libya was fully within its rights in bringing before the Court, with a view to its judicial settlement, the dispute concerning extradition, just as the United Kingdom and the United States were fully within their rights in bringing before the Security Council, with a view to its political settlement, the dispute on the international responsibility of Libya. The respective missions of the Security Council and the Court are thus on two distinct planes, have different objects and require specific methods of settlement consistent with their own respective powers. Such a situation, involving two distinct procedures before two principal organs of the United Nations having parallel competences, is, I might add, not an unusual one, as I observed in paragraph 2 above. But the difficulty in the present case lies in the fact that the Security Council not only has decided to take a number of political measures against Libya, but has also demanded from it the *extradition of its two nationals. It is this specific demand of the Council that creates an overlap with respect to the substance of the legal dispute with which the Court must deal, in a legal manner, on the basis of the 1971 Montreal Convention and international law in general.* The risk thus arose of the extradition question receiving two contradictory solutions, one legal, the other political, and of an inconsistency between the decision of the Court and that of the Security Council.

7. Such an inconsistency between the decisions of two United Nations organs would be a matter of serious concern. For it is as a rule not the Court's role to exercise appellate jurisdiction in respect of decisions taken by the Security Council in the fulfilment of its fundamental mission of maintaining international peace and security, no more than it is the role of the Security Council to take the place of the Court, thereby impairing the integrity of its international judicial function. But, at this stage of provisional measures requested by Libya, the present case compels us to confront this possibility of inconsistent decisions inasmuch as one of the Security Council's demands creates a 'grey area' in which powers may overlap and a jurisdictional conflict comes into being. For the facts of this case give the Court the power to indicate provisional measures to preserve the possible right of the Applicant to refuse the extradition of two of its nationals, whereas the Security Council has just taken a decision that is mandatory under Chapter VII of the Charter calling for the extradition of these two individuals.

[...]

12. The rights in question are neither non-existent, nor illusory, nor indeterminate. Article 7 of the 1971 Montreal Convention, the provision that gave rise to the most discussion and is at the heart of the Libyan Application, categorically imposes on every State party to the Convention the obligation either to extradite or to prosecute before its courts the alleged perpetrators of an offence, in keeping with the traditional option to which the maxim *aut dedere aut judicare* refers. Without entering into the merits of the case, I would point out that, as is well known, there does not exist in international law any rule that prohibits, or, on the contrary, imposes the extradition of nationals. All that the régime laid down by the Montreal Convention does is to complement general international law by, on the one hand,

rendering the various national laws applicable and, on the other hand, imposing on States an 'obligation to take action', in accordance with their internal law, by either extraditing or arranging for prosecution before their own courts. This option is now valid, if not under general international law, at least between all the States parties to the 1971 Montreal Convention. This being so, it has been contended that the right to be protected here is illusory, since what we are dealing with is rather an obligation. But could it possibly be that a State is not authorized to claim the right, which it derives, fundamentally, from its sovereignty, not to be hindered in the fulfilment of its international duty? Furthermore, it has been maintained that the 1971 Montreal Convention does not confer on a State party any right under Article 7 that it does not already possess by virtue of general international law, so that even if the 1971 Montreal Convention did not exist or Libya had not become a party to it Libya would remain free to deny extradition by virtue of international law. From this observation, which is correct, an erroneous conclusion has been drawn, namely, that the treaty right to be protected is non-existent, or illusory, inasmuch as Article 7 does not confer an additional right on a State. But is it conceivable that a right recognized by general international law and confirmed by an international convention would cease to exist altogether and no longer be entitled to protection as a result merely of its confirmation, which, on the contrary, would, it appears, strengthen it? In truth, this line of reasoning is based on the implicit view that in this case the Court could only apply the 1971 Montreal Convention, to the exclusion of general international law, whereas, obviously, the Court's Statute and its general mission spontaneously oblige it to apply that law.

[...]

29. The situation thus characterized, with rights which deserve protection by the indication of provisional measures but have also been annihilated by a Security Council resolution that should be deemed prima facie to be valid, does not fall completely within the framework of Article 103 of the Charter, but in fact goes slightly beyond it. That Article, which gives precedence to obligations under the Charter (i.e., Libya's obligation to comply with resolution 748 (1992)) as compared to obligations 'under any other international agreement' (here the 1971 Montreal Convention) is aimed at 'obligations'—whereas we are dealing with alleged 'rights' such as, in my view, are protected by provisional measures—and, in addition, does not cover such rights as may have other than conventional sources and be derived from general international law.

30. Subject to this minor nuance, it is clear that the Court could do no more than take note of that situation and hold that, at this stage of the proceedings, such a 'conflict', governed by Article 103 of the Charter, would ultimately deprive the indication of provisional measures of any useful effect. However, the operative part of the two Orders places itself at the threshold of the whole matter and decides that the Court, in the circumstances of the case, is not required to exercise its power to indicate provisional measures. I take the rather different view that the facts of the case do indeed justify the effective exercise of that power, while I would point out that its effects have been nullified by resolution 748 (1992). This means that I arrive, concretely, at the same result as the Court, albeit by means of a quite different approach, but also with the important difference that I am not led to reject the request for provisional measures, but rather to say that its effects have ceased to exist. [...]

IV. Commentary

Thomas Franck, the pre-eminent international jurist, saw the end of the Cold War as ushering in a new liberal democratic era in international law, which included a 'right to democracy'.[11] He also saw in the *Lockerbie* cases of 1992 a *Marbury v Madison* moment when,[12] reflecting a true separation of powers, the ICJ would seize the chance and assert a power of judicial review over the executive body of the United Nations—the UNSC.[13]

The recipe for judicial review in the *Lockerbie* cases seemed to have been present with Libya using the ICJ to defend its right to try the two suspects under the terms of the Montreal Convention 1971, to which all three states were parties, while the US and the UK resorted to the UNSC to override that criminal justice regime and force Libya to hand the two suspects over, on the basis that Libyan support for terrorism was a continuing threat to international peace and security. In fact, the provisional measures order of 1992 (extracted above) was a more nuanced judgment that could be seen either as a gentle move towards constitutionalism, or as a plea from the Court for the UNSC not to tread on its toes or, more realistically, as an indication that, if the case progressed to the merits, the ICJ would re-consider the effects of Resolution 748, but not its legality (and, presumably, come to the same conclusion). Ultimately, the ICJ denied the Libyan request for provisional measures of protection against coercive actions by the US and UK, reasoning that the obligations created by UNSC Resolution 748 applied to all parties to the dispute and that these obligations prevailed over any other treaty obligation, including those found in the Montreal Convention of 1971, by virtue of arts. 25 and 103 of the UN Charter.

At least for the purposes of denying provisional measures, the ICJ accepted that UNSC resolutions imposed obligations that prevailed over the rights and duties of state parties under the Montreal Convention 1971. The question remained whether this prima facie finding of the ICJ, made at the provisional measures stage, would be affirmed at the merits stage. There were some crumbs for those hoping for judicial scrutiny of UNSC decisions in the separate and dissenting opinions, examples of which are extracted above. Judge Oda hinted at things to come when he stated that the 'Court has at present no choice but to acknowledge' the pre-eminence of UNSC Resolution 748, while Judge Lachs spoke eloquently of the Court being the 'guardian of legality' not only of the Charter, but for the international community more broadly. Judge Bedjaoui (dissenting), however, was more critical of the Court for not asserting its competence to award provisional measures, even though he recognized that they were nullified by UNSC Resolution 748, which was imposed after the Court had been seized of the case. His criticisms of the UNSC may have been guides as to where the

---

[11] T.M. Franck, 'The Emerging Right to Democratic Governance', (1992) 86 *American Journal of International Law* 46.

[12] *Marbury v Madison*, 5 US 137 (1803) is seen as the constitutional moment when the US Supreme Court asserted its judicial review competence.

[13] T.M. Franck, 'The "Powers of Appreciation": Who is the Ultimate Guardian of UN Legality?' (1992) 86 *American Journal of International Law* 519.

Court might have gone in terms of judicial review at the merits stage, had the case reached that point. For instance, he questioned whether there was a threat to the peace in 1992 when the Lockerbie bombing had occurred in 1988. He also pointed to the lack of evidence before the UNSC, excusable if it were acting as a political organ, but not when it encroached on the competence of the judicial organ. He also suggested that art. 103 of the UN Charter was being over-interpreted to cover 'rights' in a treaty rather than duties and that, in any case, it could not overrule what he asserted was also a principle of customary international law.

The hint of promise in the 1992 order was made stronger in the 1998 judgment on admissibility and jurisdiction.[14] The US and UK, relying on art. 103 of the UN Charter, both argued that the UNSC Resolutions demanding that Libya provide a 'full and effective response' to the requests that Libya extradite the suspects to the UK or US[15] rendered the application without object (as they superseded the Montreal Convention) and inadmissible. However, the Court, relying on a narrow interpretation of its jurisprudence,[16] found that Libya's application was admissible[17] and that the Court had jurisdiction, notwithstanding the Resolutions that had been passed since the date of filing.[18]

The UK and US also argued that no dispute existed between the parties regarding the application and interpretation of the Montreal Convention, as required by art. 14 in order for a party to invoke the jurisdiction of the Court. Instead, the two states asserted that any dispute, if one existed, was between Libya and the UNSC on the effects of that body's resolutions. However, the Court found that the parties were in dispute over the applicability of the Montreal Convention to the case in hand, over Libya's asserted right to prosecute its own citizens (art. 7 of the Montreal Convention 1971) and over Libya's allegation regarding the lack of assistance by the respondents in Libya's prosecutorial investigations (art. 11 of the Montreal Convention 1971).

Although the majority upheld the Court's jurisdiction, there were significant disagreements on the impacts of the aforementioned UNSC Resolutions. Judges Fleischhauer and Guillaume, in their joint declaration, stated that the jurisdiction of the Court was limited to the interpretation and application of the Convention and does not extend to the UNSC Resolutions. This view concurs with the arguments of the respondents that the UNSC Resolutions had rendered the case without object. However, a broader reading of the 1998 judgment would indicate that the relationship between the Montreal Convention and the UNSC Resolutions does indeed fall within the Court's jurisdiction and the Court found that this issue concerned the substance of the case. Thus, it appeared in 1998 that the Court may have been willing,

---

[14] See N.D. White, 'To Review or Not to Review? The Lockerbie Cases Before the World Court', (1999) 12 *Leiden Journal of International Law* 201.

[15] S/RES/748 (1992) and S/RES/883 (1993).

[16] That the date of filing is the relevant date for judging admissibility, *Case Concerning Questions of Interpretation and Application of the 1971 Montreal Convention Arising from the Aerial Incident at Lockerbie (Libyan Arab Jamahiriya v United Kingdom; Libyan Arab Jamahiriya v United States of America)*, Judgment of 27 February 1998, [1998] ICJ Rep 115, para. 38; *Border and Transborder Armed Actions (Nicaragua v Honduras)*, Jurisdiction and Admissibility, [1988] ICJ Rep 95, para. 66.

[17] *Lockerbie* (n. 16), paras 44–5.   [18] Ibid., paras 38–9.

had the case progressed to the merits stage, to examine the question of the UNSC Resolutions' primacy over the Montreal Convention. This approach would allow the Court to submit the UNSC Resolutions to judicial scrutiny. However, it is also arguable that, as the Court's jurisdiction was based in the Convention (a treaty), a more narrow view of jurisdiction is perhaps more appropriate, which would restrict judicial scrutiny of the UNSC Resolutions. Nevertheless, the majority judgment in 1998 contained enough promise of judicial review to provoke strong dissents from both the UK and US judges, with Judge Schwebel warning that although the UN Charter was a 'living instrument', such review would not be 'evolutionary but revolutionary' by upsetting the primacy of the UNSC in matters of peace and security.

The 1998 decision avoided the substantive issues and left them for the merits phase. From the separate judgments it is clear that there was internal disagreement as to the appropriate limits to the Court's jurisdiction—whether or not the Court is restricted to declarations on the rights and duties of the parties under the Montreal Convention, or whether its jurisdiction extends to allowing it to determine the relationship between the UNSC Resolutions and the Convention. The latter approach appears to have been favoured by the Court, which may have led to a significant confrontation between the ICJ and UNSC. However, the temporary political rapprochement between the states involved led to the suspects being extradited and tried, and the ICJ was asked to remove the case from its list.

After lengthy negotiations and a change in the international mood (caused by the perceived intransigence of the UK and US), the states agreed to a trial of the two Libyan suspects by a Scottish court sitting in The Hague. UNSC Resolution 1192[19] stated that sanctions would be suspended when the accused were handed over for trial and other conditions[20] were met.[21] Libya formally admitted responsibility for the Lockerbie bombing in a letter to the president of the UNSC in 2003, stating that it 'accepted responsibility for the actions of its officials'.[22] However, it has subsequently been claimed that Libya's actions were motivated by a desire to see the sanctions removed as they were producing devastating consequences for the Libyan people and economy.[23]

The US and UK were able, through their permanent membership of the UNSC, to utilise the Chapter VII powers of the UNSC in order to attempt to force Libya to hand over the two suspects and to bring about a result that suited both their political and security agendas.[24] These two states made the decision to follow a different path

---

[19] SC Resolution of 27 August 1998.

[20] Making evidence and witnesses available to the court upon request for the purposes of the trial (para. 4).

[21] On the establishment of this court see A. Aust, 'Lockerbie: The Other Case', (2000) 49 *International & Comparative Law Quarterly* 278. See further S.D. Murphy, 'Verdict in the Trial of the Lockerbie Bombing Suspects', (2001) 95 *American Journal of International Law* 405.

[22] Libya Letter: full text, BBC News, 16 August 2003. Available at http://news.bbc.co.uk/1/hi/scotland/3155825.stm

[23] For example Saif al-Gaddafi said that Libya had admitted responsibility in order to see the trade sanctions removed, *The Conspiracy Files: Lockerbie*, 31 August 2008, BBC2. Libyan Prime Minister Shukri Ghanem stated that Libya had paid compensation as the 'price for peace' and to secure the end of sanctions, 24 February 2004, BBC Radio 4.

[24] M.P. Scharf and A.E. Miller, 'Foreword: Terrorism on Trial', (2004) 36 *Case Western Reserve Journal of International Law* 287.

and not to pursue the process laid out by the Montreal Convention 1971. In doing so, they arguably undermined the criminal justice approach, the *aut dedere aut judicare* provisions of the 1971 Convention, and made it appear 'cumbersome' and 'ineffective'.[25] The US and UK made explicit demands from the start of the process and seemed determined to involve the UNSC if their demands were not met. Under art. 5(2) Montreal Convention 1971, Libya had the legal right, as the two men were on Libyan territory, to try the suspects in a domestic court and under its domestic law. The UK and US relied on arts. 25 and 103 of the UN Charter in seeking a UNSC resolution to thereby circumvent the established treaty regime. However, although art. 103 of the UN Charter gives UNSC Resolutions primacy over pre-existing international obligations, it does not provide that such resolutions are supreme and unquestionable. As the UNSC is not subject to effective judicial scrutiny, and the ICJ was, in the event, unable to assert its jurisdiction in this area, the *Lockerbie* cases demonstrate that influential states utilizing powerful international organizations are able to circumvent the provisions of international law.

---

[25] N.D. White, 'Terrorism, Security and International Law' in A. Hehir, N. Kuhrt, and A. Mumford (eds), *International Law, Security and Ethics* (London, Routledge 2011), 11.

3.2 *Prosecutor v Duško Tadić*, Decision on the defence motion for interlocutory appeal on jurisdiction, IT-94-1-AR72, Appeals Chamber of the International Criminal Tribunal for the former Yugoslavia, 2 October 1995

Ige F. Dekker and Ramses A. Wessel

Relevance of the case

It is a truism that the powers of international organizations are not unlimited. The principle of the attribution, or conferral, of powers is undisputed and lies at the heart of debates on the competences of international organizations. A more specific question concerns whether and to what extent organs of an international organization may establish other organs. This is not unusual, and this competence was for instance recognized by the International Court of Justice in the *Effect of Awards* case, analysed in the previous Part.

The importance of the present case is that it reveals that the competence of an organ to decide on it own competence (often referred to as the principle of *Kompetenz-Kompetenz*, or *la compétence de la compétence*) may be far-reaching. The question arose whether the UN Security Council had not exceeded its powers by establishing the International Criminal Tribunal for the Former Yugoslavia (ICTY) in 1993. After all, the Security Council was a political body with no judicial powers; yet, it had created a judicial body which could prosecute and try individuals for international crimes.[1] From the perspective of the law of international organizations, the most interesting aspect of the *Tadić* case is that the Appeals Chamber of the ICTY was asked to decide whether the Security Council acted *ultra vires* in creating the ICTY.[2]

I. Facts of the case

The ICTY (or (International) Tribunal) was established by the Security Council on 25 May 1993 for the 'sole purpose of prosecuting persons responsible for serious violations of international humanitarian law committed in the territory of the former Yugoslavia'.[3] It was the first international criminal tribunal since the Nuremberg and Tokyo Military Tribunals prosecuted and convicted major German and Japanese war criminals directly after the Second World War.

---

[1] See R. Zacklin, 'The Role of the International Lawyers in an International Organisation', in C. Wickremasinghe (ed.), *The International Lawyer as Practitioner* (London, British Institute for International and Comparative Law 2000), pp. 57–68 at p. 67.

[2] The fact that, for this book, we limit ourselves to the question of the validity of the establishment of the Tribunal does not mean that the case has no substantive relevance. See for instance C. Greenwood, 'International Humanitarian Law and the *Tadić* Case', (1996) *European Journal of International Law* 265–83.

[3] See Security Council Resolution 827, 25 May 1993. By this resolution the Security Council also adopted the Statute of the International Tribunal.

Mr Duško Tadić was the first to be tried by the ICTY. As a member of the paramilitary forces he supported the attack on the district of Prijedor in the current Republika Srpska (in Bosnia and Herzegovina) during the war in the former Yugoslavia in the first half of the 1990s. In particular, he was accused of taking part, in May 1993, in the Serbian attacks on Bosnian Muslim and Croat population centres in the region of Prijedor forcing most Muslims and Croats from their homes and confining many thousands, including more than 3,000 who were held in the Omarska camp, a former mining complex. Tadić was arrested by German police in Munich in February 1994 on suspicion of having committed offences at the Omarska camp that constituted crimes under German law.

Later that year, the ICTY issued a formal request to Germany for the transfer of Tadić to the Tribunal. He arrived in The Hague in April 1995. The indictment by the Prosecutor charged him with thirty-four counts involving grave breaches of the Geneva Conventions, violations of the laws and customs of war, and crimes against humanity.[4] In judgments on the merits of the case he was found guilty for nine counts, partially guilty for two counts and not guilty for twenty-three counts, and—in 2000— sentenced to a twenty-year imprisonment.

II. The legal question

Before the International Tribunal could go into the merits of the case, it had to decide on some preliminary but fundamental questions. Tadić confronted the Tribunal with three propositions:

a) the Tribunal was unlawfully established;

b) the Tribunal's primacy over competent domestic courts was unjustified; and

c) the Tribunal lacked subject-matter jurisdiction in this case.

For the purposes of the present case note we limit ourselves to the first point, which concerns a crucial constitutional issue, namely the powers of the Security Council to establish subsidiary organs with judicial functions. The Trial Chamber of the Tribunal dismissed Tadić's arguments on this point on the basis that the objections did not go 'so much to its jurisdiction, as to the unreviewable lawfulness of the actions of the Security Council'.[5] The Appeals Chamber of the Tribunal held otherwise and discussed extensively the constitutional issues raised by the appellant Tadić, especially (1) whether there is a legal basis for the Tribunal in the UN Charter, and (2) whether the structure and functioning of the Tribunal satisfied basic requirements of the rule of law. However, before that the Appeals Chamber had to answer the question whether it had jurisdiction to deal with these constitutional issues.

---

[4] See for the various indictments as well as the judgments: http://www.icty.org/case/Tadić/4.

[5] *Tadić* case, Decision on the Defence Motion on the Jurisdiction of the Tribunal, Case No. IT-94-1-T, 10 August 1995, para. 40.

III. Excerpts

[...]

[The following part deals with the Tribunal's jurisdiction to review its establishment by the Security Council]

[...]

15. To assume that the jurisdiction of the International Tribunal is absolutely limited to what the Security Council 'intended' to entrust it with, is to envisage the International Tribunal exclusively as a 'subsidiary organ' of the Security Council (see United Nations Charter, Arts. 7(2) & 29), a 'creation' totally fashioned to the smallest detail by its 'creator' and remaining totally in its power and at its mercy. But the Security Council not only decided to establish a subsidiary organ (the only legal means available to it for setting up such a body), it also clearly intended to establish a special kind of 'subsidiary organ': a tribunal.

[...]

17. Earlier, the [International Court of Justice] had derived the judicial nature of the United Nations Administrative Tribunal ('UNAT') from the use of certain terms and language in the Statute and its possession of certain attributes. Prominent among these attributes of the judicial function figures the power provided for in Article 2, paragraph 3, of the Statute of UNAT: 'In the event of a dispute as to whether the Tribunal has competence, the matter shall be settled by the decision of the Tribunal.' [...]

18. This power, known as the principle of '*Kompetenz-Kompetenz*' in German or '*la compétence de la compétence*' in French, is part, and indeed a major part, of the incidental or inherent jurisdiction of any judicial or arbitral tribunal, consisting of its 'jurisdiction to determine its own jurisdiction.' It is a necessary component in the exercise of the judicial function and does not need to be expressly provided for in the constitutive documents of those tribunals, although this is often done (see e.g., Statute of the International Court of Justice, Art. 36, para. 6). But in the words of the International Court of Justice: '[T]his principle, which is accepted by the general international law in the matter of arbitration, assumes particular force when the international tribunal is no longer an arbitral tribunal [...] but is an institution which has been pre-established by an international instrument defining its jurisdiction and regulating its operation.' (*Nottebohm Case* (*Liech. v. Guat.*), 1953 I.C.J. Reports 7, 119 (21 March).)

[...]

22. In conclusion, the Appeals Chamber finds that the International Tribunal has jurisdiction to examine the plea against its jurisdiction based on the invalidity of its establishment by the Security Council.

[...]

[The following part deals with issues of constitutionality]

[...]

3. The Establishment Of The International Tribunal As A Measure Under Chapter VII

32. As with the determination of the existence of a threat to the peace, a breach of the peace or an act of aggression, the Security Council has a very wide margin of

discretion under Article 39 to choose the appropriate course of action and to evaluate the suitability of the measures chosen, as well as their potential contribution to the restoration or maintenance of peace. But here again, this discretion is not unfettered; moreover, it is limited to the measures provided for in Articles 41 and 42. Indeed, in the case at hand, this last point serves as a basis for the Appellant's contention of invalidity of the establishment of the International Tribunal.

In its resolution 827, the Security Council considers that 'in the particular circumstances of the former Yugoslavia', the establishment of the International Tribunal 'would contribute to the restoration and maintenance of peace' and indicates that, in establishing it, the Security Council was acting under Chapter VII (S.C. Res. 827, U.N. Doc. S/RES/827 (1993)). However, it did not specify a particular Article as a basis for this action.

Appellant has attacked the legality of this decision at different stages before the Trial Chamber as well as before this Chamber on at least three grounds: [...]

(a) What Article of Chapter VII Serves As A Basis For The Establishment Of A Tribunal?

33. The establishment of an international criminal tribunal is not expressly mentioned among the enforcement measures provided for in Chapter VII, and more particularly in Articles 41 and 42.

Obviously, the establishment of the International Tribunal is not a measure under Article 42, as these are measures of a military nature, implying the use of armed force. Nor can it be considered a 'provisional measure' under Article 40. These measures, as their denomination indicates, are intended to act as a 'holding operation', producing a 'stand-still' or a 'cooling-off' effect, 'without prejudice to the rights, claims or position of the parties concerned.' (United Nations Charter, art. 40.) [...]

34. *Prima facie*, the International Tribunal matches perfectly the description in Article 41 of 'measures not involving the use of force.' Appellant, however, has argued before both the Trial Chamber and this Appeals Chamber, that: '... [I]t is clear that the establishment of a war crimes tribunal was not intended. The examples mentioned in this article focus upon economic and political measures and do not in any way suggest judicial measures.' (Brief to Support the Motion [of the Defence] on the Jurisdiction of the Tribunal before the Trial Chamber of the International Tribunal, 23 June 1995 (Case No. IT-94-1-T), at para. 3.2.1 (hereinafter *Defence Trial Brief*).)

It has also been argued that the measures contemplated under Article 41 are all measures to be undertaken by Member States, which is not the case with the establishment of the International Tribunal.

35. The first argument does not stand by its own language. Article 41 reads as follows: 'The Security Council may decide what measures not involving the use of armed force are to be employed to give effect to its decisions, and it may call upon the Members of the United Nations to apply such measures. These may include complete or partial interruption of economic relations and of rail, sea, air, postal, telegraphic, radio, and other means of communication, and the severance of diplomatic relations.' (United Nations Charter, art. 41.)

It is evident that the measures set out in Article 41 are merely illustrative *examples* which obviously do not exclude other measures. All the Article requires is that they do not involve 'the use of force.' It is a negative definition.

That the examples do not suggest judicial measures goes some way towards the other argument that the Article does not contemplate institutional measures implemented directly by the United Nations through one of its organs but, as the given examples suggest, only action by Member States, such as economic sanctions (though possibly coordinated through an organ of the Organization). However, as mentioned above, nothing in the Article suggests the limitation of the measures to those implemented by States. The Article only prescribes what these measures cannot be. Beyond that it does not say or suggest what they have to be.

Moreover, even a simple literal analysis of the Article shows that the first phrase of the first sentence carries a very general prescription which can accommodate both institutional and Member State action. The second phrase can be read as referring particularly to one species of this very large category of measures referred to in the first phrase, but not necessarily the only one, namely, measures undertaken directly by States. It is also clear that the second sentence, starting with 'These [measures]' not 'Those [measures]', refers to the species mentioned in the second phrase rather than to the 'genus' referred to in the first phrase of this sentence.

36. Logically, if the Organization can undertake measures which have to be implemented through the intermediary of its Members, it can a fortiori undertake measures which it can implement directly via its organs, if it happens to have the resources to do so. It is only for want of such resources that the United Nations has to act through its Members. But it is of the essence of 'collective measures' that they are collectively undertaken. Action by Member States on behalf of the Organization is but a poor substitute *faute de mieux,* or a 'second best' for want of the first. This is also the pattern of Article 42 on measures involving the use of armed force.

In sum, the establishment of the International Tribunal falls squarely within the powers of the Security Council under Article 41.

(b) Can The Security Council Establish A Subsidiary Organ With Judicial Powers?

37. The argument that the Security Council, not being endowed with judicial powers, cannot establish a subsidiary organ possessed of such powers is untenable: it results from a fundamental misunderstanding of the constitutional set-up of the Charter.

Plainly, the Security Council is not a judicial organ and is not provided with judicial powers (though it may incidentally perform certain quasi-judicial activities such as effecting determinations or findings). The principal function of the Security Council is the maintenance of international peace and security, in the discharge of which the Security Council exercises both decision-making and executive powers.

38. The establishment of the International Tribunal by the Security Council does not signify, however, that the Security Council has delegated to it some of its own functions or the exercise of some of its own powers. Nor does it mean, in reverse, that the Security Council was usurping for itself part of a judicial function which does not belong to it but to other organs of the United Nations according to the Charter. The Security Council has resorted to the establishment of a judicial organ in the form of an international criminal tribunal as an instrument for the exercise of its own principal function of maintenance of peace and security, i.e., as a measure contributing to the restoration and maintenance of peace in the former Yugoslavia.

The General Assembly did not need to have military and police functions and powers in order to be able to establish the United Nations Emergency Force in the Middle East ('UNEF') in 1956. Nor did the General Assembly have to be a judicial organ possessed of judicial functions and powers in order to be able to establish UNAT. In its advisory opinion in the *Effect of Awards,* the International Court of Justice, in addressing practically the same objection, declared: '[T]he Charter does not confer judicial functions on the General Assembly [...] By establishing the Administrative Tribunal, the General Assembly was not delegating the performance of its own functions: it was exercising a power which it had under the Charter to regulate staff relations.' (Effect of Awards, at 61.)

(c) Was The Establishment Of The International Tribunal An Appropriate Measure?

39. The third argument is directed against the discretionary power of the Security Council in evaluating the appropriateness of the chosen measure and its effectiveness in achieving its objective, the restoration of peace.

Article 39 leaves the choice of means and their evaluation to the Security Council, which enjoys wide discretionary powers in this regard; and it could not have been otherwise, as such a choice involves political evaluation of highly complex and dynamic situations.

It would be a total misconception of what are the criteria of legality and validity in law to test the legality of such measures *ex post facto* by their success or failure to achieve their ends (in the present case, the restoration of peace in the former Yugoslavia, in quest of which the establishment of the International Tribunal is but one of many measures adopted by the Security Council).

40. For the aforementioned reasons, the Appeals Chamber considers that the International Tribunal has been lawfully established as a measure under Chapter VII of the Charter.

4. Was The Establishment Of The International Tribunal Contrary To The General Principle Whereby Courts Must Be 'Established By Law'?

41. Appellant argues that the right to have a criminal charge determined by a tribunal established by law is one which forms part of international law as a 'general principle of law recognized by civilized nations', one of the sources of international law in Article 38 of the Statute of the International Court of Justice. In support of this assertion, Appellant emphasises the fundamental nature of the 'fair trial' or 'due process' guarantees afforded in the International Covenant on Civil and Political Rights, the European Convention on Human Rights and the American Convention on Human Rights. Appellant asserts that they are minimum requirements in international law for the administration of criminal justice.

[...]

43. Indeed, there are three possible interpretations of the term 'established by law.' First, as Appellant argues, 'established by law' could mean established by a legislature. Appellant claims that the International Tribunal is the product of a 'mere executive order' and not of a 'decision making process under democratic control, necessary to create a judicial organisation in a democratic society.' Therefore Appellant maintains that the International Tribunal not been 'established by law.' (Defence Appeal Brief, at para. 5.4.)

[...]

It is clear that the legislative, executive and judicial division of powers which is largely followed in most municipal systems does not apply to the international setting nor, more specifically, to the setting of an international organization such as the United Nations. Among the principal organs of the United Nations the divisions between judicial, executive and legislative functions are not clear cut. Regarding the judicial function, the International Court of Justice is clearly the 'principal judicial organ' (*see* United Nations Charter, art. 92). There is, however, no legislature, in the technical sense of the term, in the United Nations system and, more generally, no Parliament in the world community. That is to say, there exists no corporate organ formally empowered to enact laws directly binding on international legal subjects.

It is clearly impossible to classify the organs of the United Nations into the above-discussed divisions which exist in the national law of States. Indeed, Appellant has agreed that the constitutional structure of the United Nations does not follow the division of powers often found in national constitutions. Consequently the separation of powers element of the requirement that a tribunal be 'established by law' finds no application in an international law setting. The aforementioned principle can only impose an obligation on States concerning the functioning of their own national systems.

44. A second possible interpretation is that the words 'established by law' refer to establishment of international courts by a body which, though not a Parliament, has a limited power to take binding decisions. In our view, one such body is the Security Council when, acting under Chapter VII of the United Nations Charter, it makes decisions binding by virtue of Article 25 of the Charter.

According to Appellant, however, there must be something more for a tribunal to be 'established by law.' Appellant takes the position that, given the differences between the United Nations system and national division of powers, discussed above, the conclusion must be that the United Nations system is not capable of creating the International Tribunal unless there is an amendment to the United Nations Charter. We disagree. It does not follow from the fact that the United Nations has no legislature that the Security Council is not empowered to set up this International Tribunal if it is acting pursuant to an authority found within its constitution, the United Nations Charter. As set out above (paras 28–40) we are of the view that the Security Council was endowed with the power to create this International Tribunal as a measure under Chapter VII in the light of its determination that there exists a threat to the peace.

In addition, the establishment of the International Tribunal has been repeatedly approved and endorsed by the 'representative' organ of the United Nations, the General Assembly: this body not only participated in its setting up, by electing the Judges and approving the budget, but also expressed its satisfaction with, and encouragement of the activities of the International Tribunal in various resolutions. (See G.A. Res. 48/88 (20 December 1993) and G.A. Res. 48/143 (20 December 1993), G.A. Res. 49/10 (8 November 1994) and G.A. Res. 49/205 (23 December 1994).)

45. The third possible interpretation of the requirement that the International Tribunal be 'established by law' is that its establishment must be in accordance with the rule of law. This appears to be the most sensible and most likely meaning of the term in the context of international law. For a tribunal such as this one to be established according to the rule of law, it must be established in accordance with the proper international standards; it must provide all the guarantees of fairness,

justice and even-handedness, in full conformity with internationally recognized human rights instruments.[…]

46. An examination of the Statute of the International Tribunal, and of the Rules of Procedure and Evidence adopted pursuant to that Statute leads to the conclusion that it has been established in accordance with the rule of law. The fair trial guarantees in Article 14 of the International Covenant on Civil and Political Rights have been adopted almost verbatim in Article 21 of the Statute. Other fair trial guarantees appear in the Statute and the Rules of Procedure and Evidence. For example, Article 13, paragraph 1, of the Statute ensures the high moral character, impartiality, integrity and competence of the Judges of the International Tribunal, while various other provisions in the Rules ensure equality of arms and fair trial.

47. In conclusion, the Appeals Chamber finds that the International Tribunal has been established in accordance with the appropriate procedures under the United Nations Charter and provides all the necessary safeguards of a fair trial. It is thus 'established by law.'

48. The first ground of Appeal: unlawful establishment of the International Tribunal, is accordingly dismissed.

IV. Commentary

From a legal-political point of view, and in the absence (by then) of an International Criminal Court, most scholars would agree with the idea that international crimes, such as war crimes and crimes against humanity, should be dealt with by an international judicial body. The war in former Yugoslavia once more pointed to the humanitarian consequences related to such crimes. The same holds true for the other situations in which the Security Council—again in the absence of the International Criminal Court—decided to establish an international tribunal, such as the International Criminal Tribunal for Rwanda (ICTR).[6]

However, in convincing people that international organizations, once created by states, are not the Frankenstein's monsters that go their own way and develop themselves independently from their creators, the present case is not particularly helpful. While in this case the public opinion may very well have been that there was a need to prosecute the war criminals of the various conflicts in the former Yugoslavia, legal scholars certainly raised their eyebrows when the Appeals Chamber of the ICTY reached its decision. This commentary focuses on (1) the power of the Security Council to create subsidiary organs and (2) the jurisdiction of the Tribunal to review the legality of the Security Council's resolution.

Subsidiary organs. The main legal question is: What are limits to the power of an organ of an international organization to establish subsidiary organs? Two principles seem at stake here: first of all, organs cannot simply extend their own functions without a legal basis; secondly, it would be difficult to accept that an organ can

---

[6] The establishment of the ICTR was also challenged before the Tribunal itself. See *Prosecutor v Kanyabashi*, Decision on the Defence Motion on Jurisdiction, ICTR-96-15-T, 18 June 1997. See for a commentary, A. Klip and G. Sluiter (eds), *Annotated Leading Cases on International Criminal Tribunals, The International Criminal Tribunal for Rwanda*, Vol. 2 (Antwerp and Oxford Intersentia 2001), p. 23.

delegate functions to a subsidiary organ when it does not have these functions in the first place.[7] The application of at least the second principle would block the Security Council to establish international tribunals.

The Appeals Chamber seems to have solved this by arguing that the Security Council has, on the basis of arts. 39 *juncto* 41 UN Charter, an implied power to establish an international criminal tribunal since it is a measure necessary for the performance of the main function of the Security Council: the maintenance of peace and security. Indeed, on the basis of art. 39 of the UN Charter the Security Council has a wide mandate to decide on the existence of a breach of the peace, a threat to the peace, or an act of aggression. Article 41, furthermore, provides that '[t]he Security Council may decide what measures not involving the use of armed force are to be employed to give effect to its decisions, and it may call upon the members of the United Nations to apply such measures'. And, indeed, while art. 41 does not explicitly mention the establishment of a tribunal as one of the measures, it does not exclude it either. However, also according to the Appeals Chamber, the crucial aspect seems to be that the International Tribunal effectively contributes to the exercise of the Council's powers to act to maintain or to restore international peace. Not without reason, it has been argued that—while perhaps sound in legal terms—this argumentation is flawed from a more practical or empirical perspective. The 'jump' from the 'maintenance of peace and security' to setting up a judicial body dealing with international crimes may be too big, and may therefore put the validity of the act—when the contribution of the Tribunal to its main purpose is not convincing—into question.[8]

In the legal context of the establishment of subsidiary organs and delegation of powers, the creation of a judicial organ by a political organ of an international organization seems to be a special, exceptional case.[9] First, the creation of the subsidiary organ is necessary because the principal organ does not possess a judicial function. And, second, the principal organ has to respect the independent position of the subsidiary organ regarding the exercise of its functions and has to accept its decisions. Against this background, the discussion by the Appeals Chamber of the question whether the tribunal is 'established by law'—as provided for by the main human rights conventions—is of interest. While going in depth in making their point, and focusing on the question of whether the establishment of the Tribunal was in conformity with the rule of law, the Appeals Chamber surprisingly ends up—in para. 46—with a predominantly formalistic analysis in concluding that the International Tribunal has been established in accordance with the appropriate procedures under the United Nations Charter and provides all the necessary safeguards of a fair trial.

Because of the special position of the International Tribunal, the decision of the Appeals Chamber is less helpful in answering the more general question concerning

---

[7] See more extensively, D. Sarooshi, 'The Legal Framework Governing United Nations Subsidiary Organs', (1996) 67 *British Yearbook of International Law* 413, 428–31.

[8] See for instance J. Klabbers, *An Introduction of International Organizations Law* (3rd edn, Cambridge, Cambridge University Press 2015), p. 222; N. White, *The Law of International Organisations* (2nd edn, Manchester, Manchester University Press 2005), pp. 82–3.

[9] See also the *Effect of Awards* case, with regard to the establishment by the General Assembly of the United Nations Administrative Tribunal, discussed in Part 2 of this volume.

the limits of the power of the Security Council (or other organs) to establish subsidiary organs and delegate powers to them. Which other parts of the Council's
main task—the maintenance of peace and security—can be delegated to such
organs? Obviously we have seen other examples of the Security Council using subsidiary bodies to deal with tasks it cannot perform itself (e.g. military missions)[10] or
which largely deal with the implementation of earlier decisions (e.g. the Sanctions
Committee). At the same time it has been held that 'improper delegation' would
occur when the Council, for example, would '"delegate" its role in the admission,
suspension, or expulsion of members', or 'delegate to a sanctions committee of the
Secretary-General the ultimate determination of whether a "threat to the peace"
exists'.[11]

Jurisdiction. As mentioned before, the argumentation of the Trial and Appeals
Chambers differs principally. The Trial Chamber decided that Chapter VII decisions
of the Security Council are simply 'not reviewable',[12] and it is not up to the Tribunal to
'judge the reasonableness of the acts of the Security Council'.[13] The Appeals Chamber
does, by contrast, take the *Kompetenz-Kompetenz* principle as the starting point, and
argues that international tribunals are allowed to deal with challenges to their own
constitution on the basis of a broad concept of jurisdiction.

> In international law, every tribunal is a self-contained system (unless otherwise
> provided). This is incompatible with a narrow concept of jurisdiction, which pre-
> supposes a certain division of labour. Of course, the constitutive instrument of an
> international tribunal can limit some of its jurisdictional powers, but only to the
> extent to which such limitation does not jeopardize its 'judicial character', [...] Such
> limitations cannot, however, be presumed and, in any case, they cannot be deduced
> from the concept of jurisdiction itself.[14]

However, it is one thing to come up with a broad—and inherent—concept of one's
own competence, it is another thing to claim the competence to decide over one's
own *existence*. Indeed, the Frankenstein's monster image does present itself quite
clearly in this type of 'haughtiness', and the assertion that one can decide on its
own fate is certainly part of the unease of some scholars with the decision of the
Appeals Chamber. Where the Trial Chamber was much more reluctant to go there,
the Appeals judges really took the time to scrutinize a Chapter VII decision of the
UN Security Council. From a political point of view the Appeals Chamber's claim
may be comprehensible, legally it is certainly not because only a decision confirming
the validity of the Security Council's establishment act could have legal effect. For
that reason, it would have been much more adequate if the Security Council would

---

[10] See N.M. Blokker, 'Is Authorization Authorized? Powers and Practice of the UN Security Council
to Authorize the Use of Force by "Coalitions of the Able and Willing"', (2000) *European Journal of
International Law* 541–68.
[11] J.E. Alvarez, 'Nuremberg Revisited: The *Tadić* Case', (1996) *European Journal of International Law*
245–64, at 254.
[12] *Prosecutor v Tadic*, Case No. IT-94-1-T, 10 August 1995, para. 6.   [13] Ibid., para. 16.
[14] *Prosecutor v Tadic*, Case No. IT-94-1-AR72, para. 11; see also paras. 12, 14, and 18.

have asked the International Court of Justice for an advisory opinion on the lawfulness of its resolution 827(1993).[15]

Related to this point is the question what would happen if the Security Council would suddenly terminate prosecutions or even end the mandate of the Tribunal. If only for practical purposes, the autonomy of the Tribunal vis-à-vis the Council is not unrestricted. While the judges see it as 'logical' that 'if the Organization can undertake measures which have to be implemented through the intermediary of its Members, it can a fortiori undertake measures which it can implement directly via its organs',[16] the Members (and their citizens) may not necessarily agree with that logic. For instance, the point made by Tadić that UN members have the sovereign right to prosecute persons for having committed international crimes in their own courts was largely left on the table by the Appeal Chamber.[17]

Overall, the importance of the *Tadić* case seems to lie in the fact that it relates to an ongoing debate on the tensions within the Charter and between the UN organs. The judgment only implicitly deals with 'the elephant in the room': the tension between the different Purposes and Principles of the Charter, which deal with sovereign equality, respect for human rights, enforcement, and peace and security at the same time. The UN system is imperfect and a combination of diverging preferences. This is why to some the somewhat pragmatic establishment of the ICTY was a gift in human rights terms, whereas others would underline the possible *ultra vires* act of the Security Council as a result of an overstretch of its own powers. Despite the fact that no one expected the Appeals Chamber to conclude that as of the next day it would end its activities because it suddenly realized its invalid creation, the case has become a classic in the debates on the inherent powers of organs of international organizations.[18]

---

[15] Compare in this sense the approach of the ICJ in the *Lockerbie* case, also analysed in Part 3 of this Volume.

[16] Paragraph 36.

[17] Yet, see the separate opinion by Judge Sidhwa, addressing this point in paras 81–94 (http://www.icty.org/x/cases/tadic/acdec/en/510027234562.htm).

[18] Tadić is not the only case in which the legality of the ICTY—or the ICTR for that matter—was challenged. Both Milosovich and Karadic filed motions claiming the invalidity of the Tribunal on several grounds. See M. Swart, '*Tadić* Revisited: Some Critical Comments on the Legacy and Legitimacy of the ICTY', (2011) 3 *Goettingen Journal of International Law* 985–1009.

3.3 *Membership in the United Nations*

James D. Fry and Agnes Chong

Relevance of the Advisory Opinions

Statehood traditionally has been determined by reference to the Montevideo Convention criteria of 'a) a permanent population; b) a defined territory; c) government; and d) [the] capacity to enter into relations with the other states.'[1] However, over the past few decades, many commentators have come to see collective recognition through UN membership as the main avenue to statehood.[2] The extraordinary efforts emerging states undertake to gain UN membership in recent years support this perceived shift.[3] Only states can be UN members, as UN Charter art. 4 indicates, and so UN membership is the 'badge' of statehood, or so the argument goes. In light of this shift to collective recognition through UN membership, the two ICJ advisory opinions that deal with UN membership gain particular importance inasmuch as they can be seen as clarifying some of the finer points of law in this area. In responding to the political stalemate in the Security Council over admission of new UN members, the ICJ insisted on adhering to the legal rules of the UN Charter concerning admission, which is one of the main lessons of these advisory opinions. However, in the end, politics ultimately prevailed over the law when resolving the stalemate, which might be the more important lesson learned from these two advisory opinions.

---

[1] Montevideo Convention on the Rights and Duties of States, art. 1, 26 December 1933, 49 Stat. 3097, UNTS 881 (1933). See *also* J. Crawford, *The Creation of States in International Law* (2nd edn, Oxford, Oxford University Press 2006), p. 45 (referring to the traditional dominance of these criteria in determining statehood); Th. D. Grant, 'Defining Statehood: The Montevideo Convention and its Discontents', (1999) 37 *Columbia Journal of Transnational Law* 403, 413–14 (same); Restatement (Third) of Foreign Relations Law of the United States, 1987, § 201 (describing this formula for statehood as customary international law).

[2] See generally J. Dugard, *International Law: A South African Perspective* (Kaapstad, Juta & Co 1994), pp. 72–3; J. Dugard, *Recognition and the United Nations* (Cambridge, Grotius Publ 1987), p. 80; H. Mosler, 'Subjects of International Law', in R. Bernhardt (ed.), *Encyclopedia of Public International Law* (Amsterdam, North-Holland 1984) Vol. 7, pp. 442, 449–50.

[3] See, for example, J. Greenberg, 'Palestinians Stay Firm on U.N. Statehood Bid', *Washington Post*, 14 November 2012, at A12; P. Chang and K. Lim, 'Taiwan's Case for United Nations Membership', (1997) 1 *UCLA Journal of International Law & Foreign Affairs* 393; V.R. Osmani, 'Foreign Policy of the Republic of Kosovo: The Role of Parliamentary Diplomacy in State-Building', (2013) 74 *University of Pittsburgh Law Review* 621, 625–7.

I. Facts of the cases

According to the UN Charter, a state may become a UN member if it meets both the substantive and procedural requirements of UN Charter art. 4:

> (1) Membership in the United Nations is open to all other peace-loving States which accept the obligations contained in the present Charter and, in the judgment of the Organization, are able and willing to carry out these obligations;
> (2) The admission of any such State to membership in the United Nations will be effected by a decision of the General Assembly upon the recommendation of the Security Council.

Despite the putative standards contained in this provision, the Cold War reality led to a situation whereby member states cast votes in favour of admission of applicant states belonging to the same political camp and against those in the opposing camp, with the ultimate outcome being that more were rejected than admitted. This was the situation until anti-colonialism and anti-racism became more acceptable once colonies started winning their independence in the 1950s.

The inability of the Security Council's permanent members to come to an agreement to admit certain new members to the UN dates back to the 57th Meeting of the Security Council on 29 August 1946.[4] At this meeting, the Soviet Union used its veto to block the admission of Jordan, Ireland, and Portugal, while the United Kingdom and the United States vetoed the admission of Albania and Mongolia.[5] At the same meeting, the Security Council recommended Afghanistan, Sweden, and Iceland to be admitted to the UN, and subsequently the General Assembly resolved to admit the three states to the UN after receiving the report of the First Committee's approval of the Security Council's recommendation.[6] As for those states that had their application for UN membership rejected, the General Assembly recommended in the same resolution for the Security Council to reconsider these applications on their respective merits and in accordance with UN Charter art. 4. At the Security Council's 186th Meeting on 18 August 1947, and at other times, the UN Secretary General declared support for admission of all the applicants and urged the Security Council to recommend their admission.[7] At that meeting, the Security Council reconsidered the applications of Albania, Mongolia, Jordan, Ireland, and Portugal, and none were recommended for admission, with the same voting outcome as the previous year.[8] The Security Council also considered the applications of Austria, Bulgaria, Hungary, Italy, Romania, Yemen, and Pakistan.[9] The latter two states were recommended for admission and the others were not.[10]

---

[4] See UN doc. S/PV.57, 29 August 1946. See *also* A.W. Rudzinski, 'Admission of New Members: The United Nations and the League of Nations', (1952) 29 *International Conciliation* 143, 159.
[5] See UN doc. S/PV.57, 29 August 1946.   [6] See UN doc. A/RES/34(I), 9 November 1946.
[7] See UN doc. Security Council Official Records (SCOR), 206th meeting, 1 October 1947, at 2032–3.
[8] See UN doc. SCOR, 186th Meeting, Lake Success, New York, 18 August 1947.
[9] See UN doc. SCOR, 206th meeting, 1 October 1947, at 2033–55.
[10] See ibid. at 2052, 2055 (for unanimous votes recommending Yemen and Pakistan).

Following the outcome of the Security Council's 186th Meeting, the General Assembly at its 118th Plenary Meeting on 17 November 1947 determined that Ireland, Portugal, Jordan, Italy, Finland, and Austria all were peace-loving states and were willing and able to carry out the obligations of the UN, but their admission applications were nonetheless rejected based on the objection of only one permanent member (the Soviet Union), and so the General Assembly requested that the Security Council reconsider the applications of these states again.[11] The Security Council considered the applications of Hungary, Romania, Bulgaria, Italy, and Finland at its 204th, 205th, and 206th Meetings from 25 September 1947 to 1 October 1947,[12] and once again, the Security Council did not recommend admission for any of these applicants.[13]

After the failure of these applicants to secure the requisite votes for admission and the continuing differences of opinion of the Security Council and the General Assembly, a special report of the proceedings was discussed in the General Assembly and its First Committee.[14] Belgium drafted a proposal to request an advisory opinion from the ICJ on the matter, which received endorsements from El Salvador, Greece, and the United Kingdom.[15] Poland, the Soviet Union, Australia, China, and India objected to Belgium's proposal on the basis that art. 4 of the Charter was sufficiently clear and, therefore, did not warrant an advisory opinion.[16] The expectation of Belgium's proposal appears to have been that the ICJ would clarify the criteria to be considered by member states when voting on admission applications. Regardless, the General Assembly ultimately agreed to request an advisory opinion from the ICJ,[17] which eventually became the ICJ's First Admissions Advisory Opinion.

The General Assembly at the third session of its 177th Plenary Meeting on 8 December 1948 reaffirmed the ICJ's decision in the First Admissions Advisory Opinion and recommended the members of the Security Council and General Assembly vote in accordance with the opinion.[18] Unfortunately, the First Admissions Advisory Opinion was not implemented to the extent that it should have been due to the continuing tensions between the Western and Eastern blocs during this time,[19] which led to a request for another advisory opinion that eventually became the Second Admissions Advisory Opinion.[20]

---

[11] See UN doc. A/RES/113 (III), 17 November 1947.
[12] Held at Lake Success, New York on 25 September 1947, 29 September 1947 and 1 October 1947 respectively.
[13] See UN doc. SCOR, 206th meeting, 1 October 1947, at 2466–75.
[14] See Y. Liang, 'Notes on Legal Questions Concerning the United Nations, Conditions of Admission of a State to Membership in the United Nations', (1949) 43 *American Journal of International Law* 288, 290.
[15] Ibid.   [16] Ibid.   [17] See UN doc. A/RES/113 (III), 17 November 1947.
[18] See UN doc A/RES/197 (III), 8 December 1948. See also L. Gross, 'Progress Towards Universality of Membership in the United Nations', (1956) 50 *American Journal of International Law* 791, 792 (observing that notwithstanding A/RES/197(IIII) recommending voting in accordance with the ICJ advisory opinion, it 'seemed to have the effect of merely stiffening [...] opposing views and making a compromise' between the sides even less probable).
[19] See Rudzinski (n. 4), at 159; Liang (n. 14), at 291–5.
[20] See UN doc A/RES/296(IV), 22 November 1949.

II. The legal questions

In Resolution 113(III) of 17 November 1947, the UN General Assembly requested an ICJ advisory opinion that addressed the following questions:

> Is a member of the United Nations which is called upon, in virtue of Article 4 of the Charter, to pronounce itself by its vote, either in the Security Council or in the General Assembly, on the admission of a State to membership in the United Nations, juridically entitled to make its consent to the admission dependent on conditions not expressly provided by paragraph I of the said Article? In particular, can such a Member, while it recognizes the conditions set forth in that provision to be fulfilled by the State concerned, subject its affirmative vote to the additional condition that other States be admitted to membership in the United Nations together with that State?

In Resolution 296(IV), 22 November 1949, the UN General Assembly requested another advisory opinion that addressed the following question:

> Can the admission of a State to membership in the United Nations, pursuant to Article 4, paragraph 2, of the Charter, be effected by a decision of the General Assembly when the Security Council has made no recommendation for admission by reason of the candidate failing to obtain the requisite majority or of the negative vote of a permanent Member upon a resolution so to recommend?

III. Excerpts

A. First Admissions Advisory Opinion

[...][21]

[22] Having been asked to determine the character, exhaustive or otherwise, of the conditions stated in Article 4, the Court must in the first place consider the text of that Article. [...] The text of [paragraph 1 of Article 4], by the enumeration which it contains and the choice of its terms, clearly demonstrates the intention of its authors to establish a legal rule which, while it fixes the conditions of admission, determines also the reasons for which admission may be refused; for the text does not differentiate between these two cases and any attempt to restrict it to one of them would be purely arbitrary.

[23] The terms "Membership in the United Nations is open to all other peace-loving States which ..." [...], indicate that States which fulfil the conditions stated have the qualifications requisite for admission. The natural meaning of the words used leads to the conclusion that these conditions constitute an exhaustive enumeration and are not merely stated by way of guidance or example. The provision would lose its significance and weight, if other conditions, unconnected with those laid down, could be demanded. The conditions stated in paragraph 1 of Article 4 must therefore be

---

[21] The numbers between brackets before each paragraph are added to the original text, following the reprint of the advisory opinions in *Oxford Public International Law.*

regarded not merely as the necessary conditions, but also as the conditions which suffice.

[24] Nor can it be argued that the conditions enumerated represent only an indispensable minimum, in the sense that political considerations could be superimposed upon them, and prevent the admission of an applicant which fulfils them. Such an interpretation would be inconsistent with the terms of paragraph 2 of Article 4, which provide for the admission of […] 'any *such* State'. It would lead to conferring upon Members an indefinite and practically unlimited power of discretion in the imposition of new conditions. Such a power would be inconsistent with the very character of paragraph 1 of Article 4 which, by reason of the close connexion which it establishes between membership and the observance of the principles and obligations of the Charter, clearly constitutes a legal regulation of the question of the admission of new States. To warrant an interpretation other than that which ensues from the natural meaning of the words, a decisive reason would be required which has not been established.

[25] Moreover, the spirit as well as the terms of the paragraph preclude the idea that considerations extraneous to these principles and obligations can prevent the admission of a State which complies with them. If the authors of the Charter had meant to leave Members free to import into the application of this provision considerations extraneous to the conditions laid down therein, they would undoubtedly have adopted a different wording.

[…]

[29] Article 4 does not forbid the taking into account of any factor which it is possible reasonably and in good faith to connect with the conditions laid down in that Article. The taking into account of such factors is implied in the very wide and very elastic nature of the prescribed conditions; no relevant political factor—that is to say, none connected with the conditions of admission—is excluded.

[30] It has been sought to deduce either from the second paragraph of Article 4, or from the political character of the organ recommending or deciding upon admission, arguments in favour of an interpretation of paragraph I of Article 4, to the effect that the fulfilment of the conditions provided for in that Article is necessary before the admission of a State can be recommended or decided upon, but that it does not preclude the Members of the Organization from advancing considerations of political expediency, extraneous to the conditions of Article 4.

[…]

B. Second Admissions Advisory Opinion

[…]

[15] The Court is … called upon to determine solely whether the General Assembly can make a decision to admit a State when the Security Council has transmitted no recommendation to it.

[…]

[17] The Court has no doubt as to the meaning of this text [Article 4, paragraph 2 of the UN Charter]. It requires two things to effect admission: a 'recommendation' of the Security Council and a 'decision' of the General Assembly. It is in the nature of things

that the recommendation should come before the decision. The word 'recommendation', and the word 'upon' preceding it, imply the idea that the recommendation is the foundation of the decision to admit, and that the latter rests upon the recommendation. Both these acts are indispensable to form the judgment of the Organization to which the previous paragraph of Article 4 refers. The text under consideration means that the General Assembly can only decide to admit upon the recommendation of the Security Council; it determines the respective roles of the two organs whose combined action is required before admission can be effected: in other words, the recommendation of the Security Council is the condition precedent to the decision of the Assembly by which the admission is effected.

[...]

[20] The conclusions to which the Court is led by the text of Article 4, paragraph 2, are fully confirmed by the structure of the Charter, and particularly by the relations established by it between the General Assembly and the Security Council.

[21] The General Assembly and the Security Council are both principal organs of the United Nations. The Charter does not place the Security Council in a subordinate position. Article 24 confers upon it 'primary responsibility for the maintenance of international peace and security', and the Charter grants it for this purpose certain powers of decision. Under Articles 4, 5, and 6, the Security Council co-operates with the General Assembly in matters of admission to membership, of suspension from the exercise of the rights and privileges of membership, and of expulsion from the Organization. It has power, without the concurrence of the General Assembly, to reinstate the Member which was the object of the suspension, in its rights and privileges.

[22] The organs to which Article 4 entrusts the judgment of the Organization in matters of admission have consistently interpreted the text in the sense that the General Assembly can decide to admit only on the basis of a recommendation of the Security Council. [...]

[23] To hold that the General Assembly has power to admit a State to membership in the absence of a recommendation of the Security Council would be to deprive the Security Council of an important power which has been entrusted to it by the Charter. It would almost nullify the role of the Security Council in the exercise of one of the essential functions of the Organization. It would mean that the Security Council would have merely to study the case, present a report, give advice, and express an opinion. This is not what Article 4, paragraph 2, says.

[...]

[26] While keeping within the limits of a Request which deals with the scope of the powers of the General Assembly, it is enough for the Court to say that nowhere has the General Assembly received the power to change, to the point of reversing, the meaning of a vote of the Security Council.

[27] In consequence, it is impossible to admit that the General Assembly has the power to attribute to a vote of the Security Council the character of a recommendation when the Council itself considers that no such recommendation has been made.

IV. Commentary

This commentary starts by highlighting the obvious connection between these two advisory opinions—both involve the same general controversy in the UN concerning the admission of new states to the UN. Surprisingly, only a few commentators discuss both advisory opinions in detail in the same piece, with those who make a connection between the two focusing either on the fact that both advisory opinions were an attempt to circumvent the Soviet veto,[22] or on the fact that the ICJ in both advisory opinions refused to accept the argument that it could not handle the question posed because of the question's political sensitivity.[23] Commentators sometimes cite the First Admissions Advisory Opinion for the notion that the intent of a provision of the UN Charter must be given its effect, inasmuch as the ICJ required the application of all of the art. 4(1) conditions for membership, or else there would have been no point for the drafters of that provision to have inserted those conditions.[24] Commentators sometimes cite the Second Admissions Advisory Opinion for representing the teleological approach to interpreting the UN Charter.[25]

Regardless, this commentary first criticizes the ICJ for its overly narrow focus in both advisory opinions. This commentary then explores how having a broader focus—one that reflected the actual debates going on in the Security Council—could have enabled the ICJ to provide a better response to the situation. In particular, the ICJ should have focused on whether the principle of universality applied to such admissions decisions and whether UN member states should have discretion when deciding on membership applications. Indeed, these were some of the main issues of contention in the Security Council's 204th, 205th, and 206th Meetings of 1947,[26] which precipitated these advisory opinions, and so these should have been the ICJ's focus in these advisory opinions had it hoped to truly make an impact on the situation. This commentary concludes by emphasizing the political nature of the ultimate resolution of this impasse over admission, thereby helping identify the limitations of international law with these types of politically sensitive situations,

---

[22] See G. Abi-Saab, et al., *The Changing Constitution of the United Nations* (London, British Institute of International and Comparative Law 1997), p. 23.

[23] See J. Crawford, *Brownlie's Principles of Public International Law* (8th edn, Oxford, Oxford University Press 2012), p. 731; J.S. Watson, 'Autointerpretation, Competence and the Continuing Validity of Article 2(7) of the UN Charter', (1977) 71 *American Journal of International Law* 60, 83; W.C. Gordon, 'International Law: International Court of Justice—Advisory Opinions: Admission to Membership in the United Nations', (1949) 47 *Michigan Law Review* 1192.

[24] See, for example, C.F. Amerasinghe, *Principles of the Institutional Law of International Organisations* (Cambridge, Cambridge University Press 2005), pp. 105–11 (referring to it as a rule of effectiveness); H.G. Schermers and N.M. Blokker, *International Institutional Law* (3rd rev. edn., Boston/Leiden, Martinus Nijhoff Publishers 2005), pp. 76–98; N.D. White, *The Law of International Organisations* (Manchester, Manchester University Press 2005), pp. 110–12.

[25] See, for example, R. Kolb, *An Introduction to the Law of the United Nations* (Oxford, Hart 2010), p. 110.

[26] See UN doc. SCOR, 203rd and 204th Meetings, 24 and 25 September 1947; UN doc. SCOR, 205th Meeting, 29 September 1947; UN doc. SCOR, 206th Meeting, 1 October 1947.

at least when the forum refuses to consider the relevant context surrounding the questions posed.

A. Factors in connection with conditions

The ICJ in the First Admissions Advisory Opinion was asked whether a member state may make its vote dependent on additional conditions not provided in art. 4(1) of the UN Charter. In relation to this question, the ICJ decided it would not concern itself with the 'actual vote' of member states—that is, the manner in which a member state arrives at its decision to vote.[27] Rather, the ICJ expressed the question in a purely legal manner:

> [A]re the conditions stated in paragraph 1 of Article 4 exhaustive in character in the sense that an affirmative reply would lead to the conclusion that a Member is not legally entitled to make admission dependent on conditions not expressly provided for in that Article, while a negative reply would, on the contrary, authorize a Member to make admission dependent also on other conditions.[28]

By emphasizing the legal nature of the request, the ICJ established a narrow scope for the question posed. Nevertheless, as the ICJ often does in its decisions and opinions, the ICJ here showed some sophistication in examining the legal issues presented to it while also showing awareness of the associated political issues. In particular, in ruling that the enumerated conditions are exhaustive, the ICJ also decided that the consideration of factors that are connected to the conditions in art. 4 are not excluded. The ICJ explicitly distinguished factors from the enumerated conditions and excluded the consideration of relevant factors, such as political factors connected to conditions of admission. The distinction was constructive as it had identified and provided a nuanced approach on how to address these two connected issues. Furthermore, the ICJ provided a solution that did not stray from the enumerated conditions in art. 4(1), while at the same time it ensured some flexibility in practice to enable consideration of factors connected to the conditions.

However, the ICJ perhaps did not go far enough in determining the extent to which factors connected to the conditions may be relied upon when voting on admission. Dissenting Judges Basedevant, Winiarski, McNair, and Read highlighted the practical dilemma faced by members of the Security Council and the General Assembly having the freedom to give regard to any consideration upon which to base their vote but not to rely on such considerations to the extent they become conditions extraneous to the criteria in art. 4(1).[29] The distinction between the two is not at all clear, and the advisory opinion certainly would have been more helpful in guiding admission decisions had it clarified the distinction. From a layperson's perspective, the division between conditions and factors that relate to conditions would appear to be a distinction without a difference, which might denigrate the ICJ's reasoning here.

---

[27] See First Admissions Advisory Opinion [1948] ICJ Rep 57, 60 (para. 11).
[28] Ibid. at 61 (para. 14).
[29] Dissenting Opinion of Judges Basedeviat, Winiarksi, McNair, and Read, [1948] ICJ Rep 82, 83.

B. Focus on the Security Council's primary responsibility

The ICJ in the Second Admissions Advisory Opinion focused almost exclusively on the Security Council's 'primary responsibility to maintain international peace and security', as opposed to explaining how the General Assembly also has responsibilities in this area. After providing the historical background for this Second Admissions Advisory Opinion, this section explains how the ICJ's approach was overly narrow.

On 13 September 1949, the Security Council reconsidered the applications of Austria, Ceylon (modern-day Sri Lanka), Finland, Ireland, Italy, Jordan, and Portugal.[30] Nine members of the Security Council (Argentina, Canada, China, Cuba, Egypt, France, Norway, United Kingdom, and the United States) had supported the draft resolutions recommending the admission of all of the above states to UN membership, but the Soviet Union consistently vetoed these applications.[31] This created yet another political impasse within the Security Council on these admission cases. As a result of the ongoing—and seemingly irresolvable—political impasses within the Security Council on these admission cases, the General Assembly resolved at its 252nd Plenary Meeting on 22 November 1949 to request a further advisory opinion from the ICJ with regard to the competence of the General Assembly to admit applicants to the UN without a recommendation from the Security Council, thereby circumventing the Security Council and the Soviet veto.

The General Assembly at its 252nd Plenary Meeting considered the 'political impasse' as communicated through the Ad Hoc Political Committee and recommended 'permanent members of the Security Council to refrain from the use of the veto in connexion with the recommendation of States for membership in the United Nations' and that the Security Council ought to bear in mind art. 4(1) of the Charter when recommending applicants for membership.[32] Clearly, from the language of the General Assembly in its 252nd Meeting, its view was that the veto of Security Council permanent members had stalled the admissions procedure of applicant states. The challenge was how to overcome this voting impasse in the Security Council in practice, and in particular whether the General Assembly may legally proceed with the business of admitting new members given that the impasse in the Security Council did not seem to have any prospects of being resolved.[33] By seeking a second legal pronouncement from the ICJ on the matter, the General Assembly had hoped that the ICJ might endorse its preferred approach. However, as can be seen from the framing of the legal issue, the General Assembly was constrained by the legal requirements of art. 4 yet again.

The General Assembly decided at its 252nd Plenary Meeting to request an advisory opinion,[34] which would act as the basis for the Second Admissions Advisory Opinion.

---

[30] See UN doc. SCOR, 442nd and 443th Meetings, 13 September 1949.

[31] Ibid. See also Th. D. Grant, *Admission to the United Nations, Charter Article 4 and the Rise of Universal Organization* (Leiden/Boston, Martinus Nijhoff Publishers 2009), pp. 64–7 (describing the 'logjam' from 1946 to 1955, and noting the admission of certain applicants was problematic by the 1950s).

[32] See UN doc. A/RES/296(IV), 22 November 1949, sec. K.

[33] See Grant (n. 31), at 65 (observing that there were no admissions to the UN from 1950 to 1955).

[34] See UN doc. A/RES/296(IV), 22 November 1949, sec. J.

In order to provide an opinion, the ICJ first established the parameters of its competence in interpreting art. 4(2) of the UN Charter to answer such a legal question. This was intended to address the objections to the ICJ's competence to answer this question on the basis that the question was of a political nature, as had been argued in the First Admissions Advisory Opinion. The ICJ settled such objections by reaffirming its judicial competence within art. 96 of the UN Charter and art. 65 of the ICJ Statute to answer any legal question, as it had similarly established in the First Admissions Advisory Opinion.[35] Furthermore, the ICJ established the limits of its judicial competence by stating that 'it cannot attribute a political character to a request which, framed in abstract terms, invites it to undertake an essentially judicial task, the interpretation of a treaty provision.'[36] The ICJ affirmed the judicial aspects of the question and its competence to provide a judicial answer.[37]

As with the First Admissions Advisory Opinion, the ICJ in the Second Admissions Advisory Opinion showed a willingness to consider the political issues associated with the legal question presented by the General Assembly. This should not be surprising, given that the bench in the Second Admissions Advisory Opinion consisted of fourteen of the fifteen judges who were involved in the First Admissions Advisory Opinion. However, the reasoning in the Second Admissions Advisory Opinion was far less balanced than in the First Admissions Advisory Opinion. For example, the ICJ focused almost exclusively on the Security Council's 'primary responsibility to maintain international peace and security,' as provided for by UN Charter art. 24(1), and failed to even mention the General Assembly's functions and powers under art. 10 to 'discuss any questions … relating to the powers and functions of any organs' (including the Security Council) and under art. 11 to consider the 'general principles of international peace and security' and to 'discuss any questions relating to [it].' Moreover, the ICJ did not examine any role of the General Assembly under the UN Charter, thereby giving more effect to the power of the Security Council and less to the power of the General Assembly. In effect, the advisory opinion may have affirmed an unbalanced power relationship without conducting a complete analysis of UN Charter Chapter IV (dealing with the General Assembly) and Chapter V (dealing with the Security Council). In failing to do so, the ICJ gave effect to the very thing that had been causing the political impasse within the Security Council in the first place, which essentially reinforced the status quo. It is understandable that the ICJ wanted to deliberate the question in abstract terms. However, it might not have been the most helpful on this occasion to give a legal opinion in the absence of the broader context. Regardless, it would have been difficult for the ICJ to render an opinion that did not give effect to the Security Council recommendation, as it is an explicit requirement under the UN Charter.[38]

---

[35] See Second Admissions Advisory Opinion, [1950] ICJ Rep 4, 7 (para. 9); First Admissions Advisory Opinion, [1948] ICJ Rep 57, 61–2 (paras 15–16).

[36] Second Admissions Advisory Opinion [1950] ICJ Rep 4, 7 (para. 10).   [37] Ibid.

[38] See White (n. 24), at 108–9; M.D. Oberg, 'The Legal Effects of Resolutions of the UN Security Council and General Assembly in the Jurisprudence of the ICJ', (2006) 16 *European Journal of International Law* 879, 891.

The extent to which the ICJ could have gone further in analyzing the question the General Assembly had posed arguably was limited by its perceived need to follow precedent. The ICJ decided it was bound to follow practice in interpreting art. 4 in accordance with its natural meaning because the words were sufficiently clear.[39] In so doing, the ICJ felt it did not need to refer to *travaux prépartoires* of the UN Charter to find further clarification.[40] The ICJ certainly wanted to ensure that legal rules are followed and to prohibit acts that are contrary to the law. At the same time, the effect of the ICJ's decision would be that the freedom of UN member states to exercise discretionary power in the UN would be constrained. The ICJ may have felt that it had indirectly settled the questions that arose in the 204th, 205th, and 206th Meetings in relation to collective voting, discretion, and the principle of universality, although it arguably did not do so. Instead, the ICJ attempted to reconcile the practical realities faced by members—that is, the issue of having to adhere to the 'legal rule' contained in UN Charter art. 4. In hindsight, the UN would have benefited from an analysis by the ICJ of the conduct of members voting in the Security Council or General Assembly (as dissenting Judges Basedevant et al. pointed out). In particular, it may have been helpful if the ICJ could have provided concrete examples or further guidance in differentiating between what it thought were political considerations that were allowed and conditions extraneous to the criteria in art. 4 that were prohibited. The ICJ's determination unfortunately did not settle the issue—it left the criteria broad and vague. Moreover, according to the dissenting Judges Basedevant et al., the proposal for universal membership at the San Francisco Conference was rejected in favour of inserting specific conditions in the Charter with respect to the 'character and policies of governments' and to allow the United Nations (through the Security Council and General Assembly) to conduct extensive investigations of all considerations to determine the fulfilment of the criteria by candidates.[41] In effect, the fulfilment, or indeed the non-fulfilment, of the conditions in art. 4(1) would be a matter left solely to the judgment and discretion of each member state,[42] with the only limit to the exercise of this discretionary judgment being 'good faith'.[43]

The preceding two sections have evaluated the ICJ's actual approach to the questions posed in both requests for an advisory opinion. The following two sections explain how the ICJ probably would have done a better job in providing guidance that impacted the actual situation, had it been willing to broaden its focus to those issues that the Security Council had been focusing on in the lead up to these requests for advisory opinions—namely, the degree to which UN member states can exercise

---

[39] See First Admissions Advisory Opinion [1948] ICJ Rep 57, 63 (para. 26).   [40] Ibid.

[41] See Dissenting Opinion of Judges Basedeviat, Winiarksi, McNair, and Read, [1948] ICJ Rep 82, 88 (citing the Minutes of Commission I/2 of the San Fransisco Conference, Vol. VII, at 308).

[42] See Abi-Saab et al. (n. 22), at 23; White (n. 24), at 110–12 (arguing that art. 4 provides for the exercise of judgment, but this judgment must be exercised within the ambit of the legal constraints in that article).

[43] S. Jacobs and M. Poirier, 'The Right to Veto United Nations Membership Applications: The United States Veto of the Viet-Nams', (1976) 17 *Harvard International Law Journal* 581, 595 (citing French and Polish oral arguments). See *also* J. Klabbers, *An Introduction to International Organizations Law* (3rd edn, Cambridge, Cambridge University Press 2015), pp. 90–112.

discretion when deciding on such matters as membership and whether such decisions should be influenced by the principle of universality.

C. Discretion

One main subtext of these advisory opinions was the question of how much discretion member states were to have when deciding such matters as membership. The UN Charter is ambiguous concerning the amount of discretion the members of the Security Council and the General Assembly are to have when deciding on such matters. Admittedly, the first sentence of UN Charter art. 24(2) appears to limit the discretion of the Security Council with the UN Charter's purposes and principles, which are listed in UN Charter arts. 1 and 2, respectively. However, according to Hans Kelsen, the scope of the discretion to be exercised by the Security Council (and General Assembly) is not limited by provisions of the UN Charter, given that the Charter does not provide for a higher authority to determine definitively whether a decision of the Security Council (or General Assembly) is correct or not.[44] Therefore, in a situation where an applicant fulfils the conditions in art. 4(1), either organ may nevertheless refuse to admit a state to membership, at least according to Kelsen.[45] Kelsen points to the report of the Rapporteur of Committee I/2 of the San Francisco Conference that interprets the UN Charter as representing a minimum standard to be satisfied, with the possibility to take into account other considerations.[46] After all, if it were the intention of the drafters to admit all states that qualified, then the qualifications for admission would need to be accompanied by some provision guaranteeing admission to those states that qualified. Such a guarantee, Kelsen points out, is absent from the UN Charter.[47]

The same report of the Rapporteur of Committee I/2 highlighted the practical difficulties of stipulating in law the 'enumeration of elements' to use in evaluating an applicant's membership qualifications, as it might offend the principle of non-intervention in states.[48] As a result, the lack of a clear 'enumeration of elements' in law in effect gave a larger amount of discretion to UN organs and member states to determine whether the criteria were fulfilled. In the interest of promoting the rule of law, the challenge in practice arguably is to ensure that the degree of discretion is appropriate in light of the particular circumstances and that the decision is not unfair or unreasonable.[49] However, this project of ensuring a lawful and fair process of UN admission was overshadowed by the political challenges facing an increasingly bipolar world during the Cold War.

[44] See H. Kelsen, *The Law of the United Nations, A Critical Analysis of Its Fundamental Problems* (London Institute of World Affairs, London 1950, New York, Praeger 1964), p. 70.

[45] Ibid.   [46] Ibid.   [47] Ibid. at p. 71.

[48] See Report of the Rapporteur of Committee I/2 of the San Francisco Conference in Minutes of Vol. VII at 308, cited in Dissenting Opinion of Judges Basedevant, Winiarski, McNair, and Read in the First Admissions Advisory Opinion, [1948] ICJ Rep 82, 88.

[49] See T. Bingham, *The Rule of Law* (London, Penguin Books 2010), pp. 48–50 (pointing out that excessive discretion of decision-makers does not provide a means to challenge arbitrary decisions and ultimately undermines the rule of law).

The real issue in dispute during the Security Council's 204th, 205th, and 206th Meetings from 25 September 1947 to 1 October 1947 appears to have been the extent that discretion may be used to admit applicants favoured by certain member states. Unfortunately, this was not the focus of the ICJ in the First Admissions Advisory Opinion, although it did mention that the argument that the conditions in art. 4 were an 'indispensable minimum' would unacceptably lead to 'unlimited power of discretion in the imposition of new conditions' inasmuch as it would be 'inconsistent with the very character of paragraph 1 of Article 4 ...'.[50] As explained in Section 5.1. above, the ICJ's main focus in the First Admissions Advisory Opinion was whether a member state may make its vote dependent on additional conditions not provided in art. 4(1) of the UN Charter, which is somewhat different from the question whether states have unbridled discretion when deciding on admission applications. Likewise, the ICJ in the Second Admissions Advisory Opinion did not focus on the amount of discretion a member state may use when deciding to admit applicants favoured by certain member states. Instead, the ICJ focused almost exclusively on the Security Council's primary responsibility to maintain international peace and security. Only the dissenting judges in the First Admissions Advisory Opinion focused significantly on discretion, interpreting art. 4(2) of the Charter to suggest that there was scope for the use of discretion to arrive at a Security Council recommendation and General Assembly decision and asserting that admission was not a procedure of accession.[51] This point relates to the principle of universality, which is the focus of the next section, inasmuch as it might influence the way that member states use their discretion in admitting applicants to the UN.

D. Principle of universality

Another main subtext of these advisory opinions was whether UN membership was supposed to be universal or selective. Currently, UN membership is virtually universal, with the Cook Islands, the Holy See, and Niue as the only bona fide states that lack UN membership. However, on 17 November 1947, when the request for this advisory opinion was made,[52] there were only fifty-five UN member states,[53] which left a large number of non-members in the world. In short, it was not entirely clear at that time whether the UN was supposed to be a universal international organization. The Moscow Conference of 1943 affirmed that the UN would open its membership to all states in order to maintain peace and security and gather peace-loving states together.[54] However, the final arrangement provided for in the UN Charter turned out to be far more complicated than this, inasmuch as the concept of openness and

---

[50] First Admissions Advisory Opinion, [1948] ICJ Rep 57, 62–3 [para. 24].
[51] See Dissenting Opinion of Judges Basedeviat, Winiarksi, McNair, and Read, [1948] ICJ Rep 82, 83–4.
[52] See UN doc. A/RES/113 (III), 17 November 1947.
[53] See UN doc., Member States of the United Nations, *at* http://www.un.org/en/members
[54] See Moscow Declaration of 1943, cl. 4. See also, P. Marshall, 'Smuts and the Preamble to the UN Charter', (2001) 358 *The Roundtable* 55, 56.

universality of membership was paradoxically at odds with the selection procedure ultimately adopted.

Upon reading the two paragraphs of UN Charter art. 4, two points stand out. First, the state being considered for membership must be peace-loving and must adhere to the obligations of membership under UN Charter art. 4(1). Second, a successful membership application must have the requisite affirmative decision of the General Assembly upon the recommendation of the Security Council, according to UN Charter art. 4(2). When interpreting these provisions, it is important whether the intent of the framers of the UN Charter was universal or selective membership, inasmuch as this intent influences how these provisions should be interpreted and applied. The principle of universality in the UN, affirmed at the 1943 Moscow Conference, means that all states are equal and would in practice require the admission of all peace-loving states to UN membership.[55] Syria and France argued in the Security Council that the political division within the UN and the use of discretionary power to decide admission cases based on subjective determinations undermined the openness of admission they saw as inherent in UN Charter art. 4.[56] Unfortunately, the ICJ did not address the principle of universality in either advisory opinion, although it should have since this arguably was at the heart of the debates within the Security Council and it possibly could have helped resolve the impasse.

When considering universality within the context of UN membership, it is necessary to ask what is meant by 'peace-loving state'. A state's preparedness to join the UN could be evidence of its peace-loving nature and its willingness to carry out the obligations of the UN Charter.[57] In practice, however, 'peace-loving' ironically may have required a declaration of war on the Axis powers before the end of the Second World War.[58] The openness and broadness of the language 'all other peace-loving states' referred to in art. 4(1) would support the ideal of inclusiveness and universality of membership. However, as one commentator points out, the UN appears to have rejected 'universality as a basis for membership'.[59] Indeed, it became clear at the San Francisco Conference in 1945 that a state's own declaration of peace-loving status would not be enough for UN admission.[60] Instead, UN member states were to use their discretion to decide if an applicant state was peace loving and if it was likely to observe the obligations under the UN Charter.[61] Permanent members of the Security Council even enjoy their veto privileges on substantive and procedural issues such as admission, which emphasizes the selective nature of admission decisions.[62] With regard to procedural issues, there had been attempts at the conference to clarify those procedural issues that were not subject to veto powers, as provided in UN Charter art.

---

[55] See UN doc. SCOR, 203rd and 204th Meetings, 24 and 25 September 1947, at 2416–17.

[56] Ibid. at 2416–17, 2423–4.   [57] See Rudzinski (n. 4), at 146.

[58] See, for example, D.F. Vagts, 'Neutrality Law in World War II', (1998) 20 *Cardozo Law Review* 459, 459 (discussing Turkey's declaration of war being connected to UN membership).

[59] Rudzinski (n. 4), at 147. The proposal from Argentina to the First Assembly of the League of Nations in 1920 for membership to be accepted on a universal basis was rejected by a vote of twenty-nine to five. Ibid., at 149.

[60] Ibid., at 154.   [61] Ibid.

[62] See Th. R. Van Dervort, *International Law and Organization* (Thousand Oaks/London, Sage Publications 1998), p. 43.

27(3), which limits the veto to non-procedural matters, although the exact contours of what constitutes non-procedural matters appears to have been left intentionally ambiguous by the drafters.[63] Nevertheless, the Security Council documented the following in response to 'the question whether the recommendation of the Security Council [with regard to admission] is subject to the voting procedure prescribed by art. 27(3) of the Charter':

> The practice of the Security Council in this respect has continued unchanged. In particular, abstentions by permanent members have continued to be regarded as not affecting the requirement of concurring votes of those members.[64]

In effect, this provided an inordinate amount of discretion to the permanent members when it came to their use of the veto, including in connection with issues of membership, which emphasizes the selective nature of UN membership. These points should have been raised in the advisory opinions, yet they were not.

In sum, the ICJ did not focus on the amount of discretion member states have when making their decisions, nor did it focus on the principle of universality, although both could have helped it answer the questions raised in these two advisory opinions and had a real impact on the actual situation at issue. Indeed, the ICJ looked at the abstract questions posed by the General Assembly without the context in which they arose, and therefore, it should not come as a surprise that these two advisory opinions had minimal impact on the resolution of the impasse. Instead, as the following section shows, the impasse ultimately was resolved through political means.

E. Political resolution

These two advisory opinions both attempted to resolve the political impasse within the Security Council and provide a legal opinion that clarified the ambiguous issues associated with UN admission. Even though the Court's advisory opinions provided legal guidance in an attempt to overcome the political stalemate, ultimately this effort was unsuccessful. Indeed, after the Second Admissions Advisory Opinion, the UN entered a period of 'logjam' over membership, inasmuch as it did not admit any new members from 1950 to 1955.[65] After obtaining the ICJ's advisory opinions, the UN attempted to take measures to overcome the political stalemate on the matter of admission of new members, with the General Assembly establishing a nineteen member state Special Committee at its 7th Session to study proposals on the question of admission of new members.[66] This Special Committee failed to provide concrete recommendations or agree on a solution.[67] Then, at its 8th Session, the General Assembly attempted to explore 'possibilities of a solution along political lines' through the Good Offices Committee.[68] The committee consisted of representatives from Egypt,

---

[63] Ibid.   [64] UN doc. art. 4, Repertory, Supplement 1, Vol. 1 (1945–55), para. 10, at 86.
[65] Grant (n. 31), at 65.
[66] See L. Gross, *Essays on International Law and Organization*, vol. 1, (Dordrecht, Kluwer 1984), pp. 585–6.
[67] Ibid.   [68] Ibid. at 586.

The Netherlands, and Peru, and was tasked with consulting members of the Security Council to '[reach] an agreement which would facilitate the admission of New Members in accordance with Article 4 of the Charter.'[69] This included the favouring of the 'widest possible membership of the United Nations,' for the Security Council to consider recommending the membership applications of eighteen states and to report those applications to the General Assembly.[70] Then Brazil and New Zealand submitted a joint draft resolution to the Security Council at its 701st Meeting that took into account General Assembly Resolution 918(X), which noted that the General Assembly would consider the eighteen applications separately.[71] The President (the representative of New Zealand) explained that the applications were to be voted upon separately in the proceedings and then on the draft resolution as a whole.[72] During the Security Council's 703rd Meeting, the Soviet Union proposed that the eighteen applications were to be voted upon as a whole, even though it may be '[legalizing a] package deal'.[73] There was further resistance to voting on the applications as a whole during the Security Council's 704th Meeting (at this point, there were twenty applicants being considered after China added two applicants, although four of the original applicants were not put to the vote as they were presented as part of the whole).[74] There was no outcome at this stage.

The turning point came at the Security Council's 705th Meeting on 14 December 1955 when the Soviet Union proposed that sixteen states would be recommended to the General Assembly for membership, but when the United States tried to add Japan to the list of states and the Soviet Union vetoed the vote on Japan, the Security Council proceeded to vote on the sixteen states separately and then on the Soviet Union's draft resolution as a whole.[75] The sixteen successful states were Albania, Jordan, Ireland, Portugal, Hungary, Italy, Austria, Romania, Bulgaria, Finland, Ceylon (modern-day Sri Lanka), Nepal, Libya, Cambodia, Laos, and Spain.[76] Subsequently, having received the requisite recommendation from the Security Council, the General Assembly decided to admit all sixteen states.[77] Notably, at this stage, the Security Council made no recommendations on the applications of South Korea, Vietnam, Mongolia, or Japan, even though they were the subject of the proposals voted upon for the recommendation of the Security Council.[78] However, having successfully had its draft resolution voted upon in the manner the Soviet Union advocated and passed through during the Security Council's 705th Meeting, the Soviet Union proceeded with submitting a further draft resolution on the following day recommending the admission of Mongolia and Japan to the General Assembly at the Security Council's

[69] UN doc. A/RES/718(VIII) of 23 October 1953.
[70] UN doc. A/RES/918(X) of 8 December 1955.
[71] See UN doc. art. 4, Repertory, Supplement 1, Vol. 1 (1945–55) at 84, para. 10; UN doc. Practices Relative to Recommendations to the General Assembly Regarding the Admission of New Members, Repertory (1952–55), ch. VII, at 97.
[72] Ibid.   [73] Ibid.
[74] UN doc. Practices Relative to Recommendations to the General Assembly Regarding the Admission of New Members, Repertory (1952–55), ch. VII, at 97–8.
[75] See UN doc. S/3509 of 14 December 1955.   [76] Ibid.
[77] See UN doc. A/RES/995(X) of 14 December 1955.
[78] See UN doc. art. 4, Repertory, Supplement 1, Volume 1 (1945–55), at 80, para. 10.

706th Meeting on 15 December 1955.[79] Subsequently, the Soviet Union's draft resolution was voted upon as a whole but was not adopted due to only one state being in favour and ten abstentions.[80] Notably, at this 706th Meeting, the President (speaking as the representative of New Zealand) said he would abstain on both the Soviet proposal as well as the United Kingdom proposal (which only contained the name of Japan) on 'constitutional grounds,' which was due to the view that 'the Council is not permitted by the Charter to attach conditions to any kind of recommendations.'[81] Further to this, the Soviet Union submitted an amendment to the United Kingdom's draft resolution to add Mongolia to be voted upon at the 708th Meeting on 21 December 1955, but the United Kingdom representative decided to postpone voting on its draft resolution.[82] There were further attempts by the Soviet Union to propose for Security Council recommendation the admission of North Korea and South Korea simultaneously at the 789th and 790th Meetings on 9 September 1957 and at the 843rd Meeting in December 1958, but these drafts were rejected due to there being only one vote in favour, with nine against and one abstention for the first occasion, and one vote in favour and eight against with two abstentions for the second occasion.[83] The United States cast the single veto vote against recommending North Vietnam to be admitted to the UN on 15 November 1976 in spite of support by fourteen members of the Security Council,[84] stating that 'Vietnam did not meet the standards established by Article 4 of the Charter ... [due to] Vietnam's failure to observe human rights with respect to American service men [...]'.[85] By this point, it became obvious that the effect of the package deal struck at the 705th Meeting had set a new precedent for admitting members as a whole, even though the development had been met with resistance from the President of the 706th Meeting, who opposed such a voting method on principle and due to the fact that the United Kingdom and the United States were simply obstructing the admission of their enemy states. Thus we see how political considerations, not legal considerations, led to the eventual resolution of the impasse over admission to the UN.

F. Conclusion

When assessing the effectiveness of these advisory opinions on the UN admissions process, it is important to keep in mind that the UN most likely was relatively distracted away from admission issues during this period by complaints of Yugoslavia, Albania, and Bulgaria threatening peace and security in Greece and the security threats associated with the Korean War, among other pressing issues.[86] It was not

---

[79] See UN doc. Practices Relative to Recommendations to the General Assembly Regarding the Admission of New Members, Repertory (1952–55), Chapter VII, at 98.

[80] Ibid.   [81] Ibid. at 98, 101.   [82] Ibid. at 98.

[83] See UN doc. Practices Relative to Recommendations to the General Assembly Regarding the Admission of New Members, Repertory (1956–58), Chapter VII, at 88.

[84] See UN doc. A/RES/31/21 of 26 November 1976.

[85] UN doc. art. 4, Repertory, Supplement 5, Vol. 1 (1970–78), at 73, para. 21.

[86] See L.M. Goodrich, 'Expanding the Role of the General Assembly, The Maintenance of International Peace and Security', (1951–52) 29 *International Conciliation* 231, 269–72.

until 1955 when the 'package deal' was negotiated that allowed the admission of sixteen states, which ended the deadlock in the Security Council.[87] It has been suggested that the 1955 package deal only managed to stay within the letter of the ICJ's advisory opinions by dealing with each applicant state separately.[88] However, the more accurate view seems to be that the entire package deal contradicts the UN Charter concerning admission, at least in light of the ICJ's interpretation of these provisions in the two advisory opinions analyzed in this case comment. In the end, it would appear that politics prevailed when it came to UN membership applications. Recent applicants for UN membership undoubtedly have noticed a similar attitude. Therefore, the ultimate significance of these advisory opinions might lie in helping understand the limits of international law when it comes to politically sensitive situations, which lesson is not entirely without value.

To end on a more positive note, the package deal arguably complied 'with the spirit of the United Nations,' inasmuch as it was a significant step towards the 'realization of universality' in UN membership.[89] Even though universalism was not the stated goal of the United Nations,[90] the package deal of 1955 dovetailed nicely with the period of decolonization at the end of the 1950s and a shift of membership policy in favour of universalism in the UN.[91] Gradually art. 4 waned in importance when deciding on admission, and admission became a mere procedural matter without significant regard to the conditions of membership established in the UN Charter.[92] Unfortunately for aspiring UN member states in modern states, the shift away from the conditions in art. 4 towards political considerations has not been accompanied by a policy in favour of universalism, as was observed in the 1950s, thus opening up the United Nations to criticism involving unfairness and illegitimacy, at least with regard to admission decisions.

---

[87] See B. Simma/D. Khan/G. Nolte/A. Paulus (eds), *The Charter of the United Nations: A Commentary* (Oxford, Oxford University Press 2002), p. 180; Kolb (n. 25), at 108–9.

[88] See Kolb (n. 25), at 109.   [89] Simma (n. 87), at 180.   [90] See Rudzinski (n. 4), at 147.

[91] See Kolb (n. 25), at 109.   [92] Ibid.

4

Legal Acts

It is undisputed that international organizations can take decisions that are binding upon their Member States and that they can even exercise sovereign powers.[1] This is evident in such organizations as, for example, the United Nations (UN), the European Union (EU), the World Health Organization (WHO), the International Civil Aviation Organization (ICAO), the Organization of American States (OAS), the North-Atlantic Treaty Organization (NATO), the Organisation for Economic Co-operation and Development (OECD), the Universal Postal Union (UPU), the World Meteorological Organization (WMO), and the International Monetary Fund (IMF).[2] Traditionally, analyses of the law-making powers of international organizations started from three propositions: (1) member states provide the international organizations they establish with the law-making powers as they see fit, laid down in the constituent instrument of the organization (constituent treaty); (2) international organizations have only the law-making powers that have been attributed to them in the constituent treaty by their member states (doctrine of attributed powers); and (3) the law-making powers of international organizations are generally limited to internal matters.[3] Recent developments suggest, however, that these traditional propositions no longer hold true.[4]

This applies in the first place to the constituent instruments establishing international organizations. Like all national and international norms, they are subject to interpretation by the parties and organs applying it. It is possible, therefore, that these constituent instruments, including their provisions pertaining to the law-making powers of the organization, will be construed in a different way than was originally intended by the drafting nations, as it proves very difficult to draft an instrument in such a manner as to effectively preclude any other possible interpretation.[5] As Boisson de Chazournes and Gadkowsky observe in their annotation of the International Court

---

[1] Part of the analysis in this introduction relies on J. Wouters and Ph. De Man, 'International Organizations as Law-Makers', in J. Klabbers and Å. Wallendahl (eds), *Research Handbook on International Organizations Law: Between Functionalism and Constitutionalism* (Cheltenham, Edward Elgar Publishing 2011), pp. 190–224.

[2] R.A. Wessel and J. Wouters, 'The Phenomenon of Multilevel Regulation: Interactions Between Global, EU and National Regulatory Spheres' in A. Follesdal, R.A. Wessel, and J. Wouters (eds), *Multilevel Regulation and the EU. The Interplay Between Global, European and National Normative Processes* (Leiden, MNP 2008), p. 13. See further, D. Sarooshi, *International Organizations and their Exercise of Sovereign Powers* (Oxford, Oxford University Press 2005) and C.F. Amerasinghe, *Principles of the Institutional Law of International Organizations* (Cambridge, Cambridge University Press 2005).

[3] J.E. Alvarez, *International Organizations as Law-makers* (Oxford, Oxford University Press 2006), pp. 120–1.

[4] See also Introduction to Part 2—Legal Powers—of this volume.

[5] See, more generally, D.C. Smith, 'Beyond Indeterminacy and Self-contradiction in Law: Transnational Abductions and Treaty Interpretation in *U.S. v. AlvareZ-Machain*', (1995) 6 *European Journal of International Law* 1.

of Justice's (ICJ) 1986 judgment in *Military and Paramilitary Activities in and against Nicaragua*, resolutions of international organizations constitute an important tool for such treaty interpretation.

Secondly, (certain) acts of international organizations are increasingly having normative repercussions beyond their concrete scope of application. A good example is the manner in which UN General Assembly resolutions are seen as evidence of customary international law by the ICJ in *Military and Paramilitary Activities in and against Nicaragua* (Boisson de Chazournes and Gadkowski) and in other cases.

Thirdly, the stronger frequency, intensity, and impact of law-making by international organizations has given rise to unprecedented dynamics before international, supranational, and national courts. The least one can say in this respect is that supremacy clauses do not, or not any longer, inspire enough awe in order for international and national courts to stay passive in the face of international institutional action when constitutional values are at stake. In particular, courts may refrain from giving effect to art. 103 of the UN Charter, which provides that '[i]n the event of a conflict between the obligations of the Members of the United Nations under the present Charter and their obligations under any other international agreement, their obligations under the present Charter shall prevail', where rival obligations pertain to the protection of fundamental rights. At the international level, one of the first cases in a UN context in this respect was the ICJ's 1971 *Advisory Opinion on the Legal Consequences for States of the Continued Presence of South Africa in Namibia*. The opinion touches upon the role of the ICJ in exercising a review over the factual and legal determinations of other principal UN organs, including the General Assembly and the Security Council (McGonigle Leyh).

Especially before European domestic and EU courts, a more intense awareness of the implications of acts of international organizations for the legal position of individuals and for deeply-held constitutional values of domestic legal orders has given rise to interesting judicial dynamics since the mid-1970s. Various strings of cases have generated true 'sagas' in which a critical constitutional dialectic between norms of international organizations and a domestic legal order unfolded before the courts. The most classical example of such a saga in the relationship between EU law and national law has been, since the 1970s, the *Solange* case-law of the German Constitutional Court, the *Bundesverfassungsgericht* (Hilpold). But over the past ten years, an even more fascinating saga sent shockwaves through the relationship between the legal orders of two important international organizations: the UN and the EU. These were the *Kadi* cases (Tzanakopoulos), in which—in a manner not dissimilar to the attitude of the German Constitutional Court vis-à-vis EU law—the ECJ refused to relinquish its control power over EU acts implementing UN Security Council decisions on terrorist blacklisting as long as the UN cannot assure comparable fundamental rights guarantees. Last but not least, the Security Council's terrorist blacklisting practice also gave rise to a clash with the Swiss Federal Tribunal in its 2007 decision in *Nada*, one of the first cases to challenge Security Council sanctions under Chapter VII before a national court, and which found an extension in the European Court of Human Rights 2012 Grand Chamber judgment in this case (Hilpold).

4.1 *Legal Consequences for States of the Continued Presence of South Africa in Namibia (South West Africa) notwithstanding Security Council Resolution 276 (1970), Advisory Opinion, [1971] ICJ Rep 16*

Brianne McGonigle Leyh

Relevance of the case

The *Advisory Opinion on the Legal Consequences for States of the Continued Presence of South Africa in Namibia* touches upon the role of the International Court of Justice (ICJ) in exercising a review over the factual and legal determinations of other principal UN organs, including the UN General Assembly (GA) and the UN Security Council (SC). In its opinion, the ICJ held by thirteen votes to two that South Africa's continued presence in the territory of South West Africa (Namibia) was illegal and that South Africa was obliged to withdraw its administration and end its occupation of the territory. It further found by eleven votes to four that member states of the UN must recognize the illegality of South Africa's occupation of Namibia and refrain from any and all acts implying recognition of the illegal occupation including the lending of support to the South African government. Finally, it called upon non-member states of the UN to acknowledge the illegality of the occupation and decline assistance to South Africa with regard to Namibia. Ultimately, the Court emphasized that UN member states are bound by their legal obligations and are required to recognize illegal conduct and refrain from providing assistance or support to the violating state. The relevance of the case, with regard to international organizations and legal acts, hinges on the findings related to the role of the ICJ as a judicial institution vis-à-vis its more political counterparts within the UN organization, the dissolution and succession of international organizations, and the power and limits of international organizations to ensure compliance with their rules and standards.

I. The facts

South West Africa, the former name for modern-day Namibia, fell under German colonial control in 1884. However, after the First World War, under the Treaty of Versailles, it was declared a League of Nations Mandate, with South Africa responsible for its administration. A League of Nations Mandate was a legal term assigned to territories that were transferred from the control of one country to another after the end of the war, often with one country administering the territory on behalf of the League until independence could be gained. When the League of Nations dissolved after the Second World War, it was agreed at the Yalta Conference that any remaining mandates should be placed under the trusteeship of the UN. All of the remaining mandates, with the sole exception of South West Africa, became UN Trust Territories.

In the case of South West Africa, South Africa refused to place it under trusteeship and instead requested that it be allowed to annex the territory. Indeed, it took steps to do so, enforcing apartheid practices and allowing white citizens to represent the territory in the South African Parliament. The refusal of South Africa to turn South West Africa into a trusteeship resulted in a 1950 ruling by the ICJ. In this brief ruling, the Court held that South Africa was not obliged to convert South West Africa into a trust territory. However, it was still obliged to act in accordance with the League of Nations Mandate, for which the GA assumed the supervisory role, and that South Africa would need to file periodic reports on the mandated territory as requested. Nevertheless, South Africa did not file reports and continued its actions of annexing the territory. Prior to the issue coming before the ICJ in the form of a request by the SC for an advisory opinion in 1970, the question of South Africa's controversial presence in Namibia continued to arise before both the GA and the SC as well as the ICJ.

In 1966, the ICJ found that Ethiopia and Liberia lacked the required legal standing to obtain a decision on whether South Africa violated its obligations under the mandate for South West Africa. Shortly afterwards, the GA passed Resolution 2145 (XXI), declaring South Africa in breach of its obligations as an administrator of a mandate and terminating the mandate. It then placed South West Africa under the direct responsibility of the UN and in 1967 created a UN Council for South West Africa responsible for administering the territory until independence.

In 1968, the SC passed Resolutions 245 and 246 endorsing the GA's Resolution 2145 (XXI). Thereafter, in 1969, the SC, in Resolution 269, requested South Africa to withdraw its administration from South West Africa. The South African government refused and the SC passed Resolution 276 (1970), declaring its continued presence illegal and noting that 'all acts taken by the Government of South Africa on behalf of or concerning Namibia after the termination of the Mandate are illegal and invalid'. It then called on all states, including those that were not member states to the UN, 'to refrain from any dealings with the Government of South Africa which are inconsistent with [the declaration]'. This resolution, and the preceding resolutions endorsing the GA's resolution, were adopted with France and the United Kingdom abstaining.

In order to help resolve the legal (and political) questions surrounding the various resolutions, the SC asked the ICJ, in Resolution 284, for an advisory opinion on what the legal consequences would be for states concerning the continued presence of South Africa in Namibia notwithstanding SC Resolution 276 (1970). South Africa objected to the proceedings.

II. The legal question

The main legal question posed by the SC to the ICJ was 'What are the legal consequences for States of the continued presence of South Africa in Namibia notwithstanding Security Council Resolution 276 (1970)?'

III. Excerpts

[...]

25. The question of Namibia was placed on the agenda of the Security Council as a 'situation' and not as a 'dispute'. No member State made any suggestion or proposal that the matter should be examined as a dispute, although due notice was given of the placing of the question on the Security Council's agenda under the title 'Situation in Namibia'. Had the Government of South Africa considered that the question should have been treated in the Security Council as a dispute, it should have drawn the Council's attention to that aspect of the matter. Having failed to raise the question at the appropriate time in the proper forum, it is not open to it to raise it before the Court at this stage.[...]

27. In the alternative the Government of South Africa has contended that even if the Court had competence to give the opinion requested, it should nevertheless, as a matter of judicial propriety, refuse to exercise its competence.[...]

29. It would not be proper for the Court to entertain these observations, bearing as they do on the very nature of the Court as the principal judicial organ of the United Nations, an organ which, in that capacity, acts only on the basis of the law, independently of all outside influence or interventions whatsoever, in the exercise of the judicial function entrusted to it alone by the Charter and its Statute. A court functioning as a court of law can act in no other way.[...]

32. Nor does the Court find that in this case the Security Council's request relates to a legal dispute actually pending between two or more States. It is not the purpose of the request to obtain the assistance of the Court in the exercise of the Security Council's functions relating to the pacific settlement of a dispute pending before it between two or more States. The request is put forward by a United Nations organ with reference to its own decisions and it seeks legal advice from the Court on the consequences and implications of these decisions.

[...]

40. The Government of South Africa has also expressed doubts as to whether the Court is competent to, or should, give an opinion, if, in order to do so, it should have to make findings as to extensive factual issues. In the view of the Court, the contingency that there may be factual issues underlying the question posed does not alter its character as a 'legal question' as envisaged in Article 96 of the Charter. The reference in this provision to legal questions cannot be interpreted as opposing legal to factual issues. Normally, to enable a court to pronounce on legal questions, it must also be acquainted with, take into account and, if necessary, make findings as to the relevant factual issues.

[...]

As to the position of the League, the Court found in its 1950 Advisory Opinion that: 'The League was not, as alleged by [the South African] Government, a "mandatory" in the sense in which this term is used in the national law of certain States'. The Court pointed out that: 'The Mandate was created, in the interest of the inhabitants of the territory, aid of humanity in general, as an international institution with an international object—a sacred trust of civilization'. Therefore, the Court found, the League 'had only assumed an international function of supervision and control' (I.C.J. *Reports 1950,* p. 132).

[...]

52. Furthermore, the subsequent development of international law in regard to non-self-governing territories, as enshrined in the Charter of the United Nations, made the principle of self-determination applicable to all of them. The concept of the sacred trust was confirmed and expanded to all 'territories whose peoples have not yet attained a full measure of self-government' (Art. 73). Thus it clearly embraced territories under a colonial régime. Obviously the sacred trust continued to apply to League of Nations mandated territories on which an international status had been conferred earlier. A further important stage in this development was the Declaration on the Granting of Independence to Colonial Countries and Peoples (General Assembly resolution 1514 (XV) of 14 December 1960), which embraces all peoples and territories which 'have not yet attained independence'.

[...]

55. [...] the League of Nations was the international organization entrusted with the exercise of the supervisory functions of the Mandate. Those functions were an indispensable element of the Mandate. But that does not mean that the mandates institution was to collapse with the disappearance of the original supervisory machinery. To the question whether the continuance of a mandate was inseparably linked with the existence of the League, the answer must be that an institution established for the fulfilment of a sacred trust cannot be presumed to lapse before the achievement of its purpose. The responsibilities of both mandatory and supervisor resulting from the mandates institution were complementary, and the disappearance of one or the other could not affect the survival of the institution.

[...]

89. Undoubtedly, the Court does not possess powers of judicial review or appeal in respect of the decisions taken by the United Nations organs concerned. The question of the validity or conformity with the Charter of General Assembly resolution 2145 (XXI) or of related Security Council resolutions does not form the subject of the request for advisory opinion. However, in the exercise of its judicial function and since objections have been advanced the Court, in the course of its reasoning, will consider these objections before determining any legal consequences arising from those resolutions.

90. [...] The mandatory Powers while retaining their mandates assumed, under Article 80 of the Charter, vis-à-vis all United Nations Members, the obligation to keep intact and preserve, until trusteeship agreements were executed, the rights of other States and of the peoples of mandated territories, which resulted from the existing mandate agreements and related instruments, such as Article 22 of the Covenant and the League Council's resolution of 31 January 1923 concerning petitions. The mandatory Powers also bound themselves to exercise their functions of administration in conformity with the relevant obligations emanating from the United Nations Charter, which member States have undertaken to fulfil in good faith in all their international relations.

91. One of the fundamental principles governing the international relationship thus established is that a party which disowns or does not fulfil its own obligations cannot be recognized as retaining the rights which it claims to derive from the relationship.

[…]

94. In examining this action of the General Assembly it is appropriate to have regard to the general principles of international law regulating termination of a treaty relationship on account of breach. For even if the mandate is viewed as having the character of an institution, as is maintained, it depends on those international agreements which created the system and regulated its application. […] The rules laid down by the Vienna Convention on the Law of Treaties concerning termination of a treaty relationship on account of breach [art. 60, para 3] (adopted without a dissenting vote) may in many respects be considered as a codification of existing customary law on the subject. […]

95. General Assembly resolution 2145 (XXI) determines that both forms of material breach had occurred in this case. […]

96. It has been contended that the Covenant of the League of Nations did not confer on the Council of the League power to terminate a mandate for misconduct of the mandatory and that no such power could therefore be exercised by the United Nations, since it could not derive from the League greater powers than the latter itself had. For this objection to prevail it would be necessary to show that the mandates system, as established under the League, excluded the application of the general principle of law that a right of termination on account of breach must be presumed to exist in respect of all treaties, except as regards provisions relating to the protection of the human person contained in treaties of a humanitarian character (as indicated in Art. 60, para. 5, of the Vienna Convention). The silence of a treaty as to the existence of such a right cannot be interpreted as implying the exclusion of a right which has its source outside of the treaty, in general international law, and is dependent on the occurrence of circumstances which are not normally envisaged when a treaty is concluded.

[…]

122. For the reasons given above, and subject to the observations contained in paragraph 125 below, member States are under obligation to abstain from entering into treaty relations with South Africa in all cases in which the Government of South Africa purports to act on behalf of or concerning Namibia. With respect to existing bilateral treaties, member States must abstain from invoking or applying those treaties or provisions of treaties concluded by South Africa on behalf of or concerning Namibia which involve active intergovernmental co-operation. With respect to multilateral treaties, however, the same rule cannot be applied to certain general conventions such as those of a humanitarian character, the non-performance of which may adversely affect the people of Namibia. It will be for the competent international organs to take specific measures in this respect.

123. Member States, in compliance with the duty of non-recognition imposed by paragraphs 2 and 5 of resolution 276 (1970), are under obligation to abstain from sending diplomatic or special missions to South Africa including in their jurisdiction the Territory of Namibia, to abstain from sending consular agents to Namibia, and to withdraw any such agents already there. They should also make it clear to the South African authorities that the maintenance of diplomatic or consular relations with South Africa does not imply any recognition of its authority with regard to Namibia.

124. The restraints which are implicit in the non-recognition of South Africa's presence in Namibia […] impose upon member States the obligation to abstain from

entering into economic and other forms of relationship or dealings with South Africa on behalf of or concerning Namibia which may entrench its authority over the Territory.

125. In general, the non-recognition of South Africa's administration of the Territory should not result in depriving the people of Namibia of any advantages derived from international co-operation. In particular, while official acts performed by the Government of South Africa on behalf of or concerning Namibia after the termination of the Mandate are illegal and invalid, this invalidity cannot be extended to those acts, such as, for instance, the registration of births, deaths and marriages, the effects of which can be ignored only to the detriment of the inhabitants of the Territory.

126. As to non-member States, although not bound by Articles 24 and 25 of the Charter, they have been called upon [...] to give assistance in the action which has been taken by the United Nations with regard to Namibia. In the view of the Court, the termination of the Mandate and the declaration of the illegality of South Africa's presence in Namibia are opposable to all States in the sense of barring *erga omnes* the legality of a situation which is maintained in violation of international law: in particular, no State which enters into relations with South Africa concerning Namibia may expect the United Nations or its Members to recognize the validity or effects of such relationship, or of the consequences thereof.

IV. Commentary

There is likely no single political issue that has involved the ICJ more than the situation in South West Africa (Namibia).[1] From 1949 through 1971, the advisory and contentious capacities of the ICJ were sought after on various aspects of the situation, with South Africa appearing six times before the Court concerning South West Africa.[2] In total, the Court issued four advisory opinions and two judgments. Today, the Court's jurisprudence continues to be relevant. This case deserves attention because it deals with a number of complex issues pertinent to the development of international law and international organizations, including the League of Nations mandate system and powers and functions of the Court as well as the political organs of the UN.[3]

Therefore, in addition to its important contribution concerning the right of self-determination,[4] the case is relevant for a number of reasons related to the theme of international organizations and legal acts. First, it sheds light on the roles of the various organs of the UN and how they interact with and reinforce one another. Second, its approach towards dissolution and succession of the League of Nations and its mandate system tested commonly held notions but succeeded in gaining support. Finally, the advisory opinion seeks to strengthen the position of the international organization by emphasizing the importance of the duty to co-operate. It has generated debate

---

[1] M. Pomerance, 'The ICJ and South West Africa (Namibia): A Retrospective Legal/Political Assessment', (2004) 12 *Leiden Journal of International Law* 425, 435.

[2] For a chronology of the case, see J. Dugard, 'The Opinion on South-West Africa (Namibia): The Teleologists Triumph', (1971) 88 *South African Law Journal* 460–77.

[3] O.J. Lissitzyn, 'International Law and the Advisory Opinion on Namibia', (1972) 11 *Columbia Journal of Transnational Law* 50–73, at 50.

[4] [1971] ICJ Rep 16 at 31.

over the powers and functions played by the various law-making and law-interpreting organs within the UN, and can be viewed as a progressive approach towards the interpretation of the law.

A. Roles of UN organs and their relationship with one another

The UN Charter lays out the roles and responsibilities of the various bodies falling under the UN. Unlike in many domestic systems, the ICJ does not have the power of judicial review. In other words, strictly speaking, the Charter does not give it the power to review the legality of decisions taken by other organs of the UN. However, it is, nonetheless, the principal judicial organ of the UN and in a request for an advisory opinion it may be asked to decide upon the validity of certain action in accordance with international law.

In this case, the Court was asked to look into the legal consequences for states related to the continued presence of South Africa in Namibia. While the SC did not ask the Court to specifically pronounce upon the validity of the actions of the SC or GA, both France and South Africa raised the issue by arguing that the GA acted *ultra vires* in adopting Resolution 2145 (XXI) terminating South Africa's mandate. As a result of it being raised, the Court did examine the validity of SC and GA resolutions underlying the request for an advisory opinion. It allotted a good portion of the opinion to justify its conclusion that the resolutions were valid, though it based this power on some rather weak argumentation.[5] Nevertheless, the opinion now lends strong support to the ability of the Court to review the validity of actions taken by political organs of the UN even when it is merely asked to pronounce upon their legal consequences.[6] Consequently, political organs should be on notice that a question concerning the meaning or legal consequence of their actions can lead to the Court exercising review. Indeed, this decision is significant because it contributed to the development of the power of judicial review of the actions of international organs of the UN.

In reviewing the validity of the relevant resolutions, the Court dealt with a number of issues related to the powers and functions of the UN. It also addressed the powers and functions of the League of Nations with respect to mandates. A key question that the Court addressed was the power of the League of Nations to revoke or terminate a mandate, without the mandatory's consent, as well as the succession of the UN to have such a power.

B. Dissolution and succession of international organizations

Parallel with the development of the modern nation-state is the growth of international organizations, to the point where they have become indispensable.[7] International

---

[5] [1971] ICJ Rep 16 at 45. The separate opinions of Judges Petrén, Onyeama, and Dillard provide stronger statements in support of the Court's actions. Judge Padilla Nervo's separate opinion opposes the position taken by the Court.

[6] Lissitzyn (n. 3), 53.

[7] M.N. Shaw, *International Law* (6th edn, Cambridge, Cambridge University Press 2008), p. 1282.

organizations facilitate co-operation amongst states, often providing an important forum for conflict resolution. Foremost among the global, international organizations is the UN. The emergence and growth of the UN system, built upon its predecessor, the League of Nations, has enabled the law to develop and grow at a rapid pace.

Every so often a major international organization is dissolved and its operations are assumed by another, often times newer, organization. When the League of Nations dissolved in 1946 the international community made practical arrangements for the transfer of its property as well as many of its functions to the UN. However, there was no automatic transfer and according to Brownlie the 'element of continuity depended on the consent of the UN'.[8] With regard to functions under treaties, any transfer of functions to the UN required the consent of the parties to the relevant treaty. With regard to the Permanent Court of International Justice (which dissolved in 1946), instruments containing acceptances of the jurisdiction of the PCIJ were deemed to be acceptances of the jurisdiction of the new ICJ by specific provisions in the new Statute.

The present case deals with the legal consequences of the dissolution of the League of Nations, which had specific organs responsible for supervising the execution of the mandate for South West Africa, and South Africa's refusal to enter into a trusteeship agreement with the successor organization, the UN. Ultimately, the Court found that the mandate agreement continued to exist despite the dissolution of the League but it did not base this decision on any principle of succession between organizations.[9] Instead, it concluded that UN organs (namely the GA) were to exercise supervisory functions despite the fact that these functions 'were neither expressly transferred to the UN nor expressly assumed by the organization'.[10] The Court took the position that the mandate itself constituted an international status for the territory which continued irrespective of the existence of the League. Moreover, the Court concluded that the resolution dissolving the League of Nations declared that the League's supervisory functions of the mandates were ending, not the mandates themselves.

Since the mandates did not end, the Court decided that the obligation of the mandatory power to submit to supervision also did not end. The supervision was being performed by the UN and the Court found that the GA was legally qualified to exercise these supervisory functions. The reasoning provided by the Court is not easy to reconcile with accepted principles of succession between organizations. Succession between international organizations occurs when the functions, rights, and obligations are transferred from one organization to another. This may occur in various ways, including by way of replacement, absorption, merger, effective secession of a party, or by a simple transfer of certain functions from one organization to another. An agreement must be reached and depends upon competence of the successor organization to perform the functions transferred from the former organization. These principles suggest that upon dissolution of the League of Nations, the UN could only have been invested with the powers to supervise the mandates if specific arrangements to that effect had been made, if such a succession had been implied in some way, or if the mandatory

---

[8] I. Brownlie, *Principles of Public International Law* (7th edn, Oxford University Press 2008), p. 669.
[9] [1950] ICJ Rep 128 at 134–7; this was reaffirmed in [1971] ICJ Rep 16 at 37.
[10] [1950] ICJ Rep 136.

power (in this case, South Africa) consented to the succession by, for example, carrying out its reporting obligation to the new entity.[11]

Instead, the main basis for the Court's finding was 'the necessity for supervision', which continued regardless of the dissolution of the supervisory organ under the mandates system. According to Judge Fitzmaurice, who dissented, the advisory opinion supports the position that an 'automatic devolution' of functions from one organization to another may occur and that in certain situations there may even be a presumption that such a devolution takes place.[12] As such, the opinion embraces the idea that cases of 'automatic succession' are not prohibited in cases of necessity.

Once the Court found that the UN had legally succeeded to the League's supervisory powers over the mandate, it ruled that the mandate would be terminable, without the mandatory's consent, if there had been a serious breach of the mandatory's obligations. In this case, the Court found that the GA was permitted to terminate the mandate since South Africa, as the mandatory, caused a serious breach by not reporting to the new supervisory power, the GA.

The fact that the GA has no power to make binding decisions and is not a judicial organ did not matter. The Court found that the mandate system itself was an institution and stressing the right to self-determination as well as the 'sacred trust of civilization' underlying the mandates, adopted a rather liberal construction of the law. The GA was not acting under its regular functions under the Charter. Instead, the Court found that it was acting within its rights as the supervisory power of the mandates and therefore could make binding decisions with regard to the mandates. This decision is quite extraordinary. It supports the notion that the GA can exercise powers outside of the context of the UN Charter.[13] It also gives some weight to the argument that GA declarations can be more than recommendatory.[14] The implications for international law and the role and function of the GA are significant.

In finding a serious breach, the Court did not go into the serious human rights violations related to the *apartheid* policies, though some brief mention is made of them. Instead, using treaty law and general principles of law, the serious breach found by the Court rested on the failure of South Africa to report to the UN on the status of the mandate. Despite requests from South Africa, it found it unnecessary to carry out a factual investigation, into the alleged failure to fulfil its obligations under the mandate. It is interesting in this regard to note that today the findings would have likely hinged on the violations of *apartheid* practices as a material breach of the mandate agreement, which at that time were not yet ripe.

Several important points emerge from the findings of the Court. First, it reinforced the idea that a treaty can be terminated on account of a material breach, and, second, it relied on the Vienna Convention on the Law of Treaties (VCLT) for its finding on termination, not in the context of two states but rather in the context of a state and

---

[11] [1971] ICJ Rep 227.

[12] I. Brownlie, *Principles of Public International Law* (7th edn, Oxford University Press 2008), p. 670.

[13] P.H. Kooijmans, 'The Advisory Opinion on Namibia of the International Court of Justice', (1973) 20 *Netherlands International Law Review* 17, 21.

[14] Lissitzyn (n. 3), 58.

an international organization.[15] This second point is remarkable because according to the VCLT it is applicable only to agreements between states and had not yet achieved the arguable status of customary international law since so few states had at that time ratified it. Having concluded that the actions of the SC and GA were valid, the Court then determined the legal consequences of the continued presence of South Africa in Namibia.

C. Reinforcing the moral authority of the international organization

Like the GA and the SC before it, the ICJ, perhaps unsurprisingly, found South Africa's actions in Namibia were illegal on the grounds of a material breach of a treaty, namely the mandate agreement. It also added, somewhat confusingly, that 'a binding determination made by a competent organ of the UN to the effect that a situation is illegal cannot remain without consequence'. As a result, the ICJ found that South Africa needed to withdraw its administration from the territory and required that other states had a duty to co-operate with the UN by prohibiting them from recognizing the acts of South Africa in Namibia as legal or valid and a duty to 'bring that situation to an end'.[16]

The non-recognition requirements found in this case appear to make collective non-recognition a precondition for any group response and arguably is the minimum required by states to serious breaches of a mandate in this particular case or those referred to in art. 40 of the UN Charter. Notwithstanding this non-recognition, the Court recognized the negative consequences that could result from non-recognition and purported to minimize these. In fact, throughout the opinion, the Court appears to regard the people of Namibia as having rights under international law, most notably with the recognition of self-determination as a legal right rather than simply a moral claim. In addition to non-recognition, the Court goes on to specifically prohibit states from entering into economic and other dealings with South Africa which could assist South Africa in its illegal occupation of Namibia and asserts a duty of states to 'bring [the] situation to an end'.[17] This latter consequence is interesting as it goes beyond simple non-recognition and seems to require positive action by states—some of whom did take diplomatic action to help negotiate an agreement later on.

The opinion setting out the legal consequences and the Court's attempts at remedying the situation show the relative limits provided under international law.[18] However, it also illustrates the moral force behind such actions when three main bodies within the UN organization call for a collective state response. Though there was no further judicial action in the case, other UN organs,[19] together with a number of states, continued to push for the withdrawal of South Africa. However, another seven years would pass until South Africa announced that it accepted proposals negotiated by

---

[15] Lissitzyn (n. 3), 61.   [16] [1971] ICJ Rep 16 at 54.   [17] [1971] ICJ Rep 16 at 54.

[18] E. Coleman Jones, 'Limitations of the International Legal Mechanism: Namibia (South West Africa) A Case Study', (1971–73) 17 *Howard Law Journal* 637–60, at 637.

[19] The advisory opinion was later approved that same year by another SC resolution, which once again endorsed the territorial integrity of Namibia, see SC Res. 301 (1971).

five Western powers, including the UK, the US, France, Canada, and West Germany, for Namibian independence via a UN supervised election and peace-keeping force.[20] After further difficulties,[21] another twelve years would pass before Namibia would finally obtain its independence on 23 April 1990. Though a long and difficult process, the situation in Namibia provides an excellent example of how three main bodies of the UN, the SC, the GA, and the ICJ, worked in parallel to achieve a common, desired result. Although the impact of the opinion is hard to measure, the Court's decision likely bolstered the resolve of the UN political organs to continue to push for a withdrawal.[22]

It is clear that international organizations, and the UN in particular, make increasingly significant contributions to international law. In addition to the decisions and judgments of international judicial bodies, state practice within international organizations is becoming an important element when looking at the process of customary law formation or discerning general principles of law. There remains, however, a great deal of debate over the powers and functions played by the various law-making and law-interpreting organs. While some have criticized the stretching of legal concepts,[23] others view it as a 'progressive, policy-oriented approach' towards interpretation of the law, which opposes strict state sovereignty and the exclusion of domestic affairs from the UN organization's sphere of influence.[24] Undoubtedly, it seems to lend weight to the importance of legal consensus within an international institution and how this may result in a new legal force of 'law-generating' capabilities.[25]

---

[20] SC Res. 435 (1978).   [21] See S/14459; S/14460/Rev.1; S/14461; and S/14462.
[22] Pomerance (n. 1), at 432.
[23] See M. Wiechers, 'South West Africa: The Background, Content and Significance of the Opinion of the World Court of 21 June 1971', (1972) 5 *Comparative and International Law Journal of South Africa* 123–70.
[24] M. Wiechers, 'The South West Africa Cases', (2010) 26 *South African Journal on Human Rights* 320–5, at 323.
[25] Pomerance (n. 1), at 434.

4.2 *Solange I*, BverfGE 37, 291, 29 May 1974; *Solange II*, BverfGE 73, 339, 22 October 1986; *Solange III*, BverfGE 89, 155 12 October 1993; and *Solange IV*, BverfGE 102, 147, 7 June 2000

Peter Hilpold

Relevance of the cases

The *Solange* case-law stands for a specific form of interaction between the legal order of the European Union (EU) and the legal orders of the member states or, respectively, between the European Court of Justice (ECJ) and the national Constitutional Courts of the member states. At the start of this line of cases the German Constitutional Court (Bundesverfassungsgericht—BverfG) first upheld its power to consider the compatibility of Community law rules with fundamental rights of the Basic Law (Grundgesetz) 'as long as the integration process has not progressed so far that Community law receives a catalogue of fundamental rights' (*Solange I*). Afterwards, when fundamental rights protection had become sufficiently strong within the EC/EU the BVerfG declared to refrain from such a control activity 'as long as the European Communities ensure effective protection of fundamental rights' (*Solange II*). Subsequently, this case-law was further clarified and extended to the delimitation of the respective competences (*Solange III* and *IV*). More specifically, it dealt with the question whether the EU was acting *ultra vires*.

The attitude taken by the BVerfG was criticized for endangering the unity of EC/EU law and for being in contrast with the principle of supremacy and unity of EC/EU law but on the final count there was nonetheless virtue in this approach.

In fact, thereby, the BVerfG managed not only to defend the high standard of fundamental rights protection in Germany but also to give a decisive contribution to the integration of a highly evolved system of fundamental rights protection into EC/EU law. In many member states the *Solange* case-law influenced heavily the domestic approach taken in this regard. This form of interaction, of a 'dialogue' between institutions on questions of fundamental rights, became exemplary also beyond the EC/EU context.

Solange I, BverfGE 37, 291, 29 May 1974

I. The facts

A German import/export firm made an application to the Administrative Court (Verwaltungsgericht) of Frankfurt am Main for annulment of a decision of the Einfuhr- und Vorratsstelle für Getreide und Futtermittel in which an export deposit of DM 17,0026.47 was declared to be forfeited after the firm had only partially used an export licence granted to it for 20,000 tons of ground maize. This decision was based on Council regulations. In a preliminary ruling the ECJ confirmed the legality of the disputed regulations. The Administrative Court then stayed the proceedings and requested the BverfG to decide whether the rule that the deposit is to be released only in a case of force majeure (and otherwise is forfeited if an export licence is not or not fully used) is compatible with the Basic Law.

In the first years of the European integration process Germany had taken a decisively pro-European stance that also characterized the attitude of its courts and, in particular, of the BVerfG. This seemed to translate into an unconditional acceptance of EU law autonomy and supremacy.[1] This attitude began to change at the beginning of the 1970s due to a broader disillusionment with European integration and an exacerbated dispute between leading German public lawyers. Some of them warned of an endangerment of the high fundamental rights protection standard by the ever-increasing importance of EC law which seemed to be widely unscathed by the fundamental rights debate.[2] Starting with Stauder in 1969[3] the ECJ recognized fundamental rights as general principles of law and therefore as part of EC law. In 1970, in Internationale Handelsgesellschaft,[4] the ECJ ruled that 'respect for fundamental rights forms an integral part of the general principles of Community law'. In the same case, however, the ECJ also proclaimed the principle of the supremacy of EC law over national constitutional law and therefore also over fundamental rights enshrined in national constitutions. After this preliminary ruling, that to many seemed too far-reaching, this question was referred to the BVerfG. In 1974 the latter issued a decision that widely diverged from that of the ECJ.

II. The legal question

The legal question referred to the BVerfG boils down to the following: did Germany have to accept EC law that stood in contrast to fundamental rights provisions of the German Constitution? The influential Mainz law Professor Hans Heinrich Rupp had asserted the existence of a far-reaching structural incongruence between EC law and national constitutional law that stood in the way of EC law supremacy.[5] The BVerfG seemed to accept at least some of his criticism.

III. Excerpts

4. The part of the Basic Law dealing with fundamental rights is an inalienable, essential feature of the valid Basic Law of the Federal Republic of Germany and one which forms part of the constitutional structure of the Basic Law.[6] Article 24 of the Basic Law does not without reservation allow it to be subjected to qualifications.

---

[1] See Decision of 18 October 1967, BVerfG 22, 293ss. (298).
[2] See for further detail B. Davies, *Resisting the European Court of Justice* (Cambridge, Cambridge University Press 2012), pp. 180ss.
[3] Case 29/69, *Stauder v Ulm* [1969] ECR 419.
[4] Case 11/70, *Internationale Handelsgesellschaft* [1970] ECR 1161.   [5] B. Davies (n. 2).
[6] English translation at The University of Texas at Austin, School of Law, Institute for Transnational Law, Foreign Law Translation, http://www.utexas.edu/law/academics/centers/transnational/work_new/german/case.php?id=588.

In this, the present state of integration of the Community is of crucial importance. The Community still lacks a democratically legitimate parliament directly elected by general suffrage which possesses legislative powers and to which the Community organs empowered to legislate are fully responsible on a political level; it still lacks, in particular, a codified catalogue of fundamental rights [...]

    c) [...]

[...] as long as the integration process has not progressed so far that the Community also receives a catalogue of fundamental rights decided on by a parliament and of settled validity, which is adequate in comparison with the catalogue of fundamental rights contained in the Basic Law, a reference by a court in the Federal Republic of Germany to the Federal Constitutional Court in judicial review proceedings, following the obtaining of a ruling of the European Court under Article 177 of the Treaty, is admissible and necessary if the German court regards the rule of Community law which is relevant to its decision as inapplicable in the interpretation given by the European Court, because and in so far as it conflicts with one of the fundamental rights in the Basic Law.

Solange II, BverfGE 73, 339, 22 October 1986

I. The facts

The starting point of this case was a dispute between a German importer of preserved mushrooms from Taiwan and the German import authorities. In application of EEC Regulation 2107/74 laying down protective measures against the import of mushrooms from non EEC-countries the (German) Federal Office for Food and Licence refused to issue an import licence. After unsuccessfully contesting the lawfulness of Regulation 2107/74 before the Frankfurt Administrative Court with reference to art. 39 of the EEC Treaty the importer appealed before the Federal Supreme Administrative Court (Bundesverwaltungsgericht). The proceedings were suspended and the Federal Supreme Administrative Court referred the question as to the lawfulness of the contested EEC import regime to the ECJ. For this Court, however, the Commission had correctly used its discretion in making its assessments when the disputed regulations were adopted.

In further proceedings before the Supreme Administrative Court the appellant objected that there had been a breach of various constitutional rules and requested either a referral of the question to the Federal Constitutional Court under art. 100(1) of the Basic Law or a fresh reference to the ECJ for further clarification in view of the specific content of the case. After both applications had been rejected the importer appealed on constitutional grounds against the judgment of the Federal Supreme Administrative Court before the Federal Constitutional Court, claiming *inter alia* that the Supreme Administrative Court should have referred the question of the alleged infringement of fundamental rights to the Constitutional Court. For the BVerfG, however, '[t]he appellant's complaints, that the European Court's ruling and Commission Regulations 1412/76 and 2284/76 as interpreted by that Court infringed the fundamental rights under the Basic Law and therefore ought not to have been applied by German authorities or courts during the period in question within the sphere to which the Basic Law applies, are inadmissible; a reference of the regulations to this Court by the Supreme Administrative Court under art. 100(1) of the Basic Law would have been inadmissible.'

The central question concerned the interpretation of the principles set out by the BVerfG in *Solange I*.

II. The legal question

The *Solange I* decision was cause for satisfaction for one group, for deep disappointment and even enragement for the other. As one commentator had it: 'In one short decision, the BVerfG had shifted dramatically to favour the side of the legal-academic spectrum which it had angered with its 1967 decision. As a result, it now faced the wrath of those scholars, with whom it had previously sided.'[7] Nonetheless, the decision was also a kind of wake-up call, in particular for the ECJ. In fact, the ECJ was well aware of the threat for the integration project originating in Karlsruhe. In extremis, Luxemburg tried to soothe Karlsruhe: two weeks before the *Solange I* decision was issued the ECJ delivered the judgment in the *Nold* case[8] where the Court stated the following:

> As the Court has already stated, fundamental rights form an integral part of the general principles of law, the observance of which it ensures.
>
> In safeguarding these rights, the Court is bound to draw inspiration from constitutional traditions common to the Member States, *and it cannot therefore uphold measures which are incompatible with fundamental rights recognized and protected by the Constitutions of those States.*[9]

As a consequence, member states should take confidence that the EC would not and could not infringe fundamental rights enshrined in their constitutions. However, this reassurance could not impress the BVerfG, at least not immediately.

III. Excerpts

II, 1 f)[10]

In view of those developments it must be held that, so long as the European Communities, in particular European Court case law, generally ensure effective protection of fundamental rights as against the sovereign powers of the Communities which is to be regarded as substantially similar to the protection of fundamental rights required unconditionally by the Basic Law, and in so far as they generally safeguard the essential content of fundamental rights, the Federal Constitutional Court will no longer exercise its jurisdiction to decide on the applicability of secondary

---

[7] See B. Davis (n. 2) with reference to, *inter alia*, H.-P. Ipsen who in 'BVerfG versus EuGH re "Grundrechte"' (1979) 14 Europarecht 3, pp. 223–8) had qualified this decision as 'wrong ... deceptive, superficial and legally erroneous' (transl. by Davis).

[8] Case 4/73, *Nold v Commission* [1974] ECR 491.   [9] Ibid., para. 13 (emphasis added).

[10] See n. 6.

Community legislation cited as the legal basis for any acts of German courts or authorities within the sovereign jurisdiction of the Federal Republic of Germany, and it will no longer review such legislation by the standard of the fundamental rights contained in the Basic Law; references to the Court under Article 100 (1) for that purpose are therefore inadmissible.

II, 1 g)

The question must, therefore, remain unanswered whether the appellant is correct in its accusation that the disputed Commission regulations in the interpretation given by the European Court infringe its fundamental rights as recognized in Article 12 (1) and 2 (1) in conjunction with Article 20 (3) of the Basic Law. It does not appear either from the appellant's submissions or from the preliminary ruling of the European Court that the Court under its interpretation of the law is in general simply not prepared or not in a position to recognize or protect the fundamental rights claimed by the appellant and that, therefore, the degree of protection of such rights required by the Basic Law has in general clearly not been reached at the level of Community law. For those reasons the present case does not give any occasion to consider a review of the disputed Commission regulations in respect of their compatibility with fundamental rights under the Basic Law. A reference of the Commission regulations under Article 100 (1) by the Federal Supreme Administrative Court in the main action would, therefore, have been inadmissible.

IV. Commentary

In the years following the *Solange I* decision the message by the BVerfG was heard and well-understood. The EC together with the member states and assisted by the ECJ tried hard to build up a sophisticated system of fundamental rights protection.

When the BVerfG was again seized with the question whether and to what extent this Court would exercise its jurisdiction to control the compatibility of EC law with fundamental rights provisions of the Basic Law it could therefore take this change of circumstances into account and withdraw, although under certain conditions, its announcement made in *Solange I*, to exercise such a control power. Therefore, in 1986, in *Solange II*, supremacy of EC law seemed to be fully restored. A reactivation of this control power was relegated to the absolutely hypothetical case that the fundamental rights standard achieved would again decline 'to an extent that makes it impossible on constitutional grounds to regard a reasonable protection of fundamental rights as being generally available'. With a control power whose exercise was made dependent on such a remote condition the EC could surely live.

Solange III, BverfGE 89, 155 12 October 1993

I. The facts and the legal question

The Treaty of Maastricht of 7 February 1992 brought about the most far-reaching reform of EC law since its inception by creating an EU with widely enlarged competences and strengthened supranational traits. This development did not meet with unconditional applause, as some feared an undue encroachment upon national sovereignty. Such fears materialized in particular in Germany, where the creation of a Monetary Union, for which the Treaty of Maastricht also laid the foundations, was seen by many as a step backwards in respect to the stable hard currency system painstakingly created with the D-Mark. [11] On the political level the Treaty of Maastricht was approved in Germany by a great majority: in the Bundestag it reached a majority of 526 out of 543 and the Bundesrat approved it unanimously.[12] In spite of this nearly plebiscitary voting Germany could not ratify the Maastricht Treaty as several complaints were filed against the federal statute ratifying the Treaty. The complaints were lodged by four German members of the European Parliament of the Green Party and by Manfred Brunner. According to the complainants the amendments to the Basic Law resulting from the ratification of the Maastricht Treaty as well as the law transforming this treaty into national law violated a series of constitutional provisions. All but one of the complaints (presented by Manfred Brunner) were dismissed.[13] Only with regard to art. 38 of the Basic Law, guaranteeing the subjective right for every German voter to take part in the election of members of the German Bundestag, the Constitutional Court had some doubts. These doubts arose from a very broad interpretation of the right to vote and the principle of democracy: the BVerfG did not want to exclude that the right to vote could potentially be affected by an extensive transfer of competences by the German parliament to another institution: 'The complainant's right arising from Art. 38 of the GG can therefore be violated, if the exercise of the responsibilities of the German Federal Parliament is transferred so extensively to one of the governmental institutions of the European Union or the European Communities formed by the governments, that the minimum, inalienable requirements of democratic legitimation pursuant to Art. 20, paras 1 and 2 in conjunction with Art. 79, para. 3 of the GG relating to the sovereign power to which the citizen is subject can no longer be complied with.'[14]

At the end, this complaint was also dismissed as unfounded as the BVerfG found no infringement of the principle of democracy in the sense described. The BVerfG used, however, the opportunity to define the limits of European integration from the viewpoint of German constitutional law.

II. Excerpts

Headnote

1. Art. 38 GG [Grundgesetz] forbids the weakening, within the scope of Art. 23 of the GG, of the legitimation of State power gained through an election, and of the influence on the exercise of such power, by means of a transfer of duties and responsibilities of the Federal Parliament, to the extent that the principle of democracy, declared as inviolable in Art. 79, para. 3 in conjunction with Art. 20, paras. 1 and 2 of the GG, is violated.

---

[11] See extensively on this subject P. Hilpold, 'Eine neue europäische Finanzarchitektur' in P. Hilpold/ W. Steinmair (eds), *Neue europäische Finanzarchitektur* (2013), pp. 3–82.

[12] See J. Wieland, 'Germany in the European Union—The Maastricht Decision of the Bundesverfassungsgericht', (1994) 5 *European Journal of International Law* 259–66, 259.

[13] Ibid., p. 261.   [14] III, b).

2. The principle of democracy does not prevent the Federal Republic of Germany from becoming a member of a compound of States [Staatenverbund] which is organised on a supranational basis. However, it is a precondition of membership that the legitimation and influence which derives from the people will be preserved within an alliance of States.

[...]

5. Art. 38 of the GG is violated if a law which subjects the German legal system to the direct validity and application of the law of the supranational European Communities does not give a sufficiently precise specification of the assigned rights to be exercised and of the proposed programme of integration (see BVerfGE 58, 1<37>). This also means that any subsequent substantial amendments to that programme of integration provided for by the Maastricht Treaty or to its authorisations to act are no longer covered by the Act of Consent to ratify this Treaty. The German Federal Constitutional Court must examine the question of whether or not legal instruments of European institutions and Governmental entities may be considered to remain within the limits of the sovereign rights accorded to them, or whether they may be considered to exceed those limits (see BVerfGE 75, 223).

[...]

9. c)

The Federal Republic of Germany is not, by ratifying the Maastricht Treaty, subjecting itself to an uncontrollable, unforeseeable process which will lead inexorably towards monetary union; the Maastricht Treaty simply paves the way for gradual further integration of the European Community as a community of laws. Every further step along this way is dependent either upon conditions being fulfilled by the parliament which can already be foreseen, or upon further consent from the Federal Government, which consent is subject to parliamentary influence.

III. Commentary

In the 'Maastricht' judgment the BVerfG reasserted its control power in the relationship with the ECJ and extended it in two directions. First of all, this power was no longer limited to fundamental rights in the traditional, stricter sense but it was extended more generally to the EC legislative power. Second, the control power should now also encompass Union acts.

As to the first aspect, the normative gateway to this new approach was found in the principle of democracy or, respectively, the right to vote. This right must not be voided by a transfer of legislative powers to a European Union not yet endowed with corresponding and sufficient democratic participatory rights of its citizens. According to the BVerfG the EU remains a 'compound of States' ('Staatenverbund'), a term introduced by the judge rapporteur Paul Kirchhof to convey the notion that the EU is neither a confederation, nor an international organization, nor a federal state but something in between. Democratic legitimation is conveyed via the national parliaments and therefore the extension of the functions and powers of the European Communities must not be limitless. The German Federal Parliament 'must retain functions and powers of substantial import'. The BVerfG takes note of the dynamic integration process but at the same time it admonishes that the national parliaments must remain in control of the 'integration programme' set by these democratically elected bodies. The implications of this statement are twofold:

— First of all, a law ratifying a treaty which transfers legislative powers to a supra-national institution like the European Union has to 'give a sufficiently precise specification of the assigned right to be exercised by the European Communities and of the proposed programme of integration'. A ratification law without such a programme would be in violation of the Basic Law.
— Secondly, the BVerfG wants to preserve a control power also over the subsequent integration process:

'[A]ny subsequent substantial amendments to that programme of integration provided for by the Maastricht Treaty or to its authorization to act are no longer covered by the Act of Consent to ratify this Treaty.'

'Accordingly, the German Federal Constitutional Court must examine the question of whether or not legal instruments of European institutions and governmental entities may be considered to remain within the limits of the sovereign rights accorded to them, or whether they may be considered to exceed those limits'.

This second assertion has met with strong criticism by legal doctrine as it implies nothing else than the control of EU law by a national constitutional court. Thereby the primacy of EU law, uncontested since Costa/ENEL,[15] and the proposition that this law has to find uniform application within all member states, has been jeopardized.

This attitude by the BVerfG was qualified as 'aggressive' and 'confrontational' and the statement by this Court that it would exercise its control power 'in cooperation' with the ECJ as deceiving and presumptuous.[16] As will be seen in the final evaluation this vision by the BVerfG was shaped to a large extent by personal approaches of individual judges to the relationship between national law and EC law. And foremost it was also a stratagem to further the acceptance of the Maastricht Treaty on the internal level.

Solange IV, BverfGE 102, 147, 7 June 2000

I. The facts and the legal question

The 'Banana judgment' of 2000 by the BVerfG represents the fourth main chapter of a long judicial controversy pitting Germany and its banana importers against the EU.[17] This controversy took place at the GATT/WTO level, at the level of the EU, and finally before the BVerfG.

Until mid-1993 each EC member state had its own banana import regime. Germany imported bananas mostly from the dollar area, while other member states, in particular France and Great Britain, preferred their former and actual colonies. This situation

---

[15] Case 6/64, *Costa v ENEL*, [1964] ECR 585.
[16] See for more details R. Ch. V. Ooyen, *Die Staatstheorie des Bundesverfassungsgerichts und Europa* (2013), pp. 31ss.
[17] See P. Hilpold, *Die EU im GATT/WTO-System* (Innsbruck: Innsbruck University Press 2009), pp. 356ss.

was terminated by Regulation No. 404/93, which established a common import regime for bananas, favouring trade from the EC area and from ACP countries, while import from the dollar areas was heavily restricted. German banana traders suffered extensive economic losses as they had to restructure their business relations. The ECJ dismissed complaints both by individuals and by Germany. Individual complaints by German banana traders before the ECJ were rejected as the complainants were not able to demonstrate that the Community had incurred non-contractual liability by manifestly and gravely disregarding the limits on the exercise of its powers.[18] Germany's complaint was rejected by the ECJ *inter alia* by stating that the right to property and the freedom to pursue a trade or business of the operators on the German market may be restricted. Furthermore, the Council had to reconcile conflicting interests by the different member states.[19] Subsequently, nineteen operators of the so-called Atlanta group brought a complaint before the BVerfG sustaining that the common market order for bananas conflicted with fundamental rights provisions of the German Constitution. Now, the BVerfG was called upon to further specify the Maastricht judgment. It took the BVerfG nearly four years to come to a decision. Some authors speculate that the Court waited for the retirement of the judge rapporteur in the Maastricht case, Paul Kirchhof.[20] The Court declared the submission inadmissible.

II. Commentary

The BVerfG considered that this submission was based on a misunderstanding of the Maastricht decision. This decision of 1993, according to the BVerfG, was not to be understood as an announcement that the BVerfG would, contrary to the *Solange II* decision, explicitly exercise its power of review again, albeit in co-operation with the ECJ. The applicants should rather have noted that in the Maastricht decision the BVerfG had quoted the statements in the *Solange II* decision which show that it exercises its jurisdiction to a limited extent.

In the Banana decision of 2000 the BVerfG, now with a different composition and confronted with a widely changed national attitude towards the European integration process, re-read and re-interpreted its own decision of 1993 in a clearly more integration-friendly fashion.

In this decision, the BVerfG has not totally relinquished its pretension for a power of review of secondary EC (EC) law as to possible infringements of fundamental rights guaranteed by the Basic Law but it has made clear that it will be highly unlikely that it will exercise this power in the future. While in the 'Maastricht' decision it was associated with a warning towards the EU not to overstretch its powers, after Lisbon, this power of review is nothing else than a safeguard for an extrema ratio situation that is very unlikely to happen. No longer, the BVerfG speaks about a 'relationship of cooperation' with the ECJ in regard to the exercise of its power of review, giving thereby

---

[18] Case C-286/93, Judgment of 11 December 1996, para. 83.
[19] Case C-280/93, Judgment of 5 October 1994.
[20] See A. Peters, 'The Bananas Decision (2000) of the German Federal Constitutional Court' (2000) 43 *German Yearbook of International Law* 277–82, 277.

further proof of its acceptance of the ECJ's prerogative when EU law and its implementation come into play.

Conclusions

The *Solange* line of cases mirrors a series of different developments:

— First of all, it can be seen as reflecting the ups and downs of the integration process. Starting boldly in a period of strong EEC scepticism the BVerfG softened its approach when the integration climate improved—only to become sceptical again when the winds changed. It is remarkable, however, that the BVerfG never stated that a national measure to implement EU law (and even less so EU law itself) had violated the required standard of fundamental rights.[21] Thereby, European integration could proceed making it ever more unlikely that such a violation would be contested.

— This case-law is also an expression of the BVerfG's personal composition. In this context, judge Paul Kirchhof, judge rapporteur of the 'Maastricht' decision, has already been mentioned. Kirchhof has been notoriously critical towards a European integration process transforming the 'compound of states' ('Staatenverbund') into a European state. According to Kirchhof such a development would be against the European legal tradition; it would be something 'unnatural'.[22] The 'Banana' judgment was issued after Paul Kirchhof had left the BVerfG[23] and was proof of a new orientation within the Court.

— The *Solange* case-law reflects also the changing attitudes towards the relationship between national law, international law, and EC/EU law. Still in the 'Maastricht' decision the relationship between national constitutional law and EC/EU law was portrayed in a 'traditional' 'international law' perspective, a perspective that visibly clashed with that of the ECJ since *van Gend & Loos*.[24] The BVerfG ostensibly tried to retain control of the integration process. While in the relationship with international law this control power is fully in place, with regard to EC/EU law this battle has since long been lost.

— At the same time, the *Solange* case-law gives evidence of profound changes in German public law doctrine moving from a traditional 'dualist' perspective towards a 'communitarian' view with pronounced monist traits.

Now a presumption is in force that fundamental rights protection within the EU is equivalent with that of the Basic Law. This presumption operates also with regard to any further development of EU fundamental rights protection even though the

---

[21] In the *European Arrest Warrant* case (BVerfGE, 2 BvR 2236/04, judgment of 18 July 2005) the BVerfG found that the national provisions implementing the Framework Decision on the European arrest warrant were unconstitutional. This finding was, however, limited to the extent that Germany had exercised its discretion within the margins left by the EU. See J. Baquero Cruz, 'The Legacy of the Maastricht-Urteil and the Pluralist Movement', (2008) 14 *European Law Journal* 389–422, 396.

[22] See R. Ch. Von Ooyen (n. 16), pp. 71ss. (82).

[23] According to an article in the German journal 'Focus' (48/2000, p. 66) when Kirchhof left his office, an internal strategy paper was drafted within the BVerfG on the basis of which the question whether ultra vires acts of the EC/EU were at hand should be decided in future by the ECJ.

[24] Case 26/62, *van Gend & Loos* [1963] ECR 1.

presumption is rebuttable. The presumption has been confirmed by the BVerfG in the Lisbon judgment of 2009[25] in view of the eminent proclamation of the Charter of Fundamental Rights.

In the Honeywell decision of 2010[26] the BVerfG has declared that the BVerfG exercises an ultra vires review only if the breach of the competences by EU bodies is sufficiently qualified. This requires a manifest breach of competences and a structurally significant shift in the structure of competences to the detriment of member states.[27] It is not sufficient to demonstrate that fundamental rights protection is substantially deficient in one specific area in comparison to that guaranteed by the Basic Law; rather, these deficits have to be of a general nature.[28]

In any case, prior to any statement by the Court that an ultra vires act is at hand, the ECJ is to be afforded the opportunity to pronounce itself on the question.

Thereby the 'Banana' decision was confirmed and further specified. A conflict between EU law and national fundamental rights is still considered to be a possibility, though a very remote one.

With regard to the accusation that the BVerfG had taken, in particular in the 'Maastricht' decision, an 'aggressive' and 'confrontational' attitude, it should also be noted that an intense dialogue was going on between Karlsruhe, Luxemburg, and Brussels which was not only directed at the preservation of subjective positions but at the development of a sustainable relationship between states, courts, and supranational institutions that should contribute to the consensual construction of a highly evolved fundamental rights area. Without doubt, over the years this dialogue has brought about the desired result. It should not be forgotten that the conflict portrayed in *Solange I–IV* was real and not a merely hypothetical one. Had the BVerfG unconditionally accepted the precedence of EC/EU law from the very beginning, it is doubtful whether Brussels and Luxembourg would have shown so much dedication to the development of such a sophisticated EC/EU fundamental rights protection as is now in place. The concept of '*Solange*' has become emblematic for a difficult dialogue between legal areas with highly different standards of fundamental rights protection. These different legal areas are connected over communicating vessels and the *Solange* principle operates like a regulator impeding this connection to excessively watering down the fundamental rights protection within one sub-system. Lately, in the Lisbon decision (2009), the BVerfG extended its approach from the protection of core fundamental

---

[25] BVerfGE 30 June 2009–2 BvE 2/08 et al. In the Lisbon decision also terminological changes demonstrated a new attitude. The BVerfG no longer spoke of 'outbreaking acts' ('ausbrechende Rechtsakte') but used the more sober term of 'ultra vires acts'. See F. Mayer/M. Wendel, 'Die verfassungsrechtlichen Grundlagen des Europarechts', in A. Hatje/P.-Ch. Müller-Graff, *Europäisches Organisations- und Verfassungsrecht* (2014), p. 234.

[26] BVerfGE 12b, 286.

[27] Mayer/Wendel (n. 25), p. 234, speak in this context of a new 'double test'. For M. Bleckmann, *Nationale Grundrechte im Anwendungsbereich des Rechts der Europäischen Union* (2011), p. 158, the BVerfG judgment with regard to the Lisbon Treaty (BVerfGE 123, 267) represents again a retreat in respect to this requirement as now also the continuing, repeated, or substantial disregard of single fundamental rights may re-activate the BVerfG's control power.

[28] '[Dass der] unabdingbar gebotene Grundrechtsschutz generell nicht gewährleistet ist'. See BVerfGE 102, 147 (164) and M. Bleckmann (n. 27), with further references.

rights to the 'constitutional identity' according to which member states should have 'sufficient leeway to determine their own economic, cultural and social living conditions'. This concept remains, however, vague.[29]

It has to be remembered that an absolute and unconditional precedence of EU law has been recognized only by a small group of member states (in particular The Netherlands and Austria). Another group (France and Poland) have adopted a dualist approach. The large majority of Constitutional Courts seem to be influenced by the *Solange* line of cases even though no Court has so far developed case-law that has become so renowned on its own in dealing with this question (in this, only the Italian Corte Costituzionale[30] is coming near to the BVerfG). Sweden has developed a so-called sä länge case-law in direct correspondence to the *Solange* cases. An attitude similar to that of the BVerfG was taken by the Hungarian Constitutional Court.[31] All in all it can be said that the protection of core constitutional values (be it fundamental rights, or the rule of law as was the case in the Czech Republic) has been an important concern for nearly all member states. The *Solange* case-law has been extremely influential as to the way this challenge may be handled. It has shown its usefulness not only in the relationship between member states and the EU but also in that between the EU and UN law, as is demonstrated by the *Kadi* case.[32] In the *Kadi* case the ECJ refused to relinquish its control power over acts transforming UN resolutions as long as the UN cannot assure comparable fundamental rights guarantees.[33] Again, this approach met on the one hand with criticism because it implied (at least indirectly) the challenge of UN law by the EU, but on the other hand it had as a consequence that the UN tried to upgrade fundamental rights protection when applying individual sanctions that stood at the centre of the *Kadi* case. In the *Bosphorus* case, to name a further example, the European Court of Human Rights (ECtHR), applying a test similar to that of the *Solange* case-law, came to the conclusion that fundamental rights protection by the EU was comparable to that of the ECHR.[34]

On the whole it can be said that the *Solange* case-law may raise a series of political and legal problems, in particular as far as it asserts a subsidiary competence by the BVerfG to identify 'outbreaking' or 'ultra vires' acts by the EU.[35] Also the 'reserve competence'

---

[29] See M. Nettesheim, in: Europarecht, 2014, p. 152, para. 26.

[30] See the judgments in the cases *Frontini* (Cort. Cost. 183/1973), *Granital* (Cort. Cost. 170/1984), and *Fragd* (Cort. Cost 232/1989).

[31] For a comprehensive comparison of the respective national positions see F. Mayer/M. Wendel (n. 25), pp. 222ss.

[32] See P. Hilpold, 'EU Law and UN Law in Conflict: The Kadi Case', (2009) 13 *Max Planck Yearbook of United Nations Law* 141–82 and idem, 'UN Sanctions Before the ECJ: the Kadi Case', in A. Reinisch (ed.), *Challenging Acts of International Organizations Before National Courts* (Oxford, Oxford University Press 2010), pp. 18–53.

[33] Ibid.

[34] *Bosphorus v Ireland* (ECHR) Reports 2005-VI 107. Therefore, the ECtHR did not exercise its control power over the acts of the Irish government. The ECtHR also, however, made it clear that this case-law applies only where state action is completely predetermined by international obligations (as it was here the case for Ireland in respect to EU acts). The ECtHR would resume its control power also in such situations, if, 'in the circumstances of a particular case, it is considered that the protection of convention rights was manifestly deficient' (para. 156).

[35] See F. Mayer, 'Grundrechtsschutz gegen europäische Rechtsakte durch das BVerfG: Zur Verfassungsmäßigkeit der Bananenmarktordnung', (2000) *Europäische Zeitschrift für Wirtschaftsrecht* 685–89.

to decide on the applicability of EU legislation cited as the legal basis for any acts of German courts or authorities in Germany by the standard of fundamental rights contained in the Basic Law has raised fears of a potential conflict between Germany's constitutional order and the EC/EU legal system. It seems, however, that the BVerfG has consequently shied away from a direct confrontation with the ECJ by considering such conflicts as merely hypothetical. In the years following the 'Maastricht' judgment the BVerfG made the probability of such a conflict even more remote. On this basis, the *Solange* case-law has become less a position expressing (potential) conflict and distrust and more a useful instrument of dialogue between different legal orders in need of co-operation with regard to core constitutional values. In this, *Solange* exerts an exemplary role in an international legal order characterized on the one hand by fragmentation and on the other by strong tendencies to improve and consolidate fundamental rights protection.

4.3 *Military and Paramilitary Activities in and Against Nicaragua* (*Nicaragua v United States of America*), Merits, Judgment, [1986] ICJ Rep 14

Laurence Boisson de Chazournes and Andrzej Gadkowski

Relevance of the case

The present case addresses numerous questions with respect to the interpretation and development of international law, such as issues relating to the sources of international law, the relationship between treaty and customary law, and the contribution of international organizations to the formation of international law. The latter—being the focus of this contribution, the case is analysed with reference to resolutions of the United Nations General Assembly, to resolutions of the Organization of American States, and to the Final Act of the Conference on Security and Co-operation in Europe (also known as the Helsinki Final Act).

I. The facts of the case

After the fall of the Government of President Anastasio Somoza Debayle in July 1979, a Junta of National Reconstruction and a new government were installed by the Frente Sandinista de Liberación Nacional (FSLN). The favourable attitude of the United States Government towards the new 'democratic coalition government' had changed by 1981 given the alleged intervention of the Government of Nicaragua in the provision of logistical support, including the supply of arms, for guerillas in El Salvador.[1] Thus, the United States Government activity against the FSLN and in support of those fighting against the then Nicaraguan Government—commonly named *contras*—ceased to be covert and was carried out openly; for example, specific provisions were inserted in US budgetary legislation for funds to be used by intelligence agencies in order to support 'directly or indirectly, military and paramilitary operations in Nicaragua'.[2]

Such activities aimed at supporting *contras* consisted of, for example, air and naval attacks on targets within the territory of Nicaragua, mining of Nicaraguan ports, supporting an army of mercenaries, etc. Other activities were particularly aimed at hindering the Nicaraguan economy through, for instance, reducing the import of Nicaraguan goods or the suspension of economic aid.[3]

---

[1] *Military and Paramilitary Activities in and against Nicaragua (Nicaragua v United States of America)*, Merits, Judgment, [1986] ICJ Rep 14, para. 19.

[2] Ibid., para. 20.

[3] *Military and Paramilitary Activities in and against Nicaragua (Nicaragua v. United States of America)*, Pleadings, Oral Arguments, Documents, vol. IV, Memorial of Nicaragua, para. 412.

On 9 April 1984, Nicaragua filed an application with the International Court of Justice alleging the United States had engaged in military and paramilitary activities in and against Nicaragua in violation of international law. In its submissions, Nicaragua requested the Court to adjudge and declare that the United States had violated its obligations under international law, to call on the United States to bring to an end the breaches of international law, and, hence, to declare that compensation was due to Nicaragua. The Court was requested to award 370,200,000 US dollars to the Republic of Nicaragua.[4]

II. The legal question

The *Military and Paramilitary Activities in and against Nicaragua* case, being as it was one of the most complex filed in the Court, raised numerous legal questions. One of them was the contribution of international organizations to the formation of international law. The issues of the legal nature and effects of legal acts of international organizations—in relation to the principles on non-intervention and the non-use of force—were discussed having regard to the resolutions of the United Nations General Assembly (GA) and of the Organization of American States as well as to the Helsinki Final Act.

The Court, while discussing the contribution of acts of international organizations to customary international law, stressed various facets of this phenomenon. On the one hand the Court found that particular provisions of a GA resolution may be treated as evidence of customary international law ('may be taken to reflect customary international law')[5] and emphasized in another passage of the judgment their impact on the creation of customary international law ('effect of consent to the text of such resolutions [...] may be understood as an acceptance of the validity of the rule or set of rules declared by the resolution by themselves').[6]

III. Excerpts

[...]

72. The declarations to which the Court considers it may refer are not limited to those made in the pleadings and the oral argument addressed to it in the successive stages of the case, nor are they limited to statements made by the Parties. Clearly the Court is entitled to refer, not only to the Nicaraguan pleadings and oral argument, but to the pleadings and oral argument submitted to it by the United States before it withdrew from participation in the proceedings, and to the Declaration of Intervention of El Salvador in the proceedings. It is equally clear that the Court may take account of public declarations to which either Party has specifically drawn attention, and the text, or a report, of which has been filed as documentary evidence. But the Court considers that, in its quest for the truth, it may also take note of statements of representatives of the Parties (or of other States) in international organizations, as well as the

---

[4] Ibid., para. 507.   [5] Merits, para. 195.   [6] Ibid., para. 188.

resolutions adopted or discussed by such organizations, in so far as factually relevant, whether or not such material has been drawn to its attention by a Party.

[...]

188. The Court thus finds that both Parties take the view that the principles as to the use of force incorporated in the United Nations Charter correspond, in essentials, to those found in customary international law. The Parties thus both take the view that the fundamental principle in this area is expressed in the terms employed in Article 2, paragraph 4, of the United Nations Charter. They therefore accept a treaty-law obligation to refrain in their international relations from the threat or use of force against the territorial integrity or political independence of any State, or in any other manner inconsistent with the purposes of the United Nations. The Court has however to be satisfied that there exists in customary international law an *opinio juris* as to the binding character of such abstention. This *opinio juris* may, though with all due caution, be deduced from, *inter alia*, the attitude of the Parties and the attitude of States towards certain General Assembly resolutions, and particularly resolution 2625 (XXV) entitled 'Declaration on Principles of International Law concerning Friendly Relations and Co-operation among States in accordance with the Charter of the United Nations'. The effect of consent to the text of such resolutions cannot be understood as merely that of a 'reiteration or elucidation' of the treaty commitment undertaken in the Charter. On the contrary, it may be understood as an acceptance of the validity of the rule or set of rules declared by the resolution by themselves. The principle of non-use of force, for example, may thus be regarded as a principle of customary international law, not as such conditioned by provisions relating to collective security, or to the facilities or armed contingents to be provided under Article 43 of the Charter. It would therefore seem apparent that the attitude referred to expresses an *opinio juris* respecting such rule (or set of rules), to be thenceforth treated separately from the provisions, especially those of an institutional kind, to which it is subject on the treaty-law plane of the Charter.

189. As regards the United States in particular, the weight of an expression of *opinio juris* can similarly be attached to its support of the resolution of the Sixth International Conference of American States condemning aggression (18 February 1928) and ratification of the Montevideo Convention on Rights and Duties of States (26 December 1933), Article 11 of which imposes the obligation not to recognize territorial acquisitions or special advantages which have been obtained by force. Also significant is United States acceptance of the principle of the prohibition of the use of force which is contained in the declaration on principles governing the mutual relations of States participating in the Conference on Security and Co-operation in Europe (Helsinki, 1 August 1975), whereby the participating States undertake to 'refrain in their mutual relations, *as well as in their international relations in general,*' (emphasis added) from the threat or use of force. Acceptance of a text in these terms confirms the existence of an *opinio juris* of the participating States prohibiting the use of force in international relations.

[...]

191. As regards certain particular aspects of the principle in question, it will be necessary to distinguish the most grave forms of the use of force (those constituting an armed attack) from other less grave forms. In determining the legal rule which applies to these latter forms, the Court can again draw on the formulations contained

in the Declaration on Principles of International Law concerning Friendly Relations and Co-operation among States in accordance with the Charter of the United Nations (General Assembly resolution 2625 (XXV), referred to above). As already observed, the adoption by States of this text affords an indication of their *opinio juris* as to customary international law on the question. Alongside certain descriptions which may refer to aggression, this text includes others which refer only to less grave forms of the use of force.

[...]

192. Moreover, in the part of this same resolution devoted to the principle of non-intervention in matters within the national jurisdiction of States, a very similar rule is found:

> 'Also, no State shall organize, assist, foment, finance, incite or tolerate subversive, terrorist or armed activities directed towards the violent overthrow of the régime of another State, or interfere in civil strife in another State.'

In the context of the inter-American system, this approach can be traced back at least to 1928 (Convention on the Rights and Duties of States in the Event of Civil Strife, Art. 1 (1)); it was confirmed by resolution 78 adopted by the General Assembly of the Organization of American States on 21 April 1972. The operative part of this resolution reads as follows:

'*The General Assembly Resolves:*

1. To reiterate solemnly the need for the member states of the Organization to observe strictly the principles of nonintervention and self-determination of peoples as a means of ensuring peaceful coexistence among them and to refrain from committing any direct or indirect act that might constitute a violation of those principles.
2. To reaffirm the obligation of those states to refrain from applying economic, political, or any other type of measures to coerce another state and obtain from it advantages of any kind.
3. Similarly, to reaffirm the obligation of these states to refrain from organizing, supporting, promoting, financing, instigating, or tolerating subversive, terrorist, or armed activities against another state and from intervening in a civil war in another state or in its internal struggles.'

193. The general rule prohibiting force allows for certain exceptions. In view of the arguments advanced by the United States to justify the acts of which it is accused by Nicaragua, the Court must express a view on the content of the right of self-defence, and more particularly the right of collective self-defence. First, with regard to the existence of this right, it notes that in the language of Article 51 of the United Nations Charter, the inherent right (or 'droit naturel') which any State possesses in the event of an armed attack, covers both collective and individual self-defence. Thus, the Charter itself testifies to the existence of the right of collective self-defence in customary international law. Moreover, just as the wording of certain General Assembly declarations adopted by States demonstrates their recognition of the principle of the prohibition of force as definitely a matter of customary international law, some of the wording in those declarations operates similarly in respect of the right of self-defence (both collective and individual). Thus, in the declaration quoted above on the Principles of International Law concerning Friendly Relations and Cooperation among States in accordance with

the Charter of the United Nations, the reference to the prohibition of force is followed by a paragraph stating that:

'nothing in the foregoing paragraphs shall be construed as enlarging or diminishing in any way the scope of the provisions of the Charter concerning cases in which the use of force is lawful'.

This resolution demonstrates that the States represented in the General Assembly regard the exception to the prohibition of force constituted by the right of individual or collective self-defence as already a matter of customary international law.[...]

195. In the case of individual self-defence, the exercise of this right is subject to the State concerned having been the victim of an armed attack. Reliance on collective self-defence of course does not remove the need for this. There appears now to be general agreement on the nature of the acts which can be treated as constituting armed attacks. In particular, it may be considered to be agreed that an armed attack must be understood as including not merely action by regular armed forces across an international border, but also 'the sending by or on behalf of a State of armed bands, groups, irregulars or mercenaries, which carry out acts of armed force against another State of such gravity as to amount to' *(inter alia)* an actual armed attack conducted by regular forces, 'or its substantial involvement therein'. This description, contained in Article 3, paragraph *(g)*, of the Definition of Aggression annexed to General Assembly resolution 3314 (XXIX), may be taken to reflect customary international law. The Court sees no reason to deny that, in customary law, the prohibition of armed attacks may apply to the sending by a State of armed bands to the territory of another State, if such an operation, because of its scale and effects, would have been classified as an armed attack rather than as a mere frontier incident had it been carried out by regular armed forces. But the Court does not believe that the concept of 'armed attack' includes not only acts by armed bands where such acts occur on a significant scale but also assistance to rebels in the form of the provision of weapons or logistical or other support. Such assistance may be regarded as a threat or use of force, or amount to intervention in the internal or external affairs of other States. It is also clear that it is the State which is the victim of an armed attack which must form and declare the view that it has been so attacked. There is no rule in customary international law permitting another State to exercise the right of collective self-defence on the basis of its own assessment of the situation. Where collective self-defence is invoked, it is to be expected that the State for whose benefit this right is used will have declared itself to be the victim of an armed attack.

[...]

203. The principle has since been reflected in numerous declarations adopted by international organizations and conferences in which the United States and Nicaragua have participated, e.g., General Assembly resolution 2131 (XX), the Declaration on the Inadmissibility of Intervention in the Domestic Affairs of States and the Protection of their Independence and Sovereignty. It is true that the United States, while it voted in favour of General Assembly resolution 2131 (XX), also declared at the time of its adoption in the First Committee that it considered the declaration in that resolution to be 'only a statement of political intention and not a formulation of law' *(Official Records of the General Assembly, Twentieth Session, First Committee, A/C. 1 /SR. 1423, p. 436)*. However, the essentials of resolution 2131 (XX) are repeated in the Declaration approved by resolution 2625 (XXV), which set

out principles which the General Assembly declared to be 'basic principles' of international law, and on the adoption of which no analogous statement was made by the United States representative.

204. As regards inter-American relations, attention may be drawn to, for example, the United States reservation to the Montevideo Convention on Rights and Duties of States (26 December 1933), declaring the opposition of the United States Government to 'interference with the freedom, the sovereignty or other internal affairs, or processes of the Governments of other nations'; or the ratification by the United States of the Additional Protocol relative to Non-Intervention (23 December 1936). Among more recent texts, mention may be made of resolutions AG/RES.78 and AG/RES. 128 of the General Assembly of the Organization of American States. In a different context, the United States expressly accepted the principles set forth in the declaration, to which reference has already been made, appearing in the Final Act of the Conference on Security and Co-operation in Europe (Helsinki, 1 August 1975), including an elaborate statement of the principle of non-intervention; while these principles were presented as applying to the mutual relations among the participating States, it can be inferred that the text testifies to the existence, and the acceptance by the United States, of a customary principle which has universal application.

[...]

264. The Court has also emphasized the importance to be attached, in other respects, to a text such as the Helsinki Final Act, or, on another level, to General Assembly resolution 2625 (XXV) which, as its name indicates, is a declaration on 'Principles of International Law concerning Friendly Relations and Co-operation among States in accordance with the Charter of the United Nations'. Texts like these, in relation to which the Court has pointed to the customary content of certain provisions such as the principles of the non-use of force and non-intervention, envisage the relations among States having different political, economic and social systems on the basis of coexistence among their various ideologies; the United States not only voiced no objection to their adoption, but took an active part in bringing it about.

IV. Commentary

The present case addresses the legal nature and effects of the acts of international organizations.[7] This is an issue that needs to be examined in a wide context, including international law-making and the sources of international law, and especially

---

[7] This issue attracted a great deal of attention in international law doctrine in the 1970s, see for example J. Castañeda, *Legal Effects of United Nations Resolutions* (New York, Columbia University Press 1969); the same author, 'Valeur juridique des résolutions des Nations Unies', (1970) 129 *Recueil des cours de l'Académie de droit international* 205–332; I. Detter, 'The Effects of Resolutions of International Organizations', in J. Makarczyk (ed.), *Theory of International law at the Threshold of the 21st Century: Essays in Honour of Krzysztof Skubiszewski* (The Hague, Kluwer 1996), pp. 381–92; R.-J. Dupuy, 'Coutume sage et coutume sauvage', in *Mélanges offertes à Charles Rousseau* (Paris, Pedone 1974), pp. 75–87; K. Skubiszewski, 'The Elaboration of General Multilateral Conventions and of Non-Contractual Instruments Having a Normative Function or Objective', *Yearbook of the Institute of International Law, Session of Helsinki 1985*, Vol. 61, Part I, Pedone, Paris, pp. 29–358; B. Sloan, *United Nations General Assembly Resolutions in our Changing World* (New York, Transnational Publishers 1991); M. Virally, 'Les actes unilatéraux des organisations internationales', in M. Bedjaoui (ed.), *Droit international. Bilan et perspectives* (Paris, Pedone 1991), pp. 253–76; and others.

in relation to art. 38(1) of the Statute of the International Court of Justice (ICJ). International organizations adopt acts with effect to the internal sphere of their functioning as well as their external activity.[8] The focus in this commentary will be on the latter, by which international organizations 'may gain a position of authority with regard to its own founders'[9] and contribute to the formation of international law. The rapidly growing importance of international organizations within the last decades resulted in a particular focus on the various acts they adopt. These acts are of a diverse legal nature and may play a role in the development of international law.

Unilateral acts adopted by international organizations, which were traditionally beyond the scope of art. 38(1), have even been considered by some as a separate source of international law. M. Bedjaoui argues that '[i]f custom, treaties and general legal principles are in danger of contributing too little, all that is left is the resolution or, in more general terms, the legal standard elaborated in international organizations, in order to attain the sought-after goal' and describes resolutions of international organizations as a modern source of international law.[10]

Generally, the status and the interaction of acts of international organizations with the sources of international law are considered as illustrating new trends in the formation and development of customary international law. It is in this context that the normative value of legal acts that are referred to in the *Military and Paramilitary Activities* case were looked at. The impact of legal acts of international organizations on the codification and formation of international law should also be highlighted.

It is recognized that normative acts of international organizations such as resolutions and recommendations contribute to the formation of international law, especially when adopted by plenary bodies. This is in particular the case for the resolutions of the General Assembly. The United Nations Charter does not grant the General Assembly with legislative powers, although there was an attempt to vest the General Assembly with such competence.[11] This does not mean that the General Assembly lacks 'law-making' capacity and that acts it adopts do not have a normative vocation. On the contrary, as stated by K. Skubiszewski, 'organs not equipped with legislative powers, are not yet regulative, yet they aim at, and contribute to, the making of law'.[12] Resolutions of the General Assembly that lay down general and abstract rules of conduct for States may, *inter alia*, be described as law-declaring and law-generating resolutions.[13]

---

[8] This is the classical distinction, according to which the former would produce legal effects only in the internal sphere of the organizations, and the latter would be deprived of any legal significance. This is, however, a scant division, taking into consideration the effects of some 'internal' resolutions produced on States and the legal effect of 'external' resolutions vis à vis member States and third States. For a critical view on this classical division, see: G. Abi-Saab, 'Cours général de droit international public', (1987) 207 *Recueil des cours de l'Académie de droit international* 156 *et seq.*

[9] Detter (n. 7), p. 382.

[10] M. Bedjaoui, *Towards a New International Economic Order* (New York, Holmes & Meier Publishers 1979), pp. 129 *et seq.*

[11] The Philippine proposal to vest the General Assembly with legislative authority was rejected by the Committee II/2 of the Conference of San Francisco by a vote of twenty-six to one, see: Documents of the U.N. Conference on International Organization, vol. 9, pp. 70 and 316.

[12] K. Skubiszewski (n. 7), p. 30.   [13] Ibid., pp. 314–15.

In the *Military and Paramilitary Activities in and against Nicaragua* case the ICJ found that GA resolutions might be treated as evidence of customary law. With reference to art. 3(g) of the Definition of Aggression, annexed to GA resolution 3314 (XXIX), the ICJ stated that it 'may be taken to reflect customary international law'.[14] In addition the ICJ went a step further in somehow piercing the veil of the process of formation of customary norms. The Court indicated that '*opinio juris* may, though with all due caution, be deduced from, *inter alia*, the attitude of the Parties and the attitude of States towards certain General Assembly resolutions, and particularly resolution 2625 (XXV) entitled "Declaration on Principles of International Law concerning Friendly Relations and Co-operation among States in accordance with the Charter of the United Nations"'.[15] It continued that '[t]he effect of consent to the text of such resolutions cannot be understood as merely that of a "reiteration or elucidation" of the treaty commitment undertaken in the Charter. On the contrary, it may be understood as an acceptance of the validity of the rule or set of rules declared by the resolution by themselves'.[16] Here, the Court evidently emphasized the impact of the GA resolutions on the creation of customary international law. In the opinion of the Court resolutions not only 'reflect' customary international law, nor should they be treated as 'merely a reiteration or elucidation of the treaty commitment'. They by themselves can shape the content of customary international law and can contribute to the formation of international law. Further, while referring to the principles of non-use of force and non-intervention as enshrined in resolution 2625, the Court found that 'the adoption by States of this text affords an indication of their *opinio juris* as to customary international law on the question'.[17] The focus of attention of the Court is placed on only one element of the custom—*opinio juris*, not really touching upon the question of State practice.

In the same vein, in its 1996 *Legality of the Threat or Use of Nuclear Weapons* advisory opinion the ICJ stated: 'General Assembly resolutions, even if they are not binding, may sometimes have normative value. They can, in certain circumstances, provide evidence important for establishing the existence of a rule or the emergence of an *opinio juris*. To establish whether this is true of a given General Assembly resolution, it is necessary to look at its content and the conditions of its adoption; it is also necessary to see whether an *opinio juris* exists as to its normative character. Or a series of resolutions may show the gradual evolution of the *opinio juris* required for the establishment of a new rule'.[18] In the latter case, the Court once more underlined the 'normative value' of GA resolutions in that they provide 'evidence important for establishing the existence of a rule or the emergence of an *opinio juris*'. In order to establish the normative value of a resolution, the Court pointed to particular criteria that need to be examined—content, conditions of adoption, and *opinio juris* as to its normative character. In other words, according to Georges Abi-Saab, the criteria are: the degree of consensus ('le degré de consensus'), the degree of concreteness ('le degré de concrétisation'), and the follow-up ('le suivi institutionnel').[19] It is important to note that

---

[14] Merits, para. 195.   [15] Ibid., para. 188.   [16] Ibid.   [17] Ibid., para. 191.
[18] *Legality of the Threat or Use of Nuclear Weapons*, Advisory Opinion [1996] ICJ, para. 70.
[19] For an elaboration of these criteria, see: G. Abi-Saab (n. 8), pp. 160–1.

these criteria are interdependent. Where there is a strong support for the adoption of a text, the content of the text will often be phrased in strong terms. On the contrary, if there is little consensus for the adoption of the text, the latter is likely to be watered down. What should be emphasized in the present case, and in reference to the conditions of adoption of GA resolution 2625 (XXV), is the Court's finding as to the United States stance, which 'not only voiced no objection to [its] adoption, but took an active part in bringing it about'.[20]

In the *Military and Paramilitary Activities* case, the ICJ in its quest for finding evidence of *opinio juris* as to the principle of non-intervention also referred to the Final Act of the Conference on Security and Co-operation in Europe.[21] The latter, signed in 1975, was a declaration that was not supposed to establish an international organization but to define the framework and directions of co-operation for participating States in various areas.[22] Some authors emphasized the fact that the Helsinki Declaration constituted a non-legally binding instrument that only contained political commitments.[23] There seems to be little doubt that the Helsinki Declaration was not intended to constitute an international agreement, both in the light of customary law and of the definition formulated in art. 2(1)(a) of the 1969 Vienna Convention on the Law of Treaties. However, it was signed by the representatives of thirty-five States and contains all the fundamental principles of international law as enshrined in the United Nations Charter as well as in international conventions. The legal status of the Helsinki Final Act is thus not that clear.[24] The Court referred to it as a means of establishing general acceptance by States—and more especially the United States—of principles of international law such as the principles of the non-use of force (para. 189) and non-intervention (para. 204). In the same vein, as regards the principle of non-intervention, the ICJ referred to the resolutions of the General Assembly of the Organization of American States—resolutions AG/RES.78 and AG/RES.128.[25]

Two more remarks on the impact of legal acts of international organizations on the interpretation and formation of international law should be added. First, resolutions of international organizations constitute an important tool for treaty interpretation. While such acts may be non-binding, their weight should not be underestimated as they may provide guidance to the interpretation of international agreements.[26]

---

[20] Merits, para. 264.   [21] See: paras 189, 204, and 264.

[22] See: A. Bloed (ed.), *From Helsinki to Vienna: Basic Documents of the Helsinki Process* (Dordrecht, Martinus Nijhoff 1990), p. 43 *et seq.*

[23] See for example C. Tomuschat, 'International Law: Ensuring the Survival of Mankind on the Era of a New Century', (1999) 281 *Recueil des cours de l'Académie de droit international* 146. The author, while referring to the status of the Conference underlined that even the name—Conference on Security and Co-operation in Europe (CSCE)—'reflected precisely its nature as a loose form of co-operation among States'.

[24] On the issue of the legal status of the CSCE, see for example L. Boisson de Chazournes, 'Qu'est-ce que la pratique en droit international?', in *La pratique en droit international, Société française pour le droit international, Colloque de Genève* (Pedone, Paris, 2004), pp. 27–8; H. G. Schermers, N.M. Blokker, *International Institutional Law* (5th Revisited edn, Leiden, Martinus Nijhoff Publishers 2011), p. 30, para. 33 and p. 991, para. 1569; C. Tomuschat (n. 23), pp. 146–7; M. Sapiro, 'Changing the CSCE into the OSCE: legal aspects of a political transformation', (1995) 89 *American Journal of International Law* 631–7.

[25] Merits, paras 192 and 204.

[26] See for example the recent ICJ decision in the *Whaling* case: *Whaling in the Antarctic (Australia v Japan: New Zealand Intervening)*, Judgment, [2014] ICJ Rep 226. In this case, with reference

Secondly, normative resolutions of international organizations contribute to the formation of international law, as codifying instruments.[27]

Certainly, in order to assess the normative value of legal acts adopted by international organizations, each legal act has to be assessed *in concreto* in terms of its content as well as the procedure under which it was adopted. One should also examine whether there exists an *opinio juris* as to its normative value. A series of similar resolutions may evidence a practice accepted by law, thereby demonstrating the *opinio juris* required for the emergence of a customary rule. Thus, such acts play a role in the formation of customary law, whether by confirming the existing rules or crystallizing new ones.[28] They can also constitute an important means of interpretation of international agreements.

---

to the non-binding resolutions of the International Whaling Commission (IWC), the Court found that 'when they are adopted by consensus or by a unanimous vote, they may be relevant for the interpretation of the Convention' (para. 46) and that the fact that the IWC has amended the Convention many times has 'made the Convention an evolving instrument' (para. 45). For a comment on this question, see: J. Arato, *Subsequent Practice in the Whaling Case, and What the ICJ Implies about Treaty Interpretation in International Organizations*, EJIL:Talk!, published on 31 March 2014.

[27] On this role, see: G. Abi-Saab (n. 8), pp. 165 *et seq.*

[28] On the 'crystallizing' effect and the relation between international conventions and customary international law, see *North Sea Continental Shelf*, Judgment, [1969] ICJ Rep 3, paras 60 *et seq.* In its decision, the ICJ pointed out three ways in which international conventions may reflect customary international law. E. Jiménez de Aréchaga presented these three modalities as follows: declarative effect on existing customary rules, crystallizing effect for customary rules *in statu nascendi*, as well as the generative effect of new customary rules, see E. Jiménez de Aréchaga, 'International Law in the Past Third of a Century', (1978) 159 *Recueil des cours de l'Académie de droit international* 1–35.

4.4 *Youssef Nada v State Secretariat for Economic Affairs and Federal Department of Economic Affairs*, Administrative Appeal Judgment, Case No. 1A 45/2007, Switzerland, Federal Tribunal, 14 November 2007, 133 BGE II 450; ILDC 461 (CH2007)

*Antonios Tzanakopoulos**

Relevance of the case

The *Nada* case before the Swiss Federal Tribunal is one of the first cases to challenge Security Council sanctions under Chapter VII before a domestic court. Its significance lies in the fact that the Swiss Federal Tribunal, instead of refusing jurisdiction to review, essentially if only indirectly, a Security Council decision, proceeded to deal with the issue head-on, putting forward an argument regarding the proper law and standard of review against which Security Council decisions could be controlled by domestic courts. In doing that, it was also the first court to adopt the European Union's (then) Court of First Instance reasoning in *Kadi I*.[1] The decision of the Swiss Federal Court led to a challenge by Nada before the European Court of Human Rights, which was decided by the Grand Chamber at the end of 2012.

I. Facts of the case

A. The sanctions regime

The 1267 sanctions regime was established by the Security Council by means of Resolution 1267 (1999), a resolution adopted under Chapter VII of the UN Charter, and in particular art. 41.[2] When the Security Council determines that there exists a threat to the peace, under art. 39 of the Charter, it has the power under art. 41 to take measures not involving the use of armed force in order to maintain or restore international peace and security. The sanctions regime in this case originally targeted the Taliban regime in Afghanistan and its prominent members, but after the collapse of the regime following the military intervention in the aftermath of the 11 September 2001 attacks on the US it was extended to cover also Osama bin Laden and persons and institutions associated with Al-Qaida.[3] Various other Security

---

* Many thanks are due to Eleni Methymaki for truly helpful comments and excellent research assistance. All errors remain, of course, my own.

[1] On this case see further ch. 4.5 in this collection.

[2] 1945 UN Charter, 1 UNTS XIV, art. 41 provides: 'The Security Council may decide what measures not involving the use of armed force are to be employed to give effect to its decisions, and it may call upon the Members of the United Nations to apply such measures. These may include complete or partial interruption of economic relations and of rail, sea, air, postal, telegraphic, radio, and other means of communication, and the severance of diplomatic relations.'

[3] The regime was split up in 2011, with two separate regimes being established for the Taliban and Al-Qaida respectively. See: UNSC Res 1988, UN Doc S/RES/1988 (17 June 2011); UNSC Res 1989, UN Doc S/RES/1989 (17 June 2011).

Council resolutions maintained the regime in force, while updating it and occasionally refining it.[4]

Under the 1267 regime, member states of the UN are directed to impose asset freezes, travel bans, and arms embargoes on individuals and legal entities associated with the Taliban, Osama bin Laden, and Al-Qaida. The persons to be targeted, whether natural or legal, are identified by a UN Security Council 'Sanctions Committee' established under the 1267 regime (the '1267 Sanctions Committee') and included in a relevant 'Consolidated List'. The imposition of the sanctions on the persons identified by the Sanctions Committee is an obligation of member states under the UN Charter in accordance with art. 25.[5] It is thus an obligation that enjoys the 'primacy' vested on obligations arising from the UN Charter by virtue of art. 103.[6]

Member states implement art. 41 sanctions imposed by the Security Council in accordance with their domestic law.[7] For example, the United Kingdom has adopted the UN Act 1946, which allows the Government to pass administrative acts (Orders in Council) in order to implement the Resolution. In Switzerland, the Federal Council (the Executive) adopted a relevant regulation ('Verordnung') to implement the sanctions, to which it annexed a list that would reflect the UN Sanctions Committee's Consolidated List and would be updated accordingly.

B. *Nada's* case

In the case at hand, Youssef Nada was identified by the Sanctions Committee as a person to be targeted and his name was included in the Consolidated List on 9 November 2001.[8] Switzerland implemented this on 30 November by including Nada's name in the annex to the relevant regulation and thus subjecting him (and certain legal persons associated with him) to an asset freeze and travel ban.

Nada responded by challenging his listing in the annex to the Swiss regulation before the competent administrative authorities, relying on the fact that the criminal process commenced against him in Switzerland had been closed in 2005, as accusations were found to be baseless. The State Secretariat for Economic Affairs (SECO) denied his challenge in early 2006, arguing that Switzerland had no authority to remove a name from the annex to the regulation as long as this name appeared on the Security Council's Consolidated List.

---

[4] The most pertinent among them being UNSC Res 1333, UN Doc S/RES/1333 (19 December 2000); UNSC Res 1730, UN Doc S/RES/1730 (19 December 2006); UNSC Res 1904, UN Doc S/RES/1904 (17 December 2009); S/RES/1988 (2011) and S/RES/1989 (2011) splitting the regime up (n. 3).

[5] Article 25 UN Charter provides: 'The Members of the United Nations agree to accept and carry out the decisions of the Security Council in accordance with the present Charter.'

[6] Article 103 UN Charter provides: 'In the event of a conflict between the obligations of the Members of the United Nations under the present Charter and their obligations under any other international agreement, their obligations under the present Charter shall prevail.'

[7] See generally V. Gowlland-Debbas (ed.), *National Implementation of United Nations Sanctions: A Comparative Study* (The Hague, Martinus Nijhoff 2004).

[8] This section relies largely on the 'Regeste' section of the Federal Tribunal's decision and on the 'Facts' section of the decision of the European Court of Human Rights Grand Chamber, to which Nada eventually complained: *Nada v Switzerland*, App No 10593/08, (Grand Chamber 12 September 2012), available at http://hudoc.echr.coe.int/sites/eng/pages/search.aspx?i=001-113121.

Nada brought an administrative appeal against SECO's refusal to remove him from the Swiss list before the Federal Department of Economic Affairs, but this was again unsuccessful. The Federal Ministry responded that Nada could only be removed following removal from the UN list, and that a special delisting procedure existed to that effect on the UN level. However, that procedure could only be pursued on behalf of the person listed by the state of their nationality or residence, of which Switzerland was neither. Nada was indeed not a Swiss national, and was resident in Campione d'Italia, an Italian enclave surrounded by Swiss territory in the canton of Ticino. This however made his travelling from the tiny enclave through Switzerland to Italy impossible due to the travel ban.

The case finally reached the Swiss Federal Tribunal, the supreme judicial instance of Switzerland. In the meantime, Resolution 1730 (2006) had created a 'Focal Point' where listed individuals could bring delisting requests without going through their State of nationality or residence. Nada had submitted a request but had heard nothing in response by the time the question fell to be decided by the Federal Tribunal. Before the Federal Tribunal, Nada argued that the Swiss regulation went beyond what was required by the 1267 sanctions regime. By imposing a travel ban on him, Swiss authorities prevented him from leaving the tiny Italian enclave to travel to Italy in order to get medical attention for various ailments and in order to tend to administrative and legal matters. To that extent, the Swiss regulation should be annulled, as it effectively had put him under house arrest for almost six years (by 2007).

II. The legal questions

The crucial legal questions before the Swiss Federal Tribunal were numerous. The first issue was whether the Tribunal could review a domestic measure implementing Security Council sanctions, when this would in effect mean that the Tribunal would also be indirectly reviewing decisions of the Security Council, over which it does not have jurisdiction. A second question was against what law the Tribunal would review the domestic decision, and thus also (indirectly) the decision of the Security Council. The overarching issue in the case was to what extent the Security Council can set aside international obligations for the protection of human rights binding on Switzerland in order to sanction individuals in the exercise of its primary responsibility for the maintenance of international peace and security.[9]

III. Excerpts

2.1 … Through [his] inclusion in Annex 2 of the Taliban Regulation, the claimant is subjected to the sanctions provided for in [that] Regulation and is thus directly and specifically affected in his enjoyment of fundamental rights. For this reason, he must be allowed to seek to legally protect these rights [before a court] …[10]

---

[9] See art. 24(1) UN Charter.
[10] These excerpts have been translated from the German text of the decision by the author. This is not an official translation of the decision. Most references of the Court have been omitted, which is signified by ellipses in square brackets [...].

2.2 Administrative court complaints are however barred against decisions [administrative acts] whose subject-matter is that of internal or external security of the State ... as well as other matters of foreign affairs. The decision of the [Federal Ministry to refuse Nada's request for the removal of his name from the administrative act freezing assets] refers to measures for the implementation of international sanctions and belongs thus to those decisions dealing with matters of foreign affairs for which the Federal Council [the Executive] has in principle [exclusive] competence. However, the exceptions [from judicial scrutiny described above ...] do not apply when the complaint refers to rights which must be granted judicial protection in accordance with Article 6(1) of the European Convention of Human Rights (ECHR) ... The inclusion of the claimant and his organisation in Annex 2 of the Taliban Regulation results in all his [assets] in Switzerland being frozen. On account of this, and on account also of the prohibition of making any payments to him or to his organisation, it is impossible for the claimant to conduct any business in Switzerland. Thus, the Taliban Regulation directly interferes with economic and business rights of the claimant. These are not precautionary measures taken to secure [the implementation] of a decision, against which judicial protection would be possible, but rather measures that have been adopted independently [of such a decision]. These independent measures have been in force now for 5 years already and there is no end in sight ...

[After the Federal Tribunal established thus its jurisdiction to hear the complaint, it considered Nada's allegation that the adoption of the measures against him was an autonomous act of Switzerland, which was not bound by Security Council decisions in 2000–2001, that is before it had become a UN Member State. However, that position had changed by the time the Federal Tribunal came to hear the complaint.]

5. In accordance with Article 25 of the UN Charter ... Member States have assumed the obligation to accept and carry out the decisions of the Security Council in accordance with the present Charter. Decisions of the Security Council are thus binding for Member States (to the extent that they do not take the form of non-binding recommendations). For decisions of the Security Council taken under Articles 41 or 42 for the maintenance or restoration of international peace and security, this also emerges from Article 48(2) of the Charter.

5.1 The obligations of the Member States under the Charter take precedence not only over their domestic law, but also, in accordance with Article 103 of the Charter, over obligations under other international treaties. In accordance with the jurisprudence of the ICJ, this precedence applies to all bilateral, regional, and multilateral treaties ... and indeed irrespective of whether these were adopted before or after the [adoption of the] Charter ...

5.2 This precedence is enjoyed not only by obligations contained in the Charter, but also by obligations which arise for the Member States under a binding Resolution of the Security Council. [...]

5.3 Even the Security Council is bound by the Charter and must thus act in accordance with the purposes and principles [of the United Nations] (Article 24(2) UN Charter), which include respect for human rights and fundamental freedoms (Article 1(3) UN Charter). However, Member States are in principle not competent to disobey an obligation with the justification that a (formally lawful) Resolution of the Security Council is materially not in accordance with the Charter. [...] This applies namely to

Resolutions which the Security Council adopts under Chapter VII of the Charter for the maintenance or restoration of international peace and security. [...]

5.4 [The Federal Tribunal then discusses the decisions of the European Court of First Instance (CFI) (as it then was) in *Yusuf* and *Kadi*, as well as *Ayadi* and *Hassan* and concludes:] The CFI assumed that the only limit to the binding force of Security Council Resolutions is posed by *jus cogens*, that is by peremptory fundamental norms that apply to all subjects of international law, including the organs of the United Nations, and from which no derogation is permitted. The CFI then reviewed the sanctions Resolutions against this benchmark and reached the conclusion that these had not violated *jus cogens*. [...] ...

5.5 In accordance with the jurisprudence of the European Court of Human Rights (ECtHR), Member States are responsible for the implementation of obligations imposed on them through international organisations, to the extent that they retain some measure of discretion [margin of appreciation] [in their implementation]. When this is not the case, the ECtHR will only review whether the relevant organisation provides for equivalent protection of rights to that of the ECHR, and whether the protection of Convention rights was manifestly deficient in the case at hand. [The Federal Tribunal refers here to the *Bosphorus* decision of the ECtHR]. The ECtHR has however not decided whether this also applies to obligations stemming from binding Resolutions of the Security Council under Chapter VII of the Charter ...

[In paras 6. and 6.1 the Federal Tribunal establishes that international law, which includes binding decisions of the Security Council, is binding on all Swiss organs].

6.2 Article 190 of the Constitution, however, does not include a rule regarding potential conflicts between different norms of international law that are both binding on Switzerland, such as, in the case at hand, sanctions Resolutions of the Security Council on the one hand and guarantees of the ECHR and of the International Covenant on Civil and Political Rights (ICCPR) on the other. If the conflict cannot be removed through interpretation, it will be the hierarchy of norms under international law that will apply. In accordance with that [hierarchy], obligations under the UN Charter take precedence. [...] The global uniform application of UN sanctions would be imperiled if the courts of each Member State could refuse the implementation of sanctions against certain individuals or legal entities on account of potential violations of fundamental rights under the ECHR or the ICCPR—which overlap to a large extent with fundamental rights protected by national constitutions.

7. However, the obligation to implement Security Council Resolutions is limited by *jus cogens*, as peremptory law that is binding on all subjects of international law. It must thus be considered whether the sanctions decisions violate *jus cogens*, as the claimant alleges.

7.1 Norms of *jus cogens*, or peremptory norms of international law, are these norms of international law from which no derogation is permitted, even when there is mutual agreement [between states]. International treaties that conflict with these norms are thus void (cf. Articles 53, 64, and 71 of the Vienna Convention on the Law of Treaties). Accordingly, States could not have dispensed with compliance with such norms even in the UN Charter. [...] Indicators of the absolute character of a norm are provisions in treaties that characterise certain rights and obligations as indispensable, for example by disallowing any contrary agreements on the part of the parties, by prohibiting the invocation of necessity as a justification for their suspension, or by excluding the possibility of making reservations to them. [...]

7.2 The CFI did not find, in the aforementioned cases, any violation of *jus cogens*. For one, it found that the fundamental rights invoked by the claimants (right to property, rights of defence, right to effective judicial protection) were not absolute, and particularly not when it came to decisions of the Security Council under Chapter VII of the Charter. For another, the Court pointed out that the relevant measures were of a limited duration, whose continuation in force is reviewed by the Security Council every 12–18 months, for which humanitarian exemptions are provided in cases of hardship, and for which there exists a formal process for the review of individual cases through the Sanctions Committee. [...]

7.3 [The Federal Tribunal] must agree with this assessment. In general, basic human rights such as the right to life, the protection from torture and inhuman or degrading treatment, the freedom from slavery and trafficking, the prohibition of collective punishment, the principle of individual criminal responsibility, as well as the rule of *non-refoulement* are considered norms of *jus cogens*. [...] Further, the protection from arbitrary detention and certain related procedural rights are also considered norms of *jus cogens*. [...] However, other human rights do not constitute peremptory norms of international law, even if they are of particular preeminence for Switzerland. [...] This is particularly the case for the fundamental rights to property and to economic freedom, which have been invoked by the claimant. [...] But even the invoked procedural guarantees (the right to a fair trial under Article 6(1) ECHR and Article 14(1) ICCPR; the right to an effective remedy under Article 13 ECHR and Article 2(3) ICCPR) do not belong to the non-derogable core of international human rights conventions (cf. Article 15(2) ECHR and Article 4(2) ICCPR) and thus in principle also not to the norms of *jus cogens*. [...]

7.4 Namely, in the area of sanctions imposed by the Security Council under Chapter VII of the Charter, there appears to be no consensus on the part of States to recognize internationally peremptory procedural guarantees for the protection of individuals. These sanctions provide for far-reaching economic limitations for the targets; however, the necessary means for basic maintenance are subject to exemptions (cf. Resolution 1452 (2002), para 1(a)), which means that there is no danger to life or health or a violation of the prohibition of inhuman or degrading treatment. The travel ban limits the freedom of movement of targeted individuals but does not in principle constitute a deprivation of their liberty: targeted individuals may still move freely within their State of residence [...]; and travelling to the State of nationality is also expressly permitted (cf. Resolution 1735 (2006) para 1(b)). Traditionally, sanctions are imposed by the Security Council without granting an individual [target] the opportunity to be heard whether in advance or after the imposition, or to challenge the imposition before an international or national court. The introduction of the delisting-procedure and the adoption in 2006 of [relevant] improvements ([description of improvements including direct requests for delisting, description of criteria for listing and delisting, notification of the targeted individual etc.]) constitute essential progress compared to the earlier situation. Even if this system falls significantly short of the requirements from the perspective of fundamental rights protection [...], there is still no violation of *jus cogens*.

[In section 8 of the decision, the Federal Tribunal examines to what extent Switzerland, bound as it is by the decisions of the Security Council, has any room for manoeuver/margin of discretion in their implementation. It finds that the Council has imposed strict obligations on member states through Resolution 1267 (1999) in that it has described the sanctions in detail and has identified the individuals and entities to be subjected to the regime, thus leaving no margin of discretion in the implementation of the decision. In conjunction with the provision of a special delisting-procedure, it is forbidden for member states to independently decide not to apply the sanctions against a designated individual; contrary conduct would constitute a violation of the Charter. The Federal Tribunal then concedes that the procedure falls short of the requirements of the right to a fair trial and to an effective remedy under both ECHR and ICCPR, but maintains that this can only be remedied by the introduction of a control mechanism at UN level, which the Federal Council and the Swiss Permanent Mission to the UN are trying to achieve. Section 9 of the decision then establishes the obligations of Switzerland to actively support the claimant in his attempt to achieve delisting by the Security Council. Section 10 determines that Switzerland has not gone beyond what the Council requires with respect to the imposition of the travel ban and thus has no independent margin of discretion in this regard as well. In section 11 the Federal Tribunal rejects the complaint.]

IV. Commentary

A. The decision

Though somewhat complicated in its structure, the Swiss Federal Tribunal's decision has a clear and logical red thread running through it, and raises many of the problems that would plague courts and tribunals as well as scholars dealing with UN targeted sanctions in years to come. The first, though implicit, point raised by the Tribunal is that of attribution of conduct and indirect review of Security Council decisions ((i) below); the Tribunal however also picks up, necessarily, on the question of conflict of norms and normative hierarchy in international law ((ii) below), as well as the question of the 'equivalent protection' doctrine of the European Court of Human Rights ((iii) below).

(i) Attribution of conduct and indirect review

The first question with which the Tribunal must grapple is that of its jurisdiction to review the impugned act. The act being challenged in the instance is a domestic act. However, it is a domestic act implementing a 'strict' international obligation, that means an obligation of result which leaves no room for manoeuver (margin of discretion in its implementation) to the implementing state. As such, the Tribunal understands that by reviewing the domestic implementing act, it will be indirectly reviewing the international act which constitutes the domestic act's basis and which defines its content. This has a twofold implication for international law. The first is the recognition that the domestic act is attributable to the state, because it is an act of one of its organs, and it can thus be reviewed by a domestic court. But at the same time, the

Tribunal recognizes that the state is not free in promulgating this act: it is controlled by the international obligation imposed by the Security Council. The Tribunal thus needs to deal with this lack of autonomy on the part of the acting state, a problem that many courts have found difficult to deal with. This is evident in the case law of the European Court of Human Rights in the cases of *Behrami* and *Al-Jedda*,[11] as well as in the various *Kadi* decisions in the Courts of the European Union,[12] and the *Ahmed* decision of the UK Supreme Court.[13]

In general public international law terms, the courts (including the Federal Tribunal) could relatively easily side step the issue (as some of them have done) by focusing on the fact that the act is an act of a state organ and thus automatically attributable to the state. Whether it may also be attributable to another subject of international law, such as the UN, need not be discussed, especially in view of the fact that the court's *ratione personae* jurisdiction would not extend to that entity anyway. Further, parallel attribution to the UN need not necessarily preclude attribution of an act of a state organ to the state.

However, courts have felt uneasy in focusing solely on this simple attribution link and proceeding with review 'as usual'. The fact that the state is normatively controlled[14] in its conduct leads the court to be reticent to review the domestic act against domestic law. On the other hand then, the Federal Tribunal agrees to review the domestic act, but only against law that would regulate both the domestic act and the international act which 'conditions' the domestic act. This leads the Federal Tribunal to questions of conflict of norms and normative hierarchy in international law.

(ii) Conflict of norms and normative hierarchy

The Federal Tribunal needs to deal with international obligations binding on two different subjects of international law, namely Switzerland on the one hand and the United Nations (of which the Security Council is an organ) on the other. Starting with Switzerland, the Federal Tribunal notices that it is faced with an apparent conflict of obligations incumbent on Switzerland (see para. 6.2): on the one hand, Switzerland is bound to comply with binding Security Council decisions under art. 25 of the UN Charter (which also take precedence over other obligations of Switzerland under international treaties, in accordance with art. 103 UN Charter). On the other hand, Switzerland is also

---

[11] ECtHR: *Behrami and Behrami v France and Saramati v France, Germany and Norway*, App No 71412/01 and 78166/01, Admissibility (Grand Chamber 2 May 2007), paras 128–44; *Al-Jedda v UK*, App No 27021/08 (Grand Chamber 7 July 2011), paras 76–86.

[12] Case T-315/01, *Yassin Abdullah Kadi v Council of the European Union and Commission of the European Communities*, [2005] ECR II-3649; Joined Cases C-402/05 and C-415/05 P, *Yassin Abdullah Kadi and Al Barakaat International Foundation v Council of the European Union and the Commission of the European Communities*, [2008] ECR I-6351; Case T-85/09, *Yassin Abdullah Kadi v European Commission*, [2010] ECR II-5177; Joined Cases of C-584/10 P, C-593/10 P and C-595/10 P, *European Commission and Others v Yassin Abdullah Kadi* [2013] ECR-0000. See further ch. 4.5 in this collection.

[13] *Her Majesty's Treasury (Respondent) v Mohammed Jabar Ahmed and Others (FC) (Appellants)* [2010] UKSC 2.

[14] On the issue of normative control over state conduct, see generally Antonios Tzanakopoulos, *Disobeying the Security Council: Countermeasures Against Wrongful Sanctions* (Oxford, Oxford University Press 2011) pp. 40–5.

bound to protect fundamental human rights under the ECHR and the ICCPR. In order to avoid the inevitable resolution of the conflict by granting precedence to the obligation to comply with Security Council decisions in accordance with art. 103 UN Charter, the Federal Tribunal shifts the focus to the other subject of international law at play, the Security Council (by which of course it means the UN, of which the Council is an organ) (see all of section 7): whatever the situation regarding Switzerland's obligations, even the Security Council is limited by norms of *jus cogens*. As such, *jus cogens* being binding on both Switzerland and the Security Council, and *jus cogens* constituting peremptory (supreme) law, the Federal Tribunal feels safe in reviewing the domestic act (and indirectly the international act) against the norms of *jus cogens*.

This approach of the Federal Tribunal is internally consistent, and also respects in principle the rules regarding conflict of norms and normative hierarchy in international law, even though parts of the reasoning could be criticized. The most serious problem in the Federal Tribunal's decision however is its identification of norms of *jus cogens*. Despite its apparent agreement with the CFI in the first *Kadi* (and related) case(s) (whose identification of *jus cogens* can and has also been criticized), the Federal Tribunal proceeds to find that such fundamental rights as the right to a fair trial or the right to an effective remedy are not *jus cogens* simply because they can be derogated from in times of emergency and are otherwise not absolute. Irrespective of whether the relevant rights, or some part of them, can be characterized as *jus cogens*, derogability and the lack of absolute character are not enough to deny a particular norm the character of *jus cogens*. Even derogable rights retain a non-derogable core, and this core could be *jus cogens*—if the international community of states has recognized the norm (or the core of the right) as one from which no derogation is permitted.[15] Where the CFI had been overly generous in characterizing fundamental rights as *jus cogens*, the Federal Tribunal revealed itself to be overly restrictive.

The reason for this could be the uneasiness that both courts felt in reviewing domestic (but also indirectly Security Council) acts against the vague category of norms that can considered *jus cogens*. Both the CFI and the Federal Tribunal accepted that they could undertake such review in principle, but when the time came to undertake it, they were reticent to find the Security Council as having violated *jus cogens*. This would be a particularly bold step, and one taken on very shaky ground to boot, given the inherent uncertainty regarding the identification and content of norms of *jus cogens*. Both courts avoided it, the CFI by undertaking a particularly low intensity review against the many norms of *jus cogens* it identified, and the Federal Tribunal by limiting the norms of *jus cogens* it identified to the core of the right to life and of the prohibition of torture and inhuman or degrading treatment or punishment.

(iii) *The equivalent protection doctrine*

Another interesting point that the Federal Tribunal picks up on is the equivalent protection doctrine elaborated by the European Court of Human Rights in *Bosphorus*

---

[15] See art. 53, 1969 Vienna Convention on the Law of Treaties, 1155 UNTS 331.

and other cases.[16] The equivalent protection doctrine is the ECtHR's way of dealing with the problem of attribution and normative control identified under (i) above. The ECtHR generally finds that acts of state organs are attributable to the state and thus subject to the obligations of the ECHR and controllable by the ECtHR. However, when such acts are strictly conditioned by way of an international obligation imposed by an international organization, the ECtHR understands that by holding the state responsible for a violation of the ECHR, it would also be indirectly holding the international organization to the standards of the ECHR, of which of course the organization is not a party (even though the organization may still be bound by norms of similar if not identical content under customary international law).

To avoid this, the ECtHR has elaborated a doctrine of 'equivalent protection'. According to this doctrine, which is much reminiscent of the *Solange* doctrine elaborated by the German Federal Constitutional Court in a number of cases (in particular *Solange II*) discussing the relationship of the German domestic legal order with the legal order of the European Union,[17] the ECtHR will presume that an act of a state in implementation of an obligation stemming from its membership of an international organization is in compliance with the ECHR, as long as the international organization provides human rights protection at least equivalent to that provided by the ECHR. As such, once it is established that the international organization offers equivalent protection of fundamental rights in general, the ECtHR will forgo control of the domestic implementing act of the state, unless the protection offered by the organization has been manifestly deficient in the instance at hand.

The Federal Tribunal notes this in connection with its discussion of the conflict of obligations faced by Switzerland under the ECHR and the UN Charter. It notes further, however, that while the ECtHR has established, through its case law, that certain organizations (such as the EU) do offer equivalent protection, it has not done so for the United Nations. It does not pursue the point further at this point (para. 5.5), but further below it explicitly recognizes that the UN procedure for listing and delisting of individual targets of sanctions falls far short of both ECHR and ICCPR requirements of procedural fairness. It thus concedes the lack of equivalent protection, and foreshadows a relevant analysis of the ECtHR.

B. The aftermath

The case of *Nada* inevitably reached the European Court of Human Rights, as was to be expected. In its decision,[18] the Grand Chamber of the ECtHR avoided the 'equivalent protection' analysis that many commentators had expected—and that the Swiss Federal Tribunal had indeed foreshadowed. Instead, the ECtHR 'invented' a margin of discretion in the implementation of the Security Council decision which Switzerland

---

[16] ECtHR: *Bosphorus Hava Yollari Turizm ve Ticaret Anonim Sirketi v Ireland*, App No 45036/98 (Grand Chamber 30 June 2005), paras 152–6; cf on immunity of international organizations *Waite and Kennedy v Germany*, App No 26083/94 (Grand Chamber 18 February 1999), paras 67–73.

[17] *Solange I* [1974] 37 BVerfGE 271; *Solange II* [1986] 73 BVerfGE 339. See further ch. 4.2 in this collection.

[18] ECtHR: *Nada v Switzerland*, App No 10593/08 (Grand Chamber 12 September 2012).

had not used to its full extent in order to safeguard Nada's rights under the ECHR, and thus found Switzerland in breach of the relevant obligations. This was a somewhat surprising decision, given that Switzerland had very little—if indeed any at all—such room for manoeuver, as the Federal Tribunal so clearly establishes in its own decision in *Nada*.

And yet, the wish of the ECtHR to avoid such an 'equivalent protection' analysis seems understandable, if not necessarily justifiable. It is clear that, at least at the time of the alleged violations, the UN offered nothing like equivalent protection of ECHR rights. This is confirmed by the fact that when the ECtHR (though not the Grand Chamber) did query whether the UN offered 'equivalent protection' to that of the ECHR in connection with the Iraqi sanctions regime (whose procedures for listing and delisting are currently the same as they were for Nada and the 1267 regime at the time of the alleged violations) in *Al-Dulimi*, it found that it clearly did not.[19] This latter case is now before the Grand Chamber, which, it is hoped, will offer some harmonization of the case law. It would then be interesting to see how the Grand Chamber will deal with the question of art. 103 UN Charter, which the Second Chamber clearly avoided in *Al-Dulimi*. Namely, if the UN offers no equivalent protection, and the state implementing the sanctions is to be held to the standards of the ECHR, how is that squared with the fact that the state must indeed give precedence to the UN obligation under arts 25 and 103 UN Charter?

---

[19] ECtHR: *Al-Dulimi AND Montana Management Inc. v Switzerland*, App No 5809/08 (26 September 2013), paras 117–21.

4.5 Case T-315/01, *Yassin Abdullah Kadi v Council of the European Union and Commission of the European Communities*, 21 September 2005, [2005] ECR II-3649 (*Kadi I CFI*); Cases C-402/05 P and C-415/05 P, *Yassin Abdullah Kadi and Al Barakaat International Foundation v Council and Commission*, Court of Justice of the EC [2008] ECR I-6351 (*Kadi I ECJ*); Case T-85/09, *Kadi v Commission* [2010] ECR II-5177 (*Kadi II GCEU*); Joined Cases C-584/10 P, C-593/10 P and C-595/10 P, *Commission and United Kingdom v Kadi*, Judgment of the Court (Grand Chamber) of 18 July 2013 (*Kadi II CJEU*)

*Antonios Tzanakopoulos**

Relevance of the cases

The *Kadi* cases before the Courts of the European Union (which, due to the entry into force of the Lisbon Treaty, changed their names halfway through the *Kadi* saga)[1] threw into sharp relief the question of legal effects of acts of international organizations and their relationship to (self-proclaimed) 'separate' legal orders (*ordres juridiques propres*)[2]. The *Kadi I CFI* decision was the first to review (if indirectly) Security Council decisions imposing sanctions under Chapter VII of the UN Charter, while the *Kadi I ECJ* decision was the first to actually strike down a 'domestic' (EU) act implementing Security Council sanctions, thus forcing member states of the EU to effectively disobey the Security Council. In *Kadi II*, a battle took place for the reversal or limitation of the precedent set by *Kadi I ECJ*. *Kadi II CJEU* confirmed a particularly demanding standard of review and undertook substantive control of the relevant EU act, and, indirectly, the Security Council decision to impose sanctions on Kadi.

I. Facts of the cases

The cases related to the targeting by the Security Council under the 1267 anti-terrorist sanctions regime described in the *Nada* case[3] of Yassin Abdullah Kadi, a businessman alleged to have been associated with Al-Qaida. This (brief) time-line of relevant events begins with Kadi's listing by the 1267 Sanctions Committee in 2001. The listing obligated member states of the UN to freeze Kadi's assets, and to impose on him a travel ban and arms embargo.[4] Kadi launched a series of challenges against the implementation of these measures,[5] including against

---

* This commentary draws in part from my relevant posts on EJIL: Talk!, the blog of the European Journal of International Law (http://www.ejiltalk.org). Many thanks are due to Eleni Methymaki for truly helpful comments and excellent research assistance. All errors remain, of course, my own.

[1] Hence, the Court of First Instance (CFI) was renamed he General Court of the European Union (GCEU), while the Court of Justice (ECJ) became the Court of Justice of the European Union (CJEU). The appropriate court name has been retained for each case, as is evident in the title abbreviations.

[2] See Case C-26/62, *Van Gend & Loos* [1963] ECR 1.   [3] See ch. 4.4, section 1.

[4] See art. 25 UN Charter.

[5] For example in Turkey: *Kadi v Prime Ministry and Ministry of Foreign Affairs of Turkey*, ILDC 311 (TR 2007); as well as in the US: *Yassin Abdullah Kadi v Timothy Geitner* et al, Civil Action No 09-0108

the implementing measures adopted by the European Union (at the time still the European Communities).[6]

The CFI in *Kadi I* refused to strike down the impugned Regulation (implementing the Security Council Resolution), undertaking a very low intensity review of the Regulation against what it considered to be peremptory rules of international law (*jus cogens*). Kadi appealed. In its historic decision on appeal the Grand Chamber of the ECJ found that the EU had not complied with its own primary law (i.e. EU law of constitutional ranking) regarding human rights protection, and struck down the implementing Regulation. The EU Commission then sought to remedy the shortcomings identified by the ECJ, relisting Kadi shortly before the expiry of the period during which the ECJ had suspended the effect of its *Kadi I* decision to annul.

Kadi, now relisted, challenged the fresh listing before the GCEU, mostly alleging that the decision to relist him suffered from the same shortcomings as the one that had been struck down by the ECJ in *Kadi I*. This launched the *Kadi II* cases. In *Kadi II*, the GCEU implicitly criticized *Kadi I ECJ*, but it 'grudgingly'[7] applied it, as it did not feel it was for the lower court to overturn a decision of the Grand Chamber of the Court of Justice. Applying *Kadi I ECJ* meant that the GCEU had to strike down the impugned Regulation again, thus releasing Kadi from the sanctions. The Commission and others appealed the decision, and the case ended up, for the second time, before the Court of Justice of the EU. The Grand Chamber of the CJEU confirmed the decision of the GCEU in material part, and so the *Kadi* saga reached closure. In the meantime, Kadi had been delisted by the Sanctions Committee upon the relevant recommendation of the Office of the Ombudsperson established by Security Council Resolution 1904 (2009) and refined by Resolution 1989 (2011).

II. The legal questions

The *Kadi* cases before the EU Courts raised a number of legal questions, some of which refer to the EU's competences and the Union's subjection to obligations stemming from the UN Charter. The most crucial legal question for present purposes is, however, that of respect of fundamental human rights of the target in the implementation of 'strict'[8] obligations imposed by the UN Security Council. Kadi argued consistently that his fundamental rights to a fair trial and to an effective remedy had been violated through his subjection to the draconian sanctions of the 1267 regime, as implemented

(JDB), Memorandum Opinion of 19 March 2012 (although in that latter case the challenge was against the US measures that had been adopted against him before—and independently of—his listing by the 1267 Committee).

[6] Even though UN member states that are also EU members are under an independent obligation to implement measures imposed by the UN Security Council, the EU employed EU acts (in particular Regulations, which have direct effect) in order to ensure uniform application of the sanctions in all EU member states (all of which are of course also UN member states). As such, attacking the EU implementing measures would presumably allow Kadi to access his accounts and so forth in all twenty-seven (now twenty-eight) EU member states.

[7] For the expression see Tim Stahlberg's comment on the decision available at http://courtofjustice.blogspot.gr/2010/10/case-t-8509-kadi-ii.html.

[8] See ch. 4.4, section 1 on the concept of 'strict' obligations.

by the EU. The EU argued that it could do nothing else but implement the measures as required by the Security Council on the basis of Chapter VII Resolutions. Essentially the difficulty was that the EU could not allow protection of the rights claimed by Kadi without risking violation of the Security Council Resolutions. What follows are the most pertinent parts of the EU Courts' responses to these arguments.

III. Excerpts

A. Kadi I CFI

176 The Court can properly rule on the pleas alleging breach of the applicant's fundamental rights only in so far as they fall within the scope of its judicial review and as they are capable, if proved, of leading to annulment of the contested regulation.[9][…]

178 The Court considers it appropriate to consider, in the first place, the relationship between the international legal order under the United Nations and the domestic or Community legal order, and also the extent to which the exercise by the Community and its Member States of their powers is bound by resolutions of the Security Council adopted under Chapter VII of the Charter of the United Nations.

179 This consideration will effectively determine the scope of the review of lawfulness, particularly having regard to fundamental rights, which the Court will carry out in the second place in respect of the Community acts giving effect to such resolutions.

180 Thirdly and finally, if it should find that they fall within the scope of its judicial review and that they are capable of leading to annulment of the contested regulation, the Court will rule on the alleged breaches of the applicant's fundamental rights.[…]

181 From the standpoint of international law, the obligations of the Member States of the United Nations under the Charter of the United Nations clearly prevail over every other obligation of domestic law or of international treaty law including, for those of them that are members of the Council of Europe, their obligations under the ECHR and, for those that are also members of the Community, their obligations under the EC Treaty.[…]

183 As regards […] the relationship between the Charter of the United Nations and international treaty law, that rule of primacy is expressly laid down in Article 103 of the Charter […] In accordance with Article 30 of the Vienna Convention on the Law of Treaties, and contrary to the rules usually applicable to successive treaties, that rule holds good in respect of Treaties made earlier as well as later than the Charter of the United Nations. According to the International Court of Justice, all regional, bilateral, and even multilateral, arrangements that the parties may have made must be made always subject to the provisions of Article 103 of the Charter of the United Nations […]

184 That primacy extends to decisions contained in a resolution of the Security Council, in accordance with Article 25 of the Charter of the United Nations … According to the International Court of Justice, in accordance with Article 103 of the

---

[9] References omitted.

Charter, the obligations of the Parties in that respect prevail over their obligations under any other international agreement [...]

[...]

190 It also follows from the foregoing that, pursuant both to the rules of general international law and to the specific provisions of the Treaty, Member States may, and indeed must, leave unapplied any provision of Community law, whether a provision of primary law or a general principle of that law, that raises any impediment to the proper performance of their obligations under the Charter of the United Nations.

[...]

193 [...] the Community must be considered to be bound by the obligations under the Charter of the United Nations in the same way as its Member States, by virtue of the Treaty establishing it.

194 In that regard, it is not in dispute that at the time when they concluded the Treaty establishing the European Economic Community the Member States were bound by their obligations under the Charter of the United Nations.

195 By concluding a treaty between them they could not transfer to the Community more powers than they possessed or withdraw from their obligations to third countries under that Charter [...].

[...]

199 In this context it is to be borne in mind ... that according to the case-law [...] the Community must respect international law in the exercise of its powers and, consequently, Community law must be interpreted, and its scope limited, in the light of the relevant rules of international law.

200 By conferring those powers on the Community, the Member States demonstrated their will to bind it by the obligations entered into by them under the Charter of the United Nations [...].

[...]

204 Following that reasoning, it must be held, first, that the Community may not infringe the obligations imposed on its Member States by the Charter of the United Nations or impede their performance and, second, that in the exercise of its powers it is bound, by the very Treaty by which it was established, to adopt all the measures necessary to enable its Member States to fulfil those obligations.

[...]

212 The question that arises in this instance is, however, whether there exist any structural limits, imposed by general international law or by the EC Treaty itself, on the judicial review which it falls to the Court of First Instance to carry out with regard to that regulation.

[...]

214 [...] as the institutions have rightly claimed, they acted under circumscribed powers, with the result that they had no autonomous discretion. In particular, they could neither directly alter the content of the resolutions at issue nor set up any mechanism capable of giving rise to such alteration.

215 Any review of the internal lawfulness of the contested regulation, especially having regard to the provisions or general principles of Community law relating to the protection of fundamental rights, would therefore imply that the Court is to consider, indirectly, the lawfulness of those resolutions. In that hypothetical situation, in fact, the origin of the illegality alleged by the applicant would have to be sought,

not in the adoption of the contested regulation but in the resolutions of the Security Council which imposed the sanctions [...].

216 In particular, if the Court were to annul the contested regulation, as the applicant claims it should, although that regulation seems to be imposed by international law, on the ground that that act infringes his fundamental rights which are protected by the Community legal order, such annulment would indirectly mean that the resolutions of the Security Council concerned themselves infringe those fundamental rights. In other words, the applicant asks the Court to declare by implication that the provision of international law at issue infringes the fundamental rights of individuals, as protected by the Community legal order.

[...]

221 In light of the considerations set out in paragraphs 193 to 204 above, the claim that the Court of First Instance has jurisdiction to review indirectly the lawfulness of such a decision according to the standard of protection of fundamental rights as recognised by the Community legal order, cannot be justified either on the basis of international law or on the basis of Community law.

222 First, such jurisdiction would be incompatible with the undertakings of the Member States under the Charter of the United Nations, especially Articles 25, 48 and 103 thereof, and also with Article 27 of the Vienna Convention on the Law of Treaties.

[...]

225 It must therefore be considered that the resolutions of the Security Council at issue fall, in principle, outside the ambit of the Court's judicial review and that the Court has no authority to call in question, even indirectly, their lawfulness in the light of Community law. On the contrary, the Court is bound, so far as possible, to interpret and apply that law in a manner compatible with the obligations of the Member States under the Charter of the United Nations.

226 None the less, the Court is empowered to check, indirectly, the lawfulness of the resolutions of the Security Council in question with regard to *jus cogens*, understood as a body of higher rules of public international law binding on all subjects of international law, including the bodies of the United Nations, and from which no derogation is possible.

227 In this connection, it must be noted that the Vienna Convention on the Law of Treaties, which consolidates the customary international law and Article 5 of which provides that it is to apply 'to any treaty which is the constituent instrument of an international organisation and to any treaty adopted within an international organisation', provides in Article 53 for a treaty to be void if it conflicts with a peremptory norm of general international law (*jus cogens*), defined as 'a norm accepted and recognised by the international community of States as a whole as a norm from which no derogation is permitted and which can be modified only by a subsequent norm of general international law having the same character'. Similarly, Article 64 of the Vienna Convention provides that: 'If a new peremptory norm of general international law emerges, any existing treaty which is in conflict with that norm becomes void and terminates'.

228 Furthermore, the Charter of the United Nations itself presupposes the existence of mandatory principles of international law, in particular, the protection of the fundamental rights of the human person. In the preamble to the Charter, the peoples

of the United Nations declared themselves determined to 'reaffirm faith in fundamental human rights, in the dignity and worth of the human person'. In addition, it is apparent from Chapter I of the Charter, headed 'Purposes and Principles', that one of the purposes of the United Nations is to encourage respect for human rights and for fundamental freedoms.

229 Those principles are binding on the Members of the United Nations as well as on its bodies. Thus, under Article 24(2) of the Charter of the United Nations, the Security Council, in discharging its duties under its primary responsibility for the maintenance of international peace and security, is to act 'in accordance with the Purposes and Principles of the United Nations'. The Security Council's powers of sanction in the exercise of that responsibility must therefore be wielded in compliance with international law, particularly with the purposes and principles of the United Nations.

230 International law thus permits the inference that there exists one limit to the principle that resolutions of the Security Council have binding effect: namely, that they must observe the fundamental peremptory provisions of *jus cogens*. If they fail to do so, however improbable that may be, they would bind neither the Member States of the United Nations nor, in consequence, the Community.

231 The indirect judicial review carried out by the Court in connection with an action for annulment of a Community act adopted, where no discretion whatsoever may be exercised, with a view to putting into effect a resolution of the Security Council may therefore, highly exceptionally, extend to determining whether the superior rules of international law falling within the ambit of *jus cogens* have been observed, in particular, the mandatory provisions concerning the universal protection of human rights, from which neither the Member States nor the bodies of the United Nations may derogate because they constitute 'intransgressible principles of international customary law' [...].

[...]

258 In this instance, as is apparent from the preliminary observations above on the relationship between the international legal order under the United Nations and the Community legal order, the Community institutions were required to transpose into the Community legal order resolutions of the Security Council and decisions of the Sanctions Committee that in no way authorised them, at the time of actual implementation, to provide for any Community mechanism whatsoever for the examination or re-examination of individual situations, since both the substance of the measures in question and the mechanisms for re-examination [...] fell wholly within the purview of the Security Council and its Sanctions Committee. As a result, the Community institutions had no power of investigation, no opportunity to check the matters taken to be facts by the Security Council and the Sanctions Committee, no discretion with regard to those matters and no discretion either as to whether it was appropriate to adopt sanctions vis-à-vis the applicants. The principle of Community law relating to the right to be heard cannot apply in such circumstances, where to hear the person concerned could not in any case lead the institution to review its position.

[...]

267 Admittedly, the [UN] procedure ... confers no right directly on the persons concerned themselves to be heard by the Sanctions Committee, the only authority competent to give a decision, on a State's petition, on the re-examination of their

case. Those persons are thus dependent, essentially, on the diplomatic protection afforded by the States to their nationals.

268 Such a restriction of the right to be heard, directly and in person, by the competent authority is not, however, to be deemed improper in the light of the mandatory prescriptions of the public international order [...]

[...]

283 [...] it is not for the Court to review indirectly whether the Security Council's resolutions in question are themselves compatible with fundamental rights as protected by the Community legal order.

284 Nor does it fall to the Court to verify that there has been no error of assessment of the facts and evidence relied on by the Security Council in support of the measures it has taken or [...] to check indirectly the appropriateness and proportionality of those measures. It would be impossible to carry out such a check without trespassing on the Security Council's prerogatives under Chapter VII of the Charter of the United Nations in relation to determining, first, whether there exists a threat to international peace and security and, second, the appropriate measures for confronting or settling such a threat. Moreover, the question whether an individual or organisation poses a threat to international peace and security, like the question of what measures must be adopted vis-à-vis the persons concerned in order to frustrate that threat, entails a political assessment and value judgments which in principle fall within the exclusive competence of the authority to which the international community has entrusted primary responsibility for the maintenance of international peace and security.

285 It must thus be concluded that [...] there is no judicial remedy available to the applicant, the Security Council not having thought it advisable to establish an independent international court responsible for ruling, in law and on the facts, in actions brought against individual decisions taken by the Sanctions Committee.

286 However, it is also to be acknowledged that any such lacuna in the judicial protection available to the applicant is not in itself contrary to *jus cogens*.

287 Here the Court would point out that the right of access to the courts, a principle recognised by both Article 8 of the Universal Declaration of Human Rights and Article 14 of the International Covenant on Civil and Political Rights ... is not absolute. On the one hand, at a time of public emergency which threatens the life of the nation, measures may be taken derogating from that right, as provided for on certain conditions by Article 4(1) of that Covenant. On the other hand, even where those exceptional circumstances do not obtain, certain restrictions must be held to be inherent in that right, such as the limitations generally recognised by the community of nations to fall within the doctrine of State immunity [...] and of the immunity of international organisations [...].

288 In this instance, the Court considers that the limitation of the applicant's right of access to a court, as a result of the immunity from jurisdiction enjoyed as a rule, in the domestic legal order of the Member States of the United Nations, by resolutions of the Security Council adopted under Chapter VII of the Charter of the United Nations, in accordance with the relevant principles of international law (in particular Articles 25 and 103 of the Charter), is inherent in that right as it is guaranteed by *jus cogens*.

289 Such a limitation is justified both by the nature of the decisions that the Security Council is led to take under Chapter VII of the Charter of the United Nations and by the legitimate objective pursued. In the circumstances of this case, the applicant's interest in having a court hear his case on its merits is not enough to outweigh the essential public interest in the maintenance of international peace and security in the face of a threat clearly identified by the Security Council in accordance with the Charter of the United Nations. In this regard, special significance must attach to the fact that, far from providing for measures for an unlimited period of application, the resolutions successively adopted by the Security Council have always provided a mechanism for re-examining whether it is appropriate to maintain those measures after 12 or 18 months at most have elapsed [...].

290 Last, the Court considers that, in the absence of an international court having jurisdiction to ascertain whether acts of the Security Council are lawful, the setting-up of a body such as the Sanctions Committee and the opportunity, provided for by the legislation, of applying at any time to that committee in order to have any individual case re-examined, by means of a procedure involving both the 'petitioned government' and the 'designating government' [...], constitute another reasonable method of affording adequate protection of the applicant's fundamental rights as recognised by *jus cogens*.

[...]

B. Kadi I ECJ

[Kadi appealed the CFI decision in *Kadi I*, arguing that the contested Regulation should be annulled, among others, on grounds of error of law in the CFI's interpretation of relevant principles of international law and in its assessment of the violation of his fundamental human rights.]

[...]

280 The Court will now consider the heads of claim in which the appellants complain that the Court of First Instance, in essence, held that it followed from the principles governing the relationship between the international legal order under the United Nations and the Community legal order that the contested regulation, since it is designed to give effect to a resolution adopted by the Security Council under Chapter VII of the Charter of the United Nations affording no latitude in that respect, could not be subject to judicial review of its internal lawfulness, save with regard to its compatibility with the norms of *jus cogens*, and therefore to that extent enjoyed immunity from jurisdiction.

281 In this connection it is to be borne in mind that the Community is based on the rule of law, inasmuch as neither its Member States nor its institutions can avoid review of the conformity of their acts with the basic constitutional charter, the EC Treaty, which established a complete system of legal remedies and procedures designed to enable the Court of Justice to review the legality of acts of the institutions [...].

282 It is also to be recalled that an international agreement cannot affect the allocation of powers fixed by the Treaties or, consequently, the autonomy of the Community legal system, observance of which is ensured by the Court by virtue of the exclusive

jurisdiction conferred on it by Article 220 EC, jurisdiction that the Court has, moreover, already held to form part of the very foundations of the Community [...].

283 In addition, according to settled case-law, fundamental rights form an integral part of the general principles of law whose observance the Court ensures. For that purpose, the Court draws inspiration from the constitutional traditions common to the Member States and from the guidelines supplied by international instruments for the protection of human rights on which the Member States have collaborated or to which they are signatories. In that regard, the ECHR has special significance [...].

284 It is also clear from the case-law that respect for human rights is a condition of the lawfulness of Community acts [...] and that measures incompatible with respect for human rights are not acceptable in the Community [...].

285 It follows from all those considerations that the obligations imposed by an international agreement cannot have the effect of prejudicing the constitutional principles of the EC Treaty, which include the principle that all Community acts must respect fundamental rights, that respect constituting a condition of their lawfulness which it is for the Court to review in the framework of the complete system of legal remedies established by the Treaty.

286 In this regard it must be emphasised that, in circumstances such as those of these cases, the review of lawfulness thus to be ensured by the Community judicature applies to the Community act intended to give effect to the international agreement at issue, and not to the latter as such.

287 With more particular regard to a Community act which, like the contested regulation, is intended to give effect to a resolution adopted by the Security Council under Chapter VII of the Charter of the United Nations, it is not, therefore, for the Community judicature, under the exclusive jurisdiction provided for by Article 220 EC, to review the lawfulness of such a resolution adopted by an international body, even if that review were to be limited to examination of the compatibility of that resolution with *jus cogens*.

288 However, any judgment given by the Community judicature deciding that a Community measure intended to give effect to such a resolution is contrary to a higher rule of law in the Community legal order would not entail any challenge to the primacy of that resolution in international law.

[...]

290 It must therefore be considered whether, as the Court of First Instance held, as a result of the principles governing the relationship between the international legal order under the United Nations and the Community legal order, any judicial review of the internal lawfulness of the contested regulation in the light of fundamental freedoms is in principle excluded, notwithstanding the fact that [...] such review is a constitutional guarantee forming part of the very foundations of the Community.

291 In this respect it is first to be borne in mind that the European Community must respect international law in the exercise of its powers [...] the Court having in addition stated [...] that a measure adopted by virtue of those powers must be interpreted, and its scope limited, in the light of the relevant rules of international law.

[...]

293 Observance of the undertakings given in the context of the United Nations is required [...] in the sphere of the maintenance of international peace and security when the Community gives effect, by means of the adoption of Community

measures taken on the basis of Articles 60 EC and 301 EC, to resolutions adopted by the Security Council under Chapter VII of the Charter of the United Nations.

294 In the exercise of that latter power it is necessary for the Community to attach special importance to the fact that, in accordance with Article 24 of the Charter of the United Nations, the adoption by the Security Council of resolutions under Chapter VII of the Charter constitutes the exercise of the primary responsibility with which that international body is invested for the maintenance of peace and security at the global level, a responsibility which, under Chapter VII, includes the power to determine what and who poses a threat to international peace and security and to take the measures necessary to maintain or restore them.

[...]

298 It must however be noted that the Charter of the United Nations does not impose the choice of a particular model for the implementation of resolutions adopted by the Security Council under Chapter VII of the Charter, since they are to be given effect in accordance with the procedure applicable in that respect in the domestic legal order of each Member of the United Nations. The Charter of the United Nations leaves the Members of the United Nations a free choice among the various possible models for transposition of those resolutions into their domestic legal order.

299 It follows from all those considerations that it is not a consequence of the principles governing the international legal order under the United Nations that any judicial review of the internal lawfulness of the contested regulation in the light of fundamental freedoms is excluded by virtue of the fact that that measure is intended to give effect to a resolution of the Security Council adopted under Chapter VII of the Charter of the United Nations.

300 What is more, such immunity from jurisdiction for a Community measure like the contested regulation, as a corollary of the principle of the primacy at the level of international law of obligations under the Charter of the United Nations, especially those relating to the implementation of resolutions of the Security Council adopted under Chapter VII of the Charter, cannot find a basis in the EC Treaty.

[...]

305 Nor can an immunity from jurisdiction for the contested regulation with regard to the review of its compatibility with fundamental rights, arising from the alleged absolute primacy of the resolutions of the Security Council to which that measure is designed to give effect, find any basis in the place that obligations under the Charter of the United Nations would occupy in the hierarchy of norms within the Community legal order if those obligations were to be classified in that hierarchy.

[...]

307 [...] by virtue of [art. 300(7) EC], supposing it to be applicable to the Charter of the United Nations, the latter would have primacy over acts of secondary Community law [...].

308 That primacy at the level of Community law would not, however, extend to primary law, in particular to the general principles of which fundamental rights form part.

[...]

316 [...] the review by the Court of the validity of any Community measure in the light of fundamental rights must be considered to be the expression, in a community

based on the rule of law, of a constitutional guarantee stemming from the EC Treaty as an autonomous legal system which is not to be prejudiced by an international agreement.

317 The question of the Court's jurisdiction arises in the context of the internal and autonomous legal order of the Community, within whose ambit the contested regulation falls and in which the Court has jurisdiction to review the validity of Community measures in the light of fundamental rights.

318 It has in addition been maintained that, having regard to the deference required of the Community institutions vis-à-vis the institutions of the United Nations, the Court must forgo the exercise of any review of the lawfulness of the contested regulation in the light of fundamental rights, even if such review were possible, given that, under the system of sanctions set up by the United Nations, having particular regard to the re-examination procedure which has recently been significantly improved by various resolutions of the Security Council, fundamental rights are adequately protected.

319 According to the Commission, so long as under that system of sanctions the individuals or entities concerned have an acceptable opportunity to be heard through a mechanism of administrative review forming part of the United Nations legal system, the Court must not intervene in any way whatsoever.[...]

321 [...] the existence, within that United Nations system, of the re-examination procedure before the Sanctions Committee, even having regard to the amendments recently made to it, cannot give rise to generalised immunity from jurisdiction within the internal legal order of the Community.

322 Indeed, such immunity, constituting a significant derogation from the scheme of judicial protection of fundamental rights laid down by the EC Treaty, appears unjustified, for clearly that re-examination procedure does not offer the guarantees of judicial protection.

323 In that regard, although it is now open to any person or entity to approach the Sanctions Committee directly, submitting a request to be removed from the summary list at what is called the 'focal' point, the fact remains that the procedure before that Committee is still in essence diplomatic and intergovernmental, the persons or entities concerned having no real opportunity of asserting their rights and that committee taking its decisions by consensus, each of its members having a right of veto.

[...]

326 It follows from the foregoing that the Community judicature must, in accordance with the powers conferred on it by the EC Treaty, ensure the review, in principle the full review, of the lawfulness of all Community acts in the light of the fundamental rights forming an integral part of the general principles of Community law, including review of Community measures which, like the contested regulation, are designed to give effect to the resolutions adopted by the Security Council under Chapter VII of the Charter of the United Nations.

[...]

[The Court then proceeded to annul the Regulation for infringement of Kadi's right to effective judicial protection and right to property as guaranteed by the EU legal order.]

C. Kadi II GCEU

[Upon Kadi's renewed subjection to the sanctions by a fresh Regulation in the wake of *Kadi I ECJ*, Kadi brought a challenge against that Regulation before the now renamed General Court.]

[...]

113 The institutions and intervening governments have [...] forcefully reiterated in these proceedings the concerns—already expressed by them in the case culminating in the judgment of the Court of Justice in *Kadi*—regarding the risk that the system of sanctions put in place by the United Nations in the context of the fight against international terrorism would be disrupted if judicial review of the kind advocated by the applicant in the light of the judgment of the Court of Justice in *Kadi* were instituted at national or regional level.

114 It is true that, once it is accepted that the Security Council has inherent competence to adopt sanctions targeted at individuals rather than at States or their governments (smart sanctions), such judicial review is liable to encroach on the Security Council's prerogatives, in particular with regard to determining who or what constitutes a threat to international peace or security, to finding that such a threat exists and to determining the measures necessary to put an end to it.

115 More fundamentally, certain doubts may have been voiced in legal circles as to whether the judgment of the Court of Justice in *Kadi* is wholly consistent with, on the one hand, international law and, more particularly, Articles 25 and 103 of the Charter of the United Nations and, on the other hand, the EC and EU Treaties [...]

116 In that regard, it has in particular been asserted that, even though the Court of Justice stated [...] that it was not for the Community judicature [...] to review the legality of a resolution adopted by the Security Council under Chapter VII of the Charter of the United Nations, the fact remains that a review of the legality of a Community act which merely implements, at Community level, a resolution affording no latitude in that respect necessarily amounts to a review, in the light of the rules and principles of the Community legal order, of the legality of the resolution thereby implemented.

117 It has, moreover, been observed that [...] the Court of Justice in any event carried out a review of the conformity of the system of sanctions set up by the United Nations with the system of judicial protection of fundamental rights laid down by the EC Treaty and did so in response to the Commission's argument that those fundamental rights were now sufficiently protected in the framework of the system of sanctions, in view in particular of the improvement in the re-examination procedure which afforded the individuals and entities concerned an acceptable opportunity to be heard by the Sanctions Committee. In particular, the Court of Justice held [...] that the re-examination procedure 'clearly [...] [did] not offer the guarantees of judicial protection' and that the individuals or entities concerned 'had no real opportunity of asserting their rights'.

118 Likewise, although the Court of Justice asserted [...] that any judgment of the Community judicature holding a Community measure intended to give effect to such a resolution to be contrary to a higher rule of law in the Community legal order would not entail any challenge to the primacy of that resolution in international law,

it has been pointed out that the necessary consequence of such a judgment—by virtue of which the Community measure in question is annulled—would be to render that primacy ineffective in the Community legal order.

[...]

121 The General Court acknowledges that those criticisms are not entirely without foundation. However, with regard to their relevance, it takes the view that, in circumstances such as those of the present case—which concerns a measure adopted by the Commission to replace an earlier measure annulled by the Court of Justice in an appeal against the judgment of this Court dismissing an action for annulment of the earlier measure—the appellate principle itself and the hierarchical judicial structure which is its corollary generally advise against the General Court revisiting points of law which have been decided by the Court of Justice. That is *a fortiori* the case when, as here, the Court of Justice was sitting in Grand Chamber formation and clearly intended to deliver a judgment establishing certain principles. Accordingly, if an answer is to be given to the questions raised by the institutions, Member States and interested legal quarters following the judgment of the Court of Justice in *Kadi*, it is for the Court of Justice itself to provide that answer in the context of future cases before it.

122 It should be observed, as an ancillary point, that, although some higher national courts have adopted a rather similar approach to that taken by this Court in its judgment in *Kadi* [...], others have tended to follow the approach taken by the Court of Justice, holding the Sanctions Committee's system of designation to be incompatible with the fundamental right to effective review before an independent and impartial court [...].

123 If the intensity and extent of judicial review were limited in the way advocated by the Commission and the intervening governments [...] and by the Council [...], there would be no effective judicial review of the kind required by the Court of Justice in *Kadi* but rather a simulacrum thereof. That would amount, in fact, to following the same approach as that taken by this Court in its own judgment in *Kadi*, which was held by the Court of Justice on appeal to be vitiated by an error of law. The General Court considers that in principle it falls not to it but to the Court of Justice to reverse precedent in that way, if it were to consider this to be justified in light, in particular, of the serious difficulties to which the institutions and intervening governments have referred.

124 It is true [...] that the Court of Justice recalled in *Kadi* that the Community must respect international law in the exercise of its powers [...] that observance of the undertakings given in the context of the United Nations is required in the sphere of the maintenance of international peace and security when the Community gives effect, by means of the adoption of Community measures [...] to resolutions adopted by the Security Council under Chapter VII of the Charter of the United Nations [...] that in the exercise of that latter power it is necessary for the Community to attach special importance to the fact that, in accordance with Article 24 of the Charter of the United Nations, the adoption by the Security Council of such resolutions constitutes the exercise of the primary responsibility with which that international body is invested for the maintenance of peace and security at the global level, a responsibility which, under Chapter VII, includes the power to determine what and who poses a threat to international peace and security and to take the measures necessary

to maintain or restore them [...] and that, in drawing up measures implementing a resolution of the Security Council under Chapter VII of the Charter of the United Nations, the Community must take due account of the terms and objectives of the resolution concerned and of the relevant obligations under the Charter of the United Nations relating to such implementation [...].

125 The fact remains that the Court of Justice also stated, in *Kadi*, that the implementation of resolutions adopted by the Security Council under Chapter VII of the Charter of the United Nations must be undertaken in accordance with the procedure applicable in that respect in the domestic legal order of each Member of the United Nations [...], that it is not a consequence of the principles governing the international legal order under the United Nations that any judicial review of the internal lawfulness of a Community measure such as the contested regulation in the light of fundamental freedoms is excluded by virtue of the fact that that measure is intended to give effect to such a resolution [...], that such immunity from jurisdiction for such a measure cannot find a basis in the EC Treaty [...], that the review, by the Court of Justice, of the validity of any Community measure in the light of fundamental rights must be considered to be the expression, in a community based on the rule of law, of a constitutional guarantee stemming from the EC Treaty as an autonomous legal system which is not to be prejudiced by an 'international agreement' [...], and that accordingly 'the Community judicature must, in accordance with the powers conferred on it by the EC Treaty, ensure the review, in principle the full review, of the lawfulness of all Community acts in the light of the fundamental rights forming an integral part of the general principles of Community law, including review of Community measures which [...] are designed to give effect to the resolutions adopted by the Security Council under Chapter VII of the Charter of the United Nations' [...].

126 The General Court therefore concludes that, in circumstances such as those of this case, its task is to ensure [...] 'in principle the full review' of the lawfulness of the contested regulation in the light of fundamental rights, without affording the regulation any immunity from jurisdiction on the ground that it gives effect to resolutions adopted by the Security Council under Chapter VII of the Charter of the United Nations.

127 That must remain the case, at the very least, so long as the re-examination procedure operated by the Sanctions Committee clearly fails to offer guarantees of effective judicial protection [...]

128 The considerations in this respect, set out by the Court of Justice [in] *Kadi*, in particular with regard to the focal point, remain fundamentally valid today, even if account is taken of the 'Office of the Ombudsperson', the creation of which was decided in principle by Resolution 1904 (2009) and which has very recently been set up. In essence, the Security Council has still not deemed it appropriate to establish an independent and impartial body responsible for hearing and determining, as regards matters of law and fact, actions against individual decisions taken by the Sanctions Committee. Furthermore, neither the focal point mechanism nor the Office of the Ombudsperson affects the principle that removal of a person from the Sanctions Committee's list requires consensus within the committee. Moreover, the evidence which may be disclosed to the person concerned continues to be a matter entirely at the discretion of the State which proposed that he be included on the Sanctions

Committee's list and there is no mechanism to ensure that sufficient information be made available to the person concerned in order to allow him to defend himself effectively (he need not even be informed of the identity of the State which has requested his inclusion on the Sanctions Committee's list). For those reasons at least, the creation of the focal point and the Office of the Ombudsperson cannot be equated with the provision of an effective judicial procedure for review of decisions of the Sanctions Committee [...].

129 In those circumstances, the review carried out by the Community judicature of Community measures to freeze funds can be regarded as effective only if it concerns, indirectly, the substantive assessments of the Sanctions Committee itself and the evidence underlying them [...].

[The General Court then applied the high standard of 'full review' of the contested regulation and annulled it for violation of Kadi's right to effective judicial protection and right to property.]

D. Kadi II CJEU

[The decision of the GCEU in *Kadi II* was eventually appealed by the EU institutions before the CJEU, whose Grand Chamber provided the closing act to the *Kadi* saga. First the CJEU confirmed that the Regulation could not be afforded any immunity from jurisdiction on the ground that its objective is to implement resolutions adopted by the Security Council under Chapter VII of the UN Charter. The Court then went on to consider the question of the standard of review.]

[...]

103 In this case, it is necessary to determine whether, in the light of the requirements [of EU law] relating to the maintenance of international peace and security while respecting international law, and specifically the principles of the Charter of the United Nations, the fact that Mr Kadi and the Courts of the European Union did not have access to the information and evidence relied on against him, to which the General Court draws attention [...] constitutes an infringement of the rights of the defence and the right to effective judicial protection.

104 In that regard [...] it must be emphasised that, in accordance with Article 24 of the Charter of the United Nations, the Security Council has been invested by the members of the UN with the primary responsibility for the maintenance of international peace and security. To that end, it is the task of the Security Council to determine what constitutes a threat to international peace and security and to take the measures necessary, by means of the adoption of resolutions under Chapter VII of that Charter, to maintain or restore international peace and security, in accordance with the purposes and principles of the United Nations, including respect for human rights.

105 In that context, as is apparent from the resolutions [...] governing the regime of restrictive measures such as those at issue in this case, it is the task of the Sanctions Committee, on the proposal of a UN member supported by a 'statement of case' which should provide 'as much detail as possible on the basis(es) for the listing', the 'nature of the information' and 'supporting information or documents that can be provided', to designate, applying the criteria laid down by the Security Council, the organisations,

entities and individuals whose funds and other economic resources are to be frozen. That designation, put into effect by the listing of the name of the organisation, entity or individual concerned on the Sanctions Committee Consolidated List which is maintained at the request of the Member States of the UN, is to be based on a 'summary of reasons' which is to be produced by the Sanctions Committee in the light of the material which the Member State proposing the listing has identified as capable of disclosure, particularly to the party concerned, and which is to be made accessible on its website.

106 When the European Union implements Security Council resolutions adopted under Chapter VII of the Charter of the United Nations [...] the competent European Union authority must take due account of the terms and objectives of the resolution concerned and of the relevant obligations under that Charter relating to such implementation [...].

107 Consequently, where, under the relevant Security Council resolutions, the Sanctions Committee has decided to list the name of an organisation, entity or individual on its Consolidated List, the competent European Union authority must, in order to give effect to that decision on behalf of the Member States, take the decision to list the name of that organisation, entity or individual, or to maintain such listing [...] on the basis of the summary of reasons provided by the Sanctions Committee. On the other hand, there is no provision in those resolutions to the effect that the Sanctions Committee is automatically to make available to, in particular, the European Union authority responsible for the adoption by the European Union of its decision to list or maintain a listing, any material other than that summary of reasons.

[...]

109 In the particular case of Mr Kadi, it is apparent from the file that the initial listing of his name, on 17 October 2001 in the Sanctions Committee Consolidated List followed a request by the United States on the basis of the adoption on 12 October 2001 of a decision in which the Office of Foreign Asset Control identified Mr Kadi as a 'Specially Designated Global Terrorist'.

110 As is apparent from recital 3 of the preamble to the contested regulation [...] following the *Kadi* judgment the Commission, by means of that regulation, decided to maintain the name of Mr Kadi on the list [...] on the basis of the narrative summaries of reasons which had been transmitted by the Sanctions Committee. As the General Court recorded [...] and as the Commission confirmed at the hearing before the Court, the Commission was not, for that purpose, put in possession of evidence other than such a summary of reasons.

111 In proceedings relating to the adoption of the decision to list or maintain the listing of the name of an individual [...] respect for the rights of the defence and the right to effective judicial protection requires that the competent Union authority disclose to the individual concerned the evidence against that person available to that authority and relied on as the basis of its decision, that is to say, at the very least, the summary of reasons provided by the Sanctions Committee [...] so that that individual is in a position to defend his rights in the best possible conditions and to decide, with full knowledge of the relevant facts, whether there is any point in bringing an action before the Courts of the European Union.

[...]

119 The effectiveness of the judicial review guaranteed by Article 47 of the Charter [of Fundamental Rights] also requires that, as part of the review of the lawfulness of the grounds which are the basis of the decision to list or to maintain the listing of a given person [...] the Courts of the European Union are to ensure that that decision, which affects that person individually [...] is taken on a sufficiently solid factual basis [...]. That entails a verification of the factual allegations in the summary of reasons underpinning that decision [...], with the consequence that judicial review cannot be restricted to an assessment of the cogency in the abstract of the reasons relied on, but must concern whether those reasons, or, at the very least, one of those reasons, deemed sufficient in itself to support that decision, is substantiated.

120 To that end, it is for the Courts of the European Union, in order to carry out that examination, to request the competent European Union authority, when necessary, to produce information or evidence, confidential or not, relevant to such an examination [...].

121 That is because it is the task of the competent European Union authority to establish, in the event of challenge, that the reasons relied on against the person concerned are well founded, and not the task of that person to adduce evidence of the negative, that those reasons are not well founded.

122 For that purpose, there is no requirement that that authority produce before the Courts of the European Union all the information and evidence underlying the reasons alleged in the summary provided by the Sanctions Committee. It is however necessary that the information or evidence produced should support the reasons relied on against the person concerned.

123 If the competent European Union authority finds itself unable to comply with the request by the Courts of the European Union, it is then the duty of those Courts to base their decision solely on the material which has been disclosed to them, namely, in this case, the indications contained in the narrative summary of reasons provided by the Sanctions Committee, the observations and exculpatory evidence that may have been produced by the person concerned and the response of the competent European Union authority to those observations. If that material is insufficient to allow a finding that a reason is well founded, the Courts of the European Union shall disregard that reason as a possible basis for the contested decision to list or maintain a listing.

124 If, on the other hand, the competent European Union authority provides relevant information or evidence, the Courts of the European Union must then determine whether the facts alleged are made out in the light of that information or evidence and assess the probative value of that information or evidence in the circumstances of the particular case and in the light of any observations submitted in relation to them by, among others, the person concerned.

125 Admittedly, overriding considerations to do with the security of the European Union or of its Member States or with the conduct of their international relations may preclude the disclosure of some information or some evidence to the person concerned. In such circumstances, it is none the less the task of the Courts of the European Union, before whom the secrecy or confidentiality of that information or evidence is no valid objection, to apply, in the course of the judicial review to be carried out, techniques which accommodate, on the one hand, legitimate security considerations about the nature and sources of information taken into account in the

adoption of the act concerned and, on the other, the need sufficiently to guarantee to an individual respect for his procedural rights, such as the right to be heard and the requirement for an adversarial process [...].

[...]

130 Having regard to the preventive nature of the restrictive measures at issue, if, in the course of its review of the lawfulness of the contested decision [...] the Courts of the European Union consider that, at the very least, one of the reasons mentioned in the summary provided by the Sanctions Committee is sufficiently detailed and specific, that it is substantiated and that it constitutes in itself sufficient basis to support that decision, the fact that the same cannot be said of other such reasons cannot justify the annulment of that decision. In the absence of one such reason, the Courts of the European Union will annul the contested decision.

131 Such a judicial review is indispensable to ensure a fair balance between the maintenance of international peace and security and the protection of the fundamental rights and freedoms of the person concerned [...], those being shared values of the UN and the European Union.

132 Notwithstanding their preventive nature, the restrictive measures at issue have, as regards those rights and freedoms, a substantial negative impact related, first, to the serious disruption of the working and family life of the person concerned due to the restrictions on the exercise of his right to property which stem from their general scope combined, as in this case, with the actual duration of their application, and, on the other, the public opprobrium and suspicion of that person which those measures provoke [...].

133 Such a review is all the more essential since, despite the improvements added, in particular after the adoption of the contested regulation, the procedure for delisting and *ex officio* re-examination at UN level they do not provide to the person whose name is listed [...] the guarantee of effective judicial protection, as the European Court of Human Rights, endorsing the assessment of the Federal Supreme Court of Switzerland, has recently stated in paragraph 211 of its judgment of 12 September 2012, *Nada* v. *Switzerland* [...].

134 The essence of effective judicial protection must be that it should enable the person concerned to obtain a declaration from a court, by means of a judgment ordering annulment whereby the contested measure is retroactively erased from the legal order and is deemed never to have existed, that the listing of his name, or the continued listing of his name, on the list concerned was vitiated by illegality, the recognition of which may re-establish the reputation of that person or constitute for him a form of reparation for the non-material harm he has suffered [...].

[The Court then proceeded to review the merits of the reasons for listing as they had been disclosed, found them lacking, and thus dismissed the appeals.]

IV. Commentary

A. The decisions

All EU court decisions in the *Kadi* saga revolve around the same main issues, though they (a) resolve them in different ways and (b) elaborate on different aspects of them as we move from the first to the second set of cases. In particular, the CFI in *Kadi I* adopts a particular view as to the question of 'normative control' of state organs by international organizations and the question of 'incidental' judicial review, as well as to the question of the relationship between legal orders in a setting of multi-level governance.[10] The ECJ in *Kadi I* takes a different view on the same questions, reversing the decision of the CFI and annulling the contested EU act. The *Kadi II* cases then are an attempt, on the one hand, to have the EU courts reverse the precedent of *Kadi I ECJ*, and on the other, failing such reversal, to materially limit the far-reaching impact of the precedent by seeking to establish a low-intensity standard of review. In what follows, three main issues will be discussed: (i) normative control and judicial review of Security Council decisions; (ii) standard of review; and (iii) internal and external justifications for the decisions in the *Kadi* saga, which result effectively in imposing on EU member states the obligation to disobey Chapter VII sanctions of the Security Council.

(i) Normative control, discretion, and judicial review

When a binding decision of an international organization leaves to its member states—as the 'agents of execution'—no margin of discretion as to its implementation, that is when it imposes a strict obligation, member states are under the effective 'normative' control of the organization.[11] Notwithstanding any arguments for direct attribution of such implementing acts to the organization promulgating the decision (and thus controlling the conduct of UN member states), it remains a possibility that these implementing acts will be concurrently attributed to the member states.[12] The latter has been accepted in practice by numerous courts: the ECtHR in a number of cases such as *Bosphorus*[13] and *Nada*,[14] the Canadian Federal Court in *Abdelrazik*,[15] the UK courts in *Hay*[16] and *HM Treasury v Ahmed and ors*,[17] the Swiss Federal Tribunal in *Nada*,[18] and others. The CFI and ECJ in *Kadi I*, and the GCEU and CJEU in *Kadi II* do the same and assume jurisdiction in order to review the EU act implementing the measures decreed by the Security Council.

However, the fact remains that in such circumstances state conduct is conditioned by the decision of the international organization, so that any review of state conduct by a court will *uno actu* also constitute review of the conduct of the organization. There are many ways in which courts have purported to deal with this situation, in

---

[10] A very similar approach is taken by the Swiss Federal Tribunal in *Nada*, see ch. 4.4, which explicitly endorses the *Kadi I CFI* decision (the only *Kadi* decision made at the time the Federal Tribunal was dealing with the *Nada* case).

[11] See ch. 4.4, section (4)A.(i).

[12] See Articles on the Responsibility of States for Internationally Wrongful Acts, art 4.

[13] *Bosphorus Hava Yollari Turizm ve Ticaret Anonim Sirceti v Ireland*, App No 45036/98 (Grand Chamber).

[14] *Nada v Switzerland*, App No 10593/08 (Grand Chamber).

[15] *Abdelrazik v Canada (Foreign Affairs)*, 2009 FC 580; ILDC 1332 (CA 2009).

[16] *Hay v Her Majesty's Treasury and Secretary of State for Foreign and Commonwealth Affairs* [2009] EWHC 1677 (Admin); ILDC 1367 (UK 2009).

[17] *Her Majesty's Treasury (Respondent) v Mohammed Jabar Ahmed and Others (FC) (Appellants)* [2010] UKSC 2.

[18] *Youssef Nada v State Secretariat for Economic Affairs and Federal Department for Economic Affairs*, Swiss Federal Tribunal, Case No 1A 45/2007, 133 BGE II 450. See further ch. 4.4 in this collection.

particular wishing to avoid any stringent (if indirect) review of the international act. The ECtHR for example has established a doctrine of equivalent protection: if the international organization promulgating the act that requires strict compliance protects human rights on a level equivalent to that of the ECHR, the legality of state conduct taken in implementation is presumed. While the presumption can theoretically be rebutted, this has not happened so far, except in the case of *Al-Dulimi*,[19] which is now pending before the Grand Chamber of the ECtHR.[20]

The CFI in *Kadi I* acknowledged the predicament of having to review Security Council conduct when reviewing member state or EU conduct in implementation, and—wishing also to avoid a stringent (indirect) review—opted for reviewing against the lowest common denominator, that is law binding both on the EU and on the UN when acting through the Security Council. It famously considered such law to be only that part of international law which has reached the status of *jus cogens*.[21] The resulting review of the EU and (indirectly) the Security Council act was of very low intensity. This was in part because of the vagueness of rules of *jus cogens* and in part because finding that the Security Council had violated *jus cogens* would be almost unthinkable.

The ECJ in *Kadi I*, on the other hand, radically rejected the connection between the international and the domestic/regional implementing measure, and went ahead to fully review the domestic measure for compliance with EU law. The ECJ accepted that the EU adopted the impugned domestic measure in order to give effect to a Security Council resolution. But it found that the EU was not limited in the choice of a model of implementation of the obligations enshrined in the resolution. Further, the adoption of the EU measure was an act directly attributable to the Union. As such, the EU courts would review any EU measure in light of fundamental rights guarantees under primary EU law. In the ensuing review, the EU measure was clearly found lacking in these terms, and was annulled. However, the ECJ was a bit disingenuous in *Kadi I*: the obligation to subject Kadi to the sanctions prescribed by the Security Council was strict. This meant that whatever the EU or the member states elected to do in implementing the decision (i.e., whatever 'model of implementation' they 'chose'), they would have had to achieve the outcome of sanctioning Kadi. Any other outcome would constitute a violation of the international obligation to comply with the decision of the Security Council. As expected, the issue came up again in the second round of *Kadi* cases.

In *Kadi II GCEU*, the EU institutions and the intervening states tried to re-invoke the argument that there was nothing they could do except blacklist Kadi, since their conduct was effectively conditioned by the binding Security Council measure, and they had no margin of discretion in the measure's implementation. This time, they tried to present this as an argument in favour of marginal (low intensity) review of the impugned Regulation. Their argument developed as follows: the ECJ said (in *Kadi I*) that it could review the Regulation implementing 1267 sanctions; but there is nothing

---

[19] *Al-Dulimi and Montana Management Inc. v Switzerland*, App No 5809/08, paras 117–21.
[20] See further the *Nada* commentary, ch. 4.4, section (4)A.(iii).
[21] For further analysis see ibid., sections (4)A.(i)–(ii). The CFI's decision in *Kadi* served in part as the inspiration of the Swiss Federal Tribunal's decision in *Nada*.

that the EU or the member states can do if the Security Council wants Kadi black-listed, except communicate to him the summary of the reasons for the listing (generalities and allegations for the most part), give him an opportunity to be heard (of no consequence, as the attempt to question generalities is unlikely to yield results anyway), and then go on and blacklist him as per the Security Council's command. If EU courts are going to review this, they have yet to establish a standard of review; so the institutions and the member states argued for the most marginal review to account for their lack of discretion (i.e. review only for manifest error or abuse of power).

The General Court acknowledged that the 1267 sanctions regime imposes strict obligations—as opposed to the anti-terrorist sanctions regime established under Resolution 1373 (2001), for example, which does not: while it is the Security Council, through the 1267 Sanctions Committee, that determines the natural and legal persons to be targeted by the 1267 sanctions, it is up to UN member states to independently determine the targets of the 1373 sanctions, following the criteria set down by the Security Council. This crucial distinction the GCEU had drawn already in *OMPI*[22] and other cases. It allowed the Court to engage in differentiated control of EU acts under the two regimes: in the first case, it would only review for compliance with *jus cogens*, since the obligation that member states had to implement was strict. In the second case, member states could exercise discretion in selecting targets, and this discretion was fully reviewable for compliance with EU law. But the General Court then conceded that accepting the arguments of the institutions for low intensity marginal review due to lack of EU discretion would be tantamount to reiterating its own (CFI) finding in *Kadi I*, which had already been reversed by the ECJ in *Kadi I*. It then followed the ECJ in rejecting the argument for marginal review, disassociating the international from the domestic measure, and engaging in 'full review' as required by *Kadi I ECJ*.

However, the GCEU only did so 'grudgingly',[23] because it is apparent throughout the judgment that it was not completely comfortable with the ECJ's reasoning in *Kadi I*. As mentioned, while the General Court acknowledged the different scope of the international obligations imposed on member states of the UN under the 1267 and 1373 sanctions regime respectively, it accepted the ECJ's obliteration of this distinction later on. That it did so without being fully convinced is evident both as implicit in the language used by the Court[24] and explicit when the GCEU listed the significant criticisms levelled by scholarship with respect to *Kadi I ECJ*. The Court went on to acknowledge 'that those criticisms are not entirely without foundation'. But given that *Kadi I* was rendered by the ECJ in Grand Chamber formation, that is with the intent of setting down certain principles, 'in principle it falls not to [the General Court] but to the Court of Justice to reverse the precedent'.

---

[22] T-228/02, *Organisation des Modjahedines du peuple d Iran v Council of the European Union* [2006] ECR II-4665, paras 100–2.

[23] Stahlberg (n. 7).

[24] See for example para. 41: 'Notwithstanding Articles 25 and 103 of the Charter of the United Nations … and although it observed … that observance [sic] of the undertakings given in the context of the United Nations was required when the Community gave effect to resolutions adopted by the Security Council under Chapter VII of the Charter, the Court of Justice asserted …'.

Indeed, both the institutions and some member states sought to have the CJEU's Grand Chamber reverse its position in *Kadi II*. The Commission, the Council, and the United Kingdom challenged the GCEU's decision in *Kadi II* essentially on three grounds, which the CJEU dealt with in two sets. The first ground was that the GCEU erred in law in not granting judicial immunity to Kadi's listing by the EU: the EU was under a strict obligation to impose sanctions on Kadi, flowing from the relevant decisions of the Security Council. The EU was allowed no discretion in implementing the measure, and thus the relevant act should be immune from review by the Union's judicature, lest the latter purport to review (indirectly) the decisions of the Security Council. In effect, the appellants launched a direct challenge to *Kadi I*, calling on the Court to reverse the precedent.

Perhaps the first ground of appeal was a long shot for the appellants, and the Court of Justice, which refused to reverse its position, quickly rejected it. It was on the basis of the second and third grounds where the Commission, the Council, and the United Kingdom, supported by numerous interveners, were probably hoping to limit the effects of *Kadi I ECJ*, all the while allowing the CJEU to 'save face' by pretending the precedent still held good. These grounds referred to the standard of review of EU measures implementing Security Council decisions to be applied by EU courts.

(ii) *The standard of review*

Once accepted that the EU courts can review EU acts implementing Security Council decisions, the question of the standard of review poses itself with some force. How strict should the court be in reviewing the implementing act? The CFI in *Kadi I* reasoned that the EU act was not reviewable against EU law, but against those rules of international law only that constitute *jus cogens*. As such it did not have to elaborate any specific standard of review—the rules of *jus cogens* being themselves rather disputed and vague, the review could only be of relatively low intensity. And so it was.

However, once *Kadi I ECJ* established that the EU implementing act is reviewable against EU law, the question became crucial. In *Kadi I*, the ECJ declared that it must ensure 'in principle the full review' of the EU act against EU law, and thus seemed to demand high intensity review. The question became the essential battleground in the *Kadi II* set of cases, where the EU institutions and the member states sought to mitigate the effects of *Kadi I ECJ* by arguing for low intensity review, which would allow for the EU implementing act to stand and would further allow them to continue complying with their obligations under the UN Charter.

The GCEU in *Kadi II* saw through the argument of the institutions and the member states. It opined that limiting the intensity of review would be tantamount to reversing *Kadi I ECJ*, as the ECJ had demanded 'full review', which would give guarantees of effective judicial protection, and thus rejected low intensity review. The question then came up again in *Kadi II CJEU*. The appellants challenged both the standard of review applied by the GCEU, and the manner of its application to the substantive claims by Kadi (violation of the rights of defence, the right of effective judicial protection, and the principle of proportionality as it relates to the protection of property).[25] The CJEU

---

[25] See *Kadi II CJEU*, paras 70 seq.

dealt with these two grounds in one go. In essence, the appellants and interveners again tried to mitigate the impact of EU judicial review of (in effect) Security Council measures, relying on the 'international context' of adoption of the measures and the fact that EU institutions had no discretion under the 1267 regime.

It is worth discussing this argument in some detail. The position taken by the ECJ in *Kadi I* is premised on the formality that EU judicial review does not affect the UN measure. True as that might be, it must be recalled that this move was justified by the ECJ claiming that there was still some discretion in the method in which the EU will implement the sanctions imposed by the Security Council.[26]

This is simply wrong if it is read to mean that the UN legal order necessarily allows discretion in implementing strict obligations: under the 1267 regime, the EU has no discretion whatsoever. As already shown, when the Security Council demands the listing of Kadi, all the EU can do is list Kadi. Should the EU afford Kadi any meaningful opportunity to challenge the listing, the challenge, if accepted, will lead to the EU member states disobeying the Security Council.

The CFI had clearly seen the difference when it compared the 1267 regime with the 1373 regime in *OMPI* in 2006,[27] as discussed above. The 1373 regime demands the imposition of measures, but allows UN member states significant discretion as to the identification of those to be sanctioned. This discretion, the CFI held, must be exercised in accordance with EU law. When there is no discretion, however, there is nothing to review (except compliance with the only law the CFI found binding on the Security Council, that is peremptory norms of international law).

When the ECJ demolished the distinction between the two regimes in its own *Kadi I*, the GCEU assumed, basing itself also on the language of the ECJ in *Kadi I*, that the ECJ wished to apply to 1267 measures a standard of review akin to that applied to 1373 measures (full review, and in fact even stricter than under the 1373 regime, where judicial safeguards also applied at the level of EU member states). This is what it did in *Kadi II GCEU*, and this was what the appellants were challenging in *Kadi II CJEU*: they argued that the GCEU erred in applying such a stringent standard of review; and it did, because it did not take into consideration that the EU institutions had no discretion in implementing 1267 measures. In effect then, the appellants were hoping that the same argument that failed on formal grounds in securing immunity of EU measures from EU judicial scrutiny would now succeed in at least limiting that scrutiny as much as possible.

One of the main arguments of the appellants was that the EU institutions did transmit to Kadi all the evidence in their possession, *in casu* the summary of reasons for listing. This was all they had, so that they could not meaningfully be required to adduce evidence they were not in possession of. The Court of Justice accepted as much but went on to clarify that this does not discharge the obligations of the institutions under EU law: it is the obligation of the competent authority to seek co-operation on the part of the UN and its member states if it appears that further information is required to allow the authority to discharge its duty of stating the specific and concrete

---

[26] See *Kadi I ECJ*, paras 298–9.   [27] *OMPI CFI* (n. 22), particularly paras 97–108.

reasons which justify subjection to restrictive measures. As such, the standard of review applied by EU courts will not only cover the procedural aspects of EU obligations, that is the obligation to transmit reasons for listing and to allow the targeted individual an opportunity to be heard, but will also extend to a substantive review of the reasons offered, that is whether these are sufficiently detailed and specific, whether they rest on a solid factual basis, and generally whether the reasons offered, or at least one of them, is substantiated. If the EU institutions cannot adduce additional evidence, then review will take place on the evidence at hand—since it is for the Union to prove that the reasons are well-founded, not for the individual to prove that they are not. If even one of the reasons stated, albeit in summary form, is substantiated, then the CJEU will not annul the listing.

This rather stringent review is required, according to the Court of Justice, not just because it is 'indispensable to ensure a fair balance between the maintenance of international peace and security and the protection of fundamental rights and freedoms, those being shared values of the UN and the EU', but 'all the more' so because, 'despite the improvements added' by Resolutions 1904 (2009) and 1989 (2011), the procedures at UN level, including the Office of the Ombudsperson, still do not provide the guarantees of 'effective judicial protection'. In this assessment, the CJEU not only explicitly endorses the ECtHR's decision in *Nada*,[28] but also implies that it may tone down its intensity of review should even more robust procedures be adopted at UN level. But it also goes on to tell the UN what the essence of that concept of 'judicial protection' must be.[29]

The Court of Justice then applied these principles to the reasons adduced for Kadi's listing, such as they were.[30] The CJEU took each of the reasons adduced by the EU (in effect, the Security Council), reviewed them in substance, and in light of the comments submitted by Kadi in response, proceeded to find all of them either too vague to be assessed or lacking in substantiation, so as not to be able to justify the restrictive measures.[31] It thus upheld the annulment of the listing, even if it substituted part of the GCEU's reasoning for its own.[32]

(iii) Internal and external justifications for disobedience of the Security Council

The outcome of the approach of the EU courts in *Kadi I ECJ* and in both *Kadi II GCEU* and *Kadi II CJEU*, is that by striking down the EU implementing act, they force the (now) twenty-eight member states of the EU to violate their obligations under the UN Charter. This extreme result requires, to say the least, some justification. The decisions of the EU courts do not (explicitly) provide any such justification. They pretend that the decisions in no way result in a breach of international law on the part of the EU or its member states. This argument, however, does not hold water.

From the perspective of international law, the annulment of the domestic implementing measures (*in casu* the EU Regulations) clearly results in the breach of the

---

[28] *Nada*, ECtHR (n. 14).   [29] See *Kadi II CJEU*, para. 134.   [30] Ibid., paras 137, 140 seq.
[31] Ibid., paras 141 seq.   [32] Ibid., paras 163–4.

international obligation of member states under art. 25 of the UN Charter. This was in fact raised by the EU institutions and by the (intervening) member states at all stages in both *Kadi I* and *Kadi II*. The annulment forces member states to disobey the Security Council decision, lest they disobey the decision of their own court(s).

One implicit justification for this extreme result on the part of the EU courts is the so-called *Solange* argument.[33] In situations where strict binding decisions can be made at various levels of governance (international, regional, domestic), there is significant potential for conflict between those various levels and the partial legal orders they represent. This is the case, in particular, when the power to impose certain restrictive measures on individuals has been conferred from one level to another, without similar safeguards being put on the exercise of the conferred power.[34]

When a case comes before the court of the legal order that has conferred the relevant power, a reaction is to be expected. This has so far generally taken the shape of the 'Solange argument', enunciated by the German Federal Constitutional Court when attempting to define the relationship between German constitutional law and acts of the European (Economic as it then was) Community, first in the 1970s,[35] and then modified in the 1980s.[36] A much simplified version of the argument runs thus: for as long as the exercise of the conferred powers on the (different or higher) level of governance takes place without safeguards similar to those to which it was subject before the conferral, when it was still exercised at the (lower) level, the court of the (lower) level will review the act of the (higher) level for compliance with the safeguards at the (lower) level (*Solange I*). When such safeguards are adopted at the (higher) level, the court at the (lower) level will desist, presuming conformity (*Solange II*).

The *Solange* argument has also been adopted by the ECtHR, but in its *Solange II* incarnation through the immediate acceptance of existence of equivalent protection. The *Solange* argument cuts both ways, as it may serve not as a tool for resistance—as *Solange I*, but also as a method to water down human rights protection—as *Solange II*. Its impact, this time as *Solange I*, was also clear both in the UK Supreme Court's *HM Treasury v Ahmed and ors*[37] and in *Kadi I ECJ*. In *Kadi II* the General Court of the EU was as explicit as it could be: it stated that it must ensure the 'full review' of the domestic implementing measure for compliance with fundamental rights (guaranteed under EU law), 'without affording [the measure] any immunity from jurisdiction on the ground that it gives effect to resolutions adopted by the Security Council under Chapter VII of the Charter of the United Nations'.[38] 'That must remain the case', the Court continued, 'at the very least, so long as (=*solange*) the re-examination procedure

[33] On the impact of the *Solange* jurisprudence of the German Federal Constitutional Court see generally A. Tzanakopoulos, 'Judicial Dialogue in Multi-Level Governance: The Impact of the *Solange* Argument' in O.K. Fauchald and A. Nollkaemper (eds), *The Practice of International and National Courts and the (De-)Fragmentation of International Law* (Oxford, Hart 2012) pp. 185–215.

[34] On conferral of sovereign powers by states to international organizations see generally D. Sarooshi, *International Organisations and their Exercise of Sovereign Powers* (Oxford, Oxford University Press 2007).

[35] *Solange I* [1974] 37 BVerfGE 271.   [36] *Solange II* [1986] 73 BVerfGE 339.
[37] *Ahmed and ors v HM Treasury* (n. 17).   [38] *Kadi II GCEU*, para. 126.

operated by the Sanctions Committee clearly fails to offer guarantees of effective judicial protection'.[39]

The *Solange* argument cannot, in and of itself, provide any justification for disobeying the Security Council under international law. This is because the decision to disobey is based on domestic law considerations: here on primary EU law on fundamental rights, otherwise (e.g. in the UK Supreme Court's *Ahmed and ors*)[40] on constitutionally protected fundamental rights. As such, it can only serve as some sort of 'internal' justification for disobedience, demonstrating that the court is justified in protecting fundamental human rights.

However, it can be argued that the fundamental rights customarily relied upon in *Solange*-type argumentation (leading to disobedience) are not solely guaranteed under domestic law, but are 'consubstantial' (i.e. they have the same or similar substance) with internationally protected human rights, such as those protected under the ECHR or the ICCPR.[41] This is the case in particular for the right to effective judicial review, otherwise cast as an aspect of the right to a fair trial. The 'consubstantial' nature of these rights is evident in the analysis of all rights under 'primary EU law' by EU courts, which regularly refer, even in the cases at hand, to both the ECHR and the ICCPR, and relevant case-law thereunder.

This then perhaps allows for an 'external' justification to be construed on the basis of international law. Elsewhere,[42] I have argued that court-imposed disobedience could qualify as a countermeasure against the Security Council's (i.e. the UN's) wrongful imposition of sanctions. This argument cannot be set out fully here, but should be borne in mind when considering potential justifications for the disobedience of international organization-imposed obligations which is forced upon states by court decisions such as those in *Kadi I* and *II*. More important than these justifications, however, are the real-life repercussions of the *Kadi I* and *II* decisions. The next subsection deals with their actual aftermath.

B. The aftermath

Each of the *Kadi* decisions had significant implications for Security Council sanctions under Chapter VII of the UN Charter and for the impact of acts of international organizations in domestic legal orders in general. The *Kadi I CFI* decision established a difficult *modus vivendi* which safeguarded the effect of UN Security Council decisions while giving some semblance of human rights supervision. It was taken up by other courts, notably the Swiss Federal Tribunal in *Nada*, and it sent a signal to the UN and its member states that sanctions had started to impact human rights too severely for courts to remain completely silent on the matter.

---

[39] Ibid., para. 127.   [40] *Ahmed* (n. 17).
[41] For the term see A. Tzanakopoulos, 'Domestic Courts in International Law: The International Judicial Function of National Courts' (2011) 34 *Loyola of Los Angeles International & Comparative Law Review* 133, 143.
[42] See A. Tzanakopoulos, *Disobeying the Security Council: Countermeasures Against Wrongful Sanctions* (Oxford, Oxford University Press 2011), ch. 7.

Originally, for example, those targeted by the 1267 and other sanctions regimes could not seek to be removed from the sanctions lists. This power was reserved for member states, in particular the targeted person's state of residence or nationality. But *Kadi I CFI* and its adoption by other courts led the Security Council to establish a Focal Point, where those targeted by the sanctions could petition the Security Council, in their own name and not through their state of residence or nationality, to be removed from the list.[43] But this improvement was to be considered inadequate as sanctions continued to extend in time.

The breaking point, the crossing of the Rubicon, was *Kadi I ECJ*, which forced member states to seek to considerably improve the sanctions regimes established by the Security Council, and which also forced the Security Council to seriously consider such further improvements, for fear of massive disobedience of its sanctions. This was particularly so as *Kadi I ECJ* was again followed by other courts, piling on the pressure. In response, the Security Council adopted, at the very end of 2009, Resolution 1904 (2009).

Resolution 1904 was clearly an attempt to thwart the 'challenges, both legal and otherwise, to the measures implemented by Member States' under the 1267 sanctions regime, as well as to make procedures for listing and delisting by the competent Sanctions Committee 'fair and clear', an ongoing effort.[44] It established an Office of the Ombudsperson which, being independent and impartial, would be able to make recommendations to the 1267 Sanctions Committee regarding the removal of persons from the sanctions list. However, the establishment of an Office of the Ombudsperson still did not satisfy domestic and regional courts, which kept pushing for judicial guarantees in the imposition of asset freezes and travel bans on persons identified by the Security Council as being 'associated with' the Taliban or Al-Qaida. In particular, the fact that the Office of the Ombudsperson could only make recommendations which had to elicit the consensus of the Security Council to lead to removal from the list was the 'deal-breaker'. In *Kadi II* in 2010, it was clear that the General Court of the EU remained unconvinced that the procedure at UN level offered the appropriate guarantees.

In 2011, the Security Council made even further improvements, introducing a so-called 'reverse consensus' requirement in rejecting recommendations of the Ombudsperson.[45] A recommendation would be adopted, unless there was consensus among the members of the Sanctions Committee *not* to adopt it. This made recommendations of the Ombudsperson quasi-binding, though the option remained for any member to remove the matter to the Security Council, where normal rules of decision making (including the veto) apply.

Despite these significant improvements to the 1267 sanctions regime, and especially the delisting procedures, national and regional international courts remain unconvinced and are keeping the pressure up. Indeed the CJEU can be seen to have raised the bar extremely high in its *Kadi II* decision. It seems that nothing short of a

---

[43] UNSC Res 1730 (2006).   [44] See UNSC Res 1904 (2009), preamb para. 9.
[45] See UNSC Res 1989 (2011).

full-blown court procedure will be enough to solicit the EU courts' deference in favour of review at UN level. No doubt this should be a welcome development—and a justified one at that, though one unlikely to be realistically achieved. At the same time, pressure is mounting for the 1267 regime improvements to be applied also to other sanctions regimes, which still only benefit from the Focal Point.[46]

It seems however that all this pressure, after procuring some progress, may send the Security Council into regression and end up being counterproductive. Indeed, in order to avoid challenges in domestic and other courts, the Security Council has started to make its sanctions regimes less and less targeted: in blunting the identification of those targeted, the Security Council makes it more difficult for those affected to challenge the measures in domestic or regional international *fora*. The Council re-situates the game on the intergovernmental level, where it is much stronger, no less so on account of art. 103 UN Charter. It remains to be seen what balance will be struck in the end. If there is an end—Kadi may have won his challenge, but the struggle for balance between international security and human rights protection in the context of UN Security Council sanctions still rages on.

---

[46] See *Al-Dulimi*, ECtHR (n. 19), paras 117–20.

5

Obligations of International Organizations

It is by now firmly accepted that (most) international organizations have (a degree of) international legal personality and therefore must be considered to be subjects of international law.[1] As such, they can be assumed to be bound by rules of general international law. This assumption was thankfully confirmed in the International Court of Justice's (ICJ) 1980 Advisory Opinion *Interpretation of the Agreement of 25 March 1951 between the WHO and Egypt* (Brölmann).

Still, the *extent to which* rules of general international law are binding upon international organizations remains a puzzling question. This question has notably arisen with regard to international human rights law.[2] Although there seems to be a convergence of views on the obligation of international organizations to respect at least *some* human rights,[3] controversies persist, notably as to the identification of sources of this obligation and its scope. For several authors, this obligation rests on the customary status of international human rights. The massive adoption and continuous affirmation of the fundamental human rights listed in the Universal Declaration of Human Rights[4] have, so it is submitted, transformed these rules—or at least some of them—into customary international law.[5] As customary international law can be assumed to apply to all subjects of international law, arguably such customary human rights norms are also binding upon international organizations.[6] Other authors consider that human rights have become general principles of international law through

---

[1] ICJ, *Reparations for injuries suffered in the service of the United Nations*, Advisory Opinion, [1949] ICJ Rep 173–219. See Part 1 on legal status.

[2] See J. Wouters, E. Brems, S. Smis, and P. Schmitt, 'Accountability for Human Rights Violations by International Organisations: Introductory Remarks', in J. Wouters, E. Brems, S. Smis, and P. Schmitt (eds), *Accountability for Human Rights Violations by International Organisations* (Antwerp/Oxford, Intersentia 2010), pp. 1–18.

[3] T. Meron, *Human Rights and Humanitarian Norms as Customary Law* (Oxford, Clarendon Press 1989) pp. 94–6; H. Hannum, 'The Status of the Universal Declaration of Human Rights in National and International Law', (1995–96) 25 *Georgia Journal of International and Comparative Law* 287–395; C. Tomuschat, *Human Rights: Between Idealism and Realism Actors* (Oxford, Oxford University Press 2003) p. 4; T. Ahmed and I. de Jesus Butler, 'The European Union and Human Rights: an International Legal Perspective', (2006) 17(4) *European Journal of International Law* 771–801; J. Wouters and C. Ryngaert, 'Impact on the Process of the Formation of Customary International Law', in M.T. Kamminga and M. Scheinin (eds), *The Impact of Human Rights Law on General International Law* (Oxford, Oxford University Press 2008) pp. 111–31.

[4] UN General Assembly, Resolution A/217 (III), *Universal Declaration of Human Rights*, UN Doc. A/RES/3/217 A, 10 December 1948.

[5] See notably H. Hannun (n. 3), at p. 322; C. Tomuschat (n. 3), at p. 4.

[6] H.G. Schermers, 'The Legal Bases of International Organization Action', in R.-J. Dupuy, (ed.), *Manuel sur les Organisations Internationals—A Handbook on International Organizations* (Dordrecht/Boston/London, Martinus Nijhoff Publishers 1998) p. 402; C. Tomuschat, 'International Law: Ensuring the Survival of Mankind on the Eve of a New Century: General Course on Public International Law', (2001) 281 *Recueil des Cours de l'Académie de Droit International* 134–5.

the medium of the 'general principles of law recognized by civilized nations' mentioned in art. 38(1)(c) of the Statute of the International Court of Justice.[7] Such general principles would not require state practice but rather result from 'a variety of ways in which moral and humanitarian considerations find a more direct and spontaneous "expression in legal form".'[8] Moreover, some provisions of human rights law—such as the prohibition of racial discrimination—are considered as norms of *jus cogens*.[9] It is generally admitted that peremptory rules bind international organizations.[10]

International courts are slowly but surely picking up these ideas. The decision in *Prosecutor v Simic et al. on the Motion for a Judicial Assistance to be Provided by SFOR and Other* (Van der Wilt) demonstrates that international criminal tribunals acknowledge that, as international institutions, they are called on to respect and promote the human rights of all individuals, including those charged with heinous crimes.

A related but somewhat different *problématique* is the question of 'succession' of an international organization in respect of the international obligations binding on its member states, by dint of the latter transferring relevant competences to the former. An early and very important case with regard to EU (at the time EEC) obligations under the General Agreement on Tariffs and Trade (GATT, now part of the WTO treaty instruments) was the European Court of Justice's 1972 judgment in *International Fruit Company v Produktschap voor Siergewassen*, in which the Court held that by transferring external trade competencies the member states showed their wish to bind the EU to the GATT. In his case-note, Kuijper situates this judgment in the much wider context of succession/acceptance by the EU of international legal obligations of its member states, from international trade law to human rights and customary international law.

---

[7] See B. Simma and P. Alston, 'The Sources of Human Rights Law: Custom, Jus Cogens, and General Principles', (1988–89) 12 *Australian Yearbook of International Law* 82, 102–8.

[8] Ibid., p. 105.

[9] B. Kondoch, 'Human Rights Law and UN Peace Operations in Post-Conflict Situations', in N.D. White and D. Klaasen (eds), *The UN, Human Rights and Post-Conflict Situations* (Manchester, Manchester University Press 2005) p. 36.

[10] H.G. Schermers (n. 6), p. 402.

5.1 Case 21-24/72, *International Fruit Company* *v Produktschap voor Siergewassen*, Court of Justice of the EC, [1972] ECR 1219

Pieter Jan Kuijper

Relevance of the case

The *International Fruit Company case* is rightly famous for two reasons: (1) the succession of the European Community to its member states in the General Agreement on Tariff and Trade (GATT); and (2) the lack of direct effect of art. XI (the prohibition of quantitative restrictions) and of the GATT in general. On point (2) the case has largely lost its initial relevance, since the Court of Justice (ECJ), though still of the same view with respect to the GATT's successor, the WTO, has considerably developed and refined its initial reasoning. It is on point (1) that the case has continued importance, not so much because it will easily find new application, but because it sheds light on the comparable, but different situation in which the EU effectively follows the rules of international organizations or of treaty bodies, to which all member states are parties, but *without* the possibility for the EU itself to accede to these organizations and treaty bodies.

I. Facts and legal questions

This was the first case before the ECJ in which the General Agreement on Tariffs and Trade (GATT) was at issue. It came to the Court by way of a so-called preliminary question from a national court, in this case a Dutch court (College van Beroep voor het Bedrijfsleven, CBB) that at the time was charged with ruling on certain economic disputes in first and last instance.[1] The question was inspired by the following facts. In the framework of the Common Agricultural Policy (CAP) the European market for hard fruit was semi-closed during the European season (late autumn and winter) to apples and pears from the southern hemisphere. Imports into the Community were restricted to a reference quantity based on the import level in previous years. If there was a threat that these reference quantities were about to be surpassed, the Commission could take safeguard measures by precisely fixing the reference quantities, as a consequence of which import licences going beyond these quantities would have to be rejected.

In the early 1970s the Dutch semi-public organ charged with implementing certain aspects of the CAP (the Produktschap mentioned in the title of the case) thus refused to issue licences for apples and pears from Chile to *International Fruit* and other importers. These importers regarded this refusal as contrary to art. XI of the

---

[1] It is recalled that the preliminary question procedure laid down in art. 177 of the EEC Treaty (presently art. 267 TFEU) had been created in order that the lower courts of the member states may, and the highest courts must, submit questions of interpretation or of validity of Union law to the ECJ in Luxembourg before deciding such cases. This would enhance and ensure the uniform interpretation and application of Union law.

GATT, which in their view contained an unconditional prohibition of quantitative restrictions on imports (para. 1). Exceptions to this prohibition were accepted for agricultural products, if these were linked to measures limiting national production or eliminating a temporary surplus (para. 2c).[2]

The first preliminary question submitted by the CBB to the ECJ was put in the form of an inquiry after the scope of art. 177 EEC Treaty (art. 267 TFEU): namely whether international agreements (in this case the GATT) could be used as the standard by which the validity of a Community act could be tested in the framework of a preliminary question procedure.

The second question, which would need a reply only if the first one was to be answered in the affirmative, inquired whether the Commission decisions that had been implemented by the refusal of licences by the Produktschap, were invalid as being contrary to art. XI of GATT.

II. Excerpts

The ECJ deals quickly and in a straightforward fashion with the first question. It remarks rather drily that the wording of art. 177 EEC (now 267 TFEU)[3] does not permit to limit the jurisdiction of the Court 'by the grounds on which the validity of [the] measures [at issue] may be contested'. Hence the Court is obliged to examine the second question.

It immediately continues with two underlying questions that are of much greater interest and difficulty and which are: (1) what are the obligations under the GATT by which the EU must be considered to be bound; and (2) whether an individual can invoke such obligations (if they exist) before the courts of the member states and of the EU itself in order to plead the invalidity of Community/Union rules. The Court expresses this as follows:

> Before the incompatibility of a Community measure with a provision of international law can affect the validity of that measure, the Community must first of all be bound by that provision.
>
> Before invalidity can be relied upon before a national court, that provision of international law must also be capable of conferring rights on citizens of the Community, which they can invoke before the Courts.

---

[2] Some years later a panel of the GATT found that the EEC had violated, amongst others, this exception provided by art. XI:2(c) GATT, see *EEC-Restrictions on Imports of Apples from Chile*—Report of the Panel adopted 10 November 1980 (L/5047-BISD 27S/98) available at https://www.wto.org. This Panel report was not given sufficient weight by the Court in a later (German) procedure concerning a similar case, see Case 112/80, *Dürbeck/Hza Frankfurt/Main-Flughafen*, paras 45–6.

[3] Article 267 TFEU (ex art. 234 TEC) reads in part as follows:

> The Court of Justice of the European Union shall have jurisdiction to give preliminary rulings concerning:
> (a) the interpretation of the Treaties;
> (b) the validity and interpretation of acts of the institutions, bodies, offices or agencies of the Union;
> Where such a question is raised before any court or tribunal of a Member State, that court or tribunal may, if it considers that a decision on the question is necessary to enable it to give judgment, request the Court to give a ruling thereon.

It is therefore necessary to examine whether the General Agreement satisfies these two conditions.

It is clear that at the time when they concluded the Treaty establishing the European Economic Community the Member States were bound by the obligations of the General Agreement.

By concluding a treaty between them they could not withdraw from their obligations to third countries.[4]

The Court then mentions one factual circumstance and two articles from the EEC Treaty, which bolster the view that the member states did not have the wish at all to act against this ground rule of the law of treaties.[5] After that, the Court returns to the first of the two questions, namely whether the EEC is bound by the obligations of the GATT:

The Community has assumed the functions inherent in the tariff and trade policy, progressively during the transitional period [1958–70] and in their entirety on the expiry of that period, by virtue of Articles 111 and 113 of the Treaty.

By conferring those powers on the Community, the Member States showed their wish to bind it by the obligations of the General Agreement.

Since the entry into force of the EEC Treaty and more particularly, since the setting up of the common external tariff, the transfer of powers which has occurred in the relations between the Member States and the Community has been put in concrete form in different ways within the framework of the General Agreement and has been recognized by the other contracting parties.

In particular, since that time, the Community, acting through its own institutions, has appeared as a partner in tariff negotiations and as a party to the agreements of all types concluded within the framework of the General Agreement, in accordance with the provisions of Article 114 of the EEC Treaty which provides that the tariff and trade agreements 'shall be concluded […] on behalf of the Community'.

It therefore appears that, in so far as under the EEC Treaty the Community has assumed the powers previously exercised by the Member States in the area governed by the General Agreement, the provisions of that agreement have the effect of binding the Community.[6]

III. Commentary

It is important to remark at the outset that the Court, in making the step from the conclusion relative to the first question (namely that the GATT is binding on the Community) to the second question (the decision on a possible direct effect of art. XI of GATT invalidating Commission decisions), skips two logical steps that remain

---

[4] Paragraphs 7–11 of the judgment.

[5] See art. 30 Vienna Convention on the Law of Treaties (VCLT), 23 May 1969, United Nations, Treaty Series, vol. 1155, p. 331. The fact referred to in the text is the submission of the EEC Treaty to the scrutiny of the GATT Contracting Parties under art. XXIV:6 GATTT, the exception for customs unions. The articles referred to are the present arts. 206 and 351(1) TFEU.

[6] Paragraphs 14–18 of the judgment.

implicit, namely (1) that the GATT, because it is binding on the EEC also becomes an integral part of the Community legal order,[7] and moreover (2) has supremacy over secondary Community law.[8]

The Court probably considered these two implicit steps in its reasoning to be self-evident and inherent in its argumentation laying down its so-called succession theory. As the Court argued, all the member states were parties to the GATT and bound by its provisions and could not, by becoming Members of the EEC, free themselves from their GATT obligations.[9] The member states, however, have transferred their powers in the area covered by GATT to the Community, while at the same time they made it clear that they did not want to escape their obligations by submitting the EEC Treaty to the GATT in the framework of its provision on customs unions (art. XXIV:6 GATT). Moreover, the Community itself, represented by the Commission, negotiated during this same period within the GATT about the gradual introduction of the common external tariff of the EEC. The other Contracting Parties of the GATT, by participating in these negotiations, *de facto* recognized this transfer of powers from the member states to the Community. The importance of this last mentioned aspect underpinning the Court's succession approach has been rather neglected in the later literature about the way in which the Community inherited its member states' rights and duties in the GATT. This is a unique element of the situation in the GATT as it existed at the time of the emergence of the EEC as a fully fledged customs union.

International Fruit did not clarify in an explicit manner whether international law in all its manifestations (treaty, customary law, and general principles of law) was part of the Community legal system and which rank it had in that system. Fairly quickly afterwards these questions were clarified in other cases. In the *Haegeman* case, the ECJ ruled 'that the provisions of an international agreement from their entry into force are an integral part of the Community legal order'.[10] After that it took some time before it was made clear that this was valid also for binding decisions of an Association Council because 'of their direct link' with such Association Agreements that had already themselves become an integral part of the Community legal order.[11] The *Poulsen* case in turn clarified beyond doubt that the Union was bound by customary international law, in that case by the law relating to different sea zones and to the varying degrees of sovereignty and sovereign rights that states had in such zones.[12] In the *Racke* case the Court

---

[7] See formula in art. VI US Constitution: '... all treaties made, or which shall be made, under the authority of the United States, shall be the supreme law of the land; and the judges in every state shall be bound thereby, anything in the Constitution or laws of any State to the contrary notwithstanding.'

[8] One might say that there is still another element in the reasoning of the Court that hovers in the background, but remains unsaid, namely the exclusive nature of the EEC's commercial policy powers, later decided in Opinion 1/75 [1975] ECR 1355.

[9] Pursuant to the *pacta tertiis*-rule (art. 34 VCLT), which art. 351 TFEU takes into account.

[10] Case 181/73 *Haegeman* [1974] ECR 449, para. 5.

[11] Case 30/88 *Greece v Commission* [1989] ECR 3711, para. 13. This principled decision led to a tidal wave of cases during the 1990s and thereafter, on the basis of non-discrimination and standstill clauses included in decisions by the Council of Association between the EEC and Turkey, relevant for the position of Turkish employees and their families in the Community, starting with Case C-192/89 *Sevince* [1990] ECR I-3461. It has to be assumed that binding decisions of international organizations are also part of EU law.

[12] Case C-286/90 *Poulsen v Anklagemyndigheden* [1992] ECR I-6019, para. 9

reviewed the invocation by the Community of the customary rule of *rebus sic stantibus* in the light of the precise content of that rule, when the Community had had recourse to it in order to justify the unilateral termination of the Co-operation Agreement with Yugoslavia.[13] From the cases mentioned here, it also transpires that the Court accorded higher rank to international law (whether treaty or custom) than to secondary Community law and that it shares in the supremacy of Union law over the law of the member states (including even constitutional law). In this connexion the Court referred from time to time to art. 216(2) TFEU, which states that agreements concluded by the Union are binding on the institutions of the Union and for its member states.

A. Does 'succession' amount to EU implementation without EU obligation?

It is fitting at this moment to make a few remarks about the 'succession' of the Union to existing customary law and to make a comparison to the 'succession' of the Union to treaty obligations. In the past, newly independent states issued from the decolonization movement of the 1960s and 1970s argued that 'your international law is not our international law', having never participated in the formation of 'your international law'. Accordingly they pretended to be able to choose 'their international law' *à la carte*. As far as customary international law is concerned, they have been largely unsuccessful, although they have deployed many efforts through recourse to UN General Assembly Resolutions and other soft law instruments. In respect of succession to treaties the newly independent states disposed of a larger margin of manoeuvre, although they were not able to have a complete 'clean slate approach' accepted. The Convention on the Succession of Treaties between States in the end became an awkward balance between the complete succession and the clean slate approach and it remains uncertain whether it correctly represents the actual practice of states.[14]

The 'succession' between the member states and the EU in respect of international legal rules obviously is a succession between international legal persons of an entirely different nature and for that reason alone succession might be more difficult. The contrary is the case. Historically the Union has not been under the slightest impulsion not to observe customary international law, although from early on it has been opting for an approach to customary law that suited its needs. A good example are the customary law rules on the exercise of legislative and enforcement jurisdiction in the field of anti-trust, where the Commission took the view that a moderate effects doctrine was in conformity with international law. That approach was approved by the Court, but initially reinterpreted to be within the bounds of the territoriality principle, which was less controversial.[15] The cases of *Poulsen* and *Racke* mentioned above are other

---

[13] Case C-162/96 *Racke v Hauptzollamt Mainz* [1998] ECR I-503, paras 48–59.

[14] See S.T. Korman, 'The 1978 Vienna Convention on Succession of States in respect of Treaties: an Inadequate Response to the Issue of State Succession' (1992–93) 16 *Suffolk Transnational Law Review* 174.

[15] Case C-48/69 *ICI v Commission (Dyestuffs)* [1972] ECR 619, Case C-137/92 *BASF v Commission* [1994] ECR I-2555. In the longer term the Court came 'round to the Commission's view of the moderate effects approach being in conformity with the customary international law of jurisdiction', see Case T-102/96 *GencorLtd v Commission (Gencor)* [1999] ECR II-753.

important examples of how the Union embraced existing customary international law through actions of the Commission and the Court.

As far as treaty law was concerned, historically the Commission and the Council, and later also the European Parliament when its legislative powers increased, have not had the slightest hesitation to move the implementation of the member states' obligations under international agreements to which they all were parties, to the Community (Union) level. This happened in many cases, where the Union was not and could not become a party, while its powers covered the matters regulated by the treaties in question. An early example is the OECD decision on an 'Understanding on a Local Cost Standard' that gave rise to the well-known Opinion 1/75.[16] As a consequence the EEC concluded and implemented this Understanding that was adopted in the OECD Council by the member states, whereas the EEC merely had a special observer status there. Another example of some notoriety is the constant implementation and adaptation of the lists of endangered species by the Union, following the CITES obligations of its member states, without itself being a member: a pure case of implementation without obligation.[17]

It bears pointing out that for succession to, or acceptance of, customary international law, a unilateral act of consent suffices, whereas for succession to treaty obligations this is often not sufficient; some kind of consent has to be forthcoming from the treaty partners. In the case of the Union's de facto succession to the member states' GATT obligations, the other GATT Contracting Parties had de facto accepted the EEC's presence and action in the GATT. That fitted with the very pragmatic and not very rules-bound way of operating of the GATT in the 1950s and early 1960s. In other treaty settings, and even more so in international organizations, third states were likely to insist on more formality, often requiring a change in the treaty's provisions on accession.

Fairly early after the Court's judgment in *International Fruit,* comments began to appear in the literature, which pointed out that the succession approach could also be fruitfully applied in other international organizations, especially if they were wholly or partially active in the sphere of the exclusive powers of the Union, such as the common commercial policy. It was pointed out that, according to the succession theory, the Union ought to carry out the Security Council sanctions against Southern-Rhodesia, since otherwise there was a risk that disparate implementation by the member states would undermine their effectiveness and cause distortions on the internal market.[18] Over the course of the years the Commission and the Council developed a technique which enabled the EC to implement any trade sanctions

---

[16] *Opinion 1/75* [1975] ECR 1355.

[17] It is only recently that the so-called Gaborone amendment of art. XXI of the CITES Convention with a view to permitting organizations like the EU to become a party to the CITES Convention was ratified by the required majority (fifty-four of eighty) of the members of CITES, which were members on the day the text of the amendment was adopted. This process has lasted over three decades, from 30 April 1983 to 29 November 2013. See http://www.cites.org/eng/disc/gaborone.php.

[18] P.J. Kuijper, 'Sanctions against Rhodesia: The EEC and the Implementation of General International Legal Rules', (1975) 12 *Common Market Law Review* 231.

imposed by the Security Council.[19] This practice was later laid down in a different form, consisting of successive decisions under the CFSP (art. 15 TEU) and the EC Treaty (arts. 60 and 300 ECT), and is now laid down in art. 215 TFEU (preceded by a decision under art. 29 TEU). Such implementation of UN sanctions that are binding on the member states is another example of implementation without obligation. However, when in the famous *Kadi* case the then Court of First Instance developed an elaborate argument to the effect that the Union was bound by UN Security Council trade sanctions and asset freezing as a kind of functional substitute for its member states in the field of international trade and capital movement,[20] the Court itself shot this down quite emphatically: the EU could not become a party to the UN Charter and thus not a member of the UN. It was a mere observer, and as such was not bound by Security Council Resolutions, although it was authorized by its founding treaty to carry them out.[21]

What the ECJ was willing to do—and it had already done so earlier—was to resort to UN Security Council resolutions as an aid in interpretation of the implementing regulations of UN sanctions on the EU level. Usually this resulted in a stringent interpretation of the Union act, especially because the Court took into account the objective of the resolutions—the maintenance of international peace and security.[22]

The well-known and long-standing case law of the ECJ reviewing EU acts in the light of the human rights and fundamental freedoms common to the constitutional traditions of the member states and exemplified by the European Convention on Human Rights (ECHR), which had been ratified by all member states, is another example of unilateral application of international treaty norms, formally without any corresponding obligation.[23] Over a very long period the Court, with increasing assurance, referred to articles of the ECHR and the case law of the European Court of Human Rights (ECtHR). At the same time the Court decided that, though co-operation on human rights and fundamental freedoms was possible in the framework of a development or co-operation relationship,[24] the EU was not empowered under the Treaties to conclude a human rights treaty.[25] This example of 'implementation without obligation' in the field of human rights and fundamental freedoms was originally entirely Court driven. However, in order to sustain the situation in which all member states were parties to the ECHR and so the Court could continue to rely on this fact in its case law, it became necessary for Commission and Council to declare accession to that Convention a condition

---

[19] See P.J. Kuijper, 'Sanctions Against Argentina: Lawfulness Under Community and International Law' in D. O'Keeffe and H.G. Schermers (eds), *Essays in European Law and Integration, to Mark the Silver Jubilee of the Europa Institute Leiden* (Kluwer, Deventer 1982) pp. 141–66.

[20] Case T-315/01 *Kadi v Council and Commission (Kadi I)*, [2005] ECR II-3649, paras 203–5.

[21] Joined Cases C-402/05 & C-415/05 *Kadi v Council and Commission (Kadi I)* [2008] ECR I-6351 paras 281–5; 316–17.

[22] Case C-84/95, *Bosphorus Hava Yollari Turizm v Ireland (Bosphorus)* [1996] ECR I-03953, paras 21–3; Case C-177/95, *Ebony Maritime SA and Loten Navigation Co. Ltd v Prefetto della Provincia di Brindisi and others (Loten Navigation)* [1997] ECR I-1111, para. 38.

[23] Case C-44/79, *Liselotte Hauer v Land Rheinland-Pfalz. (Hauer)* [1979] ECR-3727.

[24] Case C-268/94, *Portuguese Republic v EU Council* [1996] ECR I-6207.

[25] *Opinion 2/94* [1996] ECR I-1759.

for accession to the EU.[26] In the same fashion human rights and democracy started to appear in the first articles as essential underlying elements of co-operation agreements with Latin-American countries that had recently emerged from dictatorships or brutal military regimes. Such provisions were intended to simplify the suspension and even termination of these agreements, following the model of the *Racke* case.[27] This extreme case of disjunction between a human rights policy without underlying attribution of power in the Treaty and no treaty obligations in this domain, while the Union's court almost routinely applied the ECHR, following the ECtHR's case-law, will only be resolved, when the Union accedes to the ECHR pursuant to the new art. 6 TEU.[28]

B. Does 'succession' provide a solution to a new problem?

A new problem of disjunction between the development of the Union's internal powers in important sectors of *inter alia* transport policy and the impossiblity of the EU to become a party to long-standing international agreements of these sectors has arisen over the last two decades.[29] The basic international agreements on aviation (Chicago Convention and Warsaw Convention) and the organization (ICAO) conceiving and running these agreements, are not open to the Union, whereas there is considerable internal legislation in the field that may or may not be in conformity with the ICAO. Obviously the EU, when it is incapable of becoming a party to the international agreement or convention that covers the field of its new legislation, normally will venture to comply with the international convention in question, especially if all its member states are parties to it. In the light of the principle of sincere co-operation prevailing in the Union,[30] the Union institutions should not intentionally embarass their member states by producing legislation that goes against a convention that all of them are bound to respect. On the other hand the Union institutions may decide to develop further certain aspects of such conventions, and treaty partners and economic operators in the sector may see such developments as breaches of these conventions. This was the case of the American Airlines Association (AAA) and others, who believed that the regulation that extended the EU ETS system to aircraft and airlines infringed certain rules of the Chicago Convention. Hence they demanded that the Union regulation be reviewed and declared inapplicable in the light of these alleged breaches of the Chicago Convention.[31]

The same situation had occurred a few years earlier when the Union's legislation in the field of pollution of the seas was considered by a number of shipping companies

---

[26] Act concerning the conditions of accession and the adjustments to the Treaties—Accession of the Kingdom of Spain and the Portuguese Republic [1985] OJ L 302, 23.

[27] In general about these points: Bartels, *Human Rights Conditionality in EU's International Agreements* (Oxford, Oxford University Press 2005).

[28] Which after *Opinion 2/13*, n.y.r. probably has been put off for quite some time again.

[29] For a brief overview of the problem, see 'Editorial Comments. The Union, the Member States and International Agreements', (2011) 48 *Common Market Law Review* 1.

[30] Article 4(3) TEU. See in general M. Klamert, *The Principle of Loyalty in EU Law* (Oxford, Oxford University Press 2014).

[31] Case C-366/10, *American Airlines Association* [2011] ECR I-13755.

to be contrary to certain rules laid down in the so-called MARPOL Convention adopted within the framework of the International Maritime Organization (IMO).[32] In the *Intertanko* case the complaining parties explicitly invoked the precedent of the *International Fruit* case, arguing that all member states had ratified MARPOL and that hence it was binding on the EC. As a consequence its provisions could be invoked to set aside the relevant EC legislation. As in *International Fruit,* the Court was confronted with the same 'double whammy' argument: there is an obligation binding on the EU through succession and direct effect of this obligation should lead to a set-aside of a Union legislative rule. Whereas in *International Fruit* the fruit importers lost on the second issue, that is direct effect, the Court ventured to distinguish *Intertanko* from *International Fruit* on the first question. The Court signalled that the EU had not been able to become a party to MARPOL, which was not open to international organizations and, one might add, had never given any indication that a de facto succession to the member states would be acceptable to the states already parties. The Court also stated that the EU's competences, based on its internal legislation, did probably not cover the full scope of the MARPOL Convention. Hence the Union was not bound by the MARPOL Convention: the rules of the Convention had not become part of Union law and hence could not be invoked by private parties at all. The question of direct effect simply could not arise.

This was also the conclusion of similar cases, such as the *AAA* case in the field of air transport and the *TNT* case, which was a road transport and private international law case.[33] However, as long as all member states were parties to such international instruments as the Chicago Convention and MARPOL, the Court felt bound, pursuant to the principle of sincere co-operation, to take account of the provisions of such agreements in interpreting provisions of Union law. The words 'to take account of' seem to have been chosen carefully by the Court in order to distinguish this method of interpretation from the normal method of interpreting Union law in conformity or in harmony with international agreements to which the Union has become a party, when it is not giving direct effect to such agreements or their provisions.[34]

Some conclusions

The conclusions that remain to be drawn cannot be but mitigated, where the theory of the succession of international organizations to the international legal obligations of their member states are concerned. The succession of the EU to its member states' GATT obligations is a consequence of special circumstances in which the flexibility of the procedures in the GATT and the adaptation of the EU's treaty partners to such flexibility happily combined with a daring Court in order to bring about this result. The Court now maintains a strongly toned-down succession, which finds its

---

[32] Case C-308/06, *Intertanko* [2008] ECR I-4057.
[33] Case C-533/08, *TNT v AXA Versicherungen* [2010] ECR I-4107.
[34] See Case C-53/96 *Hermès* [1998] ECR I-3603; Joined Cases C-300/98 and C-393/98 *Christian Dior and Wilhelm Layher* [2000] ECR I-11307; and Case C-89/99 *Schieving-Nystad v Groeneveld* [2001] ECR I-5851.

expression merely in taking account of the existing treaty obligations of all the member states in interpreting Union law. This 'taking account of' such obligations is, as far as the author knows, also practiced by Commission and Council, when drafting Union legislation that possibly may touch upon existing treaty obligations of all the member states. The succession doctrine, or what is left of it, is no longer based on an international obligation characterized by de facto consent from the EU, its member states and third states, as in the *International Fruit* case. It now finds its foundation primarily in the EU constitutional duty of sincere co-operation (enhanced good faith) between EU institutions and the member states. This obligation in turn takes account of the obligation that member states have under international law vis-á-vis their third state treaty partners to continue to carry out their existing treaty obligations in good faith, if necessary through EU legislation, even if they legally, under EU law, do no longer have the power to take on those obligations.[35] There is a triangular relationship between the EU, its member states, and third states (or another international organization or regime) and good faith only operates on two sides of the triangle, that is to say between the EU (institutions) and its member states and between the member states and third states (or international organization or regime), but not on the third, linking the EU (institutions) to third states.

Between the third states and the EU such obligation does not exist, or at any rate is deemed not to exist, because the transfer of powers from member states to the EU continues to be regarded as *res inter alios acta* or as an illegitimate excuse under 'national' law that can have no consequences on the international level.[36] This is a highly unsatisfactory situation of which the Union is the victim, since it is its internal constitutional order that is distorted by this state of affairs, without much hope for change, unless the Union institutions (mainly the Commission and the Court in reality) manage to force the member states to break their good faith bond with third States and thus put the latter under pressure to open the treaty regime or international organization to the EU in a shorter period than the thirty years it took for CITES.[37] One may wonder whether this is yet another example of Antonio Gramsci's old order dying, while the new order is kept from being born. Is it not time for international law to come to an acceptance of the reality that there is a good faith lien also between third states and the EU in this situation, in recognition of the fact that one cannot have diplomatic relations with the EU (as nearly all states now have had for many years) without having to accept that this brings a good faith duty with it to accept this fact also in other contexts?

[35] However in some instances Union law obligations come in direct conflict with acts under international law. Such was the case, when the CJEU forbade the member states to continue the practice of accepting the notifications from third states of their acceptance of a Convention on private international law, which fell within EU exclusive competence, see *Opinion 1/13*, n.y.r.

[36] By analogous interpretation of art. 27 of the 1969 Vienna Convention on the Law of Treaties.

[37] It is, when this scenario is looming for member states and third states, that 'unholy' tacit alliances are created between these two groups of states to keep the Union out of the relevant treaty regime of international organization for a 'little bit longer'.

5.2 Interpretation of the Agreement of 25 March 1951 between the WHO and Egypt, Advisory Opinion, [1980] ICJ Rep 73

Catherine Brölmann

Relevance of the case

This opinion constitutes a point of reference when it comes to enunciating the sources of obligations binding upon international organizations. It is also authoritative as it elaborates on the general legal obligations governing the relation between an organization and its host state. Incidentally, the Court makes an articulate pronouncement on the possible political aspects of a question put before it.

I. The facts of the case

In 1949 the *Alexandria Sanitary Bureau* (dating from the nineteenth century) was integrated in the World Health Organization (WHO) as a 'regional organ' (ex art. 44 WHO Constitution). The *Eastern Mediterranean Regional Office* (EMRO) thus commenced operations on 1 July 1949, while in 1951 the WHO and Egypt concluded a host agreement further specifying privileges, immunities, and facilities of the organization ('the 1951 Agreement'). Following the 1978 Camp David Accord, agreed to by Egypt, Israel, and the United States, a number of Arab states severed diplomatic relations with Egypt and lobbied for the Regional Office to be transferred to Amman, Jordan, as soon as possible.[1] Different draft resolutions submitted to the World Health Assembly, reflecting contradicting views on a possible move of the Regional Office out of Egypt, and on the relevance of the 1951 Agreement for such a move, led the Health Assembly by Resolution of 20 May 1980 to submit to the International Court of Justice ('the Court') for its advisory opinion the following questions:

1. Are the negotiation and notice provisions of Section 37 of the Agreement of 25 March 1951 between the World Health Organization and Egypt applicable in the event that either party to the Agreement wishes to have the Regional Office transferred from the territory of Egypt?
2. If so, what would be the legal responsibilities of both the World Health Organization and Egypt, with regard to the Regional Office in Alexandria, during the two-year period between notice and termination of the Agreement?

Section 37 of the 1951 Agreement reads:

The present Agreement may be revised at the request of either party. In this event the two parties shall consult each other concerning the modifications to be made in its provisions. If the negotiations do not result in an understanding within one year, the present Agreement may be denounced by either party giving two years' notice.

---

[1] K. Lee and J. Fang, *Historical Dictionary of the World Health Organization* (2nd edn, Lanham MD, Scarecrow Press 2012), s v 'Eastern Mediterranean Regional Office'.

II. The legal question

The question(s) put to the Court were formulated in technical and rather narrow terms, linked to a specific provision in the 1951 Agreement. The Court, however, undertook to examine which legal principles and rules more generally were applicable to the question of a possible transfer of the WHO Regional Office from Egypt, and which rules and principles were part of the general legal relationship between the WHO and Egypt.

III. Excerpts

33. In the debates in the World Health Assembly […], on the proposal to request the present opinion from the Court, opponents of the proposal insisted that it was nothing but a political manoeuvre designed to postpone any decision concerning removal of the Regional Office from Egypt, and the question therefore arises whether the Court ought to decline to reply to the present request by reason of its allegedly political character. […] [J]urisprudence establishes that if, as in the present case, a question submitted in a request is one that otherwise falls within the normal exercise of its judicial process, the Court has not to deal with the motives which may have inspired the request. […] Indeed, in situations in which political considerations are prominent it may be particularly necessary for an international organization to obtain an advisory opinion from the Court as to the legal principles applicable with respect to the matter under debate, especially when these may include the interpretation of its constitution.

[…]

35. […] The Court points out that, if it is to remain faithful to the requirements of its judicial character in the exercise of its advisory jurisdiction, it must ascertain what are the legal questions really in issue in questions formulated in a request […]

36. The Court will therefore now proceed to consider its replies to the questions formulated in the request on the basis that the true legal question submitted to the Court is: What are the legal principles and rules applicable to the question under what conditions and in accordance with what modalities a transfer of the Regional Office from Egypt may be effected? […]

37. The Court thinks it necessary to underline at the outset that the question before it is not whether, in general, an organization has the right to select the location of the seat of its headquarters or of a regional office. On that question there has been no difference of view in the present case, and there can be no doubt that an international organization does have such a right. The question before the Court is the different one of whether, in the present case, the Organization's power to exercise that right is or is not regulated by reason of the existence of obligations vis-a-vis Egypt. The Court notes that in the World Health Assembly and in some of the written and oral statements before the Court there seems to have been a disposition to regard international organizations as possessing some form of absolute power to determine and, if need be, change the location of the sites of their headquarters and regional offices. But States for their part possess a sovereign power of decision with respect to their acceptance of the headquarters or a regional office of an organization within their territories; and an organization's power of decision is no more absolute in this respect

than is that of a State. As was pointed out by the Court in one of its early Advisory Opinions, there is nothing in the character of international organizations to justify their being considered as some form of 'super-State' [...]. International organizations are subjects of international law and, as such, are bound by any obligations incumbent upon them under general rules of international law, under their constitutions or under international agreements to which they are parties. Accordingly, it provides no answer to the questions submitted to the Court simply to refer to the right of an international organization to determine the location of the seat of its regional offices. [...]

[...]

42. [...] Whatever view may be held on the question whether the establishment and location of the Regional Office in Alexandria are embraced within the provisions of the 1951 Agreement, and whatever view may be held on the question whether the provisions of Section 37 are applicable to the case of a transfer of the Office from Egypt, the fact remains that certain legal principles and rules are applicable in the case of such a transfer. These legal principles and rules the Court must, therefore, now examine.

43. [...] The very fact of Egypt's membership of the Organization entails certain mutual obligations of co-operation and good faith incumbent upon Egypt and upon the Organization. Egypt offered to become host to the Regional Office in Alexandria and the Organization accepted that offer; Egypt agreed to provide the privileges, immunities and facilities necessary for the independence and effectiveness of the Office. As a result the legal relationship between Egypt and the Organization became, and now is, that of a host State and an international organization, the very essence of which is a body of mutual obligations of co-operation and good faith. [...] This special legal regime of mutual rights and obligations has been in force between Egypt and WHO for over thirty years. The result is that there now exists in Alexandria a substantial WHO institution employing a large staff and discharging health functions important both to the Organization and to Egypt itself. In consequence, any transfer of the WHO Regional Office from the territory of Egypt necessarily raises practical problems of some importance. These problems are, of course, the concern of the Organization and of Egypt rather than of the Court. But they also concern the Court to the extent that they may have a bearing on the legal conditions under which a transfer of the Regional Office from Egypt may be effected.

44. [...] It is also apparent that a reasonable period of time would be required to effect an orderly transfer of the operation of the Office from Alexandria to the new site without disruption to the work. Precisely what period of time would be required is a matter which can only be finally determined by consultation and negotiation between WHO and Egypt. [...]

[...]

46. [...] [D]espite their variety and imperfections, the provisions of host agreements regarding their revision, termination or denunciation are not without significance in the present connection. In the first place, they confirm the recognition by international organizations and host States of the existence of mutual obligations incumbent upon them to resolve the problems attendant upon a revision, termination or denunciation of a host agreement. But they do more, since they must be presumed to reflect the views of organizations and host States as to the implications of those obligations in the contexts in which the provisions are intended to apply. In

the view of the Court, therefore, they provide certain general indications of what the mutual obligations of organizations and host States to co-operate in good faith may involve in situations such as the one with which the Court is here concerned.

47. A further general indication as to what those obligations may entail is to be found in the second paragraph of Article 56 of the Vienna Convention on the Law of Treaties and the corresponding provision in the International Law Commission's draft articles on treaties between States and international organizations or between international organizations. Those provisions [...] specifically provide that, when a right of denunciation is implied in a treaty by reason of its nature, the exercise of that right is conditional upon notice, and that of not less than twelve months. Clearly, these provisions also are based on an obligation to act in good faith and have reasonable regard to the interests of the other party to the treaty.

48. [...] [I]n formulating its reply to the request, the Court takes as its starting point the mutual obligations incumbent upon Egypt and the Organization to co-operate in good faith with respect to the implications and effects of the transfer of the Regional Office from Egypt. The Court does so the more readily as it considers those obligations to be the very basis of the legal relations between the Organization and Egypt under general international law, under the Constitution of the Organization and under the agreements in force between Egypt and the Organization. The essential task of the Court in replying to the request is, therefore, to determine the specific legal implications of the mutual obligations incumbent upon Egypt and the Organization in the event of either of them wishing to have the Regional Office transferred from Egypt.

49. The Court considers that in the context of the present case the mutual obligations of the Organization and the host State to co-operate under the applicable legal principles and rules are as follows:

— In the first place, those obligations place a duty both upon the Organization and upon Egypt to consult together in good faith as to the question under what conditions and in accordance with what modalities a transfer of the Regional Office from Egypt may be effected.
— Secondly, in the event of its being finally decided that the Regional Office shall be transferred from Egypt, their mutual obligations of co-operation place a duty upon the Organization and Egypt to consult together and to negotiate regarding the various arrangements needed to effect the transfer from the existing to the new site in an orderly manner and with a minimum of prejudice to the work of the Organization and the interests of Egypt.
— Thirdly, those mutual obligations place a duty upon the party which wishes to effect the transfer to give a reasonable period of notice to the other party for the termination of the existing situation regarding the Regional Office at Alexandria, taking due account of all the practical arrangements needed to effect an orderly and equitable transfer of the Office to its new site.

Those, in the view of the Court, are the implications of the general legal principles and rules applicable in the event of the transfer of the seat of a Regional Office from the territory of a host State. Precisely what periods of time may be involved in the observance of the duties to consult and negotiate, and what period of notice of termination should be given, are matters which necessarily vary according to the requirements of the particular case. In principle, therefore, it is for the parties in each case to determine the length of those periods by consultation and negotiation in good faith. Some indications as to the possible periods involved, as the Court has said, can be seen in provisions of host agreements, including Section 37 of the Agreement of 25 March 1951, as well as in Article 56 of the Vienna Convention on the Law of Treaties and in the corresponding article of the International Law Commission's draft articles on treaties between States and international organizations or between international organizations. But what is reasonable and equitable in any given case must depend on its particular circumstances. Moreover, the paramount consideration both for the Organization and the host State in every case must be their clear obligation to co-operate in good faith to promote the objectives and purposes of the Organization as expressed in its Constitution; and this too means that they must in consultation determine a reasonable period of time to enable them to achieve an orderly transfer of the Office from the territory of the host State.

50. It follows that the Court's reply to the second question is that the legal responsibilities of the Organization and Egypt during the transitional period between the notification of the proposed transfer of the Office and the accomplishment thereof would be to fulfil in good faith the mutual obligations which the Court has set out in answering the first question.

IV. Commentary

This opinion constitutes a point of reference on two counts: first, it elaborates on the general legal obligations part of the relationship between an international organization and its host state, and secondly, it enunciates the sources of international legal obligations binding upon international organizations.

As to the first element, the questions put before the Court were formulated in rather narrow and technical terms, linked specifically to Section 37 of the 1951 Agreement. The Court however steered away from the question as to whether the 1951 Agreement was actually the legal foundation for the Regional Office, and whether by consequence the Agreement's terms for termination were applicable to a possible move of the Regional Office. This cautious approach was perhaps unsurprising given the fiery political context, and the ambiguous constellation of the 1949 informal agreement between the WHO and Egypt (see above, under II) and the 1951 Agreement.

A preliminary issue for the Court thus was to restate the question(s) put before it. Such rephrasing in order to capture the 'true legal question'[2] could seem remarkable, but falls within the competence of the Court and is not uncommon.[3] With the

---

[2] *Interpretation of the Agreement of 25 March 1951 between the WHO and Egypt*, Advisory Opinion, [1980] ICJ Rep 73, para. 35.

[3] As the Court itself also indicated, referring *inter alia* to *Certain Expenses of the United Nations (Article 17, paragraph 2, of the Charter)*, Advisory Opinion, [1962] ICJ Rep 151, 156–8. But see the dissenting opinion of Judge Morozov, who criticizes the reformulation by the Court which essentially changes the nature of the questions (*Interpretation of the Agreement of 25 March 1951 between the WHO and Egypt*, Advisory Opinion, [1980] ICJ Rep 73, 190–7). A more recent example of such rephrasing is the Court's opinion on *Legal Consequences of the Construction of a Wall in the Occupied Palestinian Territory*, [2004] ICJ Rep 136.

questions reformulated in more general terms, the Court then undertook to examine unwritten international law for rules and principles applicable to the situation, considering other headquarters agreements as well as common art. 56 – on denunciation of treaties - of the Vienna Conventions on the Law of Treaties (the later Vienna Convention's provision at the time of the opinion still in the form of the (identical) International Law Commission's draft art. 56).[4]

The various headquarters agreements[5] considered by the Court as evidentiary sources generally prescribe a period of notice for the revision or termination of the treaty, often with a specific reference to removal of the seat of the organization or finalization of 'operations' in the host state. The second paragraph of art. 56 of both Vienna Conventions sets a procedural rule ('not less than twelve months' notice') for the termination of treaties in general, once it is established in accordance with art. 56(1) that the treaty is susceptible to denunciation. In the case at hand the Court referred to the standard of art. 56(2) by way of an example, but it did not enter into the question whether art. 56—presumably a provision with, at least for its general spirit, customary status[6]—was applicable to the *move of the Regional Office* to begin with (this would have led the Court back to the discussion about the applicability of the 1951 Agreement). Incidentally, in its commentary to art. 56 the International Law Commission mentioned headquarters agreements as a class of treaties which 'by their nature' could be subject to withdrawal or denunciation.[7]

The Court thus found evidence for a general rule requiring a 'reasonable' notice period, while the precise time would vary depending on the circumstances. The Court held that in a legal relationship of a host State and an international organization, 'the very essence […] is a body of mutual obligations of co-operation and good faith' (para. 43, above). Proceeding therefrom, the Court concretely focused on the duty to consult in good faith, and—in relation to the actual move of the Office—on the duty to negotiate and consult, and on the relevant party's duty to give a reasonable period of notice. Interestingly, the opinion added a teleological slant to the duty of co-operation by stressing that the 'paramount consideration' must be 'to promote the objectives and purposes of the Organization as expressed in its Constitution' (para. 49, above).

The reliance on good faith[8] and reasonableness as guiding principles for the implementation of procedural norms in concrete cases is much in line with contemporary international law practice. Likewise, the 'obligation to co-operate' (with slightly varying meanings), which defers the concrete outcome to another legal setting, is found for instance in environmental law, disarmament law, or any dynamic legal regime with long-term objectives.

---

[4] UN Doc A/CN.4/L.300.

[5] The term seemingly used as synonymous with 'host agreement'; *Interpretation of the Agreement of 25 March 1951 between the WHO and Egypt*, Advisory Opinion, [1980] ICJ Rep 73, para. 45.

[6] T. Christakis, 'Article 56' in O. Corten and P. Klein (eds), *The Vienna Conventions on the Law of Treaties* (Oxford, Oxford University Press 2011), pp. 1251–76; T. Giegerich, 'Article 56' in O. Dörr and K. Schmalenbach (eds), *Vienna Convention on the Law of Treaties: A Commentary* (Berlin and Heidelberg, Springer-Verlag 2012), pp. 967–87, at 986.

[7] YBILC 1982 vol II (Part Two) at 57.

[8] S. Reinhold, 'Good Faith in International Law', (2013) (2) *UCL Journal of Law and Jurisprudence* 40–63.

The *Reparation for Injuries* case may have introduced the United Nations as an international legal actor to international life, but in the early decades of the UN era it would not have been self-evident how to construe the relationship between an organization and its host state (which is usually also a member state); for one because the conceptualization of international organizations' legal autonomy—or the negotiation of the organizations' legal identity—was a lengthy process and the subject of much debate. The 1980 WHO Opinion was possibly the first time the Court addressed in clear terms the two-sided nature of the obligations resting on the organization and its host state, and the 'contractual' relationship as between legal equals (para. 43, above). In that respect the opinion may be taken as a landmark.

The opinion is perhaps best known for the dictum on the sources of international legal obligations for international organizations. This is a short passage, whose function in the immediate context of the decision (para. 37, above) is not easy to interpret:[9] 'International organizations are subjects of international law and, as such, are bound by any obligations incumbent upon them under general rules of international law, under their constitutions or under international agreements to which they are parties.' While the conjunction 'or' rather than 'and' suggests a concrete indication for the case at hand (that is, how complete freedom of the organization—*in casu* to choose the location for its headquarters—might be limited by legal obligations), the passage has attained status as a principled enunciation on the sources of legal obligation for international organizations.[10]

Uncontroversial is the last element, that international organizations are bound by the treaties they conclude. Organizations' legal personality and their treaty-making capacity were already in 1980 uncontested. Logically this engenders fundamental treaty-making rules of becoming legally bound and *pacta sunt servanda*; at a formal level this was confirmed by the 1986 Vienna Convention on the Law of Treaties between States and International Organizations or between International Organizations[11] ('the 1986 Vienna Convention'), which, although not in force, is held as largely applicable to the—extensive—treaty practice of international organizations by virtue of its reflecting customary law. The law of treaties now is a unitary regime, in which organizations appear as one-dimensional legal actors analogous to states; member states are not as such bound to a treaty concluded by 'their' organization,[12] and, conversely, organizations are not as such bound by a treaty to which their member states are a party.[13]

---

[9] cf. E. Cannizzaro's and P. Palchetti's view that 'one can hardly draw from this dictum much indication that is useful for clarifying the issue,' in J. Klabbers and A. Wallendahl (eds), *Research Handbook on the Law of International Organizations* (Cheltenham, Edward Elgar 2011), pp. 365–97, at 370.

[10] See for example T. Ahmed and I. de Jesús Butler, 'The European Union and Human Rights: An International Law Perspective', (2006) 17 *European Journal of International Law* 771–801, at 777, where it is used to support rebuttal of the EU's claim that the obligations incumbent upon it in the area of human rights stem from its own internal legal order.

[11] *Vienna Convention on the Law of Treaties between States and International Organizations or between International Organizations*, 1986 (UN Doc A/CONF.129/15).

[12] See the hapless fate of draft art. 36*bis* which had a prominent role in the law of treaties codification process (YBILC 1982, Vol II (Part Two), at 44), but which never made it into the 1986 Convention.

[13] See for example C-308/06 *International Association of Independent Tanker Owners* (Intertanko) *and others v Secretary of State for Transport*, ECJ judgment of 3 June 2008.

Most often reference is made to the first element, about international organizations being bound 'under general rules of international law'. This boldly seems to go to the heart of the debate on whether international organizations are bound by customary international law. At the time the Health Assembly's request was before the Court, this question was far from decided. In any event there seems to have been wide agreement that international organizations could not generate legally relevant practice or *opinio juris*, as appears also from the *travaux* of the 1986 Vienna Convention dating from the same period.[14] Possible customary rules binding organizations would therefore be incidental and unaccounted for by the voluntarist *systématique* of international law. Since then, the debate has been spurred by developments in the field of human rights law, and the proposition that international organizations are fully bound by relevant customary international law arguably since at least a decade is no longer controversial.[15]

Less attention is generally paid to the middle part of the dictum: organizations *as subjects of international law* 'are bound by any obligations ... under their constitutions'. This completes the overview of normative constraints for organizations vis-à-vis their host states in the context at issue. The Court in this case seemingly takes the view that the institutional order is embedded in the international order[16] (after all, the organization is not itself a party to its constituent treaty). It is true that even 'secondary' internal rules of organizations can gain normative effect in international law,[17] but more often the doctrine and practice of international law cover and flatten out the internal institutional layer of the organization (see also above). The Court's statement touches upon the cutting face between the internal order of the organization and the general international legal order, which raises a number of questions that cannot be answered entirely within the 'contractual' international law framework[18] set out by the Court for a contemporary and fair approach to both the organization and the host state.

In the context of this opinion the dictum about the sources of obligation for organizations makes some clear statements—notably about the binding effect of unwritten international law—and it inspires further questions about the possible normative layers, and the interplay between the different sources. In a general sense the dictum functions as a reminder of how international organizations are not, or no longer, separate functional regimes and vehicles for state action, but rather fully fledged 'subjects of international law' which have 'as such' concomitant rights *and* duties. Also on this point the opinion can serve as a landmark along the same lines as indicated above.

---

[14] C. Brölmann, *The Institutional Veil in Public International Law* (Oxford, Hart 2007), pp. 197–244.

[15] cf. O. De Schutter, 'Human Rights and the Rise of International Organisations: the Logic of Sliding Scales in the Law of International Responsibility', in J. Wouters et al. (eds), *Accountability for Human Rights Violations by International Organisations* (Antwerp, Intersentia 2010), p. 51, at 56.

[16] cf. J. d'Aspremont, 'The Multifaceted Concept of Autonomy of International Organizations and International Legal Discourse' in R. Collins and N.D. White (eds), *International Organizations and the Idea of Autonomy: Institutional Independence in the International Legal Order* (Routledge 2011) pp. 63–86, at 65.

[17] cf. L. Boisson de Chazournes on the external normative effect of operational guidelines of the World Bank and the IFC ('Standards and Guidelines: Some Interfaces with Private Investments' in T. Treves, F. Seatzu, and S. Trevisanut (eds), *Foreign Investment, International Law and Common Concerns* (NY, Routledge 2013) pp. 100–14, at 107–8).

[18] C. Brölmann, *The Institutional Veil in Public International Law* (Oxford, Hart 2007), 251–71.

Two elements in the WHO Opinion remain to be mentioned. One is that the Court (in the same context of para. 37) returns to the proverbial reassurance of UN member states in the *Reparation* case[19] (which in turn echoed a concern voiced during the San Francisco conference,[20] while the notion as such had come up already in relation to the League of Nations):[21] 'there is nothing in the character of international organizations to justify their being considered as some form of "super-state"'. In the opinion at hand, this reference could be seen as a bit top-heavy, as the question whether an organization's freedom to choose a seat is restricted by certain mutual obligations in relation to the host state, appears more mundane and less in need of a grand, principled statement than did the unprecedented question of legal personality for the UN in the heydays of state-centered international law. It is noteworthy that in the present opinion the Court considered it necessary to reassure in a general sense the states about autonomous aspirations of the Organization, while at the same time the Court did not waste words on the theoretical debate about legal personality of international organizations. When the legal personality of the United Nations was pronounced by the 1949 *Reparation* Opinion, this did not naturally extend to all international organizations. The *Repertory of United Nations Practice* in the 1950s indeed envisaged—without giving examples— member states concluding international agreements with 'an international organization that is not a subject of international law' (in which case there would be no duty of registration, presumably because these would not be real international agreements).[22] After initial attempts to distinguish between organizations with legal personality and organizations without, the presumption of legal personality ultimately came to be applied to 'international organizations' as a general category, and—as exemplified by the 1980 Opinion—was never seriously challenged afterwards.

Last but not least, the Court as a preliminary issue had to address the allegedly political character of the request for an opinion. Article 65(1) of the ICJ Statute accords competence to the Court to give an opinion on legal questions, as opposed to political questions.[23] The objection that a question put before the Court was of a political nature had been raised in cases before the WHO Opinion,[24] as it would be in later ones.[25] It is

---

[19] *Reparation for Injuries Suffered in the Service of the United Nations*, Advisory Opinion, [1949] ICJ Rep 174, 179.

[20] The Committee which discussed the matter was anxious to avoid any implication that the to-be-created United Nations would in any sense be a 'super-state' (*Report to the [US] President on the Results of the San Francisco Conference*, Dept of State Publication 2349 (1945)).

[21] cf. P. Corbett, 'What is the League of Nations?', (1924) 5 *British Yearbook of International Law* 119–48, at 142, who mentions the 'invariably repudiated "super-State"'.

[22] See *Repertory of Practice of United Nations Organs*, (Publication No. 55. V. 2) New York 1955, Vol. 5 at 292–7.

[23] J. Frowein and K. Oellers-Frahm, 'Article 65' in A. Zimmermann et al. (eds), *The Statute of the International Court of Justice: A Commentary* (2nd edn, Oxford, Oxford University Press 2012) p. 1614.

[24] *Conditions of Admission of a State to Membership in the United Nations (Article 4 of Charter)*, Advisory Opinion, [1947–48] ICJ Rep 57, at 61–2; *Competence of the General Assembly for the Admission of a State to the United Nations*, Advisory Opinion, [1950] ICJ Rep 3, at 6–7; *Certain Expenses of the United Nations (Article 17, paragraph 2, of the Charter)*, Advisory Opinion, [1962] ICJ Rep 151, at 155.

[25] *Legality of the Threat or Use of Nuclear Weapons*, Advisory Opinion, [1996] ICJ Rep at 226; *Legal Consequences of the Construction of a Wall in the Occupied Palestinian Territory*, Advisory Opinion, [2004] ICJ Rep at 136, 155; *Accordance with International Law of the Unilateral Declaration of Independence in Respect of Kosovo*, Advisory Opinion of 22 July 2010, available at http://www.icj-cij.org, para. 26.

undisputed that the 1980 request of the Health Assembly came about in a deeply polit-icized context (in the end the Regional Office stayed in Egypt, and work was regu-larly resumed in 1985 after Israel transferred its regional membership to the European regional office). This said, it was and is settled jurisprudence of the Court to separate the legal character of a question put before it from the possibly political considerations which may have motivated that question. In this opinion especially the Court made it a point to state that 'in situations in which political considerations are prominent it may be particularly necessary for an international organization to obtain an advisory opinion from the Court as to the legal principles applicable with respect to the matter under debate, especially when these may include the interpretation of its constitution' (para. 33, above). This appears as a remarkable 'rule of law' statement on the part of the Court regarding the functioning of international organizations.

5.3 *Case No. IT-95-9-PT, Decision on the Motion for a Judicial Assistance to be Provided by SFOR and Others,* Trial Chamber of the International Criminal Tribunal for the former Yugoslavia, 18 October 2000

Harmen van der Wilt

Relevance of the case

This decision is a highly relevant follow-up to the *Blaskić* judgment of the ICTY Appeals Chamber on state co-operation and subpoena powers, in which the Chamber recognized the power of the Tribunal to issue binding orders to states. In the present case, the Trial Chamber extends this authority to cover multinational peace-keeping forces, like SFOR, as well. Moreover, the Chamber implicitly acknowledges that irregularities in the apprehension and detention of the suspect could in principle affect the court's jurisdiction.

I. The facts of the case

Although several accused are mentioned in this case, the central issue concerns the arrest and detention of one of them, Stevan Todorović preceding his trial before the International Tribunal for the former Yugoslavia in The Hague. Todorović had been indicted on charges of grave breaches of the 1949 Geneva Conventions, violations of the laws and customs of war, and crimes against humanity, relating to the events said to have taken place in the area of Bosanski Samac, in the north-eastern part of Bosnia-Herzegovina, during the summer of 1992. A warrant for the arrest of the accused had been issued on 21 July 1995 and Todorović, who lived in Serbia and Montenegro, had allegedly been abducted and taken against his will to Bosnia and Herzegovina. Subsequently, the accused was handed over to the Stabilisation Force (SFOR) at the Air Base at Tuzla, Bosnia and Herzegovina. Counsel for the accused had submitted a motion that sought an order from the Trial Chamber requesting the assistance of SFOR in the production of documents and witnesses that might shed a light on the forceful apprehension and transfer of the accused from his residence to the Tuzla Air Force basis. SFOR itself had countered the claim, by arguing that, in its opinion, the ICTY had no authority to order SFOR to disclose information. However, defence counsel had persisted in its request and had clarified the exact relief sought as: (i) an order and *subpoenas duces tecum* directed to the Commanding General of SFOR for the production of documents and other evidentiary material; (ii) a *subpoena ad testificandum* directed to the Commanding General of Tuzala Air Force and to the SFOR personnel involved in the seizure, abduction, and arrest of the accused; and (iii) a request for judicial assistance directed to the United States of America for the same materials.

II. The legal question

The core legal issue was whether the ICTY had the power to issue binding orders to an international peace-keeping force, such as SFOR, in order to obtain evidence on irregular arrest and detention. This question had hitherto been contested as several Trial Chambers had reached contrary conclusions. In this case the Trial Chamber gave a substantiated affirmative answer.

III. Excerpts

[…]

The Defence

9. The Defence argues that it is entitled to seek assistance in the production of evidence relating to the facts and circumstances of the detention and alleged arrest of the accused. In particular, it seeks:[2]

   (a) attendance of the individual or individuals who transported the accused by helicopter to the Tuzla Air Force base;
   (b) attendance of the individual who placed the accused under arrest and served the arrest warrant;
   (c) production of the audio and video tapes made on 27 September 1998 of the initial detention and arrest of the accused at the Tuzla Air Force base;
   (d) SFOR pre- and post-arrest operations reports relating to the arrest and detention of the accused.[…]

11. The Defence asserts[4] that individuals serving with SFOR are amenable to compulsory attendance, relying on a Decision of the Appeals Chamber of the International Tribunal in *Prosecutor v. Blaskić*.[5] The involvement of SFOR in the alleged abduction is said to be shown by the fact that, after being transported across the border from the Federal Republic of Yugoslavia (Serbia and Montenegro) into Bosnia and Herzegovina, a helicopter arrived within minutes of a radio call to transport the accused to the SFOR base at Tuzla.[6]

12. The Defence also asserts that it has described the documents and items sought with sufficient specificity to meet the requirements of the Appeals Chamber Decision in *Blaskić*. The request is not unduly onerous and sufficient time for compliance may be granted.

13. Further, the Defence argues that, even if SFOR itself is not subject to the jurisdiction of the International Tribunal, the individual member States remain liable and obligated to fulfil all of the obligations undertaken as members of the United Nations and thus to cooperate with the International Tribunal. The Defence suggests that this obviates any need for the Trial Chamber to address the issue of whether SFOR, as an entity, is subject to the jurisdiction of the International Tribunal, as its constituent members clearly are so subject.[7] The Defence notes that Security Council resolution 1088, of 12 December 1996,[8] which established SFOR, 'underlines that full cooperation by States and entities with the International Tribunal includes, inter alia, the surrender for trial of all persons indicted by the Tribunal and provision of information to assist in Tribunal investigations'.

The Prosecution

14. The Prosecution relies upon the arguments raised in previous filings in the proceedings as to the legality of the arrest.[9] In essence, the Prosecution asserts:

    (a) the Motion does not establish any prima facie basis for judicial enquiry;

    (b) even if any irregularity in the circumstances of the arrest did exist, it would
        not justify the relief sought.

15. The Prosecution argues that 'some international laws are not binding on certain
international institutions' first, because 'some international laws are exclusively designed
to regulate conduct between states and have no application to international institutions'
and, second, 'because of the fact that in the legitimate performance of its functions, the
powers of the International Tribunal prevail over traditional concerns of state sovereignty'.[10] In seeking to justify the legality of the arrest, the Prosecution notes that the
territorial jurisdiction of the International Tribunal extends throughout the territory
of the former Yugoslavia, and so there is no basis to assert any breach of sovereignty.
Furthermore, the arrest of persons pursuant to a valid warrant of arrest issued by the
International Tribunal does not constitute a breach of sovereignty as, if it did, all other
matters, such as investigation and indictment of any accused, holding hearings and
detaining accused persons, would also amount to a breach of sovereignty.[11] The actions
taken by the International Tribunal, which would, if conducted by a State, constitute
a breach of sovereignty of another State, are specifically authorised under the United
Nations Charter.[...]

SFOR

18. In its written submission of 10 July 2000 ('the SFOR Submission'),[15] SFOR has
argued: (i) further disclosure is unnecessary because the accused would not be entitled to the relief sought even if the allegations are proven because (a) relevant case law
does not mandate release of the accused, (b) the accused is not entitled to the remedy
of release from custody, and (c) the accused should not be returned to a State which
defies its legal obligations to the International Tribunal; and (ii) compelling requirements of operational security preclude further disclosure by SFOR concerning the
detention of the accused.[16][...]

1. Application of this power to SFOR

38. Article 29 of the Statute deals with cooperation between States and the International
Tribunal 'in the investigation and prosecution of persons accused of committing serious violations of international humanitarian law'. The Appeals Chamber decision in
Prosecutor v. Blaskić[48] confirms what is plain on a reading of that Article, that is, that
the International Tribunal is empowered to issue binding orders to States. The question is whether the International Tribunal is empowered under Article 29 to issue an
order to SFOR, bearing in mind that Article 29 is, on its face, confined to the issuing of
orders to States. To answer this it is necessary to examine both the establishment and
structure of SFOR and the scope of Article 29.[...]

2. Co-operation between SFOR and the International Tribunal

43. In December 1995 the North Atlantic Council agreed that copies of indictments
and arrest warrants issued by the International Tribunal would be transmitted to
IFOR and that any indicted person detained by IFOR would be taken into custody,

immediately informed of the charges against him and transferred as soon as reasonably practicable to the International Tribunal (hereafter 'NAC decision'). Reference to the NAC decision is to be found in the Order of Judge Claude Jorda of 24 December 1995, which, *inter alia,* noted as follows:

1. that the North Atlantic Council on 16 December 1995 agreed that, having regard to UN Security Council regulations (*sic*) 827 (1993) and 1031 (1995) and Annex 1-A of the General Framework Agreement for Peace in Bosnia and Herzegovina, the multinational military implementation force (IFOR) should detain any persons indicted by the International Criminal Tribunal who come into contact with IFOR in its execution of assigned tasks in order to assure the transfer of these persons to the International Criminal Tribunal;

2. that the North Atlantic Council on 16 December 1995 approved a supplemental Rule of Engagement on the detention and transfer of such indicted persons with application limited to Bosnia-Herzegovina, to be implemented once practical arrangements have been agreed with the International Criminal Tribunal for the transfer to it of such indicted persons.[54] [...]

3. *The scope of Article 29*

46. On its terms, Article 29 applies to all States, whether acting individually or collectively. In principle, there is no reason why Article 29 should not apply to collective enterprises undertaken by States, in the framework of international organisations and, in particular, their competent organs such as SFOR in the present case. A purposive construction of Article 29 suggests that it is as applicable to such collective enterprises as it is to States. The purpose of Article 29 of the Statute of the International Tribunal is to secure cooperation with the International Tribunal in the investigation and prosecution of persons accused of committing serious violations of international humanitarian law in the former Yugoslavia. The need for such cooperation is strikingly apparent, since the International Tribunal has no enforcement arm of its own—it lacks a police force. Although this cooperation would, more naturally, be expected from States, it is also achievable through the assistance of international organizations through their competent organs which, by virtue of their activities, might have information relating to, or come into contact with, persons indicted by the International Tribunal for serious violations of international humanitarian law. The existing relationship between SFOR and the International Tribunal is indicative of such cooperation in practice.

47. The International Tribunal has on several occasions had recourse to the general rule of treaty interpretation set out in Article 31 (1) of the Vienna Convention on the Law of Treaties ('the Vienna Convention') for the purpose of interpreting the Statute.[57] Article 31(1) of the Vienna Convention provides that 'a treaty shall be interpreted in good faith in accordance with the ordinary meaning to be given to the terms of the treaty in their context and in the light of its object and purpose.' The jurisprudence of the International Tribunal has repeatedly stressed the importance of giving due weight to the object and purpose of the Statute in its construction. The mere fact that the text of Article 29 is confined to States and omits reference to other collective enterprises of States does not mean that it was intended that the International Tribunal should not also benefit from the assistance of States acting through such enterprises in the investigation and prosecution of persons accused of committing serious violations of international humanitarian law.

48. A purposive construction of the Statute yields the conclusion that such an order should be as applicable to collective enterprises of States as it is to individual States; Article 29 should, therefore, be read as conferring on the International Tribunal a power to require an international organization or its competent organ such as SFOR to cooperate with it in the achievement of its fundamental objective of prosecuting persons responsible for serious violations of international humanitarian law, by providing the several modes of assistance set out therein.

49. The Trial Chamber is satisfied that SFOR is sufficiently organised and structured to receive and implement orders of the International Tribunal made pursuant to Article 29. [...]

B. The specific orders requested

(i) The order to SFOR

58. On the basis of the analysis at paragraphs 46–49, the Trial Chamber concludes that it is competent to issue a binding order under Article 29 of the Statute to the 33 participating States of SFOR and, through its responsible authority, the North Atlantic Council, to SFOR itself. Such an Order is issued to the various States concerned pursuant to Rule 54 bis (E) and a similar procedure will, by analogy, be applied in respect of the Order to SFOR and to the North Atlantic Council. Indeed a similar procedure has already been followed in this case to date, by serving the Motion on SFOR and inviting it to attend the hearing in July 2000. There are further provisions of the Rules permitting an affected State to apply to have such Order set aside on the basis that disclosure would prejudice its national security interests or to seek review of such a decision by the Appeals Chamber.

59. The purpose of the Defence Motion is to secure certain information and documents, which the accused believes to be in the custody and control of SFOR, and which will assist him in his motions challenging the legality of his arrest.[66] The main contention of both SFOR and the Prosecution in opposing this Motion is that the Motion should be dismissed because Todorović is not entitled to the relief he seeks, even if his allegations were to be accepted.[67] This argument proceeds on the assumption that the evidence is complete. That assumption is erroneous, as what Todorović is seeking is further evidence from SFOR which will assist him to obtain the relief which he seeks. Only when Todorović has had the opportunity to present all the available evidence will it be possible for the Trial Chamber to determine whether he is entitled to the relief he seeks. The Prosecution sought to argue once more that there is no basis in the evidence to date which entitled Todorović to obtain such material.[68] As the Trial Chamber, in its Order of 7 March 2000, has already held that there *is* such a basis, and as the application by the Prosecution for leave to appeal against that decision was refused, it is not open to the Prosecution to re-agitate that issue now.

60. As to the additional claim by SFOR that 'further' factual disclosure is precluded by 'compelling requirements of operational security',[69] the Trial Chamber does not accept the blanket objection which SFOR has raised. It was open to SFOR to make specific objections to the disclosure of particular documents or other material at the hearing in accordance with a procedure similar to that set forth in Rule 54 *bis* (F) but SFOR chose not to do so.

61. The Trial Chamber is satisfied that it has been adequately demonstrated that there is material in the custody or control of SFOR which is likely to assist Todorović

in obtaining the relief he seeks, and that there is a legitimate forensic purpose in having it produced. The Trial Chamber is also satisfied that, as the Prosecution has not been able to produce copies of the material, it is appropriate that SFOR now be required to disclose that material.

The Subpoena to SFOR Personnel to Testify

62. On the basis of the Appeals Chamber's decision in *Blaskić,* referred to in paragraph 51 of this Decision, the Trial Chamber has the competence to issue a *subpoena ad testificandum* to SFOR personnel. This includes General Shinseki since, in terms of that decision, he is not representing his State and is to be treated *qua* individual in respect of any event that he has personally witnessed, even if observed while performing his official functions. Thus he is compellable not in his role as Commanding General of SFOR but as an individual with personal knowledge of the events of which complaint is made. Similar considerations will apply to any other SFOR personnel who are shown to have direct knowledge of these events.

63. The Trial Chamber is satisfied that it would be appropriate to issue a subpoena to General Shinseki in due course, requiring him to testify in the ongoing evidentiary hearing in this matter.

IV. Commentary

This decision has its origin in the problematic fact that international criminal tribunals and courts have no police force at their disposal and are therefore dependent on the assistance of states for obtaining evidence and custody over suspects. Article 29 of the Statute of the ICTY obliges states to co-operate with the Tribunal in the investigation and prosecution of persons accused of committing serious violations of international humanitarian law. If states that are the most eligible to offer such assistance default on their obligations, international criminal tribunals are naturally inclined to turn to other states or multinational peace-keeping forces, when available. Both the Stabilisation Force (SFOR) and its predecessor IFOR were under an obligation to detain persons indicted by the ICTY with a view to their transfer to the Tribunal.[1] The choice of words delineating the category of persons that are to be detained and transferred— 'persons who come into contact with IFOR in its execution of assigned tasks'[2]—is interesting, as it begs the question whether SFOR/IFOR members were supposed to actively search for war criminals. It is generally held that they were not.[3] However, SFOR did not need to possess such far-reaching criminal enforcement powers if it could easily benefit from the actions of 'unknown individuals' who were prepared to do the dirty work and

---

[1] According to the Order of Judge Claude Jorda of 16 December 1995, which mentioned Security Council Resolution 1031 of 15 December 1995 in tandem with Annex 1-A of the Dayton Peace Agreement as the legal basis; *Prosecutor v Blagoje Simić* et al. IT-95-9, Order, Judge Jorda, filed 5 February 1996.

[2] Decision, § 43.

[3] Compare G. Sluiter, *International Criminal Adjudication and the Collection of Evidence: Obligations of States* (Antwerpen and Oxford, New York 2002), p. 265 who observes that 'although international forces such as SFOR/IFOR or KFOR perform tasks at the request of the ICTY in the field of "enforcement", they can as such not be considered the "enforcement branch" of the Tribunals'. However, Sluiter points at the contrary opinion of Judge Robinson who in his separate opinion (§ 6) to this Decision attributes a role to SFOR 'comparable to that of a police force in some domestic legal systems'.

put the suspects into SFOR's hands. Such abductions and 'irregular renditions' trigger new legal problems, as they both infringe on territorial sovereignty of states and violate fundamental human rights of human beings. The recurring issue in the ICTY's case law has been whether such acts could be attributed to SFOR or the Prosecutor's Office and whether the Tribunal had to divest itself of jurisdiction, thus sanctioning the unlawful practices in the pre-trial stage.[4] In inter-state relations this legal problem has gained currency under the maxim *male captus, bene detentus*. Traditionally most courts have turned a blind eye to irregular arrest, detention, and surrender in foreign countries, holding that such unlawful behavior preceding the trial did not prevent the court from exercising jurisdiction over the accused.[5] However, some courts have advanced a different view, arguing that the Prosecutor should come to the court with clean hands, that serious violations of the law in the pre-trial stage affected the integrity of the entire criminal process and that the court should consequently decline to exercise jurisdiction.[6] Trial Chambers of the ICTY have referred to this case law of domestic courts, emphasizing that the balancing of the interests of international criminal law enforcement, states, and individual suspects would yield different outcomes in the vertical context. I will return to this issue in due course.

The *male captus* theme as just expounded, while highlighted by both the Prosecutor and SFOR, did not feature in the Trial Chamber's decision, because the Defence sought to obtain the very documents from SFOR that would sustain its claim that SFOR had been involved in the alleged abduction. The crux of the matter was therefore whether the Tribunal could issue binding orders to an international body like SFOR. For obvious reasons, the Trial Chamber referred to the famous subpoena decision of the Appeals Chamber in the *Blaškić*-case, in which that Chamber, while denying the power of the Tribunal to punish a state, acknowledged its right to issue binding orders to states.[7] Should this power be extended in order to cover international organizations as well? Invoking art. 31(1) of the Vienna Convention which stipulates that treaties are to be interpreted in good faith in accordance with the ordinary meaning to be given to the terms of the treaty in their context and in the light of its object and purpose, the Trial Chamber answered the question affirmatively. That conclusion seems to be a sensible, if not inevitable one. Although the rendering of assistance to the ICTY did perhaps not constitute the *raison d'être* of IFOR/SFOR, it soon became one of its major tasks. SFOR's services would be largely pointless if the Tribunal would not be

---

[4] See *Prosecutor v Dokmanović*, Decision on the Motion for Release by the Accused Slavko Dokmanović Trial Chamber I, Case No. IT-95-13a-PT, 22 October 1997; *Prosecutor v Dragan Nikolić*, Decision on Defence Motion Challenging the Exercise of Jurisdiction by the Tribunal (Trial Chamber II), IT-94-2-AR72, 9 October 2002 and *Pros. v Nicolić*, Decision on Interlocutory Appeal Concerning Legality of Arrest, Appeals Chamber, Case No. IT-94-2-AR73, 5 June 2003.

[5] The most (in)famous example is the US Supreme Court's judgment in the case of *United States v Alvarez Machain* (1992) 504 US 655.

[6] *Regina v Horseferry Road Magistrates' Court, Ex parte Bennett*, House of Lords 25 June 1993, [1994] 1 AC 42; *State v Ebrahim*, South African Supreme Court (Appellate Division), Opinion, 16 February 1991, Int. Leg. Mat., Vol. 31, n. 4, July 1992, pp. 890–9.

[7] *Prosecutor v Blaškić*, Judgment on the Request of the Republic of Croatia for Review of the Decision of Trial Chamber II of 18 July 1997, IT-95-14-AR108bis, 29 October 1997, §26: 'The exceptional legal basis of Article 29 accounts for the novel and indeed unique power granted to the International Tribunal to issue orders to sovereign States.'

able to instruct the organization to co-operate. Moreover, it would imply that states could evade their obligations under art. 29 ICTY Statute by pooling their resources and establishing a collective. The Trial Chamber therefore ordered SFOR to disclose all material—correspondence, reports audio, and video tapes—that could shed light on the apprehension and arrest of the accused, Stevan Todorović. The order was predicated on Rule 54*bis* of the ICTY Rules of Procedure and Evidence ('Orders Directed to States for the Production of Evidence') which was applied by analogy to SFOR. While SFOR attempted to preclude disclosure, invoking 'compelling requirements of operational security', the Trial Chamber did not accept the 'blanket objection'.[8]

An interesting side-issue was whether the Tribunal could directly subpoena SFOR-personnel to testify during proceedings. In this respect the *Blaskić* precedent was quite instructive as well. In general, international criminal courts would not be entitled to pierce the veil of a state's internal organization. They would have to respect the state's decision to designate individuals as state officials and assign them specific tasks, both at the internal level and in international relations. The Appeals Chamber qualified the functional immunity of state officials as a corollary of such authority, which had to be observed by international organizations and international courts as well.[9] But the position of a state official who acted as a member of an international peace-keeping—or enforcement force, like SFOR—was different, as he was not present in Yugoslavia '*qua* a member of the military structure of his own country. His mandate stems from the same source as that of the International Tribunal, *id est*, a resolution of the Security Council, and therefore he must testify, subject to the appropriate requirements set out in the Rules.'[10] In a footnote, the Appeals Chamber clarified that such a direct approach of an SFOR official, bypassing SFOR itself, would be appropriate if he had direct knowledge of the commission or planning of a crime, by personal observation (the so called *subpoena ad testificandum*). If, on the other hand, the official was expected to produce a document or other written evidence (*subpoena duces tecum*), it would be preferable to address the organization.[11] As the Commanding General of SFOR, General Shinseki was assumed to have personal knowledge of the arrest of the accused, the Trial Chamber in the case under scrutiny gratefully followed the Blaskić precedent.

The very fact that the Trial Chamber was prepared to grant the request of the accused by issuing binding orders to SFOR and subpoena the SFOR General indicates that the Chamber opined that further information could reveal whether the accused's complaint would strike home. That point of view as such was contested by both the Prosecution and SFOR who asserted that, even if any irregularity in the circumstances of the arrest would surface, the accused would not be entitled to the relief sought.[12] The Trial Chamber did not agree: 'Only when Todorović has had the opportunity to present all the available evidence will it be possible for the Trial Chamber to determine whether he is entitled to the relief he seeks.'[13] In other words: the Chamber left the door ajar for the possibility that the accused's claim would be successful. This position comports with previous and subsequent case law of the ICTY. Addressing the

---

[8] Decision, § 60.　　[9] Ibid., § 41.　　[10] Ibid., § 50.　　[11] Ibid., § 50, fn. 68.
[12] Decision, §§ 14 and 18.　　[13] Decision, § 59.

question under what circumstances 'irregularities' in respect of arrest would require the court to decline to exercise jurisdiction, the Appeals Chamber in *Nikolić* made a sharp distinction between the violation of state sovereignty and infringements of human rights.[14] Balancing the legitimate expectation that those accused of universally condemned crimes will be brought to justice quickly with the principle of state sovereignty, the Appeals Chamber made it clear that the former should prevail. It did not matter whether the unlawful conduct of the accused's captors could be attributed to SFOR or not: even the former situation would not affect the Tribunal's jurisdiction. The Appeals Chamber made a highly interesting side note by suggesting that any state which failed to meet its obligations to co-operate had itself to blame for an incursion upon its sovereignty.[15] That makes sense. If a state flouts its commitments by refusing to co-operate, it cannot expect an international criminal tribunal to set aside jurisdiction, if others step in to repair the state's omission. It demonstrates that concerns for sovereignty are less pressing in the framework of vertical co-operation in criminal matters between tribunals and states than in the inter-state context.

In relation to the human rights of the accused that might have been affected by the abduction, the Appeals Chamber was more circumspect. It acknowledged that exceptionally cruel treatment of the accused during arrest and detention might leave a court no other option than to decline jurisdiction.[16] The Chamber referred to and concurred with the US Federal Court of Appeals in *Toscanino* which had famously held that 'we view due process as now requiring a court to divest itself of jurisdiction over the person of a defendant where it has been acquired as the result of the Government's deliberate, unnecessary and unreasonable invasion of the accused's constitutional rights.'[17] However, the Appeals Chamber found that in the case under consideration the treatment of the Appellant was not of such an egregious nature as to impede the exercise of jurisdiction.[18] Just as little as in the issue of state sovereignty, the Appeals Chamber did not attach much relevance to the question whether SFOR had been involved in the venture and that it was consequently responsible for the violations of his rights. I tend to agree with that position. Within the state context, the courts' sanctioning of unlawful police behavior symbolizes the rule of law and simultaneously reflects the separation of powers and the unity of the state, both vis-à-vis its citizens and other states. Such considerations are largely foreign to international tribunals. SFOR and other peace-keeping forces are not an extension of international criminal tribunals (see also the discussion in fn. 3) and it would therefore be far-fetched to argue that they are complicit or co-responsible for SFOR's faults, by simply reaping the benefits from those faults. The only thing that counts is that the Tribunal has to abide by the law and do justice which in these situations entails that it might in exceptional cases compensate the accused for his great losses and suffering.

---

[14] *Prosecutor v Nicolić* (n. 4), §§ 20–7 and §§ 28–33, respectively.

[15] Ibid., § 26: 'In the opinion of the Appeals Chamber, the damage caused to international justice by not apprehending fugitives accused of serious violations of international humanitarian law is comparatively higher than the injury, if any, caused to the sovereignty of a State by a limited intrusion in its territory, *particularly when the intrusion occurs in default of the State's cooperation*.' (italics HvdW).

[16] *Prosecutor v Nikolić*, § 30.   [17] 500 F.2d 267 (2d Cir. 1974), p. 275.

[18] *Prosecutor v Nikolić*, § 31.

The decision in *Nikolić* retroactively confirmed that the Trial Chamber had been correct in ordering SFOR to provide the necessary documents. The accused stood an, albeit tiny, chance that his claim would be accepted and that the Trial Chamber would consequently decline to exercise jurisdiction. Only on the basis of the scrutiny of all available evidence could the Trial Chamber determine if the accused would be entitled to such a relief.[19] One will of course be curious to learn the outcome of the case, but the end result was rather unspectacular. On 13 December 2000, Todorović entered a guilty plea on one count of the indictment, to wit persecution as a crime against humanity. Subsequently, the Prosecutor withdrew the other counts and the Defence withdrew the outstanding motions challenging the legality of the arrest of the accused. Stevan Todorović was convicted and sentenced to ten years' imprisonment.[20]

The decision in the case under scrutiny demonstrates once again that international criminal tribunals acknowledge that they are called to respect and promote the human rights of all individuals, including those charged with heinous crimes.[21] One may add that suspects are particularly in need of such support when they are stripped of the protection of their national state. However, in guaranteeing the fair trial rights of those standing trial, international criminal tribunals often require the assistance of states in a similar way as in (repressive) criminal law enforcement. If states default on their obligations, international tribunals must have the possibility to resort to international peace-keeping forces. In that sense the availability of such entities serves as a double-edged sword.

---

[19] Decision, § 59.

[20] *Prosecutor v Todorović*, Sentencing Judgement, Case No.: IT-95-9/1-S, 31 July 2001.

[21] That point was explicitly made by the Appeals Chamber in *Prosecutor v Barayagwiza*, Decision, Case No. ICTR-97-19-AR72, A.Ch., 3 November 1999, § 112.

6

Responsibility

The assumption that international organizations can indeed carry obligations under international law (see Section 6), inevitably begs the question whether their international responsibility could also be engaged. For such responsibility to be engaged, two requirements have to be satisfied: (1) the international organization has to commit an internationally wrongful act, that is it has to violate an international obligation it possesses; and (2) this wrongful act has to be attributable to it. The International Law Commission (ILC) has made a commendable effort to draw up rules governing the responsibility of international organizations, modelled on its earlier Draft Articles on Responsibility of States for Internationally Wrongful Acts:[1] the Articles on the Responsibility of International Organizations[2] (AIRO). This document is not free of controversy; notably, it is doubtful whether all its provisions are truly a codification of existing law. Still, the ARIO have set the terms of the debate. Some of its provisions have already been applied by courts.[3] This process that may fuel the ARIO's legitimacy.

One of the most fascinating issues pertaining to the responsibility of international organizations concerns the delimitation of the responsibility of the international organization and its member states. Most international organizations have separate legal personality (see Section 1), as a consequence of which ordinarily their own—and not their member states'—responsibility will be engaged for wrongful acts of their making. In some circumstances, however, international organization conduct is not entirely isolated from the conduct of member states, for example, where a member state aids, controls, or coerces an international organization (cf. arts. 58–60, AIRO), or vice versa (arts. 14–16 ARIO). In such cases, member states' responsibility could be engaged, possibly alongside the international organizations' responsibility.

Almost all judicial decisions that are relevant to international organization responsibility concern exactly the issue of the responsibility of member states for acts carried out in the framework of, or in connection with, international institutional action. This comes as no surprise, as dispute-settlement mechanisms do not normally have jurisdiction over international organizations, or at least do not have the competence to establish their international responsibility. Mechanisms such as the International Court of Justice, the European Court of Human Rights, and domestic courts do have jurisdiction over states, however. This explains why aggrieved individuals or legal persons have tended to bring claims against member states in such fora, even if the involvement of the member state in the impugned international organization act was rather tenuous.

---

[1] Adopted November 2001 (Supplement No. 10 (A/56/10), ch. IV.E.1.
[2] Adopted 9 December 2011 A/62/10.
[3] cf. Supreme Court of The Netherlands, 6 September 2013, *ECLI* NL:HR:2013:BZ9225 (*Nuhanović v The Netherlands*); Supreme Court of The Netherlands, 6 September 2013, *ECLI* NL:HR:2013:BZ9228 (*Mustafić c.s. v The Netherlands*).

Early court cases with respect to the delimitation of the responsibility of international organizations and their member states revolved around private liability rather than international responsibility questions. For example, in *Westland Helicopters*, a private corporation asked courts to hold member states liable for the debts of the defunct Arab Organization for Industrialization (*Westland Helicopters I* and *II, Ahlborn*). A similar scenario played out in the litigation initiated by various creditors against member states of the collapsed International Tin Council.[4] In these cases, courts did not reach unisonous verdicts: some courts dismissed the cases on the ground that an international organization has a separate legal personality, while others were willing to pierce the organizational veil and hold the member states responsible.

Later cases mainly related to the delimitation of international responsibility between the international organization and its member states with respect to human rights violations. A substantial number of these cases concern the allocation of responsibility for such violations committed in the framework of international military operations. In these cases, however, courts were not so much called on to decide whether member states were responsible for violations committed by, or liabilities incurred by the international organization. Rather, they had to decide whether the impugned act should be attributed to the troop-contributing state whose service-members committed the act, or instead to the international organization (often the UN) under whose auspices the military operation unfolded. This situation is governed by arts. 6 and 7 ARIO.[5] While initially the European Court of Human Rights (ECtHR) took the view that in such cases the exercise of 'ultimate control and authority' would be the yardstick (*Behrami*, Villalpando), in more recent cases, courts, including the ECtHR, have applied an 'effective operational control' standard (*Mustafic and Nuhanovic*, Spijkers; *Mukeshimana*, Ryngaert; *Al Jedda*, Sari). The latter standard is more in line with what the ILC had in mind for military operations; effectively, some of these decisions refer to the ARIO. It bears notice that the ECtHR has at times avoided dealing with the apportionment of responsibility between member states and the international organization, by holding that the applicants did not fall within the jurisdiction of the member state in the first place (*Bankovic*, Scovazzi).

Another line of cases decided by the ECtHR addresses the responsibility of a member state for human rights violations which were committed by an international organization, but, to some extent, involved the state. The *locus classicus* is the implementation of a binding sanctions regime, enacted at the level of the international organization, but implemented by its member states. The ECtHR has held that individuals who claimed that the sanctions regime breached their human rights did fall within the jurisdiction of

---

[4] The International Tin Council Case, *JH Rayner (Mincing Lane) Ltd v Department of Trade and Industry* [1989] 3 WLR 969 (CA), [1990] 2 AC 418 (HL), [1989] 3 All ER 523, [1990] BCLC 102. *Re International Tin Council, Maclaine Watson v International Tin Council* [1987] Ch 419, [1987] 2 WLR 1229, [1987] 1 All ER 890. *Re International Tin Council*, Judgment, *Maclaine Watson v International Tin Council* [1988] 3 WLR 1159 (CA).

[5] Pursuant to art. 6.1 ARIO, '[t]he conduct of an organ or agent of an international organization in the performance of functions of that organ or agent shall be considered an act of that organization under international law, whatever position the organ or agent holds in respect of the organization.' Under art. 7 ARIO, '[t]he conduct of an organ of a State or an organ or agent of an international organization that is placed at the disposal of another international organization shall be considered under international law an act of the latter organization if the organization exercises effective control over that conduct.'

the member state implementing the international organization sanctions. Nevertheless, the member state's responsibility would only be engaged in cases where the international organization does not provide human rights protection in a manner that is at least equivalent to the protection granted by the ECHR (*Bosphorus*, Lock). Under the *Bosphorus* principle, a member state's responsibility risks being engaged by the mere transfer of competences to an international organization which fails to adequately protect human rights, provided that an intervening action of the state could be proved. In later cases, this state action was relaxed to the point of even disappearing (*Gasparini*, Lock). In practice, however, in spite of a responsibility net that is prima facie cast wide, the ECtHR has never actually held a member state responsible for a wrongful act committed by an international organization under this principle. In contrast, responsibility has been found where the member state exercised discretion when acting in the context of international organization activity, for example, where it enters into a constitutive agreement that is violative of human rights (*Matthews*, Barros), or where it goes beyond the mere implementation of international organization obligations.[6]

Case-law on the responsibility of international organizations remains in a state of flux. To be true, it is hardly contested that the responsibility of international organizations, just like the responsibility of states, *can* be engaged. Similarly, as far as the relationship between member states and international organizations is concerned, it is widely accepted that membership alone does not suffice to hold member states responsible for the acts of international organizations to which they have transferred competences.[7] It remains unclear, however, under what precise circumstances member states' responsibility could nonetheless be engaged. For instance, could they be held responsible on the basis that they have 'circumvented' their international obligations by transferring competences to international organizations; and if so, what would precisely count as circumvention? (cf. art. 61 ARIO). Could they be held responsible on the ground that they 'abused' the legal personality of international organizations?[8] Even where agreement seems to have been reached on an applicable standard, for example, the effective control standard with respect to the apportionment of responsibility in military operations, the exact operational parameters may remain elusive.[9] Given the dearth of state and institutional practice regarding the contours of international organization responsibility, courts will be key actors in developing this legal category. The thickening case-law with respect to the apportionment of international responsibility in international military operations is a harbinger of more to come.

---

[6] For example *M.S.S. v Greece and Belgium* (2011) ECHR 2011.

[7] cf. Institut De Droit International, 'The Legal Consequences for Member States of the Non-fulfilment by International Organizations of their Obligations toward Third Parties', resolution adopted 1 September 1995 (Lisbon 1995).

[8] cf. Jean d'Aspremont, 'Abuse of the Legal Personality of International Organizations and the Responsibility of Member States' (2007) 4 *International Organizations Law Review* 91.

[9] In *Mothers of Srebrenica*, for instance, The Hague District Court held rather controversially, in a 2014 decision, that The Netherlands had effective control over a situation on the ground that Dutch soldiers acted *ultra vires* the orders of the UN commander. Court of Appeal 's-Gravenhage 30 March 2010, LJN BL8979 (*Mothers of Srebrenica v The Netherlands*).

6.1 *Westland Helicopters Ltd v Arab Organization for Industrialization, United Arab Emirates, Kingdom of Saudi Arabia, State of Qatar, Arab Republic of Egypt, and Arab British Helicopter Company,* Arbitration, 5 March 1984, 80 ILR 600

Christiane Ahlborn

Relevance of the case

The present case concerns the responsibility of international organizations and their member states. The *Westland Helicopters* arbitration is the first case in which a dispute settlement body had to decide on the possible responsibility of states for the wrongful acts of an international organization. While the Arbitral Tribunal in *Westland Helicopters* decided to hold the member states responsible alongside the international organization, Swiss courts later reversed this decision. The *Westland Helicopters* cases thus foreshadowed the debate, including many of the recurrent arguments, on whether and when the corporate veil of an international organization should be pierced.

I. Facts of the case

In 1975 the Arab Republic of Egypt (ARE), Saudi Arabia, Qatar, and the United Arab Emirates concluded a treaty establishing the Arab Organization for Industrialization (AOI). According to the AOI's Basic Statute, the organization was endowed with legal personality, exempt from the laws and institutions of the member states. It had its head office in Cairo, and a capital of 1,040 million US dollars. The main organ of the AOI was the Higher Committee of the AOI, which was composed of all four member states. In 1978, the Higher Committee signed a Shareholders' Agreement with Westland Helicopters Ltd (WHL) creating a joint stock company in Egypt. This joint stock company was later referred to as Arab British Helicopter Company (ABH). The purpose of the joint stock company was the manufacture, assembly, and sale of the Lynx helicopters made by WHL, which the AOI intended to construct in Egypt.

Following the signing of a peace agreement between the ARE and Israel in May 1979, Saudi Arabia, Qatar, and the United Arab Emirates decided to terminate the existence of the AOI from 19 July 1979. They also determined to stop all investments and to charge a committee composed of the four member states with the liquidation of the Organization. Being opposed to this decision, the ARE promulgated a Decree Law on 18 May 1979, providing for the continuing existence of the AOI in the form of a company governed by Egyptian law (EAOI). The Decree Law ensured the continuation of the AOI's activities and compliance with the commitments of the organization. The ARE replaced the representatives from the three Gulf States with Egyptian members on the Higher Committee.

After the failure of negotiations, WHL gave notice of its decision to claim damages of 126 million GB pounds against the dissolved AOI and its member states.

On 12 May 1980, it filed a request for arbitration with the International Chamber of Commerce (ICC) in Paris, which was directed against the AOI, the four member states of this organization, and ABH. The request was based on art. 12 of the Shareholders Agreement between the AOI and WHL, which provides as follows:

12. Arbitration and law

12.1 Any controversy or dispute which may arise between the parties in connection with the interpretation, application or effect of this Agreement which cannot be resolved amicably shall be finally settled under the Rules of Conciliation and Arbitration of the International Chamber of Commerce by one or more arbitrators appointed in accordance with the said Rules. Such arbitration shall be held in Geneva and the costs shall be borne as ordered by the arbitration court. Each party recognizes that the enforcement of the arbitration award may be made through any court having jurisdiction.

12.2 This Agreement shall be governed by and construed in accordance with the Laws of Switzerland.

12.3 The clauses of this Agreement and the Annexes hereto have been written in English and Arabic. Both texts shall be deemed equally authentic. Annex A hereto has been written in Arabic and an English translation has also been attached.

The ARE objected that it was not party to any of the agreements invoked by WHL, and the other defendants did not react to the request for arbitration. Nonetheless, the ICC Court of Arbitration set up an Arbitral Tribunal composed of three members on 29 October 1980. Geneva was determined to be the place of arbitration.

II. The legal question

The interim award mainly concerned the competence of the Arbitral Tribunal in relation to all six respondents, the AOI, its four member states, and ABH. In particular, the Tribunal had to answer the question whether art. 12 of the Shareholders Agreement was applicable to the AOI's four member states that had not signed the agreement explicitly.

III. Excerpts

(A. The existence of an arbitration clause in written form)

The *four States* never themselves directly signed any contract with Westland. This is not in itself a sufficient argument by which to reject, from the outset, the obligation of the four States to submit themselves to arbitration. [...]

The question whether the four States are bound by the arbitration clause concluded by the AOI in its own name (Shareholders Agreement contracted with Westland, Clause 12.1) is exactly the same as the substantive law question whether the four States are bound in general by the obligations contracted by the AOI. If the obligations under substantive law flowing from the Shareholders Agreement are obligations not only of the AOI, but also of the four States, if the *locus standi* to conduct the defence in relation to those obligations can be attributed not only to the AOI, but also to the four States, then the latter are therefore bound by the arbitration clause, just as they might, had they been summoned before an ordinary court, have availed themselves of this clause as a ground in their defence. The mandatory force of the arbitration clause cannot be dissociated from that of the substantive contractual commitments; the reply to the question as to whether the four States are bound by the acts of the AOI must always be the same, whether the procedural aspect of the arbitration clause is involved or that of the substantive law concerning the financial obligations of the four States.

[20] (B. The supranational status of the AOI)[…]

In the opinions submitted by the ARE it is maintained that no legal person may exist without a legal foundation within a national legal order. This confuses the legal position of legal persons created by individuals within the framework of private law with the position of the AOI, created by States. Whereas it is true that an individual cannot set up a legal entity without the authorization of a State or a State law, sovereign States may themselves dispense with such a basis. Their acts have the force of law, and if a State alone can create by its acts (even without recourse to its legislation previously in force) a legal person, several States clearly have the same power when they act together and with common intent, as the four States did in the present circumstances. […]

The later unilateral acts by Egypt, the aim of which was to 'nationalize' the AOI (see Decree Law No 30 of 1979 of the Arab Republic of Egypt of 18 May 1979, Exhibit 6), cannot in any way change the situation set out. The sovereignty of the ARE carries the possibility to exert its *imperium* over its own territory, but that sovereignty does not include a power to change the legal status of the AOI as set up by these treaties with the other States without the agreement of those States themselves, even if the 'seat' (in whatever sense of the word) was situate [sic] within Egyptian territory.

[23] (C. The consequence of the possible attribution of personality to the AOI as regards the liability of the four States)

One may be tempted to reduce the question of whether the four States are bound by the acts of the AOI to one of whether the AOI has legal personality or not. A widespread theory, deriving moreover from Roman law ('*Si quid universitati debetur, singulis non debetur, nec quod debet universitas singuli debent*' Dig. 3,4; 7,1), excludes cumulative liability of a legal person and of the individuals which constitute it, these latter being party to none of the legal relations of the legal person. This notion, which could be deemed 'strict', cannot however be applied in the present case. Nowhere is it accepted or given effect without limitation. […]

One must therefore disregard any question relating to the personality of the AOI. The possible liability of the four States must be determined by directly examining the founding documents of the AOI in relation to this problem.

[25] (D. The liability of the four States in the light of the constitution of the AOI)

Neither the Treaty nor the Basic Statute of AOI states the effects, as regards the four States, of obligations undertaken by the AOI *vis-à-vis* third parties. As to the liability of the four States, concurrent with that of the AOI, there are no provisions which either expressly stipulate it or exclude it. The fact that the AOI 'has the juridical personality', 'enjoys full administrative and financial independence' and 'has the right of ownership, disposition and litigation as mentioned in its statute' (Treaty, Article 1; in the same vein, see Basic Statute, Article 5), that is to say the express attribution of legal personality, of administrative independence and of the right to sue in the courts, does not in any respect allow one, as has been shown, to deduce an exclusion of the liability of the four States.

The same is true of the provision which states that AOI has a specified sum of capital (Basic Statute, Article 17); in the absence of any rule restricting liability to such capital, one cannot deduce therefrom any obstacle to an action against the four States. The provisions setting out capital are primarily internal to the AOI, determining the funds which its organs have at their disposal. One could perhaps infer that the four States' liability is secondary, in that they could not be proceeded against so long as the AOI performed its obligations whilst using the funds which had been granted to it; but it does not follow that the four States would have no liability whatsoever for obligations entered into by the AOI.

[26] In the absence of any rule of applicable law ['règle de droit positif'], what is to be deduced from the silence of the founding documents of the AOI as to the liability of the four States? In the absence of any provision expressly or impliedly excluding the liability of the four States, this liability subsists since, as a general rule, those who engage in transactions of an economic nature are deemed liable for the obligations which flow therefrom. In default by the four States of formal exclusion of their liability, third parties which have contracted with the AOI could legitimately count on their liability. This rule flows from general principles of law and from good faith. It can be supported if one likens the given situation to that which existed during the last century, where commercial organizations were formed without a clear legal basis (whether or not they could be considered as possessing personality).

[28] (E. Limitation on the scope of the personality of the AOI by its constitution)

a) The foregoing is all the more true given that the personality conferred upon the AOI by the founding States was expressly limited, both by Article I of the Treaty and by Article 5 of the Basic Statute, solely to operational needs, as is provided in the articles of many international organizations.

b) The AOI was designated by its founders as an 'organization' and as a 'body', as opposed to the 'joint-stock company' ABH, and the legal status of such a joint interstate enterprise ['entreprise commune interétatique']—to the extent that it can exist at all—cannot be relied upon in order to eliminate the liability of the States which are partners therein.

c) Finally, one must admit that in reality, in the circumstances of this case, the AOI is one with the States. At the same time as establishing the AOI, the Treaty set up the Higher Committee ('joint Ministerial Higher Committee') composed of the competent Ministers of the four States, charged with the responsibility not only to approve the Basic Statute, and to set up a provisional Directorate, but furthermore to direct the general policy of the AOI, and Article 23 of the Basic Statute describes this Committee as the 'dominating authority'.

[29] This Committee thus played a double role, both as organ of the AOI and as a grouping of States ['réunion d'Etats']. In fact, in its role as organ of the AOI, it had under its control the operations of the AOI and, as a grouping of States ['reunion d'Etats'], it signed the MOU (Exhibit 3). [...]

(G. Equity; abuse of law)[…]

It would be wrong if the disagreement which arose between the four States, in May 1979, were to be prejudicial to Westland, rendering all the guarantees worthless. It matters little whether the AOI had disappeared or not. Whether faced with either an Egyptian company which makes itself out as the successor of an international organization ['société internationale']—contrary to what had been stipulated—or a liquidation committee, which remains mute, Westland is justified in bringing the four States themselves before the Arbitrators. Were this not the case, there would be a real denial of justice.

[32] Equity, in common with the principles of international law, allows the corporate veil to be lifted, in order to protect third parties against an abuse which would be to their detriment (International Court of Justice, 5 February 1970, *Barcelona Traction*).[2][…]

VII *Immunity of the Four States* […]

[37] According to a view accepted in Switzerland, as elsewhere, the signing of an arbitration clause implies the waiver of this ground. The four States, in creating the AOI, whose obligations were binding on themselves, could not have overlooked the possibility of being proceeded against at law in respect of these obligations. The creation of the AOI therefore implies a waiver of immunity in respect of obligations entered into by the AOI.

IV. Commentary

The present case concerns the question whether states could potentially be held responsible for the acts of an international organization of which they are members. The arbitral award was limited to examining the competence of the Tribunal, and did thus not determine the actual liability of and possible remedies against AOI member states. Nonetheless, it addressed one of the central questions in the debate on the responsibility of international organizations: can the corporate veil of an international organization be pierced, and if so, under which conditions? The Arbitral Tribunal answered this question affirmatively. Noting that AOI member states had not explicitly excluded the liability of the organization in its constitution, the tribunal declared itself competent to arbitrate the case brought by WHL against all four respondent states (in addition to the AOI and ABH).

Since the *Westland Helicopters* arbitration was the first notable case concerning member state responsibility, the Tribunal had hardly any scholarly or judicial guidance in drafting its award. Until the 1980s, only a few scholars had discussed the responsibility of international organizations and their member states.[1] The arbitral award

---

[1] Writing in 1950, Clyde Eagleton first addressed the responsibility of international organizations on the basis of hypothetical case scenarios. See C. Eagleton, 'International Organization and the Law of Responsibility', (1950) 76 *Recueil des cours* 319. As one of the first authors, Ignaz Seidl-Hohenfeldern distinguished between the responsibility of international organizations and its members in 'Die völkerrechtliche Haftung für Handlungen internationaler Organisationen im Verhältnis zu Nichtmitgliedstaaten', (1961) 11 *Österreichische Zeitschrift für öffentliches Recht* 497. Other authors focused on specific topics such as space law (C.Q. Christol, 'International liability for damage caused by space objects', (1980) 74 *American Journal of International Law* 346; A. Bueckling, 'Die völkerrechtliche Haftung für Schäden, die durch Weltraumgegenstände verursacht werden', (1972) 21 *Zeitschrift für Luftrecht und Weltraumrechtsfragen* 213) or peace operations (K. Ginther, *Die völkerrechtliche Verantwortlichkeit*

in *Westland Helicopters* is therefore characterized by a search for the right methodology or framework to describe international organizations. Due to the lack of rules of international law on member state responsibility, the Arbitral Tribunal looked for an adequate comparator for international organizations. In this context, it was decisive for the outcome of the case that the Tribunal in *Westland Helicopters* settled on drawing analogies between international organizations and certain private business associations. As the later appeal against this arbitral award before the Swiss Federal Supreme Court illustrates, the outcome of the case would have been a different one if a different comparator had been chosen.

At the outset of its decision, however, the Arbitral Tribunal made clear that the AOI itself was not a private company but an entity created by virtue of international law. The consideration of the international legal personality of the AOI was necessary due to its unclear legal status. Although Saudi Arabia, Qatar, and the United Arab Emirates had expressed their intention to dissolve the organization, the ARE objected to this decision. In its submissions to the Arbitral Tribunal, the ARE argued that the AOI had not ceased to exist.[2] The ARE claimed that the three Gulf States could not unilaterally terminate the existence of the AOI, and in any case, the AOI continued to exist by virtue of Decree Law No. 30 in the form of the Egyptian AOI. Considering these claims, the Arbitral Tribunal decided that neither of the member states could change the status of the AOI unilaterally. As a result, it declined the ARE's first claim but agreed with its second submission. In other words, it objected to the ARE's argument that the AOI continued to exist as an Egyptian private company. However, it found that the AOI had legal personality under international law for purposes of the arbitration regardless of the Gulf States' decision to dissolve the organization.[3]

Although the Tribunal acknowledged that the AOI had legal personality, it underlined that this separate legal personality could not limit the liability of the member states of the organization. The Arbitral Tribunal thereby explicitly rejected the principle '[i]f something is owed to the whole, it is not owed each to each, nor do each individually owe what the whole owes'.[4] In justifying its conclusions, the Tribunal put decisive emphasis on analogies with certain forms of business associations in domestic law. According to the Tribunal, a Swiss co-operative ('société cooperative') or a limited partnership with share capital ('société en commandite par actions') could be endowed with legal personality without limiting the personal liability of its members.[5]

---

internationaler Organisationen gegenüber Drittstaaten (Vienna/New York, Springer 1969); J.A. Salmon, 'Les accords Spaak–U Thant du 20 février 1965', (1965) 11 *Annuaire français de droit international* 468).

[2] cf. Interim Arbitral Award (5 March 1984), p. 597.

[3] In its award of 5 March 1984, the Arbitral Tribunal found that it was competent to hear the claims brought against all four member states, the AOI, and ABH. On 28 June 1993, an arbitral tribunal decided the case in favour of WHL and against the AOI. The award has remained unpublished (see decision on the enforcement of the award in *Arab Organization for Industrialization and others v Westland Helicopters Ltd v. Arab Organization for Industrialization,* English High Court, Queen's Bench Division, 3 August 1994, 108 ILR 564).

[4] cf. A.X. Fellmeth and M. Horwitz, *Guide to Latin in International Law* (Oxford, Oxford University Press 2011) [online version], 'Si quid universitati debetur singulis non debetur, nec quod debet universitas singuli debent'.

[5] cf. Interim Arbitral Award (5 March 1984), p. 612.

In a similar vein, the members of a German co-operative and the partners in a French limited partnership ('société en nom collectif') could be held jointly and severally liable for the obligations of the partnership.[6] Against the background of these analogies, the Tribunal rejected the separate legal personality of the AOI as an indicator for the extent of the liability of its member states.

Instead, the Tribunal decided to base its award on the provisions of the constituent instruments of the AOI, noting that the AOI constitution neither explicitly excluded nor stipulated the liability of its member states. Although the Tribunal could have interpreted the silence of the constituent instruments either way, it opted for the liability of member states as a default rule. However, this finding of liability was not derived from the fact that the organization depended on its member states for financial resources, which might lead to secondary or subsidiary liability on the part of the member states. Rather, the Tribunal referred to the development of 'commercial organizations' whose members were by default liable unless they excluded liability explicitly. It explained that AOI member states never intended to disappear behind the corporate veil of the organizations but were 'members with liability' ('membres responsables').[7] Consequently, the Tribunal concluded that the AOI is more comparable to a general partnership or co-operative than to a joint stock company with limited liability.[8]

The Tribunal's choice of comparators shows the difficulties in applying domestic law analogies to international organizations. In most jurisdictions, limited liability is a privilege granted by a central state authority. The Tribunal's stance for unlimited member liability seems to take account of the lack of such recognition of limited liability in international law. Since limited liability was not expressly stated in the AOI constitution, third parties might have relied on the unlimited liability of the AOI's member states. This rationale behind the Tribunal's view becomes evident in its discussion on the scope of the legal personality of the AOI. In this regard, the Tribunal pointed out that the High Committee, composed of the four member states, signed a memorandum of understanding (MOU) with the United Kingdom to 'effective[ly] guarantee' that the AOI and the companies it controlled 'will properly execute their obligations to all the British companies participating under the provisions of this Memorandum'.[9] The MOU might thus have led third parties to rely on the four AOI member states' willingness to stand in for the organization if it could not fulfill its commitments. Considering that third parties such as WHL relied on the guarantees given by AOI member states, the Tribunal concluded that 'the AOI is one with the States'.[10]

Indeed, the law of international responsibility has long recognized that guarantees can lead to the attribution of conduct by one actor to another.[11] At the time of

---

[6] cf. Interim Arbitral Award (5 March 1984), p. 612. [7] Ibid., p. 614. [8] Ibid.
[9] Ibid., p. 615. [10] Ibid., p. 614.
[11] The commentary to the rules on the attribution of conduct in the Articles on State Responsibility explains: 'These rules are cumulative but they are also limitative. In the absence of a specific undertaking or guarantee (which would be a *lex specialis*), a State is not responsible for the conduct of persons or entities in circumstances not covered by this chapter.' Draft articles on Responsibility of States for Internationally Wrongful Acts, with commentaries, ILC Yearbook, 2001, vol. II, Part Two, p. 39 (para. 9). For a discussion of reliance in relation to member states of international organizations see P. Klein, *La responsabilité des organisations internationales dans les ordres juridiques internes et en droit des gens* (Brussels,

Westland Helicopter arbitration, the ILC had also just finalized its Draft Articles on the Law of Treaties between International Organizations and States, which allowed for the possibility of member states being bound by the obligations of an international organization as a result of reliance by third parties.[12] However, the finding that the AOI was one with its members is at least partly inconsistent with the Tribunal's previous recognition of the AOI's legal personality. What would be the added value of legal personality if the organization and its members were one and the same? It is a decisive characteristic of an international organization that it has *volonté distincte* separate from its member states.[13] Interestingly, the Tribunal acknowledged that members act in a 'double role' in relation to the organization: as an organ of the AOI and as a grouping of states. In the former capacity, the states were acting on behalf of the organization, in the latter capacity they were acting on their own behalf.

The Arbitral Tribunal attempted to address this inconsistency by arguing that the member states had intended to limit the legal personality of the organization, as evidenced by their signing of the Memorandum of Understanting with the United Kingdom. However, this argument seems unconvincing in light of the explicit attribution of legal personality to the AOI in art. 5 of the AOI constitution. It is true that the functions of international organizations are generally restricted.[14] Nonetheless, the conclusion that limited functions of international organizations also lead to limited legal personality is controversial. It could be argued that legal personality—as opposed to legal capacity—is a binary concept: an entity has or does not have legal personality.[15] Assuming *arguendo* that the legal personality of the AOI was functionally limited, the obligations concerning the dispute settlement owed to WHL still clearly fell within the functions of the organization. Art. 59 of the Shareholders Agreement explicitly allowed the AOI to enter into arbitration agreements. As the Swiss Federal Supreme Court pointed out in the later appeals decision, art. 59 of the Shareholders Agreement spoke towards the 'total legal independence of the Organization in relation to the founding States'.[16]

Bruylant 1998), pp. 596–8; and the Institut de Droit International, Institut de Droit International, 'The Legal Consequences for Member States of the Non-Fulfillment by International Organizations of their Obligations toward Third Parties', (1995) 66 *Annuaire de l'Institut de Droit International* 415 (para. 112), suggesting that member states might gives guarantees by their implicit conduct.

[12] See *Draft Articles on the Law of Treaties between States and International Organizations or between International Organizations, with Commentaries*, ILC Yearbook 1982, vol. II, Part Two, p. 43, Article 36 b is on 'obligations and rights arising for States members of an international organization from a treaty to which it is a party'. On this provision see C. Brölmann, *The Institutional Veil in Public International Law: International Organisations and the Law of Treaties* (Oxford, Hart 2007), p. 212 ff.

[13] For example, N.D. White, *The Law of International Organizations* (Manchester, Manchester University Press, 2005), pp. 30–1.

[14] These functional limitations are generally described in terms of the principle of speciality. As the ICJ stated in its Advisory Opinion on the *Legality of the Use by a State of Nuclear Weapons in Armed Conflict*: 'International organizations are governed by the "principle of speciality", that is to say, they are invested by the States which create them with powers, the limits of which are a function of the common interests whose promotion those States entrust to them.' [1996] ICJ Rep 66, 78 (para. 25).

[15] cf. T. Gazzini, 'Personality of International Organizations', in J. Klabbers and A. Wallendahl (eds), *Research Handbook on the Law of International Organizations* (Cheltenham/Northampton, Edward Elgar 2011), p. 43.

[16] cf. *Arab Organization for Industrialization and others v Westland Helicopters Ltd*, Swiss Federal Supreme Court (First Civil Court), 19 July 1988, 80 ILR 652.

In view of the difficulties in reconciling the AOI's legal personality with the unlimited liability of its member states, it is not surprising that the Arbitral Tribunal considered the piercing of the corporate veil of the AOI as an alternative argument towards the end of its award. As opposed to limited liability, the piercing of the corporate veil is a remedy, which allows creditors to hold shareholders of a corporation liable. A piercing of the corporate veil would thus only be necessary when the international organization has legal personality, which might unduly shield its members from liability. As a result of the separate legal personality of an international organization, its acts are usually not attributable to its member states (the same is true vice versa).[17] In exceptional circumstances, however, courts might pierce the corporate veil and hold member states responsible for the acts of the organization. As the Arbitral Tribunal noted with reference to the *Barcelona Traction* judgment of the International Court of Justice, such a piercing of the corporate veil might be warranted in case of a denial of justice or abuse of rights.[18]

The *Westland Helicopters* arbitration illustrates the challenges in holding international organizations and/or their members liable and raises many questions in this regard: can member states exclude their liability by virtue of the constituent instruments of the organization? How is the silence of the constituent instruments to be interpreted, in favour or against member state liability? In which situations do member states create reliance on their default liability in relation to third parties? The Tribunal in *Westland Helicopters* only partly found satisfactory answers to these questions, mainly on the basis of analogies with domestic corporate law. While the arbitral award on the competence of the Tribunal provided WHL with a procedural remedy for its damages, it also shook the foundations of the legal personality of international organizations. By holding that AOI member states had also waived their sovereign immunity by creating the AOI, the Tribunal certainly went a step too far. The far-reaching implications of the interim arbitral award were one of the reasons why the Federal Court of Justice in Geneva and the Federal Supreme Court annulled the award on appeal.[19] Nonetheless, the *Westland Helicopters* arbitration remains one of the few cases in which a tribunal has allowed for the possibility of holding member states responsible for the acts of an international organization.

---

[17] See Application of the Interim Accord of 13 September 1995 (*The Former Yugoslav Republic of Macedonia v Greece*), Judgment, [2011] ICJ Rep 644, as discussed in ch. 1.6.

[18] cf. *Barcelona Traction, Light and Power Company, Limited* (*Belgium v Spain*), Judgment, [1970] ICJ Rep 3, 39 (para. 56).

[19] See ch. 6.2.

6.2 *Arab Organization for Industrialization and others v Westland Helicopters Ltd,* Swiss Federal Supreme Court (First Civil Court), 19 July 1988, 80 ILR 652

Christiane Ahlborn

Relevance of the case

The present case deals with the responsibility of states for the acts of an international organization. The decision by the Federal Supreme Court forms part of an appeal brought by the Arab Republic of Egypt (ARE) against an earlier arbitral award against the ARE and five other respondents. In that arbitral award, the Tribunal had held that the member states of the Arab Organization for Industrialization (AOI), including the ARE, had agreed to arbitration by virtue of the AOI constitution. In the present case, the Swiss Federal Supreme Court partly reversed this award by upholding the separate legal personality of the AOI. As a result, AOI member states, in particular the appealing ARE, could not be subjected to international arbitration. The Swiss Federal Supreme Court's decision thus set the stage for the contemporary view on the question of the responsibility of member states of international organizations: due to the separate legal personality of an international organization, its member states cannot be held responsible for acts of the organization based on their membership alone.

I. Facts of the case

In 1975 the ARE, Saudi Arabia, Qatar, and the United Arab Emirates concluded a treaty establishing the AOI. According to the AOI's Basic Statute, the organization was endowed with legal personality and exempt from the laws and institutions of the member states. It had its head office in Cairo, and a capital of 1,040 million US dollars. The main organ of the AOI was the Higher Committee of the AOI, which was composed of all four member states. In 1978, the Higher Committee signed a Shareholders' Agreement with Westland Helicopters Ltd (WHL) creating joint stock company in Egypt. This joint stock company was later referred to as Arab British Helicopter Company (ABH). The purpose of the joint stock company was the manufacture, assembly, and sale of the Lynx helicopters made by WHL, which the AOI intended to construct in Egypt.

Following the signing of a peace agreement between the ARE and Israel in May 1979, Saudi Arabia, Qatar, and the United Arab Emirates decided to terminate the existence of the AOI from 19 July 1979. They also determined to stop all investments and to charge a committee composed of the four member states with the liquidation of the Organization. Being opposed to this decision, the ARE promulgated a Decree Law on 18 May 1979, providing for the continuing existence of the AOI in the form of a company governed by Egyptian law (EAOI). The Decree Law ensured the continuation of the AOI's activities and compliance with the commitments of the organization.

The ARE replaced the representatives from the three Gulf States with Egyptian members on the Higher Committee.

After the failure of negotiations, WHL gave notice of its decision to claim damages of 126 million GB pounds against the dissolved AOI and its member states. On 12 May 1980, it filed a request for arbitration with the International Chamber of Commerce (ICC) in Paris, which was directed against the AOI, the four member states of this organization, and ABH. This request was based on art. 12 of the Shareholders Agreement between the AOI and WHL, which provides as follows:

12. Arbitration and law

12.1 Any controversy or dispute which may arise between the parties in connection with the interpretation, application or effect of this Agreement which cannot be resolved amicably shall be finally settled under the Rules of Conciliation and Arbitration of the International Chamber of Commerce by one or more arbitrators appointed in accordance with the said Rules. Such arbitration shall be held in Geneva and the costs shall be borne as ordered by the arbitration court. Each party recognizes that the enforcement of the arbitration award may be made through any court having jurisdiction.

12.2 This Agreement shall be governed by and construed in accordance with the Laws of Switzerland.

12.3 The clauses of this Agreement and the Annexes hereto have been written in English and Arabic. Both texts shall be deemed equally authentic. Annex A hereto has been written in Arabic and an English translation has also been attached.

The ARE objected that it was not party to any of the agreements invoked by WHL, and the other defendants did not react to the request for arbitration. Nonetheless, the ICC Court of Arbitration set up an Arbitral Tribunal composed of three members on 29 October 1980. Geneva was determined to be the place of arbitration. In its interim award of 5 March 1985, the Arbitral Tribunal decided that it was competent to hear the claims against the AOI and all of its four member states.[1] While the three Gulf States had rejected to participate in the arbitral proceedings, the ARE (together with the ABH and the AOI) brought an appeal against the interim arbitral award before Swiss courts. The present decision by the Swiss Federal Supreme Court confirms the earlier decision by the Court of Justice in Geneva of 23 October 1987, which annulled the arbitral award.[2]

II. The legal question

The decision by the Swiss Federal Supreme Court mainly concerned the question whether, despite this absence of an arbitration agreement, the ARE was bound by an arbitration clause in the Shareholders' Agreement concluded between the AOI and

---

[1] cf. *Westland Helicopters Ltd v Arab Organization for Industrialization, United Arab Emirates, Kingdom of Saudi Arabia, State of Qatar, Arab Republic of Egypt, and Arab British Helicopter Company*, Arbitration, 5 March 1984, 80 ILR 600.

[2] cf. *Arab Organization for Industrialization and others v Westland Helicopters Ltd*, Court of Justice of Geneva, 23 October 1987, 80 ILR 622.

WHL. The other three AOI member states had not filed an appeal against the interim arbitral award, which remained in force in relation to them.

III. Excerpts

F. Acting separately, the ARE, ABH, the EAOI and WHL submitted four appeals to the Federal Supreme Court against this decision.

WHL argues for the partial annulment of the decision under appeal, to the extent that it annuls the interim award of 5 March 1984 in so far as the Arbitral Tribunal declared itself competent in respect of the ARE, returns the award to the Tribunal for a decision on the costs and fees of the arbitration relating to this respondent, and awards the ARE costs against WHL. WHL also requests that the proceedings be conducted in accordance with Article 91(2) OJ.

ABH and the EAOI argue in the first place in favour of the decision under appeal and the remission of the arbitral award of 5 March 1984 to the Cantonal Court for annulment; as a fall-back position they seek the annulment of this award. The ARE approves the annulment of the challenged award in so far as it returned the award to the Arbitral Tribunal for a decision on the costs and fees of the arbitration in regard to the ARE.

ABH, the EAOI and the ARE ask for WHL's appeal to be rejected. WHL argues in the first place for the non-admissibility of the appeals of ABH, the EAOI and the ARE; that failing it seeks their rejection. In the last resort, in the event of a total annulment of the award under appeal, it is in favour of the remission of the case to the Cantonal Court for it to make the necessary investigations. […]

3. a) An arbitration clause is not opposable to anyone who has not personally signed it, unless that person is bound by the signature of an organ or third party having the authority to act for him in matters including the acceptance of arbitration (Jolidon, *Commentaire du concordat Suisse sur l'arbitrage*, pp. 120 ff. and the decision cited at p. 121), or, again, on the basis of general or particular succession (*cf.* Jolidon, p. 140) or of special legal provisions within the meaning of Article 17(3) PCF (*cf.* ATF 102 Ia 582).

In this case, the appellants have not shown either a power of special representation or a succession to general or particular title. It is necessary also to consider whether the AOI or the persons who signed the arbitration clause on its behalf acted as organs or delegates committing the founding States of the Organization.

b) The Shareholders' Agreement is a private law contract expressly said to be governed by Swiss law. One can agree with the Cantonal Court and the appellants that the AOI, signatory of this contract, is a legal entity, an organism under public international law. Instead of referring to the domestic law of a State to determine the status and legal structure of this organism it is a matter of looking at the provisions of the instrument or treaty which is at the base of its creation.

The basic treaty, concluded by the four founding States, is the Agreement for Establishing the AOI of 29 April 1975. It provides for the creation of the Organization, which will come into being on signature of its Basic Statute (Art. 6), will have legal personality, will enjoy full administrative and financial independence, will be exempted from laws and institutions of the Member States and will have the right of acquisition and disposal and to engage in litigation (Article 1). It will have a nominal capital of $1040 million divided equally between the Member States (Article 4), a sum which may be increased with the approval of the Governments of the Member States.

The Basic Statute of the AOI of 17 August 1975 confirmed the birth or existence of the Organization (Article 2), its endowment with legal personality and full legal capacity (Article 5) and the applicability to the Organization of the provisions of the Establishment Agreement and all regulations issued in accordance with the Statute (Article 7). Article 59 provides that agreements and contracts concluded by the Organization with those with whom it has business dealings are to include provision for the settlement of any disputes which may arise concerning them.

The personality accorded to the AOI, as well as the autonomy conferred on it at the legal, financial and procedural level, even including a specific provision conferring on it the possibility of concluding arbitration clauses or agreements (Article 59, previously cited), are the obvious and unequivocable signs of the total legal independence of the Organization in relation to the founding States. This autonomy rules out the possibility of the contracts it concludes with third parties, and more particularly the arbitration clauses to which it subscribes, being regarded as acts undertaken by a delegate or an organ engaging the founding States. The predominant role played by these States and the fact that the supreme authority of the AOI is a Higher Committee composed of ministers cannot undermine the independence and personality of the Organization, nor lead to the conclusion that when organs of the AOI deal with third parties they *ipso facto* bind the founding States. […]

4. In the light of the foregoing, the grounds of appeal do not withstand examination.

a) With regard to the interpretation of the AOI's Establishment Treaty and the Basic Statutes of this Organization, the Court of Justice's finding that it is an entity endowed with legal personality is entirely correct and presents nothing which might conflict with the concept of legal personality in public law. This personality can very well derive from an international treaty and not present any significant differences with that which would result from a national law on companies.

b) The Cantonal Court's finding that the indication in the AOI's Statutes of the amount of its capital implies that the States had no other financial obligation is not conclusive. In any case, the existence of financial commitments by the founding States would not mean that they were bound by an arbitration clause signed by the AOI.

c) The appellants' views on the correctness of the analogy the Arbitral Tribunal drew with the general partnership (*société en nom collectif*) are totally irrelevant to the interpretation of the instruments relating to the AOI. The references to instruments of establishment, very different in their content, of a European group with an economic interest, and to the personal responsibility, under Swiss law, in a cooperative society and a joint stock company, are likewise irrelevant. As to the argument derived from the spirit of Article 6(2) IAC, it founders on Article 59 of the Basic Statute of the AOI, which authorizes the Organization to determine with its contractual partners the method of settling disputes which might arise. And we have seen (3(b)) that the independence entrusted to the AOI, notably by this Article, does not permit arbitration clauses subscribed to by this independent legal entity to be regarded as binding the founding States.

d) The fact that the Higher Committee of the AOI and indeed the four founding States concluded a memorandum, the MOU, for the purpose of supporting or not impeding the activity of the AOI has no effect on the arbitral clause. The Cantonal Court could thus view this as *res inter alios acta* in respect of WHL which was not involved in it.

e) Contrary to the appellants' assertions, there is nothing in the instruments establishing the AOI from which it might be concluded that the States were waiving their immunity from jurisdiction. The grounds of the appeal relating to the deductions the Cantonal Court has drawn from the principle that a sovereign State cannot be presumed to have waived its immunity from jurisdiction are thus unfounded.

f) The breach of the Shareholders' Agreement by the Member States of the AOI has no effect on the application of the arbitration clause. The arguments based on this breach are irrelevant. As to the denial by the President of the AOI of all responsibility of the three Gulf States following the breach, this cannot be taken as an indication of any commitment whatsoever of the States before the breach on the basis of the arbitration clause.

g) [...] Finally, the appellants claim, wrongly, that there has been a shocking offence to the spirit of equity with a decision that accepts that an organization with considerable capital alone is bound by an arbitration agreement to the exclusion of the States which founded it. But the fact that the States, in the absence of an arbitration clause, have to be pursued in their national courts does not constitute such an offence.

WHL's appeal is therefore rejected. [...]

7. a) The appellants criticize the Cantonal Court for not having annulled the award of 5 March 1984 in so far as the Arbitral Tribunal pronounced itself competent in respect to the three Gulf States, founders of the AOI with the ARE.

b) If the Cantonal Court did not annul the award of 5 March 1984 in so far as it concerned the three States, it is simply because these States, although duly summoned, failed to make an appearance and an arbitral decision which is not nullified binds the party not appealing.

IV. Commentary

The present decision concerns the appeal against an earlier decision by the Federal Court of Justice in Geneva, which annulled the interim award of 5 March 1984 in the *Westland Helicopters* arbitration.[3] By upholding the decision of the Court of Justice in Geneva, the Swiss Federal Supreme Court reversed the interim arbitral award on its most important point: that the AOI and its member states are one and the same.[4] Although the Arbitral Tribunal had recognized the international legal personality of the AOI, it generally dismissed legal personality as a decisive indicator for the liability of member states. Instead it argued that the extent of member state liability should be based on the constitution of the AOI. Since the AOI constitution did not explicitly exclude member state liability, the Arbitral Tribunal found that member states were liable by default. According to the Tribunal, this conclusion was also confirmed by a Memorandum of Understanding signed by all four AOI member states with the United Kingdom to guarantee that the joint venture companies with a majority of AOI shareholdings would comply with their obligations.

---

[3] See ch. 6.1 of this book.   [4] cf. Interim Arbitral Award (5 March 1984), p. 612.

Following an appeal by the ARE, among others, the Court of Justice in Geneva expressed its disagreement with the decision of the Arbitral Tribunal. Like the Arbitral Tribunal, the Court of Justice emphasized the legal personality of the AOI as laid down in arts. 5 to 9 of the Basic Statute.[5] Unlike the Arbitral Tribunal, however, the Court of Justice did not proceed by comparing the AOI with a general partnership ('société en nom collectif') in which the members intended to remain fully liable ('membres responsible'). As the Court of Justice noted, '[i]t is not clear what legal grounds the Arbitral Tribunal has for accepting that the AOI is a legal entity under international law and then assimilating it to a corporation under private law, recognized by national legislations and subject to the rules of these legislations'.[6] Both the interim arbitral award and the Court of Justice's decision thus illustrate the struggle to find the appropriate framework to conceptualize international organizations. The Arbitral Tribunal had mainly used analogies with domestic corporate law to conclude that AOI member states have unlimited liability for the acts of the organization. In contrast to the Arbitral Tribunal, the Court of Justice concluded that the obligation to arbitrate arising from the Shareholders Agreement between the AOI and WHL was not opposable to the ARE. The MOU signed between the four AOI member states and the United Kingdom could not be used to support the opposite interpretation, mainly because it was *res inter alios acta* in relation to the claimant WHL.[7]

This judgment by the Court of Justice in Geneva forms the basis for the present decision by the Federal Supreme Court. While relying on the Court of Justice's prior arguments, the Supreme Court's decision is characterized by a more detailed analysis of the separate legal personality of the AOI and its implications. The Federal Supreme Court underlined the provisions in the Basic Statute pertaining to the creation or existence of the AOI (art. 2) and its endowment with legal personality and full capacity (art. 5). More importantly, the Court emphasized the legal, procedural and financial autonomy of the AOI, which also enables the organization to conclude arbitration clauses or agreements on its own behalf (art. 59). According to the Supreme Court, the AOI's legal personality and autonomy are 'unequivocable signs of the total legal independence of the Organization in relation to the founding States'.[8] The Supreme Court thus acknowledged the *volonté distincte* of the AOI from its member states.

While declaring the analogies drawn by the Arbitral Tribunal between partnerships in domestic law and the AOI irrelevant, the Federal Supreme Court itself resorted to corporate law to support its views. More precisely, it used two arbitrations involving state-owned companies to distill principles that might be relevant for determining relationship between the AOI and its member states. In *Libya v Wetco*, the Swiss Federal Supreme Court had held that Libya was not bound by an arbitration clause concluded between the Libyan National Oil Company and a foreign corporation.[9] In a similar vein, the Paris Appeals Court vacated an arbitral award finding that Egypt had not become a party to the contract between S.P.P. and the Egyptian General Organization

---

[5] cf. Decision by the Court of Justice of Geneva, at p. 642.   [6] Ibid., p. 643.
[7] Ibid., p. 643.
[8] cf. Decision by the Federal Supreme Court, p. 658.
[9] cf. *The Arab Republic of Libya v Wetco Ltd* (published in part in SJ 1980), pp. 443 ff.

for Tourism and Hotels, which included the arbitral clause.[10] Against this background, the Swiss Federal Supreme Court in *Westland Helicopters* found that the AOI is not any less independent from its members than those companies. The Court also noted that strict control of a legal person by a state, or the close link between the two entities, does not automatically allow for the conclusion that the state is bound by an arbitration clause without having signed it.[11] Such a conclusion is objectively excluded when the entity concerned has legal personality, even if the state partly 'finances, supervises, controls and imposes on it very detailed rules of conduct'.[12]

Refining the decision of the Court of Justice in Geneva, the Federal Supreme Court explained that the legal personality and autonomy of an international organization such as the AOI excludes the imposition of the AOI's obligations on its member states. Unlike the Arbitral Tribunal, the Federal Supreme Court made clear that the legal personality of an international organization is decisive in determining the scope of liability of member states. In this context, the Federal Supreme Court also clarified that the approval of a minister of a member state to an arbitration agreement concluded by the organization does not imply a waiver of immunity on the part of the member state, which is not a party to the agreement.[13]

By discussing the implications of the legal personality and autonomy of the international organization, the Federal Supreme Court's decision set the stage for the subsequent treatment of the topic of the responsibility of member states of international organizations. One year later, the UK House of Lords held that the International Tin Council (ITC) 'is a separate legal personality distinct from its members', and that its contractual obligations could not be imposed on non-parties such as the ITC member states.[14] Both the *Westland Helicopters* and the ITC cases had a notable influence on the work of the *Institut de droit international* (IDI) on the topic of 'The legal consequences for member states of the non-fulfillment by international organizations of their obligations toward third parties'. As the first major codification effort, the IDI generally excluded the liability of member states on the basis of the separate legal personality of the organization. As noted in the Institute's 1995 resolution: there is 'no general rule of international law whereby States members are, due solely to their membership, liable concurrently or subsidiarily, for the obligations of an international organization of which they are members.'[15]

---

[10] cf. *S.P.P. (Middle East) Ltd And Southern Pacific Properties Ltd v The Arab Republic of Egypt and the Egyptian General Organization for Tourism and Hotels*; award published in (1983) 22 ILM 752; the judgment of the Paris Court of Appeal is reprinted in English in (1984) 23 ILM 1048.

[11] cf. Decision by the Federal Supreme Court, p. 659 (citing the decision of the Federal Supreme Court *Libya v Wetco*, 3(b)).

[12] cf. Decision by the Federal Supreme Court, p. 659.

[13] cf. ibid., citing decision of the Paris Court of Appeal, *Southern Pacific Properties Ltd v Egypt* (n. 9), at 138.

[14] cf. *Maclaine Watson & Co. Ltd v International Tin Council*, 26 October 1989, United Kingdom House of Lords, 81 ILR 670, at 678 (Lord Templeman).

[15] cf. Institut de Droit International, 'The Legal Consequences for Member States of the Non-Fulfillment by International Organizations of their Obligations toward Third Parties', (1995) 66 *Annuaire de l'Institut de Droit International* 249, p. 466. For a succinct criticism of this position see A. Stumer, 'Liability of Member States for Acts of International Organizations: Reconsidering the Policy Objections', (2007) 48 *Harvard International Law Journal* 553.

Nonetheless, it is significant that the IDI acknowledged certain exceptions to this general rule. A state member of an international organization may incur liability to a third party 'through undertakings by the State'.[16] Indeed, the arbitral award's finding of member state liability seemed to place decisive weight on the MOU signed between the four AOI member states and the United Kingdom, which was intended to guarantee the AOI's compliance with its commitments. Like the Court of Justice in Geneva, however, the Federal Supreme Court found this MOU was *res inter alios acta* in relation to WHL. Although WHL might have relied on the MOU, it was not a party to it. Alternatively, the arbitral award might also be interpreted in light of another one of the exceptions provided for by the 1995 IDI resolution. It could be argued that 'the international organization has acted as the agent of the State, in law or in fact'.[17] However, both Swiss courts, when finding that the AOI and its members were not one and the same, at least implicitly rejected the possibility of agency by the international organization.

While setting the stage for the contemporary debate on the responsibility of international organizations and their members, the *Westland Helicopters* decisions addressed the quite unique situation of the disappearance or liquidation of an international organization.[18] Although the legal status of the AOI remained unclear during the arbitration, the three Gulf States had pronounced their intention to dissolve the organization.[19] The only well-known comparable example is the collapse of the ITC.[20] Modern cases regarding the responsibility of member states of international organizations such as *Behrami and Saramati v France, Germany, and Norway* or *Nuhanovic and Mustafic v The Netherlands* rather focus on the attribution of conduct to the international organization and/or its member states.[21] Nonetheless, notable parallels between the Swiss *Westland Helicopters* decision and these modern cases exist. The question of whether or not the AOI had legal personality separate from its member states, thus shielding its members from the obligations to arbitrate, is ultimately also a question of attribution of conduct. Only by virtue of its legal personality is the international organization a 'centre of attribution' for the acts of its member states.[22] Since international organizations typically have immunity before domestic courts and are not subject to the jurisdiction of international tribunals, the outcome in such recent cases is also strikingly similar to that in the Swiss *Westland Helicopters* decisions: the injured party (*in casu* WHL) is left without a remedy.[23]

---

[16] cf. art. 5 (c)(i) of the 1995 IDI Resolution.   [17] Ibid.

[18] On the dissolution of international organizations see R. Wessel, 'Dissolution and Succession: The Transmigration of the Soul of International Organizations', in J. Klabbers and A. Wallendahl (eds), *Research Handbook on International Organizations* (Cheltenham/and Northampton, Edward Elgar 2011), p. 342.

[19] See the commentary on the *Westland Helicopters* arbitration in this book.

[20] See the discussion on *Maclaine Watson & Co. Ltd v International Tin Council*, 26 October 1989, United Kingdom House of Lords, 81 ILR 670 in this book.

[21] *Agim Behrami and Bekir Behrami v France*, App. No. 71412/01 and *Ruzhdi Saramti v France, Germany, and Norway*, App. No. 78166/01, 2 May 2007. *Nuhanovic v Netherlands*, Appeal Judgment, LJN: R5388, ILDC 1742 (NL 2011) and *Mustafic v Netherlands*, Appeal Judgment, LJN: BR 5386, Dutch Court of Appeals, 5 July 2011.

[22] cf. P. Klein, *La responsabilité des organisations internationales dans les ordres juridiques internes et en droit des gens* (Brussels, Bruylant 1998), p. 430.

[23] This is notwithstanding the fact that the interim arbitral award continued to bind the three non-appealing member states of the AOI.

In view of this bleak outcome of the Swiss appeals procedure, it is not surprising that the Arbitral Tribunal had previously invoked concerns of equity when deciding that AOI member states were bound by the arbitral clause in the Shareholders Agreement. As the Tribunal stated, '[e]quity, in common with the principles of international law, allows the corporate veil to be lifted, in order to protect third parties against an abuse which would be to their detriment'.[24] However, the Swiss Federal Supreme Court did not take up this argument. Not all situations that are to the detriment of injured parties can lead to a lifting of the corporate veil. The Federal Supreme Court rather pointed to the existence of objective criteria to decide when the actions of a member can be equated with those of the international organization. As discussed above, the crucial criterion for the Supreme Court was the attribution of legal personality to the organization in the AOI constitution.

Nevertheless, the mere provision of legal personality in the constituent instruments of an international organization appears to be an insufficient criterion. Member states could abuse the legal personality of the international organization by *de facto* depriving it of its autonomy, and thus degrading it to a mere sham or alter ego of themselves.[25] While explicit provision of legal personality is certainly an important indicator for the autonomy of an international organization, further criteria are needed to determine whether an international organization exists separately from its member states.

With its *Westland Helicopters* decision, the Swiss Federal Supreme Court opened the on-going debate on the responsibility of member states for the acts of an international organization. The most recent attempt to codify a rule on the piercing of the corporate veil of an international organization was made by the ILC's ARIO.[26] However, art. 61 of the ARIO on 'circumvention of international obligations of a State member of an international organization' has not been very positively received in international legal practice and scholarship.[27] Following the decision of the Swiss Supreme Court, the *Westland Helicopters* arbitration ended with an award in favour of WHL in 1993.[28] In line with the Swiss decision and the predominant view in legal doctrine, the responsible party was the AOI and not its member states.

---

[24] cf. *Barcelona Traction, Light and Power Company, Limited (Belgium v Spain)*, Judgment, [1970] ICJ Rep 3, para. 56.

[25] See, for example, J. d'Aspremont, 'Abuse of the Legal Personality of International Organizations and the Responsibility of Member States', (2007) 4 *International Organizations Law Review* 91. See also R. Sadurska and C. Chinkin, 'The Collapse of the International Tin Council: A Case of State Responsibility?', (1989–90) 30 *Virginia Journal of International Law* 845, stating at p. 878: 'It is possible that it was felt that *Westland Helicopters* represented an extreme form of member States hiding behind an organization which was really a façade.'

[26] The Report of the ILC's 63rd session, Official Record of the General Assembly, 66th Sess., Supp. 10 (A/66/10), 2011) (ARIO).

[27] See generally O. Murray, 'Piercing the Corporate Veil: The Responsibility of Member States of an International Organisation', (2011) 8 *International Organizations Law Review* 291.

[28] The award has remained unpublished (see decision on the enforcement of the award in *Arab Organization for Industrialization and others v Westland Helicopters Ltd v Arab Organization for Industrialization*, English High Court, Queen's Bench Division, 3 August 1994, 108 ILR 564).

6.3 *Matthews v United Kingdom*, ECtHR, App. No. 24833/94, 18 February 1999

Ana Sofia Barros

Relevance of the case

In judging cases involving the responsibility of state members of international organizations, the European Court of Human Rights (ECtHR) has consistently emphasized that even after having transferred competences to an international organization, state parties to the European Convention on Human Rights (ECHR) remain bound by the obligations prescribed therein. The present case lies among the first setting the tone for such jurisprudential development. Importantly, it constitutes the only example, among a significant number of cases, where a state was actually found responsible for not having secured ECHR rights when acting in compliance with its obligations flowing from membership of an international organization.

I. Facts of the case

On the occasion of the 1994 elections for the European Parliament, residents of Gibraltar, a dependent territory of the United Kingdom, were denied their right to vote under the terms of the EC Act Concerning the Election of the Representatives of the European Parliament by Direct Universal Suffrage of 1976 (1976 Act), and its Annex II, which did not include Gibraltar in the franchise for the said elections. The 1976 Act had been adopted by the United Kingdom, together with the member states of the then European Community (EC), following the requirements of art. 138(3) of the EEC Treaty and of Council Decision 76/787. Against this backdrop, the applicant argued that the United Kingdom had failed to comply with art. 3 of Protocol 1 to the ECHR, a provision that secured her right to free elections.

The United Kingdom premised its counter-argumentation on the fact that the 1976 Act, having been adopted within the EC framework, could not be imputed to the member states, together or individually, and could not be unilaterally varied or revoked. Next to this, the United Kingdom upheld the non-applicability of art. 3 of Protocol No. 1 to the facts under discussion on grounds that the ECHR did not impose upon states obligations relating to the undertakings of a supranational organization, in respect of which member states had limited their own sovereignty.

II. The legal question

Although the applicant's complaint regarded the operations of the EC, and thus, issues of an institutional nature and character, it raised the question of whether the responsibility of a member state could be engaged in respect of such concerns, notably for participating in the process of adoption of legal instruments informing the Community legal system. So as to answer this, the Court's analysis drew on the extent to which the member state remained bound to secure European Convention rights after having transferred the exercise of certain competences to the EC.

In making such an assessment, it is essential to clarify the relationship between the member state and the international organization in a context where the conduct of the former is directly related to the operations of the latter: this will determine the criteria on the basis of which state responsibility is to be established, that is, whether the member state is responsible for an act of the organization or rather for its own conduct performed in an institutional context.

III. Excerpts

26. According to the Government, the applicant's real objection was to Council Decision 76/787 and to the 1976 Act concerning elections to the European Parliament (see paragraph 18 above). That Act, which had the status of a treaty, was adopted in the Community framework and could not be revoked or varied unilaterally by the United Kingdom. The Government underlined that the European Commission of Human Rights had refused on a number of occasions to subject measures falling within the Community legal order to scrutiny under the Convention. Whilst they accepted that there might be circumstances in which a Contracting Party might infringe its obligations under the Convention by entering into treaty obligations which were incompatible with the Convention, they considered that in the present case, which concerned texts adopted in the framework of the European Community, the position was not the same. Thus, acts adopted by the Community or consequent to its requirements could not be imputed to the member States, together or individually, particularly when those acts concerned elections to a constitutional organ of the Community itself. At the hearing, the Government suggested that to engage the responsibility of any State under the Convention, that State must have a power of effective control over the act complained of. In the case of the provisions relating to the elections to the European Parliament, the United Kingdom Government had no such control.

27. The applicant disagreed. For her, the Council Decision and 1976 Act constituted an international treaty, rather than an act of an institution whose decisions were not subject to Convention review. She thus considered that the Government remained responsible under the Convention for the effects of the Council Decision and 1976 Act. In the alternative—that is, if the Council Decision and 1976 Act were to be interpreted as involving a transfer of powers to the Community organs—the applicant argued, by reference to Commission case-law, that in the absence of any equivalent protection of her rights under Article 3 of Protocol No. 1, the Government in any event retained responsibility under the Convention.

30. The Court notes that the parties do not dispute that Article 3 of Protocol No. 1 applies in Gibraltar. It recalls that the Convention was extended to the territory of Gibraltar by the United Kingdom's declaration of 23 October 1953 (see paragraph 19 above), and Protocol No. 1 has been applicable in Gibraltar since 25 February 1988. There is therefore clearly territorial 'jurisdiction' within the meaning of Article 1 of the Convention.

31. The Court must nevertheless consider whether, notwithstanding the nature of the elections to the European Parliament as an organ of the EC, the United Kingdom can be held responsible under Article 1 of the Convention for the absence of elections to the European Parliament in Gibraltar, that is, whether the United Kingdom is required to 'secure' elections to the European Parliament notwithstanding the Community character of those elections.

32. The Court observes that acts of the EC as such cannot be challenged before the Court because the EC is not a Contracting Party. The Convention does not exclude the transfer of competences to international organisations provided that Convention rights continue to be 'secured'. Member States' responsibility therefore continues even after such a transfer.

33. In the present case, the alleged violation of the Convention flows from an annex to the 1976 Act, entered into by the United Kingdom, together with the extension to the European Parliament's competences brought about by the Maastricht Treaty. The Council Decision and the 1976 Act (see paragraph 18 above), and the Maastricht Treaty, with its changes to the EEC Treaty, all constituted international instruments which were freely entered into by the United Kingdom. Indeed, the 1976 Act cannot be challenged before the European Court of Justice for the very reason that it is not a 'normal' act of the Community, but is a treaty within the Community legal order. The Maastricht Treaty, too, is not an act of the Community, but a treaty by which a revision of the EEC Treaty was brought about. The United Kingdom, together with all the other parties to the Maastricht Treaty, is responsible *ratione materiae* under Article 1 of the Convention and, in particular, under Article 3 of Protocol No. 1, for the consequences of that Treaty.

34. In determining to what extent the United Kingdom is responsible for 'securing' the rights in Article 3 of Protocol No. 1 in respect of elections to the European Parliament in Gibraltar, the Court recalls that the Convention is intended to guarantee rights that are not theoretical or illusory, but practical and effective (see, for example, the above-mentioned *United Communist Party of Turkey and Others* judgment, pp. 18–19, § 33). It is uncontested that legislation emanating from the legislative process of the European Community affects the population of Gibraltar in the same way as legislation which enters the domestic legal order exclusively via the House of Assembly. To this extent, there is no difference between European and domestic legislation, and no reason why the United Kingdom should not be required to 'secure' the rights in Article 3 of Protocol No. 1 in respect of European legislation, in the same way as those rights are required to be 'secured' in respect of purely domestic legislation. In particular, the suggestion that the United Kingdom may not have effective control over the state of affairs complained of cannot affect the position, as the United Kingdom's responsibility derives from its having entered into treaty commitments subsequent to the applicability of Article 3 of Protocol No. 1 to Gibraltar, namely the Maastricht Treaty taken together with its obligations under the Council Decision and the 1976 Act. Further, the Court notes that on acceding to the EC Treaty, the United Kingdom chose, by virtue of Article 227(4) of the Treaty, to have substantial areas of EC legislation applied to Gibraltar (see paragraphs 11 to 14 above).

35. It follows that the United Kingdom is responsible under Article 1 of the Convention for securing the rights guaranteed by Article 3 of Protocol No. 1 in Gibraltar regardless of whether the elections were purely domestic or European.

B. Whether Article 3 of Protocol No. 1 is applicable to an organ such as the European Parliament

36. The Government claimed that the undertaking in Article 3 of Protocol No. 1 was necessarily limited to matters falling within the power of the parties to the Convention, that is, sovereign States. They submitted that the 'legislature' in Gibraltar was the House of Assembly, and that it was to that body that Article 3 of Protocol No. 1 applied in the context of Gibraltar. For the Government, there was no basis upon which the Convention could place obligations on Contracting Parties in relation to elections for the parliament of a distinct, supranational organisation, and they contended that this was particularly so when the member States of the European Community had limited their own sovereignty in respect of it and when both the European Parliament itself and its basic electoral procedures were provided for under its own legal system, rather than the legal systems of its member States.

37. The applicant referred to previous decisions of the European Commission of Human Rights in which complaints concerning the European Parliament were dealt with on the merits, so that the Commission in effect assumed that Article 3 of Protocol No. 1 applied to elections to the European Parliament (see, for example, *Lindsay v. the United Kingdom*, application no. 8364/78, decision of 8 March 1979, Decisions and Reports (DR) 15, p. 247, and *Tête v. France*, application no. 11123/84, decision of 9 December 1987, DR 54, p. 52). She agreed with the dissenting members of the Commission who did not accept that because the European Parliament did not exist when Protocol No. 1 was drafted, it necessarily fell outside the ambit of Article 3 of that Protocol.

38. The majority of the Commission based its reasoning on this jurisdictional point. It considered that 'to hold Article 3 of Protocol No. 1 to be applicable to supranational representative organs would be to extend the scope of Article 3 beyond what was intended by the drafters of the Convention and beyond the object and purpose of the provision … [T]he role of Article 3 is to ensure that elections take place at regular intervals to the national or local legislative assembly, that is, in the case of Gibraltar, to the House of Assembly' (see paragraph 63 of the Commission's report).

39. That the Convention is a living instrument which must be interpreted in the light of present-day conditions is firmly rooted in the Court's case-law (see, *inter alia*, the *Loizidou v. Turkey* judgment of 23 March 1995 (*preliminary objections*), Series A no. 310, pp. 26–27, § 71, with further reference). The mere fact that a body was not envisaged by the drafters of the Convention cannot prevent that body from falling within the scope of the Convention. To the extent that Contracting States organise common constitutional or parliamentary structures by international treaties, the Court must take these mutually agreed structural changes into account in interpreting the Convention and its Protocols. The question remains whether an organ such as the European Parliament nevertheless falls outside the ambit of Article 3 of Protocol No. 1.

40. The Court recalls that the word 'legislature' in Article 3 of Protocol No. 1 does not necessarily mean the national parliament: the word has to be interpreted in the light of the constitutional structure of the State in question.

42. The Court reiterates that Article 3 of Protocol No. 1 enshrines a characteristic of an effective political democracy (see the above-mentioned *Mathieu-Mohin and Clerfayt* judgment, p. 22, § 47, and the above-mentioned *United Communist Party of Turkey and Others* judgment, pp. 21–22, § 45). In the present case, there has been no submission that there exist alternative means of providing for electoral representation

of the population of Gibraltar in the European Parliament, and the Court finds no indication of any.

43. The Court thus considers that to accept the Government's contention that the sphere of activities of the European Parliament falls outside the scope of Article 3 of Protocol No. 1 would risk undermining one of the fundamental tools by which 'effective political democracy' can be maintained.

44. It follows that no reason has been made out which could justify excluding the European Parliament from the ambit of the elections referred to in Article 3 of Protocol No. 1 on the ground that it is a supranational, rather than a purely domestic, representative organ.

63. The Court recalls that the rights set out in Article 3 of Protocol No. 1 are not absolute, but may be subject to limitations. The Contracting States enjoy a wide margin of appreciation in imposing conditions on the right to vote, but it is for the Court to determine in the last resort whether the requirements of Protocol No. 1 have been complied with. It has to satisfy itself that the conditions do not curtail the right to vote to such an extent as to impair its very essence and deprive it of effectiveness; that they are imposed in pursuit of a legitimate aim; and that the means employed are not disproportionate. In particular, such conditions must not thwart 'the free expression of the people in the choice of the legislature' (see the above-mentioned *Mathieu-Mohin and Clerfayt* judgment, p. 23, § 52).

64. The Court makes it clear at the outset that the choice of electoral system by which the free expression of the opinion of the people in the choice of the legislature is ensured—whether it be based on proportional representation, the 'first-past-the-post' system or some other arrangement—is a matter in which the State enjoys a wide margin of appreciation. However, in the present case the applicant, as a resident of Gibraltar, was completely denied any opportunity to express her opinion in the choice of the members of the European Parliament. The position is not analogous to that of persons who are unable to take part in elections because they live outside the jurisdiction, as such individuals have weakened the link between themselves and the jurisdiction. In the present case, as the Court has found (see paragraph 34 above), the legislation which emanates from the European Community forms part of the legislation in Gibraltar, and the applicant is directly affected by it.

65. In the circumstances of the present case, the very essence of the applicant's right to vote, as guaranteed by Article 3 of Protocol No. 1, was denied.

It follows that there has been a violation of that provision.

IV. Commentary

States' co-operative engagements towards the achievement of common goals grew exponentially in the post-war period, through the creation of international organizations. This evolution was accompanied by increased concern within the legal epistemic community regarding the implications of states' joint endeavours in terms of human rights protection. At the same time, the question of how to establish international responsibility for human rights violations linked to the activities of international organizations found its way in international litigation, especially within the European human rights regime. In a string of cases decided by the supervisory bodies of the ECHR, the legal analysis drew on the terms in which the Convention would apply following the transfer of portions of sovereignty to an international body.[1] Given the European Commission of Human Rights' prompt assertions of lack of jurisdiction *ratione personae* to examine complaints directed against an international organization such as the EC,[2] the inquiry was raised as to whether responsibility for acts performed in an institutional framework allegedly in violation of the ECHR would lie instead with the member states.

Early applications submitted against member states of the EC dealt with the responsibility of the former for the violation of European Convention rights in the context of the adoption and mostly of the implementation of EC measures.[3] The issue was first addressed by the European Commission of Human Rights in the case of *M. & Co. v Germany*[4] regarding the responsibility of Germany for having given effect to a decision of the European Court of Justice. Here, a principled approach was put forward by the Commission, one that would highly influence the unfolding of the *Matthews* decision and subsequent jurisprudence: the understanding that the transfer of powers to an international organization 'does not necessarily exclude a state's responsibility under the Convention with regard to the exercise of the transferred powers'.[5] Such a compromise coherently emerged as a corollary of the general principle advanced by the Commission already in 1958 whereby 'if a State contracts treaty obligations and subsequently concludes another international agreement which disables it from performing its obligations under the first treaty it will be answerable for any resulting breach of its obligations under the earlier treaty'.[6] In this vein, the Commission ascertained that the European Convention does not prohibit the transfer of the exercise of certain competences to an international organization provided that, within the organization, fundamental rights receive an 'equivalent protection'.[7]

The line of argument advanced in the case-law prior to *Matthews*, and further developed in the latter, has been used as a benchmark in subsequent cases decided by the ECtHR, such as the *Bosphorus* and *Gasparini* cases, also commented upon in this book.

---

[1] For an overview of relevant case-law prior to the *Matthews* decision (Matthews v United Kingdom, ECtHR, App. No. 24833/ 94, 18 February 1999), see: R.A. Lawson and H.G. Schermers, *Leading Cases of the European Court of Human Rights* (Ars Aequi Libri Nijmegen, 1999), pp. 677, 678; for an account of subsequent ECtHR decisions endorsing the *Matthews* approach, see: C. Ryngaert, 'The European Court of Human Rights' Approach to the Responsibility of Member States in Connection with Acts of International Organizations', (2011) *International & Comparative Law Quarterly* 997.

[2] cf. *Confédération Française Démocratique du Travail v The European Communities*, App. No. 8030/ 77, 10 July 1978, p. 240 (*CFDT* case).

[3] As noted by Kuijper and Paasivirta, there are significant differences between cases where member state responsibility is invoked with respect to the implementation of EC measures (be it the execution of a decision of the European Court of Justice or the implementation of a directive or regulation) and cases involving the responsibility of member states for the adoption of institutional acts (see: P.J. Kuijper and E. Paasivirta, 'Further Exploring International Responsibility: The European Community and the ILC's Project on Responsibility of International Organizations', (2004) *International Organizations Law Review* 1, p. 21). As will be seen below, member state responsibility for participation in the adoption of acts within the Community legal order raises further complications, in that the question seems to lead to different outcomes depending on whether the adopted act pertains to primary or secondary EC law.

[4] Decision of 9 February 1990, App. No. 13258/87, Decisions and Reports, vol. 64, p. 138.

[5] cf. *M. & Co. v Germany* (n. 4), p. 145.

[6] cf. *X v the FRG*, Decision of 10 June 1958, Application No 235/56, Yearbook 2 p. 256 (300), as quoted in the *M. & Co.* case (n. 4): at 145.

[7] cf. *M. & Co. v Germany* (n. 4), p. 145.

Although these judgements followed the same principled basis upon which the *Matthews* case was decided, member state responsibility by virtue of the transfer of powers to an international organization has not been established since the latter. The relevance of the *Matthews* case is also reflected in the work of the ILC, which grounded art. 61 on 'Circumvention of international obligations of a state member of an international organization' of its ARIO on the approach put forward by the ECtHR.[8]

In the present case, the first question to solve was whether the state of affairs complained of could actually be subjected to the Court's review. Although the applicant's contention regarded the exercise of her right to vote in European Parliament elections, and thus, a matter of Community 'nature' and 'character', the possibility to somehow engage the responsibility of the United Kingdom in the particular circumstances of the case would have to be present.[9] Essentially, this would entail categorizing the adoption of the 1976 Act and its Annex II (determining the absence of elections to the European Parliament in Gibraltar), allegedly incompatible with the ECHR, as state—and not institutional—conduct. This points to the significance of clarifying the position of member states within the Community legal system and, in particular, what constitutes conduct attributable to the former and conduct attributable to the EC.

Mindful of this prerequisite, both the applicant and the respondent centred part of their argumentation on the classification and imputability of the contentious acts at stake. The applicant maintained that the 1976 Act constituted an international treaty, and that Annex II to the Act had been included therein under the unilateral will of the respondent.[10] Against this backdrop, the conclusion of the 1976 Act, whilst an act disabling the respondent from complying with its obligations under the ECHR, could only render the latter responsible for any resulting breaches of the Convention. In its turn, the respondent insisted that the 1976 Act and Annex II could not be subjected to the ECtHR's review on grounds that they fell within the EC legal order.[11] Despite its status as an international treaty, the respondent reckoned, the 1976 Act was not an ordinary treaty but one of a 'special nature', which operationalized art. 138(3) of the EEC Treaty and Council Decision 76/787. Moreover, responsibility for Annex II could not fall upon the respondent as it could not have been revoked or unilaterally amended by the latter (Report of the European Commission, para. 30). Hence, based on the argument that the acts had been adopted by the Community or consequent to its requirements, and thus formed part of a distinct legal order, the respondent underlined that they could not be imputed to the member states, together or individually.[12]

> Inasmuch as EC conduct (and, generally, acts adopted by any international organization) as such cannot be challenged before the ECtHR,[13] as said above, the latter's competence to review acts adopted within the Community legal order is dependent

---

[8] cf. ARIO commentary to art. 61, paras 3–5 in Report of the Law Commission on the Work of its Sixty- Third Session, Official Record of the General Assembly, 66th Sess., Supp. 10 (A/ 66/ 10), 2011.

[9] cf. *Matthews* decision, para. 31.

[10] cf. European Commission of Human Rights Report, adopted on 29 October 1997, paras 43, 44 (hereinafter Report of the European Commission) and *Matthews* decision, para. 27.

[11] cf. Report of the European Commission (n. 10), para. 28.

[12] cf. *Matthews* decision, para. 26.

[13] cf. ibid., para. 32.

upon the notion of member state responsibility applied.[14] While measures adopted within such legal framework on the basis of a transfer of competences from states could generally be regarded, as advanced by the respondent, as institutional conduct which would thereby solely engage the responsibility of the EC, the ECtHR adopted a different approach. Based on the understanding that member state responsibility persists after the transfer of powers to an international organization, the Court was bound to identify a legally relevant margin for the member state to act, as a subject of international law, within the Community framework. Whilst the Commission did not take a stand on this point, the ECtHR followed the applicant's contention and vindicated, quite audaciously, that the adoption of EC primary law qualified as state conduct.[15] Indeed, as noted by the Court: 'the alleged violation of the Convention flows from an annex to the 1976 Act, entered into by the United Kingdom, together with the extension to the European Parliament's competences brought about by the Maastricht Treaty. The Council Decision and the 1976 Act [...] and the Maastricht Treaty, with its changes to the EEC Treaty, all constituted international instruments *which were freely entered into* by the United Kingdom'.[16]

The 1976 Act and its Annex II, alongside the extension of the competences of the European Parliament provided by the Maastricht treaty, were thus considered by the ECtHR to be attributable to the respondent, thereby engaging the responsibility *ratione materiae* of the latter under art. 3 of Protocol No. 1 to the ECHR for the consequences of the said instruments.[17] In this light, the respondent's contention that it did not have a power of effective control over the state of affairs complained of was rejected by the Court, as the responsibility of the United Kingdom derived from its own conduct of entering into treaty commitments.[18] Indeed, the control theory, now envisaged in art. 59 of the ARIO,[19] is only applicable in cases of derived responsibility, that is, where the member state is found responsible *for* the wrongful acts of a given international organization, and not for its own conduct performed in an institutional context. That being the case, the respondent's suggestion did not, presumably, come out of the blue, as the argument of effective control over institutional conduct had been made in a previous case, namely, in *Arab Organization for Industrialization and*

---

[14] cf. G. Cori et F. Kauff-Gazin, 'L'arrêt Matthews: une Protection Globale des Droits de L'Homme par une Vision Réductrice de L'Ordre Juridique Communautaire?', in *Europe* 1, 2000, p. 5.

[15] The ECtHR's decision to exclude the adoption of EC primary law from the category of institutional conduct is somewhat controversial. Already in his concurring opinion with the European Commission of Human Rights, had F. Martinez expressed his strong disagreement with such an understanding (see: Report of the European Commission). G. Cori and F. Kauff-Gazin view the ECtHR's approach as having been driven, to a great extent, by a purely internationalist intent and the desire to ensure the protection of fundamental rights in Europe, without taking sufficient account of the specificities inherent in the EC legal order. See: G. Cori et F. Kauff-Gazin (n. 14), pp. 2, 4.

[16] cf. *Matthews* decision, para. 33.   [17] cf. ibid., para. 33.   [18] cf. ibid., paras 26 and 34.

[19] Art. 59(1) ARIO prescribes that:

A State which directs and controls an international organization in the commission of an internationally wrongful act by the latter is internationally responsible for that act if:
(a) the State does so with knowledge of the circumstances of the internationally wrongful act; and
(b) the act would be internationally wrongful if committed by that State.

others v Westland Helicopters Ltd,[20] litigated in the Swiss Federal Supreme Court. This argument was ultimately dismissed by the Supreme Court in view of the need to preserve the legal personality of international organizations and the independence with which they are meant to operate.[21]

Having ascertained that the exclusion of Gibraltar from the European Parliament elections was the result of various international instruments freely entered into by the respondent, the ECtHR moved on to an analysis of the terms in which the United Kingdom was responsible for 'securing' the rights contained in art. 3 of Protocol No. 1. In practice, examining whether the 1976 Act entered into by the respondent would not detract it from guaranteeing its Convention obligations entailed a judgment on the compatibility of a provision pertaining to the EC legal system with the European Convention. This was the first case where an analysis of the sort was undertaken within the European human rights system, and thus, constitutes a turning point in the jurisprudence of the ECtHR.

It is important to note that, in embarking on such an assessment, although the Court did not explicitly refer to the 'equivalent protection' criteria espoused by the Commission in earlier case-law (referred to above), it presupposed such an approach in its reasoning. In fact, the ECtHR observed that the 1976 Act, while a treaty within the Community legal order, could not be challenged before the European Court of Justice, which essentially meant that the Community legal system did not offer a level of protection of the right to free elections equivalent to that required of states under art. 3 of Protocol No. 1 to the ECHR.[22]

The ECtHR's concern with states' duty to ensure the protection of European Convention rights within a given institutional context has been interpreted as being based on the principle of good faith, in particular, the principle of *pacta sunt servanda*.[23] According to this interpretation, the obligations set forth in the ECHR must be performed in good faith, which conditions the way in which state parties are to enter into subsequent treaty commitments. As explained by Judge Ress in his

---

[20] Swiss Federal Supreme Court (First Civil Court), 19 July 1988, 80 ILR 652. (also commented upon in this book)

[21] cf. ibid., p. 658.

[22] cf. *Matthews* decision, para. 33. See also para. 42 of the decision, where the ECtHR noted that, in the present case, there had been 'no submission that there exist alternative means of providing for electoral representation of the population of Gibraltar in the European Parliament, and the Court finds no indication of any'. The interpretation of para. 33 of the decision as being based on the principle of equivalent protection has been put forward by, *inter alia*, R. A. Lawson and H. G. Schermers (n. 1), p. 679 and P. Klein, 'The Attribution of Acts to International Organizations', in J. Crawford, A. Pellet, and S. Olleson (eds), *The Law of International Responsibility* (Oxford, Oxford University Press, 2010), p. 313. In contrast, Ciampi contends that the application of the 'equivalent protection' criteria in the present case would be redundant. This is explained by the fact that the author views the adoption of the acts under contention as not constituting conduct performed by the United Kingdom in light of its obligations flowing from membership of the EC. See: A. Ciampi, 'L'Union Européenne et le Respect des Droits de L'Homme Dans la Mise en Ouvre des Sanctions Devant la Cour Européenne des Droits de L'Homme', in (2006) *Révue Générale de Droit Internationale Public* 91.

[23] For a detailed analysis of the application of the good faith principle in the framework of member state participation in international organizations, see: O. Murray, 'Piercing the Corporate Veil: The Responsibility of Member States of an International Organization', (2011) 8 *International Organizations Law Review* 291–347.

concurring opinion in the *Bosphorus* decision: 'as the Court recognised in *Matthews v. the United Kingdom* [...] international treaties between the Contracting Parties have to be consistent with the provisions of the Convention. The same is true of treaties establishing international organisations. The importance of international cooperation and the need to secure the proper functioning of international organisations cannot justify Contracting Parties creating and entering into international organisations which are not in conformity with the Convention'.[24]

An alternative view contends that the principle under which member state responsibility is to be ascertained in this case is that of due diligence. More comprehensively than the good faith principle perhaps, the principle of due diligence provides a solid basis upon which to ground the ECtHR's widely cited assertion, made in the present case, that: 'The Convention does not exclude the transfer of competences to international organisations provided that Convention rights continue to be 'secured'. *Member States' responsibility therefore continues even after such a transfer.* (Cf. *Matthews* decision, para. 32 (emphasis added))'.

In this vein, it is not solely the initial act of establishing the international organization and drawing up its operational framework that is taken into account, but also the *continued* participation of member states in institutional affairs. Hence, according to the notion of due diligence, states must ensure that while entrusting an international organization with certain competences, they will still have at their disposal sufficient tools to oversee the impacts of the organization's activities on human rights.[25] In *Matthews,* this would imply a duty upon the respondent to diligently *monitor* and *oversee* EC operations, in particular, the occurrence of elections to the European Parliament, so as to make sure that these would not run counter to the protection of ECHR rights.

Underlying the ECtHR's assessment of the respondent's guaranteeing functions was the Court's realization that: legislation emanating from the legislative process of the European Community affects the population of Gibraltar in the same way as legislation which enters the domestic legal order exclusively via the House of Assembly [of Gibraltar].[26]

Accordingly, inasmuch as the ECHR was intended to guarantee practical and effective rights, the respondent's responsibility could be engaged regardless of whether the source of the violation was to be found in domestic or European

---

[24] cf. *Bosphorus Hava Yollari Turizm veTicaret Anonim Sirketi v Ireland*, App. No. 45036/98, 30 June 2005, Concurring Opinion of Judge Ress, para. 5.

[25] cf. P. Klein (n. 22), pp. 310–14. On states' duty of due diligence in an institutional framework, see also the study of the Institut de Droit International entitled, 'The Legal Consequences for Member States of the Non-Fulfilment by International Organizations of their Obligations Toward Third Parties', Annuaire de l'Institut de Droit International, Session de Lisbonne, Vol. 66-I, 1995, and the response of M. Jean Salmon to the 'Questionnaire' prepared by Rapporteur R. Higgins, pp. 340, 344, and 345.

The notion that states must act diligently when participating in institutional affairs has also been upheld by the UN Committee on Economic Social and Cultural Rights in its General Comments and Concluding Observations. See, *inter alia*, General Comment No. 19 on the Right to Social Security, UN Doc. E/C.12/GC/19 (2008), para. 58.

[26] cf. *Matthews* decision, para. 34.

legislation.[27] Certainly, the question could only merit a positive response in case the ECHR would be interpreted as imposing upon state parties obligations extending to the legal system of a supranational representative organ. The issue was addressed by the ECtHR in paras 36–44 of the decision, and mainly drew on whether the term 'legislature', in the sense of art. 3 of Protocol No. 1, could be interpreted as encompassing elections to the European Parliament.

In accordance with the respondent, the ECHR did not impose upon states obligations relating to the undertakings of a distinct supranational organization, in respect of which member states had limited their own sovereignty.[28] Art. 3 of Protocol No. 1 would therefore only apply to a purely domestic representational organ. The European Commission of Human Rights supported the respondent's approach, asserting that to apply such a provision to 'supra-national representative organs would be to extend the scope of Article 3 beyond what was intended by the drafters of the Convention and beyond the object and purpose of the provision'.[29] In the Commission's view, the purpose of art. 3 was to 'ensure that elections take place at regular intervals to the national or local legislative assembly', and not to provide any guarantees with respect to a 'non-national' institution such as the European Parliament.[30]

The ECtHR concluded for the opposite. Based on the character of the Convention as a living instrument and the need to interpret the obligations prescribed therein in light of present day conditions, the ECtHR found art. 3 to encompass electoral representation in the European Parliament.[31] The Court's reasoning brings to the fore an important message: it proves that, although human rights provisions do not immediately seem to apply to institutional contexts, it is possible to find in their scope of application the imposition, upon states, of particular obligations conditioning their participation in the operations of international organizations. International law must be able to accompany the new ways in which states decide to cooperate internationally (including the strengthening of their ties in the form of European integration). In this vein, as observed by the ECtHR, '[to] the extent that Contracting States organise common constitutional or parliamentary structures by international treaties, the Court must take these mutually agreed structural changes into account in interpreting the Convention and its Protocols'.[32] Eventually, the respondent was found responsible for failing to ensure respect for the right to vote of the residents of Gibraltar, as this right had been deprived of its essence and effectiveness.[33]

Arguably, the ECtHR would not apply the same reasoning if the issues complained of related to the adoption of 'normal' Community acts, that is, secondary EU law—and, generally, if the contention regarded member state participation in decision-making processes occurring in any other international organization. This important question was latent in the present case, but went unnoticed. In fact, the applicant referred to the respondent's responsibility under the Convention 'for the effects of the Council

---

[27] cf. ibid., para. 34.   [28] cf. *Matthews* decision, para. 36.
[29] cf. Report of the European Commission, para. 63.   [30] cf. ibid., para. 63.
[31] cf. *Matthews* decision, para. 39.   [32] cf. *Matthews* decision, para. 39.
[33] cf. ibid., paras 63–5.

Decision', apart from the 1976 Act.[34] Also, the ECtHR stated that the Council Decision, alongside with the 1976 Act and the Maastricht Treaty, constituted an international instrument 'freely entered into' by the Respondent (cf. *Matthews* decision, para. 33).

In commenting on the *Matthews* decision, Lawson and Schermers pointed to the possibility of extending the ECtHR's reasoning to genuine Community acts, noting that '[s]ince the Member States enabled the Community institutions to adopt these binding measures, they should bear the consequences if violations of the Convention occur'.[35] On the one hand, it is true that the Court has proved its readiness to assess member state responsibility where the object of the dispute regards issues of a purely institutional 'nature' and 'character' (in the present case, elections to the European Parliament). On the other hand, however, the Court would probably easily discard a contention regarding state responsibility for the adoption of institutional measures by claiming that the conduct complained of was solely attributable to the international organization, and thus, lay outside the Court's jurisdiction *ratione personae*. It should be noted, however, that the European regime will surely merit a particular approach in view of the EU's accession to the European Convention.[36]

The particular issue of member state responsibility for participation in the process of adoption of EU acts was raised in the earlier *CFDT* case, referred to above. After negating its jurisdiction *ratione personae* to consider the complaint against the EC Council's decision (not to designate the French trade union as a representative organization to submit a list of candidates for the Consultative Committee of the ECSC),[37] the Commission examined the question of whether the member states could be found individually responsible with relation to such act.[38] The Commission easily dispensed with the argument that France had unlawfully omitted to include the applicant's name in the abovementioned list by ascertaining that France had not yet recognized the right to individual petition under art. 25 of the Convention.[39] It did not, however, discard the possibility of establishing France's responsibility if that were not the case. With respect to the other eight member states, the Commission considered the matter to lie outside its jurisdiction *ratione personae* in that 'these States by taking part in the decision of

---

[34] cf. ibid., para. 27. In their dissenting opinion with the European Commission of Human Rights, M.A. Weitzel, C.L. Rozakis, M.P. Pellonpää, B. Conforti, and N. Bratza further note the applicant's argument that the Council Decision was not in any case a typical EC act, as it had been signed not only by the President of the Council but also the member states' ministers.

[35] R. A. Lawson and H. G. Schermers (n. 1), p. 679. Following the same line of thought, Cori and Kauff-Gazin note that: '[p]oussé jusqu'à ses ultimes consequences, le raisonnement de la Cour pourrait conduire à une extension ultérieure de sa compétence à l'égard des actes communautaires. En effet, en appliquant une logique de droit international quant à la paternité des actes communautaires, ces derniers, au moins les actes adoptés à l'unanimité, pourraient être considérés comme des actes pour lesquels les Etats membres restent les ultimes responsables, même s'ils les adoptent dans l'enceinte communautaire.' (See: G. Cori et F. Kauff-Gazin (n. 14), p. 4).

[36] See, *inter alia*, O. de Schutter, 'The Two Lives of Bosphorus: Redefining the Relationships Between the European Court of Human Rights and the Parties to the Convention', (2013) 4 *European Journal of Human Rights* 584, in particular pp. 596–615, discussing the various possible scenarios following the EU's accession to the ECHR when it comes to the application of the presumption of equivalent protection.

[37] cf. *CFDT* case, pp. 239–40, paras 1–3.   [38] cf. ibid., p. 240, para. 5.

[39] cf. ibid., p. 240, para. 6.

the Council of the European Communities had not in the circumstances of the instant case exercised their "jurisdiction" within the meaning of Article 1 of the Convention'.[40] Finally, the question was also raised as to whether the member states could be found jointly responsible for the acts complained of.[41] Unsurprisingly, the possibility was also discarded for lack of jurisdiction, although the Commission still remarked that 'the applicant ha[d] not defined what it mean[t] by [joint member state responsibility]'.[42] It is noteworthy that the *Matthews* case was the first one where the ECtHR seemed to be prepared to establish such collective responsibility, at least with regard to primary EU law. Following the ECtHR's reasoning, even where the acts at stake form part of the EU legal order, member states are bound to respect ECHR obligations, and thus, the respondent's responsibility for the consequences of the—*in casu*—Maastricht Treaty would be engaged 'together with all the other parties' to such treaty.[43] Importantly, this line of reasoning implies that the ECHR can generally have an extraterritorial scope of application, inasmuch as the responsibility of all the other member states would be determined with respect to the rights of the residents of Gibraltar.

The possibility of establishing state responsibility for/in connection with institutional measures has not merited a clear-cut response in the ECtHR's subsequent case-law. While the European Commission of Human Rights had peremptorily declared, in the aforementioned *CFDT* case, its lack of jurisdiction *rationae personae* to examine member state responsibility on grounds that the states parties had not acted within their jurisdiction in the sense of art. 1 of the ECHR, in the later case *Senator Lines v Austria* et. al,[44] which was filed against the then fifteen EU member states collectively, the ECtHR, interestingly, proceeded to an analysis of whether the applicant company could claim to be a victim, without actually declaring the application inadmissible at the outset.[45] Ultimately, it all depends on how the position of member states *vis-à-vis* an international organization is perceived and how certain acts can be categorized as being performed by states *within their jurisdiction* in the sense of art. 1 of the ECHR.

Conceptually, the answer to the question as to whether member state participation in the processes of adoption of institutional measures engages state responsibility *for/in connection with* institutional acts, or rather, for *its own conduct* performed in an institutional framework, leads to significantly different outcomes.[46] Accordingly, if the

---

[40] cf. ibid., p. 240, para. 7.   [41] cf. ibid., para. 4.   [42] cf. ibid.

[43] cf. *Matthews* decision, para. 33 (emphasis added). In the later case *Société Guerin Automobiles c. 15 Etats de l'Union Européenne*, App. No. 51717/99, 4 July 2000, where the applicant invoked the responsibility of all fifteen EU member states for the transfer of competences to the European Court of Justice, the opportunity to clarify the Court's position was not seized, in that the Court declared the case inadmissible for lack of jurisdiction *ratione materiae*.

[44] *Senator Lines v Austria, Belgium, Denmark, Finland, France, Germany, Greece, Ireland, Italy, Luxembourg, The Netherlands, Portugal, Spain, Sweden, and the United Kingdom*, App. No. 56672/00, 10 March 2004.

[45] cf. F. Hoffmeister, 'Litigating against the European Union and Its Member States—Who Responds under the ILC's Draft Articles on International Responsibility of International Organizations?', (2010) 21 No 3 *European Journal of International Law* 723, 730.

[46] In the first cases (i.e. cases of derived responsibility), the ARIO (n. 8) would apply and the commission of internationally wrongful conduct by the international organization would have to be established (see arts. 58 and 59); in the latter, the question of state responsibility would be analyzed independently from the international organization's conduct, and thus, the ILC's 2001 Articles on Responsibility of States for Internationally Wrongful Acts would rather apply (see: Report of the International Law Commission on the Work of Its Fifty-third Session, UNGAOR, 56th Session, Supp. 10 (A/56/10), 2001).

ECtHR were to perceive member state participation in decision-making processes—through the exercise of voting rights or the assumption of a specific position in consensus-based decision-making—as state conduct, it could more easily reason that the state had acted within its jurisdiction (see the ICJ case *Application of the Interim Accord of 13 September 1995 (The Former Yugoslav Republic of Macedonia v Greece)*, also discussed in this book, where the legality of the individual conduct of a member state in the decision-making process of an international organization was at stake).

> Following the Court's own words in *Matthews,* the adoption of an institutional act is also 'freely entered into' by member states through the discretion state representatives have when casting a vote in favour of the decision eventually adopted in the Council. This was even somehow admitted by the ECtHR—albeit unintendedly perhaps—when it claimed that the Council Decision, together with the 1976 Act and the Maastricht Treaty, constituted an international instrument freely entered into by the United Kingdom.[47] Moreover, an important nuance (already referred to above) was introduced in the *Matthews* case, notably, the ECtHR's focus on the *effects* that the contentious act had on the population of Gibraltar: having acknowledged that the latter would be affected in the same way regardless of the European or domestic source of the legislation at stake, the Court noted that: there is […] no reason why the United Kingdom should not be required to 'secure' the rights in Article 3 of Protocol No. 1 in respect of European legislation, in the same way as those rights are required to be 'secured' in respect of purely domestic legislation.[48]

In this light, by accepting, on the one hand, that states are prominent actors steering decision-making processes through the exercise of voting rights and, on the other hand, that 'genuine' Community acts (and generally, international organizations' acts) may well impact upon individuals in terms that are equivalent to national measures, it is possible to engage the responsibility of member states for failure to 'secure' ECHR rights when participating in the process of adoption of said institutional acts. Such a solution is not only legally viable but also desirable, if the ECHR is meant to protect not theoretical or illusory rights, but rights that are practical and effective.

---

[47] cf. *Matthews* decision, para. 33.   [48] cf. ibid., para. 34.

6.4 *Admissibility of the Application by Vlastimir and Borka Banković, Živana Stojanović, Mirjana Stoimenovski, Dragana Koksimović, and Dragan Suković against Belgium, the Czech Republic, Denmark, France, Germany, Greece, Hungary, Iceland, Italy, Luxembourg, The Netherlands, Norway, Poland, Portugal, Spain, Turkey, and the United Kingdom*, European Court of Human Rights, Grand Chamber Decision, [2001]

Tullio Scovazzi

Relevance of the case

The decision in the *Bankovic* case,[1] made on 12 December 2001, is mostly relevant for being one of few cases in which the European Court of Human Rights (ECtHR) took a position that without an acceptable explanation restricts the application of human rights granted by the European Convention on Human Rights (ECHR).

The seventeen respondent states belong to the North Atlantic Treaty Organization (NATO), an international organization that, following a decision of its North Atlantic Council, effected from 24 March to 8 June 1999 air strikes against the Federal Republic of Yugoslavia (FRY).

How effective is international adjudication in cases involving what historically has proved to be the most sinister way of using force, provoking many civilian casualties through aerial bombing? Apart from the legal aspects of the case, this is the main political question involved in the Court decision.

I. Facts of the case

On 23 April 1999 a missile launched from an aircraft engaged in NATO air strikes hit the television and radio station in Belgrade (*Radio Televizije Srbije*, RTS). Two of the four floors of the building collapsed. Sixteen civilian persons were killed and another sixteen were seriously injured. The daughter of the first and second applicants, the sons of the third and fourth applicants, and the husband of the fifth applicant died and the sixth applicant was injured.

As international organizations, such as NATO, are not parties to the ECHR, and it was not possible to identify the nationality of the aircraft that launched the missile, the applicants, all nationals of Yugoslavia, brought the case against all the states parties

---

[1] *Banković and others v Belgium and others, Admissibility,* App. No. 52207/99, ECHR 2001-XII. See Happold, 'Bankovic v Belgium and the Territorial Scope of the European Convention on Human Rights', (2003) *Human Rights Law Review* 77; Altiparmark, 'Bankovic: An Obstacle to the Application of the European Convention on Human Rights in Iraq?', (2004) *Journal of Conflict Security Law* 213; and, more generally, Milanovic, *Extraterritorial Application of Human Rights Treaties* (Oxford, Oxford University Press 2011).

to the ECHR involved in the air strikes, which they considered as severally liable for the attack against RTS. During the proceedings, the respondent states maintained that the Court could not decide the merits of the case, as it lacked jurisdiction *ratione loci*, and as a decision would determine the rights and obligations of Canada, the United States, and of the NATO itself, none of whom were parties to the ECHR. France also argued that the Court lacked jurisdiction *ratione personae*, as the bombardment was imputable only to the NATO, an organization with an international legal personality separate from that of the respondent states.

II. The legal question

On the merits the applicants relied on arts. 2 (right to life), 10 (freedom of expression) and 13 (right to an effective remedy) ECHR. However, before entering into the substance of the case, the Court was called to address the question of the admissibility *ratione loci* of the application under art. 1 ECHR (obligation to respect human rights), which provides that '[t]he High Contracting Parties shall secure to everyone within their jurisdiction the rights and freedoms defined in Section I of this Convention'.

The applicants maintained that the impugned acts of bombing a territory and killing people *ipso facto* brought them and their deceased relatives within the jurisdiction of the respondent states. The respondent states contended that the application was incompatible with art. 1 ECHR, because the applicants and their deceased relatives did not come under their 'jurisdiction', as the relevant facts occurred within a state, Yugoslavia, not party to the ECHR. They denied having exercised control of the airspace over Belgrade and, in any event, disputed that any such control could be equated with the exercise of effective control or legal authority that is required by art. 1 ECHR.

The main and the only question addressed by the Court in the decision related to the so-called extra-territorial application of the ECHR in the light of the specific circumstances of the case. Having found that it lacked jurisdiction, the Court did not address the issue of whether the impugned acts were attributable to the NATO member states or rather to NATO itself.

III. Excerpts

The Court reached the conclusion that the applicants and their deceased relatives were not capable of coming within the jurisdiction of the respondent states on account of the extra-territorial act in question.[2]

According to the Court, from the standpoint of public international law, the jurisdictional competence of a state is primarily territorial. Extra-territorial jurisdiction, while not altogether excluded, remains exceptional:

> The Court is of the view [...] that Article 1 of the Convention must be considered to reflect this ordinary and essentially territorial notion of jurisdiction, other bases of

---

[2] Cf. *Bankovic* case (n. 1), para. 82.

jurisdiction being exceptional and requiring special justification in the particular circumstances of each case.[3]

The Court found 'clear confirmation of this essentially territorial notion of jurisdiction' in the *travaux préparatoires* of the ECHR, since in the drafting of art. 1 the words 'all persons residing within their territories' were replaced with a reference to persons 'within their jurisdiction'. This was done 'with a view to expanding the Convention application to others who may not reside, in a legal sense, but who are, nevertheless, on the territory of the Contracting Parties'.[4] In the Court's view,

> the case-law of the Court demonstrates that its recognition of the exercise of extra-territorial jurisdiction by a Contracting State is exceptional: it has done so when the respondent State, through the effective control of the relevant territory and its inhabitants abroad as a consequence of military occupation or through the consent, invitation or acquiescence of the Government of that territory, exercises all or some of the public powers normally to be exercised by that Government.[5]

Although the text of the decision is not fully clear, it seems that the Court found that the notion of 'jurisdiction' followed by the applicant was at the same time too extensive, insofar as it could be confused with the notion of victim of a violation of rights granted by the ECHR, and too fragmentary, insofar as it could be tailored to the commission and consequences of a particular act (air bombing, in the specific case):

> They [= the applicants] claim that the positive obligation under Article 1 extends to securing the Convention rights in a manner proportionate to the level of control exercised in any given extra-territorial situation. The Governments contend that this amounts to a 'cause-and-effect' notion of jurisdiction not contemplated by or appropriate to Article 1 of the Convention. The Court considers that the applicants' submission is tantamount to arguing that anyone adversely affected by an act imputable to a Contracting State, wherever in the world that act may have been committed or its consequences felt, is thereby brought within the jurisdiction of that State for the purpose of Article 1 of the Convention.
>
> The Court is inclined to agree with the Governments' submission that the text of Article 1 does not accommodate such an approach to 'jurisdiction'. Admittedly, the applicants accept that jurisdiction, and any consequent State Convention responsibility, would be limited in the circumstances to the commission and consequences of that particular act. However, the Court is of the view that the wording of Article 1 does not provide any support for the applicants' suggestion that the positive obligation in Article 1 to secure 'the rights and freedoms defined in Section I of this Convention' can be divided and tailored in accordance with the particular circumstances of the extra-territorial act in question and it considers its view in this respect supported by the text of Article 19 of the Convention. Indeed the applicants' approach does not explain the application of the words 'within their jurisdiction' in Article 1 and it even goes so far as to render those words superfluous and devoid of any purpose. Had the drafters of the Convention wished to ensure jurisdiction as extensive as that

---

[3] Ibid, para. 61.   [4] Ibid, para. 63.   [5] Ibid, para. 71.

advocated by the applicants, they could have adopted a text the same as or similar to the contemporaneous Articles 1 of the four Geneva Conventions of 1949 [...].

Furthermore, the applicants' notion of jurisdiction equates the determination of whether an individual falls within the jurisdiction of a Contracting State with the question of whether that person can be considered to be a victim of a violation of rights guaranteed by the Convention. These are separate and distinct admissibility conditions, each of which has to be satisfied in the afore-mentioned order, before an individual can invoke the Convention provisions against a Contracting State.[6]

The Court did not find it necessary to pronounce on the meaning of similar jurisdiction provisions included in other human rights instruments[7] and, while admitting the existence of a gap in human rights protection, concluded that the ECHR, as an instrument having an essentially regional vocation within the 'European public order', was not designed to be applied throughout the world:

> The Court's obligation, in this respect, is to have regard to the special character of the Convention as a constitutional instrument of *European* public order for the protection of individual human beings and its role [...] is to ensure the observance of the engagements undertaken by the Contracting Parties. It is therefore difficult to contend that a failure to accept the extraterritorial jurisdiction of the respondent States would fall foul of the Convention's *ordre public* objective, which itself underlines the essentially regional vocation of the Convention system [...]. In short, the Convention is a multi-lateral treaty operating [...] in an essentially regional context and notably in the legal space (*espace juridique*) of the Contracting States. The FRY clearly does not fall within this legal space. The Convention was not designed to be applied throughout the world, even in respect of the conduct of Contracting States. Accordingly, the desirability of avoiding a gap or vacuum in human rights' protection has so far been relied on by the Court in favour of establishing jurisdiction only when the territory in question was one that, but for the specific circumstances, would normally be covered by the Convention.[8]

IV. Commentary

It is astonishing how such a questionable decision was rendered by the Court unanimously. The Court started with a wrong interpretation of the word 'jurisdiction' used in art. 1 ECHR. The preparatory works of the ECHR show that the states involved considered it too restrictive to grant human rights only to 'all persons residing within their territories' and agreed to enlarge the application of the future convention to all those 'within their jurisdiction'. This surely means that the application of the ECHR was extended also to anyone who occasionally is found in the territory of the parties, without being a resident therein. But this does not mean that the word 'jurisdiction'

---

[6] Cf. *Bankovic* case (n.1), para.75. Under Art. 1 of the four 1949 Geneva Conventions on the protection of war victims, the parties undertake 'to respect and to ensure respect for the present Convention in all circumstances'.

[7] Cf. *Bankovic* case (n. 1), para.78.   [8] Ibid, para. 80.

can be equated with the word 'territory', as the Court wrongly inferred from the pre-paratory works. 'Jurisdiction', whatever is its meaning (and the word in itself is far from being clear), is something different from territory.

It may be true that in international law the notion of 'jurisdiction' is often ter-ritorial. But this is not the case of human rights treaties. They do not belong to traditional international law, which regulates the relationship between sovereign states that have established themselves in a given territory. Human rights treaties regulate the completely different relationship between state agents and one or more individuals. Their provisions must be interpreted in the light of the object and pur-pose of this category of treaties, as required by art. 31, para. 1, of the 1969 Vienna Convention on the Law of Treaties. Because human rights treaties aim at regulat-ing the acts of state agents, they apply everywhere such agents happen to act in a way that could affect individuals. The notion of territory has no role to play in cases where human rights are at stake. The 'jurisdiction' of a state is dependent on an act done by its agent and not on the place where the act is done. If the agents of State party A torture an individual within the territory of State B without the knowledge of the latter, the ECHR applies to State A and not to State B, because the individual is within the jurisdiction of State A. The place where the act occurred and whether or not State B is a party to the ECHR have no relevance on the question of 'juris-diction'. As far as human rights are concerned, a person is under the jurisdiction of a state if he or she is subject to the authority and control of its agents. To be pre-cise, such 'jurisdiction' is neither territorial, nor extra-territorial. It is authority and control irrespective of territory.

In the *Banković* decision a court specifically established for the protection of human rights was not able to read a human rights treaty according to its very nature. It pre-ferred too restrictive an interpretation which is in itself contrary to the object and purpose of this category of treaty, that is to protect the weaker party in the relation-ship between a state and an individual. If the Court had given a more extended look to other human rights bodies—but it chose not to do so—it would have found, for instance, that the Inter-American Commission of Human Rights made the follow-ing clear remarks in the report of 29 September 1999 on the case *Coard and others v United States*:

> Given that individual rights inhere simply by virtue of a person's humanity, each American State is obliged to uphold the protected rights of any person subject to its jurisdiction. While this most commonly refers to persons within a state's ter-ritory, it may, under given circumstances, refer to conduct with an extraterritorial locus where the person concerned is present in the territory of one state, but sub-ject to the control of another state—usually through the acts of the latter's agents abroad. In principle, the inquiry turns not on the presumed victim's nationality or presence within a particular geographic area, but on whether, under the specific circumstances, the State observed the rights of a person subject to its authority and control.[9]

---

[9] *Bankovic* case (n. 1), para. 37.

The principle that human rights treaties apply to every person who is 'within the power and effective control' of a state party was confirmed, as regards the 1966 Covenant on Civil and Political Rights.[10]

The nature itself of human rights dictates the very conclusions that were so bluntly rejected by the Court, namely that anyone adversely affected by an act imputable to a state party to the ECHR, wherever in the world that act may have been committed, be thereby brought within the jurisdiction of that state for the purpose of art. 1 ECHR and that the notion of jurisdiction be equated with the notion of (assumed) victim of a violation of rights guaranteed by the ECHR. Human rights obligations are due by states to human beings in general.

Having assumed in the *Banković* decision that only in exceptional cases acts performed by parties outside their territories constitute an exercise of jurisdiction, the Court was bound to find a somehow logical threshold between what could be considered an exceptional case and what could not. This exercise proved to be quite a difficult one.

The Court could not disregard its previous judgment of 23 March 1995 in the case of *Loizidou v Turkey* (preliminary objections), where it held that the acts committed by Turkey in the occupied territory of northern Cyprus fell under the 'jurisdiction' of Turkey under art. 1 ECHR. In that case, the Court clearly stated that the ECHR has an extra-territorial application, without envisaging any exceptions:

> [A]lthough Article 1 sets limits on the reach of the Convention, the concept of 'jurisdiction' under this provision is not restricted to the national territory of the High Contracting Parties. [...] the responsibility of Contracting Parties can be involved because of acts of their authorities, whether performed within or outside national boundaries, which produce effects outside their own territory [...]. Bearing in mind the object and purpose of the Convention, the responsibility of a Contracting Party may also arise when as a consequence of military action—whether lawful or unlawful—it exercises effective control of an area outside its national territory. The obligation to secure, in such an area, the rights and freedoms set out in the Convention derives from the fact of such control whether it be exercised directly, through its armed forces, or through a subordinate local administration.[11]

In explaining the *Banković* decision, the Court found a difference between the *Loizidou* and the *Banković* cases in the fact that, in the former, the respondent state exercised 'effective control of the relevant territory [of Cyprus] and its inhabitants abroad as a consequence of military occupation'.[12] However, contrary to the belief of the Court, the fact that, in the case of air bombing, the authority and control exercised by the agents of a state over individuals in another state is restricted to one type of action and does not correspond to an almost complete exercise of state authority, as it happens in the case of territorial occupation has no particular relevance. Where is it written that a violation

---

[10] Cf. Human Rights Committee General Comment No. 31 of 29 March 2004 para. 10.
[11] *Loizidou v Turkey,* Admissibility, App No 15318/89, Case No 40/1993/435/514, A/310, [1995] ECHR 10, para. 62.
[12] Cf. *Banković* case (n. 1), para. 4 quoting *Loizidou v Turkey* (n. 10), para. 71.

of the ECHR exists only if the responsible state is in principle capable of violating in a given territory all the rights granted by this Convention? It is obvious that the crew of a bombing aircraft cannot violate all the range of rights granted by the ECHR (for example, they cannot arbitrarily arrest people in violation of art. 5 ECHR). But what they can do, in particular to kill and massacre people and to devastate and disrupt public and private properties, is enough (better: much more than enough) to be considered as an exercise of effective authority and control by the bombing state.[13]

The Court also remarked that, unlike Yugoslavia, Cyprus was a party to the ECHR, with the consequence that, if the application in the *Loizidou* case had been held inadmissible, 'the inhabitants of northern Cyprus would have found themselves excluded from the benefits of the Convention safeguards and system which they had previously enjoyed, by Turkey's "effective control" of the territory and by the accompanying inability of the Cypriot Government, as a Contracting State, to fulfil the obligations it had undertaken under the Convention'.[14] This situation, according to the Court was 'entirely different' from what happened in the *Banković* case, where Yugoslavia was not a party to the ECHR. However, it is difficult to accept the double standard established by the Court between the alleged victims of human rights violations committed by states parties to the ECHR, depending on where an act is committed. If the ECHR is the expression of a '*European* public order for the protection of individual human beings',[15] it should be so because it imposes its provisions to all acts wherever performed by the agents of the European states parties and not because it would condone such acts when committed in the territory of non-party states.

Without explicitly recognizing it, the Court itself was led to contradict in subsequent cases the untenable assumption that the ECHR would apply only to territories 'that, but for the specific circumstances, would normally be covered by the Convention'.[16] For instance, it did so in the decision of 30 June 2009 on the admissibility on the application *Al-Saadoon and Mufdhi v United Kingdom* and in the judgment of 7 July 2011 in the case *Al-Skeini and others v United Kingdom*, where it affirmed the 'jurisdiction' of the respondent state for acts committed in Iraq.

Having found its lack of jurisdiction *ratione loci*, the Court did not enter into the question of jurisdiction *ratione personae*, that is whether the impugned action was attributable to NATO rather than to its seventeen member states against which the application was brought. In the subsequent decision of 2 May 2007 on the admissibility of the cases *A. Behrami and B. Behrami v France and R. Saramati v France, Germany, and Norway*, the Court found that the impugned action and inaction were attributable to an international organization (the UN) that retained ultimate authority and control over its member states engaged in the KFOR (Kosovo Force)

---

[13] In the judgment of 29 March 2010 in the *Medvedyev v France* case, the Court tried to justify the *Banković* decision by assuming that the notion of effective control of area outside the national territory 'excluded situations [...] where—as in the *Banković* case—what was at issue was an instantaneous extraterritorial act, as the provisions of Article 1 did not admit of a "cause-and-effect" notion of "jurisdiction"' (para. 64). The Court did not however explain why an 'instantaneous' act such as air bombing, which can have permanent and disruptive consequences on human life and properties, is not a manifestation of effective control of a given area.

[14] Cf. *Banković* case (n. 1), para. 80.　　　[15] Ibid.　　　[16] Ibid.

and UNMIK (United Nations Interim Administration Mission in Kosovo) activities, so that operational command only was delegated.[17] Accordingly, the Court declared the applicants' complaints incompatible *ratione personae* with the provisions of the Convention.[18] Given the unclear command chain, it is highly uncertain what result the criterion of ultimate authority and control would have produced, if applied to the 1999 NATO military intervention in Yugoslavia.

More generally, the bombing of Yugoslavia by the aircraft of a number of NATO member states was done without any authorization by the Security Council and therefore constitutes a violation of the UN Charter. It is also a violation of the NATO Treaty itself.[19] However, not only the ECtHR, but also the International Court of Justice (in the judgment of 15 December 2004 on the *Legality of Use of Force*, preliminary objections, where it found the lack of jurisdiction to enter- tain the claims made by Yugoslavia against Canada, France, Germany, Italy, Netherlands, Portugal, Spain, United Kingdom, and the United States) and the Prosecutor of the International Criminal Tribunal for the Former Yugoslavia (who followed the recommendation made on 8 June 2008 by the Committee Established to Review the NATO Bombing Campaign Against the Federal Republic of Yugoslavia that no investigation be commenced in relation to such a campaign) for different reasons were not able to entertain the merits of cases relating to the bombing of Yugoslavia.

In its too legalistic and basically wrong approach to the *Banković* case, the ECtHR did not devote any attention to the victims of the bombing of the television and radio station in Belgrade. However, it is worthwhile to recall the relevant facts:

> On 23 April 1999, at 0220, NATO intentionally bombed the central studio of the RTS (state-owned) broadcasting corporation at 1 Aberdareva Street in the centre of Belgrade. The missiles hit the entrance area, which caved in at the place where the Aberdareva Street building was connected to the Takovska Street building. While there is some doubt over exact casualty figures, between 10 and 17 people are esti- mated to have been killed.
>
> The bombing of the TV studio was part of a planned attack aimed at disrupting and degrading the C3 (Command, Control and Communications) network. In co- ordinated attacks, on the same night, radio relay buildings and towers were hit along with electrical power transformer stations. At a press conference on 27 April 1999, NATO officials justified this attack in terms of the dual military and civilian use to which the FRY communication system was routinely put [...].[20]

---

[17] Cf. *Behrami v France*, 45 EHRR SE10, paras 133 and 144.   [18] Ibid., para. 152.

[19] 'This Treaty does not affect, and shall not be interpreted as affecting in any way the rights and obliga- tions under the Charter of the Parties which are members of the United Nations, or the primary respon- sibility of the Security Council for the maintenance of international peace and security' (art. 7).

[20] Paragraphs 71 and 72 of the Final Report to the Prosecutor by the Committee Established to Review the NATO Bombing Campaign against the Federal Republic of Yugoslavia. More generally, 'during the bombing campaign, NATO aircraft flew 38,400 sorties, including 10,484 strike sorties. During these sor- ties, 23,614 air munitions were released (figures from NATO). As indicated in the preceding paragraph, it appears that approximately 500 civilians were killed during the campaign. These figures do not indicate

The legality of such a bombing is highly questionable:[21]

> More controversially, however, the bombing was also justified on the basis of the propaganda purpose to which it was employed [...] In a statement of 8 April 1999, NATO also indicated that the TV studios would be targeted unless they broadcast 6 hours per day of Western media reports: 'If President Milosevic would provide equal time for Western news broadcasts in its programmes without censorship 3 hours a day between noon and 1800 and 3 hours a day between 1800 and midnight, then his TV could be an acceptable instrument of public information'.
>
> NATO intentionally bombed the Radio and TV station and the persons killed or injured were civilians. The questions are: was the station a legitimate military objective and; if it was, were the civilian casualties disproportionate to the military advantage gained by the attack?[22]

None of the international courts to which the case was presented will ever say a word on whether the civilians who died in the collapse of the radio and television station in Belgrade were legitimately killed. It appears that the states that are so able in air bombing are much less eager to agree that the effects of their bombing campaigns be discussed before an international court. Yet the name of the last bomb launched on the victims in Belgrade is 'jurisdiction'.

---

that NATO may have conducted a campaign aimed at causing substantial civilian casualties either directly or incidentally' (ibid., para. 54).

[21] NATO's co-operation with the Prosecutor was also questionable: 'The committee has conducted its review relying essentially upon public documents, including statements made by NATO and NATO countries at press conferences and public documents produced by the FRY. It has tended to assume that the NATO and NATO countries' press statements are generally reliable and that explanations have been honestly given. The committee must note, however, that when the OTP [Office of Tribunal Prosecutor] requested NATO to answer specific questions about specific incidents, the NATO reply was couched in general terms and failed to address the specific incidents' (ibid., para. 90).

[22] Ibid., paras 74 and 75.

6.5 *Bosphorus Hava Yollari Turizm veTicaret Anonim Sirketi v Ireland*, App. No. 45036/98, European Court of Human Rights, 30 June 2005

Tobias Lock

Relevance of the case

Bosphorus is relevant in that the European Court of Human Rights (ECtHR) introduced the so-called *Bosphorus* presumption: if a member state of an organization acted in compliance with an obligation arising from its membership and had no discretion, there is a rebuttable presumption that the member state has complied with its obligations under the European Convention on Human Rights (ECHR) provided that the organization itself ensures a protection of fundamental rights equivalent to what the Convention requires. If that is so, the presumption can only be rebutted if this protection was manifestly deficient.[1]

I. Facts of the case

Bosphorus Airways, a Turkish airline, brought an aircraft, which it had leased from the Yugoslav National Airlines, to Dublin for a service. Upon its arrival the Irish authorities impounded the aircraft on the basis of an EU Regulation, which was itself based on sanctions imposed on the Federal Republic of Yugoslavia by the UN Security Council.[2] The Regulation provided that all 'aircraft in which a majority or controlling interest is held by a person or undertaking in or operating from the Federal Republic of Yugoslavia (Serbia and Montenegro) shall be impounded by the competent authorities of the Member States'. Bosphorus challenged this in the Irish courts. The Irish Supreme Court requested a preliminary ruling from the Court of Justice of the European Union (CJEU), which held that the interference with Bosphorus' property rights was justified since the overall objective of the sanctions was to end the war on the Balkans. Having exhausted all remedies in the Irish courts, Bosphorus brought a case against Ireland to the ECtHR claiming a violation of its right to property guaranteed by art. 1 Protocol 1 ECHR.

II. Legal question

In *Bosphorus* Ireland found itself in a legal dilemma: it could either disobey its obligations stemming from the Regulation in order to uphold its obligations under the ECHR or (potentially) violate the ECHR and comply with its obligations under EU law.

---

[1] The author would like to thank Ariadne Panagopoulou for invaluable research assistance.
[2] cf. Council Regulation 990/93/EEC, OJ [1993] L 102/14 implementing UN Security Council Resolution 820.

The key legal question was whether Ireland could be held responsible for the alleged violation of the ECHR given that the Irish authorities had acted under a strict duty arising from Ireland's membership of the EU. The earlier *Matthews* decision[3] suggested that this would be the case considering that the Court had held that parties to the ECHR were allowed to transfer competences to international organizations, but that their responsibility continued after such a transfer.[4]

The key difference between *Matthews* and *Bosphorus* was that in *Matthews* the member state had acted under an obligation found in primary EU law, that is an obligation which had the same legal status as the EU Treaties, whereas the Regulation in *Bosphorus* constituted a piece of EU legislation, that is it had been adopted in accordance with the EU's legislative procedures. Another difference was that in *Bosphorus* the CJEU had already considered the Regulation to be in compliance with fundamental rights[5] so that by finding a violation of the ECHR, the ECtHR would indirectly find the CJEU to have wrongly upheld the Regulation. In addition, the Regulation was itself based on a Resolution by the UN Security Council so that the ECtHR was also at risk of second-guessing another august body and calling into question the primacy of obligations arising under the UN Charter as provided for by art. 103 UN Charter.

III. Excerpts

Having found that the alleged violation occurred within the jurisdiction of the Irish State and that art. 1 Protocol 1 ECHR had been interfered with, the Grand Chamber went on to discuss whether the interference was justified.

> 149. [...] there must exist a reasonable relationship of proportionality between the means employed and the aim sought to be realised: the Court must determine whether a fair balance has been struck between the demands of the general interest in this respect and the interest of the individual company concerned. In so determining, the Court recognises that the State enjoys a wide margin of appreciation with regard to the means to be employed and to the question of whether the consequences are justified in the general interest for the purpose of achieving the objective pursued [...].
>
> 150. [...] the general interest pursued by the impugned measure was compliance with legal obligations flowing from the Irish State's membership of the European Community. It is, moreover, a legitimate interest of considerable weight. [...]
>
> 154. In [...] establishing the extent to which a State's action can be justified by its compliance with obligations flowing from its membership of an international organisation to which it has transferred part of its sovereignty, the Court has recognised that absolving Contracting States completely from their Convention responsibility in the areas covered by such a transfer would be incompatible with the purpose and object of the Convention [...].

---

[3] ch. 6.3.
[4] cf. *Matthews v United Kingdom* App. No. 24833/94, ECHR 1999-I, para. 32.
[5] cf. Case C-84/95 *Bosphorus v Minister for Transport* [1996] ECR I-3953.

155. In the Court's view, State action taken in compliance with such legal obligations is justified as long as the relevant organisation is considered to protect fundamental rights, as regards both the substantive guarantees offered and the mechanisms controlling their observance, in a manner which can be considered at least equivalent to that for which the Convention provides [...]. By 'equivalent' the Court means 'comparable'; any requirement that the organisation's protection be 'identical' could run counter to the interest of international cooperation pursued (see paragraph 150 above). However, any such finding of equivalence could not be final and would be susceptible to review in the light of any relevant change in fundamental rights protection.

156. If such equivalent protection is considered to be provided by the organisation, the presumption will be that a State has not departed from the requirements of the Convention when it does no more than implement legal obligations flowing from its membership of the organisation.

However, any such presumption can be rebutted if, in the circumstances of a particular case, it is considered that the protection of Convention rights was manifestly deficient. In such cases, the interest of international cooperation would be outweighed by the Convention's role as a 'constitutional instrument of European public order' in the field of human rights (see *Loizidou v. Turkey* (preliminary objections), judgment of 23 March 1995, Series A no. 310, pp. 27–28, § 75).

157. It remains the case that a State would be fully responsible under the Convention for all acts falling outside its strict international legal obligations. [...] *Matthews* can also be distinguished: the acts for which the United Kingdom was found responsible were 'international instruments which were freely entered into' by it (see paragraph 33 of that judgment). [...].

158. Since the impugned measure constituted solely compliance by Ireland with its legal obligations flowing from membership of the European Community (see paragraph 148 above), the Court will now examine whether a presumption arises that Ireland complied with the requirements of the Convention in fulfilling such obligations and whether any such presumption has been rebutted in the circumstances of the present case.

(b) Whether there was a presumption of Convention compliance at the relevant time

159. The Court has described above (see paragraphs 73–81) the fundamental rights guarantees of the European Community which apply to member States, Community institutions and natural and legal persons ('individuals'). While the founding treaties of the European Communities did not initially contain express provisions for the protection of fundamental rights, the ECJ subsequently recognised that such rights were enshrined in the general principles of Community law protected by it, and that the Convention had a 'special significance' as a source of such rights. Respect for fundamental rights has become 'a condition of the legality of Community acts' (see paragraphs 73–75 above, together with the opinion of the Advocate General in the present case, paragraphs 45–50 above) and in carrying out this assessment the ECJ refers extensively to Convention provisions and to this Court's jurisprudence. At the relevant time, these jurisprudential developments had been reflected in certain treaty amendments (notably those aspects of the Single European Act of 1986 and of the Treaty on European Union referred to in paragraphs 77–78 above). This evolution has continued. The Treaty of Amsterdam of 1997 is referred to in paragraph 79 above.

Although not fully binding, the provisions of the Charter of Fundamental Rights of the European Union were substantially inspired by those of the Convention, and the Charter recognises the Convention as establishing the minimum human rights standards. Article I-9 of the later Treaty establishing a Constitution for Europe (not in force) provides for the Charter to become primary law of the European Union and for the Union to accede to the Convention (see paragraphs 80–81 above).

160. However, the effectiveness of such substantive guarantees of fundamental rights depends on the mechanisms of control in place to ensure their observance.

161. The Court has referred (see paragraphs 86–90 above) to the jurisdiction of the ECJ in, *inter alia*, annulment actions (Article 173, now Article 230, of the EC Treaty), in actions against Community institutions for failure to perform Treaty obligations (Article 175, now Article 232), to hear related pleas of illegality under Article 184 (now Article 241) and in cases against member States for failure to fulfil Treaty obligations (Articles 169, 170 and 171, now Articles 226, 227 and 228).

162. It is true that access of individuals to the ECJ under these provisions is limited: they have no *locus standi* under Articles 169 and 170; their right to initiate actions under Articles 173 and 175 is restricted as is, consequently, their right under Article 184; and they have no right to bring an action against another individual.

163. It nevertheless remains the case that actions initiated before the ECJ by the Community institutions or a member State constitute important control of compliance with Community norms to the indirect benefit of individuals. Individuals can also bring an action for damages before the ECJ in respect of the non-contractual liability of the institutions (see paragraph 88 above).

164. Moreover, it is essentially through the national courts that the Community system provides a remedy to individuals against a member State or another individual for a breach of Community law (see paragraphs 85 and 91 above). Certain EC Treaty provisions envisaged a complementary role for the national courts in the Community control mechanisms from the outset, notably Article 189 (the notion of direct applicability, now Article 249) and Article 177 (the preliminary reference procedure, now Article 234). It was the development by the ECJ of important notions such as the supremacy of Community law, direct effect, indirect effect and State liability (see paragraphs 92–95 above) which greatly enlarged the role of the domestic courts in the enforcement of Community law and its fundamental rights guarantees.

The ECJ maintains its control on the application by national courts of Community law, including its fundamental rights guarantees, through the procedure for which Article 177 of the EC Treaty provides in the manner described in paragraphs 96 to 99 above. While the ECJ's role is limited to replying to the interpretative or validity question referred by the domestic court, the reply will often be determinative of the domestic proceedings (as, indeed, it was in the present case—see paragraph 147 above) and detailed guidelines on the timing and content of a preliminary reference have been laid down by the EC Treaty provision and developed by the ECJ in its case-law. The parties to the domestic proceedings have the right to put their case to the ECJ during the Article 177 process. It is further noted that national courts operate in legal systems into which the Convention has been incorporated, albeit to differing degrees.

165. In such circumstances, the Court finds that the protection of fundamental rights by Community law can be considered to be, and to have been at the

relevant time, 'equivalent' (within the meaning of paragraph 155 above) to that of the Convention system. Consequently, the presumption arises that Ireland did not depart from the requirements of the Convention when it implemented legal obligations flowing from its membership of the European Community (see paragraph 156 above).

(c) Whether the presumption in question has been rebutted in the present case

166. The Court has had regard to the nature of the interference, to the general interest pursued by the impoundment and by the sanctions regime and to the ruling of the ECJ (in the light of the opinion of the Advocate General), a ruling with which the Supreme Court was obliged to and did comply. It considers it clear that there was no dysfunction of the mechanisms of control of the observance of Convention rights.

In the Court's view, therefore, it cannot be said that the protection of the applicant company's Convention rights was manifestly deficient, with the consequence that the relevant presumption of Convention compliance by the respondent State has not been rebutted.

IV. Commentary

While *Bosphorus* reaffirms the Grand Chamber's *Matthews* decision in so far as the general responsibility of the member states for actions and omissions based on their EU obligations is concerned, it introduces an important exception to this: if a member state of an organization acted in compliance with an obligation arising from its membership and had no discretion, there is a rebuttable presumption that the member state has complied with its obligations under the Convention provided that the organization itself ensures a protection of fundamental rights equivalent to what the Convention requires. Once established the presumption can only be rebutted if this protection was manifestly deficient.

The ECtHR thus introduced a two-stage test: at the first stage it examines whether an organization provides equivalent protection, which will lead to the presumption to apply but only in cases where the member state had no discretion in implementing its obligations. At the second stage, the ECtHR examines whether the presumption has been rebutted based on a manifest deficit in the protection of human rights in the actual case before it. As a rebuttal of the presumption is unlikely to occur in practice, the key implication is that it results in immunity from review for EU measures provided that there was no discretion for the member state.[6]

A. Rationale behind *Bosphorus*

What then are the reasons for the *Bosphorus* presumption? After all, it privileges the EU's legal order compared with the legal orders of the parties to the ECHR. Some of these orders equally guarantee a very high standard of human rights protection

---

[6] Note that the presumption was not accepted unanimously by all the judges. A forceful concurring opinion signed by six of the judges voiced serious doubt as to the wisdom behind it: by Judges Rozakis, Tulkens, Traja, Botoucharova, Zagrebelsky, and Garlicki.

but are still subject to a full scrutiny by the Court. The ECtHR relied on a substantive argument to justify the presumption: the protection of human rights in the EU's legal order is equivalent to what the Convention requires. It was thus formulated as an acknowledgment of the high quality of the protection of human rights in the EU legal order, which is in particular guaranteed by the ECJ. Hence the ECtHR considered itself in a position where it would be acceptable if it exercised its jurisdiction only in those exceptional cases in which the protection happened to be manifestly deficient.

The question then is why the *Bosphorus* presumption is limited to cases where the member states had no discretion. In such cases the member states had no opportunity to 'add' to a potential violation of the Convention as they were under a strict obligation to implement EU law as if they were the executive branch of the EU so that the member states are in a similar position to agents of the Union. Where the member states had discretion, there is no guarantee that the alleged violation of the Convention is found in provisions pertaining to EU law. The violation may well have been introduced by the member states in the exercise of their discretion so that the presumption of compatibility cannot apply.

It could be argued, however, that the true reasons for the presumption lie elsewhere. The first possible reason is that the ECtHR acted out of comity and deference towards the ECJ.[7] It acknowledged that the ECJ has a monopoly to declare EU legislation invalid. The ECtHR thus attempted to avoid a conflict with the ECJ and sent a signal of respect, in return for the ECJ's past receptiveness towards the ECtHR's human rights case law. Evidence for this view can be found in the subsequent case of *Michaud* where the ECtHR made it very clear that it had acted 'in the interest of international cooperation' and in order to avoid a dilemma for the member state.[8] Moreover, the fact that fundamental rights protection in EU law had been developed by the ECJ and the judicial protection given to individuals under the Treaties were central to the ECtHR's finding that the EU legal order could be considered to provide equivalent protection.[9] A second reason for the *Bosphorus* presumption is that the member states, and not the EU, would be held responsible for violations of the ECHR. The presumption is thus an acceptance of the fact that the EU, who in such cases is the potential violator of human rights, is not yet bound by the ECHR.[10]

---

[7] S. Douglas-Scott, '*Bosphorus v Ireland*' (2006) 43 *Common Market Law Review* 243; it has also been argued that the main motivation for the ECtHR was to limit the impact of its review on the effectiveness of the UN Security Council, cf. V.P. Tzevelekos, 'When Elephants Fight it is the Grass that Suffers: "hegemonic struggle" in Europe and the Side-effects for International Law' in K. Dzehtsiarou and others (eds), *Human Rights Law in Europe* (Routledge 2014).

[8] cf. *Michaud v France*, App. No. 12323/11, ECHR 2012, para. 104.

[9] cf. *Bosphorus v Ireland*, App. No. 45036/98, ECHR 2005-VI, paras 159–65.

[10] L. Besselink, 'The European Union and the European Convention on Human Rights: From Sovereign Immunity in *Bosphorus* to Full Scrutiny Under the Reform Treaty?' in I. Boerefijn and J. Goldschmidt (eds), *Changing Perceptions of Sovereignty and Human Rights, Essays in Honour of Cees Flinterman* (Antwerp, Intersentia 2008) p. 303; the EU is in the process of signing up to the ECHR, cf. T. Lock, 'End of an Epic? The Draft Accession Agreement on the EU's Accession to the ECHR' (2012) 31 *Yearbook of European Law* 162.

B. Open questions and post-*Bosphorus* case-law

In practical terms *Bosphorus* raises three questions. The first is under which circumstances a member state is deemed to have had no discretion so that the presumption applies. The second concerns the conditions for the existence of a manifest deficit. The third question is whether the *Bosphorus* presumption would only apply where the CJEU has had a chance to pronounce itself on the merits of the case.

Regarding the first question on discretion, the *Bosphorus* decision describes the situation in which a member state is deemed to have discretion 'where it does no more than implement legal obligations flowing from its membership of the organisation'.[11]

Discretion relates to the question whether the national legislator and national authorities are given a choice of how to comply with their obligations under EU law. In *Bosphorus* the ECtHR did not make it clear which exact factors it considers relevant when assessing whether the member state had discretion. There are two general possibilities: one would be to adopt a formalistic approach taking into account only the nature of the instrument implemented by the member state; the other possibility would be to make a substantive assessment of the degree of discretion. The latter approach would be in the spirit of the rationale of this aspect of the presumption as the member states should only be able to escape their responsibility where they did not have a chance of committing an additional violation of the Convention.

The ECtHR's case-law on this question is not entirely clear. For instance, in *Michaud* the Court emphasized the fact that the legal instrument at issue was a Directive which seemed to suggest that the member state had discretion when complying with its EU law obligations.[12] Rather enigmatically the ECtHR then held that the question whether the member state 'had a margin of manoeuvre capable of obstructing the application of the presumption of equivalent protection is not without relevance.' Regrettably, the ECtHR then did not elucidate on what this exactly meant, but it considered the presumption not to be applicable here. Thus the very nature of the measure being a Directive seems to have been an important factor (this is reminiscent of the Court's reasoning in the earlier case of *Cantoni v France*).[13]

In this context the treatment of Regulations is interesting. These are directly applicable and do not need to be implemented (art. 289 TFEU). However, as the ECtHR's case-law shows, it would be premature to conclude that the *Bosphorus* presumption applies whenever a Regulation is at issue. In *Coopérative des agriculteurs de Mayenne* a Regulation gave the member states a choice over which formula to use for calculating a levy for excess production of milk.[14] This choice might have suggested that the member states had some discretion in calculating the levy. However, the Court did not take this into account but focused on the method of calculating the amount of the levy, which was defined in the Regulation leading

---

[11] cf. *Bosphorus v Ireland* (n. 9), para. 156.   [12] cf. *Michaud v France* (n. 8), para. 113.
[13] [GC] App. No. 17862/91, ECHR 1996-V.
[14] *Coopérative des agriculteurs de la mayenne et la cooperative laitière Maine-Anjou v France*, App. No. 16931/04, ECHR 2006-XV; the facts are very much reminiscent of the earlier case of *Procola v Luxembourg*, App. No. 14570/89, DR 75.

the Court to conclude that the member states had no discretion.[15] The decision can be interpreted in two ways. On the one hand, it suggests that the nature of the measure at hand played a role in the ECtHR's conclusion that the member state had no discretion. On the other hand, when one considers the precise reasons given for this conclusion, it is clear that the ECtHR focused on the substantive content of the Regulation, which left the member states no choice in how to calculate the levy. The Court's tendency to use a substantive test was confirmed by the *M.S.S.* case[16] where the ECJ held that the Dublin Regulation[17] gave some discretion to the member states by allowing them to derogate from the general rule in asylum cases according to which the member state where an asylum seeker first entered the EU is responsible for processing his or her request for asylum. The ECtHR did not take into consideration what legal form the Dublin Regulation had but again looked at the substance. This was equally the case in *Povse v Austria* where the ECtHR concluded that art. 42 of the Brussels Regulation[18] left no discretion to a member state court as to the recognition and enforceability of a judgment by a court from another member state ordering the return of a child.[19] This shows that here, too, the ECtHR looked at the substance of the rule and not at the nature of the legal instrument. The case law subsequent to *Bosphorus* thus suggests that the ECtHR takes into account the substance of the EU law obligations rather than their form when determining whether a member state had discretion.

The second open question was whether the ECtHR would be willing to apply the *Bosphorus* presumption even in cases where the ECJ had not made a decision. Given that the main justification for the presumption was the high standard of fundamental rights protection in the Union and given that the finding that there was no manifest deficit in *Bosphorus* was largely based on the ECJ's decision in that same case, there would have been good reasons to assume that the ECtHR requires an ECJ decision. The ECtHR's case-law is not clear in this respect even though the latest decision in *Michaud* strongly suggests that the ECJ must have ruled on the question at some stage. *Michaud* contradicts the finding in the earlier *Coopérative des agriculteurs de Mayenne* which suggested that a previous ruling is not always necessary.[20] In that case the French *Conseil d'Etat* had not made a reference to the ECJ but decided the case based on EU law. Without addressing this specific point, the ECtHR nonetheless applied the *Bosphorus* presumption and held that there was no manifest deficiency in the protection of the applicants' Convention rights. By contrast, in *Michaud* the ECtHR suggested that it was crucial that 'the control mechanism provided for European Union law was fully brought into play'.[21] For *Bosphorus* to apply, the ECtHR

---

[15] cf. *Coopérative des agriculteurs de la mayenne* (n. 14), para. 5.
[16] *Confédération française du travail v European Communities* App. No. 8030/77, 10 July 1978.
[17] Case 29/69 *Stauder v Stadt Ulm* [1969] ECR 419.
[18] Council Regulation 343/2003/EC establishing the criteria and mechanisms for determining the member state responsible for examining an asylum application lodged in one of the member states by a third-country national OJ [2003] L 50/1.
[19] cf. *Povse v Austria*, App. No. 3890/11, para. 79.
[20] cf. *Coopérative des agriculteurs de la mayenne* (n. 14).
[21] cf. *Michaud v France* (n. 8), para. 114.

required that a preliminary reference had to be made unless the CJEU has had 'an opportunity to examine the question, either in a preliminary ruling delivered in the context of another case, or on the occasion of [another action]'.[22] This was confirmed in *Povse* where the Court observed that the Austrian Supreme Court had 'duly made use of the control mechanism provided for in EU law in that it asked the ECJ for a preliminary ruling'.[23] This strict stance on the applicability of the presumption underscores the argument made above as to the true rationale behind it. If the ECtHR were concerned with the presence of substantially equal protection only, the question of a reference would be irrelevant. After all, the EU's judicial system does not only consist of the CJEU. The courts of the member states are also Union courts so that the presumption should extend to the protection afforded by them where European Union law is at issue.[24] The Court clearly refused to do so and made it obvious that the presumption was introduced as an act of comity towards the ECJ.

The third question relates to the requirement of a manifest deficit for a rebuttal of the presumption. The *Bosphorus* case did not reveal much on how thoroughly the ECtHR would examine the substance of a claim of manifest deficiency. The following analysis of the Court's case-law will shed some light on this question. In *Bosphorus* itself the ECtHR's consideration was rather superficial. The Court took into consideration the nature of the interference, the general interest pursued, and the ruling of the ECJ. It is not clear what weight each of these points had and how thorough the ECtHR's examination would be. Given that the ECJ had only conducted a cursory proportionality test in its own *Bosphorus* ruling,[25] it came as a surprise that the ECtHR only dedicated two paragraphs to the question of manifest deficit and did not enter into a substantive discussion at all. It was thus suggested that the more impressive human rights analysis in the Advocate General's opinion might have saved the ECJ's decision from greater Strasbourg scrutiny.[26] The concurring judges' analyses equally maintain that the manifest deficit threshold was relatively low and stood in marked contrast to the scrutiny normally carried out by the Court (concurring opinion of Judges Rozakis et al). Judge Ress presented some examples, which in his eyes would constitute a manifest deficit. Most notably, he referred to a situation in which the ECJ did not follow well-established case law of the ECtHR (concurring opinion of Judge Ress).

The ECtHR has not had many opportunities to consider the existence of a 'manifest deficit'. The little case-law that exists suggests that it is generally willing to discuss the existence of a manifest deficiency in some detail. However, the ECtHR does not always draw a clear distinction between the applicability of the presumption and its rebuttal. For instance, in *Michaud* it addressed the question of whether a reference to the ECJ had been made in the context of whether the presumption applied whereas in *Povse*

---

[22] Ibid., para. 114.   [23] cf. *Povse v Austria* (n. 19), para. 81.

[24] cf. Opinion 1/09 *Creation of a unified patent litigation system* ECR [2011] I-1137; T. Lock, 'Taking National Court More Seriously? Comment on Opinion 1/09' (2011) 36 *European Law Review* 573.

[25] *Bosphorus v Minister for Transport* (n. 5), paras 25–6.

[26] cf. S. Peers, '*Bosphorus*—European Court of Human Rights' (2006) 2 *European Constitutional Law Review* 443, 454.

the ECtHR interpreted the reasoning concerning the ECJ in *Michaud* as a rebuttal of the presumption.[27]

The following brief discussion will show that the Court usually enters into a short scrutiny of the merits of the case in order to verify that the protection was not manifestly deficit. Only in *Biret* no such scrutiny was carried out. There is no apparent reason for this.[28] The ECtHR's approach was well demonstrated in *Kokkelvisserij* where the ECtHR engaged with the substantive question of whether the applicant should have a right to respond to the submissions of the Advocate General.[29] As the Court stated in *Bosphorus*, it requires a dysfunction of the mechanisms of control of the observance of Convention rights in order for a manifest deficit to exist. This is a high hurdle, as was shown in *Povse* where the fact that the ECJ had not reviewed the compatibility of the measure at issue with fundamental rights was not seen as sufficient proof for a manifest deficit. The ECtHR considered that the applicants had been in a position to challenge the compatibility with the Convention of the judgment of the Italian court. If that challenge failed, they would be in a position to bring Italy before the ECtHR rather than Austria, the courts of which merely executed the Italian court's judgment.[30]

---

[27] cf. *Michaud v France* (n. 8), para. 115 and *Povse v Austria* (n. 19), para. 83.

[28] cf. *Etahlissements Biret et CIE S.A. and Société Biret International v 15 EU Member States* App. No. 13762/04, 9 December 2008, para. 2: the Court merely unconvincingly stated that its reasoning in *Coopérative des agriculteurs de la mayenne* (n. 14) was applicable mutatis mutandis.

[29] cf. *Kokkelvisserij v Netherlands*, App. No. 13645/05, 20 January 2009.

[30] cf. *Povse v Austria* (n. 19), para. 86.

6.6 *Agim Behrami and Bekir Behrami v France*, App. No. 71412/01 and *Ruzhdi Saramati v France, Germany, and Norway*, App. No. 78166/01, European Court of Human Rights, 2 May 2007

*Santiago Villalpando**

Relevance of the case

When the European Court of Human Rights (ECtHR) rendered its *Behrami and Saramati* decision, in 2007, the responsibility of international organizations was only emerging as a topic of interest for the mainstream of international legal scholarship. Judicial precedents being scarce and the relevant practice difficult to identify, few authors ventured into the topic, which was generally perceived as somewhat abstract and out of focus. The International Law Commission (ILC) itself—which had taken up the topic for codification back in 2002—encountered obstacles in identifying relevant primary sources and relied heavily on a transposition, *mutatis mutandis*, of the rules codified in its draft articles on state responsibility.

The *Behrami and Saramati* decision constitutes a watershed precedent, insofar as it highlighted the concrete legal and logistical problems that could arise from responsibility claims, both for international organizations and their member states. Its findings served to bring the issues in this area into clearer focus, triggering a lively debate that quickly spread to other judicial fora and brought the topic to the central stage of international law.

As a precedent, however, the decision is not exempt from ambiguities. While being vested with the highest possible authority in the European judicial system of human rights protection (as it was rendered by the Grand Chamber of the ECtHR), the decision was only adopted by majority and its reasoning often reads as a patchwork of legal arguments sewn together, probably with a view to gathering the agreement of different factions in the deliberations. While ground-breaking in its statements regarding the respective roles of international organizations and their member states in peacekeeping and peace enforcement operations, the decision ultimately dismissed the claims before it on procedural grounds and did not make any determination as to the responsibility of the stakeholders involved (the respondent states, the North Atlantic Treaty Organization (NATO), or the UN). While it quickly became a *locus classicus* of international jurisprudence, being repeatedly cited by domestic and international tribunals, its reasoning contains controversial findings and has been subject to severe criticism in the legal literature.

I. Facts of the case

The decision rendered, on 2 May 2007, by the Grand Chamber of the ECtHR concerned two applications regarding events that had taken place in Kosovo subsequent to

* The views expressed herein are those of the author and do not necessarily reflect the views of the United Nations.

Resolution 1244 of 10 June 1999. By this resolution, the Security Council of the United Nations had decided the deployment in Kosovo of an international civil administration (the United Nations Interim Administration Mission in Kosovo, UNMIK) and an international security presence (the Kosovo Force, KFOR), which were active at the time of the events. The *Behrami* application, filed against France, concerned the tragic death of a young boy and serious injury inflicted to his brother from the detonation of a cluster bomb dropped by NATO forces in 1999: the applicants argued that the failure of French KFOR troops to mark or defuse such bombs, which they knew to be present on the site, constituted a breach of art. 2 of the ECHR. In the *Saramati* application, filed against Norway and France, the applicant claimed that his arrest and extrajudicial detention by UNMIK police under Norwegian and French command violated arts. 5, 13, and 6, para. 1, of the Convention.

II. The legal question

The decision was limited to the question of the admissibility of the applications. The main issue to be examined by the Court was whether there was a sufficient jurisdictional link, within the meaning of art. 1 of the Convention, between the applicants and the respondent states (para. 66). Noting that, on the relevant dates, Kosovo was under the effective control of international presences, which exercised the public powers on the territory, the Court considered that this implied determining the contribution of the respondent states to those international presences (para. 71), which would allow it to establish the compatibility *ratione personae* of the applications with the provisions of the Convention (para. 72).

III. Excerpts

As the first step of its assessment (paras 123–6), the Court determined that the issuance of detention orders fell within the security mandate of KFOR and the supervision of de-mining fell within UNMIK's mandate.

The Court then turned to the question whether the impugned action of KFOR (the detention of Mr Saramati) and inaction of UNMIK (the failure to de-mine in the *Behrami* case) could be attributed to the UN, a matter that led it to examine first the legal foundation of these international forces under Chapter VII of the UN Charter (paras 128–31). According to the Court, the Security Council, by its Resolution 1244, had 'delegated' to willing organizations and member states the power to establish KFOR, which therefore operated 'on the basis of UN delegated, and not direct, command'. The Court further considered that the Security Council had also 'delegated' civil administration powers in Kosovo, in this case to UNMIK, a subsidiary organ established by the Secretary-General.

With regard to the detention of Mr Saramati (paras 132–42), the Court interpreted Resolution 1244 as giving rise to a chain of command by which the Security Council 'was to retain ultimate authority and control over the security mission and it delegated to NATO […] the power to establish, as well as the operational command of, the international presence, KFOR' (para. 135; see also paras 138 and 140). The Court thus concluded that 'KFOR was exercising lawfully delegated Chapter VII powers of the [Security Council] so that the impugned action was, in principle, "attributable" to the UN' (para. 141).

As to the alleged failure to de-mine in the *Behrami* case (paras 142–3), the Court found that, given that UNMIK was a subsidiary organ of the UN created under Chapter VII of the Charter, 'the impugned inaction was, in principle, "attributable" to the UN' (para. 143).

Having decided (at least in principle) the issue of attribution, the Court turned to the question of its competence *ratione personae* (paras 144–52). Noting that the UN had a legal personality separate from that of its member states and that the organization was not a contracting party to the Convention (para. 144), the Court also found that it could not interpret the Convention in a manner that would interfere with the fulfilment of the mandate of the organization, including the effective control of its operations (para. 149). Given that it had considered that the impugned acts and omissions of KFOR and UNMIK could not be attributed to the respondent states and, moreover, had not taken place on their territory or by virtue of a decision of their authorities, the Court therefore concluded that the applicants' complaints were incompatible *ratione personae* with the provisions of the Convention (para. 152), which ultimately led it to declare both applications inadmissible.

IV. Commentary

The legal regime of the responsibility of international organizations constitutes the backbone of the decision of the Court in the *Behrami and Saramati* cases. From the outset, the Court framed its reasoning in terms of international responsibility with reference to the work of the ILC, and its final conclusions relied on two essential findings in this area, namely: that the impugned actions and omissions were, in principle, attributable to the United Nations; and that this attribution implied that the respondent states could not be held accountable for such actions and omissions under the Convention.

The Court's reliance on the work of the ILC is remarkable. In the section devoted to the relevant law and practice, the *Behrami and Saramati* decision described the ILC draft articles on international responsibility and their commentaries immediately after the rules on the use of force and the UN Charter, and before, for example, the Vienna Convention on the Law of Treaties or Security Council Resolution 1244. While the order is not decisive in itself, it is noteworthy that the Court seems to have accepted without hesitation that the rules codified by the ILC constituted a faithful reflection of the applicable customary rules, since it referred to them without discussion and without invoking any other relevant precedent in the area. This conviction was already widely shared by international jurisprudence (including the International Court of Justice) with respect to the ILC articles on state responsibility, which were adopted in 2001, but not as regards the draft articles on the responsibility of international organizations, which, at the time, the ILC was still considering on first reading. Furthermore, the reference to the work of the ILC provided an important legal foundation for the judicial determination of the cases. In the first steps of its assessment, the Court clarified that it used the term 'attribution' in the same way as the ILC in the draft articles, and it is the finding with regard to this issue that ultimately led to the conclusion that the applications were inadmissible.

The finding that the impugned actions and omissions were attributable to the UN played, indeed, a central role in the reasoning of the Court and constitutes one of the most significant legacies of the *Behrami and Saramati* decision. On closer analysis, however, this finding raises several issues.

First of all, the Court analyzed, under the same concept of 'delegation', the legal situation of both KFOR and UNMIK. In the decision, 'delegation' is defined as 'the empowering by the [Security Council] of another entity to exercise its function as opposed to "authorising" an entity to carry out functions which it could not itself perform' (para. 43). The Court considered that, in its Resolution 1244, the Security Council had made two 'delegations' so defined: a delegation to willing organizations and member states of the power to establish an international security presence in Kosovo, which resulted in the creation of KFOR; and a delegation of civil-administration powers on the territory to a subsidiary organ established by the Secretary-General, UNMIK. These are, however, two very different factual situations: the latter takes place exclusively within the institutional framework of the organization, while the former implies a recourse to different international legal persons, particularly NATO and the respondent states, which could be held separately accountable for their actions.

This is important from the perspective of the law of international responsibility. In the decision, the concept of 'delegation' is instrumental to the conclusions of the Court and establishes the link with the issue of attribution. The Court indeed postulates the principle that 'delegation must be sufficiently limited so as to remain compatible with the degree of centralisation of [Security Council] collective security constitutionally necessary under the Charter and, more specifically, for the acts of the delegate entity to be attributable to the UN' (para. 132). In other words, for the Court, a delegation necessarily requires that all delegated actions and omissions remain attributable to the organization under the law of international responsibility.[1]

The situations of KFOR and UNMIK are very different from the perspective of the rules on attribution. In its description of the applicable law, the decision referred to two provisions of the ILC's ARIO, as provisionally adopted on first reading: draft art. 3 (General principles) and draft art. 5 (Conduct of organs or agents placed at the disposal of an international organization by a State or another international organization).[2] These provisions are directly relevant to the attribution to the

---

[1] If one considers that the quoted passage follows the finding that the establishment of KFOR was based on a delegation by the Security Council, the statement, which introduces the section in which the Court examines the question of attribution of KFOR actions, seems to announce a foregone conclusion, since it affirms that for the delegation to remain compatible with the Charter the acts of the delegated entity need to be attributable to the United Nations.

[2] In the final version of the draft articles, as adopted by the ILC on second reading in 2011 and submitted to the General Assembly, draft art. 3 was split in two (para. 1 became draft art. 3, para. 2 became draft art. 4) and draft art. 5 became draft art. 7, with an identical text. For convenience, reference is made in the text to the draft article numbers as provisionally adopted on first reading, which are the ones used by the Court in the decision.

UN of conduct by KFOR, which is an international military presence established from organs placed at the disposal of the organization by NATO and its member states. However, the most pertinent provision to analyze UNMIK's conduct, namely draft art. 4,[3] was not quoted in the decision. According to this provision, the conduct of an organ or agent of an international organization in the performance of its functions shall be considered an act of that organization under international law, whatever position the organ or agent holds in respect of the organization (including, for example, its characterization as a subsidiary organ).

The most controversial aspect of the *Behrami and Saramati* decision lies in its application of the test of attribution to the conduct of KFOR. According to the codification by the ILC,[4] the conduct of an organ of a state or an organ or agent of an international organization that is placed at the disposal of another international organization shall be considered under international law an act of the latter organization 'if the organization exercises effective control over that conduct'. In other words, under the test identified by the ILC, an action by KFOR should have been attributed to the UN if the latter had exercised effective control over that action. In its decision, the Court describes the chain of command that resulted from Resolution 1244 in the following terms: 'The [Security Council] was to retain ultimate authority and control over the security mission and it delegated to NATO (in consultation with non-NATO member states) the power to establish, as well as the operational command of, the international presence, KFOR' (para. 135). In other words, as explicitly recognized by the Court, the Security Council did not have 'direct operational command' over KFOR (para. 136).

It follows that the application of the ILC test of attribution should have led to the conclusion that the detention of Mr Saramati was *not* attributable to the UN, since the latter did not exercise effective control over that action. This conduct should have been attributed, on the contrary, either to NATO or to the troop-contributing nations (particularly the respondent states in this case), depending on the answer given to the question of which of these entities had exercised effective control over the detention. The Court devoted some analysis to this question, concluding that 'effective command of the relevant operational matters was retained by NATO' (paras 135–40), but this did not alter its ultimate finding that the impugned action was, 'in principle, "attributable" to the UN' (para. 141).

It is unclear how the decision of the Court should be interpreted on this point. Taking into account that the Court makes explicit reference to the ILC provision, without voicing any criticism to the criterion codified therein, one is tempted to conclude that the decision makes a mistake in its application of the test requiring effective control over the relevant conduct. Alternatively, it could be argued that the Court is applying a different test of attribution (one of 'ultimate authority and control'), but in

---

[3] Draft art. 4, as provisionally adopted on first reading, became draft art. 5 in the final version of the draft articles on the responsibility of international organizations.

[4] As it results from draft art. 5, as provisionally adopted on first reading, and draft art. 7, in the final version of the draft articles.

this case there is no evidence of any legal analysis by the Court supporting the adoption of such a test.

Besides the matter of attribution, the *Behrami and Saramati* decision contains another finding regarding international responsibility, namely that the fact that the impugned conduct was, in principle, attributable to the UN implied that the respondent states could not be held accountable for such conduct and thus settled the matter.

The Court did devote some elaboration to the argument, based on its *Bosphorus* precedent, that a state party to the Convention, which had transferred sovereign power to an international organization in order to pursue co-operation in certain fields of activity, could remain responsible under art. 1 of the Convention for all acts and omissions of its organs (paras 145–51). However, the Court considered that this implied that it needed to determine whether it was competent *ratione personae* 'to review the acts of the respondent States carried out on behalf of the UN' (para. 146), and it disposed of the argument on account of the imperative of not interfering with the fulfilment of the UN key mission in the field of international peace and security (para. 149). The Court also rejected the applicants' argument that the substantive and procedural protection of fundamental rights provided by KFOR was not 'equivalent' to that under the Convention, noting that, in the present instance (contrary to the *Bosphorus* case), the impugned acts and omissions 'cannot be attributed to the respondent States' (para. 150–1).[5]

What the Court did not take into account is the possibility that more than one entity could be held responsible for the same internationally wrongful act.

First of all, the Court did not explore the eventuality that the impugned actions or omissions could simultaneously be attributed to more than one entity, that is, in this case, not only to the UN, but also to the respondent states or NATO. As noted by the ILC in its commentary to the ARIO, dual or even multiple attribution of conduct, although it may not frequently occur in practice, cannot be excluded.[6] The specific question whether dual attribution would be possible where the organ of the state (or of an international organization) is placed at the disposal of an international organization remains open to debate.[7]

Second, and in any event, the Court did not inquire whether the respondent states could be held accountable for the impugned actions or omissions, even if these were

---

[5] These findings, in themselves, may be subject to discussion in light of subsequent judicial decisions, particularly by the European Court of Justice in the *Kadi (I)* case, which considered that the protection of fundamental human rights was to be preserved even when the implementation of the mandate of the United Nations in the field of international peace and security is involved.

[6] Commentary to Chapter II, para. 4, in Report of the International Law Commission on the work of its 63rd session (2011), p. 16.

[7] In its commentary to draft art. 7, as adopted on second reading, the ILC seems sometimes to assume that, in such cases, the conduct of the organ placed at the disposal of the organization could be attributed to only one entity, either the state (or organization) or the recipient organization (see commentary to draft art. 7, paras 1 (*in fine*) or 4, in ibid., p. 20). All would depend on which entity, the state (or organization) of origin or the recipient international organization, had the effective control of the conduct. However, the ILC also distinguishes this hypothesis from that of an organ that is 'fully seconded' to the organization, thus recognizing that when an organ is placed at the disposal of an organization, the state (or organization) of origin retains some degree of control.

only attributable to the UN. In its work, the ILC has indeed envisaged several situations in which a state could engage its responsibility in connection with the conduct of an international organization, namely: the aid or assistance of the state in the commission of an internationally wrongful act of the organization; the direction or control exercised by the state over the commission of an internationally wrongful act of the organization; the coercion of an organization by a state; and the circumvention of international obligations of the state member of an international organization.[8] The latter hypothesis is of particular interest, insofar as it is largely based on the case law of the ECtHR itself, including the *Bosphorus* precedent referred to above.[9] In this case, according to the ILC, the state could be held responsible if three conditions are met: (i) that the organization has competence in relation to the subject matter of an international obligation of the state; (ii) that there be a significant link between the conduct of the circumventing member state and that of the international organization; and (iii) that the organization commits an act that, if committed by the state, would have constituted a breach of the obligation.[10] Furthermore, a state member of an international organization could also be held responsible for an act of the organization if it has accepted responsibility for that act towards the injured party or it has led the injured party to rely on its responsibility.[11] Without prejudice to the question whether one or more of these circumstances were present in the *Behrami* and *Saramati* cases, one could have expected the Court to at least consider this eventuality, particularly taking into account that it rejected the applications on the sole ground of inadmissibility.

The *Behrami and Saramati* decision had a kindling effect on the debate regarding the responsibility of international organizations and their member states, drawing attention to the concrete logistical and legal problems that may arise in the area. It has also left a contrasting legacy.

On the one hand, the *Behrami and Saramati* decision has had a loyal following in international and domestic case-law. As could be expected from a decision of the Grand Chamber, the precedent was confirmed in subsequent rulings of the European Court itself. In *Kasumaj v Greece*[12] and *Gajic v Germany*,[13] on matters relating to property occupied or used by contingents of KFOR, the Court found the applications inadmissible on the grounds, once again, that KFOR actions were, in principle, attributable to the United Nations. In *Berić v Bosnia and Herzegovina*[14], the Court considered that the impugned action by the High Representative in Bosnia and Herzegovina was

---

[8] In the final version of the draft articles, see Part Five (Responsibility of a State in connection with the conduct of an international organization), draft arts. 58–61.

[9] The ILC refers, in particular, to the following case law of the European Court: *Waite and Kennedy v Germany*, Judgment of 18 February 1999, *ECHR Reports*, 1999-I, para. 67; *Bosphorus Hava Yollary Turizm ve Ticaret Anonim Sirketi v Ireland*, Judgment of 30 June 2005, *ECHR Reports*, 2005-VI, para. 154; and *Gasparini v Italy and Belgium*, App. No. 10750/03, Decision of 12 May 2009.

[10] See commentary to art. 61, paras 6–8, in the Report of the International Law Commission on the work of its 63rd session (2011), p. 95.

[11] Draft art. 62 of the final version of the draft articles.

[12] App. No. 6974/05, Judgment of 5 July 2007.

[13] App. No. 31446/02, Judgment of 28 August 2007.

[14] App. No. 36357/04, Judgment of 16 October 2007.

also, in principle, attributable to the UN, thus extending the *Behrami and Saramati* reasoning to the case of acceptance by the respondent state of an international civil administration in its territory. The decision has also influenced other jurisdictions. In the decision of 12 December 2007, *R (on the application of Al-Jedda) (FC) v Secretary of State for Defence* Judgment (Grand Chamber),[15] which concerned actions by the Multi-National Force in Iraq, the House of Lords of the United Kingdom made reference, with approval, to the test of attribution identified in the *Behrami and Saramati* decision, while distinguishing the instant case from such precedents. Later, in the *Al-Jedda v United Kingdom* judgment[16] on the same matter, the European Court also referred to this precedent to reach the conclusion that the acts and omissions of foreign troops within the Multi-National Force were not attributable to the UN, because the Security Council had 'neither effective control nor ultimate authority and control' over such acts and omissions.

On the other hand, the *Behrami and Saramati* decision has been widely criticized in the legal literature, which highlighted the ambiguities of its reasoning, its practical and legal implications, and its departure from the rules codified by the ILC.[17] In its subsequent work on the responsibility of international organizations, the ILC took note of the fact that the European Court had relied on its draft articles, as preliminarily adopted on first reading, without formulating any criticism, but further noted that it had in fact not used the proposed test in the way that had been envisaged. It observed, in this regard, that 'when applying the criterion of effective control, "operational" control would seem more significant than "ultimate" control, since the latter hardly implies a role in the act in question'.[18] On second reading, the ILC decided to maintain its draft article unchanged, reaffirming the rule according to which the conduct of an organ placed at the disposal of an international organization shall be attributable to the latter only if it had effective control over such conduct.

As pointed out by the ILC, other authorities also distanced themselves from the criterion applied by the Court in the *Behrami and Saramati* decision. In his report of June 2008 on the United Nations Interim Administration Mission in Kosovo, the UN Secretary-General affirmed that 'the international responsibility of the United Nations will be limited in the extent of its effective operational control'.[19] Moreover, the District Court of The Hague, in its *Mothers of Srebrenica* decision, found the respondent state (The Netherlands) responsible for its involvement in the events at Srebrenica on the basis of the criterion of 'effective control', closer to the ILC test.[20]

In sum, with respect to the issues of responsibility addressed in the *Behrami and Saramati* decision, one is faced with the curious situation in which the jurisprudence

---

[15] App. No. 27021/08, Judgment of 7 July 2011.

[16] App. No. 27021/08, Judgment of 7 July 2011 (Grand Chamber).

[17] For a comprehensive list of scholarly articles on the decision, see: commentary to draft art. 7, para. 10, note 115, in the Report of the International Law Commission on the work of its 63rd session (2011), p. 23.

[18] Ibid., p. 23.   [19] UN Doc. S/2008/354, para. 16.

[20] District Court (The Hague), Judgment of 10 September 2008, Case No. 265615/HA ZA 06-1671 (English translation available at http://www.asser.nl/upload/documents/20120905T111510-Supreme%20Court%20Decision%20English%2013%20April%202012.pdf).

of international judicial bodies and the United Nations organs involved in the codification of international law and a majority of the legal literature have held different views as to the state of customary international law. The situation of uncertainty that ensues regarding the rules applicable to attribution and joint responsibility is a matter of concern, particularly as it may have a very practical impact on the UN and the accountability of the organization and member states in cases of peacekeeping and peace-enforcement operations conducted by a coalition of the willing. This matter may, of course, resolve itself with the consolidation of a clear practice and *opinio juris*, but may also (and preferably) be addressed by the General Assembly if it were to decide to follow up on the draft articles submitted by the ILC.[21]

---

[21] While the ILC submitted its draft articles on the responsibility of international organizations to the General Assembly in 2011, the Assembly only took note of the draft articles, deciding to postpone to its sixty-ninth session the decision as to the form to be given to them (see Resolution 66/100 of 9 December 2011). In 2014, the General Assembly again took note of the articles and, while requesting the Secretary-General to prepare an initial compilation of decisions of international courts, tribunals, and other bodies referring to them and inviting Governments and international organizations to submit information on their practice in this regard and comments on any future action regarding the articles, postponed once again its consideration of the matter to its seventy-second session (see Resolution 69/126 of 10 December 2014). The matter will thus be revisited in 2017. Given the hesitation shown by the Assembly, since 2001, on the fate of the articles of state responsibility, it is unlikely that a decision will be made at that time.

6.7 *Gasparini v Italy and Belgium*, App. No. 10750/03, Admissibility Decision, European Court of Human Rights, 12 May 2009

Tobias Lock

Relevance of the case

Gasparini is relevant in that it extended the *Bosphorus* presumption to the North Atlantic Treaty Organization (NATO).[1] It also refined the requirement that the violation must have occurred within the jurisdiction of the member state by introducing the notion of a 'structural lacuna'.

I. Facts

The applicant was an employee of the NATO. He had brought proceedings before the NATO Appeal Board (NAB) concerning an increase in his pension contributions, which he contested. These proceedings remained unsuccessful. Before the European Court of Human Rights (ECtHR) the applicant did not challenge the substantive outcome of the proceedings but complained that the procedure before the NAB was incompatible with art. 6(1) European Convention on Human Rights (ECHR), which guarantees a fair trial. He claimed in particular that the proceedings had not been held in public even though art. 6(1) ECHR expressly stipulates that everyone is entitled to a public hearing. He also claimed that the members of the NAB were not impartial as they had been chosen by the North Atlantic Council, the decision making body of NATO.

II. The legal question

The main legal questions in this case were whether the alleged violation of the ECHR stemming from the NAB's rules of procedure were attributable to the respondent states given that none of their institutions had been involved in the case at hand and, if so, whether the presumption formulated in *Bosphorus* was applicable to NATO.

III. Excerpts

The Court recalled its decisions in *Bosphorus v Ireland*[2] and *Behrami and Behrami v France* and *Saramati v France, Germany, and Norway*[3] before embarking on a discussion whether the *Bosphorus* presumption could be applied.[4] It held:

---

[1] The author would like to thank Ariadne Panagopoulou for invaluable research assistance.
[2] App. No. 45036/98, ECHR 2005-VI.   [3] [GC] App. Nos. 71412/01; 78166/01 (2 May 2007).
[4] cf. discussions in ch. 6 on the *Bosphorus* and *Behrami* cases.

La Cour constate qu'en l'espèce, contrairement à la situation dans les affaires Boivin et Connolly précitées, le requérant allègue expressément que le mécanisme de règlement des conflits du travail interne à l'OTAN n'accorde pas aux droits fondamentaux une protection « équivalente » à celle assurée par la Convention. En effet, l'intéressé conteste des caractéristiques intrinsèques à ce système, à savoir l'absence de publicité des débats devant la Commission de recours de l'OTAN, prévue par l'article 4.71 de l'annexe IX au règlement applicable, ainsi que la procédure de nomination des membres de cette Commission telle que décrite par l'article 4.11 du même instrument (voir la partie « Droit international pertinent » ci-dessus). Dès lors, contrairement aux affaires Boivin et Connolly, où il n'y avait pas lieu de se livrer à un tel examen puisque les requérants mettaient en cause, non pas une lacune structurelle du mécanisme interne concerné, mais une décision particulière prise par l'organe compétent de l'organisation internationale en cause, la Cour considère qu'il lui faut rechercher si le mécanisme de règlement des conflits contesté dans la présente affaire, à savoir la voie de recours devant la CROTAN, est entaché d'une « insuffisance manifeste », ce qui renverserait en l'espèce la présomption de respect par les Etats défendeurs de leurs obligations au titre de la Convention.

La Cour estime qu'elle doit examiner la question en tenant compte des principes développés dans sa jurisprudence concernant les juridictions nationales des Etats défendeurs. A cet égard, elle observe cependant que son contrôle en vue de déterminer si la procédure devant la CROTAN, organe d'une organisation internationale ayant une personnalité juridique propre et non partie à la Convention, est entachée d'une insuffisance manifeste est nécessairement moins ample que le contrôle qu'elle exerce au regard de l'article 6 sur les procédures devant les juridictions internes des Etats membres de la Convention, lesquels se sont obligés à en respecter les dispositions. Pour la Cour, il lui faut en réalité déterminer si, au moment où ils ont adhéré à l'OTAN et lui ont transféré certains pouvoirs souverains, les Etats défendeurs ont pu, de bonne foi, estimer que le mécanisme de règlement des conflits du travail interne à l'OTAN n'était pas en contradiction flagrante avec les dispositions de la Convention.

Quant au grief relatif à la publicité des débats, la Cour a rappelé à de nombreuses reprises dans sa jurisprudence relative aux procédures devant les juridictions nationales des pays membres que la tenue d'une audience publique constitue un principe fondamental consacré par l'article 6 § 1. Cela étant, cette disposition n'exige pas nécessairement la tenue d'une audience dans toutes les procédures. [...]

Quant à la présente affaire, la Cour constate que l'article 4.71 de l'annexe IX au règlement du personnel civil de l'OTAN prévoit expressément que « les séances de la Commission de recours ne sont pas publiques ». Cette disposition est cependant fortement nuancée par l'article suivant, qui dispose que les parties au litige peuvent « assister aux débats et développer oralement tous arguments à l'appui des moyens invoqués dans leurs mémoires [ainsi que] se faire assister ou représenter à cet effet soit par un membre du personnel civil ou militaire de l'OTAN soit par un conseil choisi par eux ». De manière générale, la Cour observe que la CROTAN a à connaître du contentieux du travail entre les instances dirigeantes de l'OTAN et le personnel civil employé par cette organisation. Il s'agit donc de litiges en matière civile qui, en général, portent sur des questions d'ordre technique et exigent une décision rapide, ainsi que l'illustre du reste l'affaire du requérant dans laquelle celui-ci contestait l'augmentation du taux de sa contribution au régime de pensions des agents de l'OTAN. Enfin, la Cour relève que, dans sa décision du 4 septembre 2002 déboutant le requérant, la CROTAN a justifié l'absence de caractère public des débats par la nécessité d'« en préserver la sérénité dans le contexte spécifique d'une organisation telle que l'OTAN (…) ».

Au vu de l'ensemble de ces éléments, la Cour estime que les deux Etats défendeurs, au moment où ils ont approuvé le règlement sur le personnel civil, ont pu considérer à bon droit que le type d'affaires dont la CROTAN a à connaître pouvaient être examinées et tranchées par elle de manière adéquate dans le cadre de la procédure prévue par le règlement applicable, et, qu'eu égard à l'ensemble des dispositions de ce règlement, notamment à l'article 4.72 précité, les exigences d'équité étaient satisfaites sans la tenue d'une audience publique. Sans examiner plus avant le cas d'espèce, elle relève qu'il ressort de la décision de la CROTAN et des autres éléments du dossier que l'absence de publicité n'a en rien nui à l'équité de l'ensemble de la procédure.

Quant au grief du requérant tenant à la partialité alléguée des membres de la Commission, la Cour remarque d'emblée, à la lecture de l'article 4.11 du règlement pertinent que les trois membres de la CROTAN, qui sont désignés pour trois ans par le Conseil de l'Atlantique Nord, doivent être des personnes entièrement extérieures à l'OTAN et dont la compétence est « établie ». Elle observe par ailleurs que, contrairement à ce qu'affirme le requérant, il ressort clairement de l'article 4.21 que les recours soumis à la CROTAN doivent être dirigés contre des décisions des chefs des organismes de l'OTAN, qu'ils appliquent ou non des décisions du Conseil de l'Atlantique Nord (voir la partie « Droit international pertinent » ci-dessus). Dans la décision dont le requérant fait grief en l'espèce, la CROTAN rappelle d'ailleurs expressément qu'elle « ne peut connaître directement d'une décision du Conseil de l'Atlantique Nord ». La Cour observe par ailleurs que tout requérant peut, conformément à l'article 4.16 de l'annexe IX au règlement sur le personnel civil, invoquer une présomption de partialité et demander que la composition de la Commission de recours soit modifiée. Elle constate à titre incident que le requérant ne s'est prévalu, à aucun moment, de cette possibilité au cours de la procédure devant la Commission. Quoi qu'il en soit, elle considère ici aussi que, eu égard à l'ensemble des dispositions réglementaires pertinentes, les deux Etats défendeurs ont pu juger au moment de l'adoption du règlement applicable que celui-ci instituait un tribunal conforme aux exigences posées par l'article 6.

Compte tenu de ce qui précède, la Cour estime que les deux Etats mis en cause ont pu à bon droit considérer, au moment où ils ont approuvé le règlement sur le personnel civil et ses annexes par l'intermédiaire de leurs représentants permanents siégeant au Conseil de l'Atlantique Nord, que les dispositions régissant la procédure devant la CROTAN satisfaisaient aux exigences du procès équitable. Aucun élément susceptible de contredire ce constat n'a été porté à la connaissance de la Cour. Elle en conclut que la protection offerte au requérant en l'espèce par le mécanisme de règlement interne des conflits de l'OTAN n'était donc pas entachée d'une « insuffisance manifeste » au sens donné à ce terme dans l'arrêt Bosphorus, particulièrement dans le contexte spécifique d'une organisation telle que l'OTAN. Dès lors, elle considère que le requérant n'est pas fondé à faire grief à l'Italie et à la Belgique d'avoir souscrit à un système contraire à la Convention, et que la présomption de respect de celle-ci par ces deux Etats n'a pas été renversée.

IV. Commentary

A remarkable aspect of *Gasparini* is that it was the first judgment in which the Court was willing to hold Convention parties responsible for an act by an international organization with members that are not bound by the Convention. The USA and Canada are not bound by the Convention, but the alleged procedural deficit in the Staff Rules of NATO would be attributable to them as well. If the Court had found a violation of the Convention, it would thus have held these countries indirectly responsible for the violation of a human rights treaty to which they are not parties. This would have raised interesting issues concerning the extraterritoriality of the Convention.

However, the true significance of the *Gasparini* judgment lies elsewhere. Despite its brevity, it is a decision which is difficult to follow as it is neither well-drafted nor well-reasoned. It is significant for the manner in which it applies the *Bosphorus* presumption to an organization that is not the EU. Furthermore, it introduces important distinctions regarding the requirement of state involvement as a pre-condition for an alleged violation to have arisen within the jurisdiction of the respondent state.

A. Application of the *Bosphorus* case-law

It is recalled that in *Bosphorus* the ECtHR considered the responsibility of a member state of the EU for state action triggered by its obligations under EU law. The Court introduced a rebuttable presumption that a member state has complied with its obligations under the Convention provided that the organization itself ensures a protection of fundamental rights equivalent to what the Convention requires and if that member state had no discretion when carrying out its obligations. The presumption can only be rebutted if this protection was manifestly deficient.[5]

The Court's extension of the *Bosphorus* presumption to NATO came as a surprise. While it must be admitted that in *Bosphorus* the Court had deliberately not restricted the presumption to the EU by making repeated references to international organizations in general, it must be considered that it was adopted very much in recognition of the EU's supranational character and the high level of human rights protection afforded by the CJEU (cf. discussion on *Bosphorus*). This is also evident from subsequent decisions concerning the applicability of the presumption. In particular, in *Michaud* the Court seemed to consider it as almost indispensable that the ECJ had made a ruling in the same case and approved of the measure at hand.[6] There has hitherto been not much evidence of the fact that NATO offers an equivalent protection to what is required by the ECHR, yet the Court seemed to take this as a given. Interestingly, in a more recent decision the

---

[5] cf. *Bosphorus v Ireland* (n. 2), paras 155–7.
[6] cf. *Michaud v France* App. No. 12323/11, ECHR 2012; see also the discussion in ch. 6.5.

Court refused to extend the presumption to the UN Security Council's Sanctions Regime.[7]

Apart from the question whether it is appropriate to extend *Bosphorus* to NATO, the Court's decision was doctrinally unsound in that the Court did not fully apply the two stages of the *Bosphorus* test. Rather, the Court only considered the second stage of the test concerning the rebuttal of the presumption by asking whether in the present case the mechanism for conflict resolution was manifestly deficient. At no point in the judgment did the Court state that NATO generally offers a protection equivalent to that offered by the Convention. This is striking as the test of whether there was a manifestly deficient protection is designed to be a difficult one to meet. As the Court made it clear in *Bosphorus*, it requires a dysfunction of the mechanisms of control of the observance of Convention rights.[8] Such a high threshold is only justified where the organization normally offers an equivalent protection, so that the ECtHR can relax the intensity of its oversight. Only then can the ECtHR tolerate deficiencies in the human rights protection, which are not manifest. When establishing that the EU offered such an equivalent protection in *Bosphorus*, the ECtHR argued at length that this was the case (see discussion of *Bosphorus* case). No such argument was made in *Gasparini*.

Moreover, the Court seems to have ignored the more general principle of responsibility of members of an international organization formulated in *Matthews v United Kingdom*.[9] It is recalled that *Bosphorus* is only applicable to secondary EU legislation and only where the member state has no discretion. The main reason why the *Bosphorus* presumption does not apply to violations originating in the EU Treaties itself is that there is no judicial remedy against them under EU law. The ECJ only has jurisdiction to declare acts of secondary EU law to be incompatible with the EU's founding Treaties and the EU Charter of Fundamental Rights. Considering that there is no possibility to challenge the Staff Rules of NATO within NATO, the Court ought to have applied the *Matthews* doctrine whereby it has full jurisdiction to review whether the rule complained of is in violation of the Convention.

In addition, *Gasparini* seems to introduce a different rationale for the *Bosphorus* presumption. The Court stated that it would have to determine in reality if the defendant states, when joining NATO, were able to consider in good faith that the internal mechanism for the solution of labour conflicts was not in flagrant contradiction to the Convention. This suggests that it would no longer be necessary that the human rights protection provided by an international organization is actually equivalent to that under the Convention at the time of the alleged violation, but rather that the test would be whether at the moment of joining an organization, the Convention Parties concerned had acted in good faith. The crucial time for the Court's assessment thus seemed to be the moment of accession to NATO. However, this is in contradiction to *Bosphorus*, where the Court clearly assumed that the crucial time for the Court's assessment of whether the presumption applies is the time of the alleged violation and

---

[7] cf. *al-Dulimi and Montana Management Inc. v Switzerland* App. No. 5809/08 (26 November 2013).
[8] cf. *Bosphorus v Ireland* (n. 2), para 166.
[9] App. No. 24833/94, ECHR 1999-I (cf. discussion in ch. 6.3).

not the time of accession to the organization. Whether or not a member state had *bona fide* considered that the protection offered would not be in violation of the Convention should thus not determine the applicability of the presumption.

B. The requirement of state involvement

A further important aspect of the *Gasparini* decision concerns the requirement of state involvement in order to satisfy art. 1 ECHR, which contains a threshold requirement limiting the applicability of Convention rights to persons within the jurisdiction of one of the contracting states.[10] It is argued here that the Court's finding of state involvement in *Gasparini* has made this area of the case law even more complex. A brief overview of some cases preceding and some cases following *Gasparini* follows to demonstrate this point.

The Court distinguished *Gasparini* from two of its earlier decisions, *Boivin v 34 Member States of the Council of Europe*[11] and *Connolly v 15 Member States of the EU*.[12] Boivin was an employee of Eurocontrol, an international organization of which the thirty-four respondent states were members. He complained of his removal from the post of head accountant before the International Labour Organization Administrative Tribunal, which had jurisdiction to hear the case. Claiming violations of arts, 6, 13, and 14 ECHR he alleged a number of procedural violations, such as inequality of arms, lack of an effective examination of his claim, and insufficient reasoning in the judgment. His case remained unsuccessful. The ECtHR distinguished the case from *Bosphorus* because '[a]t no time did [the respondent states] intervene directly or indirectly in the dispute, and no act or omission of those States or their authorities can be considered to engage their responsibility under the Convention'. It held that the applicant's complaints were directed against the decision of the Administrative Tribunal and not against a measure by the respondent states so that the applicant could not be considered to have been 'within the jurisdiction' of these states for the purposes of art. 1 ECHR.[13] The Court thus established a requirement of state involvement in order to be able to hold a member state of an international organization responsible for the acts and omissions of that organization.

Connolly confirmed this approach in respect of member states of the EU and with regard to a court which is an institution of the organization. Connolly had been dismissed from his post as an official of the European Commission for having published a book that was highly critical of the European Monetary Union and its underlying political motivation. He unsuccessfully took his case to the EU's courts before complaining to the ECtHR.[14] He argued that in the proceedings before the Court of Justice he should have been allowed to respond to the submissions of the Advocate General.

---

[10] It is phrased: 'The High Contracting Parties shall secure to everyone within their jurisdiction the rights and freedoms defined in Section I of this Convention.'

[11] App. No. 73250/01, 9 September 2008.   [12] App. No. 73274/01, 9 December 2009.

[13] cf. *Boivin* (n. 11).

[14] cf. Case T-203/95 *Bernard Connolly v Commission of the European Communities* [1999] ECR II-443; Case C-273/99 P *Bernard Connolly v Commission of the European Communities* [2001] ECR I-1575.

The ECtHR ruled that the alleged violation could not be attributed to the member states since the applicant had not been in their jurisdiction as art. 1 ECHR requires. It is thus clear from *Connolly* that for a member state to be responsible for violations of the ECHR rooted in EU law, there has to be member state action (the approach in *Connolly* and *Boivin* was later confirmed in *Rambus Inc. v Germany*[15] and *Beygo v 46 Member States of the Council of Europe*).[16]

The requirement of state involvement is an important clarification of the basic tenets of *Matthews*, the leading case in this field (cf. chapter 6.3 on the *Matthews* case). In *Matthews* the ECtHR's Grand Chamber had held that parties to the ECHR were allowed to transfer competences to international organizations, but that their responsibility continued after such a transfer.[17] By considering some degree of state involvement as a requirement for this responsibility to arise, *Boivin* and *Connolly* created a gap in the protection of fundamental rights reminiscent of that in *Behrami and Saramati*.[18]

Interestingly, in *Gasparini* the Court distinguished *Boivin* and *Connolly* and found sufficient state involvement. It drew a line between actual decisions by the organization and deficiencies in the protection of fundamental rights, rooted in a structural lacuna of the internal mechanism for conflict resolution. Where a structural lacuna exists, the violation is attributable to the member state. This distinction is very subtle and fails to fully convince given that the differences between the cases are minimal. For instance, *Connolly* could have also been interpreted to involve a structural lacuna in the procedure of the Court of Justice given that the Statute of the Court of Justice is part of EU primary law. In this connection it is an obvious flaw of *Gasparini* that the Court did not further define what it meant by a structural lacuna.[19] It thus added considerable confusion to the case law in this area. It remained unclear what exact parameters would be used to determine the existence of state involvement.

Moreover, in drawing this distinction, the ECtHR failed to consider its earlier decision in *Biret*.[20] In that case the Court had held that the lack of access to a court or tribunal before which directives could be directly challenged was due to an alleged deficit in the Community judicial order and thus could not be attributed to the respondent states. This should have been considered a structural lacuna so that *Gasparini* can hardly be squared with *Biret*. Moreover, as pointed out above, even if one accepted the approach in *Gasparini*, the further question of differentiating it from *Matthews* arises.

Gasparini has been cited in a number of subsequent decisions concerning the requirement of state involvement for an alleged violation to have occurred within the jurisdiction of the respondent state according to art. 1 ECHR. *Chapman v Belgium* concerned another labour dispute between NATO and one of its former employees. In contrast to Gasparini, Chapman brought his labour case before a Belgian court. For

---

[15] App. No. 40382/04, 16 June 2009.   [16] App. No. 36099/06, 16 June 2009.
[17] cf. *Matthews v United Kingdom* para. 32.   [18] cf. ch. 6.6 on the *Behrami* case.
[19] cf. C. Ryngaert, 'The European Court of Human Rights' approach to the responsibility of Member States in connection with acts of international organizations' (2011) 60 *International & Comparative Law Quarterly* 997, 1005.
[20] See *Etahlissements Biret et CIE S.A. and Société Biret International v 15 EU Member States* App. No. 13762/0, 9 December 2008.

this reason, the Court was able to hold that 'the impugned decision was taken by an organ of the respondent State, namely the Brussels Employment Appeal Tribunal' so that there was sufficient state involvement to satisfy art. 1 ECHR.[21] In a similar vein, the Court had decided in *Kokkelvisserij* that a request for a preliminary reference from a court of an EU member state was sufficient state involvement allowing the applicant to invoke deficits in the procedure before the CJEU.[22] This suggested a rather low threshold for the requirement of state involvement. However, the Court did not consider the conclusion by The Netherlands of an agreement with the UN, that the headquarters of the International Criminal Tribunal for the former Yugoslavia be based in The Hague, sufficient involvement to bring decisions of that tribunal within the jurisdiction of The Netherlands.[23] A perhaps useful distinction from the former cases could be that there was no direct relationship between the fact that an international organization or court was based in a country and the decisions of that court, whereas both in *Chapman* and *Kokkelvisserij* the very case on which the complaint was based had been heard by a domestic court.

The preceding discussion has thus shown that the case-law on the responsibility of member states for violations of the Convention by international organizations is not yet fully settled. Moreover, the Court in *Gasparini* displayed some insecurity in the application of the *Bosphorus* presumption. It can only be hoped that the uncertainties and contradictions identified will be removed in the future.

---

[21] cf. *Chapman v Belgium* App. No. 39619/06, 5 March 2013, para. 44.
[22] cf. *Kokkelvisserij v Netherlands* App. No. 13645/05, 20 January 2009.
[23] cf. *Galić v Netherlands* App. No. 22617/07, 9 June 2009, para. 46.

6.8 *Mukeshimana-Nguilinzira and ors. v Belgium and ors.*, Brussels Court of First Instance, ILDC 1604 (BE 2010), 8 December 2010

*Cedric Ryngaert**

Relevance of the case

The present (interim) decision addresses the relationship between international organizations and their member states for the purposes of establishing responsibility for internationally wrongful acts, in particular in the context of UN peace operations to which UN member states contribute troops. The Dutch Supreme Court's decision in *Nuhanovic*, with respect to the genocide in Srebrenica (1995), is the most well-known domestic court decision in this context. In this case, the Dutch Supreme Court upheld the validity of the 'effective control' standard in apportioning responsibility between an international organization and its member states. This Belgian decision applies a similar standard in a case concerning Belgian UN peacekeepers withdrawing from a compound in Rwanda (1994), after which scores of Rwandans were massacred by extremist militia.

I. The facts of the case

On 5 October 1993, the UN Security Council established a peacekeeping operation in Rwanda, the *Mission des Nations Unies pour l'Assistance au Rwanda* (MINUAR). MINUAR, which commenced its deployment in late October 1993, operated under a Chapter VI mandate to keep peace and security in Rwanda's capital, Kigali. According to MINUAR's rules of engagement, it was to remain impartial in the Rwandan civil war and in particular to refrain from any favourable or hostile act vis-à-vis the Rwandan army or the troops of the exiled Tutsi (FPR). Its mandate and rules of engagement strictly limited its capacity to resort to force in cases of self-defence against persons or groups who threatened protected sites and populations. Only on 17 May 1994 did the UN Security Council, on the basis of Resolution 918 expand the mission's mandate to the protection of displaced persons, refugees, and civilians in danger.

The military division of MINUAR was composed of different sectors, of which the Kigali sector was commanded by the Belgian Colonel Marchal. Belgium contributed a batallion under the command of Lieutenant-Colonel Dewez. This batallion was spread over different encampments in Kigali. One encampment was based at the Official Technical School (*Ecole Technique Officielle*, ETO). It was placed under the order of captain Lemaire.

Between 7 and 11 April 1994, about 2,000 Tutsi and some moderate Hutu sought refuge in the ETO. Colonel Marchal initially attempted to refuse access to the

---

* [This Commentary is based on the author's commentary for the ILDC, mentioned above.].

encampment, but finally access was permitted. Accordingly, the ETO was *de facto* transformed into a refugee camp under the protection of Belgian MINUAR soldiers.

On 11 April 1994, French soldiers passed by the ETO to evacuate foreign citizens, after which the Belgian MINUAR soldiers started evacuating their encampment by firing into the air to prevent the Rwandan refugees from hindering their departure. No measures were taken to guarantee the security of the Rwandan refugees. Shortly after the departure of the Belgian soldiers, the Interahamwe militias entered the ETO and killed the refugees. Most were killed in the hours following the departure of the Belgian soldiers.

Eight survivors and relatives of those killed brought a civil lawsuit against Belgium and the commanders Marchal, Lemaire, and Dewez before the Brussels Court of First Instance on 7 April 2004. Another survivor brought a suit on 4 December 2007. They requested the court to hold the defendants tortuously liable and to order them to indemnify them for the damages suffered by their relatives during the massacre which followed the evacuation of the ETO by Belgian soldiers on 11 April 1994. The plaintiffs argued that control over the troops stationed at the ETO was withdrawn from MINUAR and was placed under the exclusive responsibility of the Belgian State.

The Belgian State and the military commanders contested the jurisdiction of the Belgian State, arguing that the complaint in reality targeted the UN and its members. They also observed that the Belgian contingent encamped at the ETO was still subject to the authority of MINUAR.

II. The legal question

This case concerns the attribution and apportioning of international responsibility with respect to a UN peacekeeping operation in which Belgian troops participated. In particular, the Court was called on to rule, firstly, whether the decision to evacuate Belgian UN peacekeepers from the Belgian/UN compound where Rwandan refugees had sought protection was attributable to Belgium or to the UN, and secondly, whether there was a causal link between the decision to evacuate the compound and the massacre of the Rwandan refugees.

III. Excerpts [translation ILDC]

As the victims did not invoke the responsibility of the UN or other UN member states, but only the responsibility of the Belgian State, Belgian courts had jurisdiction over acts committed by Belgian MINUAR peace-keepers. No analogy could be drawn to the case of Kosovo, where Belgium, as a NATO member, consented to and provided operational support to a military operation decided by NATO (para. 26).

The victims had *prima facie* established that the acts in question amounted to crimes under international law (para. 35).

Article 136 quater of the Penal Code, which rendered war crimes punishable in Belgian law, also applied to offences committed in a non-international armed conflict, which opposed the forces of the Rwandese army and organized armed groups against the Tutsi troops. Caught in this conflict, the refugees at the ETO were protected persons under the Geneva Conventions (para. 34).

In order for the statute of limitations of war crimes to be determined, it sufficed that the acts in question could qualify as war crimes, without having to verify whether the massacre at the ETO was punishable as a crime against humanity or genocide prior to the entry into force of the Act of 10 February 1999, as repealed in 2003 (Belgium) (which made war crimes punishable under Belgian law) or whether the principle of non-retroactivity of criminal law constituted an obstacle to this determination (para. 34).

At no time was the concrete decision to evacuate the ETO the subject of a dialogue between the Belgian commander and the UN commander. Instead, there was a permanent dialogue between Marchal and the chiefs of staff of the Belgian army, which did not hesitate to carry on regardless of consultations with the MINUAR. Therefore, the decision to evacuate the ETO was a decision taken by Belgium and not by the MINUAR (para. 38).

The complaints regarding the Belgian State's general attitude, such as the failure to take measures to stop the genocide, the decision to withdraw the blue helmets of the MINUAR, Belgium's restriction of its operations to the protection of its nationals, and a fortiori the policy conducted in this context by the UN, did not concern commanders Marchal, Dewez, and Lemaire. The latter did not have the capacity to influence the general course of events in Rwanda, the decision to withdraw the Belgian blue helmets from MINUAR, or the commitment of soldiers to operation Silver Back. For those commanders, the only relevant question was whether the evacuation of the ETO constituted failure to act in the face of war crimes taking place. The commanders should perhaps have considered the decision to evacuate illegal and should have resisted it, as they lacked means of protecting the refugees. This question had specific relevance for Mr Lemaire in respect of Mr Ngulinzira, the former having been entrusted with a mission to protect the latter, according to the plaintiffs (paras. 40–2).

The Belgian commanders could not have been ignorant of the war crimes committed on a large scale in Rwanda before the evacuation of the ETO, and of the fact that such crimes would be perpetrated against the ETO refugees once the protection by the Belgian soldiers came to an end. The commanders could have had no illusion as to the fate that awaited the refugees after the departure of the Belgian blue helmets. The commission of the crime proscribed in art. 136septies, 5° PC did not require additional knowledge of official orders given with a view to perpetrating the crimes (para. 46).

The fact that the commanders obeyed orders did not absolve them as such of their potential responsibility; nor did the fact that prior to the evacuation they searched in vain for alternative solutions for the protection of the refugees, because those orders could lead to the commission of war crimes (para. 47).

The mere passive presence of Belgian soldiers sufficed to guarantee the Rwandan refugees' security. Besides, the rules of engagement of their mandate authorized them to use force in self-defence in case their encampment had been attacked (para. 48).

It had not been proven that the harm suffered by the refugees at the ETO was necessary to prevent harm to other persons (para. 49).

It was undeniable that the refugees were not endangered as long as the Belgian blue helmets were at the ETO, and that they were massacred after the Belgian blue helmets' departure. The fact that a number of refugees were killed outside the ETO, on the hill of Nyanza, or that Rwandan soldiers or policemen participated in the killings of the militia, did not break the chain of causality. Different witness statements demonstrated that the majority of those who continued to enjoy the protection of the UN were saved. Accordingly, the immediate incidence of the evacuation of the ETO on the massacres of the refugees was sufficiently established, without the plaintiffs being required to adduce proof that their relatives would have survived the war, had there been no massacre on 11 April 1994. There was no proof that, without the evacuation of the ETO, they would have been killed anyway (para. 51).

Decisions on the blameworthiness of the commanders and the evaluation of the damages to be awarded were reserved for a later date. The screening of a film Shooting Dogs, to which the parties could react, would in all likelihood allow for the drawing of a clearer picture of the situation prevailing in Rwanda at the time (paras. 48, 52).

IV. Commentary

While this decision was only an interim decision ('jugement avant dire droit'), it nevertheless raised a number of interesting legal issues. Some related to the admissibility of the complaints (e.g., jurisdiction, statute of limitations, and attribution); others related to the merits (notably the question of whether there was a causal link between the decision to evacuate the ETO and the ensuing massacre of the refugees). For our purposes of international institutional law, the main legal question was to whom the decision to evacuate the ETO should be attributed: to Belgium or rather to the UN (or to both)? The Court held that this decision was taken by Belgium, and not by the UN, as the Belgian UN peacekeepers were de facto under Belgian command and control. Thus, the acts of the peacekeepers were attributable to Belgium, and could engage Belgium's responsibility. While the court did not cite the ILC's Draft Articles on the Responsibility of International Organizations for Internationally Wrongful Acts[1] (ARIO 2009), its decision seemed to be inspired *a contrario* by what is now art. 7 in ARIO 2011.[2] This provision stipulates that '[t]he conduct of an organ of a State or an organ or agent of an international organization that is placed at the disposal of another international organization shall be considered under international law an act of the latter organization if the organization exercises effective control over that conduct'. As there was no effective control on the part of the UN, but instead on the part of the state, the court went on to apply the law of state responsibility.

It is noted that, at the time of the decision, the ILC in its Commentary to then art. 6 ARIO had clarified that the article had specific relevance 'in the case of military contingents that a State places at the disposal of the United Nations for a peacekeeping

---

[1] UN GAOR, 64th Session, Supp 10, UN Doc A/64/10 (2009).   [2] UN Doc A/66/100.

operation'.[3] It is also noted that at that time, in a somewhat similar situation, a Dutch court had held that the acts of Dutch peace-keepers in Bosnia Herzegovina could not be attributed to The Netherlands,[4] and the European Court of Human Rights (ECtHR) did not consider the acts of NATO member state troops acting under the authority of the UN in Kosovo to be attributable to the member states.[5]

The Belgian court seemed to distinguish the MINUAR case from *Behrami*, but why precisely both cases should conceptually be distinguished remained elusive. Arguably, both cases should have been decided by reference to the 'effective control' standard as set forth in art. 6 ARIO 2009/art. 7 ARIO 2011. It is well-known, however, that the ECtHR applied a standard of 'ultimate control' in *Behrami*. According to the ECtHR, the UN Security Council had 'delegated to NATO the power to establish, as well as the operational command of, the international presence, KFOR,' and thus that the UN 'was to retain ultimate control over the security mission'.[6] The Belgian MINUAR case implicitly rejected this 'ultimate control' standard, and instead emphasized the standard of *de facto* operational control. The Dutch Court of Appeal (2011) and the Dutch Supreme Court (2013) later applied the same standard in the Srebrenica cases of *Mustafic* and *Nuhanovic*.[7]

A major part of the decision was devoted to technical questions of prescription under Belgian law. From an international law perspective, it was notable that the court reaffirmed the imprescriptibility of international crimes. However, due to a peculiarity of Belgian law, the court ruled that the statute of limitations as regards the complaint against the Belgian State had run out. Under Belgian law, the statute of limitations for a civil action, which was normally five years, could be extended if the wrongful act could be considered a criminal offence. This would normally have meant that, if the criminal offence amounted to an international crime, no statute of limitations at all would be applicable. But as the Belgian State could technically not commit a criminal offence, the statute of limitations for the civil action against the Belgian State could not be extended. The court left it open whether the statute of limitations could nevertheless be extended as regards the vicarious liability of the Belgian State, that is the liability of the state for the wrongful acts of its agents rather than for its own acts. This was to be decided at a later stage in the proceedings.

As the civil suits against the Belgian commanders were not subject to a statute of limitations, the court went on to consider the merits as regards those suits. The court set out at great length that there was a causal link between the commanders' decision to evacuate the ETO compound and the massacre of the refugees by the Interahamwe militias, but stopped short of holding the commanders liable for a failure to act in this phase of the proceedings. In order to shed additional light on the circumstances

---

[3] ARIO Commentary 2009, p. 62.

[4] *HN v Netherlands* (Ministry of Defence and Ministry of Foreign Affairs), First instance judgment, LJN: BF0181/265615; ILDC 1092 (NL 2008), 10 September 2008.

[5] ECtHR, *Behrami and Behrami v France and Saramati v France, Germany, and Norway*, Decision (Grand Chamber) of 2 May 2007 on the admissibility of App. Nos. 71412/01 and 78166/01.

[6] *Behrami*, para. 135.

[7] Supreme Court (HR), *State of The Netherlands v Mustafic* et al., ECLI:NL:HR:2013:BZ9228; *State of The Netherlands et al. v Nuhanović*, ECLI:NL:HR:2013:BZ9225—see also ch. 6.9 in this volume.

prevailing in Rwanda at the time, the court, somewhat unusually, acceded to a request to order the screening of a movie (rather than a documentary) on the Rwandan genocide. This was supposed to help the court in its determination of whether the commanders were blameworthy. Still, it was notable that some initial determinations as to the blameworthiness of the commanders were already made by the court in this interim decision: the court rejected the defence of superior orders,[8] ruled that the doctrine of superior responsibility/failure to act[9] applied to commanders in respect of international crimes committed by militias over which the former did not exercise formal authority, and held the mental element of the crime of failure to act in the face of the crimes committed by the militias, to be established, at least in part.

At the time of publication, the decision was still under appeal.

---

[8] cf. art. 33 of the Rome Statute of the International Criminal Court (17 July 1998), UN Doc A/CONF.183/9, entered into force 1 July 2002 (Rome Statute).

[9] cf. art. 28 of the Rome Statute.

6.9 *Nuhanović v Netherlands*, Judgment, BZ9225, and *Mustafić v Netherlands*, Judgment, BZ9228, Supreme Court of The Netherlands, 6 September 2013

Otto Spijkers

Relevance of the case

The *Nuhanović* and *Mustafić* cases deal with the legal responsibility of The Netherlands for acts committed by a battalion of Dutch soldiers, placed at the disposal of the UN to take part in a peacekeeping mission.[1] In its judgment, the Dutch Supreme Court made extensive use of the Draft Articles on the Responsibility of States for Internationally Wrongful Acts (DARS),[2] and the Draft Articles on the Responsibility of International Organizations (ARIO) of the International Law Commission (ILC).[3] While the question of attribution is decided on the basis of international law, the wrongfulness of the conduct of the Dutch peacekeepers is assessed mainly on the basis of local domestic (Bosnia-Herzegovina) private law. Nonetheless, as an *obiter dictum*, the Supreme Court also had something interesting to say about the extraterritorial application of international human rights law in a case such as this one.

I. Facts of the case

The war in the former Yugoslavia began in the early 1990s, when Slovenia and Croatia, soon followed by Bosnia-Herzegovina, declared themselves independent, and the central authorities of Yugoslavia reacted with violence.[4] The response of the UN was the establishment of the United Nations Protection Force (UNPROFOR)[5] Part of the UN's peacekeeping or peace-enforcement strategy was to designate so-called 'safe areas', enclaves of peace where civilians could hide from the war. Srebrenica became such a 'safe area' in April 1993.[6] Around 200 lightly armed troops, placed at the disposal of UNPROFOR by The Netherlands, were stationed in a compound near a village called Potočari, situated less than ten kilometres from Srebrenica. Their mission was to protect the civilians from the warring parties. In exchange, the civilians had to surrender their weapons, if they had any, to the UN. Unfortunately, the Dutch peacekeepers could not prevent the fall of Srebrenica into the hands of the

---

[1] From a legal point of view at least, the two cases—*Nuhanović* and *Mustafić*—are very much alike, and thus the focus in this comment will be on just one of them: the case of Hasan Nuhanović.

[2] Report of the ILC's fifty-third session, Y.I.L.C. Vol. II, Part Two.

[3] Report of the ILC's sixty-third session (2011), UN Doc. A/66/10.

[4] For an analysis of the facts, see especially *The Fall of Srebrenica* (Report of the UN Secretary-General), 15 November 1999, UN Doc. A/54/549; *Rapport sur les événements de Srebrenica* (Report of the Assemblée Nationale of France), 22 November 2001; *Srebrenica—A 'Safe' Area* (Report of The Netherlands Institute for War Documentation), 10 April 2002 (available at http://213.222.3.5/srebrenica); *Missie zonder vrede* (Report of Dutch Parliament), January 2003.

[5] SC Resolutions 758 of 8 June 1992 and 981, 982, and 983 of 31 March 1995.

[6] SC Resolution 819 (1993) of 16 April 1993, para. 1.

Bosnian-Serb Army in July 1995. Thousands of Muslims hiding in the 'safe area' were killed by the Bosnian-Serbs almost as soon as the Dutch peacekeepers evacuated. Not long after this Srebrenica genocide, the war ended with a cease-fire signed in November 1995 in Dayton, Ohio (USA).

Hasan Nuhanović worked as an interpreter for the UN Military Observers. In this capacity, he provided assistance to 'Dutchbat', the name commonly used to refer to the battalion of Dutch UN peacekeepers stationed near Srebrenica. When the enclave fell, the peacekeepers all left the area. Hasan Nuhanović was permitted to leave with the soldiers of Dutchbat. Dutchbat refused to take the relatives of Hasan Nuhanović with them as well. These relatives were basically handed over to the Bosnian-Serb Army, and Hasan's brother and father were killed together with thousands of other Bosnian Muslims.

II. The legal question

Nuhanović asked the Dutch Court to declare that The Netherlands had committed a wrongful act by Dutchbat's refusal to take his relatives along when Dutchbat evacuated after the fall of Srebrenica. This refusal ultimately led to their death, and Dutchbat did know or should have known this. The legal questions are thus the following: Can Dutchbat's conduct be attributed to the state of The Netherlands? And if so, was Dutchbat's conduct wrongful, in the sense that it was in breach of an existing legal obligation of The Netherlands?

III. Excerpts

Can Dutchbat's conduct be attributed to the State?

3.8.2 It follows from articles 4 and 8 DARS that Dutchbat's conduct can be attributed to the State if Dutchbat should be considered as an organ of the State (art. 4 (1) DARS) or if Dutchbat in fact acted on the instructions or under the direction or control of the State (art. 8 DARS).

3.9.1 In the proceedings before the Court of Appeal the debate between the parties focused on the question of whether the circumstance that Dutchbat had been placed at the disposal of the United Nations by the State meant that Dutchbat's conduct could be attributed not to the State pursuant to article 4 (1) or article 8 DARS but only to the United Nations. The provisions of the ARIO are of relevance in connection with the latter point.

[The Court then lists the relevant provisions in ARIO, esp. arts. 6, 7, and 48, and cites from the ILC Commentary to these articles.]

3.9.4 The Commentary on Part Two, Chapter II ARIO notes that articles 6–9 ARIO do not necessarily mean that conduct must be exclusively attributed to an international organization—thereby resulting in exclusive responsibility of the international organization—but instead leave open the possibility of conduct being attributed to an international organization and a State, which would then result in dual attribution to the international organization and the State concerned [...] Article 48 (1) ARIO [...] expressly leaves open the possibility of more than one State or organization being held responsible for the consequences of an internationally wrongful act. [...]

3.10.2 It is apparent from the Commentary on article 7 ARIO [...] that this attribution rule applies, *inter alia*, to the situation in which a State places troops at the disposal of the United Nations in the context of a UN peace mission, and command and control is transferred to the United Nations, but the disciplinary powers and criminal jurisdiction (the 'organic command') remain vested in the seconding State. It is implicit in the findings of the Court of Appeal that this situation occurs in the present case. After all [...] the Court of Appeal has held—and this has not been disputed in the cassation appeal—that it is not at issue that The Netherlands, as the troop-contributing State, retained control over the personnel affairs of the military personnel concerned, who had remained in the service of The Netherlands, and retained the power to punish these military personnel under disciplinary and criminal law. [...]

3.11.3 [...] For the purpose of deciding whether the State had effective control it is not necessary for the State to have countermanded the command structure of the United Nations by giving instructions to Dutchbat or to have exercised operational command independently. It is apparent from the Commentary on article 7 ARIO [...] that the attribution of conduct to the seconding State or the international organization is based on the factual control over the specific conduct, in which all factual circumstances and the special context of the case must be taken into account. In the disputed findings of law the Court of Appeal has examined, in the light of all circumstances and the special context of the case, whether the State had factual control over Dutchbat's disputed conduct. The Court of Appeal has not therefore interpreted or applied the law incorrectly.

3.13 The above findings lead to the conclusion that parts 2 and 3 of the cassation appeal oppose in vain the Court of Appeal's ruling that the State had effective control over the conduct of which Dutchbat—and hence the State as well—is accused by Nuhanović. Given this position, the Court of Appeal was able to find on the basis of the attribution rule of article 7 ARIO, which is applicable to this case, partly in view of what is provided in the attribution rule of article 8 DARS—that Dutchbat's disputed conduct can be attributed to the State.

<u>Was Dutchbat's conduct wrongful?</u>

[The Supreme Court first explains that the application of the relevant domestic law of Bosnia and Herzegovina already leads the Court to the conclusion that the State acted wrongfully towards Nuhanović. Nonetheless ...]

3.16 The Supreme Court would observe, by way of *obiter dictum* [...] as follows.

3.17.1 Part 5 [of the grounds of appeal] submits that any assessment of Dutchbat's disputed conduct by reference to the legal principles implicit in articles 2 and 3 ECHR [European Convention on Human Rights] and articles 6 and 7 ICCPR [International Covenant on Civil and Political Rights] is prevented by the fact that the State did not have jurisdiction as referred to in article 1 ECHR and article 2 (1) ICCPR either in Srebrenica or in the compound in Potočari. This submission fails.

3.17.2 According to the case law of the European Court of Human Rights (ECtHR), the possibility is not excluded that a Contracting State may, in exceptional circumstances, have the jurisdiction referred to in article 1 ECHR even outside its territory (cf. ECtHR 7 July 2011, no. 55721/07, NJ 2012/430 (*Al-Skeini and Others v. the United Kingdom*)).

3.17.3 In this case Dutchbat's presence in Srebrenica and in the compound in Potočari resulted from the participation of The Netherlands in UNPROFOR, and UNPROFOR derived its right to take action in Srebrenica from the Agreement on the status of the United Nations Protection Force in Bosnia and Herzegovina concluded between the United Nations and Bosnia and Herzegovina [...]. This means that the State was competent, through Dutchbat, to exercise jurisdiction within the meaning of article 1 ECHR in the compound. Nor can it be said that, after the fall of the enclave on 11 July 1995 and, in particular, at the moment of Dutchbat's disputed conduct, it was *de facto* impossible for the State to exercise jurisdiction as referred to above in the compound. According to the facts on which it has based its judgment, the Court of Appeal has assumed that the Bosnian Serb army respected Dutchbat's authority over the compound to which it had withdrawn until the departure of Dutchbat on 21 July 1995. These facts provide a sufficient basis for the view that the State, through Dutchbat, was actually able to ensure compliance with the human rights enshrined in articles 2 and 3 ECHR and articles 6 and 7 ICCPR in relation to Muhamed and Ibro Nuhanović.

IV. Commentary

In this commentary, the most interesting parts of the judgment will be evaluated critically. The Dutch Supreme Court judgment in *Nuhanović* will also be compared with a more recent judgment of The Hague District Court, in a case between the *Mothers of Srebrenica* (Foundation) and The Netherlands.[7] In this most recent judgment, the state of The Netherlands was essentially held responsible for the deaths of the male refugees that were deported by the Bosnian Serbs from the compound in Potočari after the fall of Srebrenica.

For a state to be legally responsible, the conduct must be attributable to the state, and that conduct must constitute a breach of a legal obligation.[8] The Dutch Supreme Court dealt with attribution and the wrongfulness of the acts separately. In this commentary, this approach will be followed.

A. Attribution

When examining the question of attribution, the Dutch Supreme Court applied only international law. In doing so, it uncritically followed the Dutch Appeals Court. Both Courts held that the question of attribution was closely related to the interpretation of the agreement between The Netherlands and the UN on the provision of Dutch troops. And since this was an international agreement, the attribution question had to be answered on the basis of international law.[9]

What does international law say about attribution in this context? It is the view of the UN Legal Counsel and Secretariat that, when soldiers replace their

---

[7] *Mothers of Srebrenica v Netherlands*, Judgment, The Hague District Court, 16 July 2014, ECLI:NL:RBDHA:2014:8748.

[8] Article 2, DARS.   [9] *Nuhanović v Netherlands*, para. 3.6.2.

own helmets with the blue helmets of a UN peacekeeping mission, their actions should normally be attributable to the UN. The UN generally affirms that 'as a subsidiary organ of the United Nations, an act of a peacekeeping force is, in principle, imputable to the Organization'.[10] The ILC acknowledges that this has been the practice of the UN since the very early days (United Nations Operation in the Congo (ONUC) in 1960s), a consistent practice which is reflected in the many agreements made between the UN and troop-contributing states.[11] This practice is different when it comes to peace-*enforcement* operations, where the UN Security Council authorizes states to take military action. In such operations, the soldiers do not wear blue helmets but instead keep their own national helmets on. And the leadership on the ground over the military operation is left to the states that take part in such so-called 'coalitions of the willing'. With regard to such peace-enforcement missions, it is the UN's view that 'the conduct of the operation is imputable to the State or States conducting the operation'.[12]

> But the ILC disagrees with the UN Secretariat's rigid distinction between peace*keeping* and peace-*enforcement* missions. It is the ILC's view that the same rule, that is that it all depends on who has effective control over the specific acts concerned,[13] 'should also apply to peacekeeping operations, insofar as it is possible to distinguish in their regard areas of effective control respectively pertaining to the United Nations and the contributing State'.[14] The use of the word 'should' is interesting, because it suggests that the ILC is here proposing a change in the law. And it explains its reasons to do so, as follows: While it is understandable that, for the sake of efficiency of military operations, the UN insists on claiming exclusive command and control over peacekeeping forces, attribution of conduct should also in this regard be based on a factual criterion.

All this suggests that, in view of the ILC, the UN and the troop-contributing states ought to change their fifty years of consistent practice of holding the UN, in principle, responsible for the acts of peacekeeping operations, and that they should instead base responsibility as from today on a factual criterion.

The ILC did not find much support in existing case law for this new approach. The judgments of the ECtHR, discussed elsewhere in this book, to which the ILC referred in its commentary, either chose a different criterion altogether (primarily *Behrami*),[15] or were related to peace-enforcement missions, or even to acts of a multinational occupying force (*Al-Jedda*).[16] In fact, the only example that the ILC could find, in its ARIO commentary of 2011, of a case in which the effective control criterion was applied to a peacekeeping mission, was the Court of Appeal's judgment in this very same *Nuhanović* case.

---

[10] UN Doc. A/CN.4/545, section II.G, p. 17, as cited in A/66/10, § 6, at 88.
[11] See A/66/10, § 6, at 88. [12] See UN Doc. A/CN.4/545, section II.G, at 18.
[13] Article 7 ARIO. [14] See A/66/10, § 9, at 90.
[15] ECtHR (Grand Chamber), App. Nos. 71412/01 and 78166/01, 2 May 2007, Decision as to the Admissibility of App. No. 71412/01 by Agim Behrami and Bekir Behrami against France and App. No. 78166/01 by Ruzhdi Saramati against France, Germany, and Norway, available at http://www.echr.coe.int.
[16] ECtHR (Grand Chamber), App. No. 27021/08, 2 May 2007, Judgment (Merits and Just Satisfaction), Case of *Al-Jedda v United Kingdom*, available at http://www.echr.coe.int.

It is noble of the UN that it so generously accepts legal responsibility for the conduct of its peacekeepers. In a way, the organization thereby protects the troop-contributing state from all sorts of lawsuits. If a troop-contributing state finds itself confronted with a claim for reparation of damages caused by the conduct of peacekeepers, it can simply refer the claimant to the UN. However, as evidenced by an earlier ruling of the Dutch Supreme Court in the case between the *Mothers of Srebrenica* and *The Netherlands*, which is discussed elsewhere in this book, due to the UN's immunity before domestic courts and its reluctance to create an alternative legal remedy within the UN system, it is actually very difficult for an individual to hold the UN responsible before a court of law.[17] And thus, in the absence of a legal remedy against the UN, one cannot be surprised that persons claiming to be the victim of a wrongful act allegedly committed by a UN peacekeeper will begin proceedings against the troop-contributing state.[18]

This unfortunate situation of claimants having nowhere to go might have motivated the ILC to disagree with the UN that the conduct of peacekeepers should always be attributed to the organization. The ILC's rejection of the categorical distinction between peacekeeping missions and peace-enforcement missions that the UN makes can also be defended on the basis that peacekeeping forces are sent into conflict zones with mandates which are more and more robust, and on the basis that troop-contributing states insist on having more and more control over 'their' peacekeepers. From a policy perspective, the better view is that the question of who is responsible—the UN and/or the troop-contributing state—must be answered by considering which of the two in fact had the *effective control* over the specific conduct for which responsibility is disputed. But this view is not (yet) supported in actual UN peacekeeping practice, and this of course is no minor detail at a moment when a Court of law is asked to identify the applicable customary international law at the time the acts took place.

What did the Dutch Courts do? Did they side with the UN, the ILC, or did they decide a different approach altogether? First of all, the Dutch Supreme Court accepted that the same conduct could in principle be attributed both to The Netherlands and to the UN.[19] In reaching this decision, the Court made use of art. 48 ARIO, but its interpretation of this article has been convincingly challenged elsewhere.[20] Moreover, any references to evidence of a consistent state practice supporting Rule 48 ARIO are absent in the Dutch Supreme Court judgment.

---

[17] See Aleksandar Momirov's commentary of *Mothers of Srebrenica v The Netherlands & the UN*, LJN: BW1999, Dutch Supreme Court, 13 April 2012; and *Stichting Mothers of Srebrenica and Others against The Netherlands*, App. No. 65542/12, European Court of Human Rights, 11 June 2013.

[18] *Mothers of Srebrenica* judgment of 16 July 2014, at para. 4.35.

[19] For a recent commentary on how the Dutch Supreme Court dealt with the attribution issue, see also O.F. Direk, 'Responsibility in Peace Support Operations: Revisiting the Proper Test for Attribution Conduct and the Meaning of the "Effective Control" Standard', in The *Netherlands International Law Review*, Vol. 61, Issue 1, May 2014, pp. 1–22.

[20] See A/66/10, pp. 144–5. For a critique, see Cedric Ryngaert's case note in The *Netherlands International Law Review*, Vol. 60, Issue 3, December 2013, pp. 441–6.

Now that the same conduct is in principle attributable to both the UN and to The Netherlands, the Dutch Supreme Court can assess the responsibility of The Netherlands without having to look at the responsibility of the UN as well. This is important, because the UN was not a party to the proceedings in *Nuhanović*, and thus the Dutch Court could not make any pronouncements, direct or indirect, on the legal responsibilities of the UN.

The Supreme Court based its decision on attribution primarily on art. 7 ARIO, which states that the conduct of an organ placed at the disposal of an international organization by a state must be considered to be the conduct of that international organization, when the organization has effective control over the conduct.[21] The Netherlands argued that art. 6 ARIO was the relevant provision, and not art. 7. Article 6 ARIO simply states that the conduct of an organ of an international organization is attributable to that international organization. The argument of the state was thus that the peacekeepers were a UN organ. This, as explained above, is also the view of the UN itself. But the Supreme Court followed the ILC Commentary to ARIO, according to which a battalion of peacekeepers is not a UN organ, because the battalion to a certain extent still acts as an organ of the state supplying the soldiers. Important is the fact that the troop-contributing state retains disciplinary powers and criminal jurisdiction over its peacekeepers.[22]

Interestingly, the Dutch Supreme Court also referred to art. 8 DARS. Strictly speaking, art. 7 ARIO says nothing about the attribution of conduct of an organ placed at the disposal of an international organization by a state to that state. All it says is that, if the international organization does not have effective control over the conduct of the organ, then it is not responsible for that conduct. But that does not mean that, by definition, this makes the state responsible in such cases. In theory, it could very well be that neither of the two is responsible. And so to complete the picture, the Dutch Supreme Court relied on art. 8 DARS. According to this provision, the conduct of a group of persons shall be considered an act of a state if the group is in fact acting under the effective control of that state in carrying out the conduct. This provision was meant to make it possible to attribute acts of persons not formally part of the state system to the state in exceptional circumstances. One may wonder why the Supreme Court did not instead make use of art. 4 DARS, according to which the conduct of any state organ shall be considered an act of that state. If peacekeepers are not UN organs, as the UN itself claims, then it would be logical to consider the peacekeeping force as a state organ. They are not the mercenaries, militants, or band of irregulars for which art. 8 DARS was designed. If we follow the Dutch Supreme Court, the peacekeepers are nobody's organ; and whoever happens to be in control of them at the relevant time is responsible for their actions.[23]

---

[21] *Mothers of Srebrenica* (n. 7): para. 4.33 where the Hague District Court followed this route.

[22] A/66/10, at para. 7 and pp. 88–9.

[23] The exact opposite has also been suggested, that is that a peacekeeping force can be both a state organ *and* a UN subsidiary organ at the same time. See p. 180 of M. Tondini, 'The "Italian Job": How to make International Organisations Compliant with Human Rights and Accountable for their Violation by Targeting Member States', in J. Wouters, E. Brems, S. Smis, and P. Schmitt (eds), *Accountability for Human Rights Violations by International Organisations* (Antwerp, Intersentia 2010).

B. Wrongfulness

When assessing the wrongfulness of the acts attributable to The Netherlands, the Dutch Supreme Court situated itself primarily in the domestic legal order of Bosnia-Herzegovina—the rules of private international law require that the Court applies the *lex loci delicti commissi*. Interestingly, in the *Mothers of Srebrenica* case, the Hague District Court held that the rules of private international law prescribe that, when a state exercises sovereign powers over a particular area outside its territorial jurisdiction, that the law of that state applies.[24] Because the Hague District Court was convinced that The Netherlands had effective control over the compound in Potočari at the relevant time, it held Dutch—as opposed to Bosnia-Herzegovinian—private law applicable to the events in the compound.

Nuhanović had argued that The Netherlands (Dutchbat) had committed a wrongful act (tort) by not making every possible effort to avoid the death of his two relatives. The existence of such an obligation in the legal order of Bosnia-Herzegovina could be based on domestic provisions of private (tort) law, but also on international law, as international law has direct effect within the Bosnian legal order. And thus international law re-emerged on the scene through the backdoor. The most relevant international obligation is the state's responsibility to guarantee to all within its jurisdiction the enjoyment of the right to life. This human right is codified in art. 6 ICCPR, and art. 2 ECHR.

In view of the Supreme Court, Bosnian tort law alone could suffice to establish the wrongfulness of the acts.[25] Nonetheless, as an *obiter dictum*, the Court wished to say something about the applicability of international human rights law to the situation. The Supreme Court held that the international human rights provisions mentioned may indeed be invoked against The Netherlands, because the acts concerned did fall within the jurisdiction of The Netherlands in the sense of art. 1 ECHR and art. 2(1) ICCPR. Earlier, the Dutch District Court in *Nuhanović* had referred to the *Bankovic* case of the ECHR in support of the argument that the term 'jurisdiction' in art. 1 ECHR should 'be interpreted as an essentially territorial concept', and the acts took place in Bosnia and not in The Netherlands.[26] But the Supreme Court, relying on the *Al-Skeini* judgment of the same ECtHR, noted that the jurisdiction of a party to the ECHR extends, in exceptional circumstances, also to areas outside its own territory.[27]

When determining whether the acts of Dutchbat fell within the Dutch 'human rights jurisdiction', the Supreme Court looked closely at the formal legal arrangements *and* at the facts and the situation on the ground. It implicitly distinguished a *de jure* and *de facto* basis of extraterritorial jurisdiction. The Netherlands formally (*de jure*) had jurisdiction because the territorial entity, the state of Bosnia-Herzegovina,

---

[24] *Mothers of Srebrenica* (n. 7), para. 4.167.

[25] *Nuhanović v Netherlands*, paras 3.15.4 4 and 3.15.5.

[26] *Nuhanović v Netherlands*, para. 4.12.3. Reference was made to ECtHR (Grand Chamber), App. No. 52207/99, 12 December 2001, Decision as to the Admissibility, *Case of Bankovic and Others v Belgium and Others*, available at http://www.echr.coe.int.

[27] ECtHR (Grand Chamber), App. No. 55721/07, 7 July 2011, Judgment (Merits and Just Satisfaction), *Case of Al-Skeini and Others v United Kingdom*, available at http://www.echr.coe.int

had surrendered its competence to govern in the area to UNPROFOR.[28] Clearly, UNPROFOR cannot be equated with The Netherlands, but considering the Supreme Court's answer to the attribution question (see above), this was nonetheless relevant. The Netherlands also had *de facto* jurisdiction, because an examination of the facts had shown that it was not impossible for The Netherlands to exercise jurisdiction through Dutchbat, and prevent the human rights violations from happening. It could have done so, but it did not.[29]

C. Conclusion and policy implications

This case is unique in many ways. It is one of the first cases in which ARIO is applied to a UN peacekeeping mission. It is also unique in the sense that the acts concerned were not examples of isolated misconduct by individual soldiers acting *ultra vires*, or peacekeepers causing car accidents or something in that category. Instead, this case dealt with a failure of the peacekeepers to protect some of the individuals they were supposed to protect. It is especially because of the latter aspect that the judgment caused a lot of concern. The Dutch Minister for Defence was asked recently if a Srebrenica type-situation, in which the UN loses control of a UN peacekeeping mission and the troop contributor is obligated to step in, could occur again in the future. She replied that a change in the situation in the area where a peacekeeping mission operates, for example the outbreak of large-scale hostilities or a general deterioration of the situation, may always lead to the situation in which the UN is no longer able to control the execution of the mission. This, said the Minister, may be a reason for the troop-contributing state to fill in the void and take effective control.

If The Netherlands' approach for the future is to take over control from the UN much sooner and with much more confidence than was done in Srebrenica, then the responsibility of The Netherlands is of course much sooner engaged. This is a consequence of the application of the 'effective control' criterion. Applying art. 7 ARIO and/or 8 DARS—or perhaps even art. 4 DARS—will then quickly lead to the conclusion that The Netherlands exercises effective control over the peacekeepers, and that The Netherlands is responsible for their conduct. The Netherlands is thus not trying to avoid responsibility in the future by prohibiting the Dutch authorities in The Hague from ever getting involved in the direction and control of peacekeeping missions. Instead, The Netherlands has chosen the exact opposite strategy: in order not to be held responsible for a failure of Dutch peacekeepers in the future, The Netherlands will prevent such failures, by involving itself more intensely in the way peacekeeping missions are conducted.[30]

---

[28] *Nuhanović v Netherlands*: para. 3.17.3.   [29] Ibid.

[30] Answers provided on 11 March 2014 by Hennis-Plasschaert, Minister of Defense of The Netherlands, to questions raised by Dutch Parliamentarians on 29 January 2014. The document is available at http://www.tweedekamer.nl/kamerstukken/, under 'Kamerstuk' 29521-235.

6.10 *Al-Jedda v United Kingdom*, App. No. 27021/08, European Court of Human Rights, 7 July 2011

Aurel Sari

Relevance of the case

The judgment delivered by the Grand Chamber of the European Court of Human Rights (ECtHR) in the *Al-Jedda* case in 2011 touches on a broad range of questions concerning the application of the European Convention on Human Rights (ECHR) to multinational military operations and the Convention's relationship with other rules of public international law. Many of these questions, such as the relationship between the Convention and international humanitarian law, have been the subject of detailed attention in the literature.[1] The focus of the present chapter is on the judgment's contribution to the law of international responsibility, in particular the rules governing the attribution of wrongful conduct in the context of military operations conducted jointly by states and international organizations. The relevance of the *Al-Jedda* case in this context is twofold. First, it highlights the continued confusion surrounding the relationship between jurisdiction as a threshold requirement for the applicability of the ECHR and attribution as an element of international responsibility for a breach of the Convention, as well as the difficulties entailed by allocating responsibility between states and international organizations involved in the conduct of peace-support operations more generally. Second, the decision marks an evolution in the European Court's approach to the attribution of wrongful conduct compared to its earlier decision in the joined cases of *Behrami* and *Saramati*.[2] In particular, the European Court now appears to accept that the relevant test governing the attribution of wrongful conduct is that of 'effective control'.

I. Facts of the case

The *Al-Jedda* case arose out of the detention of the applicant, Mr Hilal Abdul-Razzaq Ali Al-Jedda, by British armed forces operating as part of the Multinational Force in Iraq (MNF).

---

[1] See J. Pejic, 'The European Court of Human Rights' *Al-Jedda* Judgment: The Oversight of International Humanitarian Law', (2011) 93 *International Review of the Red Cross* 837; H. Krieger, 'After *Al-Jedda*: Detention, Derogation, and an Enduring Dilemma', (2011) 50 *Military Law and the Law of War Review* 419; M. Kashgar, 'The ECtHR's Judgment in *Al-Jedda* and its Implications for International Humanitarian Law', (2011) 24 *Humanitäres Völkerrecht* 229. For more general comments, see F. Messineo, 'Things Could Only Get Better: Al-Jedda beyond *Behrami*', (2011) 50 *Military Law and the Law of War Review* 321; M. Milanović, 'Al-Skeini and Al-Jedda in Strasbourg', (2012) 23 *European Journal of International Law* 121; M. Zgonec-Rozej, 'Al-Jedda v. United Kingdom—Application No. 27021/08', (2012) 106 *American Journal of International Law* 830.

[2] cf. *Behrami and Behrami v France and Saramati v France, Germany, and Norway*, App. Nos 71412/01 and 78166/01 (2007) 45 EHRR SE10.

On 20 March 2003, a coalition led by the United States of America and the United Kingdom invaded Iraq with the aim of removing Saddam Hussein from power. Following the end of major combat operations, the United Kingdom became an occupying power and jointly exercised the powers of government in Iraq with other members of the coalition under the law of belligerent occupation.[3] The legal framework governing the presence and activities of British forces in Iraq changed with the adoption of Security Council Resolution 1511 on 16 October 2003.[4] The resolution authorized the establishment of 'a multinational force under unified command to take all necessary measures to contribute to the maintenance of security and stability in Iraq'.[5] It further urged all member states of the UN to contribute assistance, including military forces, to the multinational force 'under this United Nations mandate'.[6] On 8 June 2004, the Security Council adopted Resolution 1546 to extend the mandate of the MNF after the end of the occupation at the request of the Iraqi authorities.

The claimant held dual Iraqi-British citizenship and had lived in the United Kingdom since 1972. In September 2004, he travelled to Iraq where he was detained by coalition forces and later held in a British-run detention facility in Basrah. His detention was justified and upheld at periodic reviews on the basis that it was necessary for imperative reasons of security in Iraq. He was eventually released in December 2007, having been deprived of his British citizenship.

II. The legal question

On 8 June 2005, Al-Jedda brought judicial review proceedings before the English courts against the Secretary of State to challenge his detention. The Secretary of State accepted that Al-Jedda fell within the jurisdiction of the United Kingdom for the purposes of art. 1 of the ECHR and thus benefitted from the right to liberty and security of person guaranteed in art. 5 of the Convention. Whilst the Secretary of State conceded that Al-Jedda's detention could not be justified with reference to any of the exceptions enumerated in art. 5 and as such prima facie breached his right to liberty, he argued that Security Council Resolutions 1511 and 1546, applied in conjunction with art. 103 of the UN Charter,[7] rendered his detention lawful. These submissions were upheld by the lower courts.[8]

On the claimant's appeal to the House of Lords, the Secretary of State introduced a new argument. Relying on the recently decided *Behrami* case, he submitted that the conduct of British forces participating in the MNF had to be attributed to the UN

---

[3] See Letter dated 8 May 2003 from the Permanent Representatives of the United Kingdom of Great Britain and Northern Ireland and the United States of America to the United Nations addressed to the President of the Security Council, 8 May 2003, S/2003/538.

[4] cf. C. Stahn, *The Law and Practice of International Territorial Administration: Versailles to Iraq and Beyond* (Cambridge, Cambridge University Press 2008), pp. 363–81.

[5] cf. Operative para. 13.   [6] cf. Operative para. 14.

[7] Article 103 of the UN Charter reads as follows: 'In the event of a conflict between the obligations of the Members of the United Nations under the present Charter and their obligations under any other international agreement, their obligations under the present Charter shall prevail.'

[8] See *R. (Al-Jedda) v Secretary of State for Defence* [2005] EWHC 1809 (Administrative Court); *R. (Al-Jedda) v Secretary of State for Defence* [2006] EWCA Civ 327 (Court of Appeal).

rather than to the United Kingdom. The majority of the House of Lords rejected this claim, but found that the Security Council resolutions authorizing the presence and activities of British forces in Iraq displaced art. 5 of the Convention to the extent that a conflict arose between them.[9] Consequently, the House of Lords affirmed that Al-Jedda's detention did not entail a violation of art. 5 of the ECHR.

The parties revisited these points in their submissions before the ECtHR. The Government contended that the legal position of the British MNF contingent was essentially identical with that of national contingents forming part of Kosovo Force (KFOR), so that the *Behrami* case applied.[10] In detaining the applicant, British forces were not exercising the sovereign authority of the United Kingdom but the international authority conferred upon the MNF by the relevant Security Council resolutions. The Government submitted that as a result Al-Jedda did not fall within its jurisdiction and his detention could not be attributed to the United Kingdom. Endorsing the majority view of the House of Lords, the claimant replied by suggesting that the legal circumstances of the MNF differed from that of KFOR in material respects.[11] His legal position was clearly distinguishable from that of the applicants in *Behrami*, with the effect that his detention had to be attributed to the United Kingdom and not to the UN.[12]

The question confronting the ECtHR therefore was this: did the applicant fall within the jurisdiction of the United Kingdom and was the conduct of British troops attributable to the United Kingdom or to the UN?

III. Excerpts

1. Article 1 of the Convention reads as follows: 'The High Contracting Parties shall secure to everyone within their jurisdiction the rights and freedoms defined in Section I of [the] Convention.' As provided by this Article, the engagement undertaken by a Contracting State is confined to 'securing' ('*reconnaître*' in the French text) the listed rights and freedoms to persons within its own 'jurisdiction' (see *Soering v. the United Kingdom*, 7 July 1989, § 89, Series A no. 161; *Banković*, cited above, § 66). 'Jurisdiction' under Article 1 is a threshold criterion. The exercise of jurisdiction is a necessary condition for a Contracting State to be able to be held responsible for acts or omissions imputable to it which give rise to an allegation of the infringement of rights and freedoms set forth in the Convention (see *Ilaşcu and Others v. Moldova and Russia* [GC], no. 48787/99, § 311, ECHR 2004-VII).

2. The Court notes that, before the Divisional Court and the Court of Appeal in the first set of domestic proceedings brought by the applicant, the Government

---

[9] *R. (Al-Jedda) v Secretary of State for Defence* [2007] UKHL 58 (House of Lords). For a commentary on the House of Lords decision, see A. Orakhelashvili, '*R (On the Application of Al-Jedda) (FC) v. Secretary of State for Defence*' (2008) 102 *American Journal of International Law* 337; A. Sari, 'The *Al-Jedda* Case before the House of Lords', (2009) 13 *Journal of International Peacekeeping* 181; F. Messineo, 'The House of Lords in *Al-Jedda* and Public International Law: Attribution of Conduct to UN-Authorized Forces and the Power of the Security Council to Displace Human Rights', (2009) 56 *Netherlands International Law Review* 35.

[10] cf. *Al-Jedda* (n. 9), paras 64–8.   [11] cf. *Al-Jedda* (n. 9), paras 69–72.

[12] cf. *Al-Jedda* (n. 9), para. 73.

accepted that he fell within United Kingdom jurisdiction under Article 1 of the Convention during his detention in a British-run military prison in Basrah, South East Iraq. It was only before the House of Lords that the Government argued, for the first time, that the applicant did not fall within United Kingdom jurisdiction because his detention was attributable to the United Nations rather than to the United Kingdom. The majority of the House of Lords rejected the Government's argument and held that the internment was attributable to British forces (see paragraphs 16–18 above).

3. When examining whether the applicant's detention was attributable to the United Kingdom or, as the Government submit, the United Nations, it is necessary to examine the particular facts of the case. These include the terms of the United Nations Security Council Resolutions which formed the framework for the security regime in Iraq during the period in question. In performing this exercise, the Court is mindful of the fact that it is not its role to seek to define authoritatively the meaning of provisions of the United Nations Charter and other international instruments. It must, nevertheless, examine whether there was a plausible basis in such instruments for the matters impugned before it (see *Behrami and Saramati*, cited above, § 122). The principles underlying the Convention cannot be interpreted and applied in a vacuum and the Court must take into account relevant rules of international law (ibid.). It relies for guidance in this exercise on the statement of the International Court of Justice in § 114 of its advisory opinion '*Legal consequences for States of the continued presence of South Africa in Namibia*' (see paragraph 49 above), indicating that a Security Council resolution should be interpreted in the light not only of the language used but also the context in which it was adopted.

4. The Court takes as its starting point that, on 20 March 2003, the United Kingdom together with the United States of America and their coalition partners, through their armed forces, entered Iraq with the aim of displacing the Ba'ath regime then in power. At the time of the invasion, there was no United Nations Security Council resolution providing for the allocation of roles in Iraq in the event that the existing regime was displaced. [...]

5. The first Security Council resolution after the invasion was Resolution 1483, adopted on 22 May 2003 (see paragraph 29 above). [...] Resolution 1483 did not assign any security role to the United Nations. The Government does not contend that, at this stage in the invasion and occupation, the acts of its armed forces were in any way attributable to the United Nations.

6. In Resolution 1511, adopted on 16 October 2003, the United Nations Security Council, again acting under Chapter VII, underscored the temporary nature of the exercise by the Coalition Provisional Authority of the authorities and responsibilities set out in Resolution 1483, which would cease as soon as an internationally recognised, representative Iraqi government could be sworn in. In paragraphs 13 and 14, the Security Council authorised 'a multinational force under unified command to take all necessary measures to contribute to the maintenance of security and stability in Iraq' and urged Member States 'to contribute assistance under this United Nations mandate, including military forces, to the multinational force referred to in paragraph 13' (see paragraph 31 above). The United States, on behalf of the multinational force, was requested periodically to report on the efforts and progress of the

force. The Security Council also resolved that the United Nations, acting through the Secretary General, his Special Representative, and the United Nations Assistance Mission in Iraq, should strengthen its role in Iraq, including by providing humanitarian relief, promoting the economic reconstruction of and conditions for sustainable development in Iraq, and advancing efforts to restore and establish national and local institutions for representative government.

7. The Court does not consider that, as a result of the authorisation contained in Resolution 1511, the acts of soldiers within the Multi-National Force became attributable to the United Nations or—more importantly, for the purposes of this case—ceased to be attributable to the troop-contributing nations. The Multi-National Force had been present in Iraq since the invasion and had been recognised already in Resolution 1483, which welcomed the willingness of Member States to contribute personnel. The unified command structure over the force, established from the start of the invasion by the United States and United Kingdom, was not changed as a result of Resolution 1511. Moreover, the United States and the United Kingdom, through the Coalition Provisional Authority which they had established at the start of the occupation, continued to exercise the powers of government in Iraq. Although the United States was requested to report periodically to the Security Council about the activities of the Multi-National Force, the United Nations did not, thereby, assume any degree of control over either the force or any other of the executive functions of the Coalition Provisional Authority.

8. The final resolution of relevance to the present issue was no. 1546 (see paragraph 35 above). It was adopted on 8 June 2004, twenty days before the transfer of power from the Coalition Provisional Authority to Interim Government and some four months before the applicant was taken into detention. Annexed to the resolution was a letter from the Prime Minister of the Interim Government of Iraq, seeking from the Security Council a new resolution on the Multi-National Force mandate. There was also annexed a letter from the United States Secretary of State to the President of the United Nations Security Council, confirming that 'the Multi-National Force [under unified command] is prepared to continue to contribute to the maintenance of security in Iraq' and informing the President of the Security Council of the goals of the Multi-National Force and the steps which its Commander intended to take to achieve those goals. It does not appear from the terms of this letter that the Secretary of State considered that the United Nations controlled the deployment or conduct of the Multi-National Force. In Resolution 1546 the Security Council, acting under Chapter VII, reaffirmed the authorisation for the Multi-National Force established under Resolution 1511. There is no indication in Resolution 1546 that the Security Council intended to assume any greater degree of control or command over the Multi-National Force than it had exercised previously.

[...]

9. In the light of the foregoing, the Court agrees with the majority of the House of Lords that the United Nations' role as regards security in Iraq in 2004 was quite different from its role as regards security in Kosovo in 1999. The comparison is relevant, since in the decision in *Behrami and Saramati* (cited above) the Court concluded, *inter alia,* that Mr Saramati's detention was attributable to the United Nations and

not to any of the respondent States. It is to be recalled that the international security presence in Kosovo was established by United Nations Security Council Resolution 1244 (10 June 1999) in which, 'determined to resolve the grave humanitarian situation in Kosovo', the Security Council 'decide[d] on the deployment in Kosovo, under United Nations auspices, of international civil and security presences'. The Security Council therefore authorised 'Member States and relevant international organizations to establish the international security presence in Kosovo' and directed that there should be 'substantial North Atlantic Treaty Organization participation' in the force, which 'must be deployed under unified command and control'. In addition, United Nations Security Council Resolution 1244 authorised the Secretary General of the United Nations to establish an international civil presence in Kosovo in order to provide an interim administration for Kosovo. The United Nations, through a Special Representative appointed by the Secretary General in consultation with the Security Council, was to control the implementation of the international civil presence and coordinate closely with the international security presence (see *Behrami and Saramati,* cited above, §§ 3, 4 and 41). On 12 June 1999, two days after the Resolution was adopted, the first elements of the NATO-led Kosovo Force (KFOR) entered Kosovo.

10. It would appear from the opinion of Lord Bingham in the first set of proceedings brought by the applicant that it was common ground between the parties before the House of Lords that the test to be applied in order to establish attribution was that set out by the International Law Commission, in Article 5 of its draft Articles on the Responsibility of International Organisations and in its commentary thereon, namely that the conduct of an organ of a State placed at the disposal of an international organisation should be attributable under international law to that organisation if the organisation exercises effective control over that conduct (see paragraphs 18 and 56 above). For the reasons set out above, the Court considers that the United Nations Security Council had neither effective control nor ultimate authority and control over the acts and omissions of troops within the Multi-National Force and that the applicant's detention was not, therefore, attributable to the United Nations.

11. The internment took place within a detention facility in Basrah City, controlled exclusively by British forces, and the applicant was therefore within the authority and control of the United Kingdom throughout (see paragraph 10 above; see also *Al-Skeini and Others v. the United Kingdom* [GC], no. 55721/07, § 136 and *Al-Saadoon and Mufdhi v. the United Kingdom* (dec.), no. 61498/08, § 88, ECHR 2010 ...; see also the judgment of the United States Supreme Court in *Munaf v. Geren,* paragraph 54 above). The decision to hold the applicant in internment was made by the British officer in command of the detention facility. Although the decision to continue holding the applicant in internment was, at various points, reviewed by committees including Iraqi officials and non-United Kingdom representatives from the Multi-National Force, the Court does not consider that the existence of these reviews operated to prevent the detention from being attributable to the United Kingdom.

12. In conclusion, the Court agrees with the majority of the House of Lords that the internment of the applicant was attributable to the United Kingdom and that during his internment the applicant fell within the jurisdiction of the United Kingdom for the purposes of Article 1 of the Convention.

IV. Commentary

The ECtHR dealt with the parties' submissions in two steps. Citing its earlier decision in *Ilaşcu*, the Court made it clear at the outset that the exercise of jurisdiction within the meaning of art. 1 of the ECHR is a necessary pre-condition for a potential finding of international responsibility.[13] This is so because jurisdiction operates as a threshold criterion for the applicability of the ECHR: a state party owes no obligations under the Convention to anyone outside its jurisdiction and in such circumstances the question whether its international responsibility is engaged for a possible breach of the Convention does not arise at all. However, the Government denied that Al-Jedda fell within its jurisdiction because the troops detaining him acted in an international rather than a national capacity. In a second step, the Court therefore investigated whether Al-Jedda's detention should be attributed to the United Kingdom or to the UN. However, at this point of the Court's reasoning a finding on attribution turns into a precondition for a finding on jurisdiction. Whether or not the United Kingdom exercised jurisdiction over Al-Jedda within the meaning of art. 1 of the ECHR now suddenly depends on the question whether the control exercised by British forces over him was to be attributed to the United Kingdom or not. This reversal of preliminary considerations emerges clearly from the concluding observations of the Court, which suggest that the Court considered the applicant to fall within the United Kingdom's jurisdiction precisely *because* his detention was to be attributed to the United Kingdom.[14]

As a result of this reversal, the clear conceptual distinction between jurisdiction as a primary matter of substantive law and attribution as a secondary matter of responsibility—the Court's initial starting point—collapses almost completely. The Court could have avoided this outcome with relative ease. In an extra-territorial setting, the requirement of jurisdiction pursuant to art. 1 of the Convention is satisfied whenever a state party exercises effective physical control over an individual.[15] The legal basis for the exercise of such control[16] or indeed the absence of any valid legal basis,[17] has no bearing on this requirement. Consequently, whether or not Al-Jedda was detained on the basis of national or international competences is irrelevant for the purposes of establishing that his detention crossed the jurisdictional threshold under art. 1.[18] Moreover, whatever international functions British forces assumed as part of the MNF, they did not thereby lose their legal character and identity as British soldiers and thus their character as agents and organs

---

[13] *Ilaşcu v Moldova and Russia*, App. No. 48787/99, 8 July 2004 (2004) 40 EHRR 46.

[14] cf. *Al-Jedda* (n. 9), para. 86.

[15] cf. *Al-Skeini v United Kingdom*, App. No. 55721/07, 7 July 2011 (2011) 53 EHRR 18, paras 131–40.

[16] cf. *M. & Co. v Germany*, App. No. 13258/87, 9 February 1990 (1990) 64 Eur. Comm. H.R. Dec. & Rep. 138; *Bosphorus v Ireland*, App. No. 45036/98, 30 June 2005 (2006) 42 EHRR 1, para. 153; *Nada v Switzerland*, App. No. 10593/08, 12 September 2012 (2013) 56 EHRR 18, para. 168.

[17] cf. *Loizidou v Turkey*, Preliminary Objections, App No 15318/89, 23 March 1995 (1995) ECHR 10, para. 62.

[18] Thus in *Bosphorus* (n. 16), the European Court affirmed Ireland's jurisdiction regardless of the fact that the wrongful act in question was adopted by the Irish authorities pursuant to European Community law (paras 135–8).

of the United Kingdom.[19] It follows, therefore, that Al-Jedda did fall within the jurisdiction of the United Kingdom for the purposes of art. 1 of the ECHR and that the United Kingdom was bound to guarantee to him the rights and freedoms recognized by the Convention.[20] Whether or not the United Kingdom failed to comply with this obligation is a separate question which depends, amongst other matters, on whether the conduct of British forces should be attributed to the United Kingdom or not.

In determining whether the applicant's detention was to be attributed to the United Kingdom or to the UN, the ECtHR followed the logic of its earlier reasoning in *Behrami*. In that case, the Court famously attributed the acts of KFOR to the UN on the basis that the Security Council retained ultimate authority and control over the military operation in Kosovo.[21] This reasoning has attracted widespread criticism in the literature, as the Court seemed to confuse the legality of the delegation of Security Council powers under the UN Charter with the attribution of internationally wrongful conduct.[22] Although both questions entail a test of control, the law of international responsibility imposes a test of 'effective control',[23] for the purposes of attributing wrongful conduct, while the delegation of Security Council powers is subject to the more relaxed standard of 'overall authority and control' under the institutional law of the UN.[24]

By confusing these two bodies of law, the ECtHR has manoeuvred itself into something of a tight spot. To comply with the internal law of the UN, the Security Council will at all times retain at least 'ultimate authority and control' over any mandates it issues under Chapter VII of the UN Charter. Consequently, if this test is used as a basis for attribution, it follows that wrongful acts carried out by national contingents participating in Security Council mandated operations, such as the MNF in Iraq, will always have to be attributed to the UN rather than to their respective sending states. Coupled with the reversal of preliminaries in *Al-Jedda*, whereby a finding of attribution has become a precondition for a finding of jurisdiction and therefore the applicability of the Convention, this means that, in principle, the ECHR will never apply to state parties contributing troops to Security Council mandated

---

[19] *Attorney-General v Nissan* [1970] AC 179, at 198 and 222. cf. F. Messineo, '"Gentlement at Home, Hoodlums Elsewhere?" The Extra-territorial Exercise of Power by British Forces in Iraq and the European Convention on Human Rights', (2012) 71 *Cambridge Law Journal* 15, 15–16.

[20] In favour of a broad approach to jurisdiction see M. Andenas and E. Bjorge, 'Human Rights and Acts by Troops Abroad: Rights and Jurisdictional Restrictions', (2012) 18 *European Public Law* 473, at 492.

[21] cf. *Behrami* (n. 2), paras 128–44.

[22] For example K.M. Larsen, 'Attribution of Conduct in Peace Operations: The "Ultimate Authority and Control" Test', (2008) 19 *European Journal of International Law* 509; A. Sari, 'Jurisdiction and International Responsibility in Peace Support Operations: The *Behrami* and *Saramati* Cases', (2008) 8 *Human Rights Law Review* 151; H. Krieger, 'A Credibility Gap: The *Behrami* and *Saramati* Decision of the European Court of Human Rights', (2009) 13 *Journal of International Peacekeeping* 159; M. Milanović and T. Papić, 'As Bad as It Gets: The European Court of Human Rights's *Behrami* and *Saramati* Decision and General International Law', (2009) 58 *International and Comparative Law Quarterly* 267.

[23] cf. *Application of the Convention on the Prevention and Punishment of the Crime of Genocide* (*Bosnia and Herzegovina v Serbia and Montenegro*), [2007] ICJ Rep 15, para. 406.

[24] On the delegation of Chapter VII powers, see D. Sarooshi, *The United Nations and the Development of Collective Security* (Oxford, Oxford University Press 1999).

operations. This outcome is hardly correct as a matter of law or desirable as a matter of policy.[25]

The *Al-Jedda* case presented the ECtHR with an opportunity to address the unhappy implications of its decision in *Behrami*. The Court could have done so on a principled basis and formally overturn *Behrami* in response to its overwhelmingly negative reception. Instead, it decided to follow the House of Lords in distinguishing *Al-Jedda* from *Behrami* on the facts. Although there are obvious differences between KFOR and the MNF, the material facts are identical and point to the conclusion that the Security Council retained overall authority and control over both operations.[26] By overemphasizing the differences and neglecting the similarities between KFOR and the MNF,[27] the Court managed to arrive at the right conclusion: it declared that the acts of British forces participating in the MNF could not be attributed to the UN and that Al-Jedda therefore fell within the United Kingdom's jurisdiction.[28] However, it arrived at this conclusion at the cost of preserving, if not deepening, the conceptual confusion in its case-law.[29] Although *Behrami* therefore remains a valid, albeit unconvincing precedent, it is interesting to note that the Court concluded its analysis in *Al-Jedda* by declaring that the Security Council had 'neither effective control nor ultimate authority and control' over the acts of British forces.[30] The simultaneous reference to the misplaced 'ultimate authority and control' standard and to the correct 'effective control' test is puzzling.[31] At best, it may be understood as an implicit acknowledgement that *Behrami* was wrongly decided.[32] At worst, it may be a sign that the Court continues to view *Behrami* as a good authority.

In any event, the Court's reasoning raises a broader question whether the effective control test is the sole or even the most appropriate principle of attribution during international military operations. The effective control test focuses on factual subordination at the expense of legal and institutional relationships.[33] By adopting this

---

[25] cf. E. Katselli, 'International Peace and Security, Human Rights and the Courts: A Critical Reappraisal', (2011) 16 *International Journal of Human Rights* 257, at 259–60.

[26] See Lord Rodger's powerful dissent on this point in *Al-Jedda* (n. 9), paras 58–105. See also Messineo (n. 9) at 43–7.

[27] For example the Court emphasized that KFOR was created by Security Council Resolution 1244, whereas the MNF was a pre-existing force. Ignoring for the moment the fact that the MNF was established by Resolution 1511, it is difficult to see the significance of this factor. But see M.I. Papa, 'Le autorizzazioni del Consiglio di sicurezza davanti alla Corte europea dei diritti umani: dalla decisione sui casi *Behrami* e *Saramati* alla sentenza Al-Jedda', (2012) 6 *Diritti umani e diritto internazionale* 229, 252–3.

[28] Some commentators have suggested that in declining to attribute Al-Jedda's detention to the UN, the Court accepted the possibility of dual or multiple attribution of wrongful conduct: for example M.C. Lopez, 'Towards Dual or Multiple Attribution: The Strasbourg Court and the Liability of Contracting Parties' Troops Contributed to the United Nations', (2013) 10 *International Organizations Law Review* 193, 214–15; Papa (n. 27), p. 254–5. Whatever the Court did, it did implicitly.

[29] cf. M. Milanović, 'Al-Skeini and Al-Jedda in Strasbourg', (2012) 23 *European Journal of International Law* 121, 136; see also *Serdar Mohammed v Ministry of Defence* [2014] EWHC 1369 (QB), para. 178.

[30] cf. *Al Jedda* (n. 9), para. 86.

[31] cf. V. Zambrano, 'State Responsibility for Human Rights Violations: The Ultimate Control Test and the Interpretation of UN Security Council Resolutions', (2013) *European Human Rights Law Review* 180, at 184.

[32] cf. M. Szydło, 'Extra-Territorial Application of the European Convention on Human Rights after *Al-Skeini* and *Al-Jedda*', (2012) 12 *International Criminal Law Review* 271.

[33] cf. A. Sari, 'UN Peacekeeping Operations and Article 7 ARIO: The Missing Link', (2012) 9 *International Organizations Law Review* 77, 80.

perspective, the Court failed to seriously engage with the Government's argument concerning the legal identity of its forces operating as part of the MNF. Should the fact that national contingents act in an international capacity have any bearing on the attribution of their conduct? There are some indicators in domestic jurisprudence[34] and Convention case-law[35] suggesting that it should. Nor is the effective control test free from difficulties. Different actors involved in a peace-support operation may exercise effective control over different aspects of a national contingent's activities. Attributing wrongful conduct to only one actor may be artificial in the face of multiple levels of control.[36] The Government called attention to this when it pointed out that Al-Jedda's continued detention was decided and authorized jointly by the Government of Iraq and the Commander of the MNF.[37] It is worth noting in this respect that it is unclear whether a relationship of factual dependency must be established with reference to physical factors alone or whether normative factors may also serve as evidence of factual subordination, although practice does not appear to be settled.[38]

While it would be too much to expect the ECtHR to resolve these open questions of the law of international responsibility, one may expect it to demonstrate a more coherent attitude to a subject so pivotal to its judicial mandate. While *Al-Jedda* thus marks an evolution in Court's jurisprudence, its contribution to greater clarity is modest.

---

[34] For example *N. K. v Austria* (1979) 77 ILR 470, 472; *Kunduz Case*, 26 K 5534/10, ILDC 1858 (DE 2012), 9 February 2012, para. 78.

[35] For example *Ilse Hess v United Kingdom* (*Admissibility*), App. No. 6231/73, 28 May 1975, ECommHR (1975) 2 DR 125.

[36] cf. C. Leck, 'International Responsibility in United Nations Peacekeeping Operations: Command and Control Arrangements and the Attribution of Conduct', (2009) 10 *Melbourne Journal of International Law* 346. See also Papa (n. 27), at 255.

[37] *Al-Jedda* (n. 9), para. 67.

[38] cf. *Nuhanović v Netherlands*, LJN:BR5388, 5 July 2011, ILDC 1742 (NL 2011), para. 5.18.

7

Immunity

Immunities are procedural impediments to the exercise of jurisdiction by courts, ordinarily domestic courts. It is a mainstay of international law that states are entitled to immunity under customary international law (see for an attempt at codification: United Nations Convention on Jurisdictional Immunities of States and Their Property (UN Convention Jurisdictional Immunities).[1] This immunity finds its justification in the principle of the sovereign equality of states, according to which no state can sit on judgment of another state, which after all is formally its peer under international law.

Immunities have also been accorded to international organizations. This has happened on the basis of constituent documents rather than customary international law or general principles of law (*League of Arab States*, Ryngaert).[2] The rationale for such immunities also differs: they do not serve to protect international organizations from interference by their peers—other international organizations—but rather by the domestic courts of states, including their member states. Therefore, international organization immunity is essentially geared to protecting the autonomy of the international organization vis-à-vis states.

As immunity is an issue that plays out in domestic courts, there is a wealth of domestic decisions on the issue. Moreover, there is a limited number of international decisions ruling on the immunity determinations made by domestic courts, in particular those of the European Court of Human Rights (ECtHR), but also of the International Court of Justice (ICJ).

Formally speaking, the immunity of international organizations has never been considered as absolute, unlike the immunity of states. Only insofar as international organizations act within the powers conferred on them by the member states, can they rely on immunities.[3] In practice, however, this 'functional' immunity has become quasi-absolute, as international organizations do not normally act *ultra vires*. However, two movements in the case-law have tended to erode this immunity: the importation of restrictive immunity from the law of state immunity, and the application of human rights, the right of access to a court in particular. Obviously, international organizations could also decide to waive their immunity.

The first movement can mainly be associated with US courts, v of which have ruled that there is a commercial exception to the immunity of international organizations

---

[1] Adopted 2 December 2004, opened for signature 17 January 2005 until 17 January 2007, UN Doc. A/RES/59/38.

[2] But see Supreme Court 20 December 1985, *LJN* AC9158 (*AS v Iran-United States Claims Tribunal*) (conferring immunities on the Iran-US Claims Tribunal, considered as an international organization, on the basis of customary international law).

[3] See, for example, art. 105(1) Charter of the United Nations (adopted 26 June 1945, entered into force 24 October 1945) 1 UNTS XVI (UN Charter): 'The Organization shall enjoy in the territory of each of its Members such privileges and immunities as are necessary for the fulfilment of its purposes.'

similar to the exception to state immunity featuring in the US Foreign Sovereign Immunities Act (*Nokalva*, Boon). Not all US courts have been taking this path, however, and have affirmed the international organizations' quasi-absolute immunity (see, e.g. *Askir*, Ruys).[4]

The second movement, inspired by procedural human rights, can be associated with Europe, but again, its application is not uniform. As early as the 1960s, claimants began to advance the argument that international organizations should offer them a right to a remedy, in the absence of which they should be allowed to sue the international organization in domestic courts. This argument was initially dismissed and the quasi-absolute immunity of international organizations was confirmed; it was even recognized that international organizations such as the UN did not offer proper remedies via internal mechanisms (*Manderlier*, Schmitt). In 1999, however, in *Waite and Kennedy* and *Beer and Regan* (note Neumann and Peters), the ECtHR ruled, regarding an employment case brought against the European Space Agency (ESA) before German courts, that 'a material factor in determining whether granting ESA immunity from German jurisdiction is permissible under the Convention is whether the applicants had available to them reasonable alternative means to protect effectively their rights under the Convention.'[5] After these decisions, it remained unclear, however, whether contracting states to the European Convention on Human Rights (ECHR) were *required* to dismiss an international organization immunity claim in case the relevant international organization did not make reasonable alternative means available to guarantee a claimant's right to a remedy. Some Belgian courts have turned out to be the strictest, by going as far as to reject an international organizations' immunity in case its dispute-settlement mechanism did not meet the quality guarantees required by art. 6 ECHR, which enshrines the right to a remedy (*Siedler*, Schmitt). In this approach, the mere existence of a dispute-settlement mechanism does not suffice for an international organization to plead its immunity before domestic courts. Most courts have not interpreted the *Waite and Kennedy* principle too strictly, however. This deferential approach to the international organization may well be in keeping with what the ECtHR meant, as also borne out by its follow-up judgment in *Chapman v Belgium* (2013) ECHR 2013, whereby the NATO Appeals Board appeared to satisfy itself with a level of internal protection that is equivalent rather than identical to the protection offered by art. 6 ECHR. Some courts have even taken the view that art. 6 ECHR does not apply where international law limits the scope of jurisdiction of a domestic court (*Entico*, Wickremasinghe), although such a view is in tension with the *Waite and Kennedy* principle. Still, the ECtHR itself has held that *Waite and Kennedy* does *not* apply in procedures against the UN in respect of peace operations. According to the Court, given the UN's special status as a collective security organization, its quasi-absolute functional immunity cannot be abrogated by human rights considerations (*Mothers of Srebrenica*, Momirov).

---

[4] In *Askir*, the Court found it unnecessary to decide whether the restrictive immunity doctrine applied; it eventually applied the functional immunity doctrine and granted immunity to the UN. *Askir v Boutros-Ghali*, 933 F. Supp. 368 (S.D.N.Y 1996).

[5] cf. *Waite and Kennedy v Germany* (1999) ECHR 1999–I 393, para. 68.

Aside from case-law on the immunities of international organizations as such, there is some case-law on immunities of international organization officials. In principle, international organization officials, like state agents, enjoy immunity *ratione materiae* for acts performed in an official capacity, as deciding otherwise would allow courts to circumvent the immunity of the organization. Some higher-ranking international organization officials also enjoy immunity *ratione personae* during their term of office, for acts performed in both an official and a private capacity, just like diplomats or some high-ranking state officials.[6]

It may not always be clear whether an international organizations' official acts in an official or a private capacity. A thorny question in this respect is whether the domestic court hearing the case against the official, or rather the international organization can make this determination. The leading ICJ case on the issue is the Advisory Opinion in *Cumaraswamy* (officially known as *Difference relating to Immunity from Legal Process of a Special Rapporteur of the Commission on Human Rights*, Wickremasinghe). In this opinion, the Court did justice to the demands of both the UN and the member state hearing the case, by entitling the UN's view on the immunity of its officials to 'a presumption, which can only be set aside by a national court for the most compelling reasons and is thus to be given the greatest weight by the national courts'.[7] *Cumaraswamy* also constituted the first 'binding advisory opinion' of the Court in the sense of art. VIII Section 30 of the 1946 UN Convention on Privileges and Immunities, which stipulates that an advisory opinion given by the Court on a difference arising out of the interpretation or application of the Convention will be accepted as binding by the parties.

A final issue that is worth mentioning in an immunity context concerns the availability of service of process regarding international organizations. Domestic legal systems often require that the defendant is provided with actual notice of a suit. This process is not self-evident when it comes to serving international organizations: in many states consent of the international organizations' Head is required. Where consent is not secured, the international organization is formally not put on notice, and cannot appear in court (*Prewitt*, Boon). In such cases, the immunity question will not even be addressed by the court.

---

[6] See the Convention on the Privileges and Immunities of the United Nations (adopted 13 February 1946) 90 UNTS 327, art. V. and art. 105(2) UN Charter.

[7] cf. *Difference Relating to Immunity from Legal Process of a Special Rapporteur of the Commission on Human Rights*, Advisory Opinion, [1999] ICJ Rep 62, para. 61.

7.1 *Manderlier v Organisation des Nations Unies and Etat Belge* (*Ministre des Affaires Etrangères*), Tribunal Civil de Bruxelles, 11 May 1966, Journal des Tribunaux, 10 December 1966, No. 4553, 121

Pierre Schmitt

Relevance of the case

This 1966 case, brought by a Belgian citizen—Mr Manderlier—against the UN and the Belgian State before the Brussels Civil Tribunal (the Tribunal) is particularly interesting because it is one of the first cases in which UN immunity from jurisdiction was challenged. Most of the legal questions raised by the plaintiff in relation to the scope of the UN's immunity are still debated nowadays before domestic jurisdictions. Among these questions, the Tribunal examined whether the UN's immunity was conditional upon the latter's respect of art. VIII, Section 29 of the Convention on Privileges and Immunities of the United Nations (CPIUN). Moreover, the Tribunal assessed whether the immunity could be rejected in favour of a human rights argument based on the right of access to justice and whether it could only be invoked in relation to actions or situations that were necessary for the UN to achieve its goals. Finally, it evaluated whether the UN had waived its immunity in this particular case. Secondly the Tribunal also discussed whether the UN had legal personality under domestic law necessary to appear before it.

I. Facts of the case

On 5 December 1961, Mr Manderlier, a Belgian citizen settled in the Congo, saw his flat extensively damaged in the course of fighting involving UN troops situated there. He lodged a first claim on 15 February 1962 against the UN for compensation of the damage that he estimated at 336,710 Belgian francs (i.e. more than 8,000 euros). In December 1962, his property was looted and burnt by UN troops and he was victim of acts of violence committed upon his person. He lodged a second claim for compensation for the loss on 10 January 1963 against the UN through the Belgian Minister for Foreign Affairs and External Trade for the compensation of a damage that he estimated at 3,799,675 Belgian francs (i.e. almost 100,000 euros).

Mr Manderlier's situation was not unique. Many Belgians settled in the Congo launched similar claims for compensation of damages to persons and properties that they considered as attributable to the UN. They turned towards their state—Belgium—to exercise diplomatic protection. Most of these claims—in total, there were 1,298 files brought against the UN—were centralised by the Belgian Ministry for Foreign Affairs and transmitted to the UN seat in New York.[1]

---

[1] cf. Belgian House of Representatives, *Documents parlementaires*, session 1964–65, 1009, no. 2, Annex 3. For further information, see J. Salmon, 'De quelques problèmes poses aux tribunaux belges par les actions de citoyens belges contre l'O.N.U. en raison de faits survenus sur le territoire de la République démocratique du Congo', *Journal des Tribunaux* (1966), p. 713.

The UN disputed the facts but after intercessions by the Belgian Government it declared itself prepared to 'accept financial liability where the damage is the result of action taken by agents of the United Nations in violation of the laws of war and the rules of international law'.[2] After selecting those cases in which individuals had been victims of internationally wrongful acts by the UN, the UN considered that approximately 580 claims were entitled to compensation. The UN Secretary-General agreed that, 'without prejudice to the privileges and immunities which the United Nations enjoys, he will pay the Belgian Government the sum of one million five hundred thousand United States dollars ($1,500,000) in an outright and final settlement of all claims'[3] filed against the UN by Belgians for damage to persons and property caused by the UN Force in the Congo. This agreement was incorporated in an exchange of letters of 20 February 1965 between the Belgian Minister for Foreign Affairs and the UN Secretary-General[4] and enacted in a Belgian Law of 7 May 1965.[5]

A list was drawn up by the UN of individual claims for which the UN accepted liability. The Belgian Government divided this lump sum and informed the victims of their right to receive part of the UN settlement payment. Acceptance of this sum would not prevent them from receiving any further compensation from the Belgian State but would waive any further rights of action against the UN. The Government proposed an amount of 140,000 Belgian francs (i.e. approximately 35,000 euros) out of the financial contribution by the UN. In addition, the Government declared that the material damage of Mr Manderlier could lead to a complementary contribution by the Belgian State. Yet, Mr Manderlier considered the amount too low and brought an action before the Belgian courts against both the UN and the Belgian State, claiming a total sum of 6,119,350 Belgian francs (i.e. approximately 150,000 euros). The UN pleaded its immunity from the jurisdiction of the Belgian Tribunal.

II. The legal question

The arguments raised by the plaintiff engendered several legal questions to be assessed by the Tribunal. A preliminary issue examined by the Tribunal focused on the legal personality of the UN to appear before the Brussels Civil Tribunal. The other legal

---

[2] cf. *Manderlier v Organisation des Nations Unies et l'État Belge* (*Ministre des Affaires Etrangères*), Brussels Civil Tribunal, 11 May 1966, (1972) 45 ILR 446–55, 465.

[3] cf. *Manderlier* case (n. 2), p. 465.

[4] Exchange of letters constituting an Agreement between the United Nations and Belgium relating to the settlement of claims filed against the United Nations in the Congo by Belgian nationals: New York, 20 February 1965, *United Nations Juridical Yearbook* (1965) p. 39; 1 *Revue belge de droit international* (1965) p. 558.

[5] Loi du 7 Mai 1965 portant approbation des actes internationaux suivants: 1° Accord entre le Royaume de Belgique et l'Organisation des Nations-Unies, relatif au règlement des comptes nés de l'administration par les Nations-Unies des anciennes bases militaires belges au Congo; 2° Accord entre le Royaume de Belgique et l'Organisation des Nations-Unies relatif au règlement du problème des réclamations introduites auprès de l'Organisation des Nations-Unies par des ressortissants belges, ayant subi des dommages au Congo, conclus par échanges de lettres, datées à New York, le 20 février 1965, *Moniteur Belge*, 29 July 1965, 9069.

questions analyzed mainly concerned the nature and the scope of the UN immunity from jurisdiction:

1) Is the UN's immunity from jurisdiction absolute or functional?

2) Is the UN's immunity conditional upon the respect by the latter of art. VIII, Section 29 of the CPIUN?

3) Is the UN's immunity conditional upon the respect by the latter of the United Nations Declaration for Human Rights of 10 December 1948 and the European Convention on Human Rights?

4) Did the UN waive its immunity from jurisdiction in this case?

In addition, the plaintiff put the question of the extent of the diplomatic protection exercised by the state to the Tribunal.

III. Excerpts

The United Nations was set up by the San Francisco Charter of 26 January 1945, approved in Belgium by the Law of 14 December 1945. By Article 104 of the Charter the Organization enjoys in the territory of each of its Members such legal capacity as may be necessary to it. The defendant is consequently competent to appear in legal proceedings in Belgium. Nevertheless, by Article 105 of the Charter the Organization enjoys in the territory of each of its members such privileges and immunities as are necessary for the fulfilment of its purposes.

The defendant, while competent to appear in legal proceedings in Belgium, rejects the jurisdiction of this Court, invoking the immunity from jurisdiction accorded to it by Section 2 (Article II) of the Convention on the Privileges and Immunities of the United Nations, approved by the General Assembly on 13 February 1946. In effect, under these provisions the U.N. enjoys immunity from jurisdiction, except in so far as it has expressly waived it in a particular case. This provision is both general and absolute. It follows necessarily that the Organization is an independent entity which places itself above the nations, acting according to its own free will, without being subject to any national, judicial, or other authority. […]

Section 29 of the Convention lays down that the Organization is to provide for appropriate methods of settlement for disputes of a private law character to which it may be a party. It would normally follow that the defendant was bound to draw up regulations to govern its relations in private law and set up courts to decide disputes arising from the latter.

It is true that the U.N. has set up certain courts of special jurisdiction, such as the Administrative Tribunal of the United Nations. However, it is an undisputed fact that it has not set up any court with a general or unlimited jurisdiction. In fact, no independent and impartial court has been set up, before which the plaintiff could bring the defendant to have the claim decided which he has brought before the present Court.

The General Assembly of the United Nations, it is true, adopted the Universal Declaration of Human Rights on 10 December 1948, (published in the *Moniteur belge* of 31 March 1949). In Article 10 this Declaration lays down the principle that everyone is entitled to a public hearing by an independent and impartial tribunal in the determination of his rights and obligations or of any criminal charge against him. In spite of this provision of the Declaration which the U.N. proclaimed on 10 December 1948, the Organization has neglected to set up the courts which it was in fact already bound to create by Section 29 of the Convention [on Privileges and Immunities] of 13 February 1946.

However, the Universal Declaration does not have the force of law. Its sole aim is to express the common ideal to be attained by all peoples and all nations, in order that by instruction and education respect for these rights and freedoms may be developed and that measures may be taken progressively to ensure that they are recognized and universally and effectively applied in the future. The principles of the Universal Declaration are already contained in general in the Belgian Constitution of 7 February 1831. The Declaration, which is merely a collection of recommendations, without binding force, has not been submitted for approval to the Belgian legislature.

The plaintiff invokes in vain Article 10 of the Universal Declaration in order to claim that in the absence, within the framework of the U.N., of an international court qualified to hear him and to judge his claim, he must be entitled to bring the defendant before a national court qualified to do so. From this the plaintiff makes bold to argue that Article 10 made the immunity from jurisdiction decreed by Section 2 of the Convention of 13 February 1946 conditional.

That immunity is unconditional, and has been so since the conclusion of the Convention in 1946. It was not abrogated, either conditionally or finally, by the Declaration of 1948. It is true that the European Convention for the Protection of Human Rights and Fundamental Freedoms, concluded at Rome on 4 November 1950, contains in Article 6 a provision more or less similar to that of Article 10 of the Universal Declaration. The Law of 13 May 1965 approved the Rome Convention and decided that it should have full and complete effect; the Convention has thus been incorporated into Belgian Law. However, that Convention was concluded between fourteen European States only, and cannot be applied to and imposed upon the United Nations. Section 2 of the Convention [on Privileges and Immunities] of 13 February 1946 is binding and has full force, even though no court has been set up in pursuance of Section 29.

The defendant considers quite wrongly that the previously mentioned Agreement, reached between the U.N. and Belgium on 20 February 1965, constitutes the appropriate method of settlement provided for by Section 29. The defendant had the claims addressed to it, and in particular those of the plaintiff, examined by its own authorities, without argument of any kind. It then took a unilateral decision by which, according to its letter of 20 February 1965, it believed itself bound to limit its spontaneous intervention. The defendant has thus in reality been judge in its own case. Such a procedure in no sense constitutes an appropriate method of settlement for deciding a dispute.

Be that as it may, it is for the United Nations, and for it alone, to set up the courts which would produce an appropriate method of settlement for the disputes which it may have with third parties. Immunity from jurisdiction has been conferred upon it, however inconvenient may be its results for litigants.

In the Senate, on 8 April 1965, the Minister for Foreign Affairs declared that the U.N. had waived its immunity from jurisdiction. But the Minister for Foreign Affairs cannot bind the United Nations, nor its Secretary-General, through declarations he makes in the Belgian Legislative Chamber. His view of the situation cannot bind the judge in his interpretation of international law. The plaintiff has not produced proof that the defendant has expressly waived its right to invoke immunity from jurisdiction in this particular case in which they are opposed.

Article 105 of the San Francisco Charter of 26 June 1945 accords the United Nations only those privileges and immunities that are necessary to it for the fulfilment of its purposes. Those purposes, as enumerated in Article I of the Charter, do not include acts against private citizens such as are the subject of the plaintiff's complaints. The provisions of Section 2 of the Convention [on Privileges and Immunities] of 13 February 1946 are wider than those of Article 105 of the Charter. They grant a general immunity from jurisdiction and do not limit it to what necessity strictly demands for the fulfilment of the defendant's purposes. These two international conventions have equal force, and the less widely drawn one of 26 June 1945 cannot restrict the field of application of the more widely drawn one of 13 February 1946.

The United Nations Organization is not a sovereign power. It has neither territory nor population. It follows that it cannot invoke rights of sovereignty different from the similar, but partial, rights which the Conventions have expressly and with limited effect given to it. Immunity from jurisdiction is the absolute privilege of whoever enjoys it. It can be withdrawn only by a properly effected change in the law which granted it; and the courts are not judges of when it is expedient for the beneficiary to invoke it. [...]

The plaintiff in addition levels charges against the Belgian State apart from the actual acts committed in the Congo. He accuses it in particular of not having properly defended his interests. [...]

In fact, to protect its nationals and their property, the second defendant negotiated with the first defendant in a way that was partially successful, and arrived at the Agreement of 20 February 1965, approved by the Law of 7 May 1965. That Agreement and the Law approving it are an act of the legislature, which neither the executive nor the judiciary can sanction, modify or squash. It cannot avail the plaintiff to attack the executive on account of the acts of the legislature. [...]

It is equally unavailing for the plaintiff to attack the defendant for not having brought the case before the International Court of Justice. The procedure provided for by Section 30 of the aforementioned Convention of 13 February 1946 is not intended to cover actions brought by private individuals; it concerns only disputes which have arisen between the United Nations and one of its Member States. The plaintiff has no personal right to compel the second defendant to embark upon proceedings in international law against the first defendant. No agreement of any kind was concluded between the plaintiff and the second defendant, and the latter did not undertake any express obligation towards the plaintiff with a view to obtaining on his behalf full compensation for his loss. [...]

It is open to the plaintiff not to accept the benefit of the international Agreement of 20 February 1965 and the Law of 7 May 1965 and to act directly against the U.N.; but in the absence of any appropriate court set up in pursuance of Section 29 of the Convention of 13 February 1956,[6] then, as the Minister of Foreign Affairs has most

---

[6] Sic. Although the date of 13 February 1956 is mentioned in the English translation of the decision provided in *Manderlier v Organisation des Nations Unies et l'État Belge (Ministre des Affaires Etrangères)*, Brussels Civil Tribunal, 11 May 1966, (1972) 45 ILR 446–55, the correct date of the Convention is 13 February 1946. This footnote has been added and does not appear in the original version of the decision.

judiciously pointed out, one cannot see where the U.N. could be sued, nor how, nor on what legal basis (*Annales parlementaires, Chambre*, 6 April 1965, p. 4), so long as it shelters behind its immunity from jurisdiction.

For these reasons the Court:

Declares that the plaintiff's claim is inadmissible before the present court in so far as it is brought against the first defendant, the United Nations Organization, which invokes the immunity from jurisdiction acknowledged by Belgium and by the Convention on the Privileges and Immunities of the United Nations of 13 February 1946, approved by the Law of 28 February 1948;

Declares that the plaintiff's claim against the second defendant, the Belgian State, is admissible but that the claim fails;

Accordingly dismisses the plaintiff's claim;

Orders him to pay the costs of the action.[7]

IV. Commentary

This is one of the first cases in which a national court was confronted with the argument of UN immunity from jurisdiction in a dispute relating to peacekeeping operations.[8] The decision of the Tribunal as to the absolute character of UN immunity is still valid nowadays, as is its cautious approach in accepting waivers of such immunity and verifying whether these are expressly made by the competent organ, that is in the case of the UN, the Secretary-General.

Among the legal questions analyzed by the Tribunal, the first one concerned the legal personality of the UN. The Tribunal noted that the UN was set up by the UN Charter, as approved by Belgian law.[9] Given that art. 104 of the UN Charter granted such legal capacity as may be necessary for the UN in the territory of each of its members, the defendant was competent to appear in legal proceedings in Belgium. The question of UN legal personality has similarly been discussed in other cases before national jurisdictions in the 1950s. In another Belgian case of 1952, *United Nations v B,* the UN brought an action against a former employee to recover undue money paid to the dissolved UN Relief and Rehabilitation Administration (UNRRA). The employee counter-argued that both UNRRA and the UN did not have legal personality. However, the Civil Tribunal of Brussels dismissed this argument on the basis that both the Washington Agreement setting up UNRRA and the UN Charter were 'ratified' (sic) by Belgian Laws—respectively of 3 August 1944 and of 14 December 1945.[10] In 1954, the Canadian Superior Court of Montreal analyzed the UN's legal personality in *United Nations v Canada Asiatic*

---

[7] *Manderlier v Organisation des Nations Unies et l'État Belge (Ministre des Affaires Etrangères),* Brussels Civil Tribunal, 11 May 1966, (1972) 45 ILR 446–55. The French version of the decision is available at *Pasicrisie Belge*, 1966, II, 103 and *Journal des Tribunaux* (1966) p. 721.

[8] See J. Salmon (n. 1), at 713.

[9] cf. Loi du 14 Décembre 1945 approuvant la Charte des Nations Unies et le Statut de la Cour Internationale de Justice, signée à San Francisco le 26 Juin 1945, *Moniteur Belge*, 1 January 1946, 1.

[10] See also *UNRRA v Daan,* Cantonal Court Amersfoort, 16 June 1948, District Court Utrecht, 23 February 1949, Supreme Court (Hoge Raad) of The Netherlands, 19 May 1950, (1951) NJ 150; (1955) 82 *Journal de droit international* (Clunet) 855–87; (1949) 16 ILR 337–8.

Lines Limited.[11] It decided that the UN possessed legal personality and had the right to institute legal proceedings. Nowadays, the legal personality of the UN is generally accepted by national jurisdictions. As noted by August Reinisch, '[a]lthough they usually stop short of de-recognizing or failing to recognize the legal personality of international organizations, [the courts'] reasoning clearly demonstrates the essential importance of the personality of an international organization in order to enable a domestic court to adjudicate the underlying dispute'.[12]

One of the core legal questions examined in the *Manderlier* case concerned the scope of the immunity from jurisdiction of the UN and the distinction between functional and absolute immunity. It is recalled that the immunity of the UN and its personnel is governed by two main sources: art. 105 of the UN Charter and the CPIUN. The former provides that the UN and its officials shall enjoy in the territory of its member states such privileges and immunities as necessary for the fulfilment of its purposes. The 'necessity' standard expresses the UN's functional immunity, as affirmed by the International Court of Justice in *Reparation for Injuries Suffered in the Service of the United Nations*.[13] Furthermore, the CPIUN, and more specifically its art. II, Section 2, provides that '[t]he United Nations, its property and assets wherever located and by whomsoever held, shall enjoy immunity from every form of legal process except insofar as in any particular case it has expressly waived its immunity. It is, however, understood that no waiver of immunity shall extend to any measure of execution.' The Tribunal recalled that according to art. 105 of the UN Charter, the UN only enjoys privileges and immunities which are necessary for the fulfilment of its purposes enumerated in art. 1 of the Charter. This does not comprise acts against private citizens. The Tribunal's statement could be taken as a hint that it would not have granted immunity if it had applied functional immunity, given that it qualified the disputed acts of the UN as outside of its functions.[14] However, the Tribunal added that the provisions of Section 2 of the CPIUN 'grant a general immunity from jurisdiction and do not limit it to what necessity strictly demands for the fulfilment of the defendant's purposes'.

Furthermore, the plaintiff argued that art. II, Section 2 and art. VIII, Section 29 of the CPIUN were closely linked in the way that the UN's immunity from jurisdiction should be conditional upon the availability of an appropriate method of settlement for disputes of a private law character. Given that no appropriate method of settlement had been established, the plaintiff argued that the Tribunal could not grant immunity to the UN. The Civil Tribunal of Brussels rejected the argument raised by the plaintiff and affirmed the general and absolute character of the immunity granted by art. II, Section 2 of the CPIUN, except for an express waiver by the UN itself. The Tribunal noted that '[i]mmunity from jurisdiction is the absolute privilege of whoever enjoys it'.

[11] Superior Court Montreal, 2 December 1952, *Rapports de Pratique du Québec* (1954) 158–60; (1954) 48 AJIL 668; (1958 II) 26 ILR 622.

[12] cf. A. Reinisch, *International Organizations Before National Courts* (Cambridge, Cambridge University Press 2000), p. 39.

[13] ICJ, 11 April 1949, Advisory Opinion, [1949] ICJ Rep 174.

[14] cf. A. Reinisch (n. 12), p. 346.

It is remarkable that the Tribunal did not examine the question whether the UN is bound by the CPIUN and bears an obligation to set up appropriate methods of settlement for disputes of a private law character prior to analyzing the question whether the UN's immunity is conditional upon the availability of an appropriate method of settlement for disputes of a private law character. The UN is not a party to the CPIUN, which has been ratified so far by 160 states. Hence, it has no direct obligations stemming from the convention. Nonetheless, in its Advisory Opinion in *Difference Relating to Immunity from Legal Process of a Special Rapporteur of the Commission on Human Rights,* the ICJ noted that claims against the UN 'shall not be dealt with by national courts but shall be settled in accordance with the appropriate modes of settlement that "[t]he United Nations shall make provisions for" pursuant to Section 29'.[15] Thus, the ICJ recognized the obligation of the UN under Section 29 of the CPIUN to establish appropriate methods of settlement for disputes of a private law character, which was implicitly taken for granted in the *Manderlier* case by the Civil Tribunal of Brussels.

While considering that the UN's immunity was absolute, the Tribunal seemed uncomfortable with its decision and recognized that 'it is an undisputed fact that it has not set up any court with a general and unlimited jurisdiction. In fact, no independent and impartial international court has been set up, before which the plaintiff could bring the defendant to have the claim decided which he has brought before the present Court.' This observation of a deficiency led the Tribunal to analyze the following legal argument raised by the plaintiff, namely a violation of art. 10 of the Universal Declaration of Human Rights and art. 6 of the ECHR, which both consecrate the right of access to justice, that is the right to a public hearing by an independent and impartial tribunal in the determination of his rights and obligations. The Tribunal considered that these provisions were not binding on the UN since the Universal Declaration was merely a 'collection of recommendations' and the European Convention on Human Rights 'was concluded between fourteen European states only, and cannot be applied to and imposed upon the United Nations'. Such argumentation—as to the legal status of the right of access to justice—would probably be more questionable nowadays.[16] Indeed, most legal systems include the right of access to independent dispute-settlement mechanisms providing fair hearings to plaintiffs[17] and numerous observers assert that the right of access to justice could be considered as customary law.[18] Dinah Shelton, for whom the right of access to

---

[15] *Difference Relating to Immunity from Legal Process of a Special Rapporteur of the Commission on Human Rights,* Advisory Opinion, [1999] ICJ Rep 62, para. 66. See also A. Reinisch, 'The Immunity of International Organizations and the Jurisdiction of their Administrative Tribunals', (2002) 7(2) *Chinese Journal of International Law* 285–306, 289.

[16] cf. A. Reinisch and U.A. Weber, 'In the Shadow of *Waite and Kennedy*: The Jurisdictional Immunity of International Organizations, the Individual's Right of Access to the Courts and Administrative Tribunals as Alternative Means of Dispute Settlement', (2004) 1 *International Organizations Law Review* 59, 77.

[17] cf. D. Shelton, *Remedies in International Human Rights Law* (2nd edn, Oxford University Press 2005), p. 8.

[18] In relation to art. 14 of the ICCPR, art. 6 of the ECHR, art. 8 of the ACHR, and arts 7 and 26 of the African Charter, L. Doswald-Beck states '[t]hese texts are very similar and, even more significantly, so is the jurisprudence of the treaties' supervisory bodies. Therefore, we can speak of principles of

justice constitutes the procedural aspect of the right to an effective remedy, stated that '[i]t is clear that the obligation to provide effective remedies is an essential component of international human rights law'.[19]

Another important legal question discussed in the *Manderlier* case concerned the waiver of immunity by the UN. The plaintiff contended that the Belgian Minister for Foreign Affairs declared on 8 April 1965 in the Senate that the UN had waived its immunity from jurisdiction. Consequently, the plaintiff argued that this waiver permitted the Brussels Civil Tribunal to decide on the case. The Tribunal however found that the Minister 'cannot bind the United Nations, nor its Secretary-General, through declarations he makes in the Belgian Legislative Chamber ... His view of the situation cannot bind the judge in his interpretation of international law'. This view is in conformity with both art. II, Section 2 and art. V, Section 20 of the CPIUN which respectively require all waivers to be express and grant the discretion to waive the immunity to the Secretary-General. This case illustrates the prudence of national jurisdictions in accepting waivers of immunity by international organizations and verifying whether these are expressly made by the competent organ. Another example of such a cautious approach may be found in the *Mendaro v World Bank* case, where the US Court of Appeals for the DC Circuit held in 1983 that '[t]his policy underlying the immunity of an international organization also suggests that the court should be slow to find an "express" waiver ... Courts should be reluctant to find that an international organization has inadvertently waived immunity when the organization might be subjected to a class of suits which would interfere with its functions'.[20]

This case is also interesting because it refers to a specific practice for settlement of claims by the UN, namely the compensation of victims for the damages caused during UN operations through the payment of a lump sum. The UN considered that approximately 580 claims were entitled to compensation and a lump-sum agreement of 1,500,000 US dollars was agreed. The Belgian Government distributed the sum among the claimants. The choice of a lump sum as a mode of settlement seems to have been based on political considerations in 1965. Indeed, a majority of states within the General Assembly would not have accepted compensation of Belgian citizens, as they were considered by many as principally responsible for the situation in Congo. Consequently, the agreement reached between the Secretary-General and Belgium— based on the international responsibility of the UN—appeared to be a pragmatic[21] though not ideal solution. It does not guarantee an effective right of access to justice to

---

customary law'. L. Doswald-Beck, 'ILO: The Right to a Fair Hearing Interpretation of International Law', in L. Doswald-Beck and R. Kolb, *Judicial Process and Human Rights: United Nations, European, American and African Systems: Text and Summaries of International Case-Law* (2004), pp. 119 ff. Theodor Meron noted that the 'right to be tried by a competent independent and impartial tribunal established by law as customary law'. T. Meron, *Human Rights and Humanitarian Norms as Customary Law* (Oxford, Clarendon Press 1989), pp. 96–7.

[19] cf. D. Shelton (n. 17), p. 8.

[20] cf. *Mendaro v World Bank*, US Court of Appeals, 27 September 1983, DC Cir, 717 F2d 610 (DC Cir 1983).

[21] Case note by J. Salmon, 'De quelques problèmes poses aux tribunaux belges par les actions de citoyens belges contre l'O.N.U. en raison de faits survenus sur le territoire de la République démocratique du Congo' *Journal des Tribunaux* (1966), p. 713.

individuals. 'Claimants are therefore likely to prefer remedies which they are entitled to pursue in their own name, whether under an individual complaints mechanism or at the international level or through civil litigation.'[22]

Mr Manderlier appealed the decision, which was confirmed by the Court of Appeal of Brussels on 15 September 1969.[23] Notwithstanding its decision, the Court of Appeal recognized that 'in the present state of international institutions there is no court to which the appellant can submit his dispute with the United Nations', which 'does not seem to be in keeping with the principles proclaimed in the Universal Declaration on Human Rights'.

Given that the *Manderlier* case dates from 1966, one may wonder whether it is still relevant today. Indeed, recent cases—notably rendered by Belgian jurisdictions— have engendered a new perspective in favour of the right of access to courts[24] inspired by the ECtHRs' *Waite and Kennedy* jurisprudence, in which the Court considered it a 'material factor' in determining whether granting an international organization immunity from domestic jurisdiction was permissible under the Convention, 'whether the applicants had available to them reasonable alternative means to protect effectively their rights under the Convention'.[25] Nevertheless, this evolution of jurisprudence has mainly occurred in cases concerning staff-related disputes. Moreover, a review of national cases involving the UN demonstrates that its immunity is still considered unconditional and absolute, except for an express waiver.[26] This has notably been confirmed by the Dutch Supreme Court on 13 April 2012 in a case brought by a group called the 'Mothers of Srebrenica' against the UN before Dutch jurisdictions to hold the UN responsible for its failure to prevent the massacre in the Bosnian town of Srebrenica and to obtain financial compensation.[27] The lawyers brought the case before the ECtHRs, arguing the violation

---

[22] M.C. Zwanenburg, *Accountability under International Humanitarian Law for United Nations and North Atlantic Treaty Organization Peace Support Operations* (Leiden, Martinus Nijhoff Publishers 2004) p. 273; C. Wickremasinghe and G. Verdirame, 'Responsibility and Liability for Violations of Human Rights in the Course of UN Field Operations', in C. Scott (ed.), *Torture as Tort: Comparative Perspectives on the Development of Transnational Human Rights Litigation* (Oxford, Hart 2001), pp. 465–90, p. 465.

[23] *Manderlier v Organisation des Nations Unies et l'État Belge* (*Ministre des Affaires Etrangères*), Court of Appeal of Brussels, 15 September 1969, (1969) 69 ILR 139; case note by P. De Visscher, 'De l'immunité de juridiction de l'Organisation des Nations Unies et du caractère discrétionnaire de la compétence de protection diplomatique', (1971) 25 *Revue critique de jurisprudence belge* 456, 460.

[24] *Western European Union v Siedler*, Belgian Court of Cassation, 21 December 2009, Cass. No. S.04.0129.F, ILDC 1625 BE 2009; see also *General Secretariat of the ACP Group v Lutchmaya*, Belgian Court of Cassation, Cass. Nr. C.03.0328.F, ILDC 1573 BE 2009. Judgments of the Court of Cassation and selected decisions of other Belgian courts are available at http://www.belgiumlex.be/. See also J. Wouters, C. Ryngaert, and P. Schmitt, 'Case-Note to Belgian Court of Cassation, *Western European Union v. Siedler; General Secretariat of the ACP Group v. Lutchmaya; General Secretariat of the ACP Group v. B.D.*', (2011) 105 *American Journal of International Law* 560.

[25] *Waite and Kennedy v Germany*, European Court of Human Rights, 18 February 1999, App. No. 26083/94, para. 68; *Beer and Regan v Germany*, European Court of Human Rights, 18 February 1999, App. No. 28934/95, para. 59. See ch. 7.2 in this book.

[26] J. Wouters and P. Schmitt, 'Challenging Acts of Other United Nations' Organs, Subsidiary Organs and Officials', in A. Reinisch (ed.), *Challenging Acts of International Organizations before National Courts* (Oxford, Oxford University Press 2010) pp. 77–110.

[27] *The Association of Citizens Mothers of Srebrenica v The Netherlands and the UN* (*Appeal*), Dutch Supreme Court, 10/04437, 12 April 2012. See also *The Association of Citizens Mothers of Srebrenica v*

of the right of access to justice and the right to a remedy. A decision of inadmissibility was rendered unanimously on 11 June 2013 against the Mothers of Srebrenica on
the basis of UN's immunity.[28] The Court decided that the granting of immunity to
the UN served a legitimate purpose and it could not bring military operations under
Chapter VII of the UN Charter within the scope of national jurisdictions because
this would allow states, through their Courts, 'to interfere with the key mission of
the UN [to secure international peace and security], including with the effective conduct of its operations'. Furthermore, the Court explained that a civil claim did not
override immunity for the reason that it was alleging a particularly grave violation
of international law, even a norm of *jus cogens*. The particular mission of the UN
and the nature of applicants' claims justified the differentiation of this case from the
Waite and Kennedy jurisprudence. Hence, the view of the Brussels Civil Tribunal in
the 1966 *Manderlier* case qualifying the UN's immunity as absolute seems to be still
valid nowadays.

The Netherlands and the UN (Appeal), Court of Appeal in The Hague, 200.022.151/01, 30 March 2010;
The Association of Citizens Mothers of Srebrenica v The Netherlands and the UN (Incidental Proceedings),
District Court in The Hague, 295247/HA ZA 07-2973, 10 July 2008.

[28] *Stichting Mothers of Srebrenica and Others against The Netherlands*, European Court of Human
Rights, 11 June 2013, App. No. 65542/12. See ch. 7.10.

7.2 *Abdi Hosh Askir v Boutros Boutros-Ghali, Joseph E. Connor et al.*, US District Court SDNY, 29 July 1996, 933 F. Suppl. 368 (SDNY 1996)

Tom Ruys

Relevance of the case

The present case affirms the immunity from legal process of the UN and UN personnel acting in their official capacity in procedures before national courts (regardless of allegations of malfeasance). Although the Court refrains from explicitly pronouncing on the consequences of possible discrepancies between immunities granted under domestic law and international law, it acknowledges that the 1946 General Convention on the Privileges and Immunities of the United Nations provides immunity from 'every form of legal process', the only exception being express waiver by the UN itself. In the margin, it sheds light on the scope of the doctrine of 'restrictive immunity', by holding that acts that form part and parcel of military and humanitarian peacekeeping operations (including the occupation of property to house troops etc.) involve the exercise of governmental functions rather than private commercial activity and thus benefit from immunity.

I. Facts of the case

Following the downfall of President Siad Barre in 1991, civil war broke out in Somalia between followers of Interim President Ali Mahdi Mohamed and followers of General Mohamed Farah Aidid. With nearly one million refugees and almost five million people threatened by hunger, the Security Council stepped in. In January 1992, it imposed an arms embargo on Somalia.[1] Subsequently, on 24 April 1992, the Council decided to establish the United Nations Operation in Somalia (UNOSOM I).[2] The UNOSOM I peacekeeping operation lasted from April 1992 until March 1993. As of November 1992 it operated alongside the US-led Unified Task Force (UNITAF), which was authorized by the UN Security Council to use 'all necessary means' to establish a secure environment for relief efforts. In March 1993, the Council decided on a transition from UNITAF to a new UN peacekeeping operation (UNOSOM II), which was eventually withdrawn in March 1995.[3]

In the wake of the UN peacekeeping operation, Abdi Hosh Askir, a Somalian citizen, brought an action for damages before the United States District Court of New York. Abdi Hosh Askir was the owner of a compound in Mogadishu encompassing nearly one million square meters and containing *inter alia* an office complex, a hotel, recreational facilities, and restaurants. Claiming that the UN had

---

[1] cf. SC Res. 733(1992) of 23 January 1992; SC Res. 746(1992) of 17 March 1992,
[2] cf. SC Res. 751(1992) of 24 April 1992.   [3] cf. SC Res. 814(1993) of 26 March 1993.

wrongfully and without proper authorization occupied approximately one quarter of the compound for a period of about eighteen months, he sought over 190 million US dollars in damages, allegedly equivalent to the fair rental value of the compound, as well as exemplary damages of 750 million US dollars plus interest.

The action was brought against UN Secretary-General Boutros Boutros-Ghali and Under-Secretary-General for Administration and Management Joseph Connor, both in their individual and official capacities, as well as several UN agents, including the construction company and private military contractor Brown & Root Services Corp. The plaintiff eventually dropped UN Secretary-General Boutros-Ghali as a defendant in the case in order to remedy a jurisdictional defect.

II. The legal question

The key question before the US District Court was whether or not Under-Secretary-General for Administration and Management Joseph Connor enjoyed immunity from legal process in the context of the action for damages lodged by Mr Abdi Hosh Askir. The claimant raised several arguments as to why no immunity should be accorded, relating both to US domestic law (in particular the International Organizations Immunities Act (IOIA) and the Foreign Sovereign Immunities Act (FSIA)) and international law (in particular the 1946 General Convention on the Privileges and Immunities of the United Nations). The different arguments were ultimately dismissed by the Court in its judgment of 29 July 1996.

III. Excerpts

The plaintiff offers three arguments against dismissal based on immunity.

First, with respect to the U.N. Convention, the plaintiff argues that the immunity afforded under article 2 is coextensive with the immunity provided to international organizations under the International Organizations Immunities Act ('IOIA'), 22 U.S.C. § 288a. The plaintiff argues that the IOIA affords the United Nations the same immunity provided to foreign governments under the Foreign Sovereign Immunities Act ('FSIA'), 28 U.S.C. § 1602 *et seq.* The plaintiff takes the position that the FSIA, and therefore for the purpose of the United Nations the IOIA, provides only restrictive immunity.

The Supreme Court recently explained the distinction between restrictive and absolute immunity: 'Under the restrictive, as opposed to the "absolute," theory of foreign sovereign immunity, a state is immune from the jurisdiction of foreign courts as to its sovereign or public acts (*jure imperii*), but not as to those that are private or commercial in character (*jure gestionis*) [...] [A] state engages in commercial activity under the restrictive theory when it exercises "only those powers that can also be exercised by private citizens," "as distinct from those" "powers peculiar to sovereigns." Put differently, a foreign state engages in commercial activity for purposes of the restrictive theory only where it acts "in a manner of a private player within" the market.'
Saudi Arabia v. Nelson, 507 U.S. 349, 359–60, 113 S.Ct. 1471, 1478–79, 123 L.Ed.2d 47 (1993) (citations omitted). The plaintiff argues that this action arises from the

commercial activities of the United Nations, namely the leasing and occupation of property, and therefore falls outside the bounds of restrictive immunity.

It is unnecessary to decide, *first,* whether the restrictive immunity doctrine of the FSIA applies to the United Nations through the IOIA, or *second,* whether that restrictive immunity would trump the otherwise absolute immunity afforded by the U.N. Convention itself. Neither of these questions are necessary to determine because even if the more limited restrictive immunity doctrine applied, the claims in this case do not arise out of commercial activity by the United Nations. *Compare Tuck v. Pan American Health Org.,* 668 F.2d 547, 550 (D.C.Cir. 1981) (declining to decide whether international organization governed by IOIA was granted restrictive or absolute immunity by virtue of the FSIA because activity was not commercial); *Broadbent v. Organization of American States,* 628 F.2d 27, 32–33 (D.C.Cir.1980) (same).

The scope of restrictive immunity is determined by the nature of the activity rather than its motivation or purpose. *See Saudi Arabia,* 507 U.S. at 360, 113 S.Ct. at 1479; *Broadbent,* 628 F.2d at 33; *Friedar v. Government of Israel,* 614 F.Supp. 395, 399 (S.D.N.Y. 1985). In this case, the plaintiff complains that his property was seized and occupied by the United Nations as part of its military and humanitarian peace-keeping mission in Somalia. A military operation, even one directed at ensuring the delivery of humanitarian relief, is not an endeavor commonly associated with private citizens—indeed, military operations are a distinctive province of sovereigns and governments. The occupation of property during such an operation to house troops, store and distribute supplies and ordinance, or manage the logistics and planning of peacekeeping and humanitarian relief efforts is part and parcel of such an operation. The United Nations mission in Somalia provided 'a military force to enable relief agencies to deliver food and other supplies to the Somali people.' (Compl. ¶ 11.) This is not a case of the United Nations arranging for one of its officials to lease a residential apartment in a foreign state and providing heat, hot water, and electricity this is a case of an armed military occupation in a country where the government had been overthrown and no administration had taken its place. (Compl. ¶ 8.) Indeed, the perimeter of the compound in Mogadishu was secured with 'sandbags, land mines, barbed wire, and other anti-personnel weapons.' (Compl. ¶ 22.) There is no doubt that the operation of a military logistics and supply base was not commercial activity of the sort contemplated under the restrictive immunity doctrine. *See Saudi Arabia,* 507 U.S. at 361, 113 S.Ct. at 1479 ('[A] foreign state's exercise of the power of its police has long been understood for purposes of the restrictive theory as peculiarly sovereign in nature.'); *Friedar,* 614 F.Supp. at 399 (acts relating to recruiting for armed forces and determining veterans benefits were 'purely governmental').

Accordingly, even if the immunity available to the United Nations and its officials is only restrictive immunity, the immunity still applies because the nature of the acts complained of by the plaintiff are the exercise of governmental functions rather than private commercial activity.

The plaintiff's second argument is that the interpretation of the term 'immunity' in the U.N. Convention itself should exclude commercial activities. The plaintiff makes this argument by pointing out that judicial decisions involving the interpretation of the scope of the U.N. Convention have related principally to employment disputes between former employees and the United Nations or its agencies. *See De Luca v. The United Nations Organization,* 841 F.Supp. 531 (S.D.N.Y.), *aff'd without opinion,*

41 F.3d 1502 (2d Cir.1994), *cert. denied*, 115 S.Ct. 1429, 131 L.Ed.2d 310 (1995); *Klyumel v. United Nations*, No. 92 Civ. 4231, 1992 WL 447314 (S.D.N.Y. Dec. 4, 1992) (report and recommendation by Grubin, M.J.), *aff'd and adopted*, 1993 WL 42708 (S.D.N.Y. Feb. 17, 1993); *Boimah*, 664 F.Supp. 69; *see also Shamsee v. Shamsee*, 74 A.D.2d 357, 428 N.Y.S.2d 33 (2d Dep't 1980) (appeal of contempt order against U.N. Joint Staff Pension Fund).

None of these cases limit their respective interpretations of the immunity afforded by the U.N. Convention. Indeed, in *De Luca* the Court observed that the U.N. Convention contained no exceptions to its immunity provisions obviating any need to consider whether the FSIA or the IOIA applied. *See De Luca*, 841 F.Supp. at 533 n. 1. The U.N. Convention by its terms provides immunity from 'every form of legal process', the only exception being express waiver by the United Nations itself.

In any event, even if there is an exception to the immunity provided by article 2 of the U.N. Convention based on a distinction between commercial and noncommercial activity, as explained above, the activities upon which this lawsuit is based are not commercial.

Accordingly, the immunity provided by the U.N. Convention applies in this case.

The plaintiff's third and final argument is based on the allegedly wrongful nature of the acts of the United Nations and Connor. The plaintiff argues that the United Nations did not have the authority to adopt the resolutions passed in connection with the peacekeeping operations in Somalia. The plaintiff also alleges that Connor was not authorized to refuse to pay the plaintiff rent for the use of the compound or to refuse to pay him because of racial animus or bias based on the plaintiff's national origin. The plaintiff also makes allegations of fiscal improprieties relating to the operation of the United Nations generally and the operation in Somalia in particular, attributing the mismanagement to defendant Connor. (Compl. ¶ 46–50.)

The plaintiff's allegations of malfeasance do not serve to strip the United Nations or Connor of their immunities afforded under the U.N. Convention. *See De Luca*, 841 F.Supp. at 535 (defendant remained immune under the IOIA notwithstanding allegations of illegality and wrongdoing); *Tuck*, 668 F.2d at 550 n. 7 (IOIA immunity still applied notwithstanding allegations of race discrimination); *Donald v. Orfila*, 788 F.2d 36, 37 (D.C.Cir.1986) (allegations of improper motive did not strip individual of immunity under IOIA).

The allegation that the United Nations did not properly adopt its own resolutions authorizing its actions in Somalia is equally unavailing. The plaintiff has done nothing more than offer conclusory allegations that the missions in Somalia were beyond United Nations authority because they were interventions in civil wars. This allegation stands in direct contradiction to a series of duly adopted United Nations Security Council Resolutions ('UNSC'), including UNSC Resolution 794 (Dec. 3, 1992) and UNSC Resolution 814 (Mar. 26, 1993), each adopted pursuant to Chapter VII of the United Nations Charter.

Accordingly, the plaintiff's allegations of misconduct by Connor and lack of authority by the United Nations do not overcome Connor's assertion of immunity in this case.

[In conclusion] For the reasons explained in this Opinion, the Court dismisses *sua sponte* the claims against defendant Connor in his official and individual capacities pursuant to Fed. R.Civ.P. 12(b)(1) for lack of subject matter jurisdiction because, as described above, Connor is immune from being sued in this action.

IV. Commentary

The essence of the case concerns the jurisdictional immunity of the United Nations and its personnel before national courts. While the UN defendants had not been served with the summons and complaint, the UN legal counsel submitted papers asserting the absolute immunity of the UN defendants and requesting the Court to dismiss the complaint—a position that was supported by the United States government.[4]

Although the claim was originally brought against Connor *both* in his official and individual capacities, the Court notes at the outset (in a footnote) that the plaintiff acknowledges that the claim against Connor in his official capacity may be treated as an action against the UN itself. As for the claim against Connor in his individual capacity, the Court observes that the plaintiff failed to explain in any way why the alleged actions would fall outside the scope of his official duties (which clearly they did not). Obviously, 'the mere allegation that the United Nations did not possess the authority to undertake its missions in Somalia' (as the plaintiff suggested) did not imply that Connor's alleged actions would somehow be less a part of his official function. For the sake of completeness, the Court recalls that, 'in any case', the immunities provided under art. V, Section 18 of the 1946 General Convention on the Privileges and Immunities of the United Nations (cf. UNTS vol. 1, 15)—which entered into force in respect of the United States upon its accession on 29 April 1970—'are applicable here and would afford [Connor] protection *in his individual capacity*' (emphasis added). Even if the outcome seems correct, this *obiter dictum* is somewhat puzzling in that art. V, Section 18 refers to the immunity from legal process of UN officials 'in respect of words spoken or written and all acts performed by them *in their official capacity*' (emphasis added).[5] The remainder of the judgment focuses on the immunity of the UN as an international organization as such.

Before the US District Court, the plaintiff submitted three arguments against dismissal based on immunity. First, the plaintiff argued that the US 'International Organizations Immunities Act' ('IOIA', 22 U.S.C. §288a) provides only restrictive immunity to international organizations, similar to the immunity granted to states under the 'Foreign Sovereign Immunities Act' ('FSIA', 28 U.S.C. § 1602 et seq.).

---

[4] As Reinisch observes, 'as a matter of practice, most international organizations find ways to communicate their legal point of view to courts either by the official way of informing the forum state's foreign ministry or by directly communicating with the courts, since—even if immunity does not have to be claimed by the defendant—it is frequently useful to communicate the organization's legal opinion on the matter' (cf. A. Reinisch, *International Organizations before National Courts* (Cambridge, Cambridge University Press 2000), p. 139).

[5] It might have been more sensible to refer instead to art. V, Section 19 which affirms that the Secretary-General and all Assistant Secretaries-General shall enjoy the privileges and immunities accorded to diplomatic envoys. This provision was applied, for instance, in *Brzak v United Nations* (US Court of Appeals for the Second Circuit, 2 March 2010, 597 F.3d 107, 111–12) and in *Delama Georges v United Nations* (US District Court, Southern District of New York, 9 January 2015, 13-CV-7146 (JPO), available at http://www.ijdh.org/wp-content/uploads/2011/11/Dkt62_Opinion_and_Order_01_09_15.pdf, at 7–8).

Second, the plaintiff argued that the interpretation of the term 'immunity' in the 1946 General Convention on the Privileges and Immunities of the United Nations itself should exclude commercial activities. Third, the plaintiff relied on the allegedly wrongful nature of the acts of the UN and of Connor.

As far as the first argument is concerned, the case fits within a broader series of cases brought before US national courts against various international organizations and/or their employees, and in which the relationship between the International Organizations Immunities Act and the Foreign Sovereign Immunities Act was at stake. Indeed, when in 1945 the United States adopted the IOIA, it was stipulated that international organizations would enjoy 'the same immunity from suit and every form of judicial process as is enjoyed by foreign governments, except to the extent that such organizations may expressly waive their immunity [...]' (Section 2(b)). In 1976, however, the United States adopted the Foreign Sovereign Immunities Act, which provides for a series of exceptions to the jurisdictional immunity of a foreign state (§1605), for instance, when 'the action is based upon a commercial activity carried on in the United States by the foreign state; or [...] upon an act outside the territory of the United States in connection with a commercial activity of the foreign state elsewhere and that act causes a direct effect in the United States [...].' US Courts, including the US Supreme Court, have moreover repeatedly confirmed that the FSIA accords only 'restrictive immunity', as opposed to 'absolute immunity', to foreign states, and that this extends to sovereign or public acts (*acta de jure imperii*), but not to those that are private or commercial in character (*jure gestionis*).[6]

Against this background, a controversy has developed in US legal doctrine and in judicial opinion as to whether the immunity granted to international organizations under the IOIA should be determined by reference to the standard of absolute immunity prevailing at the time of the IOIA's adoption, or rather by reference to the standard of restrictive immunity subscribed to (in respect of foreign governments) in the FSIA and in US judicial decisions.[7]

On the one hand, in a number of cases, and in particular in a variety of employment-related cases, US Courts have simply circumvented this conundrum by holding that even under a restrictive immunity standard, the international organizations concerned would still enjoy immunity.[8] Thus, in *Tuck v Pan American Health Organization*, the Court held that even under the restrictive standard, the PAHO enjoyed immunity since the action forming the basis of Tuck's complaint, viz. the supervision of its employees, was no commercial activity in the sense of the FSIA.[9] Similarly, in *Morgan v IBRD*, the District of Columbia district court dismissed a tort action against the World Bank for libel, slander, and false imprisonment, *inter alia* because the claims

---

[6] For example US Supreme Court, *Saudi Arabia v Nelson*, 507 US 349 (1993); US Supreme Court, *Alfred Dunhill of London v Republic of Cuba*, 425 US 682 (1976).

[7] cf. A. Reinisch (n. 4), pp. 197–203.

[8] For example *Marvin R. Broadbent et al. v OAS et al.*, US District Court DC, 25 January 1978, 28 March 1978; US Court of Appeals DC Cir., 8 January 1980; *Weidner v International Telecommunications Satellite Organization*, DC Court of Appeals, 21 September 1978.

[9] cf. US District Court DC, 13 September 1990, 752 F. Supp. 492 at 494 (DDC 1990).

arose 'directly from the World Bank's employment practices, which do not constitute 'commercial activity' within the meaning of the [FSIA]'.[10]

By contrast, in several other cases, US Courts have interpreted the IOIA as according only restrictive immunity, in line with the immunity granted by the FSIA. If this position was hinted at, rather cautiously, in *De Luca v United Nations* (another employment case), it was adopted more explicitly in *Dupree Associates Inc v US*[11] and *Margo Rendall-Speranza v Edward A. Nassim and the International Finance Corp.*[12]

Thus, in *Dupree Associates*, for instance, the District Court unequivocally held that 'international organizations are entitled only to restricted immunity. It is this court's opinion that this is the proper interpretation of the IOIA'.[13]

If the latter approach is followed, the question may arise to what extent the restrictive immunity allegedly granted by the IOIA (*juncto* the FSIA) is trumped by the more specific privileges and immunities granted to individual international organizations and their employees in separate conventions and headquarters agreements. In particular, in the case of the UN, the question arises to what extent such restrictive immunity is trumped by the broad immunity apparently envisaged by the 1946 General Convention on the Privileges and Immunities of the United Nations (which the US ratified in 1970). In *De Luca v United Nations,* the District Court of New York confirmed in passing that the broader immunity granted by the latter Convention should take precedence. According to the Court, even if the immunity granted by the IOIA was subject to exceptions, similar to those provided for in the FSIA, '[w]e need not consider the application of these exceptions to the instant case, for the U.N. Convention, which contains no such exceptions, provides sufficient ground for finding the U.N. immune from plaintiff's claims'.[14] In a 'statement of interest' in a distinct procedure similarly arising from the occupation by UN peacekeepers of certain premises in Mogadishu,[15] the US government expressed support for the position in

---

[10] cf. *Morgan v IBRD* US District Court DC, 17 November 1980, US Court of Appeals DC Cir., 13 November 1981.

[11] US District Court DC, 31 May 1977, 22 June 1977, (1982) 63 ILR 95.

[12] cf. *De Luca v. United Nations Organization, Perez de Cuellar, Gomez, Duque, Annan* et al., US District Court SDNY, 10 January 1994, 841 F. Supp. 531 (1994), fn. 1 ('Under IOIA, designated international organizations receive the same immunity as that "enjoyed by foreign governments, except to the extent that such organizations may expressly waive their immunity for the purpose of any proceedings or by the terms of any contract." 22 U.S.C.A. § 288a(b). [...] The immunity of foreign governments is now governed by the Foreign Sovereign Immunities Act ("FSIA"), 28 U.S.C.A. § 1602 et seq. (Supp. 1993). The FSIA confers on foreign governments general jurisdictional immunity subject to several exceptions. 28 U.S.C.A. § 1604. We need not consider the application of these exceptions to the instant case, for the U.N. Convention, which contains no such exceptions, provides sufficient ground for finding the U.N. immune from plaintiff's claims.'), *Dupree Associates Inc v US* US District Court DC, 31 May 1977, 22 June 1977, (1982) 63 ILR 95, *Margo Rendall-Speranza v Edward A. Nassim and the International Finance Corp* US District Court DC, 18 March 1996, 3 July 1996.

[13] cf. *Dupree Associates* (n. 12).

[14] cf. *De Luca v United Nations Organization, Perez de Cuellar, Gomez, Duque, Annan* et al., US District Court SDNY, 10 January 1994, 841 F. Supp. 531 (1994), fn. 1 (n. 12).

[15] According to statement of interest, the claims over the occupation by UN peacekeepers of certain premises in Mogadishu were allegedly settled through an arbitral procedure, with an arbitral award of February 2001 allegedly ordering to pay the claimants a compensation of 757,452.26 US dollars.

De Luca. In particular, the US government (correctly) emphasized that 'the immunity standards of [the] more generalized law' of the FSIA and IOIA could not override the UN Convention's treatment of the narrow, precise, and specific subject of the immunities of the UN.[16]

The same result was reached in the judgment of the US Court of Appeals in *Brzak v United Nations*.[17] While leaving aside whether the immunity granted by the IOIA is broader than that accorded by the FSIA or not, the Court of Appeals held in this case that the 1946 Convention is a self-executing treaty, which 'unequivocally grants the United Nations absolute immunity without exception'.[18]

Finally, at least one Court of Appeals case has explicitly dismissed the suggestion that the immunity granted to international organizations under the IOIA should be determined by reference to the standard of restrictive immunity subscribed to (in respect of foreign governments) in the FSIA. In particular, in light of the text and legislative history of the IOIA, the US Court of Appeals for the District of Columbia Circuit in *Atkinson v the Inter-American Development Bank* held that 'despite the lack of a clear instruction as to whether Congress meant to incorporate in the IOIA subsequent changes to the law of immunity of foreign sovereigns, Congress' intent was to adopt that body of law only as it existed in 1945—when immunity of foreign sovereigns was absolute'.[19]

In *Askir v Boutros-Ghali*, however, the District Court of New York followed the first of the aforementioned approaches—that is, the Court deemed it unnecessary to decide (1) whether the restrictive immunity doctrine of the FSIA applied to the United Nations through the IOIA, and, if so, (2) whether that restrictive immunity would trump the otherwise absolute immunity afforded by the UN Convention itself.

As in previous cases, the reason for this resided in the fact that, even if the UN and its officials were to enjoy only restrictive immunity, the immunity would still apply 'since the nature of the acts complained of […] are the exercise of governmental functions rather than private commercial activity'. In accordance with established US case-law, the Court recalled that the scope of restrictive immunity is determined by the nature of the activity, rather than its motivation or purpose.[20] *In casu*, there

---

[16] cf. Statement of interest of the United States of America, US District Court, DC, *John Kamya v the United Nations*, Civil No. 1:02CV01176(TFH), at 4, available at http://www.state.gov/documents/organization/38812.pdf

[17] 2 March 2010, 597 F.3d 107.

[18] The Court of Appeals nonetheless adds a further argument, noting that 'the plaintiffs have not presented any argument […] which would suggest that one of FSIA's exceptions to immunity would apply'.

Note: in the more recent case of *Delama v United Nations* (US District Court, 13-CF-7146 (JPO), 9 January 2015), the District Court simply recalls the self-executing character of the 1946 Convention, as affirmed in *Brzak v United Nations*, without even mentioning the IOIA.

[19] *Atkinson v Inter-American Development Bank and Kestell*, Appeal judgment, 156 F 3d 1335 (DC Cir 1998), No 97-7181, [1998] USCADC 237, 332 U.S.App.D.C. 307, ILDC 1766 (US 1998), 9 October 1998, Court of Appeals (DC Circuit) [D.C. Cir.], Section III. According to the Court of Appeals, 'Congress was content to delegate to the President the responsibility for updating the immunities of international organizations in the face of changing circumstances.'

[20] This corresponds by and large to the approach adopted in art. 2(2) of the UN Convention on jurisdictional immunities of States and their property (not yet in force).

was no doubt 'that the operation of a military logistics and supply base was not commercial activity of the sort contemplated under the restrictive immunity doctrine'. Indeed, according to the Court, a military operation, even if directed only at ensuring the delivery of humanitarian aid, is not an endeavour commonly associated with private citizens. Crucially, the court found that the occupation of property during such an operation to house troops, store and distribute supplies and ordinance, or manage the logistics and planning of peacekeeping and humanitarian relief efforts 'is part and parcel of such an operation'. The Court contrasted such activities to the UN arranging for one of its officials to lease an apartment in a foreign state. In all, the Court's reasoning sheds further light on the application of the restrictive immunity doctrine to military and police operations abroad (by states or international organizations) and confirms that conduct associated to such operations will normally benefit from immunity from suit.[21]

With regard to the plaintiff's second argument, concerning the interpretation of the term 'immunity' in the 1946 General Convention, the Court notes that the plaintiff adduces no evidence to support a narrow interpretation of the term, but instead confines himself to pointing out that previous US judgments involving the Convention related principally to employment disputes. Against this, the Court rightly observes that none of these cases supports a restrictive interpretation of the immunity provided for in the Convention. Quite the contrary, the Court draws attention to *De Luca*, where it was previously held that the Convention provides immunity from 'every form of legal process' without any exception (save for an express waiver by the UN itself).[22] While it is perhaps regrettable that the Court did not affirm in more explicit/stronger wording that the *lex specialis* rules of the 1946 Convention take precedence over the general domestic rules of the IOIA (regardless of the interpretation of the latter rules), the outcome remains the same: the Court implicitly affirms that the UN in principle enjoys absolute immunity from suit. For the sake of completeness, the Court recalls, that even if the immunity provided for in the General Convention would not apply to commercial activities, the activities upon which the claim is based are not commercial in any case.

Finally, the Court gives short shrift to the third (and ostensibly poorly developed) argument concerning the allegedly wrongful nature of the acts of the UN, and of Connor, and dismisses it without much ado. On the one hand, the Court confirms that allegations of malfeasance—viz. the suggestions that the UN did not have the authority to set up the peacekeeping operation in Somalia or that Connor was not authorized to refuse to pay rent for the use of the compound—did not remove the immunity from suit accorded to the UN and to Connor. The Court is of course stating the obvious: immunity from legal process would surely be of little avail if it would not

---

[21] Compare to ICJ, *Jurisdictional Immunities of the State (Germany v Italy: Greece intervening)*, Judgment, [2012] ICJ Rep 99, at §§ 65–78. Consider also art. 11 of the European Convention on State Immunity and art. 12 of the UN Convention on Jurisdictional Immunities of States and their Property.

[22] cf. *De Luca v United Nations Organization, Perez de Cuellar, Gomez, Duque, Annan et al.*, US District Court SDNY, 10 January 1994, 841 F. Supp. 531 (1994).

extend to (allegedly) wrongful conduct. It is noted that *in casu* the allegedly wrongful conduct did not take place in the country where the claim was brought. As a result, the case does not offer any insight into the question whether there exists in general international law a 'territorial tort exception' for official acts, and, if so, under what conditions said exception would apply.[23] On the other hand, the Court dismisses in passing the allegation of the plaintiff that the missions in Somalia were beyond the UN's authority because they were interventions in civil wars. Instead, the Court finds that the operations were established pursuant to a series of 'duly adopted' UN Security Council resolutions, 'each adopted pursuant to Chapter VII of the United Nations Charter'. Again, while this is hardly a revolutionary finding, it remains interesting to note that the Court implicitly confirms that the UN Security Council's Chapter VII jurisdiction undoubtedly extends to civil war scenarios. Seen from this perspective, the judgment—adopted several years before the emergence of the 'Responsibility to Protect' doctrine—adds to the substantial body of evidence in state practice confirming that non-international armed conflicts and large-scale human rights violations within a state can give rise to a 'threat to the peace' in the sense of art. 39 of the UN Charter.

---

[23] cf. for example (in the context of *state* immunity) ICJ, *Jurisdictional Immunities of the State (Germany v Italy: Greece intervening)*, Judgment, [2012] ICJ Rep 99, para. 65 where the Court considered that it was 'not called upon [...] to resolve the question whether there is in customary international law a 'tort exception' to State immunity applicable to acta jure imperii in general'; see also: A. Dickinson, '*Germany v. Italy* and the Territorial Tort Exception—Walking the Tightrope', (2013) 11 *Journal of International Criminal Justice* 147.

7.3 Difference relating to Immunity from Legal Process of a Special Rapporteur of the Commission on Human Rights, Advisory Opinion, [1999] ICJ Rep 62

Chanaka Wickremasinghe*

Relevance of the case

The Advisory Opinion on the *Difference Relating to Immunity from Legal Process of a Special Rapporteur of the Commission on Human Rights* is one of the relatively few cases that have required the International Court of Justice to consider directly issues related to the immunity of an international organization (in this case the UN). It provides important guidance on how to delineate between activities that are pursued by the UN and its officials in an official capacity and are therefore entitled to immunity, and activities which are pursued in some other capacity and therefore are subject to national jurisdiction.

At a procedural level the case is significant as the first occasion on which the process of so-called 'binding advisory opinions' under art. VIII, Section 30[1] of the 1946 Convention on the Privileges and Immunities of the United Nations (General Convention) has been invoked, leading in itself to some interesting questions about the adaptation of the Court's advisory jurisdiction to a more formal mode of dispute settlement.

I. Facts of the case

The case arose from a media interview given by Dato' Param Cumaraswamy, a Malaysian lawyer and a Special Rapporteur on the 'Independence of Judges and Lawyers' to the UN Human Rights Commission. The Special Rapporteur was reported to point to a recent case before the Malaysian courts and saying that it appeared to be a case of 'judge choosing', but also adding that he had not yet made up his mind. As a result a number of companies in Malaysia made claims against the Special Rapporteur for defamation seeking very substantial sums by way of damages and exemplary damages against him.

The UN Secretary-General determined that, as a Special Rapporteur of the Human Rights Commission, Cumaraswamy was an expert on mission for the purposes of the

---

* Legal Counsellor, Foreign and Commonwealth Office. This article is written in his personal capacity.

[1] 'Section 30. All differences arising out of the interpretation or application of the present convention shall be referred to the International Court of Justice, unless in any case it is agreed by the parties to have recourse to another mode of settlement. If a difference arises between the United Nations on the one hand and a Member on the other hand, a request shall be made for an advisory opinion on any legal question involved in accordance with Article 96 of the Charter and Article 65 of the Statue of the Court. The opinion given by the Court shall be accepted as decisive by the parties.' The use of the advisory jurisdiction of the Court is necessary in this respect since only states may be parties before the Court under its contentious jurisdiction (see art. 34 of the Statute of the International Court of Justice).

General Convention, and that since the media interview had been given by him in the performance of his mission on behalf the UN, he was entitled to immunity from legal process of any kind in accordance with art. VI, Section 22 of the Convention.[2] The Secretary-General informed the Government of Malaysia of this determination and asked that the Government advise the Malaysian courts of the Special Rapporteur's immunity.

However, when the Special Rapporteur sought to have the claims against him struck out, the Government of Malaysia provided a certificate simply observing that he enjoyed immunity 'only in respect of words spoken or written or acts done in the course of performance of his duties'. The Government made no mention of the Secretary-General's determination that the interview in question had been in performance of his official mandate. The Malaysian courts found that the Secretary-General's determination was only a statement of opinion, and that the question of the capacity in which the interview had been given, and therefore also the question of immunity, could be considered with the merits of the dispute. Effectively the Special Rapporteur would be forced to defend himself on the merits, before the question of immunity could be determined. This would of course be to deny much of the effectiveness of immunity, which provides its holder with a preliminary plea to bar immunity, without having to address the merits of a claim.

The UN Secretary-General therefore invoked the procedure under art. 30 of the General Convention, and advised the UN's Economic and Social Council (ECOSOC) to make a request to the International Court of Justice for an advisory opinion[3] which would be decisive of the dispute as between the UN and Malaysia.

II. The legal question

The Secretary-General proposed that the broad question of principle be referred to the Court, that is whether the Secretary-General had exclusive authority to determine whether or not acts of officials and experts of the UN were performed in an official capacity and therefore immune. However, in the event, ECOSOC asked the ICJ to give an advisory opinion on the more focused question of the applicability of art. VI, Section 22 of the General Convention to the Special Rapporteur, and secondly on the legal obligations of Malaysia in this case.

In response to the legal question about the applicability of the General Convention in the context of the particular case, the answers urged by the various participants in their pleadings can be broadly categorized into three different approaches.

---

[2] Section 22. Experts (other than officials coming within the scope of article V) performing missions for the United Nations shall be accorded such privileges and immunities as are necessary for the independent exercise of their functions during the period of their missions, including the time spent on journeys in connection with their missions. In particular they shall be accorded [...] (b) in respect of words spoken or written and acts done by them in the course of the performance of their mission, immunity from legal process of every kind. This immunity from legal process shall continue to be accorded notwithstanding that the persons concerned are no longer employed on missions for the United Nations [...]'

[3] The Secretary-General is not empowered to request advisory opinions of the Court, for discussion see S. Rosenne, *The Law and Practice of the International Court, 1920–2005*, (4th edn, 2006), pp. 326–7.

On the one hand, the UN, with support of some member states (notably Costa Rica, Germany, and Sweden), took the position of principle that the Secretary-General had the exclusive authority to determine whether the words or acts of UN officials and experts were spoken or done in performance of their official functions. For the Secretary-General the determination was one of *fact*, which he was in a unique position to make, and this was implicit in the scheme of the General Convention.

On the other hand Malaysia submitted that the Secretary-General's approach was an unwarranted attempt to place limitations on both the executive authority of Malaysia and the jurisdiction of its courts. For Malaysia the issue was primarily a *legal* determination as to the scope of immunity, which, in line with the practice of other national courts and the writings of authors, was a matter for the national court to determine.

However a third group of states (namely Italy, the United Kingdom, and the US) urged a more nuanced approach. They recognized that the Secretary-General's determination of whether a given act was official or not should be given full weight by the national court, but ultimately they submitted the extent of immunity was a legal question for determination by the national court. For those states in the group who addressed the merits, they urged the court to find that the Special Rapporteur was in fact immune in respect of what he said during the media interview in question.

III. Excerpts

50. In the process of determining whether a particular expert on mission is entitled, in the prevailing circumstances, to the immunity provided for in Section 22 *(b)*, the Secretary-General of the United Nations has a pivotal role to play. The Secretary-General, as the chief administrative officer of the Organization, has the authority and the responsibility to exercise the necessary protection where required [...]

51. Article VI, Section 23, of the General Convention provides that 'privileges and immunities are granted to experts in the interests of the United Nations and not for the personal benefit of the individuals themselves'. In exercising protection of United Nations experts, the Secretary-General is therefore protecting the mission with which the expert is entrusted. In that respect, the Secretary-General has the primary responsibility and authority to protect the interests of the Organization and its agents, including experts on mission. In that respect, the Secretary-General has the primary responsibility and authority to protect the interests of the Organization and its agents, including experts on mission. As the Court held:

> 'In order that the agent may perform his duties satisfactorily, he must feel that this protection is assured to him by the Organization, and that he may count on it. To ensure the independence of the agent, and, consequently, the independent action of the Organization itself, it is essential that in performing his duties he need not have to rely on any other protection than that of the Organization [. . .]' *(Reparation for Injuries Suffered in the Service of the United Nations, Advisory Opinion, I.C.J. Reports 1949, p. 183.)*

52. The determination whether an agent of the Organization has acted in the course of the performance of his mission depends upon the facts of a particular case. In the present case, the Secretary-General, or the Legal Counsel of the United Nations on his behalf, has on numerous occasions informed the Government of Malaysia of his finding that Mr. Cumaraswamy had spoken the words quoted in the article in *International Commercial Litigation* in his capacity as Special Rapporteur of the Commission and that he consequently was entitled to immunity from 'every kind' of legal process [...]

56. The Court is not called upon in the present case to pass upon the aptness of the terms used by the Special Rapporteur or his assessment of the situation. In any event, in view of all the circumstances of this case, elements of which are set out in paragraphs 1 to 15 of the note by the Secretary-General, the Court is of the opinion that the Secretary-General correctly found that Mr. Cumaraswamy, in speaking the words quoted in the article in *International Commercial Litigation,* was acting in the course of the performance of his mission as Special Rapporteur of the Commission. Consequently, Article VI, Section 22 (b), of the General Convention is applicable to him in the present case and affords Mr. Cumaraswamy immunity from legal process of every kind.

57. The Court will now deal with the second part of the Council's question, namely, 'the legal obligations of Malaysia in this case' [...]

59. The Court wishes to point out that the request for an advisory opinion refers to 'the legal obligations of Malaysia in this case'. The difference which has arisen between the United Nations and Malaysia originated in the Government of Malaysia not having informed the competent Malaysian judicial authorities of the Secretary-General's finding that Mr. Cumaraswamy had spoken the words at issue in the course of the performance of his mission and was, therefore, entitled to immunity from legal process (see paragraph 17 above). It is as from the time of this omission that the question before the Court must be answered.

60. As the Court has observed, the Secretary-General, as the chief administrative officer of the Organization, has the primary responsibility to safeguard the interests of the Organization; to that end, it is up to him to assess whether its agents acted within the scope of their functions and, where he so concludes, to protect these agents, including experts on mission, by asserting their immunity. This means that the Secretary-General has the authority and responsibility to inform the Government of a member State of his finding and, where appropriate, to request it to act accordingly and, in particular, to request it to bring his finding to the knowledge of the local courts if acts of an agent have given or may give rise to court proceedings.

61. When national courts are seised of a case in which the immunity of a United Nations agent is in issue, they should immediately be notified of any finding by the Secretary-General concerning that immunity. That finding, and its documentary expression, creates a presumption which can only be set aside for the most compelling reasons and is thus to be given the greatest weight by national courts. The governmental authorities of a party to the General Convention are therefore under an obligation to convey such information to the national courts concerned, since a proper application of the Convention by them is dependent on such information.

Failure to comply with this obligation, among others, could give rise to the institution of proceedings under Article VIII, Section 30, of the General Convention.

62. The Court concludes that the Government of Malaysia had an obligation, under Article 105 of the Charter and under the General Convention, to inform its courts of the position taken by the Secretary-General. According to a well-established rule of international law, the conduct of any organ of a state must be regarded as an act of that state [...]

Because the Government did not transmit the Secretary-General's finding to the competent courts, and the Minister for Foreign Affairs did not refer to it in his own certificate, Malaysia did not comply with the above- mentioned obligation.

63. Section 22 *(b)* of the General Convention explicitly states that experts on mission shall be accorded immunity from legal process of every kind in respect of words spoken or written and acts done by them in the course of the performance of their mission. By necessary implication, questions of immunity are therefore preliminary issues which must be expeditiously decided *in limine litis*. This is a generally recognized principle of procedural law, and Malaysia was under an obligation to respect it. The Malaysian courts did not rule *in limine litis* on the immunity of the Special Rapporteur (see paragraph above), thereby nullifying the essence of the immunity rule contained in Section 22 (b). Moreover, costs were taxed to Mr. Cumaraswamy while the question of immunity was still unresolved. As indicated above, the conduct of an organ of a State—even an organ independent of the executive power—must be regarded as an act of that State. Consequently, Malaysia did not act in accordance with its obligations under international law.

64. In addition, the immunity from legal process to which the Court finds Mr. Cumaraswamy entitled entails holding Mr. Cumaraswamy financially harmless for any costs imposed upon him by the Malaysian courts, in particular taxed costs.

65. According to Article VIII, Section 30, of the General Convention, the opinion given by the Court shall be accepted as decisive by the parties to the dispute. Malaysia has acknowledged its obligations under Section 30.

Since the Court holds that Mr. Cumaraswamy is an expert on mission who under Section 22 *(b)* is entitled to immunity from legal process, the Government of Malaysia is obligated to communicate this advisory opinion to the competent Malaysian courts, in order that Malaysia's international obligations be given effect and Mr. Cumaraswamy's immunity be respected.

66. Finally, the Court wishes to point out that the question of immunity from legal process is distinct from the issue of compensation for any damages incurred as a result of acts performed by the United Nations or by its agents acting in their official capacity.

The United Nations may be required to bear responsibility for the damage arising from such acts. However, as is clear from Article VIII, Section 29, of the General Convention, any such claims against the United Nations shall not be dealt with by national courts but shall be settled in accordance with the appropriate modes of settlement that '[t]he United Nations shall make provisions for' pursuant to Section 29.

Furthermore, it need hardly be said that all agents of the United Nations, in whatever official capacity they act, must take care not to exceed the scope of their functions, and should so comport themselves as to avoid claims against the United Nations.

IV. Commentary

The findings of the Court on the merits constitute a powerful vindication of the immunity of the UN and its officials. The rationale of that immunity is clearly set out as to enable the UN to achieve the performance of its internationally agreed functions independently of undue interference by national authorities. The immunity is therefore a vital technique for the UN, to achieve its ends in an international system that allocates jurisdiction primarily to sovereign states. For the main part, the allocation of jurisdiction relies on considerations of territoriality and nationality. By contrast an international organization will have to carry out its activities on the territory of a state, and through its officials and experts who will be linked to a state through the bond of nationality. Indeed the facts of the case are rather well illustrative of this, concerning the activities of a Malaysian Special Rapporteur, giving an interview pursuant to his mandate in Malaysia, and expressing his concerns about the functioning of the Malaysian courts.

On the other hand, implicit in the judgment is a concern for the rule of law, and in particular for ensuring accountability of the exercise of public power, as is of course appropriate for the principal judicial organ of the UN. Recognizing that there should be a proper balance between the broad public (international) interest and the individual case, the Court therefore did not answer the question as to who has 'the final say' on matters of immunity quite as the Secretary-General had argued. Instead it found that the Secretary-General's views establish 'a presumption, which can only be set aside by a national court for the most compelling reasons and is thus to be given the greatest weight by the national courts'.[4]

At a practical level, the advisory opinion provides important guidance to the national court in handling questions of immunity. In particular in this respect, the finding that there is requirement for questions of immunity to be dealt with *in limine litis,* which arises from the nature of immunity itself. In other words, since the purpose of immunity is to prevent any unwarranted interference that impinges on the functioning of the holder of the immunity, the issue of immunity when raised should be dealt with expeditiously at the outset of proceedings.

At the level of procedure, this is the first instance of a so-called 'binding advisory opinion' (i.e. an advisory opinion which the parties have accepted in advance as being 'decisive' of their difference).[5] It is interesting to note that despite the consent to the jurisdiction of the Court in this matter through art. 30 of the General Convention, and its invocation by ECOSOC, the Court nevertheless applied its usual criteria in deciding at the outset whether or not to comply with the request for an advisory opinion (cf. paras 24–30). In particular it might be noted that one of these criteria stresses the institutional link between the Court and the UN, and that answering a request for an advisory opinion represents the Court's participation in the activities of the

---

[4] cf. Advisory Opinion, para. 61.

[5] cf. R. Ago '"Binding" Advisory Opinions of the International Court of Justice' (1991) 85 *American Journal of International Law* 439; see also Rosenne (n. 3), p. 77, fn. 7.

Organization.[6] This statement of course cannot take away from the judicial nature or function of the Court, but perhaps in providing a binding resolution of a difference between the UN and a member state, it is not so much the Court's institutional links with the UN that should be the focus, as the consent of the parties to the Court's process.[7]

The advisory opinion also points out a potential procedural tension in the process, in that the question put to the Court by ECOSOC was slightly different from the question of principle which the primary parties wished to address. In the event the Court was able to address both aspects in this case satisfactorily, but it is perhaps an issue to be borne in mind when seizing the Court in this way in future cases.

---

[6] In this respect the Court frequently refers to its statement to this effect in its Advisory Opinion on *Interpretation of Peace Treaties with Bulgaria, Hungary and Romania, First Phase*, [1950] ICJ Rep 71.

[7] On a related note, Rosenne suggests that the present advisory opinion was in relation to a '"normal" bilateral dispute between the United Nations, represented by the Secretary-General, and Malaysia', and queries the decision of the Court to allow all states parties to the General Convention to participate, rather than limiting participation to the parties to the dispute in exercise of its discretion under art. 68 of its Statute. See Rosenne (n. 3), p. 1001.

7.4 *Beer and Regan v Germany*, App. No. 28934/95 and *Waite and Kennedy v Germany*, App. No. 26083/94, European Court of Human Rights, 18 February 1999

Thore Neumann and Anne Peters

Relevance of the case

The two decisions were the first in which an international human rights court commented on the conflict between immunities of international organizations before domestic courts and the human rights-based obligation of states to provide individuals with access to a court. The ECtHR reviewed the domestic court's act of granting immunity to an international organization against art. 6(1) ECHR. It employed an 'alternative means test', that is, it inquired whether the aggrieved party had means other than access to state courts at its disposal to pursue its claims. In performing a human rights review, the ECtHR departed from the traditional paradigm of international organizations' absolute immunity which would dispense international organizations under all possible circumstances from domestic judicial proceedings and enforcement, typically on the basis of broad treaty provisions (in statutes, headquarter agreements, etc.) to that effect.

Since the rendering of the two judgments, the alternative means-test has become a key concept in the law of organizational immunities in Europe. The ECtHR's judgments have considerably influenced domestic case-law in this area. At the same time, the relative openness and ambiguity of the judgments as to some core aspects of the alternative means rationale have prevented the development of a homogeneous domestic case-law in this field.

I. The facts of the case

The cases were launched by two computer experts, respectively, who had, over a couple of years, performed services at the European Space Agency's (ESA) Operations Centre in Darmstadt, Germany. The applicants had not been hired directly by ESA. Rather, they had been placed at ESA's disposal as part of a scheme of contractual relations between ESA, a sub-company controlled by ESA, and external service providers. When contracts were cancelled between the external service providers, this scheme broke down. This would have terminated the applicants' work at ESA.

The applicants hence tried to avail themselves of the benefits of the German Provision of Labour (Temporary Staff) Act (*Arbeitnehmerüberlassungsgesetz*), a statute which is meant to protect workers who are hired out by one legal entity to another. This law contains a provision according to which, under certain circumstances, an employment relationship between the transferee of the employees, that is the receiving legal entity, and the transferred employee is created by means of a legal fiction. The applicants argued that they had become staff members of ESA on the basis of this provision.

Their action for declaratory relief to this effect before the German courts was rejected as inadmissible on the basis of ESA's immunity from jurisdiction. This was confirmed in last instance by the German Federal Employment Court (*Bundesarbeitsgericht*). The applicants hence argued before the European Commission of Human Rights that the German courts' refusal to entertain their claims due to ESA's immunity from jurisdiction violated their right of access to a court under art. 6 (1) ECHR. When the European Commission of Human Rights rejected their application in its reports of 2 December 1997, the applicants filed a suit before the ECtHR.

II. The legal questions

The main legal questions of this case were (1) whether and under what conditions a domestic court's act granting immunity from jurisdiction to an international organization violates a private party's right of access to a court under art. 6 (1) ECHR, (2) which role the availability of a reasonable alternative means of dispute settlement for private parties should play in this context, and (3) which type of alternative means could satisfy the requirements of art. 6 (1) ECHR in the face of organizational immunities.

III. Excerpts

[...]

59. The Court recalls that the right of access to the courts secured by Article 6 § 1 of the Convention is not absolute, but may be subject to limitations; these are permitted by implication since the right of access by its very nature calls for regulation by the State. In this respect, the Contracting States enjoy a certain margin of appreciation, although the final decision as to the observance of the Convention's requirements rests with the Court. It must be satisfied that the limitations applied do not restrict or reduce the access left to the individual in such a way or to such an extent that the very essence of the right is impaired. Furthermore, a limitation will not be compatible with Article 6 § 1 if it does not pursue a legitimate aim and if there is not a reasonable relationship of proportionality between the means employed and the aim sought to be achieved [...].

[...]

63. Like the Commission, the Court points out that the attribution of privileges and immunities to international organisations is an essential means of ensuring the proper functioning of such organisations free from unilateral interference by individual governments.

The immunity from jurisdiction commonly accorded by States to international organisations under the organisations' constituent instruments or supplementary agreements is a long-standing practice established in the interest of the good working of these organisations. The importance of this practice is enhanced by a trend towards extending and strengthening international cooperation in all domains of modern society.

Against this background, the Court finds that the rule of immunity from jurisdiction, which the German courts applied to ESA in the present case, has a legitimate objective.

64. As to the issue of proportionality, the Court must assess the contested limitation placed on Article 6 in the light of the particular circumstances of the case.

[…]

67. The Court is of the opinion that where States establish international organisations in order to pursue or strengthen their cooperation in certain fields of activities, and where they attribute to these organisations certain competences and accord them immunities, there may be implications as to the protection of fundamental rights. It would be incompatible with the purpose and object of the Convention, however, if the Contracting States were thereby absolved from their responsibility under the Convention in relation to the field of activity covered by such attribution. It should be recalled that the Convention is intended to guarantee not theoretical or illusory rights, but rights that are practical and effective. This is particularly true for the right of access to the courts in view of the prominent place held in a democratic society by the right to a fair trial […].

68. For the Court, a material factor in determining whether granting ESA immunity from German jurisdiction is permissible under the Convention is whether the applicants had available to them reasonable alternative means to protect effectively their rights under the Convention.

69. The ESA Convention, together with its Annex I, expressly provides for various modes of settlement of private-law disputes, in staff matters as well as in other litigation […].

Since the applicants argued an employment relationship with ESA, they could and should have had recourse to the ESA Appeals Board. In accordance with Regulation 33 § 1 of the ESA Staff Regulations, the ESA Appeals Board, which is "independent of the Agency", has jurisdiction "to hear disputes relating to any explicit or implicit decision taken by the Agency and arising between it and a staff member" […].

[…]

70. Moreover, it is in principle open to temporary workers to seek redress from the firms that have employed them and hired them out. Relying on general labour regulations or, more particularly, on the German Provision of Labour (Temporary Staff) Act, temporary workers can file claims in damages against such firms. In such court proceedings, a judicial clarification of the nature of the labour relationship can be obtained. […]

71. The significant feature of the instant case is that the applicants […] attempted to obtain recognition of permanent employment by ESA on the basis of the above-mentioned special German legislation for the regulation of the German labour market.

72. […] [B]earing in mind the legitimate aim of immunities of international organisations […], the test of proportionality cannot be applied in such a way as to compel an international organisation to submit itself to national litigation in relation to employment conditions prescribed under national labour law. To read Article 6 § 1 of the Convention and its guarantee of access to court as necessarily requiring the application of national legislation in such matters would, in the Court's view, thwart the proper functioning of international organisations […].

73. In view of all these circumstances, the Court finds that, in giving effect to the immunity from jurisdiction of ESA on the basis of section 20(2) of the Courts Act, the German courts did not exceed their margin of appreciation. Taking into account in particular the alternative means of legal process available to the applicants, it cannot be said that the limitation on their access to the German courts with regard to ESA impaired the essence of their "right to a court" or was disproportionate for the purposes of Article 6 § 1 of the Convention.

74. Accordingly, there has been no violation of that provision.

IV. Commentary

A. *Waite and Kennedy* and the 'human rights approach' to organizational immunities

The centrepiece of *Waite and Kennedy*[1] is the notion that an international organization should *in principle* only enjoy immunity before domestic courts if it provides an alternative means of dispute settlement for individuals seeking redress against it. This solution provides an escape to the structural dilemma[2] of (in the context of international organizations usually sweeping) immunities versus the human rights law-based obligations of states to grant individuals access to a court.[3] Admittedly, an alternative means cannot be a fully fledged substitute for state courts reviewing a claim by an aggrieved individual.[4] However, in view of the significant public interests associated with granting immunities to international organizations, it may be an acceptable disadvantage for a claimant to be referred to an alternative means of dispute settlement. The ECtHR did not apply or refer to any *règlement des litiges* clause (i.e. treaty obligations which require an organization to establish a dispute settlement mechanism for certain disputes) when *identifying* the alternative means question as a basic proportionality factor. It referred to the *règlement des litiges* clause only when checking ESA's alternative means against its previously stated requirement. This suggests the applicability of the alternative means test independently of whether positive legal obligations require an organization to set up an internal dispute settlement mechanism in a given case or not.

The ECtHR's approach has both procedural and substantive legal consequences. Procedurally, domestic courts must engage in an incidental scrutiny of whether an alternative means exists, is available, and fulfils certain quality criteria.[5] Plaintiffs

---

[1] For the sake of abbreviation we refer to *Waite and Kennedy* only.

[2] S. Tauchmann, *Die Immunität internationaler Organisationen gegenüber Zwangsvollstreckungsmassnahmen* (Baden-Baden, Nomos 2005), pp. 209, 216, 217.

[3] A. Reinisch, *International Organizations Before National Courts* (Cambridge, Cambridge University Press 2000), pp. 366–9; R. Pavoni, 'Human Rights and the Immunities of Foreign States and International Organizations', in E. de Wet/J. Vidmar (eds), *Hierarchy in International Law* (Oxford, Oxford University Press 2012), pp. 71–113, 73, 103 et seq.

[4] M. Kloth, *Immunities and the Right of Access to Court Under Article 6 of the European Convention on Human Rights* (Leiden, Nijhoff 2010), p. 19.

[5] ECtHR, *Waite and Kennedy*, para. 68. See A. Reinisch/U.A. Weber, 'In the Shadow of *Waite and Kennedy*: The Jurisdictional Immunity of International Organizations, the Individual's Right of Access to the Courts and Administrative Tribunals as Alternative Means of Dispute Settlement', (2004) 1 *International Organizations Law Review* 59–110, 78–9, 93 et seq.; C. Ryngaert, 'The Immunity

are advised to first exhaust remedies within an organization before turning to state courts.[6] Moreover, the ECtHR's approach should be interpreted as establishing a presumption of a disproportionate restriction of the applicant's right to a remedy where an alternative means does not exist, is not available, or lacks core quality standards.[7] Arguably, the functions of such a presumption would not be limited to an allocation of the burden of proof. At ECtHR level, the proportionality of an interference with the Convention must be substantiated by the state anyway. The presumption would also substantively guide the judicial margin of appreciation (of the ECtHR or domestic courts) when applying the proportionality principle and weighing the conflicting interests.

In terms of substance, *Waite and Kennedy* suggests that when an alternative means is not available and other aspects do not militate in favour of upholding immunity, the domestic act granting immunities violates the Convention. This appears to imply that in such a case, the obligations of the forum state emanating from art. 6 ECHR should supersede the state's (treaty- or customary-law-based) obligations to respect the immunity of the organization.[8] However, the ECtHR has so far never found a domestic act awarding immunity to an international organization to actually violate the Convention. Hence, the Court so far did not need to explain and construe any possible overriding effect of state obligations flowing from art. 6(1) ECHR over those emanating from the law of immunities. Neither has the Court, so far, decided on the type of remedies to be granted by the state for a violation of art. 6 ECHR (restitution in form of granting access to a court? Monetary compensation?).[9]

The ECtHR did not tread unchartered territory in 1999. The existence and quality of an alternative means of legal protection as part of a human rights based review of domestic acts granting immunity had been—with nuances and in more or less concrete terms—already examined prior to *Waite and Kennedy* by domestic courts, for

---

of International Organizations Before Domestic Courts: Recent Trends', (2010) 7 *International Organizations Law Review* 121, 132.

[6] E.J. Habscheid, 'Immunität internationaler Organisationen und Art. 6 I EMRK (insbesondere zum Rechtsschutz der Bediensteten)', in R.A. Schütze (ed.), *Einheit und Vielfalt des Rechts: Festschrift für Reinhold Geimer* (München, Beck 2002), pp. 255–76, 272. See also ECtHR, *Chapman v Belgium*, App. No. 39619/06, 5 March 2013, paras 54, 55.

[7] T. Neumann/A. Peters, 'Switzerland', in A. Reinisch (ed.), *The Privileges and Immunities of International Organizations in Domestic Courts* (Oxford University Press 2013), pp. 241–74, 252, with reference, *inter alia*, to E. Gaillard/I. Pingel-Lenuzza, 'International Organisations and Immunity from Jurisdiction: To Restrict or to Bypass', (2002) 51 *International and Comparative Law Quarterly* 1–15, 15. But see J.F. Flauss, 'Droit des immunités et protection internationale des droits de l'homme', (2009) 10 *Revue Suisse de droit international et de droit européen* 299, 322, who interprets the ECtHR's perfunctory review of the alternative means in *Waite and Kennedy* as being tantamount to a 'de facto presumption of conventionality' of granting immunity.

[8] See C. Ryngaert (n. 5), 134. *Contra* such an interpretation N. Angelet/A. Weerts, 'Les immunités des organisations internationales face à l'article 6 de la Convention européenne des droits de l'homme', (2007) *Journal du Droit International* 26, 5: it is not within the ECtHR's competence to decide the conflict. See further, for example, C. Dominicé, 'Observations sur le contentieux des organisations internationales avec des personnes privées', (1999) 45 *Annuaire français de droit international* 623, 638–9, 646, who (normatively) argues that the right of access to a court has attained *ius cogens* status and thereby makes immunities provisions inapplicable (not null and void) in case of a violation.

[9] Pavoni (n. 3), 110.

example in Argentina, Germany, Greece, Italy, or Switzerland.[10] It cannot be ascertained to what degree, or if at all, the ECtHR (or the European Commission of Human Rights) in fact took notice of domestic 'precedents'.[11] Insights into this issue cannot be gleaned from the party submissions before the ECtHR,[12] as they do not make explicit references to any domestic case law in this regard. The only identifiable source of influence is the preceding German Federal Employment Court's judgment in *Waite and Kennedy* of 1993.[13] That court had examined whether the German implementing law of the ESA Convention (and ESA's immunity) infringed upon core requirements of German constitutional law (including the constitutional guarantee of judicial protection). The German Federal Employment Court, just like the ECtHR later, *inter alia* found that ESA's employees could turn to ESA's appeals board, and that hired-out workers could possibly pursue claims against the companies which had hired them out to ESA. This satisfied the minimum requirements of German constitutional law. That part of the German Federal Employment Court's decision stands in the tradition of the German Federal Constitutional Court's *Eurocontrol II* decision of 1981, relating to a different international organization.[14]

B. The merits and de-merits of *Waite and Kennedy*

What, then, if not the novelty of the basic idea, accounts for the immense attention *Waite and Kennedy* has received? Arguably, the decision's merits are both of a doctrinal and of a sociological nature. First, one relative innovation can be seen in the ECtHR's doctrinal reconceptualization of the long-existing *quid pro quo*-rationale (immunity in exchange for an alternative means of dispute settlement) as a pivotal consideration of proportionality in the context of a human rights screening of organizational immunities cases. Integrating the alternative means question into the proportionality test is arguably advantageous from the perspective of the Court. First, it provides a convincing doctrinal peg upon which to hang its review of the *règlement des litiges* clauses in headquarter agreements and other rules governing the establishment and organization of an alternative means.[15] Such norms do not belong to the pool of law formally applicable by the Court. Second, this provided the Court with a flexible tool to tackle very different types of organizational immunities cases.[16] The proportionality solution may amount to a justificatory scheme for 'balancing away', in a given case, the non-availability or the qualitative flaws of an alternative means of redress. If the

---

[10] A. Reinisch/R. Janik, 'The Personality, Privileges, and Immunities of International Organizations before National Courts—Room for Dialogue', in A. Reinisch (ed.) (n. 7), pp. 329–37, 334 and the individual country contributions in the book; Pavoni (n. 3), 104; Ryngaert (n. 5), 135.

[11] See for example R. Vinuesa, 'Argentina', in: Reinisch (ed.) (n. 7), pp. 17–30, 23.

[12] On file with authors.

[13] German Federal Labour Court, *W. and K. v European Space Agency*, 7 AZR 600/92, judgment of 10 November 1993.

[14] German Federal Constitutional Court, 2 BvR 1107, 1124/77 and 195/79, decision of 10 November 1981, BVerfGE 59, 63 ('*Eurocontrol II*').

[15] cf. also Reinisch/Weber (n. 5), 79.

[16] See also ICJ, *Jurisdictional Immunities of the State, Germany v Italy*, Judgment of 3 February 2012, [2012] ICJ Rep 99 et seq., Dissenting Opinion of Judge Antônio A. Cançado Trindade, para. 215.

ECtHR (or a domestic court in the ECtHR's footsteps) finds an alternative mechanism to be non-existent, unavailable, or at fault with basic quality requirements, it can still negate an art. 6 ECHR violation and uphold immunity if other proportionality factors warrant this.[17]

Making the alternative means test a question of proportionality can also be criticized—both conceptually and in the context of this concrete case. In conceptual terms, it may be inadequate to squeeze such an important aspect as the (alternative) protection for individuals into a 'give-and-take'—or compromise-based balancing scheme. This may lead to dubious statements about the alternative means and its qualities. For example, as indicated above, a manifest lack of independence of an alternative body can be outbalanced by important reasons supporting immunity (i.e. where an international organization fulfils particularly important tasks of the public interest, etc.). Thereby, however, a core value of international due process and of good adjudicatory governance, namely the independence of (quasi-)adjudicatory bodies, is *de facto* subjected to a single case-dependent relativism. As an element of proportionality, the independence of the alternative means becomes more or less important, hinging on individual case-related factors. This could translate into the following proposition: the more important an international organization for the fulfilment of elementary public tasks at the international level is, etc., the less independent its administrative tribunal may be. Such conclusions may seem a natural consequence of the application of the proportionality principle and the entanglement of immunity and the alternative means under this principle's auspices. Still, such possible inferences may send the wrong message to certain international organizations and devalue international procedural guarantees.

As to this concrete case, the Court has (rightly) attracted criticism, *inter alia,* for having generally weighted too lightly the individuals' right of access to a court, given its importance for the rule of law and the right's universal normative status.[18] Also, the Court was too perfunctory in the performance of the alternative means test.[19] The ECtHR's rather limited review of the alternative means appears to echo, in some respects, the German Federal Employment Court's limited scrutiny of the alternative means in its *Waite and Kennedy* decision of 1993.[20] While this demonstrates that the ECtHR's approach respects the margin of appreciation, it can also be criticized with the argument that the ECtHR should interpret the Convention autonomously.

In any case, the open-endedness of the ECtHR's proportionality approach makes it vulnerable for a misuse by domestic courts. The vaguer the general standards for an alternative means, the greater is the danger that courts use the test to (unduly) justify immunities by declaring them compatible with whatever standard suits the particular

---

[17] See in detail below, text/notes at n. 42 to 52 and, in particular, Angelet/Weerts (n. 8), 26.

[18] H. Tigroudja, 'L'immunité de juridiction des organisations internationales et le droit d'accès à un tribunal', (2000) 11 *Revue trimestrielle des droits de l'homme* 77–106, 89–93.

[19] The competence of ESA's administrative board to hear claims by temporary workers appeared doubtful. Also, the Court failed to review core qualitative attributes of ESA's administrative board. See, *inter alia*, A. Reinisch, 'Case of *Waite and Kennedy v. Germany*, Application No. 26083/94; Case of *Beer and Regan v. Germany*, Application No. 28934/95, European Court of Human Rights, 18 February 1999', (1999) 93 *American Journal of International Law* 933–8, 937; Flauss (n. 7), 322–3; Tauchmann (n. 2), 229–31, Tigroudja (n. 18), 104–6; critically also Habscheid (n. 6), 270.

[20] See n. 13.

case and the particular organization.[21] Typically, states have strong political interests in hosting international organizations, and this is evidenced by the usually intense competition between states for the position as host state. The concomitant desire to provide a smooth working environment for an organization may lead to a certain bias on the part of the host state government in favour of immunity. In states built on a separation of powers, domestic courts may not necessarily adopt such governmental biases. Still, due to domestic courts' possible deference to their government's conduct of foreign affairs, courts might also suffer from a certain predisposition in favour of immunity. Reference to the *Waite and Kennedy* case-law, in its openness and flexibility, may then serve as a vehicle for masking up political motives for upholding immunities with legal considerations. Coated in the lacquer of purportedly neutral proportionality rhetoric,[22] domestic decisions in favour of immunity which are based on an incomplete, result-oriented, or biased review of an alternative means could represent a novel (and more subtle) variant of 'absolute immunity'.

From a sociology of law-perspective, the ECtHR at least stabilized the trend and catalyzed the already ongoing discourses among academics, practitioners, and some domestic courts to attach to an organization's status before domestic courts its own provision of alternative (quasi-)judicial protection to individuals.[23] In the succeeding years, a number of European domestic courts took over and/or adapted the basic approach of the ECtHR and entered into a 'vertical' judicial dialogue with the ECtHR.[24] The authority of *Waite and Kennedy* flows from the ECtHR's role as the highest organ to review Convention-based claims, and is maybe also owed to the fact that the court (indirectly) judged on a matter of international institutional life of which it forms a part itself and on which it is therefore particularly knowledgeable and credible.

C. *Waite and Kennedy* as a motor for the constitutionalization of international organizations?

From a systemic perspective, the ECtHR's *dicta* can be understood as fuelling compensatory constititionalization processes of international organizations.[25] The conferral of powers to international organizations creates the risk that those may curtail and violate individual rights. At the same time, the exercise of such powers falls outside the scope of domestic constitutional confines or, for the sake of the functioning of the organization, is immunized against domestic control measures. The control and accountability vacuum thus created normatively calls for compensatory measures, preferably in form of an adequate own accountability infrastructure of international organizations.[26] Such calls are more than mere policy arguments where domestic

---

[21] cf. Neumann/Peters (n. 7), 253.

[22] See generally S. Tsakyrakis, 'Proportionality: An Assault on Human Rights?', (2009) 7 *International Journal of Constitutional Law* 468.

[23] C. Ryngaert (n. 15), 121–48, 135; from an ex-ante perspective Flauss (n. 7), 318.

[24] See the various contributions and the conclusions in A. Reinisch (ed.) (n. 7).

[25] A. Peters, 'Compensatory Constitutionalism: The Function and Potential of Fundamental International Norms and Structures', (2006) 19 *Leiden Journal of International Law* 579.

[26] A. Peters, 'The Constitutionalisation of International Organisations', in: N. Walker/J. Shaw/S. Tierney (eds), *Europe's Constitutional Mosaic* (Oxford, Hart 2011), pp. 253–85.

constitutional requirements and obligations arising from constitution-supplementing international treaties such as the ECHR legally condition (immunity-granting) acts by domestic authorities. Via the 'hinge' of a domestic conferral of immunities to an international organization—in itself an exercise of domestic public power—Convention-based and possibly domestic constitutional standards are indirectly projected upon the organization. If the latter wants to keep its immunity, it must adapt its dispute settlement procedures accordingly and create and maintain a compensatory accountability infrastructure.[27]

Whether the constitutionalization impulse given by *Waite and Kennedy* has—in an empirically measurable fashion—triggered a general, pan-institutional amelioration of organizational standards of internal review cannot easily be determined. On the one hand, comprehensive data on institutional reforms of dispute settlement systems in international organizations is lacking so far. On the other hand, other factors may influence processes of institutional remodelling of administrative tribunals (or other mechanisms of dispute settlement), such as the desire or need to adapt to (emerging or consolidating) general principles of international adjudication. It would hence be difficult to prove that an organization has adopted reforms in reaction to *Waite and Kennedy* and/or domestic follow-up case-law. At least as far as ESA's administrative board is concerned, certain moderate changes have been made after *Waite and Kennedy*. These modifications did not broaden or clarify the board's competences *ratione personae* to hear claims by temporary workers (as one might have expected or wished after *Waite and Kennedy*). However, the appeals board has implemented qualitative changes. It has significantly enhanced its transparency by proactively granting access to all case-law since 1976 via the internet.[28]

D. Critical reception and doctrinal debates

While the ECtHR has confirmed the alternative means approach in subsequent case-law,[29] it has only marginally further concretized the conditions of its application. In the following, we focus on five issues which have been left in vagueness by the ECtHR in *Waite and Kennedy* and which have kept commentators busy during the different reception phases of the judgment:

(1) Lack of a precise standard of review: The ECtHR failed to explicitly state the precise standard of review for the test of the alternative means, and, in particular, to provide a comprehensive catalogue of necessary minimum qualities.[30] Domestic courts are thus on their own in defining the material standard of review of an alternative

---

[27] Ryngaert (n. 5), 139; Pavoni (n. 3), 110, 111; Council of Europe, Parliamentary Assembly, Committee on Legal Affairs and Human Rights, Accountability of International Organisations for Human Rights Violations, Report by José Maria Beneyto, Doc. 13370, 17 December 2013, para. 32.

[28] See http://www.esa.int/About_Us/Law_at_ESA/Appeals_Board

[29] ECtHR, *Prince Hans-Adam II of Lichtenstein v Germany*, App. No. 42527/98, judgment of 12 July 2001, para. 48; *Chapman v Belgium* (n. 6), paras 45 et seq.

[30] A. Reinisch, 'The Immunity of International Organizations and the Jurisdiction of their Administrative Tribunals', (2008) 7 *Chinese Journal of International Law* 285, 292; Angelet/Weerts (n. 8), 9.

means. This has led to considerable variances in the quality and rigour of domestic courts' performances of the alternative means test.[31] The existing imbroglio might be further exacerbated by the Court's *dictum* in *Stichting Mothers of Srebrenica*.[32] Here, the Court confirmed that the lack of an alternative means does not necessarily lead to an art. 6 ECHR violation in cases of organizational immunities.[33] Since no competent alternative means existed at all in the UN for the claimants,[34] the court did not engage in any qualitative review. While some courts might stick to a practice of thoroughly reviewing an alternative means, others might be motivated by *Stichting* to put more energy into identifying and defining factors which could outbalance any non-existence or flaws of an alternative means in a given case. As a consequence, they could deem any (further) qualitative review obsolete (once such factors have been identified).

The inhomogeneous domestic case-law is problematic from the perspective of legal certainty. Also, it is the ECtHR's very own task to safeguard the coherent interpretation of the Convention. It should fulfil this task not only *ex post* by rectifying domestic applications of the Convention,[35] but also *ex ante* by giving clear guidelines which domestic authorities and courts may follow in the first place. In any case, the *de facto* incoherent domestic case law has so far prevented the crystallization of the alternative means requirement into an obligation of regional customary law.

(2) **The scope *ratione materiae*:** Is the alternative means approach transferrable to all types of organizational immunities cases? The ECtHR merely decided a concrete dispute in employment-related matters over the immunity of jurisdiction of an international organization. Yet, nothing in the judgments militates against a transfer of the approach to cases not involving employment disputes, or to immunities from execution.[36] In fact, domestic courts have explicitly carried out *Waite and Kennedy*-inspired alternative means tests, or referred to this case-law in cases involving construction contracts with an international organization,[37] involving an organization's immunity of enforcement,[38] etc. Also, in *Stichting*, the Court itself appears to have applied the *Waite and Kennedy* rationale to a complaint against the UN by outsiders, that is not employees of the organization. This demonstrates and confirms the universalizability and versatility of *Waite and Kennedy*.

(3) **Evidence problems:** With regard to the actual implementation of the alternative means test by domestic courts, aggrieved individuals might be structurally

---

[31] See in detail Ryngaert (n. 5), 123, 136 et seq.

[32] ECtHR, *Stichting Mothers of Srebrenica and Others v The Netherlands*, App. No. 65542/12, judgment of 11 June 2013.

[33] Ibid., para. 164. See also below.   [34] Ibid., para. 163 *in fine*.

[35] See for a (*Waite and Kennedy*-based) ECtHR review of a *domestic* court's performance of the *Waite and Kennedy* test ECtHR, *Chapman v Belgium* (n. 6), paras 52–4.

[36] Kloth (n. 4), 154; Pavoni (n. 3), 112; I.F. Dekker/C. Ryngaert, 'Immunity of International Organizations: Balancing the Organization's Functional Autonomy and the Fundamental Rights of Individuals', (2011) 138 *Mededelingen van de Nederlandse Vereniging voor Internationaal Recht* 83, 99.

[37] Swiss Federal Supreme Court, *A.SA et consorts v Conseil Fédéral*, 4A.1/2004/ech, judgment of 2 July 2004, ATF 130 I 312, ILDC 344 (CH 2004) (with note by A.R. Ziegler), para. 4.1.

[38] Swiss Federal Supreme Court, *NML Capital Ltd et al. v. BIS and Debt Enforcement Office Basel-Stadt*, 5A_360/201, judgment of 12 July 2010, ATF 136 III 379, ILDC 1547 (CH 2010) (with note by T. Neumann), para. 4.5.

disadvantaged. Depending on the applicable procedural law, it may be upon the individual claimant to furnish evidence that an alternative means does not exist or is insufficiently organized.[39] This may pose serious problems because information especially on the concrete functioning of an alternative means may be hard to obtain.[40] Where possible, courts should hence adopt a lenient approach and interpret domestic rules of evidence in light of the applicant's rights under art. 6 ECHR and the (difficult procedural) circumstances of the case. Furthermore, technically, until immunity is formally waived by the organization or discarded by a (domestic) court, domestic courts are not in a position to summon an organization before them for evidentiary issues or otherwise request information from an organization.[41] This leads, in some situations, to an additional infringement of the applicant's procedural basic rights such as the principle of equality of arms.

(4) **Rigid or flexible link between alternative means and (dis-)proportionality**: One of the most important questions concerns the potential consequences of the non-existence and/or non-availability of a reasonable alternative means. For the ECtHR, the alternative means argument was (merely) 'a material factor' within the proportionality examination. This cautious wording had led to the conclusion by parts of the literature[42] and by some domestic courts (albeit typically not in employment disputes)[43] that the non-availability of an adequate alternative means did not invariably entail disproportionality.[44] As mentioned above, in its ruling in *Stichting*,[45] the ECtHR confirmed this flexible interpretation of *Waite and Kennedy*. The Court stated that 'in the absence of an alternative remedy the recognition of immunity is [not] ipso facto constitutive of a violation of the right of access to a court' and underlined that its 'judgments in Waite and Kennedy and Beer and Regan [could not] be interpreted in such absolute terms either.'[46] Admittedly, the Court's clarifications in *Stichting* concerned the immunity of the UN, and, moreover, not an employment-related dispute. Due to the particularly important tasks of the UN with regard to securing peace, the UN's immunities are considered in principle more far-reaching than those of other organizations.[47] Still, the ECtHR's unqualified and general confirmation of the flexible interpretation of the alternative means rationale must be understood to apply to all types of organizational immunities cases.

---

[39] See on this issue also (with a discussion of relevant German case-law) Reinisch (n. 30), 301–2.
[40] See Neumann/Peters (n. 7), 261–2.   [41] Ibid.
[42] Angelet/Weerts (n. 8), 9–10, 12; A. Reinisch (n. 30), 292; A. Peters, 'Die funktionale Immunität internationaler Organisationen und die Rechtsweggarantie', (2011) 21 *Revue Suisse de droit international et de droit européen* 397, 425.
[43] UK High Court of Justice, *Entico v UNESCO*, [2008] EWHC 531 (Comm), judgment of 18 March 2008, para. 27 (see Pavoni (n. 3), 105–6); cf. Swiss Federal Supreme Court, *NML Capital Ltd. et al. v BIS and Debt Enforcement Office Basel-Stadt* (n. 38), para. 4.5.3.
[44] This latter (rigid) reading of *Waite and Kennedy* seems to have been espoused, however, for example by L. Caflisch, 'Immunité des États et droits de l'Homme: Évolution récente', in J. Bröhmer et al. (eds), *Internationale Gemeinschaft und Menschenrechte: Festschrift für Georg Ress* (Cologne, C. Heymanns 2005), pp. 935–48, 935. See on the debate also Pavoni (n. 3), 104–8, arguing that domestic case-law before and after *Waite and Kennedy* backs the 'strict' interpretation, and Ryngaert (n. 5), 134–5.
[45] ECtHR, *Stichting Mothers of Srebrenica v The Netherlands* (n. 32).   [46] Ibid., para. 164.
[47] The Hague Court of Appeals, *Stichting Mothers of Srebrenica v The Netherlands and United Nations*, Case No. 200.022.151/01, judgment of 30 March 2010, LJN: BL8979, para. 5.10 (see Dekker/Ryngaert (n. 36), 99–101); Beneyto Report (n. 27), para. 36; cf. Kloth (n. 4), 149 et seq.

On the one hand, the confirmation of the flexible approach could be positive. There may indeed be extreme cases where individual legal protection must cede to other considerations, and where immunity should be upheld.[48] These may be cases where the organization is the structurally weaker part (i.e. in disputes with large enterprises), where the existence of the organization would be at stake, etc. Furthermore, with the flexible approach, domestic courts are not tempted to pretend that a substandard alternative means meets the requirements when in reality, they want to uphold immunity for other important reasons. This may generally foster an honest and transparent jurisprudential evaluation of the alternative means in the face of immunities.

On the other hand, the recent repudiation by the Court of a strict[49] reading of *Waite and Kennedy* can be criticized. For example, a strict understanding appears preferable for employment-related disputes.[50] Also, if only for the sake of legal certainty, it would have behoved the Court to define the circumstances under which the lack of an alternative means will be without consequence for the immunity of an organization.[51] In any case, where factors can be identified which justify upholding immunity despite a non-existent or flawed alternative means, courts arguably must still perform the alternative means test and flag any shortcomings of the organization's internal mechanism in their judgments (and be this in form of an *obiter dictum*). This is due to the ECtHR's request to take all relevant factors into account. Authority for this conclusion can also be drawn from *Stichting*, where the Court explicitly mentioned the non-availability of an alternative means although it did not find a violation of art. 6 ECHR.[52] Thereby, courts may give a shot across the bows of international organizations and/or internal dispute settlement bodies that they make improvements even in cases where immunity is upheld.

(5) Lack of influence of the immunity-granting state over the alternative means: May the incriminated state defend itself by pointing to its alleged lack of influence over the establishment and organization of an alternative means? Governmental influence is usually limited to (1) obliging an international organization to institute alternative means of dispute settlement in the headquarter agreements, etc., (2) working, on the basis of a host state's membership status, towards the establishment of an adequate alternative means through internal decision-making mechanisms of the organization itself,[53] (3) diplomatic efforts and related 'soft' means of persuasion. Beyond these options, it is precisely the organization's independence from singular member states which precludes influence by the immunity-granting state. Even more so, the fulfilment of core standards of 'adequacy' of the alternative means such as requirements of impartiality of the internal judges or decision-makers, etc. must *per definitionem* be

---

[48] Cf. Dekker/Ryngaert (n. 36), 99 (in the context of the *Stichting Mothers of Srebrenica* case); Ryngaert (n. 5), 144

[49] Reinisch (n. 30), 292.

[50] Recent Swiss case-law could point in that direction, Neumann/Peters (n. 7), 264–6, 267.

[51] cf. in a different context Neumann (n. 38), A6. *Contra,* possibly, Angelet/Weerts (n. 8), 10, 18; on possible criteria the Court might take into account ibid., 13–19.

[52] ECtHR, *Stichting Mothers of Srebrenica* (n. 32), para. 163.

[53] C. Janik, 'Die EMRK und internationale Organisationen—Ausdehnung und Restriktion der *equivalent protection*-Formel in der neuen Rechtsprechung des EGMR', (2010) 70 *Zeitschrift für ausländisches öffentliches Recht und Völkerrecht* 127–79, 162.

outside the range of influence of states: if an internal appeals board, etc. was susceptible to external interference, its adequacy as an alternative means in the very terms
of the *Waite and Kennedy* standard would be questionable. Governments might thus
argue that to the extent that they have attempted to persuade the organization to
establish an alternative means via the mentioned admissible channels, or lack influence in the first place, any absence or shortcomings of an alternative means can in no
way be imputed to them.

In fact, domestic decisions prior *and* subsequent to *Waite and Kennedy* sometimes
content themselves to (merely) enumerate and cite legal obligations of international
organizations to instigate means of settlement. They do not inquire further into the
actual setup and functioning of the alternative means.[54] This suggests that states fulfil their human rights-based obligations simply by including so-called *règlement des
litiges*-clauses in their headquarter agreements. It was precisely *Waite and Kennedy*
which raised that standard. Arguably, the judgment required that an adequate alternative means must *in fact* have been instituted,[55] regardless of whether the state did
exert or even could have exerted influence on the organization's internal organization in this regard. As indicated above, in *Stichting*, the Court possibly took a step
back and emphasized the fact that the UN's failure to establish an alternative means
for external complainants was 'not imputable to The Netherlands'.[56] However, the
Court also pointed out that the case differed from other organizational immunities
cases and thereby relativized (also) its statement on the imputability.

The lack of remedies within an international organization in the face of immunity
leads to a possible *déni de justice* for individuals through a combination of four elements, only two of which lie in the sphere of influence of the defendant state: (1) the
transferral of powers to international organizations, (2) the invocation or non-waiver
of immunity by the organization, (3) the actual granting of immunity in domestic proceedings as a legal act of the defendant state's court, and (4) the failure to establish an
alternative means, an omission (and possibly a violation of international law) in many
cases attributable to the international organization in question. However, this mul-
tiplicity of causes for the purported *déni de justice* should not lead to a disadvantage
for the individual. Generally speaking, the ECtHR's 'equivalent protection'-formula
doctrinally 'implies [...] dragging the [trigger point of] material responsibility to a
point in time before the actual act violating the Convention.'[57] Material responsibility is triggered by the state's transferral of powers to an international organization
and/or its failure to withdraw those powers in case the organization's legal order is
in tension with the Convention.[58] It is precisely this legal conceptualization which
does justice to the fact that an individual state is often not in a position to influence
the decisions of an organization.[59] In the specific case of organizational immunities,
however, such conceptualizations are not even necessary. According to the ECtHR,
the act of upholding of immunity by a state court (in full awareness or reproach-
able unawareness) of the *factual* non-existence or non-availability of an adequate

---

[54] Reinisch (n. 3), 275 et seq.   [55] Cf. Habscheid (n. 6), 275.
[56] ECtHR, *Stichting Mothers of Srebrenica* (n. 32), para. 165.
[57] Janik (n. 53), 165 (our translation); Pavoni (n. 3), 82, 100 (discussing ECtHR, *Gasparini v Italy and
Belgium*, App. No. 10750/03, decision of 12 May 2009).
[58] Janik (n. 53), 162.   [59] Ibid.

alternative means of redress) fully qualifies as trigger of the Court's jurisdiction and—in a given case—as *déclencheur* of state responsibility.[60] These considerations show that any actions, omissions, or lack of influence of the forum state with regard to the alternative means should not affect the question of state responsibility where immunity is granted in the absence of an adequate alternative means.

Despite the mentioned open questions, *Waite and Kennedy* has powerfully shaped the law of organizational immunities.

---

[60] ECtHR, *Chapman v Belgium* (n. 6), para. 44. See also Tigroudja (n. 18), 100–2.

7.5 *League of Arab States v T M.*, Belgian Court of Cassation, ILDC 42 (BE 2001), 12 March 2001

*Cedric Ryngaert**

Relevance of the case

An international organization ordinarily only enjoys privileges and immunities on the basis of specific international conventions, for example, as entered into by the organization and the host state (headquarters agreements). The question may arise whether an organization also enjoys immunity in the absence of a convention, or when a convention has not entered into force. Such immunity could be based on customary international law or on a general principle of law. In the *Spaans* case, the Dutch Supreme Court held that an international organization, in the case the Iran-US Claims Tribunal, was entitled to immunity from jurisdiction against an employee's claim in an employment dispute, even though no agreement between The Netherlands and the Tribunal provided for immunity of the latter.[1] This decision is an outlier, however. There are no other known cases of a domestic court granting immunity to an international organization on the basis of customary international law. The judgment that is the subject of this commentary addressed the question whether an international organization could be entitled to immunity on the basis of a *general principle of law*, in the absence of due approval of a headquarters agreement between the international organization and the host state.

I. Facts of the case

TM had brought an employment case against the League of Arab States (League) in a Belgian labour court. The case was eventually heard by the Court of Cassation (Supreme Court). The precise material conflict of the employment dispute cannot be inferred from the Court of Cassation's judgment, since the court limited itself to answering the contentious legal questions. The particular facts of the dispute were, in any event, not relevant to the international law dimension of the case.

TM argued that the League—an international organization—was not entitled to immunity from jurisdiction under international law. The Court of Appeals concurred, and held that the League did not enjoy immunity from jurisdiction in Belgium, on the ground that the federal parliament had failed to approve the Headquarters Agreement between Belgium and the League of Arab States, adopted

---

* [This Commentary is based in part on the author's commentary for ILDC, mentioned above.]

[1] See *Spaans v Iran-United States Claims Tribunal*, Final appeal judgment, Case No 12627, Decision No LJN: AC9158, NJ 1986, 438, (1987) 18 NYIL 357, ILDC 1759 (NL 1985), 20 December 1985, Supreme Court [HR].

on 16 November 1995 (1995 Headquarters Agreement), which provided for immunity of the organization (in spite of the fact that the 'communities' and 'regions', which are the devolved entities in Belgium's federal system, had approved the agreement). The Court of Appeals considered *in eventu* that the dispute was in fact about an *actum iure gestionis* (of commercial nature), which was not covered by the immunity from jurisdiction.

The League thereupon filed a cassation appeal, arguing that approval of the 1995 Headquarters Agreement by the federal parliament was not required (since, in particular, the 1995 Headquarters Agreement could enter into force on the basis of the mere signature), and that immunity from jurisdiction of international organizations was a general principle of international law. As far as the treaty law claims were concerned, the League argued that approval was in fact not required, as Belgium and the League had purportedly given their consent to be bound by the 1995 Headquarters Agreement by their mere signature, and alternatively, that the 1995 Headquarters Agreement could be given provisional application.

To that effect, the League relied on the Vienna Convention on the Law of Treaties between States and International Organizations or between International Organizations (21 March 1986 25 ILM 543), not yet in force (1986 VCLT), providing for such consent to be bound (arts. 11 and 12 of the 1986 VCLT) and provisional application (art. 25 of the 1986 VCLT).

II. The legal question

Whether a bilateral treaty concluded with an international organization that had not been approved by parliament could give rise to legal consequences in the Belgian legal order. Whether the League of Arab States was immune from jurisdiction in the Belgian courts.

III. Excerpts [translation ILDC]

The 1986 VCLT had not yet entered into force. The argument based on the binding effect of the mere signature, as codified in Article 11 of the 1986 VCLT was therefore dismissed. (paragraph 10)

The failure on the part of the Belgian federal parliament to approve the text of the 1995 Headquarters Agreement between Belgium and the League had domestic legal consequences. A treaty had no binding force in the domestic legal order in the absence of approval by the federal parliament, even when the treaty had entered into force for Belgium under international law. Under Belgian constitutional law (Article 167 of the Constitution, 17 February 1994 (Belgium)), treaties could only give rise to legal consequences in the domestic legal order if the competent parliaments had given their approval. Thus, if the parliaments of Belgium's federal entities (communities and regions) had given their timely approval, whereas the federal parliament had not, the treaty had no binding force. The fact that the treaty partly related to matters within the competency of the entities of the federation (whose parliaments had approved the treaty) did not subtract from this. (paragraph 22)

There was no general principle of public international law in the sense of Article 38(1)(c) of the Statute of the International Court of Justice (26 June 1945) to the effect of there being immunity from jurisdiction of international organizations with respect to the states that had established or recognized them. (paragraph 24)

The request of the League was rejected; and jurisdiction over the League was upheld. (paragraph 25)

IV. Commentary

Cases before domestic courts against international organizations often relate to employment matters, as exemplified by this Belgian case against the Arab League. The central aspect of this case is the Court of Cassation's holding that there is no general principle of international law recognizing immunity from jurisdiction of international organizations with respect to states having established or recognized them. This appears to be in keeping with Amerasinghe's observation, in relation to the immunity of international organizations for employment disputes, that '[t]he decisions of national courts do not reflect a uniform approach', and that, in cases where domestic courts did not uphold immunity and thus exercised jurisdiction, '[i]t is not clear whether these courts would exercise jurisdiction in the case of all international organizations or whether the exercise of jurisdiction was restricted only to specific organizations in specific cases'.[2]

The gist of the parties' and the court's argument did, however, not relate to general international institutional law, but rather to the 1995 Headquarters Agreement. Pursuant to art. 1 of the 1995 Headquarters Agreement, the goods and assets which the League uses for the exercise of its official activities in Belgium enjoy immunity from jurisdiction (except if this immunity is waived). Possibly, this could imply that Belgian courts indeed have to recognize the immunity of the League. Yet it could be argued that this provision only related to immunity from enforcement, and not to immunity from jurisdiction. The court did not deal with this substantive question.

The main problem in this case related to the Belgian federal parliament's failure to approve the treaty at the time the case was brought (approval was only given in 1999). Somewhat oddly, the parliaments of Belgium's federal entities (communities and regions) had given their timely approval, whereas the federal parliament had not.

As noted, the argument that ratification was not necessary, and that mere signature would suffice on the basis of the 1986 VCLT, was dismissed by the court, as the 1986 VCLT had not yet entered into force. Even at the time of writing of this comment, there were insufficient ratifications for the treaty to enter into force (see art. 85.1 of the 1986 VCLT; Belgium had deposited its ratification on 1 September 1992. However, the provision for consent to be bound in the 1986 VCLT was analogous to a similar provision in the Vienna Convention on the Law of Treaties (23 May 1969),[3] which entered into force 27 January 1980 (1969 VCLT).

---

[2] See C.F. Amerasinghe, *Principles of the Institutional Law of International Organizations* (2nd edn, Cambridge University Press 2005), pp. 326–7 ('Amerasinghe'), giving, at p. 327, two examples of immunity being denied.

[3] 1155 UNTS 331; 8 ILM 679 (1969); 63 AJIL 875 (1969).

The court conspicuously failed to ascertain whether the provisions of the 1986 VCLT reflected customary international law.[4] It left open the question of whether the 1995 Headquarters Agreement could indeed be binding at the international level. If the relevant provisions of the treaty could be considered as customary international law, the court could have found that there was insufficient evidence that the parties wanted the 1995 Headquarters Agreement to enter into force on the basis of mere signature, or that they wanted to have it provisionally applied.

As the substance of the 1995 Headquarters Agreement undeniably falls within the constitutional competence of the federal state, the inevitable result of the federal parliament's failure to approve the 1995 Headquarters Agreement is that it is not binding in domestic courts and that the courts cannot apply it. Quite reasonably, the approval of the 1995 Headquarters Agreement by the parliaments of the federal entities was found to be immaterial. Deciding otherwise would have been incompatible with the guarantees outlined in art. 167 of the Constitution, which clearly provides that an international agreement only has domestic consequences when it is approved by the parliaments of the federal entities within whose competence the agreement falls.

It is finally noted that the distinction between *acta iure gestionis* and *acta iure imperii*, which is often made in the law of state immunity, did not play a role before the court, which refused to discuss its relevance as it had already found jurisdiction on other bases (namely the absence of parliamentary approval of the relevant agreement). In contrast, the Brussels Court of Appeal had argued, *a fortiori*, that a dispute relating to an employment contract was an *actum iure gestionis* and not an *actum iure imperii*. Immunity would not apply to the former act. The League, however, argued that art. 1 of the 1995 Headquarters Agreement did not draw a distinction between different acts of the international organization. Under general international law, it appears that the distinction may not be relevant to the immunities of international organizations.[5] The Court of Cassation, for its part, was probably wise not to enter into an *a fortiori* discussion on the existence of the said distinction.

On a comparative note, whereas the Belgian Court of Cassation held that there was no general principle on the basis of which an international organizations enjoyed immunity, the Dutch Supreme Court (*Hoge Raad*), in the 1985 *Spaans* case, took the view that the immunity of international organization is governed by customary international law in the absence of a specific treaty. This case concerned the immunity from jurisdiction of the Iran-US Claims Tribunal in an employment dispute brought against it by a former employee, Spaans. The Court characterized the Tribunal as an international organisation that borrows its legal personality from international law.[6]

At the time of the suit, no headquarters agreement or other treaty on privileges and immunities had been concluded between the Tribunal, or by Iran and the United States, with The Netherlands. Such an agreement only materialized in 1990, with an Exchange of Letters between the Government of the Kingdom of The Netherlands and the President of the Iran-United States Claims Tribunal on granting privileges and immunities to the Tribunal, No 004282, 24 September 1990,[7] which provided for the immunity of the Tribunal.

---

[4] Custom can be applied in the Belgian legal order; see Drecoll, 25 January 1906, Pas 1906, L 109.
[5] See Amerasinghe (n. 2), 328.   [6] NJ 1986, 438.
[7] Published in the Dutch *Tractatenblad*, 1990, p. 150.

The absence of a valid treaty at the time of the judgment did not stop the Supreme Court from inquiring whether immunity could be based upon customary international law, concluding that '[a]ccording to unwritten international law as it currently stood, an international organization was in principle not subject to the jurisdiction of the courts of the host state in respect of disputes which were immediately connected to the fulfilment of the tasks assigned to that organization. Possible exceptions did not need to be explored in this case'.[8] The Court proceeded to find that '[d]isputes which might have arisen between an international organization and those who played an essential role in the performance of its tasks belonged to the category of disputes which were immediately connected with the performance of these tasks'.[9] In so doing, the Court distanced itself from the lower courts' determination that the immunity of international organizations was customarily governed by the distinction between *acta jure imperii* and *acta jure gestionis*, a distinction borrowed from the law of state immunity. The lower courts for that matter diverged in the characterization of the organization's acts with regard to the employment dispute before them: the District Court considered it as *actum jure gestionis*, but the Court of Appeal as *actum jure imperii*. By ruling that the categories of the law of state immunity do not apply with respect to the law of international organization immunity, the Dutch Supreme Court did not have to characterize the organization's acts. Commentators have astutely observed that '[t]he dismissal by the Supreme Court of this distinction in relation to international organizations underscored the special character and independence of international organizations as legal actors'.[10]

It remains curious, however, that a court looked for immunity of an international organization beyond treaty law in the first place. There are no other reported cases of domestic courts recognizing the immunity of an international organization on the basis of customary law, or general principles—although this may just be so because almost in all cases a treaty is indeed available. There are however some reported court cases which explicitly *reject* the existence of international organization immunities under customary international law.[11] In a 1999 Italian case involving the European University Institute, the court ruled that customary rules on immunity only apply to states, not to international organizations, as international organizations enjoy only limited international legal personality.[12] Another Italian court confirmed in 2007 that the immunity of international organizations could only be based on conventional instruments, such as headquarters agreements, and not on alleged customary international law.[13] In a 1993 case, the Paris Court of appeal similarly found that there was no international organization immunity under customary international law.[14]

---

[8] Paragraph 3.3.4—translation from ILDC 1759.

[9] Paragraph 3.3.5—translation from ILDC 1759.

[10] R. Peeters and C. Brölmann, ILDC 1759, A2.

[11] See also I. Dekker and C. Ryngaert, 'Immunity of International Organizations: Balancing the Organization's Functional Autonomy and the Fundamental Rights of Individuals', preadvies, 'Making Choices in Public and Private International Immunity Law', (2011) *Mededelingen van de Nederlandse Vereniging voor Internationaal Recht* 138, 83–109.

[12] *EUI v Piette*, Italian Yearbook of International Law (1999), p. 156.

[13] Corte Suprema di Cassazione [Court of Cassation], 19 February 2007 (unpublished) (Italy), *ILDC* 827 (IT 2007), *ILDC* 297 (IT 2005), H4 (refusing to uphold a general customary international law rule of *par in parem non habet imperium/jurisdictionem*, as exists in the law of state immunity).

[14] *CEDAO v BCCI*, 13 January 1993, Court of Appeals of Paris, 120 *JDI* 353 (1993).

Domestic courts may generally only recognize *treaties* as the basis for immunity of international organizations, but such treaties need not necessarily be formal treaties that have been approved by Parliament. Also 'simplified' treaties that confer immunity on the organization may pass muster. In another, more recent case (2010) against the Iran-US Claims Tribunal,[15] the court held that the aforementioned 1990 exchange of letters between The Netherlands and the President of the Tribunal regarding the accordance of privileges and immunities to the Tribunal and its process participants, contained 'an international agreement between a State and an international organisation governed by international law, and thus a treaty, a source of international law' (*Iran U.S. Claims Tribunal Den Haag,* para. 3.3: 'ligt in voormelde briefwisseling een internationale, door het volkenrecht beheerste overeenkomst tussen een Staat en een internationale organisatie besloten en is er sprake van een verdrag, zijnde een bron van volkenrecht'). The District Court held it to be irrelevant that this treaty had not been submitted to Parliament for approval, on the ground that 'under customary international law, a state may not invoke the fact that its consent to be bound by a treaty has been expressed in violation of a provision of its internal law regarding competence to conclude treaties as invalidating its consent'.[16]

---

[15] The District Court of The Hague (Rechtbank den Haag), *Iran U.S. Claims Tribunal Den Haag,* 23 June 2010 (not published).

[16] *Iran U.S. Claims Tribunal Den Haag,* para. 3.4 '(Naar het oordeel van de rechtbank kan in het midden blijven of ten aanzien van het hier aan de orde zijnde verdrag, waarbij feitelijk wordt afgeweken van artikel 17 van de Grondwet (inhoudende dat niemand tegen zijn wil kan worden afgehouden van de rechter die de wet hem toekent), op basis van de Rijkswet goedkeuring en bekendmaking verdragen al dan niet de (stilzwijgende of uitdrukkelijke) goedkeuring van de Staten-Generaal was vereist en/of verkregen. Naar internationaal gewoonterecht immers mag het feit dat de instemming van een Staat door een verdrag gebonden te worden is gegeven in strijd met een bepaling van zijn nationale recht betreffende de bevoegdheid tot het sluiten van verdragen, in beginsel door die Staat niet worden aangevoerd ter ongeldigverklaring van die instemming.').

7.6 *Prewitt Enterprises, Inc. v Org. of Petroleum Exporting Countries*, 353 F.3d 916 (11th Cir. 2003)

*Kristen Boon**

Relevance of the case

The present case addresses effective service of process of an international organiza-tion which the state is not party to. The US Court of Appeals for the Eleventh Circuit relied upon the Federal Rules of Civil Procedure (FRCP) because the Organization of Petroleum Exporting Countries (OPEC) did not fall within the purview of the International Organizations Immunities Act (IOIA) and no other applicable treaty existed regarding the treatment of OPEC in a United States domestic court. The deci-sion's reliance upon FRCP and application of foreign law resulted in the inability of the plaintiffs to bring a claim against OPEC without its express consent.

I. Facts of the case

Prewitt Enterprises, Inc. (Prewitt), an Alabama corporation, bought large quantities of gasoline for resale. OPEC is an intergovernmental organization established in 1960 and presently headquartered in Vienna, Austria. The principal aim of OPEC is 'the co-ordination and unification of the petroleum policies of Member Countries and the determination of the best means for safeguarding their interests, individually and collectively'.[1]

OPEC's relationship with the Austrian government is set forth in the Agreement Between the Republic of Austria and the Organization of the Petroleum Exporting Countries Regarding the Headquarters of the Organization of the Petroleum Exporting Countries[2] (Headquarters Agreement). The Austrian Parliament enacted this agree-ment into law by resolution and the agreement was published in the Austrian Official Gazette.

Prewitt filed a complaint in the Northern District of Alabama, Southern Division on behalf of itself and as representative of all other entities who directly purchase gas-oline products in the United States, against OPEC for violations of US antitrust law.[3] Specifically, Prewitt claimed that OPEC's co-ordination agreements amongst member and non-member states to fix world prices for oil violated the Sherman Act and the Clayton Act. OPEC objected to the district court's jurisdiction on several grounds, including insufficient service of process. The district court dismissed the case finding

* Thanks to Marissa Mastroianni for her excellent research assistance.
[1] cf. OPEC Statute, art. 2(A), 10 October 1960, 443 U.N.T.S. 247.
[2] eb. 18, 1974, BGBL 1974/38.
[3] cf. *Prewitt Enterprises, Inc. v Org. of Petroleum Exporting Countries*, 224 FRD 497 (N.D. Ala. 2002); however, note that this judgment vacated an earlier judgment in *Prewitt Enterprises, Inc. v Org. of Petroleum Exporting Countries*, CV-00-W-0865-S, 2001 WL 624789 (N.D. Ala. 22 March 2001).

that Prewitt did not serve OPEC in accordance with the FRCP. Prewitt appealed the district court's dismissal. The Eleventh Circuit affirmed the district court's decision on the same reasoning.

II. The legal question

The question raised by the present case is the following: did the claimant effectively serve OPEC under the FRCP by sending the complaint through international registered mail, which provided OPEC with actual notice of the suit?

III. Excerpts

[...]

Prewitt claimed that as a result of OPEC's illegal conduct, its own acquisition and inventory costs for gasoline have increased significantly. Consequently, Prewitt requested that the court declare the OPEC-coordinated agreements illegal under United States law, enjoin implementation of the agreements, grant any other appropriate equitable relief, and award costs of the suit against OPEC for injuries sustained by Prewitt.

Prewitt attempted service on OPEC by requesting that the trial court send a copy of the complaint to OPEC by international registered mail, return receipt requested. The court clerk did so, mailing Prewitt's summons and complaint to OPEC at its headquarters in Vienna. The pleadings were signed for, stamped 'received' by OPEC's Administration and Human Resources Department, and forwarded to the Director of OPEC's Research Division as well as other departments including the Secretary General's office. Ultimately, the Secretary General decided that the OPEC Secretariat would not take any action with regard to the summons and complaint.

[...]

The threshold issue in this case is whether OPEC has been effectively served under the Federal Rules of Civil Procedure. If it has not, we must then determine whether extraterritorial service of process on OPEC may be effectuated at all under the circumstances here. By definition, 'service of summons is the procedure by which a court having venue and jurisdiction of the subject matter of the suit asserts jurisdiction over the person of the party served.' *Miss. Publ'g Corp. v. Murphree*, 326 U.S. 438, 444–45, 66 S.Ct. 242, 90 L.Ed. 185 (1946). A court is required to have personal jurisdiction under the Due Process Clauses of the Fifth and Fourteenth Amendments to the United States Constitution 'as a matter of individual liberty' so that 'the maintenance of the suit [...] [does] not offend "traditional notions of fair play and substantial justice."' *Ins. Corp. of Ir. v. Compagnie des Bauxites de Guinee*, 456 U.S. 694, 702–03, 102 S.Ct. 2099, 72 L.Ed.2d 492 (1982) (quoting *Int'l Shoe Co. v. Washington*, 326 U.S. 310, 316, 66 S.Ct. 154, 90 L.Ed. 95 (1945)).

[...]

Thus an 'unincorporated association' headquartered outside of the United States that is (1) subject to suit under a common name and (2) has not waived service may be served in any manner authorized under Fed.R.Civ.P. 4(f) for individuals in a foreign country except for personal delivery.

[...]

In this case, no other means of service has been 'otherwise provided by federal law' nor is there an 'internationally agreed means reasonably calculated to give notice such as those means authorized by the Hague Convention on the Service Abroad of Judicial and Extrajudicial Documents ...' The federal laws pertaining to service of process on a foreign entity are codified in 28 U.S.C. §§ 1602 et seq., the Foreign Sovereign Immunities Act (FSIA), and 22 U.S.C. §§ 288 et seq., the International Organizations Immunities Act (IOIA). The parties agree that neither of these federal laws apply to OPEC in this case. The parties likewise agree that there is no international agreement that stipulates the appropriate means of service.

Thus we must look to the remainder of Fed.R.Civ.P. 4(f), which provides for other methods by which an unincorporated association may be served in the absence of relevant federal law or international agreements:

> (2) if there is no internationally agreed means of service or the applicable international agreement allows other means of service, provided that service is reasonably calculated to give notice:
> (A) in the manner prescribed by the law of the foreign country for service in that country in an action in any of its courts of general jurisdiction; or
> (B) as directed by the foreign authority in response to a letter rogatory or letter of request; or
> (C) unless prohibited by the law of the foreign country, by
> (i) delivery to the individual personally of a copy of the summons and the complaint; or
> (ii) any form of mail requiring a signed receipt, to be addressed and dispatched by the clerk of the court to the party to be served; or
> (3) by other means not prohibited by international agreement as may be directed by the court.

Fed.R.Civ.P. 4(f)(2) and (3).

Prewitt originally chose to attempt service of process on OPEC under Fed.R.Civ.P. 4(f)(C)(ii). However, the method set forth under that provision applies only if it is not prohibited by the law of the foreign country. Based on the evidence presented, the district court correctly found that service on OPEC was prohibited by the law of Austria. Article 5(2) of the Austrian/OPEC Headquarters Agreement provides that: 'the service of legal process [...] shall not take place within the [OPEC] headquarters seat except with the express consent of, and under conditions approved by, the Secretary General.' Since the Headquarters Agreement was enacted into law by resolution of the Austrian Parliament and published in the Austrian Official Gazette pursuant to the Austrian Constitution, the district court found it to be an integral part of Austrian law. Thus, because service was prohibited by Austrian law, Prewitt could not have effectively served OPEC under Fed.R.Civ.P. 4(f)(C)(ii).

Prewitt nonetheless suggests that we should liberally construe the formal requirements for service under the Federal Rules because OPEC received actual notice but simply chose to 'ignore the whole thing.' Br. of Appellant at 23. However, we find no support for such an argument. Due process under the United States Constitution requires that 'before a court may exercise personal jurisdiction over a defendant, there must be more than notice to the defendant [...] [t]here also must be a basis for the defendant's amenability to service of summons. Absent consent, this means there must be authorization for service of summons on the defendant.' *Omni Capital Int'l v. Rudolf Wolff & Co.*, 484 U.S. 97, 104, 108 S.Ct. 404, 98 L.Ed.2d 415 (1987) (emphasis added). In other words, an individual or entity "is not obliged to engage in litigation unless [officially] notified of the action [...] under a court's authority, by formal process." *Murphy Bros., Inc. v. Michetti Pipe Stringing, Inc.*, 526 U.S. 344, 347, 119 S.Ct. 1322, 143 L.Ed.2d 448 (1999). In this case, Fed.R.Civ.P.(f)(2)(C)(ii) clearly states that service of process by registered mail is only authorized where it is not prohibited by foreign law. Here, the Headquarters Agreement constitutes Austrian law and, under Article 5(2), expressly prohibits all service of process upon OPEC within the headquarters seat that has not been consented to by its Secretary General. Thus, we agree with the district court that even though OPEC had actual notice of the filing of the suit, service of process was ineffective because it was clearly not in substantial compliance with the requirements of Fed.R.Civ.P. 4(f)(2)(C)(ii).

Alternatively, Prewitt argues that even if service failed under Fed.R.Civ.P. 4(f)(2)(C)(ii), service by registered mail upon OPEC nonetheless complied with Fed.R.Civ.P. 4(f)(2)(A), which permits service if it is effectuated "in the manner prescribed by the law of the foreign country for service in that country in an action in any of its courts of general jurisdiction." The provisions of Austrian law that Prewitt references from Austria's Civil Procedure Code and regulations for service of process by mail relate to service by Austrian courts on persons resident in Austria and abroad. None of these Austrian law provisions directly pertain to service mailed from abroad upon international organizations resident in Austria. [...] Section 11(2) (as amended 1998) of the Austrian Services Act directly addresses service from abroad upon international organizations such as OPEC requiring that:

the mediation of the Federal Ministry for Foreign Affairs shall be enlisted in undertaking service of process on foreigners or international organizations that enjoy privileges and immunities under international law, regardless of their place of residence or headquarters.

There would be no way for Prewitt to serve OPEC under § 11(2) of the Austrian Service Act because we must assume that if it had gone to the Austrian Federal Ministry of Foreign Affairs, the Ministry would have applied the laws of its own country and obeyed the dictates of the Austrian/OPEC Headquarters Agreement prohibiting service without OPEC's consent.

[...]

Finally, Prewitt contends that even if its service by registered mail on OPEC could not be effectuated pursuant to any of the provisions of Fed.R.Civ.P. 4(f)(2), the district court still had the discretion to order service of process pursuant to Fed.R.Civ.P. 4(f)(3), which provides that service may be effected 'by other means not prohibited by international agreement as may be directed by the court.' (emphasis added). We agree with Prewitt that a district court's denial of relief under 4(f)(3) is reviewed under an abuse of discretion standard. However, there is no abuse of discretion here; on the contrary, any circumvention of 4(f)(2)(C)(ii) by the district court in directing service again by registered mail would constitute such an abuse. On these facts, we cannot read 4(f)(3) as permitting that which has already been specifically prohibited under 4(f)(2).

[...]

However, the 1993 Advisory Committee Notes to Fed.R.Civ.P. 4(f)(3) instruct that:

Paragraph (3) authorizes the court to approve other methods of service not prohibited by international agreements [...] Inasmuch as our Constitution requires that reasonable notice be given, an earnest effort should be made to devise a method of communication that is *consistent with due process* and *minimizes offense to foreign laws.*

Rather than minimizing offense to Austrian law, the failure to obtain OPEC's consent would constitute a substantial affront to Austrian law. We can find no support permitting such a consequence in the face of Austria's direct prohibition of service on OPEC without its consent.

[...]

Austrian law clearly provides protection to OPEC as an international organization from all methods of service of process without its consent and also requires that any service of process from abroad be effected through Austrian authorities. In this case, OPEC has made clear that it refuses to consent expressly to service of process by Prewitt; thus, the district court did not abuse its discretion in denying Prewitt's motion to authorize alternative means of service.

IV. Commentary

There has been disagreement regarding how to effectuate service of process in claims brought against an international organization that does not fall within the scope of any federal statute or treaty. The lack of a controlling international convention that applies to all international organizations uniformly creates widely varied case law from state to state.[4] Thus, domestic law often plays a significant role in determining effective service of process of an international organization.[5]

In general, international organizations with broad regional power enjoy a wide range of immunity from every form of legal process.[6] In *Prewitt*, the District Court recognized the tension between the plaintiff's right to bring the claim against OPEC due to violations of US law and OPEC's immunity from legal service of process.[7] The district court realized that the decision would preclude United States claimants from effectively serving OPEC; thereby, giving OPEC a way around being held liable for

---

[4] The International Law Commission (ILC) spent more than thirty-one years trying to reach a consensus on the topic of relations between states and international organizations, but abandoned its efforts in 1992. See M. Möldner, 'International Organizations or Institutions, Privileges and Immunities', in *Max Planck Encyclopedia of Public International Law* (2008), p. 2.

[5] Not only does domestic law play an important role in implementing international agreements, but in the absence of such an international agreement, domestic law can directly grant privileges and immunities to international organizations. See Möldner (n. 4), p. 3.

[6] See C. Wickremasinghe, 'International Organizations or Institutions, Immunities Before National Courts', in *Max Planck Encyclopedia of Public International Law* (2009), p. 2 (this also includes the African Union, Council of Europe, and Organization of American States).

[7] Prewitt Enterprises, 224 FRD, p. 502 ('The notion of wholly insulating from service of process an entity such as OPEC—whose decisions surely affect the daily lives of most Americans—is, for many, a bitter pill to swallow. But the Court must apply the rules as they are written. The rules reflect a clearly expressed diplomatic policy choice of Congress to respect the normative and, ultimately, the legislative, decisions of foreign sovereigns.').

its violations of US law. However, the district court opined that the FRCP reflects Congress' respect for the legislative decisions of other states.

Although the decision would, in effect, insulate OPEC from suit in the United States,[8] the Eleventh Circuit affirmed the District Court's dismissal because service did not comport with US domestic law. As a preliminary matter, no international agreement or federal statute governed in *Prewitt* because OPEC is not considered an international organization under the IOIA.[9] Moreover, the US is not a member of OPEC.[10]

Thus, the court turned to the FRCP to determine whether service of process was effectuated.[11] The court first applied Fed. R. Civ. P. 4(h)(2) that provided for legal service of OPEC in any manner authorized by Fed. R. Civ. P. 4(f).[12] To satisfy the rule, the court noted that plaintiffs must have served OPEC in accordance with the law of the foreign country it was located in.[13] Thus, in holding that the plaintiff did not effectively serve OPEC under the FRCP, the court made various determinations regarding what is proscribed as effective service of process in Austrian law.[14] Specifically, the Austrian/OPEC Headquarters Agreement precludes service of process without the express consent of OPEC's Secretary General.[15] Due to the fact that the Austrian/OPEC Headquarters Agreement was enacted into law by the Austrian Parliament, the court deferred to Austrian law.[16] The court also rejected plaintiffs' arguments regarding OPEC's actual notice of the suit, thus applying the FRCP's language in a strict sense.[17]

In 2013, the United States District Court for the District of Columbia was faced with a similar situation.[18] In that case, the plaintiffs also sued OPEC for violations of the Sherman Act and the Clayton Act and the court was again called on to dismiss the motion for insufficient service of process.[19] The court adopted *Prewitt* and dismissed the case because Austrian law prohibits any form of service of process to OPEC without its consent.[20]

---

[8] Unless OPEC expressly consented to service, pursuant to art. 5(2) of the Headquarters Agreement.

[9] cf. *Prewitt Enterprises*, 353 F.3d at 922.

[10] It is important to note that US courts have not treated all cases against an international organization of which it is not party to in the same manner. For example, in *International Tin Council v Amalgameet, Inc.*, the state court pointed out that there was no basis to extend the immunities the International Tin Council (ITC) enjoyed under its Headquarters Agreement with the United Kingdom. 524 N.Y.S.2d 971, 975 (N.Y. Sup. Ct. 1988) *aff'd*, 529 N.Y.S.2d 983 (1988).

[11] cf. *Prewitt Enterprises* (n. 9), p. 923.   [12] cf. *Prewitt Enterprises* (n. 9), p. 922.

[13] Ibid., pp. 922–4.   [14] Ibid., p. 928.   [15] Ibid., p. 923.   [16] Ibid., p. 924.

[17] Ibid., pp. 924–9.

[18] cf. *Freedom Watch, Inc. v Org. of Petroleum Exporting Countries*, 288 F.R.D. 230 (D.D.C. 2013).

[19] Ibid., pp. 230–1.

[20] cf. Ibid., p. 232. However, the court in *Freedom Watch* did consider an argument that was not made in *Prewitt* regarding the service of process on OPEC's attorneys who were located in the United States. The court held that OPEC did not authorize its attorneys to accept service of process on its behalf. Ibid., p. 233.

7.7 *Entico Corporation Ltd v UNESCO*, 18 March 2008, [2008] EWHC 531 (Comm), [2008] 2 All ER (Comm) 97

*Chanaka Wickremasinghe**

Relevance of the case

This case provides the most detailed examination to date by a United Kingdom court of the relationship between the immunity of an international organization, UNESCO, and the right of access to a court, as it is implied in the interpretation of art. 6 of the European Convention on Human Rights (ECHR). It raises an interesting question about the applicability of the much-cited judgment in *Waite and Kennedy*[1] in the context of a UN Specialised Agency.

I. Facts of the case

The claimant, a British company, sought to enter into a contract with UNESCO for the printing and production of a calendar. Draft contract terms were proposed by the claimant, and discussed by the parties, including a provision for the settlement of disputes by arbitration under the UNCITRAL rules. However before the contract had been formally concluded UNESCO indicated that it did not wish to proceed with the project. The claimant alleged that the cancellation was contrary to the implied contract between them and sued for compensation in the Commercial Court in London. UNESCO did not take part in the proceedings, and the claimant sought a judgment in default.

II. The legal question

In seeking to enter a default judgment, the claimant sought to overcome the immunity enjoyed by UNESCO under art. III, Section 4 of the 1947 Convention on the Privileges and Immunities of the Specialised Agencies (1947 Convention). In this respect, the claimant challenged the UK legislation which implemented the 1947 Convention in UK law on the basis that it was incompatible with the right of access to a court implicit under art. 6 of the ECHR. The Secretary of State for Foreign and Commonwealth Affairs intervened to submit that there was no incompatibility.

III. Excerpts

Mr Justice Tomlinson:
>   [...]
>   17. At the outset it should be stressed that the immunity given to UNESCO in this jurisdiction has been given solely in order to comply with the UK's obligations under

---

* Legal Counsellor, Foreign and Commonwealth Office. This piece is written in a personal capacity.
[1] See ch. 7.4.

public international law. I have already set out the source of this obligation at paragraph 2 above, the 1947 Convention. It is an obligation owed to virtually the entire international community. I have already set out Sections 4 and 5 of Article III which is headed 'PROPERTY, FUNDS AND ASSETS'. It should be noted that Section 4 makes no provision for any waiver whatsoever so far as concerns the immunity from execution. Article IX, headed 'SETTLEMENT OF DISPUTES' includes Section 31 which provides:

> 'Each specialised agency shall make provision for appropriate modes of settlement of: (a) Disputes arising out of contracts or other disputes of private character to which the specialised agency is a party; (b) Disputes involving any official of a specialised agency who by reason of his official position enjoys immunity, if immunity has not been waived in accordance with the provisions of section 22.'

It necessarily follows that an 'appropriate' mode of settlement does not include within it submission to the process of execution. A specialised agency cannot waive its immunity in that regard. There is nothing in the Convention to make enjoyment of the privileges and immunities conferred by Sections 4 and 5 dependent upon compliance with section 31. Section 31 itself offers no criteria pursuant to which the appropriateness of a mode of settlement is to be judged. Importantly, section 31 does not say that the mode of settlement for which provision is made must be effective. It would be wholly inimical to the international scheme envisaged if individual States party arrogated to themselves the power to determine whether the provision made by each specialised agency for the settlement of disputes is adequate, whether considered generally or by reference to the facts of a particular case.

18. The 1947 Convention must be interpreted in accordance with the principles codified in Articles 31-33 of the Vienna Convention on the Law of Treaties, 1969, which require that a treaty be interpreted in good faith, in accordance with the ordinary meaning to be given to the terms of the treaty in their context and in the light of the treaty's object and purpose. Sections 4 and 5 of the 1947 Convention are clear, unequivocal and unconditional. They plainly require the parties to recognise and to give effect to a broad jurisdictional immunity possessed by each specialised agency. There is in my judgment no room for 'reading down' [i.e. limiting by process of interpretation] the provisions of the 1947 Convention in order to take account of the provisions of the subsequent ECHR, a treaty which is binding upon only a minority of the parties to the 1947 Convention.

19. Article 31.3(c) of the Vienna Convention provides:

> 'There shall be taken into account, together with the context: . . . (c) any relevant rules of international law applicable in the relations between the parties . . .'

As was pointed out by the ECt.HR in *Bankovic v. Belgium* 123 ILR 94 at paragraph 57 of the judgment, the ECHR is itself an instrument which must be construed in the light of this article. Moreover Article 30.4(b) of the Vienna Convention has the effect that the need to comply with the requirements of the ECHR does not excuse compliance with an earlier convention to which more states are party than are party to the ECHR. As Mr Greenwood QC, for the Secretary of State, submitted, it is in the highest degree implausible that when the states party drafted and acceded to the ECHR they intended thereby to place themselves in violation of their existing international obligations. Their existing international obligations, owed to many more states than were or are party to the ECHR, required them to recognise and to give effect to a broad and unqualified jurisdictional immunity enjoyed by each specialised agency. It would therefore be surprising if Article 6 of the ECHR was intended to render this regime non-compliant, thereby plunging all states party to both the ECHR and the 1947 Convention into a position in which their obligations conflicted.

[...]

23. It is unnecessary for me to decide whether Article 6 of the ECHR is in these circumstances in fact engaged at all. In the context of State immunity Lord Millett in *Holland v. Lampen-Wolfe* [2000] 1 WLR 1573 at 1588 pointed out that while Article 6 'forbids a contracting state from denying individuals the benefit of its powers of adjudication it does not extend those powers'. In *Jones v. Saudi Arabia* [2007] 1 AC 270 both Lord Bingham at paragraph 14 and Lord Hoffmann at paragraph 64 expressed their agreement with Lord Millett's approach. As Lord Hoffmann put it, 'there is not even a *prima facie* breach of Article 6 if a State fails to make available a jurisdiction which it does not possess'. When the UK became party to the ECHR it possessed no jurisdiction over UNESCO unless UNESCO chose to waive its immunity.

24. Since recognition of the immunity of an international organisation is equally required by international law, there can be no reason for regarding this approach as not equally applicable to recognition of organisational immunity as it is to recognition of State immunity. Certainly when considering whether the grant of immunity to an international organisation pursues a legitimate aim, the ECt.HR has drawn no distinction—see *Waite and Kennedy v. Germany* [1999] 30 EHRR 261 at paragraph 63. In that case however Germany conceded that Article 6 was engaged and the court proceeded on the basis that it was applicable. That case was moreover concerned with the European Space Agency ('the ESA'), an international organisation created by a small group of European States all of which were parties to the ECHR and had been so for some years before the establishment of the ESA.

25. In the present case it makes no difference to the outcome of this application whether Article 6 is regarded as engaged or not. I turn therefore to consider whether, on the assumption that Article 6 is engaged, the grant of immunity to UNESCO pursues a legitimate aim and if there is a reasonable relationship of proportionality between the means employed and the aim sought to be achieved.

26. In relation to the first question, it was as I understood it the submission of Ms Fatima [i.e. Counsel for the claimant] that the court is concerned with the question whether the grant of immunity to UNESCO and similar organisations is itself a legitimate aim in the sense of being necessary to its or their proper functioning. In my judgment jurisprudence of which I must take account demonstrates that this is not the appropriate question. In its separate judgments in the trilogy of cases *Al-Adsani v. United Kingdom* (2001) 34 EHRR 273, *Fogarty v. United Kingdom* (2001) 34 EHRR 302, and *McElhinney v. Ireland* (2001) 34 EHRR 323, the Grand Chamber of the ECt. HR included, in identical terms, the following passage:

'The Court must first examine whether the limitation pursued a legitimate aim. It notes in this connection that sovereign immunity is a concept of international law, developed out of the principle *par in parem non habet imperium*, by virtue of which one State shall not be subject to the jurisdiction of another State. The Court considers that the grant of sovereign immunity to a state in civil proceedings pursues the legitimate aim of complying with international law to promote comity and good relations between States through the respect of another State's sovereignty.

The Court must next assess whether the restriction was proportionate to the aim pursued. It recalls that the Convention has to be interpreted in the light of the rules set out in the Vienna Convention of 23 May 1969 on the Law of Treaties, and that Article 31(3)(c) of that treaty indicates that account is to be taken of "any relevant rules of international law applicable in the relations between the parties." The Convention, including Article 6, cannot be interpreted in a vacuum. The Court must be mindful of the Convention's special character as a human rights treaty, and it must also take the relevant rules of international law into account. The Convention should so far as possible be interpreted in harmony with other rules of international law of which it forms part, including those relating to the grant of State immunity.

It follows that measures taken by a High Contracting Party which reflect generally recognised rules of public international law on State immunity cannot in principle be regarded as imposing a disproportionate restriction on the right of access to a court as embodied in Article 6 section 1. Just as the right of access to a court is an inherent part of the fair trial guarantee in that Article, so some restrictions on access must likewise be regarded as inherent, an example being those limitations generally accepted by the community of nations as part of the doctrine of State immunity.'

It follows in my judgment that compliance with obligations owed in international law is of itself pursuit of a legitimate aim. Furthermore, insofar as the 1974 Order reflects generally recognised rules of public international law on organisational immunity, which in my judgment it does, it cannot in principle be regarded as imposing a disproportionate restriction on the right of access to court as embodied in Article 6(1).

27. It is true that in the earlier case of *Waite and Kennedy*, which was concerned with organisational rather than State immunity, the ECt.HR did not express itself in quite such stark terms. However as I have also already pointed out, there can in fact be no principled basis upon which the approach can in the two situations be different. The Commission was in that case almost equally divided, a bare majority, 17–15, finding that Germany had not exceeded its margin of appreciation in limiting the applicants' rights of access to the national courts in relation to an employment dispute with the ESA. The dissentients pointed out that the Commission was there concerned only with the immunities of international organisations created after the coming into force of the ECHR—see page 281. It is true that in considering proportionality the Court said that it regarded as a material factor whether the applicants had available to them means of redress which were a reasonable alternative to access to the German national courts—see paragraph 68 at page 287. At paragraph 73 of the judgment the Court said that it took into account in particular the alternative means of legal process available to the applicants, which involved an internal tribunal. However I note that the Court did not approach the matter upon the basis that it is a pre-requisite to the compatibility with Article 6 of

organisational immunity that the organisation provide an alternative forum for dispute resolution. Furthermore the conceded applicability of Article 6 in that case to disputes involving the ESA created no possibility of conflict of international obligations. The Court was concerned only with the obligations of an ECHR State owed to other ECHR States and to an organisation created by such States long after they had acceded to the ECHR. In the light of the approach of the ECt.HR in the subsequent trilogy of State immunity cases it is not in my judgment safe to assume that the ECt.HR would in a case involving the immunity of a global organisation created prior to the ECHR adopt reasoning similar to that to be found in *Waite and Kennedy*. Indeed it is worth setting out in full what the Court did on that occasion say about the immunity of international organisations in the context of legitimate aim. At paragraph 63, a passage to which I have already drawn attention above, the Court said this:

> 'Like the Commission, the Court points out that the attribution of privileges and immunities to international organisations is an essential means of ensuring the proper functioning of such organisations free from unilateral interference by individual governments.
>
> The immunity from jurisdiction commonly accorded by States to international organisations under the organisations' constituent instruments or supplementary agreements is a long-standing practice established in the interest of the good working of these organisations. The importance of this practice is enhanced by a trend towards extending and strengthening international co-operation in all domains of modern society.
>
> Against this background, the Court finds that the rule of immunity from jurisdiction, which the German courts applied to ESA in the present case, has a legitimate objective.'

One can understand why in that case there was an argument for the applicability of Article 6, which was of course conceded. By contrast I can find no justification for reading a convention concluded some years before the ECHR, the majority of whose parties are not bound by that later Convention, in the light of the later principles espoused by only a small sub-set of the parties to the earlier convention.

28. If however, contrary to my view, it is relevant to take into account the availability of an alternative forum, it is clear that there is in the present case an available mode of dispute resolution, i.e. arbitration under UNCITRAL Rules. For the reasons already stated I find it inappropriate to assess its adequacy and likely efficacy, although I should record that it has certainly not been established that it is an inadequate remedy. It is the remedy which Entico itself put forward for acceptance. The immunity from execution of UNESCO is not incompatible with Article 6—see *Kalogeropolou v. Greece* 129 ILR 537, and is in any event irrelevant, UNESCO having stated that it will comply with any award. [...]

29. In my judgment therefore if Article 6 is engaged there is no violation of Entico's Article 6 rights. It has of course already been held by the Court of Appeal in *Stretford v. The Football Association* [2007] 2 Lloyd's Rep 31, that voluntarily entering into an arbitration agreement amounts to a waiver of rights under Article 6. However my principal conclusion is that the 1974 Order is not incompatible with Article 6 [...]

IV. Commentary

The judgment represents a rather careful assessment of the relationship of immunity of an international organization and the individual right of access to a court. In line with UK case-law the judgment starts by questioning whether art. 6 is engaged at all in cases where immunity is a requirement of international law. The position of the House of Lords, in the context of state immunity, is that where international law limits the scope of the jurisdiction of the national court, art. 6 cannot of itself extend the jurisdiction of the court beyond those limits.[2] However in this respect the position in UK law appears to diverge from the approach of the Strasbourg Court.[3] In the present case the Judge found that he did not have to come to a definitive conclusion on the point, since he found that maintaining immunity was compatible with art. 6 in any event.

As regards the compatibility of immunity with art. 6, the starting point is of course that the right of access to a court is not an unlimited right, but that any limitation must pursue a legitimate aim and be proportionate in the circumstances. The Judge had little difficulty in finding that the immunity deriving from the 1947 Convention, a treaty with a broad take up by states around the world, met these requirements. On the question of proportionality, it is interesting to note that the Judge resisted the approach, which is sometimes urged in the literature, of reading *Waite and Kennedy* as *ipso facto* requiring the provision of alternative remedies as prerequisite for the enjoyment of immunity by international organizations.[4] The judgment suggests that a more nuanced or contextual approach needs to be taken to the question. Whilst the provision of alternative remedies was undoubtedly an important factor weighed by the Court in *Waite and Kennedy*, that was in relation to the ESA, an organization established by European states, established after they had acceded to the ECHR. The judgment suggests that other considerations may weigh in the context of a global organization with its own established and widely followed regime of immunities. In this connection the judgment of the Strasbourg Court in the *Mothers of Srebrenica* case appears to bear this out.[5]

The huge variety of international organizations, including as regards their membership, structures, powers, and activities, means that the extent of their immunities must be fashioned in the case of each organization to meet their particular functional needs.[6] This suggests that the national court, as here, needs to approach generalizations in this area of the law with appropriate care, and with a full appreciation of the international legal context that governs the international organization in question.

---

[2] cf. *Holland v Lampen-Wolfe*, [2000] 1 WLR 157.

[3] cf. *Jones and Mitchell v UK*, judgment of 14 January 2014, paras 164–5.

[4] See, e.g., A. Reinisch 'Transnational Judicial Conversations on the Personality, Privileges and Immunities of International Organizations—an Introduction', in A. Reinisch (ed.) *The Privileges and Immunities of International Organizations in Domestic Courts* (Oxford, Oxford University Press 2013), pp. 10–15.

[5] cf. *Stichting Mothers of Srebrenica and others v The Netherlands*, decision of 11 June 2013, paras 161–5.

[6] cf. Commentaries to the ILC's Articles on the Responsibility of International Organisations, paras 1–9.

7.8 *Western European Union v Siedler,* Belgian Court of Cassation, 21 December 2009

Pierre Schmitt

Relevance of the case

This decision was rendered on 21 December 2009 by the Belgian Court of Cassation, that is the Supreme Court in civil and penal matters, simultaneously with two other decisions concerning the immunity of jurisdiction and execution of international organizations established in Belgium. The three decisions concerned employment-related disputes between individuals and international organizations—the Western European Union (WEU) in the decision commented, the African, Caribbean, and Pacific Group of States (ACP Group) in the two other decisions. All three decisions are relevant, as only very few Supreme Courts in the world have tackled the question of the immunity of international organizations, and even fewer have examined the tension between the immunity of the organization and the individual's right of access to a court. Moreover, the Belgian Supreme Court confirmed the *Waite and Kennedy* jurisprudence of the ECtHR, which set out a method to negotiate the said tension, and applied it in a concrete case. Among the three decisions, the judgment in *Western European Union v Siedler* is particularly relevant because the Court examined the *quality* of the dispute-settlement mechanism within the WEU, and proved willing to reject the immunity of the organization when such quality was insufficient. Furthermore, the Court ruled that, in case of rejection of immunity, the internal law of the organization was to be applied to the dispute, as opposed to domestic law.

I. The facts of the case

Ms Siedler had worked since 1991 for the WEU when her employment was terminated in 2000. In accordance with WEU staff rules, she petitioned the WEU internal appeals commission to obtain a compensation. However, the compensation granted by the internal appeals commission would have been substantially higher pursuant to Belgian labour legislation, which is why she subsequently sued the WEU at the Labour Tribunal of Brussels.

In its decision of 7 March 2002, this Tribunal granted higher compensation—equivalent to six months' salary—but Ms Siedler appealed on grounds of insufficiency. The WEU filed an incidental appeal, invoking its immunity from jurisdiction before the Belgian courts and arguing alternatively that the Belgian Act on Labour Contracts was not applicable to this case. Indeed, civil servants whose position was governed by a personnel statute were excluded from its scope of application pursuant to art. 1 of the Act on Labour Contacts.

On 17 September 2003, the Labour Appeals Court set aside the WEU's immunity from jurisdiction on the ground that it contradicted the right of access to justice enshrined in art. 6(1) of the European Convention for the Protection of Human Rights and Fundamental Freedoms (ECHR) and art. 14(1) of the International Covenant on Civil and Political Rights (ICCPR).[1] Although the WEU had made an internal procedure available to individuals aggrieved by its acts, the quality of that procedure did not correspond to the guarantees inherent in the notion of a fair trial, in particular an independent dispute-settlement mechanism. Furthermore, the Court of Appeals considered that the Council of the WEU did not have the power to adopt a personnel statute pursuant to the treaty for collaboration in economic, social, and cultural matters and for collective self-defence (17 March 1948) and the agreement on the status of WEU, national representatives and international staff (11 May 1955). Consequently, the WEU Staff Rules did not constitute a personnel statute and the Belgian Act on Labour Contracts was applicable.

The WEU subsequently brought the case to the Court of Cassation claiming that the Court of Appeals had wrongly rejected its immunity from jurisdiction and applied Belgian labour law. It asserted that the grant of immunities to international organizations before national jurisdictions pursued a legitimate goal and constituted an admissible limitation to art. 6(1) ECHR. Moreover, it considered that in its *Waite and Kennedy* jurisprudence, the ECtHR merely requested the existence of a reasonably available means—that is characterized by its constituent instrument as independent—to protect one's rights without assessing its quality. Finally, the WEU argued that its Staff Rules were supranational and directly applicable rules in the Belgian legal order. Hence, WEU Staff Rules would prevail over the Belgian Act on Labour Contracts.

II. The legal question

In *Western European Union v Siedler*, the Belgian Court of Cassation was confronted with the conflict between the immunity from jurisdiction of an international organization and the right to a fair trial as contained in art. 6(1) of the ECHR. The specificity of this case was that an internal procedure was available for individuals aggrieved by WEU acts in employment related disputes—the internal appeals commission. However, the question arose whether its quality corresponded to the guarantees inherent to the notion of a fair trial, notably with regard to its independence. Hence, the Court of Cassation had to decide whether the mere existence of a reasonably available means to protect one's rights was sufficient to guarantee the right of access to justice or whether the latter required an assessment of the quality of this means in order to be effective. Finally, the Court had to decide which material rules apply to the conflict, which required a clarification as to whether the internal staff regulations had direct effect in the Belgian legal order.

---

[1] *Siedler v Western European Union*, Brussels Labour Court of Appeals, 17 September 2003, *Journal des Tribunaux*, 2004, p. 617; case note by E. David, 'L'immunité de juridiction des organisations internationales', *Journal des Tribunaux*, 2004, p. 619; ILDC 53 (BE 2003).

III. Excerpts

The grant of privileges and immunities to international organizations is necessary to permit the good functioning of these organizations without any unilateral interference by a national government. The fact that states generally grant immunity from jurisdiction to international organizations in their constitutive instruments or in additional agreements constitutes a long-dated practice, aimed to ensure the good functioning of international organizations. The importance of this practice is reinforced by the tendency to enlarge and intensify international cooperation, which is illustrated in all domains of contemporary society. In these conditions, the rule of immunity from jurisdiction of international organizations pursues a legitimate aim (para. 47).[2]

The question of whether the immunity was proportionate to the aim pursued should be evaluated in light of the particular circumstances of each case. To determine whether the restriction of fundamental rights flowing from such immunity was compatible with art. 6(1) of the ECHR, it was important to examine, in accordance with the jurisprudence of the ECtHR, whether the individual against whom such immunity was invoked had access to other reasonably available means to protect his or her rights. Article 6(1) of the ECHR did not prevail over the WEU's immunity (paras. 48–9).

When determining whether the immunity invoked by the international organization could be reconciled with art. 6(1) of the ECHR, the court was not to limit itself to merely taking note of the characterization of an internal appeals commission as independent by the instrument which established that commission. The mode of designation—by an intergovernmental committee—and the short term of the mandate—two years—of the members of the commission were to be taken into account as well. These features of the internal appeals commission involved the risk that the members would be closely tied to the organization, thereby lacking independence (para. 53).

The WEU Staff Regulations that determined the mode of calculating the indemnity allowance in case of breach of contract had direct effect in the domestic legal order and therefore prevailed over any other applicable domestic law provisions of the Act on Labour Contracts (para. 61).

The immunity of the WEU before the Belgian court was rejected but the WEU Staff Regulations were applied.[3]

IV. Commentary

In this case, the Court of Cassation acknowledged that certain limitations to the right of access to justice could be accepted, as long as they did not annihilate this right, as they had a legitimate purpose and as there was a reasonable proportionality.[4] The

---

[2] This excerpt has been translated by the author from French into English.

[3] cf. *Western European Union v Siedler*, Belgian Court of Cassation, 21 December 2009, Appeal Judgment, Cass No S 04 0129 F, ILDC 1625 (BE 2009).

[4] For more information, see J. Wouters, C. Ryngaert, and P. Schmitt, 'Case-Note to Belgian Court of Cassation, *Western European Union v Siedler; General Secretariat of the ACP Group v Lutchmaya; General Secretariat of the ACP Group v. B.D.*', (2011) 105 *American Journal of International Law* 560.

Court recognized the legitimate aim of immunities of international organizations in order to secure the good functioning of these organizations without any unilateral interference by a national government.[5] The Court of Cassation also mentioned the long-standing practice that states generally grant immunity from jurisdiction to international organizations in their constitutive instruments or in additional agreements. This reference implicitly confirms the prior jurisprudence of the Belgian Court of Cassation that privileges and immunities of international organizations do not have a customary nature but are entirely treaty-based.[6]

In order to examine the proportionality, the Court of Cassation referred to the *Waite and Kennedy* jurisprudence of the ECtHR and applied it to the concrete case. The ECtHR had declared that a material factor in determining if the immunity of an international organization before domestic courts was permissible was to examine whether individuals had available to them 'reasonable alternative means to protect effectively [their] rights under the Convention'.[7] This rather vague statement has given rise to intense debates among scholars as to its exact meaning.

The Court of Cassation considered that the mere existence of a dispute-settlement mechanism within the international organization was not sufficient to pass the *Waite and Kennedy* test. A number of qualitative due process criteria—especially to guarantee its independence—had to be met before the international organization could effectively rely on such a mechanism to justify its immunity. In the Court of Cassation's view, the independence of the internal appeals commission could not be guaranteed since it was composed of members designated by the WEU's intergovernmental committee and who only served for terms of two years, which was insufficient to secure their independence.

This finding may be open to criticism.[8] As observed by Maarten Vidal in his comments on the appellate judgment in the *Siedler v the Western European Union* case, the Court 'seems to have been overzealous in transposing the qualitative criteria of art. 6(1) of the ECHR to the level of international administrative

---

[5] At the previous stage of the procedure, the Labour Court of Appeals noted that international organizations had a broader immunity than states because of several reasons: as opposed to states, international organizations have only restricted competences as a result of their institutional functions. They have to fulfil these functions without any interference. Hence, their immunity from jurisdiction has no other limit than the mandate that they have received. Moreover, international organizations are disarmed in front of states since they cannot invoke reciprocity when their immunity is impinged. Finally, the cases of abuse of immunity from jurisdiction are considered as theoretical and member states could revise the regime of the immunity. *Siedler v Western European Union*, Brussels Labour Court of Appeals, 17 September 2003, *Journal des Tribunaux*, 2004, p. 617; case note by E. David, 'L'immunité de juridiction des organisations internationales', (2004) *Journal des Tribunaux* 619; ILDC 53 (BE 2003).

[6] cf. *League of Arab States v TM*, Belgian Court of Cassation, 12 March 2001, *Journal des Tribunaux*, 2001, at 610, ILDC 42 (BE 2001).

[7] *Waite and Kennedy v Germany*, European Court of Human Rights, 18 February 1999, App. No. 26083/94, para 68; *Beer and Regan v Germany*, European Court of Human Rights, 18 February 1999, App. No. 28934/95, para. 59.

[8] See for instance E. De Brabandere, 'Belgian Courts and the Immunity of International Organizations', (2013) 10 *International Organizations Law Review* 464–504; P. Sands and P. Klein, *Bowett's Law of International Institutions* (6th edn, London, Sweet & Maxwell 2009); A. Weerts and N. Angelet, 'Les immunités des organisations internationales face à l'article 6 de la Convention européenne des droits de l'homme', (2007) 134 *Journal du droit international* 21.

tribunals' when reviewing the WEU's internal dispute-settlement mechanism.[9] As noted by this author, the due process quality of the WEU's procedure 'is not substantially inferior to the general practice in international organizations'.[10] For instance, members of the former UN Administrative Tribunal and members of the Administrative Tribunal of the ILO were appointed to renewable three-year terms. Hence, the application of the *Siedler* review test could potentially lead to the rejection of immunity in most cases brought against international organizations before national jurisdictions.

However, certain international organizations have recently reviewed their dispute-settlement mechanisms, such as the new UN Dispute Tribunal, whose judges are appointed for a non-renewable term of seven years by the General Assembly on the recommendation of the Internal Justice Council, and may be removed by the General Assembly only in case of misconduct or incapacity. This evolution reinforces the independence of the members of the UN Dispute Tribunal in comparison to other administrative jurisdictions in international organizations. It should in principle be recognized under the Court of Cassation's review standard. Yet, the Court did not clearly indicate the required minimum length of the mandate of judges sitting on an organization's dispute-settlement mechanism. Hence, court rulings on this issue will be difficult to predict.[11]

The *Siedler* case is not the only example in which a national jurisdiction has conducted a qualitative review of an internal mechanism in an international organization. In a 2007 case, the Italian Court of Cassation considered that the obligation of an international organization—the International Plant Genetic Resources Institute (IPGRI)—to provide an independent and impartial remedy was a *conditio sine qua non* for maintaining its immunity from jurisdiction. The IPGRI's headquarters agreement stated that IPGRI had to 'establish suitable procedures for resolving disputes with its employees'.[12] In accordance with this provision, IPGRI joined the ILO and engaged the jurisdiction of the ILO Administrative Tribunal in 1991, but the facts in this case pre-dated its membership. Hence, employees were left with only an internal remedy that was not considered independent and impartial. In its decision, the Court of Cassation ruled that IPGRI was not entitled to immunity and that such disputes fell within Italian jurisdiction.

Yet, one must admit that these two examples are rather isolated and that the vast majority of national jurisdictions have adopted a much more cautious approach. This is equally true in Belgium, where lower tribunals have refrained from following the approach advocated by the Court of Cassation in *Siedler*. For instance, in its 2011 judgment in *SA Energies Nouvelles et Environnement v Agence Spatiale Européenne*, the Brussels Court of Appeals found three reasonable alternative means, which could be combined, to effectively protect the plaintiff's rights, that is seeking support from the national delegate within the ESA Industrial Policy Committee,

---

[9] cf. M. Vidal, ILDC 53 (BE 2003), para. A5.   [10] Ibid., para. A4.
[11] J. Wouters, C. Ryngaert, and P. Schmitt (n. 4), at p. 565.
[12] *Drago v IPGRI*, Italian Court of Cassation, 19 February 2007, No. 3718, ILDC 827 (IT 2007) (quoting art. 17 of the headquarters agreement).

resorting to the ombudsman procedure and launching a claim against other companies on grounds of civil liability and/or abuse of dominant position. The Court of Appeals did not analyze the quality of the internal dispute-settlement procedure, which only permitted the claimant to call for support from the Belgian representative to the organization's committee on industrial policy and to resort to an ombudsman procedure. Instead, the Court concentrated most of its decision on examining the possible claims against the two companies instead of against the ESA. Hence, the Court of Appeals—as opposed to the Court of Cassation in the *Siedler* case— adopted a broad interpretation of the reasonable alternative test and took into consideration several means which did not all meet the guarantees prescribed by art. 6 of the ECHR. Indeed, the possibility to call for support from the Belgian delegation resembles a diplomatic means a far cry from the conditions of art. 6 of the ECHR and the Ombudsman had no competence to hear employment-related disputes and its decisions were non-binding.[13]

Furthermore, the ECtHR itself seems to reject the interpretation given by the Belgian Court of Cassation in *Siedler* to its reasonable alternative means test stated in *Waite and Kennedy*. In the *Chapman v Belgium* decision of 2013 concerning an employment-related dispute with NATO, the ECtHR decided that the national jurisdiction—the Brussels Labour Court of Appeals—had rightly considered the NATO Appeals Board as an effective internal mechanism.[14]

In this case, Mr Chapman had sued NATO before the Brussels Tribunal of First Instance without trying to solve the dispute before the NATO Appeals Board. The Tribunal accepted his claim and ordered his reinstatement as a NATO staff member. On appeal, the Belgian Government intervened and sustained that an alternative mechanism was available, that is the NATO Appeals Board. The Court of Appeals followed the Belgian Government and rejected Mr Chapman's claim. After a negative opinion from an attorney at the Court of Cassation, Mr Chapman brought the case before the ECtHR. In March 2013, the latter confirmed the Belgian Labour Court of Appeals' view that Mr Chapman would have had an effective internal procedure before the NATO Appeals Board. Mr Chapman had failed to use an available remedy and he was consequently unable to demonstrate how the failings he attributed to that procedure had deprived him of the safeguards of art. 6(1). For these reasons, the Court rejected his complaint. It is interesting to note that the Court did not analyze the Appeals Board but merely noted that the plaintiff did not demonstrate that the Appeals Board would not fulfill the guarantees of art. 6. This deferential approach contradicts the Court of Cassation's interpretation in *Siedler*.

In another recent case at the ECtHR involving NATO, *Gasparini v Italy and Belgium*, the plaintiff asserted that the internal dispute-settlement mechanism was incompatible with the requirements of the ECHR, notably because the NATO Appeals

---

[13] For further information, see *SA Energies Nouvelles et Environnement v European Space Agency*, Brussels Court of Appeals, 23 March 2011, Appeal judgment, No. 2011/2013, 2006/AR/1480, ILDC 1729 (BE 2011).

[14] cf. *Richard Chapman v Belgium*, App. No. 39619/06, 5 March 2013.

Board sessions were not public. As a consequence, Belgium—host state of NATO—and Italy—the state of nationality of the plaintiff—had failed to ensure the creation of a dispute-settlement mechanism offering an equivalent protection when transferring competences to NATO. In its decision, the ECtHR held that it could review a structural lacuna in rights protection caused by the failure of the NATO Appeals Board to hold its sessions in public.[15] However, it further explained that its power to determine whether the procedure before the NATO Appeals Board was manifestly deficient was necessarily less ample than its power to review the procedures before the contracting states' domestic jurisdictions.

This analysis of recent jurisprudence of the ECtHR seems to indicate that the requirements of internal procedures within international organizations may not be strictly similar to the requirements of the European Court vis-à-vis its member states' domestic jurisdictions.[16] A certain level of 'equivalent protection' (although not necessarily identical) to the one of art. 6 ECHR seems to suffice to meet the requirements of the ECHR.[17] This approach has already been adopted by certain national jurisdictions, such as a Dutch Court of Appeals which held in 2007 that it sufficed that the international organization, the European Patent Office, provided comparable legal protection, to meet the requirements of art. 6. This was guaranteed in the particular instance by the possibility of submitting the case to the ILO Administrative Tribunal.[18] This requirement of a comparable or equivalent protection should prevent the claimant's right of access to courts from becoming illusory.[19] In a decision issued by the Court of Appeal in The Hague on 17 February 2015 in a case opposing trade unions of employees of the European Patent Office to the European Patent Organization, the Court of Appeal confirmed that the central question is whether alternative judicial process offers a 'comparable' protection to art. 6 ECHR. The determinant factor consists in the assessment of whether the right of access to court is impaired in its essence and that the protection of ECHR rights is 'manifestly deficient'. In this case, the Court found such manifest deficiency as a result of the absence of any alternative judicial process to the plaintiffs, which did not result in a presumption of a violation of art. 6 ECHR *per se* except that it was combined with a number of additional factual circumstances including the assertion by the plaintiffs that their right to strike and their right to participate in collective

[15] cf. *Gasparini v Italy and Belgium*, App. No. 10750/03, 12 May 2009. For discussion, see C. Ryngaert, 'The Responsibility of Member States in Connection with Acts of International Organizations: Assessing the Recent Case Law of the European Court of Human Rights', (2011) 60 *International Law and Comparative Law Quarterly* 997.

[16] See also E. De Brabandere (n. 8), p. 492.

[17] cf. J. Wouters, C. Ryngaert, and P. Schmitt (n. 4), pp. 560–7.

[18] cf. *Bertrand v European Patent Organization*, Dutch Court of Appeals of The Hague, 28 September 2007, No. BB5865, 06/1390.

[19] cf. *Stavrinou v United Nations and Commander of the United Nations Force in Cyprus*, Supreme Court of Cyprus, ILDC 929 (CY 1992). In this decision, the Cyprus Court upheld the immunity of the United Nations Peacekeeping Force in Cyprus (UNFICYP) because a special dispute-settlement mechanism for local personnel was organized by the UNFICYP Agreement. Yet, as indicated by Artistotle Constantinides in his comments on the decision, the Court refrained from examining the mechanism which 'was no more than an administrative procedure to be determined by the Commander of the UNFICYP'. *Bertrand v European Patent Organization* (n. 18), para. A6.

bargaining were systematically restricted. The Court concluded that there was a disproportionate restriction of the right of access to justice and ignored the organization's immunity from jurisdiction.[20]

This being said, both the *Gasparini* and the *Chapman* case concerned NATO, which is an international organization whose members are not all state parties to the ECHR. Hence, one may not exclude a stricter application of the requirements with respect to an international organization whose members are all state parties to the ECHR, such as the WEU. However, even in this case, it seems hardly defendable to require that the dispute-settlement mechanisms established by international organizations should meet all the conditions of art. 6 since international organizations—with the possible exception in the future of the EU—are not parties to the ECHR.

Another interesting aspect of the *Siedler* case is that once the Court of Cassation had decided to reject the immunity and to take the case, it applied the internal law of the WEU to the conflict instead of Belgian labour law. Indeed, the WEU Staff Regulations had direct effect in the domestic legal order and therefore prevailed over any other applicable domestic law provisions of the Act on Labour Contracts. The Court of Cassation concluded that the WEU Staff Regulations would determine the amount of the indemnity allowance to which the claimant was entitled. For this particular aspect, the Court of Cassation disagreed with the Court of Appeals, which had applied the Belgian Act on Labour Contracts to the conflict. As a consequence, the Court of Cassation quashed the judgment of the Court of Appeals.

Given that only few national jurisdictions rejected the immunity from jurisdiction of an international organization, there is scarce jurisprudence on the applicable law to such conflict. In the literature, certain scholars have suggested that the host state's (domestic) law should apply as the default position.[21] Yet, if the international organization has developed its own rules with respect to a specific situation, those rules should apply. In the *Siedler* case, the WEU Staff Rules determined the mode of calculating the indemnity allowance for breach of contract very precisely.

To a certain degree, the application of the internal substantive law of the WEU by the Court of Cassation seems to counter-balance the rejection of the immunity of the international organization, as if the Court of Cassation had searched to find an equilibrium between, on the one hand, the autonomy of the international organization and, on the other hand, the individual's right of access to a court. Nevertheless, one has to admit that the Court of Cassation has gone very far—probably too far in light of the other decisions of national jurisdictions and of the posterior jurisprudence of the ECtHR—in its qualitative review of the dispute-settlement procedures established within international organizations to handle employment related disputes.

---

[20] cf. *Vakbondsunie van het Europees Octrooibureau ('VEOB, The Hague Department) & SUEPO (Staff Union of the European Patent Office) v European Patent Organization*, Court of Appeal in The Hague, Case No. 200.020.173/01, 17 February 2015.

[21] cf. J. Klabbers, *An Introduction to International Institutional Law* (2nd edn, Cambridge, Cambridge University Press 2009), p. 137; A. Reinisch, 'Accountability of International Organizations According to National Law', (2005) *Netherlands Yearbook of International Law* 119.

7.9 *OSS Nokalva, Inc. v European Space Agency,* United States Third Circuit decision, 617 F.3d 756 (3d Cir. 2010)

*Kristen Boon**

Relevance of the case

In this case, the US Court of Appeals for the Third Circuit rejected the long-held assumption that international organizations are entitled to absolute immunity under the domestic International Organizations Immunities Act (IOIA). The court applied the same concept of restrictive immunity to international organizations as has been developed and applied to sovereign states. This case therefore has important implications for the evolution of immunities of international organizations over time.

I. Facts of the case

OSS Nokalva, Inc. ('OSSN') is a software and technology service company based in New Jersey. Headquartered in Paris, the European Space Agency (ESA) is an international organization composed of eighteen member states created to further space research and technology in Europe. Between 1996 and 2004, ESA and OSSN executed four sets of Licensing and Software Maintenance Agreements with the goal of helping ESA develop its own software. A forum selection clause in later agreements stated that disputes would be subject to the jurisdiction of New Jersey courts or the Federal court for the district of New Jersey.

Alleging that ESA had violated their Agreements by distributing OSSN software to third parties and by failing to provide adequate compensation, OSSN filed suit in the Superior Court of New Jersey, which was then removed to the United States District Court for the District of New Jersey at the request of ESA. ESA then moved to dismiss the case for lack of subject-matter jurisdiction, claiming that it was granted absolute immunity under the IOIA. The IOIA is a federal statute, enacted in 1945, which grants certain designated international organizations (of which ESA is one) 'the same immunity from suit and every form of judicial process as is enjoyed by foreign governments, except to the extent that such organizations may expressly waive their immunity for the purpose of any proceedings or by the terms of any contract'.[1]

The District Court denied ESA's motion to dismiss after making a determination that ESA was entitled to absolute immunity but had expressly waived its immunity in the Agreements. ESA appealed the decision. OSSN cross appealed the decision that ESA was entitled to absolute immunity in the first place.

* Professor of Law, Seton Hall Law School. Thanks to Amy Cuzzolino for her excellent assistance in preparing this commentary.
[1] cf. 22 U.S.C. § 288a(b).

II. The legal question

This case looks at the evolution of the immunities of international organizations over time. At the time the IOIA was enacted, states enjoyed 'virtually absolute' immunity and, by the statute, international organizations were given the same immunities as states. However, the immunities of states have since been modified and restricted, most notably by the 1976 Foreign Sovereign Immunities Act 28 U.S.C. § 1605(a)(2), which stated that immunity would not be granted in situations 'in which the action is based upon a commercial activity carried on in the United States by the foreign state; or upon an act performed in the United States in connection with a commercial activity of the foreign state elsewhere'.

The legal question raised by this case is: does the language of the IOIA allow for the incorporation of subsequent changes to sovereign state immunity thereby conferring a restrictive, not absolute, immunity upon international organizations?

III. Excerpts

[...]

A federal statute enacted in 1945, the international organizations Immunities Act, 22 U.S.C. § 288, *et seq.* ('IOIA'), applies to those international organizations which the President designates as entitled to the benefits of the Act. *See* 22 U.S.C. § 288. The IOIA provides that designated international organizations, to the extent consistent with the instruments creating them, have the capacity to enter into contracts. *Id.* § 288a(a)(i). The IOIA also provides that designated organizations 'enjoy the same immunity from suit and every form of judicial process as is enjoyed by foreign governments, except to the extent that such organizations may expressly waive their immunity for the purpose of any proceedings or by the terms of any contract.' *Id.* § 288a(b). ESA's predecessor was designated as an international organization by President Johnson in 1966. *See* Exec. Order No. 11,318, 31 Fed.Reg. 15307 (Dec. 5, 1966), as amended by Exec. Order No. 11,351, 32 Fed.Reg. 7561 (May 22, 1967), superceded by Exec. Order No. 11,760, 39 Fed.Reg. 2343 (Jan. 17, 1974), as amended by Exec. Order No. 12,766, 56 Fed.Reg. 28463 (June 18, 1991).

The ESA Convention ('Convention') governs ESA's policies, procedures, and internal rules. A council of representatives ('Council') from ESA's member states oversees its governance. The Convention provides that ESA is immune from 'jurisdiction and execution,' except to the extent that it shall, by decision of the Council, have expressly waived such immunity in a particular case; the Council has the duty to waive this immunity in all cases where reliance upon it would impede the course of justice and it can be waived without prejudicing the interests of the Agency[.]

Convention, Annex I, Art. IV ¶ 1(a).

[...]

In its complaint, OSSN asserts that ESA: (1) breached the Agreements by distributing OSSN software to third parties; and (2) failed to compensate OSSN for certain software, as well as for the distribution of OSSN's software to third parties. As a result, OSSN filed contract claims as well as claims for unjust enrichment, conversion, negligence, collection of debt payable, and a claim asserting that ESA 'tortiously and unlawfully interfered with [OSSN's] customer relationships and prospective economic advantage […]' App. at 33–37.

ESA moved to dismiss the complaint under Federal Rule of Civil Procedure 12(b)(1), contending that the District Court lacked subject matter jurisdiction because the IOIA grants it absolute immunity. OSSN countered first that ESA's immunity is not absolute and does not bar suit in this case, and alternatively, that even if ESA's immunity is absolute, it waived such immunity both by the Convention and by ESA's execution of the Agreements with the aforementioned forum selection clauses.

[…]

The District Court denied ESA's motion to dismiss. The Court relied primarily on a decision of the United States Court of Appeals for the District of Columbia, *Atkinson v. Inter–American Development Bank,* which held that the Inter–American Development Bank, a financial institution designated as an international organization under the IOIA, was entitled to 'virtually absolute' immunity, 'contingent only upon the State Department's making an immunity request to the court […]' 156 F.3d 1335, 1340 (D.C.Cir.1998) (quoting *Verlinden B.V. v. Cent. Bank of Nigeria,* 461 U.S. 480, 486, 103 S.Ct. 1962, 76 L.Ed.2d 81 (1983)). Following that reasoning, the District Court found 'that ESA[, like the Inter–American Development Bank,] is entitled to absolute immunity' pursuant to the IOIA.App. at 14.

Nevertheless, the District Court continued, '[a]n international organization's absolute immunity […] is subject to […] limitation [by] […] express waiver by the international organization […]' App. at 14 (citing *Mendaro v. World Bank,* 717 F.2d 610, 613–14 (D.C.Cir. 1983)). Focusing on the language in the Convention stating that 'the Council has the duty to waive […] immunity in all cases where reliance upon it would impede the course of justice and it can be waived without prejudicing the interests of the Agency,' App. at 15 (quoting Convention, Annex I, Art. IV ¶ 1(a)), the District Court denied ESA's motion to dismiss on the ground that ESA waived its immunity for 'both the contract and tort claims' brought by OSSN, App. at 22. The District Court reasoned that although such non-specific waivers are disfavored, a waiver of immunity here 'would provide ESA with [a] corresponding benefit […].' App. at 16. Such benefit, decided the District Court, is 'the ability to participate in the international commercial marketplace.' App. at 21. ESA appeals that decision. OSSN cross appeals the finding that ESA is entitled to absolute immunity.

[…]

It is an accepted tenet of appellate jurisdiction that we 'may affirm a judgment on any ground apparent from the record, even if the district court did not reach it.' *See Kabakjian v. United States,* 267 F.3d 208, 213 (3d Cir.2001) (citing *Resolution Trust Corp. v. Fidelity and Deposit Co. of Maryland,* 205 F.3d 615, 635 (3d Cir.2000)). We cannot accept the District Court's decision that ESA is entitled to absolute immunity and therefore need not address whether ESA waived its immunity. We believe there is a more generally applicable basis on which to decide the relevant issue, and proceed therefore to discuss OSSN's cross-appeal.

We begin with an analysis of the IOIA. That Act provides that international organizations such as ESA 'shall enjoy the *same* immunity from suit and every form of judicial process *as is enjoyed by foreign governments* […]' 22 U.S.C. § 288a(b) (emphases added). As the text makes clear, 'Congress was legislating in shorthand, referring to another body of law—the law governing the immunity of foreign governments—to define the scope of the new immunity for international organizations.' *Atkinson,* 156 F.3d at 1340. The effect of 'legislating in shorthand' was to link the immunity of international organizations to that of foreign governments. As a 'reference statute,' it raised whether the IOIA should be understood to codify for international organizations the extent of immunity that foreign governments enjoyed in 1945 when the IOIA was enacted, or whether it should be understood to require incorporation of subsequent changes in the law of foreign sovereign immunity. *See id.* The D.C. Circuit in *Atkinson,* and the District Court in reliance thereon, took the former view, determining that the IOIA provided that international organizations were to have indefinitely the same level of 'virtually absolute' immunity as foreign sovereigns enjoyed in 1945—later changes to foreign sovereign immunity notwithstanding. *Id.* at 1340 (quoting *Verlinden,* 461 U.S. at 486, 103 S.Ct. 1962).

Even if the *Atkinson* court were correct that foreign sovereigns always enjoyed absolute immunity in 1945, and we recognize that there may be some question about that proposition, it does not follow that subsequent changes to the extent of immunity accorded to foreign sovereigns should not be reflected in the immunity to which international organizations are entitled under the IOIA. The language of the IOIA suggests the contrary.

The most important change to the immunity of foreign sovereigns occurring since 1945 was the enactment of the Foreign Sovereign Immunity Act of 1976 ('FSIA'). *See* 28 U.S.C. §§ 1330, 1602, *et seq.* That Act affords foreign governments immunity from the jurisdiction of United States courts, *see id.* § 1604, except in specific circumstances, including those:

(1) in which the foreign state has waived its immunity either explicitly or by implication [...] [and] (2) in which the action *is based upon a commercial activity carried on in the United States by the foreign state; or upon an act performed in the United States in connection with a commercial activity of the foreign state elsewhere;* or upon an act outside the territory of the United States in connection with a commercial activity of the foreign state elsewhere and that act causes a direct effect in the United States[.]

Id. § 1605(a)(1)–(2) (emphasis added).

[...]

ESA points to nothing in the statutory language or legislative history that suggests that the IOIA provision delegating authority to the President to alter the immunity of international organizations precludes incorporation of any subsequent change to the immunity of foreign sovereigns. Indeed, ESA acknowledged at oral argument that the State Department has expressed support for OSSN's contention that the same restrictive immunity conferred on foreign governments in the FSIA should be applied to ESA. The State Department's view was reflected in a 1980 letter, where a State Department Legal Adviser wrote 'The [FSIA] amended [U.S.] law by codifying a more restrictive theory of immunity subjecting foreign states to suit in U.S. courts [...] By virtue of the FSIA [...] *international organizations are now subject to the jurisdiction of our courts in respect of their commercial activities* [...]' Letter from Roberts B. Owen, Legal Adviser, State Department, to Leroy D. Clark, General Counsel, Equal Employment Opportunity Commission (June 24, 1980) (emphasis added), *reprinted in* Marian L. Nash, *Contemporary Practice of the United States Relating to International Law,* 74 Am. J. Int'l L. 917, 917–18 (1980). The State Department's direct pronouncement of IOIA immunity is persuasive, particularly because the State Department played an important role in drafting the IOIA. *See* OSSN Br. at 47 n. 6 (citing Letter from Harold D. Smith, Director, Bureau of the Budget, to James Francis Byrnes, Secretary of State, (Nov. 6, 1945), H.R.Rep. No. 1203 at 7).

[...]

ESA's contrary position leads to an anomalous result. If a foreign government, such as Germany, had contracted with OSSN, it would not be immune from suit because the FSIA provides that a foreign government involved in a commercial arrangement such as that in this case may be sued, as ESA acknowledged at oral argument. We find no compelling reason why a group of states acting through an international organization is entitled to broader immunity than its member states enjoy when acting alone. Indeed, such a policy may create an incentive for foreign governments to evade legal obligations by acting through international organizations. *See* Steven Herz, *International Organizations in U.S. Courts: Reconsidering the Anachronism of Absolute Immunity,* 31 Suffolk Transnat'l L.Rev. 471, 521–22 (2008). For these reasons, we conclude that ESA is not entitled to immunity as it stood for foreign sovereigns in 1945.

As noted, the FSIA grants foreign governments immunity from the jurisdiction of United States courts, except when, *inter alia*, 'the action is based upon a commercial activity carried on in the United States [...]' 28 U.S.C. § 1605(a)(2). It is undisputed that the Agreements at issue here constituted such 'commercial activity' and, because we construe the IOIA to incorporate the exceptions to immunity set forth in the FSIA, we will affirm the District Court's order denying ESA's motion to dismiss.

[...]

IV. Commentary

When this case came before the US Third Circuit, it had been presumed by the court below that the ESA held absolute immunity under the domestic IOIA albeit an immunity that had been waived by ESA's actions.[2] This followed from a long line of case history supporting absolute immunity.[3] The Third Circuit has offered the first challenge to this assumption, determining that the IOIA did not grant absolute immunity to international organizations, only restrictive immunity. The court made its determination by analogizing the immunities of international organizations to the immunities enjoyed by sovereign states. This analysis is fitting because the immunities of international organizations, enshrined in international organization charters,

---

[2] The district court relied primarily on *Atkinson v Inter-American Development Bank*, 156 F.3d 1335 (D.C. Cir. 1998), in which the three-judge panel (including now Chief Justice of the United States Supreme Court John Roberts) had held that the Inter-American Development Bank was 'entitled to "virtually absolute" immunity' under the IOIA. Immunity was limited only by situations in which international organizations are obligated to waive their immunity so as not to 'impede the course of justice'.

[3] The D.C. Circuit has seen the majority of legislation regarding the immunities of international organizations, many of which are headquartered in Washington, D.C. See *Broadbent v. Org. of Am. States*, 628 F.2d 27 (D.C. Cir. 1980) which first raised the debate over absolute versus restrictive immunity; *Mendaro v World Bank*, 717 F.2d 610 (D.C. Cir. 1983); *Atkinson*, 156 F.3d 1335; *Vila v Inter-American Investment Corp.*, 570 F.3d 274 (D.C. Cir. 2009).

conventions,[4] headquarter agreements, and domestic legislation, were originally formulated by borrowing from the law that gave immunity to states.[5] As Charles Brower writes, although this case has the appearance of a landmark decision, 'it may have few practical effects on immunities determinations even if widely followed'.[6]

Sovereign state immunity developed from an earlier era in which actual sovereigns agreed not to prosecute each other without express consent. Over time this concept of immunity transferred from the person of the sovereign to the state itself.[7] The IOIA was enacted in 1945, the same year as the UN Charter, when international organizations were in their infancy. In the wake of two World Wars, countries recognized the need for co-operation in order to build peace.[8] The newly formed international organizations were considered fragile, and this conception of them was the primary motivator behind the development of protection for international organizations in the form of privileges and immunities.[9] Granting international organizations immunities helped them evolve and become functional actors on the world stage; supporting whatever was 'necessary for the fulfillment of [their] purposes'.[10] When the IOIA was enacted, states enjoyed absolute immunity.[11] By virtue of the new statute that granted them 'the same immunity from suit and every form of judicial process as is enjoyed by foreign governments', so did international organizations. In 1976, the Foreign Sovereign Immunities Act 28 U.S.C. § 1602 et seq. (1979) (FSIA) was passed, which allowed that foreign states would not be immune to actions that were based on commercial activity conducted in the US or that concerned property rights involving the US. Sovereign states no longer benefitted from absolute immunity under US law.[12] What this meant for international organizations depended on the intent of Congress as interpreted from the wording of the IOIA. The D.C. Circuit Court determined that the intent was to give international organizations the same immunity as *was* enjoyed by foreign governments at the time the IOIA was adopted, holding that any subsequent limitations to state immunities should not be applied to international organizations.[13]

---

[4] E.g., the Convention on the Privileges and Immunities of the United Nations, 13 February 1946, 1 UNTS 15.

[5] E.g., G.L. Rios & E.P. Flaherty, 'International Organization Reform or Impunity? Immunity Is the Problem', (2010) 16 *ILSA Journal of International & Comparative Law* 433, 436.

[6] cf. C. Brower, 'United States', in A. Reinisch, (ed.), *The Privileges and Immunities of International Organizations in Domestic Courts* (Oxford, Oxford University Press 2013), p. 319.

[7] cf. Rios and Flaherty (n. 5), p. 435; quote from U.N. Charter art. 105(1).

[8] cf. S. Herz, 'International Organizations in U.S. Courts: Reconsidering the Anachronism of Absolute Immunity', (2008) 31 *Suffolk Transnational Law Review* 471, 488.

[9] cf E. Gaillard and I. Pingel-Lenuzza, 'International Organisations and Immunity from Jurisdiction: To Restrict or to Bypass', (2002) 51 *International and Comparative Law Quarterly* 1.

[10] cf. Rios and Flaherty (n. 5), p. 454.

[11] How absolute state immunity was at the time is debated by some scholars. See Herz (n. 8), p. 502. Prior to the drafting of the IOIA, the Supreme Court opined that the immunities of foreign governments should be determined not by the courts but by the executive and legislative branches. See *Republic of Mexico v Hoffman*, 324 US 30 (1945).

[12] FSIA was the codification of more than a decade of state practice of not recognizing immunity for the private acts of foreign sovereigns. See Letter from Jack B. Tate, Acting Legal Advisor to the Dep't of State, to Philip B. Perlman, Acting Att'y Gen., 19 May 1952, *in* 26 Dep't St. Bull. 969 (1952).

[13] The *Nokalva* court pointed to statements by officials from the State Department indicating that subsequent changes to state immunity should also apply to international organizations. The Court found this persuasive as 'the State Department played an important role in drafting the IOIA'. *OSS Nokalva v European Space Agency*, 617 F.3d 756, 764 (3d Cir. 2010).

As the *Nokalva* decision suggests, this meant that international organizations were given greater immunity than states. The Third Circuit foresaw a problem with this as a matter of principle: states would have greater immunity acting through an international organization than acting alone. This might encourage states to form and act through international organizations in order to get around their legal obligations.[14] That the Third Circuit could make this prediction belies a fundamental shift in the understanding of international organizations: they are no longer fledgling enterprises in need of protection but powerful international actors in their own right.

To date, the *Nokalva* case has not driven a significant shift in the law: in US jurisprudence, the Third Circuit remains an outlier.[15] Courts in several European countries have declined to analogize international organization and state immunity, upholding the absolute character of the former.[16] In general, national courts base the immunities of international organizations on their founding treaties and headquarter agreements between the organization and the state.[17] This is true even in the US, where the Second Circuit has found the debate over absolute and restrictive immunity inapplicable to the UN, which the court determined is governed by the UN's own Convention on Privileges and Immunities.[18] However, in keeping with the IOIA's linkage of international organization immunities to the immunities of states, international organizations may be following in states' footsteps. Two centuries ago, it was deemed 'incompatible with [the] dignity' of a state to subject it to a domestic legal process.[19] Today, numerous disputes involving states and 'the reinforcement of the principle of legality' have produced an entirely different outlook.[20] As international organizations have grown in power and influence this has led to a similar increase in disputes. In the absence of effective alternative mechanisms for dispute resolution, the scope of immunity of international organizations will become increasingly restricted.[21]

---

[14] cf. *OSS Nokalva v European Space Agency*, 617 F.3d at 764. In this regard, there is an interesting analogy with regards to the responsibility of international organizations, and the fear that states may avoid responsibility by acting through the corporate form.

[15] See *Price v Unisea, Inc.*, 289 P.3d 914, 920 (Alaska 2012), 'This new interpretation contradicts the precedent established by *Atkinson,* and we decline to follow it.'; *Lempert v Rice*, 956 F. Supp. 2d 17, 25 (D.D.C. 2013), 'Plaintiff's heavy reliance on case law outside of this Circuit is misplaced.'; *Garcia v Sebelius*, 867 F. Supp. 2d 125, 141 (D.D.C. 2012) The Circuit has held that 'Congress' intent' in regards to the IOIA 'was to adopt th[e] body of law only as it existed in 1945—when immunity of foreign sovereigns was absolute'.

[16] *Consortium X v Switzerland*, Switzerland Federal Supreme Court, 2 July 2004, ILDC 344 (CH 2004); *Firma Baumeister Ing. Richard L. v O*, Austrian Supreme Court, 14 December 2004, ILDC 362 (AT 2004). See also *Beer and Regan v Germany*, App. No. 28934/95, 18 February 1999 and *Waite and Kennedy v Germany*, App. No. 26083/94, which held that the ESA's immunity against suit in Germany did not violate the ECHR.

[17] cf. C. Ryngaert, 'The Immunity of International Organizations Before Domestic Courts: Recent Trends', (2010) 7 *International Organizations Law Review* 121, 125.

[18] cf. *Brzak v United Nations*, 597 F.3d 107 (2d Cir. 2010).

[19] *The Schooner Exchange v McFaddon*, 7 Cranch 116 (1812).

[20] cf. Gaillard and Pingel-Lenuzza (n. 9), p. 2.

[21] cf. ibid., p. 4.

7.10 *Mothers of Srebrenica v The Netherlands and the UN*, LJN: BW1999, Dutch Supreme Court, 13 April 2012 and *Stichting Mothers of Srebrenica and Others against The Netherlands*, App. No. 65542/12, European Court of Human Rights, 11 June 2013

Aleksandar Momirov

Relevance of the cases

The present decision of the Dutch Supreme Court and the non-admissibility decision of the ECtHR, which in effect confirmed the reasoning of the Dutch Supreme Court, are part of the jurisprudential developments concerning the law on immunities of international organizations (the Supreme Court judgement, and the ECtHR decision, respectively). Increasingly, domestic and regional courts have started reinterpreting the law on immunities as a response to human rights-based critiques. Whether or not international organizations enjoy immunity before a domestic court should, according to this developing approach, depend on a balancing act between, on the one hand, the functional interests of the international organization and, on the other hand, the individuals' right of access to court. The decisions discussed in this section illustrate this development as well as the limits of this developing line of jurisprudence by confirming that the immunity of the UN, as a *sui generis* international organization, shall not be subjected to the aforementioned balancing act.

I. The facts of the cases

In what is considered to be one of the darkest pages of the Yugoslav wars, the Bosnian town of Srebrenica—previously declared a demilitarized 'safe area' under the protection of the UN forces deployed in Bosnia and Herzegovina (UNPROFOR)—was ran over by the Bosnian Serb Army in July 1995. The ensuing expulsion of women and children from the enclave and the killing of more than 7000 men and boys have been qualified as genocide by the International Court of Justice (ICJ) and the International Criminal Tribunal for the Former Yugoslavia (ICTY).[1] The failure of UNPROFOR and in particular Dutchbat—the Dutch component bearing primary responsibility in the Srebrenica region—to demilitarize the enclave and protect the civilians from the 'safe area' has been the subject of numerous political debates and legal proceedings in various states and at the international level.

In 2007, Mothers of Srebrenica, a Dutch foundation established in order to represent the relatives of the individuals killed during the Srebrenica massacres, initiated

---

[1] cf. ICJ, *Case Concerning the Application of the Convention on the Prevention and Punishment of the Crime of Genocide* (*Bosnia and Herzegovina v Serbia and Montenegro*), Judgment, 26 February 2007 and, amongst others, ICTY, *Prosecutor v Krstić*, (IT-98-33), Appeals Chamber, Judgment, 19 April 2004.

proceedings against the state of The Netherlands and against the UN before the District Court in The Hague. With respect to the UN, the foundation held that it was partly responsible for the fall of the enclave and for the consequences thereof, including the failure to prevent the mass killings. The foundation sought, on behalf of the surviving relatives, a judgment declaring that the UN (as well as The Netherlands) acted wrongfully. The foundation based its arguments, which will be touched upon in the following sections, both on Dutch civil law and on international law.

Amongst the various legal matters raised during the proceedings, this contribution addresses the question of immunity of the UN. Both the Dutch Supreme Court as well as the ECtHR had to decide whether the grant of immunity to the UN under the present circumstances was justified, that is whether upholding the UN's immunity would amount to a violation of the right of access to court.

II. The legal questions

Both decisions deal with the extent of immunities enjoyed by international organizations before domestic courts. The two decisions acknowledge the ongoing doctrinal and jurisprudential calibration of the relationship between human rights (the right of access to courts in particular) and the immunity of international organizations. Two particular aspects of the cases characterize the significance of the decisions: firstly, the cases relate to activities of the UN, carried out under Chapter VII of the UN Charter and secondly, it is generally assumed that the allegations brought against the UN in the case before the Dutch Supreme Court relate to peremptory norms of international law.

Hence, the decisions address the following legal questions: does the grant of immunity to the UN infringe upon an individual's right of access to court *and* should this right prevail in situations where claims are based on alleged violations of norms of *jus cogens*?

III. Excerpts

Mothers of Srebrenica v The Netherlands & the UN, LJN: BW1999, Dutch Supreme Court, 13 April 2012 [...]

3.1 The central question in this case is whether the appeal court was right to rule that the UN is entitled to immunity from jurisdiction, and consequently that the Dutch courts are not competent to hear the action brought by the Association et al. in so far as it is directed against the UN. [...]

Basis for and scope of the UN's immunity

4.2 The basis for the UN's immunity (to be distinguished from the immunity granted to its officials and to experts performing missions for the UN) is article 105 of the UN Charter and article II, § 2 of the Convention. The court of appeal was correct to interpret the latter provision—which is an elaboration of article 105, paragraph 1—in the light of article 31 of the Vienna Convention on the Law of Treaties, to mean that the UN enjoys the most far-reaching immunity from jurisdiction, in the sense that the UN cannot be summoned to appear before any domestic court in the countries that are party to the Convention.

Both the basis for and the scope of this immunity, which is aimed at ensuring that the UN can function completely independently and thus serves a legitimate purpose, are therefore different from those underlying the immunity from jurisdiction enjoyed by foreign states. As stated in section 13a of the General Legislative Provisions Act, the latter, after all, stems from international law *(par in parem non habet imperium)*, and applies exclusively to acts of a foreign state performed in a governmental capacity *(acta iure imperii)*.

UN immunity and access to the courts

4.3.1 As stated in 4.1.1, the appeal court examined, on the basis of the criteria set out by the ECtHR in *Beer and Regan v. Germany* (ECtHR 18 February 1999, no. 28934/95) and *Waite and Kennedy v. Germany* (ECtHR 18 February 1999, no. 26083/94), whether the invocation of UN immunity is compatible with the right of access to the courts enshrined in article 6 ECHR and article 14 ICCPR. In the cassation proceedings the State is no longer contesting the argument that this right—which is not an absolute right—also constitutes a rule of customary international law.

4.3.2 Both the cases cited above involved proceedings before the German courts against the European Space Agency (ESA) in which the claimants wanted the court to establish that they had become employees of ESA under German law. ESA, an international organisation, pled immunity from jurisdiction under article XV, §2 of the Convention for the establishment of a European Space Agency of 30 May 1975 in conjunction with Annex I to the same Convention (Dutch Treaty Series 123). The German court had accepted that plea. The ECtHR held that this did not constitute a violation of article 6 ECHR. [...][...]

4.3.4 The UN occupies a special place in the international legal community, as expressed by the ECtHR in its decision in the cases of *Behrami and Behrami v. France and Saramati v. France, Germany, and Norway*, ECtHR 2 May 2007, no. 71412/01 and 78166/01.[...]

4.3.5 The interim conclusion must be that the appeal court erred in examining, on the basis of the criteria formulated in *Beer and Regan* and *Waite and Kennedy*, whether the right of access to the courts as referred to in article 6 ECHR prevailed over the immunity invoked on behalf of the UN.

4.3.6 That immunity is absolute. Moreover, respecting it is among the obligations on UN member states which, as the ECtHR took into consideration in *Behrami, Behrami and Saramati*, under article 103 of the UN Charter, prevail over conflicting obligations from another international treaty.

4.3.7 However, this does not answer the question of whether, as argued by the Association et al. with reference to the dissenting opinions in the ECtHR's judgment of 21 November 2001 in the case of *Al-Adsani v. the United Kingdom* no. 35763/97 concerning state immunity, the right of access to the courts should prevail in the present case over UN immunity because the claims are based on the accusation of involvement in—notably in the form of failing to prevent—genocide and other grave breaches of fundamental human rights (torture, murder and rape). On this matter, the Association et al. argue in 5.13 of their writ of summons in cassation: 'There is no higher norm in international law than the prohibition of genocide. This norm in any event takes precedence over the other norms at issue in this legal dispute. The enforcement of this norm is one of the main reasons for the existence of international law and for the most important international organisation, the UN. This means that in cases of failure to prevent genocide, international organisations are not entitled to immunity, or in any event the prohibition should prevail over such immunity. The view that the UN's immunity weighs more heavily in this instance would mean *de facto* that the UN has absolute power. For its power would not be subject to restrictions and this would also mean that the UN would not be accountable to anyone because it would not be subject to the rule of law: the principle that no-one is above the law and that power is curbed and regulated by the law. Immunity of so far-reaching a kind as envisaged by the appeal court is incompatible with the rule of law and furthermore undermines the credibility of the UN as the champion of human rights'. [...]

4.3.10 Even more important than the fact that [the *Al-Adsani v. the United Kingdom* opinion] does not reflect even the current status of the view accepted by the ECtHR, is the ruling by the International Court of Justice (ICJ), cited by the State in its response to the Advocate-General's advisory opinion, in its judgment of 3 February 2012 in the case *Jurisdictional Immunities of the State (Germany vs. Italy: Greece intervening)*. At issue in this case was, *inter alia*, the question of whether the Italian courts should have respected Germany's immunity in cases in which compensation was claimed from Germany for violations of international humanitarian law committed by German forces during the Second World War. The ICJ concluded that they should have. [...]

4.3.14 Although UN immunity should be distinguished from State immunity, the difference is not such as to justify ruling on the relationship between the former and the right of access to the courts in a way that differs from the ICJ's decision on the relationship between State immunity and the right of access to the courts. The UN is entitled to immunity regardless of the extreme seriousness of the accusations on which the Association et al. base their claims.

Concluding considerations

4.4.1 The foregoing considerations lead to the conclusion that the complaints on grounds of law in grounds of appeal 3 to 7 in the appeal in cassation are untenable. Nor can the complaints in grounds of appeal 1, 2, 8 and 9—the sees no reason to request a preliminary ruling from the Court of Justice of the European Union on ground of appeal 8—result in cassation. Under section 81 of the Judiciary (Organisation) Act no further reasons for this decision need be given, since the complaints do not warrant the answering of questions of law in the interests of the uniform application or development of the law.

4.4.2 According to the considerations set out in 4.3.1 to 4.3.13 above, the complaints in grounds of appeal 2 and 3 in the cross-appeal are largely well-founded, but this does not result in cassation. Nor do the remaining grounds of appeal result in cassation. Under section 81 of the Judiciary (Organisation) Act no further reasons for this decision need be given, since the complaints do not warrant the answering of questions of law in the interests of the uniform application or development of the law. [In this two-tiered case, the Dutch Supreme Court rendered its judgment in 2012 with respect to the UN.]

Stichting Mothers of Srebrenica and Others against The Netherlands, **App. No. 65542/12, European Court of Human Rights, 11 June 2013** [...]

118. The applicants alleged violations of Article 6 of the [Convention]. [...]

(b) The Court's assessment [...]

140. The applicants' argument rests on three pillars. The first is the nature of the immunity from domestic jurisdiction enjoyed by international organisations, which is, in their submission, functional; in this, they argue, it contrasts with the sovereign immunity enjoyed by foreign States, which is grounded on the sovereign equality of States among themselves. The second is the nature of their claim, which derives from the act of genocide committed at Srebrenica and is in their view of a higher order than any immunity which the United Nations may enjoy. The third is the absence of any alternative jurisdiction competent to entertain their claim against the United Nations. The Court will consider each of these in turn.

α. *The nature of the immunity enjoyed by the United Nations* [...]

149. Previous cases before the Court in which the question of the immunity from domestic jurisdiction of international organisations has come up have, until now, concerned disputes between the organisation and members of its staff (see *Waite and Kennedy* and *Beer and Regan*, both cited above; see also *Lopez Cifuentes v. Spain* (dec.), no. 18754/06, 7 July 2009). [...]

152. The present case is different from all those mentioned. At its root is a dispute between the applicants and the United Nations based on the use by the Security Council of its powers under Chapter VII of the United Nations Charter.

153. Like resolutions of the Security Council, the United Nations Charter and other instruments governing the functioning of the United Nations will be interpreted by the Court as far as possible in harmony with States' obligations under international human rights law.

154. The Court finds that since operations established by United Nations Security Council resolutions under Chapter VII of the United Nations Charter are fundamental to the mission of the United Nations to secure international peace and security, the Convention cannot be interpreted in a manner which would subject the acts and omissions of the Security Council to domestic jurisdiction without the accord of the United Nations. To bring such operations within the scope of domestic jurisdiction would be to allow individual States, through their courts, to interfere with the fulfilment of the key mission of the United Nations in this field, including with the effective conduct of its operations (see, *mutatis mutandis, Behrami and Behrami v. France and Saramati v. France, Germany and Norway*, cited above, § 149).

[β. *The nature of the applicants' claim*]

158. However, unlike *Jorgić*, the present case does not concern criminal liability but immunity from domestic civil jurisdiction. International law does not support the position that a civil claim should override immunity from suit for the sole reason that it is based on an allegation of a particularly grave violation of a norm of international law, even a norm of *ius cogens*. In respect of the sovereign immunity of foreign States this has been clearly stated by the ICJ in *Jurisdictional Immunities of the State (Germany v. Italy: Greece intervening)*, judgment of 3 February 2012, §§ 81–97. In the Court's opinion this also holds true as regards the immunity enjoyed by the United Nations.

159. Notwithstanding the possibility of weighing the immunity of an official of the United Nations in the balance, suggested in paragraph 61 of the ICJ's Advisory Opinion concerning the *Difference Relating to Immunity from Legal Process of a Special Rapporteur of the Commission on Human Rights*, the Court sees no reason

to reach a different finding as regards the immunity enjoyed by the United Nations in the present case, especially since—unlike the acts impugned in the *Jurisdictional Immunities* case—the matters imputed to the United Nations in the present case, however they may have to be judged, ultimately derived from resolutions of the Security Council acting under Chapter VII of the United Nations Charter and therefore had a basis in international law.

[γ. The absence of any alternative jurisdiction] [...]

163. As the applicants rightly pointed out, in *Waite and Kennedy* (cited above, § 68)—as in *Beer and Regan* (cited above, § 58)—the Court considered it a 'material factor', in determining whether granting an international organisation immunity from domestic jurisdiction was permissible under the Convention, whether the applicants had available to them reasonable alternative means to protect effectively their rights under the Convention. In the present case it is beyond doubt that no such alternative means existed either under Netherlands domestic law or under the law of the United Nations.

164. It does not follow, however, that in the absence of an alternative remedy the recognition of immunity is *ipso facto* constitutive of a violation of the right of access to a court. In respect of the sovereign immunity of foreign States, the ICJ has explicitly denied the existence of such a rule (*Jurisdictional Immunities of the State (Germany v. Italy: Greece intervening)*, § 101). As regards international organisations, this Court's judgments in *Waite and Kennedy* and *Beer and Regan* cannot be interpreted in such absolute terms either. [...]

169. The above findings lead the Court to find that in the present case the grant of immunity to the United Nations served a legitimate purpose and was not disproportionate.

170. It follows that this part of the application is manifestly ill-founded and must be rejected in accordance with Article 35 §§ 3 (a) and 4 of the Convention.

IV. Commentary

The Supreme Court judgment and the non-admissibility ECtHR decision concern the tragic events which occurred in and around Srebrenica in 1995. Numerous legal proceedings, both domestic as well as international, have ever since engaged in establishing the facts. Also in terms of law, courts and tribunals have been assessing legally relevant relationships pertaining to the events in Srebrenica in various fields of international law, including international criminal law and the law on state responsibility. The decisions discussed in this section focus on a different body of law and address the scope of immunities enjoyed by international organizations before domestic courts.[2] As previously stated, the decisions shed light on two questions in particular: does the grant of immunity to the UN infringe upon an individual's right of access to court *and* should

---

[2] Both decisions are intrinsically linked—and share the same factual backdrop—with two other judgments which are discussed in this volume, namely *Nuhanovic v Netherlands*, Appeal Judgment, LJN: R5388, ILDC 1742 (NL 2011) and *Mustafic v Netherlands*, Appeal Judgment, LJN: BR 5386, both rendered by the Dutch Court of Appeals on 5 July 2011.

this right prevail in situations where claims are based on alleged violations of norms of *jus cogens*? As both decisions deal with the same questions, and considering the fact that the ECtHR decision in essence confirmed the Supreme Court's judgment, this commentary will primarily focus on the Supreme Court judgment, referring to the ECtHR decision where required.[3]

With respect to the first question, international law generally accepts that international organizations enjoy immunity from legal proceedings based on the theory of functional necessity. This functional immunity differs from state immunity, which has been construed as an absolute immunity enjoyed by one sovereign vis-à-vis another—*par in parem non habet imperium*.

As opposed to state immunity, functional immunity is not based on any conception of sovereignty but on the necessity of international organizations to be able to exercise their duties and fulfil their purpose in a way unhindered by, possibly malevolent, domestic jurisdictions. Worded differently, functional immunity is an indispensable shield against 'unilateral interference by individual governments'.[4] The legal foundation of immunities enjoyed by international organizations is generally founded on a combination of constitutive documents of international organizations, various bilateral and multilateral treaties, as well as domestic legislation.[5] Turning to the UN, immunity is governed by the Convention on Privileges and Immunities of the United Nations (General Convention), which in effect implements the immunity provided to the UN by art. 105 of the UN Charter. The preamble of this convention states that the UN is granted 'such privileges and immunities as are necessary for the fulfillment of its purposes'. As argued by the applicants in the ECtHR proceedings, this would imply that 'whenever the United Nations invoked its immunity, the courts had to determine whether a functional need for such immunity existed' (ECtHR decision, para. 122). However, art. II, Section 2 of the General Convention grants the UN 'immunity from every form of legal process', a provision interpreted widely so as to confer absolute immunity on the UN and its subsidiary bodies.[6]

Such an all-encompassing conception of immunity has given rise to human rights concerns. Simply put, in carrying out their activities, international organizations increasingly affect individuals directly. At times, individuals' human rights might even be violated. Indeed, the invocation and subsequent grant of immunity might bar individuals from having their claims examined by a court. Consequently, it has been

---

[3] As the Strasbourg court stated, it had 'only to decide whether The Netherlands violated the applicants' right of "access to a court", as guaranteed by Article 6 of the Convention, by granting the United Nations immunity from domestic jurisdiction', ECtHR decision, para. 137.

[4] cf. *Waite and Kennedy v Germany*, App. No. 26083/94, 18 February 1999, para. 63 (*Waite and Kennedy*).

[5] cf. United States International Organizations Immunities Act, 29 December 1945, 22 U.S.C., Section 288, however, the customary status of functional immunity of international organizations has been disputed.

[6] cf. A. Reinisch & U.A. Weber, 'In the Shadow of Waite and Kennedy. The Jurisdictional Immunity of International Organizations, the Individual's Right of Access to the Courts and Administrative Tribunals as Alternative Means of Dispute Settlement', (2004) 1 *International Organizations Law Review* at 60, fn. 5, quoting the UN Office of Legal Affairs.

argued that when applied in a near-absolute manner, granting immunity leads to a breach of the right to an effective remedy that is the right of access to court.[7]

The two present decisions add to a broader jurisprudential development through which courts, both at the domestic as well as at the international level, have started to question the scope of immunity enjoyed by international organizations—or rather the unconditionality thereof. In so doing, courts engage in a balancing act in which they consider whether upholding the jurisdictional immunity of an international organization is proportionate in relation to the right of access to court and a possible denial thereof. Indeed, the ECtHR, for example, has recognized that the rights at stake are not absolute, but that restrictions on the basis of immunity need to pursue a legitimate aim and have to be proportionate.[8]

In assessing this proportionality, the existence of alternative mechanisms through which recourse and redress would be provided to the adversely affected individuals has proven to be a decisive factor. More specifically, according to this approach, a court would be willing to assume jurisdiction over an international organization if this organization does not provide for a mechanism through which a level of human rights protection can be upheld which is similar to that of the court's own legal system.[9] A pioneer when it comes to developing this approach, the German Bundesverfassungsgericht held in the third decision amongst its famed *Solange* judgments, in relation to the European Community, that:

> Acts done under a special power, separate from national powers of Member States, exercised by a *supra*-national organization also affect the holders of basic rights in Germany. They therefore affect the guarantees of the Constitution and the duties of the Constitutional Court, the object of which is the protection of constitutional rights in Germany—in this respect not merely as against German state bodies.[10]

The ECtHR upheld this so-called 'equivalent protection' approach and, in *Waite and Kennedy,* added that:

> a material factor in determining whether granting [the European Space Agency] immunity from German jurisdiction is permissible under the [ECHR] is whether the applicants had available to them reasonable alternative means to protect effectively their rights under the Convention.[11]

---

[7] This right is for example guaranteed by art. 2(3) of the International Covenant on Civil and Political Rights. This right should be understood broadly and as related to such adjacent rights dealing with access to court and fair trial. See for example the American Convention on Human Rights (art. 8) and the ECHR (art. 6). The right to access to court is implied in these documents and has been recognized by the ECtHR as implicit to art. 6 ECHR, as restated in *Waite and Kennedy*, para. 50.

[8] cf. *Al-Adsani v the United Kingdom*, App. No. 35763/97, 21 November 2001, paras 52–67 (*Al-Adsani*). See also for example F. Francesco (ed.), *Access to Justice as a Human Right* (Oxford University Press 2007).

[9] Reinisch and Weber conclude, however, that even when such alternative mechanisms do exist, they generally fall short of respecting most of the accepted fair trial standards, see Reinisch and Weber (n. 6), pp. 109–10.

[10] cf. Germany, Federal Constitutional Court, BverfGE 89, 155 12 October 1993 (*Solange III*), in 1 *Common Market Law Review* 57 at 253. Various courts from other jurisdictions have at times adopted this approach, see for example Switzerland, Federal Supreme Court, *Consortium X v Switzerland*, BGE 130 I 312, 2 July 2004, ILDC 344 and France, Court of Cassation, *La Banque Africaine de Développement v Mr X*, 04-41012, 25 January 2005, ILDC 778.

[11] cf. *Waite and Kennedy*, para. 68. The reasoning was further embraced in key decisions: *Bosphorus Hava Yollari Turizm ve Ticaret Anonim Sirketi v Ireland*, App. No. 45036/98, 30 June 2005 (*Bosphorus*) and European Court of Justice (ECJ), Joined Cases C-402 and 415/05P, *Kadi & Al Barakaat International Found. v Council of the European Union & Commission of the European Communities*, ECR I-6351, 3

Adding to this developing line of jurisprudence, the two present decisions are characterized by two particular features: firstly, the underlying facts relate to activities of the UN, carried out under Chapter VII of the UN Charter and secondly, the allegations brought against the UN in the case before the Dutch Supreme Court relate to peremptory norms of international law, albeit that this last feature is disputed as will be discussed below.

The first point of interest is, thus, whether the described balancing act should also be applied to UN immunity. At the outset of the first instance proceedings, the UN clearly invoked its immunity, rather than making use of the possibility to waive it.[12] Hence, before reaching the cassation phase, in 2008 the District Court in The Hague had rejected the claims against the UN on the basis that it lacked jurisdiction.[13] The Court of Appeal then upheld the judgment of the District Court,[14] Civil Law Section, Judgment in the incidental proceedings, 10 July 2008 (District Court judgment). The Dutch Supreme Court had to assess whether the lower instance courts were right in granting the UN immunity and rendered its judgment in 2012 confirming the grant of immunity of the UN, albeit for reasons surprisingly different from the ones relied on by the Court of Appeal.

Although the Court of Appeal had granted the UN immunity, it had done so only after weighing the ramifications of such a decision in terms of human rights-related implications. In the words of the court, 'the Court of Appeal believes that article 103 of the Charter does *not* preclude testing the immunity from prosecution against article 6 ECHR and article 14 ICCPR'.[15] The Court went on to apply these standards. With respect to whether there were alternative mechanisms available to the Mothers of Srebrenica, the Court of Appeal held that the plaintiffs had various alternatives at their disposal. The court specified that these were alternatives through which the *actual* perpetrators could be held criminally responsible.[16] This reasoning of the court is rather unconvincing, as it emphasizes the existence of *other* legal mechanisms through which *other* involved actors could be held to account, rather than mechanisms which could assess the responsibility of the UN. In fact, the court disregarded the fact that the General Convention links the privileges and immunities of the UN with an obligation for *the UN itself* to establish alternative mechanisms, which would address the possible wrongdoings of the UN, rather than any other actors. As this

---

September 2008 (*Kadi I*). For a critical view of the piercing of absolute immunity, see for example G. De Búrca, 'The European Court of Justice and the International Legal Order after Kadi', (2010) 51(1) *Harvard International Law Journal* 1–50.

[12] In a letter dated 17 August 2007, the UN had informed the Dutch Permanent Representative to the UN that it would not waive its immunity in this particular case (cf. Supreme Court judgment, para. 3.2.2).

[13] District Court in The Hague, *Association Mothers of Srebrenica et al. v The Netherlands and the United Nations*, (2995247/HA ZA 07-2973, LJN: BD6796), Civil Law Section, Judgment in the incidental proceedings, 10 July 2008.

[14] cf. ibid.

[15] cf. ibid., at paras 5.2–5.5 (emphasis added). See also references in the Supreme Court judgment, para. 4.3.1.

[16] cf. District Court judgment, at paras 5.11–5.13 (emphasis added). See also Supreme Court judgment, para. 4.1.1.

issue was also brought up by the applicants in the subsequent ECtHR proceedings, the Strasbourg court briefly touched upon the question of alternative mechanisms. However, it did not engage in an assessment of possible alternative mechanisms, or a lack thereof. Rather, it concluded that it 'does not follow, however, that in the absence of an alternative remedy the recognition of immunity is *ipso facto* constitutive of a violation of the right of access to a court'.[17]

In terms of whether granting immunity would serve a legitimate aim, the Court of Appeal found that in this particular context, immunity 'is closely connected to the public interest pertaining to keeping peace and safety in the world [and] that only compelling reasons should be allowed to lead to the conclusion that the United Nations' immunity is not in proportion to the objective aimed for', *quod non* according to the Court.[18] In sum, by applying the *Waite and Kennedy* criteria, the Court of Appeal had expanded the reach of these criteria to the UN—erroneously so, as the Dutch Supreme Court held in its judgment.

The Dutch Supreme Court quashed the reasoning of the Court of Appeal. In several to-the-point paragraphs, the Supreme Court points to the fact that the 'UN occupies a special place in the international legal community'.[19] While confirming the immunity of the UN, the court rejects boldly that the *Waite and Kennedy* criteria—or as it seems any other criteria, for that matter—should be applied in cases concerning the UN. As the court states, '[t]he interim conclusion must be that the appeal court erred in examining, on the basis of the criteria formulated in *Beer and Regan* and *Waite and Kennedy*, whether the right of access to the courts as referred to in article 6 ECHR prevailed over the immunity invoked on behalf of the UN', concluding unequivocally '[t]hat immunity is absolute'.[20] In the proceedings before the ECtHR, the Strasbourg court upheld this view by holding that the present case was fundamentally different from previous cases pertaining to the immunity of international organizations, emphasizing the importance of the UN, especially when acting under Chapter VII of the UN Charter.[21]

As to the second characteristic feature of the proceedings, the Supreme Court also dismissed the gravity of the underlying claims as a possible limitation to immunity. The Court first generously cites the Mothers of Srebrenica's writ of summons in cassation:

> There is no higher norm in international law than the prohibition of genocide. This norm in any event takes precedence over the other norms at issue in this legal dispute. The enforcement of this norm is one of the main reasons for the existence of international law and for the most important international organisation, the UN. This means that in cases of failure to prevent genocide, international organisations are not entitled to immunity, or in any event the prohibition should prevail over such

---

[17] cf. ECtHR decision, para. 164.   [18] cf. Court of Appeal judgment, para. 5.7.
[19] cf. Supreme Court judgment, para. 4.3.4.
[20] cf. ibid., paras 4.3.5–4.3.6. The applicants in the ECtHR proceedings argued that this distinction between the UN and other international organizations was flawed (cf. ECtHR decision, paras 130–2).
[21] cf. ECtHR decision, paras 149–54.

immunity. The view that the UN's immunity weighs more heavily in this instance would mean *de facto* that the UN has absolute power. [...][22]

The Supreme Court went on to reject this argumentation and reinforced the parallel between state immunity and the immunity of international organizations by basing its argument on several key decisions in which the vast scope of state immunity had previously been upheld despite allegations of violations of *jus cogens* norms. In so doing, the court relied heavily on the ECtHR *Al-Adsani* decision, where state immunity was upheld despite allegations of violations of the prohibition of torture.[23] Similar emphasis was placed on the 2012 *Jurisdictional Immunities of the State* judgment of the International Court of Justice.[24]

In the subsequent proceedings before the ECtHR, the nature of the underlying proceedings was also dismissed as a factor which could inform a decision on whether or not to grant immunity. Furthermore, the Strasbourg court, just like the Dutch Supreme Court, left aside the question of whether the obligation to prevent genocide had *jus cogens* status to begin with. Rather, the ECtHR essentially dismissed the gravity-argument by emphasizing the fact that the proceedings before the Dutch courts concerned civil claims: '[i]nternational law does not support the position that a civil claim should override immunity from suit for the sole reason that it is based on an allegation of a particularly grave violation of a norm of international law, even a norm of *ius cogens*'.[25]

In sum, the two decisions should be placed in the context of two developments within the body of law that regulates immunities of international organizations. Firstly, both decisions fortify the link between the traditionally functional immunity of international organizations and state immunity. In their decisions, both courts rely heavily on several judgments of the ECtHR and the International Court of Justice which, in previous years, have restated the rigid nature of state immunity; a development most recently reconfirmed by the ECtHR's much discussed *Jones* decision.[26] This linkage gives impetus to the jurisprudential development according to which the grant of immunity, at least when it comes to states and the UN, does not depend on the nature of the underlying allegations in a particular case. Secondly, by granting the UN seemingly absolute immunity, the Dutch Supreme Court remains loyal to a fault to a rigid conception of immunity. Leaving aside possible further developments of the equal protection-line of argumentation and the *Waite and Kennedy* criteria with respect to other actors, these two decisions put a hold on such possible developments with respect to the immunity of the UN, as a *sui generis* international organization, for activities carried out under Chapter VII.

---

[22] cf. Supreme Court judgment, para. 4.3.7.
[23] cf. ibid., paras 4.3.8–4.3.9.
[24] cf. ICJ, *Jurisdictional Immunities of the State (Germany v Italy; Greece intervening)*, Judgment, 3 February 2012, para. 93; see Supreme Court judgment, paras 4.3.10–4.3.14.
[25] cf. ECtHR decision, para. 158.
[26] cf. *Jones and others v the United Kingdom*, App. No. 34356/06 and 40528/06, 14 January 2014.

Index